TEA THER

D1350005

France

France

A Phaidon Cultural Guide

With over 800 colour illustrations
and 20 pages of maps

Phaidon

Author: Jacques-Louis Delpal

Phaidon Press Limited, Littlegate House, St Ebbe's Street, Oxford, OX1 1SQ

First published in English 1985

Second impression 1986

Originally published simultaneously in French as *Guide Nathan: France*
and in German as *Knaurs Kulturführer in Farbe: Frankreich*
© Droemersche Verlagsanstalt Th. Knaur Nachf. Munich/Zurich 1978
English translation ©Phaidon Press Limited 1985.

British Library Cataloguing in Publication Data

France. — (A Phaidon cultural guide)
  1. France — Description and travel — 1975-
  — Guide-books
  914.4'04838   DC29.3

  ISBN 0-7148-2353-8

Translated from the French and edited by Babel Translations, London
Typeset by Electronic Village Limited, Richmond, Surrey
Printed in Spain by H. Fournier, S.A.-Vitoria

Cover illustration: interior view of the Basilica of St. Remi, Reims
(photo: Giraudon, Paris)

Preface

France, the hub of western Europe, is a country of stunning contrasts. Stretching from the shores of the Atlantic to the Mediterranean, its climate and scenery vary dramatically. Its architecture, adapted to suit both climate and landscape, is of a marked diversity reflecting periods of royal, imperial and republican patronage: hence the history of France can be traced in its buildings, in proud cathedrals and humble wooden churches, in romantic castles, neat manor-houses, palaces and fine country-houses.

The art of the master-builder (sometimes a famous architect, sometimes a genius whose name is unknown) is enhanced by the works of painters, decorators, sculptors, glass-makers, weavers and cabinet-makers. Often their work can be seen in its original setting; but sometimes it is transferred for safekeeping to one of France's numerous museums. And while Paris naturally has gathered together thousands of masterpieces of every period, the visitor to France will also discover many treasures on display in the provinces – in small towns as well as cities. French museums are no longer dreary warehouses of art, but complement the richly furnished and decorated churches and châteaux for which the country is justly famed.

This tourist guide to the monuments and culture of France presents a digest for visitors, concentrating on representative items of interest. It covers, of course, all the major attractions which no tourist must miss, but it also explores many out-of-the-way places and unusual items which are worthy of inclusion. The vastness of the subject has resulted in concise descriptions of France's great treasures, but significant facts of history have been included, and an attempt has been made to evoke atmosphere and put the subject in its cultural context.

As with the other guides in this series, the entries are arranged in alphabetical order for easy reference. The illustrations – which are all in colour – are placed next to the relevant text. More than 800 churches, castles, chateaux, museums, theatres and works of art are shown, including ground-plans of many important buildings.

The heading to each entry gives the name of the town, and immediately below the name and number of its geographical region (department); on the right is the number of inhabitants and a reference to the map section (pp. 410-29).

The Publishers would be grateful for notification of any errors or omissions.

Abbeville
80 Somme

(26,600 inhab.)

p.410□I 2

A seaport, on the banks of the Somme, Abbeville has undergone considerable change as a result of the war. Devastated in the battles of May 1940 (during which the then Colonel de Gaulle distinguished himself at the head of his tanks), it has subsequently been carefully rebuilt so that it now combines architectural unity with uncongested streets. The former collegiate church, *Saint-Wulfram*, stands in the centre of the town, where the restoration work is still continuing. It has a tall, Flamboyant Gothic façade with two square towers and an open gable. This monumental façade is extensively sculpted and dates from the 15C. The splendid Renaissance leaves of the central portal were lovingly worked by craftsmen from Picardy. Other traces of the town's history can be seen in the former Rames factory, the town library, which has a Carolingian evangeliary, and the *museum*, named after Boucher de Perthes, the 'father' of pre-history'. *Château Bagatelle*, the sumptuous country house of an 18C industrialist, lies on the road to Paris. Inside it is tastefully furnished and has delicate panelling, whilst outside the façade of red brick and white stone combines with the French park to produce an image of luxury and grace.

Agde
34 Hérault

(11,800 inhab.)

p.424□K 15

The ancient town of Agde was originally a Phocaean colony and is situated on the Hérault some 4 km. from the Mediterranean. Several ancient houses, as well as other vestiges of its Graeco-Roman past, have survived. The fortified former cathedral of *Saint-Étienne* was built of hard black lava at the end of the 12C. Its machicolations and strong square towers make it look like a castle. The large nave was originally very dark but most of the windows were enlarged in the 17C. In the broken barrel vault there is an opening which gave the watchmen on the parapet access to the inside.

Black lava was also used to build the 17C *Hôtel de Ville* (town-hall). The church of *Saint-Sever* has been altered and restored time and again but retains its 15C polygonal apse. It houses the *Saint-Christ*, also 15C, a wooden sculpture, believed to have miraculous properties. The *Musée Agathois* contains finds from local and regional excavations, together with old costumes and

examples of the Romanesque. Like Cahors Cathedral, the semicircular apse is flanked by three radiating apsidal chapels, to produce an arrangement that appears beautifully balanced from the outside. The Gothic nave is very short and its builders undoubtedly planned to add a row of domes; however, they were unable to do so. Several Renaissance houses have been made into a richly stocked *museum*: collections of French and foreign ceramics; faience by Bernard Palissy (who came from the SW); a remarkable series of paintings by Goya; and works by the Impressionists. Pride of place is taken by a *Venus*, a Greek marble sculpture found by a local peasant in his field near Le Mas d'Agenais.

Environs: Moirax (9 km. S.): *Notre-Dame de Moirax* is a large, elegant priory church dating from the end of the 11C. It rises above the roofs of the village and retains a Romanesque appearance, although it now has ribbed vaults and is surmounted by an incongruous bell-tower. 17C panelling. **Aubiac** (9 km. SW): The small but exquisite church of *Sainte-Marie* blends perfectly with the village, whose houses (with roofs of round tiles) cluster tightly around it. The church is a Romanesque masterpiece, although parts of the apse are earlier; it has strong 12C towers, that above the choir shows Carolingian influence.

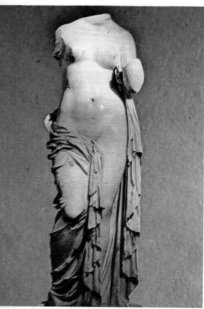

Agen, museum, Vénus du Mas

head-dresses, religious works of art and various collections.

On the coast, a holiday resort has been built at Cap-d'Agde.

| **Agen** | (35,900 inhab.) |
| 47 Lot-et-Garonne | p.423□G 13 |

On the river Garonne, Agen is a modern town with broad streets. It is the centre of a fertile region devoted to growing early vegetables and fruits (the prunes of Agen are famous). During the Renaissance, in particular, Agen flourished and attracted numerous scholars. The former collegiate church of *Saint-Caprais*, which dates mainly from the 11&12C, became a cathedral after the Revolution. The apse and, to a lesser extent, the transept are perfect

| **Aigle (L')** | (10,300 inhab.) |
| 61 Orne | p.410□G 5 |

A small industrial town between the districts of Ouche and Perche, with two attractive churches. *Saint-Martin,* which is built in a mixture of styles, combines the Gothic and a touch of Renaissance with its original Romanesque (12,15&16C). A magnificent Flamboyant tower with statues overshadows the simple 12C limestone bell-tower. The high altar has an important altarpiece dating from 1656. Modern stained glass by Max Ingrand. *Saint-Jean-Baptiste* is also Romanesque in origin, though Renaissance in style. It has a Louis XIII high altar and interesting statues. The *Musée Juin 1944*, devoted to the battle of Normandy, is housed in the outbuildings of a 17C Castle (designed by Hardouin Mansart).

Aigueperse	(2,700 inhab.)
63 Puy-de-Dôme	p.420□K 10

Birthplace of the Lord Chancellor and jurist Michel de l'Hospital (1506–73). It was capital of the Duchy of Montpensier (the most famous holder of this title was the unruly 17C Grande Mademoiselle), and a stage on the route taken by French kings when returning from Italy. It is a town which is steeped in its own past. The castle's former *Saint-Chapelle* (Flamboyant Gothic) is richly panelled and houses two 16C white marble statues of the Virgin and Louis XII. In *Notre-Dame*, only the choir and transept date from the 13C. A funerary chapel, flanked by a Renaissance chapel, has been added in the angle of the crossing, S. of the 16C nave. The church possesses a beautiful 15C *Nativity* painted on wood, by Benedetto Ghirlandaio. The Hôtel de Ville (town hall) is a former convent of the Poor Clares (17C). The belfry has a jack above the entrance and there is a statue of Michel de l'Hospital in the courtyard.

Environs: Château de la Roche (3 km. NW): A formidable castle built in the 12&13C, with a watch-tower and a square keep, which dominates Aigueperse; in the 16C it became the splendid residence of the l'Hospital family. Its main courtyard is surrounded on three sides by buildings and on the fourth side it is closed by a 16C Volvic stone balustrade. The castle houses

Aigues-Mortes, towers and ramparts

fine Louis XIV and Louis XV furniture and Aubusson tapestries. In the keep, one room is devoted to de l'Hospital, the Lord Chancellor celebrated by Ronsard. **Château d'Effiat** (5 km. NE): Rebuilt with enthusiasm in 1627 by the Marquis d'Effiat, Marshal of France. The main section of the building has a high roof and is finely adorned with pilasters. The remarkable, monumental portal, at the front of the building, bears the Marshal's arms.

Aigues-Mortes	(4,600 inhab.)
30 Gard	p.425□L 14

A quiet town surrounded by 13C walls. Isolated, in an area of pools and salt pans, Aigues-Mortes owes its foundation to St. Louis, who set off from here on the Cru-

Aïnhoa, Basque village

sade of 1248 and the disastrous Tunisian expedition (1270). He had the harbour, which is now silted up, dredged and the magnificent *Tour de Constance* built. The circular keep is 121 ft. tall and commands an extensive view. Louis' son, Philip the Bold, ordered the construction of the walls, which are flanked by twenty towers. The church of *Notre-Dame-des-Sablons* is 13C.

Aïnhoa   (540 inhab.)
64 Pyrénées-Atlantiques   p.422☐D 15

An old and unusual *bastide*, this pleasant, white village lies close to the Spanish frontier and is composed of typical Basque houses. Some are purely Labourdin in character (Labour is the name of the small coastal region), whilst the style of others is that of Basse-Navarre. The church is Romanesque in origin but has been altered. It too is typical of the region, with its galleried nave. The monument to the dead at the entrance to the old cemetery is in the style of Basque discoidal tombs.

Aire-sur-l'Adour   (7,000 inhab.)
40 Landes   p.422☐F 14

This town on the edge of the rich Chalosse region was called *Atura* by the Romans and was the seat of an early bishop. The former *cathedral* has been altered many times since the 11C and its nave is now 15C. The furnishings are essentially 18C. The Bishop's Palace (16&17C) now houses the Hôtel de Ville.

In the suburb of Mas-d'Aire, the church

Aire-sur-l'Adour, church portal

Airvault, church façade, detail

of *Sainte-Quitterie* dates from various periods (12–18C). Inside: *Christ* by Poussin, decorated capitals in the choir and a Merovingian sarcophagus in the crypt.

Environs: Geaune (14 km. SW): 15C church with an impressive bell tower and porch. **Vielle-Tursan** (7 km. from Geaune): Church partly 12C, with interesting Romanesque details.

Airvault	(2,500 inhab.)
79 Deux-Sèvres	p.418□F 8

Airvault is a large, peaceful village on the borders of Haut-Poitou and Gâtine, at the point where the river Thouet is spanned by an old bridge. It was the seat of a college of regular Augustinian canons, founded in the 2nd half of the 10C.

Saint-Pierre: One of Haut-Poitou's major monuments; like the nearby and architecturally related Saint-Jouin-de-Marnes, it is an eloquent example of regional monastic art. The church is a mixture of Poitevin Romanesque (12C) and Angevin (13C) styles. The façade has a triangular gable flanked by column buttresses, but its decoration has been depleted by time and vandalism (there are only mutilated remains of an equestrian statue, the *Cavalier Poitevin*). In front of the façade, a fine half-recessed porch forms a narthex. The square bell tower has a tall 13C stone spire. There is a fine semicircular choir and the Romanesque nave and side aisles blend perfectly with the Angevin Gothic vault. The decoration of the pillar capitals alternates between plant motifs and depictions of monsters and various scenes. On each side of the half-columns supporting the nave's vault, there are primitively worked statuettes on corbels representing monsters. A recess in the chapel of the N. transept houses the remains of the first Abbot of Airvault; nine statuettes decorate this Romanesque tomb. The 12C chapterhouse and part of the cloister's arcades are all that remain of the priory's monastery buildings.

The town's narrow alleys lead to the remains of a granite fortress, which overlooked the valley. Of the ruined wall, only three square towers remain.

Aix (île d')   (210 inhab.)
17 Charente-Maritime   p.418□E 10

A flat island nearly two miles long lying a short way off the Aunis coast opposite La Rochelle. It is covered with low, white houses and its streets are lined with tamarisks and hollyhocks. L'île d'Aix owes its fame to a distinguished guest, Napoleon, who stayed there in 1815 before surrendering to the English. The village was forti-fied by Vauban and access is via a gate with a drawbridge. Laid out like a town, the streets, which bear such evocative names as Rue Napoléon, Rue Marengo and Place d'Austerlitz, cross at right angles. The fine residence of the commander, where Napoleon stayed, has become the *Musée Napoléon* and its ten rooms are full of mementoes of the Emperor (portraits, arms, clothes, various documents). The *Muséum Africain* houses the fine collection of Baron Gourgaud's trophies (Baron Gourgaud was a descendant of Napoleon's companion in exile). In addition to specimens of African wildlife there is also the stuffed camel which Bonaparte rode during the Egyptian campaign.

Aix-en-Provence   (114,100 inhab.)
13 Bouches-du-Rhône   p.425□M 14

Springs, sparkling or mossy, houses of buff-coloured stone, the green shadows of the Cours Mirabeau, the cathedral museum. 'The most beautiful town in France

Ile d'Aix, Musée Napoléon   *Aix-en-P., Fontaine de la Rotonde* ▷

Aix-en-P., Pavillon de Vendôme, atlantes

Aix-en-P., Pavillon de Vendôme

after Paris,' declared the great traveller De Brosse in the 18C. Noble and welcoming, here secret and aristocratic, there rejuvenated by students and the crush of festival crowds, Aix is one of the most important cities of of the vast region of Provence. It was united to the Crown in 1481 and before long was the seat of a Parliament. It is the birthplace of the moralist Vauvenargues, the painters Jean-Baptiste Van Loo, François Granet, and Paul Cézanne, as well as Emile Zola and Darius Milhaud. The turbulent Count Mirabeau, who in 1789 was elected as representative of the Third Estate, lived here.

The *Cours Mirabeau* (17C Hôtel Maurel de Pontevès, the family house of Cézanne) separates the irregularly laid out medieval and Renaissance towns from the well-ordered 18C quarters. The cathedral

stands in the oldest part of Aix, which is now a mixture of buildings from various periods. Close to the Hôtel de Ville, which has a baroque 17C façade, there is the *Tour Communal*; a medieval base surmounted by a Renaissance top housing an astronomical clock dating from 1661. In the square there is an 18C fountain (with likenesses of Louis XIV and local figures). At the heart of old Aix, the Saint-Sauveur district remains medieval in character, having quiet, narrow streets and houses with heavy, closed doors and only the occasional window. The 17&18C former *Évêché* (Bishop's Palace) has magnificent *tapestries* hanging in the bishop's apartments.

Cathedral of Saint-Sauveur: The cathedral, which adjoins a Romanesque cloister, comprises the remains of a Romanesque church, a main building dat-

Aix-en-P., Fondation Vasarely

ing from the 13&14C, 14&15C side chapels and a 4&5C Baptistry, with capitals taken from a Roman building. In keeping with the diversity of the cathedral, the façade's main door (1510) retains fine half Gothic, half Renaissance *leaves* (prophets and sibyls). The nave is hung with remarkable tapestries woven at the beginning of the 16C for Canterbury Cathedral. The famous triptych, *The Burning Bush*, was painted in 1476 by Nicolas Froment, who belonged to the Provençal school. Near the cathedral, the charming *Musée du Vieil-Aix* has Moustiers faience, old Provençal cribs, figures, and unusual puppets.

Surrounded by old houses and elegant mansions, the 17C church of **Sainte-Marie-Madeleine** houses the central panel of another famous triptych, this time an *Annunciation*. Painted in the 1440s by

an unknown artist, it is a mixture of Flemish and Provençal styles.

The *Quartier Mazarin* is an open, spacious area, crossed by roads which intersect each other at right angles; work on it began in 1646, at the instigation of Archbishop Michel Mazarin, the brother of the Cardinal who succeeded Richelieu. The *Musée Paul-Arbaud* is named after the collector whose treasures, amassed in the course of a lifetime, it houses: these include manuscripts and early printed works, paintings and drawings, old furniture and Provençal faience.

Musée Granet: This museum too bears the name of the collection's donor, François Granet of Aix. He was a neoclassical painter and pupil of David. Among the most outstanding museums in the province, it boasts one of the last self-portraits

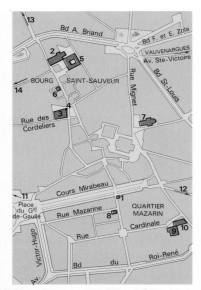

Aix-en-Provence 1 Hôtel Maurel de Pontevès **2** cathedral of Saint-Sauveur **3** Hôtel-de-Ville **4** tower **5** former bishop's palace **6** Musée du Vieil-Aix **7** church of Sainte-Marie-Madeleine **8** Musée Paul-Arbaud **9** Musée Granet **10** church of Saint-Jean-de-Malte **11** Fondation Vasarely **12** Sainte-Victoire **13** Atelier de Cézanne **14** Pavillon de Vendôme

of Rembrandt, dating from 1665, and the bulk of Cézanne's engravings. It has departments of painting (Italian and Dutch schools of the 17,18&19C), sculpture and archaeology (Celto-Ligurian sculpture from the *Oppidum d'Entremont*, a fortified camp, and religious and political capital, which was destroyed by the Romans), as well as a permanent gallery of contemporary art. The museum is particularly rich in 18C and early-19C portraits, and it exhibits the work of painters of the Provençal school, which was composed of painters from the N. who were attracted by the light of the Midi, as well as local painters such as Fragonard.

The 13C, Gothic, fortified church of *Saint-Jean-de-Malte* stands beside the museum.

Pavillon de Vendôme: A 17C folly with a façade, which was heightened in the 18C, and a fine iron staircase. Display of objets d'art and Provençal furniture.

Fondation Vasarely: A living museum, a centre for information, research and meeting. The foundation was devised by Victor Vasarely (see **Gordes**) and inaugurated in 1975. Hexagonal units are grouped in an original and functional manner. It is partly open to the public but its main function is as a meeting place for various artists. Set in the *Jas du Bouffant* (Bergerie des Vents, 4 km. W. of the town centre), it displays the works of Vasarely.

Cézanne et la Sainte-Victoire: Like Zola, his childhood friend, who described him in *L'Oeuvre*, Cézanne came from Aix. He ended his life here alone, dying in 1906. (A storm took him by surprise whilst he was out painting on a hill, he was caught in the rain for several hours and was brought back unconscious.) The long limestone spine of the Montagne Sainte-Victoire, a symbol of the Aix region, was one of his favourite subjects. The *Atelier de Cézanne*, on the street bearing his name, displays various mementoes of him.

Environs: Vauvenargues (14 km. N. of Sainte-Victoire) The 16&17C château, which stands alone on a hillock, has had two famous owners, the 18C author and moralist Vauvenargues and Pablo Picasso, who bought it in 1958.

Aqueduc de Roquefavour (14 km. W.): Beautiful 19C structure recalling the Pont du Gard. 4 km. away, the village of **Ventabren** forms a picturesque group with castle ruins.

Aix-les-Bains   (22,300 inhab.)
73 Savoie   p.421 □ N 10

The name Aix-les-Bains (from *acquae*

Le Bourget-du-Lac, rood-screen in the church

meaning waters) does not refer to the Lake Bourget of Lamartine's poems but to the thermal springs that have been exploited since antiquity. The seat of Romanticism in the 19C and an important spa, Aix also has the *Arch of Campanus*, a defaced funerary monument built in the 3C or 4C by a patrician. The former *Château des Marquis d'Aix*, the most interesting part of which dates from the early 16C, houses the Town Hall. A Roman building known as the 'Temple of Diana' contains the *Musée Lapidaire*, which displays archaeological finds made in Aix and the surrounding areas. The *Musée Faure* has a collection of faience, various memorabilia connected with Lamartine, and a fine group of Impressionist paintings.

Environs: Le Bourget-du-Lac (9 km. S.): An old village that has become a cen-

tre for holidays and sailing on the lake. Le Bourget was the seat of the Dukes of Savoy (11 – 13C). The castle-priory, once a daughter house of Cluny, dates from 1030 (a gallery of the two-storey cloister survives). The priory church stands on a pre-Romanesque crypt and has been extensively rebuilt. It contains an extraordinarily expressive 13C frieze.

Ajaccio: see **Corsica**

Albi	(49,500 inhab.)
81 Tarn	p.423☐I 13/14

Albi is famous for its formidable cathedral, which expresses both power and refine-

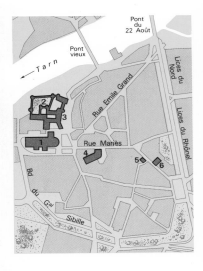

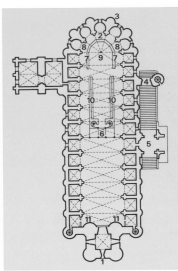

Albi 1 Cathedral of Sainte-Cécile **2** Palais de la Berbie **3** Musée Toulouse-Lautrec **4** collegiate church of Saint-Salvi **5** Maison Enjalbert **6** Hôtel de Reynès.

Albi, cathedral of Sainte-Cécile 1 Bell tower-keep **2** apse **3** former watchtower **4** Domenico of Florence's portal **5** canopy **6** choir screen **7** choir enclosure **8** ambulatory **9** choir **10** stalls **11** fresco of the Last Judgement

Albi, cathedral of Ste-Cécile

ment, and whose red brick glows in the setting sun. The bishop's residence is fortified, while the rest of the town is made up of timber-framed houses with successive overhangs, narrow lanes, staircases and vaults, and hanging gardens. A town of the ancient province of Languedoc, Albi has the air of a Lombard city, being both sophisticated and powerful at the same time. The fortifications of the cathedral and the bishop's residence assert the dominance of the Church in the land of the Cathars. The Albigensian heresy was only put down with difficulty by a cruel and ruthless crusade in the 13C.

Cathedral of Sainte-Cécile: The immense and magnificent church replaced an old cathedral, the cloisters of which now

Albi, cathedral portal ▷

grace a garden. Begun in 1482, the construction of this brick building spanned two centuries. The vertical emphasis of the fortress is made more striking by the lack of flying-buttresses (buttresses are built into the mass of the walls for greater support). The church is dominated by a powerful bell tower-keep, which passes from a square plan to an octagonal one (the top three storeys are 15C). Like a minaret, an old watch tower rises from the apse. The highly decorated portal by Domenico of Florence opens between a tower and the church, and dates from the very beginning of the 15C. Steps lead up to the S. porch, which, with its extravagantly chiselled canopy of white stone (16C), stands out against the plain red brickwork. The body of the church, which is both broad and high, is divided by the stone choir screen, a marvel of Flamboyant tracery. The *choir* lies behind this screen and is surrounded by a richly decorated enclosure so as to form an ambulatory. Whereas virtually all the statuary has disappeared from the screen, the enclosure still retains its polychrome statues. The first part of the choir,

dating from the 15C, was reserved for the bishop and chapter, which explains the presence of stalls, surmounted by statues of angels. The figures in the choir display Burgundian influence. *Wall paintings*: 'Illuminated church': the church was completely decorated with wall paintings by Italian artists at the beginning of the 15C. However, the fresco of the *Last Judgement* on the W. wall is entirely French. This immense composition (66 ft. by 45 ft.) was defaced in the 17&18C, but two large and original views of Heaven and Hell have survived.

Palais de la Berbie (from *besbié*, a Romance word meaning bishop): Dominated by a strong keep and protected by curtain walls, this fortress-palace is 13–15C. Terraces overhanging the Tarn were turned into a garden and promenade in the 17C. Inside: fine main staircase; 13C chapel, heavily restored in the 17C (coloured stucco, paintings); and magnificent apartments with remarkable ceilings.

Musée Toulouse-Lautrec: The Palais de

Albi, Musée Toulouse-Lautrec   *Alençon, Notre-Dame, nave* ▷

la Berbie houses the Musée Toulouse-Lautrec. The crippled painter of concerts, dances and smoke-filled cafès was born in Albi in 1864. Numerous works of contemporaries (Rodin, Bourdelle, Maillol, Despiau, Utrillo, Marquet, Rouault, Touchagues, Vuillard, Vlaminck, and Matisse in particular) are displayed alongside his paintings, drawings, lithographs and posters.

The former collegiate church of **Saint-Salvi** was built mainly in the 13C on the site of an existing building. Altered in the 15C, it is still partly Romanesque (apse with apsidioles, capitals). The bell tower has an 11C base, a 14C top storey and a watch turret, from which it takes its name, Tour de la Gâche (*gachole* means watch turret in the dialect of Languedoc). The cloisters were rebuilt in 1270.

The ancient streets of Albi are lined by numerous picturesque buildings, the top storeys of which are often open—for the drying of provisions. The *Maison Enjalbert* is a remarkable timber-framed corner residence which dates from the 16C, as does the Hôtel de Reynès, with its large, embossed doorway.

Alençon	(34,700 inhab.)
61 Orne	p.414□G 5

Noble and charming in its verdant setting, this old Norman city preserves its reputation as the 'capital of lace'. It has for long been famous for its fine and enchanting point-lace, and this is still made by nuns and their pupils. The *Musée-École Dentellière* displays old pieces and explains the twelve stages in the meticulous working of a *point d'Alençon* motif. Lace-making was actively encouraged by Henri IV and by Colbert, Minister to Louis XIV, who established a factory.

Notre-Dame d'Alençon: Built between the end of the 14C and the beginning of the 16C. It has a carved porch with finely worked upper parts (1506–8). The tall nave is lightened by a well-proportioned triforium and roofed by a highly decorated Flamboyant vault of complex design. There is also a 16C organ chest, an unusual pulpit (1536) and fine 16C stained glass in the clerestory. Thérèse Martin, the future St.Teresa of Lisieux, was baptized in the first chapel of the left aisle. The *Maison d'Ozé*, a fine 15C residence, houses a small museum principally devoted to local history. Several streets in this district are partly closed to traffic and retain much of their historical character.

The Hôtel de Ville is an elegant, curved building dating from the 18C. It houses a wide-ranging *Museum*, which concentrates on the 17,18&19C (Restout, Philippe de Champaigne, Géricault, Courbet, Boudin); there are several superb examples of local and foreign lace (16 – 19C). The birthplace of St.Theresa, the former Hôtel des Intendants (17C), faces the *Préfecture*, a remarkable Louis XIII building of brick and granite (*c.* 1630).

Environs: Saint-Céneri-le-Gérei (13 km. SW) possesses a most attractive Romanesque church (late-11C–early-12C). Set on a spur above the Sarthe, it retains frescos, which date mainly from the 14C, although for the most part they were heavily restored during the last century.

Aléria: see **Corsica**

Alès	(45,800 inhab.)
30 Gard	p.425□L 13

A gateway to the mountains and a frontier town between the arid garrigues and the watery freshness of the Auvergne, Alès lies in a loop of the Gardon and in the shelter of a citadel built by Vauban in 1688. The *Cathedral of Saint-Jean* rises from the crowded old city close to the river. It is a mixture of styles from different centuries; the majority of the building is 18C, the W. front Romanesque and its porch Gothic. Ribbed vaults have been retained. Some interesting paintings decorate the transept, including an 18C *Assumption* by Mignard. The *Musée du Colombier* is housed in the restored buildings of the Château du Colombier. It contains a series of remarkable 16,17&18C canvases, including a beautiful triptych by Jean Bellegambe (*c.* 1470–1534).

Alise-Sainte-Reine	(710 inhab.)
21 Côtes-d'Or	p.415□L 7

On the summit of Mont Auxois, a monumental statue of Vercingétorix recalls the fact that the fate of the Gauls was decided here. The name Alise-Sainte-Reine comes from *Alésia*, the stronghold besieged by Caesar's legions and a saint, Regina, to whom many miracles are attributed. The two parts of the village meet on the side of the hill where the Gauls were entrenched. The extremely old church of *Saint-Léger* dates back to the 8C, and has been restored. The *Musée Alésia* was founded by Napoleon III and displays the finds of digs (mainly statuettes and coins), which have been undertaken at various periods.

In 52 BC Alésia was the Gauls' Waterloo. Elected by the representatives of the various Gallic tribes, Vercingétorix, from Arverne, led a large-scale uprising against the Roman invaders. After his cavalry had been defeated, he withdrew to the oppidum of Alésia, a Mandubian stronghold. Caesar surrounded the Gallic earthwork fortifications. Anticipating the arrival of a relief force, he built two contravallations, defensive lines against sorties by the besieged, and a circumvallation to protect the Roman rear. The Gallic cavalry was unable to impede the work and the blockade

Alise-Sainte-Reine, the excavations of Alésia

Amboise, chapel of St-Hubert

well as a 7C Merovingian church and Gallic 'huts'.

Environs: Flavigny-sur-Ozerain (12 km. through Les Laumes, SE): Perched on a wooded spur, the village, which is medieval in character, owes its existence to the abbey housing the relics of St.Regina. The Carolingian crypts and 18C buildings of this monastic establishment survive. The 13C Church of Saint-Genest was altered in the 15&16C.

Ambert	(8,100 inhab.)
63 Puy-de-Dôme	p.420☐K 11

This quiet, old town lies between wooded slopes on a small 'limagne' (the local word for plain) drained by the river Dore. A paper-making industry has been established here since the 15C. The old town with its tortuous streets has several fine 15&16C houses, as well as an unusual 19C circular town hall, built along the lines of the Paris corn-exchange.

Saint-Jean: (late-15C, early-16C), in local granite; late Flamboyant and Renaissance (Chapelle du Sacré-Coeur and bell-tower). Formerly, the church's main entrance was on the S. side, where there is a portal decorated to a high degree of finish, bearing inscriptions on each side of the pier. Inside, the pillars lack capitals, a typical feature of late Gothic, which accentuates the elegance of the nave. The first chapel on the left, opening on to the ambulatory, houses a 16C *Pietà*, which is venerated locally.

Environs: Moulin Richard de Bas (5.5 km. E.): The art of white paper manufacture is continued here following the same methods as in the 14C. It is the only one of the region's 300 mills that is still active, making paper by hand. Upstairs, the *Musée du Papier* is devoted to the old world of paper-making (furniture, associated objects) and the history of paper.

tightened. All attempts at counter-attack were beaten off and Vercingétorix surrendered himself to Caesar. He was strangled in Rome, after six years in captivity. The Gallic oppidum became a major Gallo-Roman city, which was abandoned by its inhabitants during the Merovingian period. All trace of it disappeared under a cover of earth and grass. The 19C digs fuelled polemical debates, with certain experts doubting that it was actually the site of Alésia. However, this has now been established.

The Alésia Excavations: Traces of Caesar's earthworks for the siege of Alésia are inconspicuous to the uninitiated but the plan of the later Gallo-Roman city is clearly visible. Excavations have revealed important remains (foundations of houses and shops, a temple, a theatre, streets), as

Amboise, château

Ambierle (1,420 inhab.)
42 Loire p.420□K 10

Halfway between the granite peaks of the Madeleine and the vast basin of Roanne, on the slopes of the Côtes Roannaise, this village is still surrounded by vineyards. It is dominated by the buildings of the former Cluniac priory. Built at the end of the 15C, the *church* is a fine example of the Flamboyant style: a very high, elegant nave; delicate capitals on the supporting pillars; and slender apsidal bays with splendid 15C stained glass (Christ in the centre flanked by life-size figures of saints). The altarpiece is a *Crucifixion*, a magnificent six-panelled polyptych, which was ordered in 1466 from a Brussels studio and which combines Flemish realism with subtle interplay of colours. The panels depict the donors and are attributed to Roger van der Weyden or one of his pupils. The *Musée Forézien* has a detailed display of life in the Forez region, with exact reconstructions of interiors, as well as exhibits of ancient trades, development of dress over a century, customs and superstitions.

Amboise (11,200 inhab.)
37 Indre-et-Loire p.414□H 7

Amboise's setting is one of the most charming in the valley, consisting as it does of an island moored in the Loire, with its changing hues, a pale stone château on a flat spur, old houses and a shaded avenue (Promenade du Mail). The history of the town is closely intertwined with that of the elegant building dominating it (although of course, it goes back much further). The vast cellars hollowed out at the edge of the plateau are still known as the 'grenier de César' (the granary of Caesar). In 1434, after Amboise had been confiscated from the vassals of the Counts of Anjou, the Kings of France devoted themselves to altering, enlarging and embellishing the château, which originally had been purely a fortress. Much taken with the building so transformed by his ancestors, François I summoned Leonardo da Vinci to Amboise in 1516, and the 'universal genius' of the Renaissance spent his final years beside the Loire, dying at Clos-Lucé in 1519.

The Château: Imposing, in spite of the destruction of the 19C, and elegant to a still greater degree, the Château of Amboise was one of the first residences of the Kings of France to be built for pleasure. It is situated in the angle between the valley of the Loire and the valley of one of its tributaries. Its terrace has been turned into a garden. The *Chapelle Saint-Hubert*, an astonishingly carved Gothic jewel of a building, dates from the last decade of the 15C. The lintel of the fine portal shows St. Christopher bearing the Infant Jesus and St. Hubert kneeling before a deer (an illustration of the legend concerning the saint). The tympanum shows the Madonna and Child between Charles VIII and Anne of Brittany. The Flamboyant decoration of the interior is extraordinarily rich. The *Logis du Roi*, a Gothic building from the end of the 15C, faces the Loire. Windows of the fine Salle des États open on to the Balcon des Conjurés (balcony of the conspirators), where Protestant conspirators were hung in 1560. The two vaulted halls have been restored to their original appearance (they were altered when the Logis housed the Algerian Emir Abd-el-Kader, who was being held in France). The Tour des Minimes, which is next to the Logis du Roi, consists of a hollow central column around which a gently sloping ramp winds upwards, giving access to coaches and horses. The same is also true of the Tour d'Hurtault on the town side. The battlemented terrace offers a vast panorama of the Loire Valley and the towers of Tours Cathedral. Flanked by tur-

Amiens, cathedral

Amiens, museum, 16C painting

rets on the W., the *Aile Louis XII-François I* houses fine Gothic and Renaissance furniture and is hung with Aubusson tapestries; there are also portraits of the Orléans family (who have entrusted the château to a foundation).

Saint-Denis: The 12C church of a former Benedictine priory; it dates from the Romanesque period but is typically Angevin in style (fine ribs and curved vaults). In the 16C a secondary S. aisle was added. Many of the capitals were reworked but those of the first bay of the nave are intact, with their bizarre figures with animal heads. A recess in the wall contains a 16C marble funerary statue. Striking in its realism, this 'drowned woman' frozen by death had, according to report, the features of a mistress of François I, the frivolous wife of an obliging financier (Marie Gaudin, known as 'la belle Babou'). The *Musée de la Poste*, in the town centre, offers a complete history of the postal service, from the era of mail coaches onwards.

Clos-Lucé: 'A necessary pilgrimage of art and science'. François I gave this 15C manor to the famous painter, engineer and inventor, Leonardo da Vinci, one of the most wide-ranging geniuses of all time. He worked here at the end of his life, proposing to the King a system for regulating the untamed river Loire, and possibly outlining the plans for Chambord. Clos-Lucé still has the bed where he died; there are also some astonishing models made by IBM from his plans (water elevator, ventilation system, jack, prototype paddleboat, etc).

Environs: Pagode de Chanteloup (3 km., on the edge of the Forest of Amboise): An unusual and elegant structure standing on the edge of this vast area of forest and meres. It was built at the behest of the Minister Choiseul in the 18C, in imitation of the 'pagoda' in London. The pyramidal

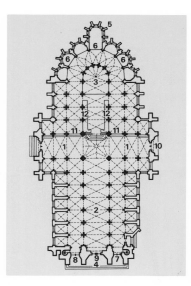

Amiens, cathedral of Notre-Dame 1 Transept **2** nave **3** choir **4** parvis **5** apse **6** radiating chapels **7** Portal of the Virgin **8** Portal of St. Firmin **9** Portal of the Beau Dieu d'Amiens **10** Portal of the Gilded Virgin **11** grille **12** stalls

tower blends Chinese and Louis XVI decoration. From its top there is a view stretching from Blois to Tours.

Ambronay   (1,270 inhab.)
01 Ain   p.421 □ M 10

A Benedictine abbey founded in the 9C made Ambronay famous. Although severely damaged, its remains are not without beauty. The *abbey church of Sainte-Marie* was built in the 13&15C. On the lintels of the portal there are depictions of the Life of the Virgin and the Resurrection of the Dead. Inside, the building is mainly Gothic and the chapel of Sainte-Catherine houses the 15C recumbent

Amiens, cathedral of Notre-Dame, detail of the Gallery of the Kings

figure of the abbot, Jacques de Mauvoisin, who was involved in the restoration of the church during his own lifetime. The choir is lit by refined 15C stained-glass windows. The restored chapterhouse is itself pure Gothic in style. The cloisters are composed of a series of openings decorated by beautiful stone tracery and they are unusual in having a gallery and a lean-to roof.

Amiens	(136,000 inhab.)
80 Somme	p.410□I 3

Amiens is the capital of Picardy and today a modern city; it has been rich since the Middle Ages thanks to its prosperous textile industry; and its velvets are famous. The 340 ft. Tour Perret dominates the town and it, together with the vast university campus and the centrally situated concrete and glass Maison de la Culture, provides evidence of this contemporary development. Often in the path of invasions, Amiens has suffered many disasters, although the works of art and objects in the richly stocked *Musée de Picardie* have escaped these. In the low-lying part of the town by the Somme, which here sluggishly divides its streams, the Marché sur l'Eau (Water Market) still receives long, black flat-bottomed boats laden with vegetables and fruit from the *hortillonages*, market gardens which are intersected by canals. Some fine, old houses, the Logis du Roi, the Maison du Sagittaire (16C) and the Hôtel des Trésoriers de France (17C), remain.

The Cathedral of Notre-Dame: War

Amiens, N.-D., statues by portal

has failed to destroy this glorious testimony to Christian faith. 476 ft. long, 230 ft., wide at the transept, and with a vault almost 140 ft. high, it is the largest cathedral in France and a jewel of Gothic art. It is not just the size that causes amazement, but the uniform style and the perfection and harmony of the proportions. Built in the purest 13C style, it is the Gothic cathedral *par excellence*. Work began in about 1220, the nave was completed in 1236 and the choir in 1268. Laid out in the form of a Latin cross on the site of a Romanesque building, it has 126 pillars and is crowned by a spire, which rises to 370 ft. Such a building was the work of audacious and accomplished builders. A broad, open space allows one to take stock of the building, to admire the rich yet rigorous arrangement, the projection of the apse and the seven radiating chapels.

FAÇADE: The magnificent W. façade, which was completed in *c.* 1236, is enlivened by the clever balance of form and space. There are three tall, majestic, imposingly vaulted portals, which are separated by powerful buttresses. Above these, there are 22 colossal statues in the gallery of the Rois de France (Kings of France), and on top of this there is an open passage. Higher still, between the bays of the towers, there is a large rose window with fine tracery, and above this there is the Galerie des Sonneurs (Bellringer's Gallery). The right portal is dedicated to the Virgin and the left one to St. Firmin, a 4C evangelist in Picardy. The pier of the central portal, at the heart of this 'bible of stone' that is the cathedral, bears the impassive, serene *Beau Dieu d'Amiens*, which is accompanied by a Last Judgement. While in the tympanum the dead experience the horrors of the Last Judgement, the majesty of this Christ seems to recall that all remains love and grace. The foundations of the three porches are decorated with quatrefoil bas-reliefs. On the left portal there is a fantastic calendar showing the signs of the zodiac and the labours of the months. The wealth of sculpture at Amiens covers a wide range of iconographical subjects. The portal in the S. transept (*c.* 1260) bears the *Vierge Dorée*. Its gilding has disappeared but she still smiles archly at the Infant Jesus and discreetly acknowledges her femininity. INTERIOR: The cathedral's marvels include a magnificent wrought-iron grill which separates the choir and the nave, an enigmatic weeping angel and the 110 Flamboyant Gothic, oak choir stalls (one of the most remarkable sets in France).

Musée de Picardie: On the ground floor are rooms containing Egyptian, Greek and Roman antiquities. On the first floor is one of the principal attractions of the museum: 15 paintings from the *Puy Notre-Dame d'Amiens*, a fraternity which had its base in the cathedral from the 14–18C and held competitions in poetry and painting there each year. In the N. picture gallery are works by 18C French masters including Fragonard, La Tour and Boucher and also sculpture by Puget, Houdon and Pigalle. In the Lavalard rooms there are Italian (Tiepolo), Dutch (Frans Hals, van Goyen) and Spanish (El Greco) works. There are also contemporary works by Matisse, Vuillard, Lurçat and Rouault among others.

Environs: Picquigny (10 km. NW): The impressive ruins of the fortress of the representatives of the Bishop of Amiens dominate the Somme Valley. A strong wall surrounds a keep.

Ancenis (7,300 inhab.)
44 Loire-Atlantique p.413☐E 7

There is a *château* at Ancenis because of its strategic position on the Loire, bordering in the E. the former Duchy of Brittany. Built at the end of the 10C, today it consists of a postern flanked by powerful round towers, which are decorated with gargoyles, a vaulted gallery and wing from the Renaissance, and some 17C pavilions. Nearby, the church of *Saint-Pierre-et-Saint-Paul* (15&16C, highly restored) contains a font under a fine 18C canopy.

Ancy-le-Franc (1,240 inhab.)
89 Yonne p.415☐L 7

The vast Château d'Ancy was built for the Clermont-Tonneau family between 1546 and 1622, probably to the plans of Primaticcio. A square, grey building with small corner pavilions, it has a severe exterior appearance, which conceals the charms of its interior. This strong, sober building encloses a square, galleried courtyard, a Renaissance masterpiece. Each of the inner façades bears the motto of the first owners, a family which was ruined by the purchase of the county of Tonnerre: *Si omnes ego non* ('Although all have disowned you, I will not'). This mysterious phrase refers to the loyalty of an ancestor to the Pope.

Anet, château

Ancy is a veritable museum of the decorative arts, with its panelling, frescos in the Salle des Nudités and the Chambre de Diane, superb ceilings and furniture from the Renaissance and other periods. The panelling of the 16C chapel was painted by a gifted artist. The Galerie de la Pharsale is decorated with pictures illustrating the defeat of Pompey by Caesar at Pharsalus. Its counterpart, the Galerie des Sacrifices, is decorated with cameos. Built by Louvois, who bought the château but scarcely visited it, the outbuildings are arranged in a horseshoe around a square courtyard (exhibitions of contemporary art). There is a charming folly dating from 1761 hidden in a clump of trees.

Andlau (1,950 inhab.)
67 Bas-Rhin p.417☐O 5

A large, typical Alsace village lying on the slopes of a valley in the Vosges, Andlau clusters around a monastic establishment, which was founded in the 9C by the wife of the Emperor Charles the Fat. Rebuilt at the end of the 17C and the beginning of the 18C, the former abbey church retains some remarkable Romanesque elements: a powerful porch with a frieze running across it, a richly decorated portal, and a large crypt which is divided into two parts, one laid out about 1050 and the other after 1080. An ancient statue represents *St. Richard's Bear*—tradition has it that in the Middle Ages a bear was fed in the abbey's courtyard. The monastery buildings date from the 17&18C. The village contains many old houses.

Anet (1,800 inhab.)
28 Eure-et-Loir p.410☐H 5

The Château d'Anet was built for Diane de Poitiers, widow of Louis de Brézé and mistress of Henri II. The King financed the work, which began in 1548, under the direction of Philibert Delorme. Confiscated as national property at the Revolution, and then sold, this beautiful building

Angers, château, aerial view

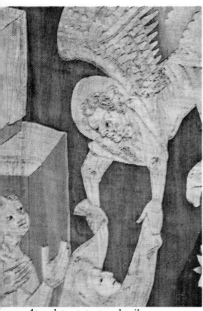

Apocalypse tapestry, detail

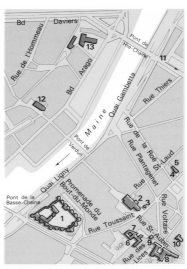

Angers 1 Château **2** cathedral of Saint-Maurice **3** Maison d'Adam **4** Logis Pincé **5** Musée Turpin de Crissé **6** Logis Barrault **7** Musée des Beaux-Arts et David d'Angers **8** Préfecture **9** Tour Saint-Aubin **10** church of Saint-Martin **11** church of Saint-Serge **12** church of the Trinité **13** Hôpital Saint-Jean

has been partly destroyed. The magnificent and monumental portal of the château is dominated by a bronze group representing a stag being attacked by hounds. The tympanum bears a cast of the *Nymphe de Fontainbleau*. This work (created for the Château de Fontainbleau, the original of which is in the Louvre) was executed in France by the great sculptor Benvenuto Cellini.

| **Angers** | (143,000 inhab.) |
| 49 Maine-et-Loire | p.413□F 7 |

A beautiful and rather severe city of wide avenues and gardens, Angers seems protected for ever by its impressive feudal fortress set above the Maine. The grey of the town centre contrasts with the whiteness of the surrounding, newer districts. The town itself, lying on the edge of the Loire Valley, still benefits from its position at the intersection of river and land routes. The Romans built baths, a circus, an amphitheatre and, in the 3C, defences. For a long period power was in the hands of a line of Counts. One of these, Geoffroi, liked to wear a sprig of broom (genêt) in his hat, and the surname Plantagenêt was passed on to his descendants. As a result of marriages, Angevin princes became powerful sovereigns, ruling in England, Normandy and almost the whole of the west of what is now France. This empire collapsed during the Hundred Years War. The last Angevin prince, the good but weak King René, bequeathed Anjou to France on his death in 1480.

Château: A massive structure which has

defied the wear of centuries, the castle was built at great speed between 1230 and 1240. Alternating layers of dark slate blocks and beds of white stone were used in the construction and the thick curtain wall is surrounded by dry moats and flanked by seventeen large, round towers. The tops of the latter were removed on the orders of Henri III. The citizens of Angers had asked for the defences to be completely dismantled but the governor delayed the work. Although the castle is rugged and austere externally, it is very different on the inside. The main courtyard contains some elegant 15C buildings: the beautifully vaulted Sainte-Geneviève chapel with its carved keystones, the Logis Royal (Royal Residence), and the Logis du Gouverneur, which was built against the ramparts and altered in the 18C.

The Tapestries: The chapel retains an original stained-glass window, and houses some remarkable Flemish tapestries from the end of the 15C. These include *The Passion* and *The Resurrection*. Panels of Angers' finest tapestries, *The Apocalypse Tapestries*, are hung along the walls of a modern gallery built half underground. This 'beau tapis' was left to the cathedral by King René. It was woven between 1373 and 1380 by the Parisian weaver Nicolas Bataille, from the cartoons of Hennequin de Bruges. Confiscated during the Revolution and cut up, this magnificent tapestry was sold in 1843 by the Administration des Domaines as worthless. It illustrates the Apocalypse of St. John in reds and blues, and originally measured 550 ft. in length, three-quarters of which has now been rehung.

Cathedral of Saint-Maurice: An elegant Romanesque-Gothic building, built in the 12&13C on the site of earlier churches. Saint-Maurice has a beautiful sculpted portal with 17C door leaves. In the tympanum there is *Christ in Majesty*

Angers, château, Porte du Châtelet

surrounded by symbols of the Evangelists, angels and the elders of the Apocalypse; the arches and piers display figures from the Old Testament. The large nave is lit from the left by fine stained glass from the end of the 12C, and the choir by iridescently coloured glass (1230–60). The beautiful rose-window of the N. transept has 15C stained glass.

Beside the cathedral stands the unusual *Maison d'Adam*, a picturesque 15C house with finely worked corbels, which is still joined to the old Bishop's Palace.

The *Logis Pincé*, Rue Lepneveu, was built from 1523 onwards for an important citizen, Jean de Pincé. It houses the varied collection of the *Musée Turpin de Crissé*. Works of art from all periods are well represented in this museum but it is particularly rich in Oriental Art, such as masks and Japanese prints. The 15C *Logis Barrault* houses the twin *Musée des Beaux-Arts et David d'Angers* in the rooms where Catherine de Medici and the governors of Anjou stayed. One section contains paintings and sculpture by artists such as Philippe de Champaigne, José de Ribera, Jordaens, Watteau, Fragonard, Tiepolo, Ingres, Delacroix, Corot, Houdon, Rodin, and Rude, whilst another section houses statues, busts and sculptures by Pierre Jean-David, known as David d'Angers (1788–1856).

The *Préfecture* occupies some former abbey buildings, which were altered considerably in the 17C but which retain some fine 12C features (beautiful Romanesque arcades decorated by Poitevin sculptors, beneath a modern gallery). The *Tour Saint-Aubin*, from the mid 12C, served as a belfry and keep for the abbey. The church of *Saint-Martin* dates from the 11&12C (with an elegant 13C Angevin Lady Chapel). The church of *Saint-Serge* has an 11&13C Angevin choir and a 15C nave.

The *Quartier de la Doutre* (across the Maine) was prosperous in the Middle Ages but subsequently gradually abandoned. The picturesque Place de la Laiterie is surrounded by fine, restored 15C houses. The church of the *Trinité*, once the monastery's dependence, dates from the 12C and has two fine Romanesque doorways. The most important building on the left bank is the *Hôpital Saint-Jean*, built 1180 – 1210. Roofed with Angevin vaults, as bold as they are light, the former Salle des Malades is full of colour. The walls are hung with the ten tapestries of *Le Chant du Monde*, an enigmatic cosmic work by Jean Lurçat. 259 ft. long and 14 ft. 5 in. high, it is full of symbols and allegories. It was woven at the Gobelins factory between 1957 and 1966, when the painter died without having produced the final cartoons. The cloisters consist of two 12C galleries and a Renaissance gallery. The chapel dates from the early 13C (remnants of paintings). Previously a barn, the grenier Saint-Jean (granary) contains fine restored woodwork.

Angoulême, cathedral, hinges   *Angles-sur-l'Anglin, ruins of the château* ▷

Angoulême, cathedral, Christ in majesty

historic sculptures have recently been discovered downstream.

Angoulême (50,500 inhab.)
16 Charente p.419□G 10

Perched on a limestone spur at the confluence of the Charente and the Anguienne, Angoulême is dominated by the white mass of its cathedral. A place of shelter in antiquity, it was integrated with Aquitaine under the Roman Empire. It was evangelized by St.Ausonius and later by the popular St.Cybard, after whom a score of churches in the region have been named. Fortified in the 13C, the capital of Charente suffered during the Wars of Religion. In the 16C, it enjoyed days of pomp and ceremony, when Marguerite de Valois, the sister of François I, surrounded herself with a court of artists and scholars.
Modern Angoulême presents two aspects. The aristocratic and bourgeois upper part (le plateau) and the commercial lower part (l'houmeau), where the hero of Balzac's *Illusions Perdues* was born. The town offers a mixture of the *Ancien Régime*, with quiet, paved streets lined by fine houses, and the variety of a medium sized industrial town.
The Ramparts: The ramparts of Angoulême, although largely demolished, still retain numerous towers, both round and square, and they offer a pleasant shaded promenade with a view over the beautiful countryside of the Charente.
The only parts of the château of the Counts of Angoulême to survive are the 13C polygonal or Lusignan tower and the 15C round or Valois tower, in which Marguerite d'Angoulême was born. These were preserved by the architect Abadie, when he built the Gothic-Renaissance Hôtel de Ville on the site of the château in the last century.

Cathedral of Saint-Pierre (12C): The

Angles-sur-l'Anglin (580 inhab.)
86 Vienne p.419□H 8/9

130 ft. above the river, the old houses of Angles-sur-l'Anglin cluster around the extensive ruins of its feudal castle. Like Chauvigny, it is evidence of the temporal power of the Bishops of Poitiers; it was abandoned in the 18C. The ruins of the fortress, which was a formidable stronghold in the Middle Ages, stand on the top of a steep spur and are over 460 ft. in length. The rectangular keep, the curtain wall with round towers, the logis ((residence) and the chapels all date from different periods (12–15C). All that remains of the Abbey of Saint-Croix is a curiously worn façade and a bay of the 12&13C church. The cemetery contains a 15C hosanna cross. Rock shelters with pre-

façade of the cathedral of Saint-Pierre is one of the most beautiful ranges of Romanesque sculpture in the W. of France. The iconographic repertoire and the plastic quality of the many figures, which were the work of various sculptors, elegantly conveys the religious intensity of the Middle Ages. Under Girard (the Papal Legate who undertook to replace the previous cathedral), sculpture, previously confined to the portals' tympanums spread to the façade. Themes used include the *Ascension* and *The Last Judgement*: There is a procession of the Apostles representing the Church triumphant, angels acting as ushers for Christ in majesty, who is surrounded by the symbols of the four Evangelists. Then there are the chosen and the damned, amongst which one can see Dives, his face torn by a serpent. The beauty of this façade contrasts with the sobriety of the interior. The nave with its row of domes poses the question raised by many other churches in the SW, namely, what is the origin of this form of vaulting? It originated in the East but how did it reach Aquitaine? The first example appeared in the 11C at Cahors. Girard, who as a canon travelled through different regions, would have seen the domes of Périgueux Cathedral, then under construction. At a time when interesecting ribs were unknown, domes were the only way to cover such a large space. Despite a certain coldness, the overall effect is not without majesty. The central drum dome is by Abadie, who restored the cathedral (1866 –85). He rebuilt the tall, five-storeyed, stepped-back tower, whose top storey is pierced by richly sculpted bays. The church of *Saint-André* has a 12C porch and a 15C nave. The hospital has an interesting chapel.

Musée Municipal: Housed in the former Bishop's Palace (12C, restored 15C), it contains a number of collections: prehistory, Romanesque art, 17,18&19C paintings, etc. *Musée de la Société d'Archéologie:* a col-

Annecy, Palais de l'Isle

lection of stones in the garden; local and regional antiquities inside.

Environs: Saint-Michel (5 km. W.): In the suburbs of Angoulême, this small industrial district has a curious 12C Romanesque church. Built on an unusual plan, resembling that of a baptistery, it is octagonal with eight apsidioles at the corners. It is roofed by a ribbed dome and lantern. The interesting carving is confined to the portal and the arcades of the sides apsidioles. The tympanum shows St. Michael slaying the dragon. It is one of the most expressive representations of the archangel and was skilfully executed by a travelling artist on a pilgrimage. According to the chronicle, the church was built 'to receive in this place the poor of Christ'; it was a chapel-refuge on the pilgrimage route to Santiago de Compostela.

Anjony (château)
15 Cantal   p.420☐J 12

Perched on a rocky spur dominating the
valley of the Doire, this 15C fortress has
undergone few alterations in the course of
the centuries and displays a perfect unity
of style. There is a large, three-storeyed rectangular keep, strengthened by four corner
towers. The low wing was added in the
18C. The residence, on the second floor
of the fortress, is decorated by 16C frescos
representing the nine Champions and it
contains some fine early 17C furniture.
The two other halls also house valuable
furniture, paintings and tapestries. The
chapel, which is in one of the corner
towers, is covered by frescos of the life and
passion of Christ. One of the niches contains Notre-Dame d'Anjony, a black Virgin of the Auvergne school.

Annecy   (55,000 inhab.)
74 Haute-Savoie   p.421☐N 10

Bonne-Fontaine, château (Antrain)

Annecy, situated on the edge of a beautiful lake, like some town out of an operetta,
can be traced back to a prehistoric lakeside
town, the remains of which have been
found close to the small Île des Cygnes (Island of Swans). A Gallo-Roman trading
centre on the Vienna-Geneva route, it
prospered on the shores of the lake but was
then abandoned during the barbarian invasions. Annecy developed around the
château, after the installation of the Counts
of Geneva (13C), followed by the Bishops
of the town. It became the capital of an important region and then part of Savoy in
the 15C. It benefited from the settlement
of the religious communities expelled from
Geneva during the Reformation. St.
Francis de Sales lived there from 1602 until
his death. He is buried in the basilica close
to St.Jane de Chantal, who founded the Order of the Visitation with him. Jean-
Jacques Rousseau was 16 years old when
he met Mme. de Warens at Annecy.

Château: An irregular group dominating
the town, built between the 12C (the Tour
de la Reine/Queen's Tower) and the 17C.
The Vieux-Logis (Old Residence) dates
from the 14C, and the Nemour and New
Residences from the 16C. Now restored,
the château houses a *Musée Régional*. Old
Annecy is centred on the Thiou, a canal-
ized outlet for the lake, where there is a
charming jumble of bright waters, passageways, arcades, coloured façades, and fine
old houses. A fortified house on an island
in the Thiou, the *Palais de l'Isle*, dates in
part from the 12C. The church of *Saint-
Maurice* was founded by the Dominicans
in the 15C; on a pillar there is a 16C fresco,
the *Descent from the Cross* by Pourbus the

elder. The nearby 17C *Church of Saint-François* was a dependency of the first Visitation monastery. The *Cathedral of Saint-Pierre* (1520–35), which is oriented N/S, has a tall nave and no transepts. Jean-Jacques Rousseau belonged to its choir. A 236 ft. spire dominates the *Basilica of the Visitation*, a large church completed in 1930. Its crypt has been hollowed out of the rock and houses a polychrome 16C wooden Virgin said to have miraculous properties. *Saint-Bernadette-d'Albigny*, in concrete, metal and wood is one of the successes of the contemporary Savoyard architect Maurice Novarina (1963).

Environs: Annecy-le-Vieux (2.5 km. NE): The church has an arcaded 12C belfry and there is a famous bell-foundry, which was established in 1796. **Château de Menthon-Saint-Bernard** (10 km. SE): Picturesque manor with keep and turrets built 13–15C. **Chateau de Montrottier** (10 km. via Lovagny): 15C keep, a feudal building with some 19C alterations; it houses a wide variety of collections belonging to the Académie Florimontane, a scholarly society founded in 1610.

Antibes	(56,400 inhab.)
06 Alpes-Maritimes	p.426☐O/P 14

Surrounded by commonplace buildings and forming a single resort with Juan-les-Pins and Cap d'Antibes, Antibes was originally a Greek settlement. 16C ramparts plunge straight into the sea. Maupassant wrote his *Sur l'Eau* here in 1885 and the writer Jacques Audiberti (1899–1966) was born here. A truly Mediterranean town, it is a captivating museum of old stone and the 'quarter ancien' is a tempting place to wander through. The *Antipolis* can be studied in the *Musée Archéologique* (Archaeological Museum) of the Bastion Saint-André, which displays the results of underwater excavations. Traces of the Roman city can be seen in the Cours Masséna. The *former cathedral* retains Romanesque features and a 12C bell tower, although the greater part of it is 17C.

Château Grimaldi and Musée Picasso: The sober, proud 14&15C Grimaldi Château houses a collection of Gallo-Roman archaeology and an important collection of the works of Pablo Picasso, mostly dating from 1946 (sketches, tapestries, sculptures, ceramics). The terrace offers a panoramic view and has a display of the forceful statues by Germaine Richier.

Cap d'Antibes. A 13–16C chapel dedicated to Notre-Dame, and the villa of the botanist Thuret, which is set in a beautiful, exotic garden. The Batterie du Graillon houses a *Musée Naval et Napoléonien*, which concentrates on the return from Elba.

Antrain	(1,650 inhab.)
35 Ille-et-Vilaine	p.413☐E 5

Set in undulating countryside, at the confluence of the Couesnon and the Loisance. A number of 15&16C houses have survived along its narrow, sloping streets. The church of *Saint-André* scarcely shows its Romanesque origins except for the semicircular portal, which is flanked by buttresses. Unusually for this region, the S. door, known as the 'porte des femmes' (ladies' door), has a tympanum beneath a saddleback roof. The interior has no aisles and is chiefly remarkable for its ribbed vault over the crossing.

Environs: Château de Bonne-Fontaine (2 km. S.): 16C château in a park of old trees (where the Duchess Anne dispensed justice). It is a fine fortified build-

Arc-et-Senans, former royal salt works designed by Ledoux

ing with battlemented round towers and machiolated turrets surrounding the main building. The latter is pierced by mullioned windows and dormer windows with stone mullions and transoms. **Château du Rocher-Portail** (10 km. SE): Near Saint-Brice-en-Coglès. A proud, classical house standing beside a pool, which supplies water for the moat. The left wing has a fine Renaissance gallery opening on to the main courtyard through semicircular arches. An elegant stone balustrade marks the site of what was a drawbridge.

Apt	(11,700 inhab.)
84 Vaucluse	p.425 □ M 14

Surrounded by hills, this small, active town was originally a Roman colony. It was the seat of a bishop until the Revolution. Since the Middle Ages it has been the main centre of preserves and crystallized fruit (Mme. de Sévigné called it a 'preserving pan'). The former cathedral of *Sainte-Anne* dates mainly from the 12C but it has lost its Romanesque appearance following alterations in the 14&17C. The chapel of Sainte-Anne, with an octagonal dome, was not quite complete when, in 1660, Anne of Austria came to pray before the relics of her patron saint (reliquary above the altar). The choir covers a double Romanesque and pre-Romanesque crypt. Rich cathedral treasure, including the famous 'veil of Saint Anne', a decorated piece of eastern cloth dating from the 11C.

Environs: Saignon (4 km. SE): A village and belvedere dominated by a crag. It has a 12C Romanesque church, formerly at-

Argenton-Château, portal of the church of Saint-Gilles

tached to an abbey, which had itself been founded before the 10C; façade 16C. Sober in style, its only decoration is in the choir.

Vieux-Pont (Old Bridge) over the Cuisance one can see the towers of the old wall. Arbois controls access to the 'reculée' or blind valley, where the river shoots over waterfalls out of a cave.

Arbois	(4,250 inhab.)
39 Jura	p.421☐N 8

Surrounded by its famous vineyard, the large village of Arbois is a picturesque sight straddling the Cuisance. Pasteur spent a studious childhood here and his family's house, which has not changed, may be visited. The church of *Saint-Just* is distinguished by its gilded yellow bell tower capped by a bulbous dome (16C). It contains a beautiful Gothic *Madonna and Child*. The Place de la Liberté has some interesting arcaded houses (18C). From the

Arbresle (L')	(4,250 inhab.)
69 Rhône	p.420☐L 10

A small town with an old centre on the edge of the Beaujolais region and the Monts du Lyonnais, L'Arbresle contains a church from the 13&15C, which has old stained glass. Houses mellowed by age cluster around the church, (remains of a medieval château at the edge of the hill). 2 km. away a cubist bell tower draws one's attention to the *Couvent de la Tourette*, built (1957–9) on a green slope in the valley of the Brévenne. All concrete, it is the work of Le Corbusier and the extreme rigour of its bare, dry style is striking, with geometrical interplay of horizontal, vertical and diagonal lines. It houses the Thomas More and Albert le Grand religious centres.

Arc-et-Senans	(1,230 inhab.)
25 Doubs	p.421 □ N 8

Arc-et-Senans entered history in the 18C with the development of a salt-works. Although some architects are content just to build, others want to change the world. Claude Nicolas Ledoux (1736–1806) was one of the latter. The former royal salt works, his grandest work (1773–9) is not just a fine, monumental group. Passing through the entrance portico of six Doric columns the visitor enters a different universe. The 'City' as built by Ledoux, in its functional organization of space, the rigour of its geometrical forms, the arrangement and decoration of the buildings, expresses a view of man, his work and leisure. A partial realization of a Utopia, Arc-et-Senans reflects the desire to found a better world. Salt-working finished at the end of the last century but the unusual complex, which Ledoux was unable to complete, remains almost intact. Combining the beautiful with the functional, the buildings are arranged in a semicircle. The buildings devoted to the various trades are arranged around the periphery and face towards the centre, where the director's residence is flanked by two factory buildings. A factory with the atmosphere of a temple, it displays both a nostalgia for the antique and a strange modernism.

The existing buildings (which are but a part of the 'new town' planned in Ledoux's scheme) house a foundation whose aims the visionary architect would have shared.

It is devoted to futurology, and its purpose is to sketch out a 'probable history' of the future.

Aregno: see **Corsica**

Argentan	(17,500 inhab.)
61 Orne	p.410 □ G 5

This peaceful town controls a communications network, and during the battles of August 1944 it suffered severely. It was the birthplace of Fernand Léger. Much of its character has been lost, but careful restoration — virtually rebuilding in certain parts — has saved *Saint-Germain*, a light and elegant church built in the 15–17C. It has a magnificent Flamboyant porch on one side and its plan is highly original. Nearby there is a severe 14C château and its former chapel, which has a pretty 15C doorway. The 15C Tour Marguerite is a remnant of the demolished fortifications. *Saint-Martin*, a restored 16C church, has fine 15&16C stained glass in the clerestory of the choir.

Environs: Interesting churches at **Écouché (9 km. SW) and at Saint-Christophe-le-Jajolet** (10 km. S.), where there is a beautiful *Burial of the Virgin*, a primitive Flemish painting. The 18&19C château of **Sassy** stands close to the latter village, surrounded by tiers of terraces.

Argenton-Château	(1,200 inhab.)
79 Deux-Sèvres	p.418 □ F 8

Protected by the remains of its walls, Argenton-Château lies on the E. edge of the Vendée. It stands on a rock at the confluence of the Argenton and the Ouère. The old château was the home of the chronicler Philippe de Commynes, the friend and historian of Louis XI. The only parts of this fortress left are the curtain wall and a chapel, which has a fresco in its Romanesque apse.

Saint-Gilles: Founded in the 11C and enlarged in the 15C, it owes its renown to the remarkable Romanesque W. doorway, which belongs to the Saintonge style of façade (see the Abbaye aux Dames in Saintes). Here, a single arch occupies the entire space between the side buttresses. Its archivolts display traditional themes, dear to the imagination of the region: angels supporting a central medallion; the battles of the Vices and the Virtues, illustrating the *Psychomachia*, a 4C poem composed by Prudentius; and the foolish and wise Virgins, another theme favoured by sculptors; these are followed by the Apostles, and the signs of the zodiac accompanied by the labours of the months. Between the archivolt and the cornice there are highly decorated spandrels; that on the left represents the banquet of Dives and on the right there is a boat carrying the

Argenton s/C., chapel of St-Benoît

damned to hell, the elect being gathered to Abraham's bosom.

Argenton-sur-Creuse   (6,800 inhab.)
36 Indre   p.419☐H 9

A modest town in the S. of Berry with old houses grouped along the river, their sloping roofs covered in slates or brown tiles. From the Pont-Vieux the town unfolds and its loggias and galleries are reflected in the Creuse. Beyond the bridge, the *Chapel of Saint-Benoît* (15&16C) has a 15C statue of the Madonna and Child. The picturesque Rue de la Coursière crosses the upper town and leads to *Notre-Dame-des-Bancs*. This pilgrimage chapel was rebuilt in the 15C; it is surmounted by a large gilded statue of Notre-Dame d'Argenton (19C).

Environs: Saint-Marcel (2 km. N.): An old village dominating the right bank of the Creuse, and standing on the site of the Gallo-Roman city of *Argentomagus*. Important finds have been recovered in the course of excavations and these are displayed in the small *Musée du Prieuré*. The church (11&12C) has a massive bell tower and contains some fine 16C statues and a 15C fresco. Church 'Treasure' includes two shrines, a carved wooden one of the 12C and the other a 14C one in gilded copper, decorated with Limoges enamel. It also houses the arm and reliquary bust of St. Marcel (14C).

Arles   (50,400 inhab.)
13 Bouches-du-Rhône   p.425☐L 14

Set in nondescript, modern surroundings, this splendid town was described by Chateaubriand as an 'open air museum'. Greek, Roman, medieval and thoroughly Provençal, Arles combines a distant Celto-

Arles, the arena

Arles 1 Musée Réattu **2** Muséon Arlaten **3** Hôtel-de-Ville **4** church of Saint-Trophime **5** cloister **6** arena **7** theatre **8** church of Notre-Dame-la-Major **9** Alyscamps **10** Saint-Honorat **11** Musée Lapidaire Païen **12** Musée Lapidaire Chrétien **13** baths

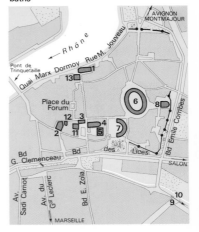

Ligurian past with the age of photography, which is well represented in the *Musée Réattu*. The city where Van Gogh painted ceaselessly (in between attacks of insanity), is a major archaeological source, ruins and monuments bearing witness to a long and enthralling history. Arles (*Arlath*: town in the marsh) was linked to the Greeks of Marseilles and subsequently became an important Roman city. A religious centre from the 4C, Arles received the Emperor Constantine on several occasions and acted as a subsidiary capital after the foundation of Constantinople. Plagued by invasions, it was the capital of a Burgundian-Provençal kingdom but in the 10C it became part of the Holy Roman Empire. Attached to Provence, in 1481 it was joined with it to France. The creation of the

Muséon Arlaten by Mistral and the activities of the Félibrige poets, made it the spiritual centre of Provence.

The *Place de la République* lies at the heart of old Arles and is dominated by an obelisk of Egyptian granite from the Roman Arena. The 16C (rear façade) and 17C *Hôtel de Ville* surround a tower (1555) bearing a statue of Mars known as the *Homme de Bronze*. The entrance hall on the ground floor is spanned by a skilfully constructed flat vault. There is a statue of Mistral in the *Place du Forum*, which occupies virtually the same site as the ancient forum.

Saint-Trophime and its cloisters: An exceptional Romanesque group, influenced by antique art. A former cathedral, it has a nave and two aisles, as is normal in Provençal Romanesque. The building dates from the 11C (transept) and 12C (the tall, narrow nave). The choir and ambulatory are 15C, whilst the Flamboyant *Chapelle des Rois* (Kings' Chapel) is 17C. In the second half of the 12C a *portal* was added to a severe façade. This famous portal of Saint-Trophime is like a monument on its own, a sort of triumphal arch. It has an important and remarkable range of statues, relating, in particular, to the Childhood of Christ, the Last Judgement and the Apocalypse. A hieratical Christ in Majesty reigns in the tympanum with the symbols of the Evangelists; the lintel depicts the wise Apostles. St.Peter and St.John, on the left, and St.Paul and St.Andrew, on the right, flank the entrance to the church. To the right of the doorway, above the statues of St.James the Less and St.Philip, there is a spectacular procession of the damned, who are being dragged naked to hell by devils, whilst on the other side there is a peaceful procession of the redeemed. A real book in stone, it would once have been read by the pilgrims gathered in Arles en route for Santiago de Compostela. The W. group shows, in overall outline, marked Roman influence. The

Arles, Les Alyscamps

cloisters are entered through a 14C doorway and are amongst the most beautiful in Provence. Half Romanesque, half Gothic (12&14C), they retain remarkable capitals and statues.

The Arena and Theatre: Today, bullfights, Provençal races and folk spectacles take place in this immense 2C oval structure. Defensive towers were added in the 12C, and in the Middle Ages the amphitheatre was filled with buildings and turned into a citadel. Impressive, though mostly in ruins, the theatre dates from the beginning of Augustus's reign. The famous *Vénus d'Arles* (now in the Louvre) was found here, as well as an important series of statues, some of which are in the Museum of Pagan Art.

Notre-Dame-la-Major dates from the

14,16,17&18C, and has a 19C bell tower. Behind the church there are the remains of the Roman ramparts (1C BC), which were also used as medieval fortifications.

Alyscamps and Saint-Honorat: A pagan and Christian burial ground which fascinated Dante, Van Gogh and Gauguin. Today, Les Alyscamps is a long path bordered by empty or defaced tombs. This cemetery, which is the subject of numerous legends, takes its name from *Campi Elissi* ('Paradise of the Ancients'). Saint-Honorat is a rather motley building, which includes some Carolingian remains and is dominated by a remarkable octagonal bell tower. The Romanesque portal and the apse over the crypt were rebuilt in the 12C.

The Museums of Arles: Thanks to a long-standing local taste for collecting, which was revived by Mistral, Arles is a town of many and varied museums. Their contents range from Gallo-Roman antiquities to Picasso. The rich collections (from the excavations at Trinquetaille, the theatre, the forum and Les Alyscamps) of the *Musée lapidaire Païen* (Museum of Pagan Art) are housed in a strange, 17C church built in the southern Gothic style. A large Jesuit chapel, also 17C, houses the sarcophagi of the *Musée Lapidaire Chrétien* (Museum of Christian Art). These quite remarkable pieces are mainly from the time of Constantine (4C). The *Cryptoportiques*, a series of mysterious underground galleries, can be entered from the museum. These were 1C store-rooms, the layout of which probably corresponded to the cryptoportiques to be seen in the Museum of Christian Art. The former 'Place des Hommes', the Place du Forum was for centuries the living heart of the city. The remains of a vanished temple, two Corinthian columns, have been added to the corner of a house.

The statue of Mistral (1969) with his Mireille inscribed on a medallion is surrounded by railings which are in the form of the tridents used by the guardians of the Camargue.

The Musée Réattu is housed in two adjacent 15C buildings, near to the extensive baths built under Constantine. It offers a pleasant and clear display of a varied set of collections, ranging from 18C Dutch seascapes to the photographs of Man Ray, Richard Avedon, and Lucien Clergue. A series of small Picasso drawings has been added to numerous modern and contemporary works. The museum bears the name of the Arles painter Jacques Réattu, and displays several of his canvases.

The Muséon Arlaten was created by Frédéric Mistral, the great Provençal writer, who received the Nobel Prize in 1904. One of the founders of the Félibrige school of Provençal literature, Mistral worked for years to establish this somewhat old-fashioned but infinitely fascinating museum, which occupies a Gothic house. It is devoted to the history, traditions, legends, and craftsmen of old Provence. Displays of costumes and furniture and a genuine Camargue hut.

Environs: Montmajour (5 km. N.): Set on a pine-covered hill, the powerful abbey of Montmajour overlooks a vast watery area of rice fields, which the monks attempted to drain in the Middle Ages. Founded in the 10C, this Benedictine establishment prospered thanks to a famous pilgrimage. Stripped after being sold as national property during the Revolution, the abbey has been restored and strengthened. The Romanesque abbey church and cloisters are 12C, whilst the elegant 18C buildings, now ruined, were the work of Pierre Mignard, the nephew of the painter. **Fontvieille** ('fontaine vieille' or old spring) dozes (9 km. NE) amidst hills and pine forests shaped by the wind. Windmills, cypresses, silver-green olive trees, egg-shell stone and sparkling light, this is

Arras, Place des Héros

the Provence of Alphonse Daudet (1840–97), the most fantastic of the naturalist writers. The 'moulin de Daudet' (Daudet's mill), which houses a small museum devoted to him, almost makes one believe the writer when he says, 'It is from there that I write to you, my door wide open, in the good sun...' In fact the *Les Lettres de mon Moulin* novels were written in Paris.

Arnay-le-Duc   (2,500 inhab.)
21 Côte-d'Or   p.420☐L 8

An old town protected by ancient ramparts, where Henri IV fought the Catholic troops of the Duke of Mayenne. There are some old houses, a church (15&16C) with a beautiful vault, and behind the church a tower, which was formerly part of an old feudal château. A stream, the Arroux, springs from a Romanesque well.

Arras   (50,400 inhab.)
Pas-de-Calais   p.411☐J 2

The former capital of Atrébates and now the capital of Artois. Although Arras is expanding rapidly into a large modern town, it retains an architectural record of its former periods of prosperity.

The Old Town: There is no other city in northern France where the monuments and houses of the 17&18C, whether rebuilt, preserved or restored, form such a fine array. It is rich in quite unusual architecture, which reflects both the intense economic and industrial activity since the

Middle Ages and also the taste of its magistrates, who, two centuries ago, acted as enlightened town planners. Two squares are the pride of Arras, the *Grande Place* and the *Place des Héros*. The latter is dominated by the noble, Flamboyant bell tower (246 ft. high) of the Hôtel de Ville (rebuilding began in 1922), a markedly homogeneous masterpiece of Flemish architecture. The tall, narrow houses characteristic of these squares are all built to the same plan, known as 'à pas de moineau' (sparrow step), with shaped gables. The fronts are supported by colonnaded arcades, which form a continuous gallery-promenade all round the squares. In the lower town there is the unusual, octagonal *Place Victor-Hugo*.

Abbey of Saint-Vaast: A former abbey church, it is now the cathedral. Rebuilt in the 18C after frequently suffering damage, the Abbey of Saint-Vaast is one of the most successful pieces of classical, monastic architecture. The rigorous yet sober form tempers the scale and immensity of a building that is astonishing in its

Arras, Palais St-Vaast

monumental and majestic appearance. Its colossal staircase exemplifies this desire for grandeur and simplicity. The abbey buildings, the *Palais Saint-Vaast*, are no less striking. The cloisters are large and soberly decorated with capitals, garlands and roses. Despite their size (sides of 164 ft.), they are a model of balance and order. Purity of line, gentle curves and lightness all contribute to the serenity of the place. Part of the Palais Saint-Vaast houses the *Musée Municipal*, which perpetuates the tradition of 'Arras, town of art', displaying work and staging annual events. (Arras, meaning tapestry, was in general use in English and *arazzi* is an Italian word for tapestries.) A beautiful marble death-mask of a young girl (early-14C), pieces of Arras porcelain and paintings by Corot are amongst the museum's finest exhibits.

Environs: Les Crêtes du Sacrifice (N.): The noise and fury of battle have never spared this quiet city. In the First World War the nearby Artois hills were the scene of bitter clashes which cost the lives of thousands of men. The Canadian memorial at Vimy and the basilica of Notre-Dame-de-Lorette with its ossuary provide a solemn reminder of the battles.

Arthous (abbey)
40 Landes   p.422□E 14

Founded by Premonstratensians in 1160, the isolated abbey of Arthous was a stop on one of the routes to Santiago de Compostela. Used as a farm, it was already badly dilapidated when major restoration work was undertaken. The outside of the Romanesque apse and apsidioles is beautifully decorated and the monastery buildings themselves contain the interesting *Musée Archéologique*, with prehistoric tools, Magdalenian horse carvings, mosaics, and a boat hollowed out of a single tree trunk).

Environs: Hastingues (4 km. NW): A bastide founded by the English in 1305, rebuilt in the 16C. Old houses.

Assy (church)
74 Haute-Savoie   p.421☐O 10

The consecration of Assy's church in 1950 was an important event for contemporary religious architecture. The building is the work of Maurice Novarina, a Savoyard who employs regional traditions without slavishly following them. Responsible for, amongst others, Sainte-Bernadette d'Annecy and the Olympic village in Grenoble, in his design for Assy, Novarina did not produce anything that was revolutionary in architectural terms; rather, he employed new decorative ideas. Some of the greatest contemporary artists worked on Assy: Fernand Léger (mosaic for the façade), Marc Chagall (decoration of the Baptistery), Lurçat (tapestry in the choir), Bazaine and Rouault (stained glass), Germaine Richier (*Christ*), Matisse (ceramics), Braque (bas-relief), Bonnard (the painting *Saint François de Sales visitant un asile*), and Lipchitz (sculptures).

Aubazines
19 Corrèze   (650 inhab.)
                                    p.419☐H 11

This village clusters around the former abbey *church*, which was founded by St. Etienne of Aubazines. It was built at the beginning of the 12C at the same time as the monastery and is pure Cistercian in style, as simple outside as in. The nave, which unfortunately lost three bays in the 18C, is barrel vaulted and supported by fine pillars. Above the crossing there is a dome on pendentives and this in turn supports an octagonal tower. The austerity of the order of St.Bernard can be seen in the

grey glass windows (12C), in which the lead armature forms the only decoration. The left transept houses a remarkable and very simple 12C oak ecclesiastical cupboard. The right transept contains the magnificent, shrine-like tomb of St. Etienne. The monastery buildings are now occupied by an orphanage and retain the former Romanesque chapterhouse, the long corridor for the monks' cells, and a large kitchen.

Aubenas
07 Ardèche   (13,800 inhab.)
                                    p.425☐L 12

Finely placed on a hill dominating the basin of the Ardèche, the capital of Bas-Vivarais offers an extensive view over the valley. Aubenas has some fine Renaissance houses (the turret of the *Maison des Chimères*, opposite the château, is decorated with splendid gargoyles). The *château* built in the 12&15C was altered in the 17&18C. Glazed, multi-coloured tiles somewhat reduce the severity of this fortress, which

Assy, church, 'Passion' by Rouault

now houses the Hôtel de Ville. It is made up of a façade flanked by round, machicolated towers, a keep with watch-towers and a parapet walk, and a Renaissance courtyard. The *Chapel of Saint-Benoît*, the former chapel of the Benedictines of Aubenas, is an elegant, hexagonal 18C building and contains the mausoleum of Marshal d'Ornano and his wife (17C).

Environs: Largentière (4 km. SW): Takes its name from the silver-mining which took place there (10–15C). A picturesque town with arched alleyways, it is entered through the austere *Porte des Récollets* (the Gate of the Recollects — reformed Franciscans), a remnant of the former walls (some sections of the wall and the *Tour de l'Argentière* are still visible). The church of the *Assumption* (13C) has a tall three-sided apse and a Carolingian sarcophagus, and is to be found between the old town and the *château*, a sober 15C building restored in the 18C.

Aubeterre-sur-Dronne   (420 inhab.)
16 Charente   p.419□G 11

Although situated in the department of Charente, Aubeterre belongs to Périgord. Dominating a loop of the Dronne, this small town of winding lanes clings to the white chalk cliff from which it takes its name (*alba terra*, meaning white earth). It was once surrounded by a fortified wall with three gates, but all that remains are the ruins of a large round tower (the Tour Saint-Jean), and a fortified gateway, which consists of a square building with an upper machicolated gallery.

Saint-Jean: An underground church from the 11&12C, hollowed out of the chalk beneath the château. It is an unusual building, resembling the monolithic sanctuary in Saint-Émilion. The vast, barrel-vaulted

nave rises 63 ft. and opens into a lower apse, at the centre of which there is a reliquary. This too is cut from the rock and is decorated with clusters of columns and blind arcades, like the Holy Sepulchre in Jerusalem. Octagonal piers separate the nave from the single aisle and the entire W. side of this is taken up by a gallery, which is linked to the château. A piscina and some tombs have been discovered cut into the ground in the middle of the nave. The church was probably built to house relics of the Holy Sepulchre collected on the Crusade by Pierre II of Castillon, who held the château at that time. At the Revolution it was transformed into a saltpetre factory to produce explosives for the armies of the Republic.

Saint-Jacques: A former abbey church with an extensive Saintonge style Romanesque façade (12C) and multifoil doorway. The latter has 4 archivolts decorated with plant motifs framed by two arches with fine capitals.

In the old town, a number of houses with wooden galleries deserve particular attention: the crenellated tower of the former convent of the Poor Clares, the Tour des Apôtres (Apostles' Tower) and its residence (15,16&17C); the residence of the Cordeliers (17C); and the convent of the Minimes with its beautiful cloisters (17C).

Aubigny-sur-Nère   (5,600 inhab.)
18 Cher   p.415□I/J 7

Pleasant, small town, which preserves traces of the Stuarts who were its Scottish lords and who fought for the French. Aubigny is proud of its timber-framed houses and former château (15&16C), which is now the town hall. The *church* dates mainly from the 13C and, apart from Bourges Cathedral, it is the most interesting Gothic building in Haut-Berry.

Aubusson, Saint-Saens tapestry (Mobilier National)

Environs: Château de la Verrerie (11 km. SE): Standing by a lake, on the edge of a pleasant village, this château (15&16C) recalls the past activities of the region's glass makers. It houses furniture and tapestries, as well as the alabaster mourners from the tomb of Jean de Berry, which was destroyed in the Revolution.

Aubigny, château de la Verrerie

Aubusson	(6,900 inhab.)
23 Creuse	p.419☐I 10

Aubusson, at the confluence of the Creuse and the Bauze, is the epitome of the small, charming towns of central France, with its numerous old houses, jumble of roofs and towers, narrow streets and background of green hills. However, it owes its fame to the production of tapestry, an industry in which it has held undisputed sway since the 15C. Woven on horizontal frames, known as 'de basse lisse' (low warp), this industry flourished in the 16&17C. In 1665 Aubusson weavers were able to call themselves a royal factory and from then on the town mark was woven on each piece. The 18C was a brilliant period. Several painters came to the town and organized a school of drawing to teach the weavers. Under the direction of the master weavers of that time, Pierre de Saiglière, François Chapelle, Jean Palisson and Picon de Laubart, and inspired by Flemish painting and the works of such well-known painters as Boucher, Aubusson produced landscapes of trees and foliage and scenes of hunting and fishing. The Revolution ruined everything. Some workshops were restarted in the 19C but the tapestry did not recover its prestige until, in 1937 Jean Lurçat came to Aubusson. He was followed by numerous contemporary artists and a real renaissance began. The finest modern pieces are displayed in the exhibition organized in the Hôtel de Ville, from July to October, in the École Nationale des Arts Décoratifs (National School of the Decorative Arts) and in the galleries in the Grand-Rue.

The *Maison du Vieux Tapissier* (16C) is the picturesque home of a weaving family and it contains a display of the industry as it was. The *Maison Vallenet* has a corner watch-turret and two façades, one 16C and the other 18C, with elegant balconies. The *Tour de l'Horloge* (Clock Tower, 16C), formerly the watch-tower of the local viscount's castle, dominates the old Pont de la Terrade. The church of *Sainte-Croix* (13C) has three low aisles and houses a reliquary of the Holy Cross (17C), a bust of St.Barbara, (wood, 17C) and a tapestry of *The Vision of Constantine* after Raphael, dated 1770.

Auch	(25,100 inhab.)
32 Gers	p.423 □ G 14

The old city of Auch is situated on the Gers, a river prone to violent flooding. Gascon through and through, Auch is

Auch, cathedral of Ste-Marie, Renaissance choir stalls

dominated by what (along with Orléans), is the last of the great Gothic cathedrals. Begun in 1489 and consecrated in 1548, *Sainte-Marie* was only finished in the 17C, when the architects had some difficulty in adapting to the original style. Standing on the steep slope of the valley, the cathedral is famous for its stained-glass windows (choir, 1507–13) in magnificent reds and purples. The Renaissance oak stalls were carved in the 1520s, their decoration repeating the iconography of the stained glass. A stone and marble choir enclosure dates from 1609 and bears statues from the old rood-screen. The former, Archbishop's Palace (18C) houses the prefecture and a former chapel contains the varied collections of the *Musée d'Art et d'Archéologie*. The high school occupies a 16C former Jesuit college. The Tour des Prisons and the remains of the Officialité date from the 14C.

Aulnay

	(1,600 inhab.)
17 Charente-Maritime	p.418 □ F 10

The church of *Saint-Pierre* of Aulnay is one of the most attractive examples of Poitevin Romanesque style. It stands isolated on the old pilgrimage route to Santiago de Compostela, at the crossing of two pre-Romanesque roads (one of which leads from Angers to Saintes), surrounded only by tombstones and cypresses. The warm colour of the stone and the perfection of the carved decoration contribute to the visual harmony of this 12C sanctuary. The classical, pure plan of Aulnay is in the form of a Latin cross: nave and aisles, transept and apsidioles, choir and semicircular apse. The capitals are all finely worked and display a splendid variety of carving (elephants, Samson and Delilah, the sacrifice of Abel). The arches of the doorway of the S. transept exhibit a magnificent display of the effervescence of the medieval imagination: the Romanesque

bestiary side by side with the 24 elders of the Apocalypse, the Apostles and prophets supported by small atlantes. The W. façade is strengthened by thick buttresses and has two lanterns in which a light once shone for pilgrims. The arches of the central portal display the region's favourite themes: the signs of the zodiac, the wise and foolish Virgins, Virtues and Vices, and angels adoring the mystic lamb. On the left-hand arches, luxuriant plant motifs frame the Crucifixion of St.Peter and on the right-hand ones they surround a Christ between St.Peter and St.Paul. A particular feature of the apse is the eastern-style carving around the central window.

Auray

	(10,400 inhab.)
56 Morbihan	p.412 □ C 7

This Breton town, perched on the banks of the Loch (river Auray) has a charming harbour. The picturesque streets of the *Quartier Saint-Gouston* (across a sturdy 18C bridge of 4 arches) have 15C Guines

Aulnay, church, S. portal, detail

Auray, church of St-Gildas

Auray, old houses

style houses. The Renaissance style church of *Saint-Gildas* stands on the right bank. It has a restrained, two-storeyed bell-tower crowned by a lantern, and an elegant S. doorway. The high altar has a very fine 17C altarpiece; the legend of Saint Gildas is retold in some modern stained glass. The chapel of the Père-Éternel (Eternal Father) contains some remarkable carved wooden stalls from the Chartreuse (Charterhouse) d'Auray.

Environs: Sainte-Avoye (4 km. SE): A hamlet, typical of the region. It has an interesting Renaissance chapel with a carved and painted wooden rood screen showing Christ and his twelve Apostles. **Sainte-Anne-d'Auray** (8 km. N.): The sanctuary of Sainte-Anne-d'Auray has been the site of the biggest Breton pilgrimage ever since 1623, when the mother of the Virgin ap-

peared to Yves Nicolazic, a peasant. (The annual Great Pardon is on the 25 and 26 July.) The only old buildings to survive are the cloisters (1640), which have small windows above the arcades. In the basilica's right transept (19C) there is a gilded wooden statue of St.Anne. Part of the face of a primitive statue burnt during the Revolution is set in the plinth. The *church treasure* contains a collection of votive paintings, the oldest dating from the 17C, in addition to numerous gifts and legacies, a relic of the saint and ornaments offered by Anne of Austria.

Aurillac	(33,400 inhab.)
15 Cantal	p.419 □ I 12

Capital of the Haute-Auvergne. The new

parts of this modern commercial town spread up the valley's slopes, but the old districts of pretty houses squeezed against the ramparts of the abbey church and the walk along the Jordanne still survive. Aurillac or *Aureliacum* undoubtedly originated as a Gallo-Roman estate, the property of a certain Aurelius. The town began to form around the abbey, which had been founded in the 10C by St.Géraud, a count from the Auvergne. Attached to the monastery was a school, one of whose pupils was Gerbert, the future Sylvester II and 'Pope of the Millennium'. His statue (1851), by David d'Angers, stands at the N. end of the Promenade du Gravier.

Saint-Géraud (15,16&17C) is a heterogeneous building standing on the site of the first abbey church. It retains some Romanesque features, such as an arcade in the S. transept and two fine 12C capitals near the entrance. The chapel of Saint-Géraud has some carved stones embedded in the wall, as well as a curious capital (Samson) supporting a reliquary. Virtually the only part of the abbey to survive is the former hostelry, a house with Romanesque arches and delicate capitals.

Chapelle d'Aurinques (late-16C) is a chapel which commemorates an incident in Aurillac during the Wars of Religion. It was built after a victory over the Huguenots, which was attributed to the intervention of the Virgin. The circular part of the building is formed by one of the towers of the town walls. There are three 18C paintings of the battle in 1581 and the annual thanksgiving procession.

Notre-Dame-des-Neiges was the chapel of a Franciscan monastery (14C, restored 18C). It houses a venerated black Virgin. Most of the monastery buildings have disappeared but the Gothic building now used as the sacristy was formerly the chapterhouse. Its ribbed vault is supported by two pillars and it opens into an elegant 15C chapel. The church contains numerous works of art.

The *Maison des Consuls* (16C) is a restored Renaissance house and the home of the *Musée du Vieil-Aurillac*. The doorway is decorated with parts of the town arms: scallop shells, referring to pilgrims travelling to Santiago de Compostela, and the Fleur de Lys. Old houses can be found along the Rue de la Coste, the Rue d'Aurinques and in many streets of old Aurillac. Here and there, behind a doorway with an emblazoned pediment one can find a monumental staircase and an inner courtyard (see the Hôtel de Noailles in particular). The *Maison des Volcans*, which is housed in a wing of the 19C Château Saint-Étienne (11C keep), displays collections of minerals and explains the science of mineralogy. The *Musée J.-B. Rames* (second floor of the Tour de l'Horloge) contains local geological collections (natural history, mineralogy, flora) as well as a reconstruction of the interior of a local house. The *Musée Hippolyte de Parieu* (third floor) possesses some sculptures and paintings of the French and Dutch schools as well as works by local artists.

Autun   (17,600 inhab.)
71 Saône-et-Loire   p.420☐

Set firmly on a hill, the former 'sister and rival of Rome' seems to lie for all eternity in the shadow of its cathedral, one of the most beautiful in France. Autun—the ancient *Augustudunum* — was founded by Rome at the beginning of the Christian era. The conquerors of the Gauls, who were on good terms with the Éduens, the local inhabitants, founded a vast city surounded by four miles of walls. Several parts of this remain, in particular two gateways, the *Porte d'Arroux* and the *Porte de Saint-*

André. The Éduens abandoned their oppidum of Mont Bibracte and flocked to the town, which flourished and was second only to Lyons. Famous for its Moenian schools (from *moeniana*: porticoes beneath which the lectures were given), Autun was converted to Christianity early. It became part of the Duchy of Burgundy and shone again in the Middle Ages. Talleyrand, the renegade churchman who became one of the greatest of French diplomats, was the Bishop just before the Revolution.

Cathedral of Saint-Lazare: A large church with a famous tympanum and capitals, the exterior of Saint-Lazare has been altered over the centuries but it retains its Romanesque interior almost intact. Begun in 1120, it was ready to receive the relics of Lazarus in 1146. It underwent major alterations in the 15&16C after a storm had destroyed the tower and shaken the choir. The audacious spire, which soars 252 ft. without any woodwork to support the masonry, was built by Cardinal Rolin. It was a point of honour amongst the canons to build highly decorated chapels. The richness of these contrasts with the restrained nave. In the 18C the cathedral suffered from being altered in line with contemporary taste: the magnificent tomb of Lazarus was demolished, the choir hidden beneath marble, and the tympanum plastered. However, in the 19C Violet-le-Duc oversaw its restoration and strengthening.

PORTAL AND TYMPANUM: A vast porch stands before the 12C façade, which has two 19C towers. It has an extraordinary tympanum (1130 – 40), originally polychrome, which was the work of Gislebertus—an artist who was referred to by Malraux as the Romanesque Cézanne. A hieratic Christ in Majesty dominates the scenes of the *Last Judgement* with numerous figures in bas-relief and the round. The lintel and the outer arches have also been sculpted with animation. The tympanum is framed by medallions illustrating the seasons, the signs of the zodiac and the labours of the days. On either side of the portal, there are three columns with historiated capitals. One of the left-hand ones

Aurillac, Place d'Aurinques

Aurillac, Chapelle d'Aurinques

shows the wolf and the crane from the fable of Aesop which inspired La Fontaine's *le Loup et la cigogne* ('The Wolf and the Stork').

NAVE AND THE CHOIR: The large nave, with its seven bays and 75 ft. high broken barrel vault, is a perfect example of the Burgundian Romanesque. Modelled on Cluny, the fluted pillars and the arcades of the high galleries give it a character of its own. The builders of Saint-Lazare were possibly influenced by the ornamentation of the Roman Porte d'Arroux (Arroux gate). The capitals illustrate scenes, including many racy ones, from the Old and New Testaments, together with foliage and palm leaves. The aisles have side chapels and one of the left-hand ones contains a *Martyrdom of St. Symphorian* by Ingres. The relics of Lazarus are enclosed in a small enamelled reliquary beneath the high altar. On the right of the choir there are statues of the President of the Parlement of Burgundy, Pierre Janin (d. 1623), and his wife in prayer. The 16C chapterhouse contains capitals from the transept

and choir which have had to be removed and replaced by copies.

Musée Rolin: Housed in an outbuilding of the old Hôtel Rolin and a 19C house, this elegantly arranged museum displays both the major and the lesser pieces from its varied collections with equal taste. These include the finds of the Bibracte excavations, splendid Roman statuary, numerous paintings and fine furniture. A marvellous 12C nude, *reclining Eve* adorns the lintel of the cathedral. This charming figure, which is probably the work of Gislebertus, is pretending to turn away from the apple. The grave and gracious *Vierge d'Autun* is an exquisite polychrome stone Virgin from the end of the 15C. Next to this there is a *Nativity* (*c.* 1480) by the Master of Moulins, a painting on wood which shows a kneeling Cardinal Rolin. The former Bishop's Palace is medieval in origin but was altered in the 18C. The Lycée Bonaparte, where the future Emperor and Lazare Carnot were pupils, is a former Jesuit college built from 1709 onwards (gate 1772). The adjacent church dates

Autun, tympanum of the cathedral portal

Autun, Nativity by the Master of Moulins

Autun, cathedral of St-Étienne, capital

from the mid 18C. Outside the Porte Saint-André and the Porte d'Arroux there are a number of Gallo-Roman remains: an important, extensively restored *theatre* from the 1C, a temple 'outside the walls', also known as the *Temple of Janus* and, 1 km. from the town, a mysterious pyramid known as the *Pierre de Couhard*, which is probably a funerary monument.

Environs: Mont-Beuvray (24 km. W.): One of the peaks of the Morvan, it bears the acropolis of the Éduens, Gallic allies of Rome whom Caesar pardoned for having followed Vercingétorix. It was abandoned at the beginning of the Christian era for Autun. The fortified camp was surrounded by a dry stone rampart some three miles long. Caesar worked on his *Commentaries on the Gallic Wars* on this plateau. Excavations have uncovered the founda-

tions of Gallic houses. **Château de Sully** (15 km. NE): The 'Fontainebleau of Burgundy' according to Mme. de Sévigné, a noble, magnificent building, the birthplace of Mac-Mahon, it dates from the 16&17C. The courtyard is a masterpiece of the Second Renaissance.

Auxerre	(40,000 inhab.)
89 Yonne	p.415☐K 7

The old centre of Auxerre, clustered around its high cathedral, is reflected in the Yonne. The chief town of Yonne remains unchanged within the lines of the two concentric walls which surrounded it, but further out there are modern districts. The walls themselves have disappeared and boulevards now run along their course. A

Autun, Musée Rolin, Eve reclining (12C lintel)

small Celtic village, which became a prosperous Gallo-Roman city and the birthplace of Saint-Germain, Auxerre was governed first by counts and then by its bishops. Part of the Duchy of Burgundy, it was joined to France after the death of Charles the Bold. Restif de La Bretonne, the author of *Monsieur Nicolas* and the *Paysan Perverti*, who was born in 1734 at Sacy, was apprenticed to a local printer.

The Tour de l'Horloge (Clock Tower) or Tour Gaillard dates from the end of the 15C. It is a remnant of the medieval fortifications and bears a 17C clock with faces which indicate the time and the movements of the sun and the moon. In the 18C Roussel, the bailiff who was the inspiration for the ridiculous figure in the song, *Cadet-Roussel*, lived nearby. The 18C Hôtel de Ville is surrounded by old houses.

The Cathedral of Saint-Étienne: The first cathedral was built in the 5C and the present one, the fifth, was begun in 1215 on the site of a Romanesque building, the crypt of which remains. Work continued until the 16C and the S. bell tower is still incomplete.

EXTERIOR: The richly decorated main façade suffered at the hands of the Huguenots. Christ reigns in the tympanum of the central portal (13&14C) whilst its piers are decorated with the wise and foolish Virgins. A curious, small bas-relief shows Aristotle carrying the mistress of Alexander on his back—an incident taken from a legend. The left portal is finely decorated with incidents from Genesis (the creation of man, the garden of Eden, and the Flood) as well as the Coronation of the Virgin. The 13C right portal tells the story of David and Bathsheba. The portal on the

Auxerre, the Yonne and the cathedral

S. side dates from the 14C and on the N. side from the 15C.

INTERIOR: The broad, soaring nave dates from the 14C, with 15C vaulting. The 14C transept is lit by fine 16C rose-windows. The quite exceptionally elegant choir (1215–34) has a bas-relief of St.Stephen on the so-called Féries altar (Holy Day), and an original monument to Bishop Nicolas Colbert (18C). The stalls were rebuilt on the orders of Bishop Jacques Amyot (d. 1593) and his bust stands on another monument. A masterpiece of lightness, the original ambulatory is 13C; the magnificent but unfortunately incomplete set of 13C historiated stained glass is a blaze of deep colours. It illustrates some three hundred and fifty scenes from the Bible and Christian legends. There are frescos in the 11C *crypt*. The cathedral treasure includes religious pieces worked in gold, 12&13C chased enamel work, and Books of Hours. On the N. side of the cathedral the former Bishop's Palace, now the Préfecture, has a 12C Romanesque gallery, which was the bishops' walk.

Saint-Germain: Mutilated in 1811 and separated from a remarkable 12C Romanesque bell tower, this former abbey church was begun in 1277 but not completed until the beginning of the 15C. A tall, bare, even severe church, it contains fragments of stone monuments. Beneath the Gothic building there is a half underground maze formed by two superimposed crypts. These date from various periods but the main part is 9C, although the 'Confessio' is earlier. This sanctuary contains frescos illustrating three episodes in the life of St.Stephen (9C). One (circular but altered) is Carolingian in origin whilst the other is

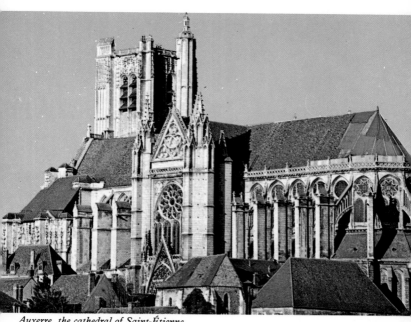

Auxerre, the cathedral of Saint-Étienne

13C. The chapel of Saint-Laurent has a 9C fresco of the *Adoration of the Magi*.

An unusual old house contains the *Musée Leblanc-Duvernoy*, which displays furniture that belonged to Soufflot (an important architect from this region), faience and fine tapestries. The 16C bell tower of the church of *Saint-Pierre* echoes that of the cathedral.

Avallon	(9,260 inhab.)
89 Yonne	p.415☐K 7

Extending into a characterless modern town, the old part of Avallon occupies a spur between ravines and the green valley of the Cousin. Originally a Gallo-Roman town and once the seat of a count, the town was an important stronghold in the Middle Ages. The ramparts, towers and bastions of its defences still exist. The old quarter is entered through the Porte de l'Horloge (Clock Gate), which is surmounted by a strong tower and a campanile.

Saint-Lazare: Standing above a deep ravine, the apse and apsidioles of this former collegiate church date from the 11C or 12C. The façade's two remaining portals are fine examples of Burgundian Romanesque but they were badly defaced in the Wars of Religion and the Revolution. The 12C nave draws its inspiration from the Vézelay region. The right aisle communicates with the 15C deconsecrated church of *Saint-Pierre*.

The small *Musée de l'Avallonnais* houses a varied collection and a *Miserere* by Rouault.

Auxerre, cathedral, tympanum

Auxerre, church of St-Germain

Avignon	(93,000 inhab.)
84 Vaucluse	p.425□M 13

Nearly three miles of battlemented walls surround this old papal city, with its churches and museums, its squares and alleys, and the formidable palace which the chronicler Froissart called, 'the most beautiful and the strongest house in the world'. An essential stop on the journey to Provence, the former fief of the Holy See has much to offer: its old stonework, 'the colour of dried leaves', and its works of art. However, it is also a centre of live, contemporary and sometimes even avant-garde culture. In 1947 a festival of theatre, ballet, opera and cinema was started in response to an idea of Jean Vilar.

Avignon owes its past glory to the Popes, who resided there in the 14C, and its region, the Comtat Venaissin, was a papal state. The town gained numerous buildings and became one of the 'capitals' of Europe, receiving prelates, ambassadors, artists and merchants. When the Popes finally returned to Rome, Avignon became a neglected papal state until it was annexed by France in 1789. The extensive 14C papal wall is still impressive even though the moats have been filled in. It protected the town against armed bands and also against the Rhône floods. This rapidly-flowing river passes under the four remaining arches of the 12C *Pont Saint-Bénezet* with its Romanesque-Gothic chapel. This is the 'Pont d'Avignon' of the famous song.

The *Place de l'Horloge*, the vital hub of the town, is dominated by a keep (1354), on top of which there is a later bell tower. In the 19C a new jack-o'the-clock replaced the old

Avignon, Palais des Papes

automatic striking mechanism, and this is now in the Musée Lapidaire. The square is 15C, enlarged in the 19C, and occupies the site of the ancient forum. The *Place du Palais* is surrounded by a spectacular array of buildings, including the former Hôtel des Monnaies (1619) and the *Petit Palais*. A former episcopal residence of the 14&15C, this remarkable and beautiful building was, until not long ago, in an appalling state. It has been transformed by major restoration and it now houses the *Musée d'Art du Moyen Age*, which contains

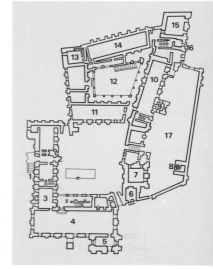

Avignon, Palais des Papes 1 Entrance **2** Aile des Grands-Dignitaires **3** Tour de la Gâche **4** Palais-Neuf **5** Tour Saint-Laurent **6** Tour de la Garde-Robe (Chambre du Cerf) **7** Tour des Anges **8** Tour du Jardin **9** Tour Saint-Jean **10** Aile du Consistoire **11** Aile du Conclave **12** cloister of the Palais-Vieux **13** Tour de la Campane **14** chapel of Benedict XII **15** Tour de Trouillas **16** Tour de la Glacière **17** gardens of Urban V

12–14C paintings and sculpture and a rich collection of Italian primitives.

Palais des Papes: (Papal Palace) A fortress-like palace and a vast residence, it is, with its clear lines, a major example of 14C Gothic architecture. Consisting of two adjacent buildings, the *Palais-Vieux* (Old Palace), and the *Palais-Neuf* (New Palace), this complex was built in less than 35 years, starting in 1334. Benedict XII, Clement VI and Innocent VI oversaw the building and decoration of this architectural masterpiece. Covering more than 161,000 square feet, the Papal Palace is most impressive with its high towers and its formidable walls. 'It looks more like the citadel of an Asian tyrant than the residence of the vicar of God', said Prosper Mérimée, then inspector of historic monuments, whilst deploring the vandalism of the soldiers billeted in the palace in the 19C. Its restoration was to take half a century of patient work. The vast main courtyard is surrounded by the Palais-Vieux of Benedict XII (mostly built 1334–8) and the more sumptuous Palais-Neuf, which was built by his successors. The two buildings are linked by the *Chambre du Cerf*, a study with beautiful frescos painted by Matteo Giovanetti in 1343. Often defaced and sometimes saved by covering washes, the remarkable paintings (1343–52) of the Papal Palace have been skilfully and authentically restored. The *fresco of the Prophets* in the *Grande Audience* (Grand Audience Hall) is also the work of Giovanetti.

Notre-Dame-des-Doms (from *domo episcopali*): This cathedral church, which now has a prominent 19C gilded-lead weeping Virgin, has partly lost its Romanesque character. The paintings of the portal, executed by Simone Martini in 1341, have been removed and are now in the Grand Tinel, a room in the Old Palace. Notre-Dame is dominated by a magnificent tower and lantern, which are unique in Provence.

Avignon, Saint-Bénezet bridge

It contains a 12C white marble chair, which served as the papal throne. A 14C side chapel has a canopied tomb (1345) of Pope John XXII, a fine Flamboyant work that was unfortunately defaced during the Revolution. On the S. side, a round chapel built in 1680 is a small architectural gem. Old houses abound in Avignon, particularly in the *Quartier de la Banasterie*, around the chapel of the *Pénitents-Noirs* (17C) and the church of *Saint-Pierre* (1358–1525, fine late 14C bell tower). The church of *Saint-Symphorien* was rebuilt in the 17C but it retains its 15C façade. The *Cloître des Carmes* (Cloister of the Carmelites) and *Saint-Jean-le-Vieux* date from the 14C, whilst the nearby domed chapel of the *Visitation* is 17C. *Saint-Didier* is a large and elegant southern Gothic church which was begun in 1325. The outline of one of its chapels is used in the altarpiece of

Notre-Dame-du-Spasme, a work ordered in 1428 by King René from the sculptor Francesco Laurana. A symmetrical chapel contains 14C frescos. The Hôtel Berton de Crillon (1625), which has a carved façade and a courtyard paved with pebbles from the Rhône, stands behind Saint-Didier. Avignon is a city of countless churches and chapels and *Saint-Agricol* is one of the most interesting of those not mentioned so far. It stands at the top of a broad staircase and was rebuilt in the Gothic style during the 14C. Subsequently altered, its façade is late 15C and the bell tower 16&17C. There is an interesting funerary chapel in the right aisle (1703–7). The *retable des Doni* (1525), the work of the Burgundian sculptor Imbert Boachon, stands at the bottom of this aisle.

Musée Calvet, Rue Joseph-Vernet: A sumptuous 18C house, with fine iron gates, houses this rich and highly eclectic museum, which was founded at the beginning of the 19C, thanks to the bequest of Esprit Calvet, a wide-ranging collector. The painting department has works of every period from P.Breugel to Vasarely: Flemish, French, Spanish, Italian and Dutch schools, Hubert Robert, David, Géricault, Corot, Manet, Toulouse-Lautrec, Renoir, Cézanne, Modigliani. The museum also houses Greek and Gallo-Roman antiquities, as well as a splendid collection of iron-work. The *Musée Lapidaire,* an annex of the Musée Calvet, occupies the former chapel of a 17C Jesuit monastery. Amongst other pieces it contains: the Venus de Pourrières, the man-eating lion known as the *Tarasque de Noves* and works from various periods up to the Renaissance. The recumbent effigy of

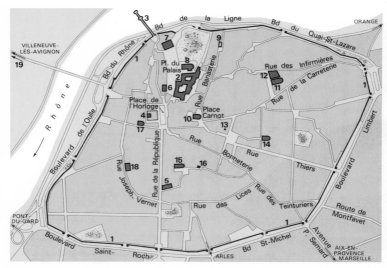

Avignon 1 Walls **2** Palais des Papes **3** Saint-Bénezet bridge **4** keep **5** Musée Lapidaire **6** Hôtel des Monnaies **7** Petit Palais (Musée d'Art du Moyen Age) **8** cathedral church of Notre-Dame des Doms **9** Chapelle des Pénitents-Noirs **10** church of Saint-Pierre **11** church of Saint-Symphorien **12** Carmelite cloister **13** Saint-Jean-le-Vieux **14** chapel of the Visitation **15** church of Saint-Didier **16** Hôtel Berton de Crillon **17** church of Saint-Agricol **18** Musée Calvet **19** former collegiate church of Notre-Dame

Cardinal de La Grange (d. 1402), depicts the dead man with startling realism.

Environs: Villeneuve-lès-Avignon (2 km. right bank): The Rhône was for long the border between Avignon, the papal city, and Villeneuve in Languedoc, a town founded by Philippe-le-Bel—whose name is still borne by a strong tower (1302). The S. Gothic former collegiate church of *Notre-Dame* contains several 17C paintings and in the sacristy there is a marvellous, smiling Virgin in ivory from the 14C. A 17C monumental door leads to the *Chartreuse du Val-de-Bénédiction* (charterhouse), founded 1356. Patiently restored, this rather unusual group includes buildings from several periods, some of which have undergone alterations (the large 14C cloisters were rebuilt in the 17&18C). The *church* has a 17C porch and two 14C naves.

It is partly ruined and, interestingly, it has amphorae and holes arranged so as to deaden the echo. There are several fine houses in the town built by cardinals when Avignon was the papal city, and there are also numerous 17&18C houses. **Fort Saint-André** stands at the top of Mont Andaon. This stronghold was begun in 1362 by the Kings of France and encloses a monastery and a small village, which today are in ruins. The pretty Romanesque church is 12C.

Avranches	(11,400 inhab.)
50 Manche	p.413☐E 5

Avranche is a city of panoramic views and it has a marvellous garden with a view of the unreal silhouette of Mont-Saint-

Avignon, Pietà of Villeneuve-lès-Avignon (Louvre)

Michel. Now a subprefecture, the former *Bishop's Palace* has some fine 15C remnants. The *Musée de l'Avranchin* is housed in its outbuildings and contains a large collection of manuscripts from the abbey of Mont-Saint-Michel. The basilica of *Saint-Gervais* partly dates from the 18C. The *Mémorial Patton* stands on an area of land regarded as American territory (the earth and the surrounding trees came from the USA).

Azay-le-Ferron (1,310 inhab.)
36 Indre p.419□H 8

Azay-le-Ferron lies on the edge of the harsh and wild Brenne. Its château combines a variety of styles, with 15C machicolations, a Renaissance logis (residence) and classical pavilions. The French gardens are surrounded by a park in various styles shaded by old trees. Inside, there are rooms in Empire and Restoration styles, furniture by the Jacob brothers, a fine Flanders tapestry, decorative paintings of the Genoese school and numerous objets d'art (Limoge enamels, Compagnie des Indes porcelain, plate, opal glasses).

Azay-le-Rideau (2,800 inhab.)
37 Indre-et-Loire p.414□G 7

A 13C lord, Ridel d'Azay, gave his name, albeit corrupted, both to the château, which replaced a feudal fortress, and the village. Built 1518–27 by a rich financier whose wife oversaw the work, this masterpiece of the Touraine Renaissance is surrounded by water and greenery. As Balzac recalled, 'climbing a ridge, I admired for the first time... this cut diamond set on the Indre and mounted on piles masked by flowers.' Standing in a park, above the widened river, it has had a varied history; it was confiscated by François I, fell to Louis XIII, possibly welcomed Louis XIV, and certainly received Frederick-Charles of Prussia (in 1870 — unfortunately for France). Azay-le-Rideau was a 'modern' house and its whiteness, so typical of the Loire, is symptomatic of a stage in the development of architecture. It was built at a time when people were beginning to want a pleasant residence rather than a grim fortress. Machicolations are no more than decorative motifs, towers become turrets, and defensive features disappear. There is still something Gothic in the silhouette but its symmetrical balance suggests Italian inspiration. The finest feature of the façade is the grand staircase, with its straight flights and barrel vault, a novelty in the age of steep spiral staircases. The house bears the seal of Claude of France and François I (represented beneath the windows by their emblems, the ermine and the salamander), and it houses tapestries, paintings and objets d'art in the *Musée de la Renaissance*.

Azay-le-Rideau, château ▷

Baccarat

Baccarat	(5,600 inhab.)
54 Meurthe-et-Moselle	p.417☐O 5

A small town, it was the base for the troops of General Leclerc when he struck into Alsace in November 1944. Baccarat owes its fame to the important glass-works founded in 1764. A *museum* devoted to crystal displays pieces from the past and present. The church of *Saint-Rémy*, which is reflected in the Meurthe, stands next to a bell tower and a signal tower. A sober 1950s building displaying a fine use of space, it should be seen when the sun enlivens the glass, which is set in concrete (stained glass depicts the creation of the world).

Bailleul	(13,500 inhab.)
59 Nord	p.411☐J 1

Flanders, which stretches from Dunkirk to Lille, begins here. The yellow brick brings lightness to the gabled façades, and the hills of Flanders overlook the treeless plain behind the monument to the dead. The perpetual victim of war, from the Norman raid of 882 up till 1944, this small and now quiet town has been rebuilt in the local architectural style. The belfry, with its 12C foundations, and the Hôtel de Ville have been built in a Flemish Renaissance style, which inspired the architects of the new church. The *Musée Benoît de Puydt* is devoted to regional art and houses Bailleul ceramics and lace and Flanders faience, furniture and tapestry.

Bailleul (château)	
76 Seine-Maritime	p.410☐G 3

A park full of statues surrounds one of the most attractive Renaissance châteaux in Normandy. It was built in the 16C by an old family whose forebears had taken part in the Conquest of England. Simple, balanced and original in its elegance, Bailleul is only decorated on its main façade. It contains remarkable furniture, fine tapestries, numerous objets d'art and paintings.

Balleroy	(750 inhab.)
14 Calvados	p.413☐F 4

The village's broad avenue frames a fine Louis XIII building, the work of the precocious architect François Mansart, who was only 28 years old when work began on the Château du Balleroy in 1626. Standing in a vast English style park surrounded by dry moats, the building is restrained on the outside and faded in colour; inside, however, it is richly decorated. Gold and purple vie in the main hall, which has a ceiling painted by François Mignard and also contains portraits by him.

Barbezieux (5,550 inhab.)
16 Charente p.418☐F 11

At the heart of the Cognac region, the capital of 'Petit Champagne', this is a quiet commercial town. The château stands on an esplanade and was built towards the end of the 15C by Marguerite de la Rochefoucault. A lover of luxury, she was, nevertheless, hospitable to the poor. At a time when corn was a luxury, this woman 'fed a multitude of people who flocked there and thus saved several from dying of hunger'.

Environs: Manoir de Maine-Giraud

(parish of Champagne-de Blanzac, 18 km.) This modest 15C manor was owned by the poet Alfred de Vigny, who had his study in the central tower. It was there that he composed *La mort du loup* in a single night.

Barcelonnette (3,250 inhab.)
04 Alpes de Haute-Provence p.426☐O 13

Lying at the heart of Ubaye, a small, once isolated Alpine region, Barcelonnette was long called Barcelonne. Before belonging to the Counts of Savoy, it was owned by the Counts of Provence, who founded its namesake in Catalonia. French since 1713, the tranquil town is surrounded by luxurious villas built by the 'Barcelonettes' — emigrants who returned after making their fortune in the New World. It retains the well-ordered layout of a former stronghold, as well as parts of its ramparts and a 15C tower, the remnant of a Dominican monastery. The Hôtel de Ville houses the *Musée de Préhistoire et d'Antiquités*.

Bailleul (Seine-Maritime), château

Bar-le-Duc (20,600 inhab.)
55 Meuse p.416☐M 5

Divided into the lower town along the Or-
nain and the upper town with steeply sloping streets, this important commercial
centre remains a quite remarkable example of urban architecture. The Rue du
Bourg, the Rue des Ducs-de-Bar, and the
Place Saint-Pierre all have 16&17C houses,
which are often decorated with sculpture;
there are also fine Renaissance mansions,
such as that now occupied by the Palais de
Justice. The principal building in the
lower town is the Church of *Notre-Dame*,
a heterogeneous building which is basically
Gothic (13C choir, 14C nave). It has a
wooden Christ by Ligier Richier, a famous
sculptor from Lorraine and a pretty bas-
relief of the *Virgin* (16C). The former collegiate church of *Gilles-de-Trèves* (1574) has
a large rectangular courtyard with covered
galleries supported by fluted pilasters and
surmounted by a delightful Renaissance
stone balustrade. The church of *Saint-*

Antoine has a vast, single aisle (14&15C)
and a five-sided apse containing interesting 14C frescos, which were revealed in
1962. The elegant 14C church of Saint-
Étienne stands at the top of the upper
town. It contains the tomb of René de Cha-
lons, the masterpiece (1545) of Ligier
Richier, an extreme realist before his time.

Barneville-Carteret (2,050 inhab.)
50 Manche p.413☐E 3/4

Barneville and Carteret, situated on the
edge of the Cotentin *bocage*, with its
manors and manor-like farms, are linked
by a major seaside resort. Barneville's
Romanesque church, *Saint-Germain*, has
been altered in the course of time. It is
flanked by a fortified tower, which has a
12C base and several historiated capitals
(Daniel in the lion's den, the Baptism of
Christ, grotesque figures, a fantastic bestiary). Carteret's small harbour owes its
defences to the strategic position it oc-

Balleroy, château   *Bar-le-Duc, tomb of R. de Châlons* ▷

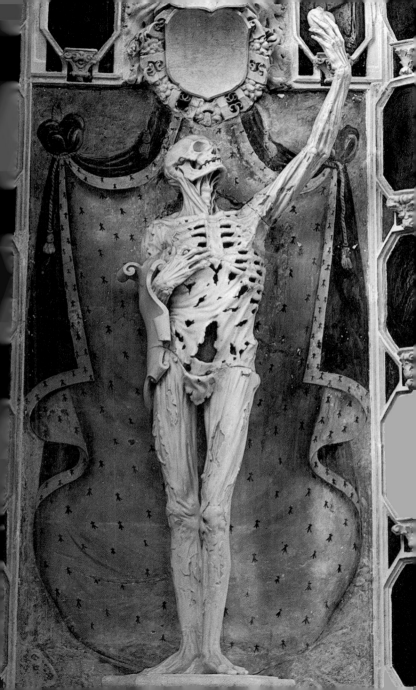

cupies opposite the Channel Islands. There are only a few remains of the military buildings, which are described in *Une Vieille Maîtresse* by Barbey d'Aurevilly, the great Cotentin writer of the last century, who as a child spent his holidays in Carteret's manor, an 18C house (now in disrepair).

Environs: Portbail (7 km. S.): Numerous Gallo-Roman remains have been found in the village and there is also a baptistery, which dates from the 6C or earlier. Dominated by a strong 15C fortified tower, the church is mainly 11C. The monks built the Abbey of Lessay on the ruins of a Roman villa, the hypocaust of which has been uncovered.

Bar-sur-Aube	(7,450 inhab.)
10 Aube	p.415□ L 6

'I was born in a region of brooks and streams in a corner of the undulating Champagne countryside,' wrote the philosopher Gaston Bachelard (1884–1962), who was born in this small, old-fashioned Vallage town. The church of *Saint-Pierre* (late-12C) is a Burgundian Gothic building, which has a fine apse with radiating chapels. To one side of the church, there is a 14C wooden gallery, a 'halloy', which housed shopkeepers' stalls. Inside, there is a fine polychrome stone *Virgin of the Bouquet*, also 14C. The former chapel of the château of the Counts of Bar, the church of *Saint-Maclou* (late 12C), has a curious belfry-porch, which was once fortified.

The treasure of the chapel of the Hôpital consists of a polychrome stone group known as the *Education of the Virgin*, a typical example of early-16C sculpture from this region.

Environs: Abbey of Clairvaux (15 km. S.): This Cistercian abbey was founded in the 12C by St.Bernard. Rebuilt in the 18C, this haven of meditation became a central prison.

Bar-sur-Aube, 'halloy' of the church of Saint-Pierre

Bar-sur-Seine (3,450 inhab.)
10 Aube p.415☐L 6

A small town on the banks of the sluggish Seine, it has had an eventful past. Sieges and fires ruined the château of the Counts of Bar and only the Tour d'Horloge (Clock Tower) remains of this powerful fortress. There are a number of good houses, including some half-timbered ones and a fine Renaissance example in brick and timber. The church of *Saint-Étienne* (built 1505–1628) combines Flamboyant and Renaissance styles and has superb 16C stained-glass windows.

Bassac (510 inhab.)
16 Charente p.418☐F 10

Founded *c.* 1002 by a Jarnac lord, the monastery housed a Benedictine community, who built the present abbey church (12C). The Romanesque bell tower (125 ft. high) is one of the most remarkable in Charente and consists of four storeys, each smaller than the one below. Severely damaged in the Hundred Years War and the Wars of Religion, the abbey church was in need of restoration. The façade, which is in the Saintonge Romanesque style, was fortified in the 15C. The single aisle has a straight-ended apse and 17C Angevin vaults. In the 18C the monks' vast choir was refurbished. The fine eagle lectern and the carved stalls are the result of the combined efforts of the Benedictine brothers and local artists.

Bassoues (510 inhab.)
Gers p.423☐G 14

Straddling a ridge between two parallel valleys, the village owes its magnificent keep to Armand Aubert, a 14C Archbishop of Auch. An imposing, beautifully built structure some 138 ft. high, it was completed in 1371. Originally, there was no entrance on the ground floor and access was through a doorway, which still exists, on the first floor. The lower hall and the first

Bassac, monastery and abbey church

and second storeys have ribbed vaults. The third and fourth levels are separated by a boarded floor. To the SE the keep protected a powerful château, which is now ruined. The basilica of Saint-Fris contains the sarcophagus of this saint, who was killed by the Saracens in 732.

Bastia: see **Corsica**

Bastie d'Urfé
42 Loire   p.420□L 10

At the beginning of the 17C, Honoré d'Urfé's precious pastoral novel *L'Astrée* met with some success, with its descriptions of the banks of a small Forez river. In the previous century, one of his ancestors had turned a simple manor house into one of the most beautiful Renaissance buildings in Forez. The most remarkable part of the *château* is the double loggia occupying the right side of the main courtyard. A ramp leads to the apartments, where the 'chambre peinte', with a magnificently decorated ceiling, should not be missed. Episodes from *L'Astrée* are illustrated in beautiful Aubusson tapestries. As in Italian *palazzi*, the grotto is closed by beautiful arbour-like grilles. It combines mosaics of coloured sands with caryatids made of shells and pebbles.

The chapel has decorated vaults coffered in stucco and an altar consisting of four white marble bas-reliefs and a series of large paintings of the Italian school, depicting scenes from the Old Testament.

Baugé
49 Maine-et-Loire   (4,000 inhab.)
                                         p.413□F 7

Baugé is a small, pleasant, farming town set amidst forests and clearings filled with heather and broom. It has some fine 16,17&18C houses.

The Hôtel de Ville is housed in the former *château*, which was rebuilt in 1430 (elegant staircase in a turret with corners cut off;

Baugé, château

small *museum* with faience, arms and old coins). Founded in the 17C, the *hôpital* still has its original, finely panelled pharmacy. It contains a remarkable collection of faience pots, herb boxes, and glass and tin vessels. The chapel has a carved and gilded wooden tabernacle (17C). The *Chapelle des Filles du Coeur de Marie* or the *Incurables* houses a relic found in Constantinople in the 13C. It is a double-armed Cross with two figures of the crucified Christ in gold and precious stones and it is supposed to have been made with pieces of the True Cross. It became the emblem of the Dukes of Anjou and it is known today as the Cross of Lorraine.

Baume-les-Messieurs (200 inhab.)
39 Jura p.421 □ M 8

The abbey was founded in the 6C on a pleasant site at the meeting point of three valleys. In 910, one of its abbots, Bernon, left with some monks to found Cluny. The monastic life continued until 1793, declin-

ing when the monks became 'gentlemen', who were less concerned with the Rule of St.Benedict and more interested in wealth and temporal power.

Parts of the monastery buildings remain, including the 13C storeroom, the main block (15&17C) and a courtyard (the galleries of the cloister have disappeared but the fountain remains); these now house the *Musée de l'Artisanat Jurassien*. The *abbey church*, originally Romanesque, dates from various periods, having been altered several times, particularly in the 13&15C. The portal is dominated by God the Father giving his blessing and there is a long arcaded nave. Inside, there are some interesting tombstones and, in the choir, an altarpiece with panels by the Flemish school.

Baux-de-Provence (Les) (370 inhab.)
13 Bouches-du-Rhône p.425 □ L/M 14

Until the 15C an eyrie of feudal lords, Les Baux (from *baou*: rock) is now ruined, but

Baume-les-Messieurs, abbey church

Baux-de-Provence, ruined castle

Bayeux, apse of the cathedral

it is still one of the sights of Provence. Blending in perfectly with its magnificent, sun-drenched site like some brightly polished old jewel, this astonishing village displays delightful Renaissance houses (Hôtels de Manville and des Porcelets). The Place Saint-Vincent is dominated by the Renaissance belfry of the church of *Saint-Vincent*, whose Romanesque nave and aisles were built half underground. Some S. chapels also were partly cut out of the rock in the 16&17C. There is contemporary stained glass by Max Ingrand. To one side is the Chapelle des Pénitents Blancs (17C), which has housed temporary exhibitions since its restoration. The Rue du Trencat, hollowed out of the rock, leads to the Tour-de-Brau (14C), with the *Musée Lapidaire*. The ruins of the château (a 13C keep and a dovecote) lie outside the town amidst strange scenery.

Bavay   (4,100 inhab.)
59 Nord   p.411 ☐ K 2

Bavay is a large village situated to the N. of the forest of Mormal. Typical of the region, it has slate roofs. The Hôtel de Ville is flanked by a 16C belfry. There would be nothing else worth mentioning had the impressive *Roman ruins* not been discovered in 1942. Standing at the hub of eight roads radiating out across Europe, the ancient *Bagacum* was one of the largest cities of Roman Belgium. The capital of the Nervii and a commercial town, it began to decline at the end of the 3C. A vast, 270,000 sq. ft. urban complex (2C) and three town walls have been uncovered, to reveal pillars and arcades, shops and baths. At the W. of the excavation site there are three galleries, one obviously a basement, stand-

Bayeux, section of the tapestry

ing in front of a rectangular, three-aisled building. A *museum* contains a rich collection of everyday objects: bronzes, pottery, glass.

| **Bayeux** | (14,600 inhab.) |
| 14 Calvados | p.413☐F 4 |

The old capital of the Bessin, miraculously spared in 1944, it is famous for its tapestry and cathedral. However, it also has a remarkable museum, some timber-framed houses and fine 18C mansions.

The Tapestry: The *Telle du Conquest* or *Toile du Duc Guillaume* is now incorrectly known as the 'Bayeux Tapestry'. It is in fact an enormous piece of embroidery in coloured wools on unbleached linen. The work of one or more artists and a number of painstaking embroidresses, it tells the story of the Conquest of England by William the Conqueror, as well as the preceding events. A 230 ft. long 'filmstrip', divided into a large number of scenes and featuring hundreds of characters, this immense embroidery was hung from the pillars of the cathedral. Dating from the 11C, its colours are astonishingly fresh and, since it was rolled up in a chest, it escaped damage and little has been cut off it.

The Cathedral: Standing on the site of a series of sanctuaries, which in turn replaced a Roman temple, *Notre-Dame de Bayeux* dates from the 12C, although it was altered subsequently: in the Gothic style in the 13C, in the 14C (side chapels) and in the 15C (central tower). The W. towers and the crypt preserve the original Romanesque and enable one to guess how it would have been elsewhere. The relatively poor main façade does not prepare one for the splendour of the nave. There is also a plethora of stone on the S. side with a riot of balustrades, pinnacles and flying buttresses. A highly decorated *portal* has a tympanum devoted to St. Thomas-à-Becket. The 15C central tower has a chiselled octagonal upper storey, which nearly collapsed completely in the 19C and was saved only with difficulty (underpinning was necessary.) The light, balanced *nave* blends the late Romanesque with the 13C. Note the unusual carved decoration, whose little scenes and figures are forcefully drawn. The pillars supporting the rebuilt tower over the crossing have a Romanesque core. The superb *Gothic choir* (*c.* 1230) has 17&18C grills and Renaissance stalls. The Louis XVI high altar was decorated by Caffieri. The 11C crypt has unusual capitals, whilst the elegant Gothic (12C) chapterhouse has a remarkable floor of 15C glazed bricks.

The Musée Baron Gérard: This wide-

ranging museum is housed in one of the buildings of the former bishop's palace. It has collections of remarkable Rouen faience, old porcelain from Bayeux and Valognes, tapestries, extremely fine lace and sculpture. Paintings include those of local artists together with Flemish and Italian primitives and French painters (17 –19C).

Environs: Abbey of Mondaye (10 km. S.): An ancient Premonstratensian monastery, rebuilt in the 18C and remarkably decorated under the direction of the prior Eustache Restout, uncle of the painter Jean Restout. The abbey church has a large terracotta *Assumption* and an organ chest with fine carvings. **Château de Brécy** (13 km. E.): Fortified building dating from end of 17C with a fine arrangement of terraces.

Creully (14 km. E.): Romanesque-Gothic church with 17C belfry, château (11–17C).

Bayeux, cathedral, S. portal

Bayonne	(44,800 inhab.)
64 Pyrénées-Atlantiques	p.422 □ D 14

A river port at the mouth of the Adour, close to the beaches of the Atlantic and on the edge of the Basque region. Fine star-shaped fortifications built by Vauban surround the town. Half Gascon and half Basque, the city's stonework reveals its long past. In the Gallo-Roman period it was known as *Lapurdum* and in the Middle Ages it became Baîona. Enriched by privateers in the 17&18C, the town owed its reputation to the 'faures', local ironworkers and arms manufacturers, who invented a knife for fixing to rifles during a charge. Adopted by the French army, this became the bayonet. The town consists of *Grand Bayonne*, around the cathedral, and *Petit Bayonne*, the former village of Neuf, originally built outside the walls but subsequently protected by one. There are significant remnants of the old defences: the *Château Vieux*, a large medieval fortress in which Du Guesclin was imprisoned; Vauban's *remparts* or ramparts (late 17C); the *Château Neuf* (late 15C) and the *Porte de Mousserolles* (18C).

The Cathedral: Sainte-Marie or Notre-Dame with its pointed 19C spires stands of the site of a Roman temple. The only important Gothic building in the region, it dates back to the 13C. However, two fires forced the work to be restarted and it continued until the 15C. The bold vaults of the nave date from the 14C, when the English were masters of the area. However, the French triumphed over the English and English leopards and French fleur-de-lys appear together on the keystones of the vaults. One of the most beautiful stained-glass windows in the cathedral is that dating from 1531, which lights the chapel of Saint-Jérome from the N. The sacristy has a 13C double portal, which is contemporary with the apse. It once opened into the cloisters but the N. part of these has been removed. The cathedral rises above Grand Bayonne, whose old streets retain great character.

Museums: The remarkable *Musée Basque et de la Tradition Populaire* occupies a 16C monastery. Extremely well organized, it mixes the serious and the anecdotal, and provides the best introduction there is to the Basque region, its history and its still vibrant folklore. A special section introduces the Basque game of pelota. There are also displays of the discoidal funerary stele so typical of the region, and makhilas (staves for walking and fighting) worked in medlar wood. The *Musée Bonnat* owes its collections to the painter Léon Bonnat, who was born in Bayonne in 1833. He assembled a collection of great, and even exceptional, works, including paintings by Botticelli, Van Dyck, Rubens, Hals, Rembrandt, El Greco, Goya, and Turner. The museum also has numerous works by Bonnat himself and carved ivory plaquettes from the 14C. The collection of drawings is especially fine.

Bayonne, cloister of the cathedral of Notre-Dame

Bazas, cathedral of Saint-Jean-Baptiste

Bazas (5,250 inhab.)
33 Gironde p.422□F 13

Birthplace of the Gallo-Roman poet Ausonius, Bazas is on a hill, close to the great
forest of the Landes, its pinky-red roofs
clustering around the former cathedral. In
the centre of the town there is a fine, old
square surrounded by arcades, which vary
in design. Note the old house containing
the Syndicat d'Initiative (Tourist Office)
and the Hôtel de Ville with its classical façade. To the side of the cathedral the
former cemetery has been turned into a
small garden with a panoramic view over
the lovely valley. On the other side of the
church, a street and then a lane lead to the
Porte Gisquet, which is flanked by two
15C towers. Of the rest of the fortifications,
only traces remain.

The Cathedral: Standing at one end of
the central square it catches the evening
sun and turns golden. A former cathedral,
it is dedicated to St.John the Baptist and
until the Revolution housed a relic. It was
once the capital of the Vasates, a tribe
which gave their name to the town. The
city's first bishop dates from the time of
Clovis; Bazas was a bishopric until the end
of the Ancien Régime. The former cathedral, which is one of the most beautiful religious buildings in Aquitaine, was
begun in 1233 on the site of a Romanesque
sanctuary. It was altered and enlarged in
the 16&17C and the curious triangular
gable was added in 1725. It boasts an extraordinary façade with innumerable
statues—indeed, it is virtually a museum
of medieval imagery in itself. The three
portals date from the 13C; there is a statue
of Christ over the central opening, with the

Beaufort, church

Beaugency, the Tour de César

Virgin and St.Peter over the side portals. All the arches are finely historiated: saints, martyrs and angels on the central portal; signs of the zodiac, the tree of Jesse, scenes from the New Testament, and angels playing instruments on the right; the life of Adam and Eve and the wise and foolish Virgins are on the left. Built in the 13C but almost entirely rebuilt subsequently, the extensive, light nave retains its Gothic character—in contrast with the Louis XV altar, which came from a Cistercian abbey.

Bazouges-sur-le-Loir   (1,370 inhab.)
72 Sarthe   p.413☐F 7

A large village, stretching along the banks of the Loir, Bazouges has some 16C houses (Maison du Pilori) and a fine church with a fortified tower dating in part from the 12C. The bridge offers a delightful view of an elegant château, which dates back to the 16C. (The two residential wings were rebuilt in the 17C; there is a 16C chapel).

Beaufort-en-Vallée   (4,100 inhab.)
49 Maine-et-Loire   p.413☐F 7

Set amidst the flowers of the Val d'Anjou, an area devoted to horticulture, this small town is dominated by the remains of a château (rebuilt in 1346) and a tower (1455), which was built on the order of King René. The church has a fine Renaissance belfry (1542) and dates mainly from the 15C. It contains an interesting 17C carved wooden altar. The town has a number of old houses and a small museum.

Beaugency (6,850 inhab.)
45 Loiret p.414□I 6/7

A small town delivered from the English in 1429 by Joan of Arc, it was demolished by Condé, burnt by the Protestants in 1567 and shelled in 1944. Despite its misfortunes, Beaugency still has several monuments, old houses and a picturesque bridge (22 arches from various periods, 6 from the 16C). The Place du Martroi in the town centre, has a humble 11C church and a 15C wooden house. The *Maison des Templiers*, Rue du Puits-de-l'Ange, has a typically Romanesque façade. The *Hôtel de Ville* includes an elegant Renaissance house, which was restored in the 19C. Beneath the first-floor windows there are the arms of Beaugency, those of the Longueville family and the salamander of François I. In the Council Chamber there are eight valuable 17C embroidered panels which illustrate the continents and pagan sacrifices.

The Church of Notre-Dame: A former abbey church (12C), it was restored in the 17C, and has false Gothic wooden vaults erected in the 1660s. Ruined in 1940, the right aisle has been rebuilt. It held the Council of 1104 (the excommunication of Philippe I) and the Council of 1152 (annulment of the marriage of Louis VII and Eleanor of Aquitaine). The *Tour de César*, a magnificent rectangular keep, the top section of which is missing, stands to the left of the church. It suffered in the Wars of Religion and the vaulting of the five storeys collapsed in 1840. Victor Hugo set the fifth act of *Marion Delorme* in the tower.

Château and Museum: Built by Dunois, the château was once linked to the keep by a covered gallery. The principal residence (15C) is built against the curtain wall and a 14C tower. It houses the charming and fascinating *Musée Régional d'Arts et Traditions de l'Orléanais* (with costume, head-dresses, furniture, etc.)

Environs: Meung-sur-Loire (7 km. NE): Quite a large village with old plane trees

Beaugency, aerial view of the town and the Loire

shading the banks of the Loire. The 13C *château* was rebuilt by Louis XIV and enlarged in the 18C by Mgr. de Jarente, who lived there in splendid exile. The fine church of *Saint-Liphard* (13C) is dominated by a strong belfry with a pale grey upper section (11&12C). The famous local poet Jean de Meung completed the allegorical *Roman de la Rose* here, a work which had been started half a century earlier by Guillaume de Lorris.

Beaulieu-sur-Dordogne (1,710 inhab.)
19 Corrèze   p.419☐I 12

In 855, lured by the freshness of a Dordogne that is now more world weary, the Archbishop of Bourges, Raoul de Turenne, decided to found an abbey in this 'beau lieu' or beautiful place. Now it is a charming and peaceful town arranged around the large church of Saint-Pierre. There are a number of fine old buildings and houses with porches; one lovely Renaissance house is decorated with statuettes and corbels.

Saint-Pierre: A large church in the Romanesque style of Limoges, it is famous for its S. portal, a masterpiece of Romanesque sculpture. Preceded by a broad open porch, it has a fine carved group of the *Last Judgement*, the large figure of Christ with extended arms dominating the whole scene. The lintel is covered with monsters and chimeras, whilst the pier is decorated with three figures of prophets. The interior layout is of the pilgrim church type: the barrel-vaulted nave is flanked by aisles surmounted by galleries and the choir is surrounded by an ambulatory with radiating chapels. The treasure comprises a 12C Virgin in wood covered with chased silver and an arm reliquary of St. Felicity in gilded silver.

The remaining former monastery buildings (Place des Pères) include the chapterhouse (12C), which has fine capitals. The chapel of the Penitents (12&15C) stands

Beaulieu, tympanum of the S. portal of the church of Saint-Pierre

apart on the edge of the river. This former parish church with a bellcote has a Romanesque apse and a nave with Gothic chapels.

Beaulieu-sur-Mer   (4,300 inhab.)
06 Alpes-Maritimes   p.426☐P 14

Perched at the foot of the mountains, Beaulieu is an lively centre for water sports. The *Villa Kerylos*, a reconstruction of a Greek villa, is rather surprising and occupies a promontory with a view of the town and Saint-Jean.

Beaumont   (1,320 inhab.)
24 Dordogne   p.419☐G 12

A bastide founded by the English. Its medieval appearance has in part been lost, although there is a fine church from the 13&14C, which has been restored. The nearby *Château de Bannes*, on the road to Bergerac, dates from the 15&16C.

Beaumont-Lomagne   (4,100 inhab.)
82 Tarn-et-Garonne   p.423☐H 14

A commercial bastide. A large 16C wooden market has survived in the middle of a galleried square. The brick church (13&15C) is a veritable fortress and has a belfry in the Toulouse style.

Beaune   (20,000 inhab.)
21 Côte-d'Or   p.420☐L 8

At the heart of the wine area of Burgundy, Beaune is full of character, having a ring of ramparts, bastions and boulevards. The former seat of a Duke, it has many fine, old houses, particularly in the Rue de Lorraine. However, tourists only have eyes for the famous Hôtel-Dieu with its brightly coloured roofs, for Notre-Dame, a Romanesque collegiate church with Gothic alterations and for the Hôtel of the Dukes of Burgundy, which houses a wine museum.

Hôtel-Dieu: Flemish splendour in the heart of Burgundy, the magnificent 'house of the poor' was built in the middle of the 15C by Nicolas Rolin, a fabulously wealthy Chancellor to the Dukes John the Fearless and Philip the Good. Entrusted to nuns, the hospital continued to receive the sick until just after the last war. Today it is both a museum and the annexe of a modern hospital. Austere externally, the Hôtel-Dieu is arranged around a magnificent and picturesque main courtyard with an old well. The buildings are submerged under vast roofs, with high, lead-pinnacled dormer windows and a wooden gallery. As was common in Burgundy in the 5C, the glazed, multi-coloured roof tiles form a geometric pattern. The tall, spacious nave, which ends in a chapel known as the 'Chambre des Pauvres' (the Chamber of the Poor), has scarcely altered since the Middle Ages. It has a superb chestnut keel vault, gargoyle-like carvings and a polychrome wooden Christ in chains (15C). Rebuilt in 15C style, carved wooden cloisters separate the Salle des Malades (Hall of the Sick) from a restored chapel. The mysterious motto 'Seulle' ('lone star') appears on the tiling and on the walls. It is Rolin's homage to Guigone, his second wife, who was the star of his life. The kitchens have a 17C automatic spit in the superb fireplace. The pharmacy, which was redecorated in the 18C, opens on to a second courtyard and contains a display of Nevers faience, pots, bronze mortars and pewter. The guided tour ends in the Salle Saint-Louis, from which the invalids' beds

Beaune, roof of the Hôtel-Dieu ▷

have been removed and which is now a museum. The superb *polyptych of the Last Judgement* was ordered from Roger van der Weyden by Nicolas Rolin in 1443. Together with Van Eyck's *Mystic Lamb*, it is one of the finest pieces of primitive Flemish painting. The panels which close over the central triptych have been sawn through their thickness and then opened out so that it is possible to see how the altarpiece appears open and closed at one and the same time. Inspired by church tympana, the pathetic *Last Judgement* shows important comtemporary figures (including Chancellor Rolin and his wife, Pope Eugenius IV and Philip the Good) on either side of Christ and St.Michael who is shown weighing souls. Beneath the dazzling upper register, the resurrected dead make tiny, pitiable figures. One enters heaven whilst others fall to hell. The side panels include portraits of Chancellor Rolin and his wife. The Hôtel-Dieu also displays furniture, the 15C hanging with a red background, which formerly decorated the 'Chambre des Pauvres' on high days, and fine sets of 16C tapestries.

The Collegiate Church of Notre-Dame: A fortified church of Romanesque structure but Gothic in style. An extensive 14C porch covers almost the whole of the church's façade. Nevertheless, it is a fine example of Cluniac art, its interior recalling that of the cathedral of Saint-Lazare in Autun. Begun right at the start of the 12C, it was nearly complete in the 13C. However, a fire in 1273 led to alterations. The porch was built 1332–48 and the chapels were opened in the 14&15C (the Chapelle de Bouton is 16C). Major restoration was carried out in the 1860s under the direction of Viollet-le-Duc. The portals in the façade, which were savagely attacked during the Revolution, retain fine 15C stained glass. In the right corner, in a chapel founded by Canon Jean-Baptiste de Bouton, note the pretty Renaissance decoration. The square central tower dates from the 12&13C and its four-cornered dome and lantern from the end of the 16C.

INTERIOR: Some capitals in the right aisle are historiated. The Chapelle de Bouton is as heavily decorated inside as it is on the

Beaune, the pharmacy of the Hôtel-Dieu   *Beaune, polyptych in the Hôtel-Dieu* ▷

outside. Frescos in the Chapelle Saint-Léger (the second in the left aisle) include the *Resurrection of Lazarus*. They were painted from 1470–3 by Pierre Spicre, a Flemish painter attached to the Burgundian court. To the left of the high altar there is a primitive picture of the Virgin in Glory in the Auvergne style (12C). The five panels of the *Tapestries of the Life of the Virgin* (*c.* 1500) surround the choir. They consist of 19 scenes depicting Mary from birth to death and her coronation. A 12C door in the right transept leads to a gallery (which was part of the former cloisters), into which the 13C chapterhouse opens.

The Hôtels des Ducs, Musée des Vins de Bourgogne: The Hôtel des Ducs became the Logis du Roy (Royal Residence) when Burgundy became part of France. It is arranged around an irregular courtyard (14,15&16C) and is the home of a remarkable museum, which traces the history of the vine and wine from antiquity to the beginning of the 20C. A visit begins in the 14C fermenting room, where there are enormous old presses (18&19C), and ends in the hall of the Ambassade des Vins de France (Embassy of the Wines of France), in front of a bacchanalian tapestry by Lurçat.

Musée des Beaux-Arts: This museum occupies part of a former Ursuline convent, which is now attached to the town hall. It contains a large number of paintings, particularly those of Félix Ziem (1821–1911), an unjustly neglected local artist, who was influenced by Impressionism. There are also exhibits devoted to old Beaune, and archaeological finds. Finally, the Salle Marey has an exhibition of early cinematography. Marey was a doctor and physiologist from Beaune and developed chronophotography (1892), which was a major step towards cinematography.

The *Place Monge* occupies the site of the former Hôtel de Ville, which was destroyed in 1790. A statue of the local geometer Gaspard Monge (1746–1818) by Rude is surrounded by several Renaissance mansions. No. 9, the Hôtel de la Rochepot, was

Beaune, tapestry of the Life of the Virgin

built about 1522 by the draper Jean Pétral; it has a Gothic façade and a Renaissance courtyard. The base of a tall belfry appears to date from the 13C but most of it is from the end of the 14C; the bell dates from 1407. The *Rue de Lorraine* has several fine mansions, whose façades have varying amounts of decoration (16–18C). The Rue de Lorraine continues as the road to Dijon and runs past *Saint-Nicolas*, a church with a wooden porch over a Romanesque portal.

Beauregard (château)
41 Loir-et-Cher   p.414□H 7

At the edge of the forest of Russy, the charming Château de Beauregard dominates the Beuvron valley. More a manor house than a castle and a former meet of the Blêsois Hunt, it dates back to the 16C, with alterations from the 18&19C (the frescoed chapel was mercilessly destroyed under the First Empire). On the first floor the *Galerie des Portraits* contains an astonishing series of 363 small portraits surrounding fifteen Kings of France. The panelling beneath these was painted by Jean Mosnier, a local artist whose work is also found at Cheverny (royal mottoes and emblems). The fine ceiling with painted beams is matched by the bright Delft tiles on the floor. These depict an army of infantry and cavalry in the uniform of Louis XIII. The Cabinet des Grelots owes its name to the arms of the du Thier family (three hawk's bells or *Grelots*), which decorate the coffered ceiling. It has fine panelling and 16C paintings on wood.

Beauvais
60 Oise   (57,000 inhab.)
                                 p.410□I 4

Capital of the Bellovac Gauls who were destroyed by the Romans, it rose again in the Middle Ages; it was also rebuilt after the last war. The modern city surrounds a colossal but incomplete cathedral, the churches of Basse-Oeuvre and Saint-Étienne, and the Gothic former Bishop's Palace, which today houses an interesting

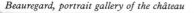

Beauregard, portrait gallery of the château

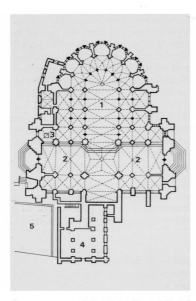

Beauvais, cathedral of Saint-Pierre 1 Choir **2** transept **3** astronomical clock **4** Basse-Oeuvre **5** cloister

Beauvais, cathedral, the choir

museum (archaeology, sculpture and paintings). The town stands on a rise at the confluence of two small rivers. One of its most famous figures was Jeanne Hachette, who galvanized the inhabitants in 1472 and forced the 80,000 soldiers of Charles the Bold to raise the siege. However, the Bishop of Beauvais, Pierre Cauchon, was less glorious, siding with the enemies of France (the English and the Burgundians) and sending Joan of Arc to the stake. For a long time the town had a famous tapestry factory and the looms are still in operation, but in Paris at the Gobelins, where they produce low warp tapestries for the State.

Cathedral: Of surprising proportions, like Cologne Cathedral; the choir appears that much more impressive since the building remains incomplete. The vast sanctu-

ary would undoubtedly have been the last word in Gothic architecture if the skilful craftsmen had been able to complete their immense programme. Striving to make it too large, too high and too light, they built vaults so daring that in 1284 they collapsed, leaving just the apse. Rebuilding (with the addition of new supporting piers) was directed by Guillaume de Roye and Aubert d'Aubigny and was completed in 1324. The windows were made of slender panels of stained glass, much of which survives. The first third of the 16C saw the completion of the transept. In the mid 16C a tower was built on the piers of the crossing. Yet again the builders were too daring, and in 1573 the 500 ft. spire collapsed, destroying the tower and seriously damaging the transept and its Flamboyant façades. The Beauvais architects were unable to find the money to carry out all the rebuilding as well as adding a nave and thus Saint-Pierre became the largest of the truncated churches. The cathedral, whose vaults reach dizzying heights (157 ft.), still has interesting stained-glass windows and a fine series of tapestries. The astronomical clock is 19C. The *Basse-Oeuvre*, a 10C church and the nave of the original cathedral, occupies the site of what would have been the 'new' nave.

Saint-Étienne: A Romanesque-Gothic church, it has a 12C nave and transept and a soaring choir built during the first third of the 16C in Flamboyant style. The N. transept has a pretty Romanesque rose-window.

Bec-Hellouin (Le)	(460 inhab.)
Eure	p.410☐G/H 4

The famous abbey of Le Bec-Hellouin stands hidden amongst the leaves beside a large stream (*bec* in Norman French); only the formidable tower with its delicate upper storey is clearly visible. The abbey was founded by the knight Herluin (Hellouin) and transferred to this site in 1073. An important religious centre in the Middle Ages, the abbey fell into disrepair and was only gradually restored by the monks of the community of Saint-Maur. Most of the surviving buildings are reconstructions from the first part of the 18C; the former refectory is now the abbey church. Abandoned at the Revolution and pillaged during the 19C, the abbey was all but razed. However, major reconstruction work has restored all its former beauty. The noble tower of Saint-Nicolas (1467) and the former chapterhouse (12,13&18C decoration) are amongst the oldest surviving buildings. The cloisters, rebuilt in the 17C, were richly decorated by Guillaume de la Tremblaye. The new abbey church is long and light and contains a lithe, stone

Beauvais, astronomical clock

Abbey of Bec-Hellouin

Virgin dating from the 13C and a sarcophagus containing the remains of Herluin.

Belfort   (57,400 inhab.)
90 Territoire de Belfort   p.417☐O 7

Belfort, in the 'gap' between the Jura and the Vosges, was the soft underbelly of France and lay open to any invasion. However, the genius of Vauban and stubborn resistance turned it into an impregnable stronghold. The 13C feudal castle dominates the town from the top of a 220 ft. cliff. In the 17C it was turned into a citadel and surrounded by an ingenious system of fortifications. At the end of the 19C these had to be levelled in order to allow urban expansion. The only part still standing, the *Porte de Brisach* (1687), was formerly a gateway through a double wall and led to the citadel, which now houses the *Musée Historique*. A colossal *Lion* in Vosges sandstone stands against the rock wall, a symbol of the invincible castle. Carved by Bartholdi (1875–80), it is an admirable tribute to the 'energy of the defence'. In the town the massive, solemn basilica of *Saint-Christophe* (18C) is austere outside but more delicately handled within: there is a frieze of angels' heads along the nave and a delicate wrought-iron grille with gold details which rings the choir. The museum has an interesting collection of regional archaeology. The Hôtel de Ville has a fine classical council chamber (Salle de Conseil).

Bellême   (1,840 inhab.)
61 Orne   p.410☐G 5

Bellême, a former walled town of 17&18C houses. Standing on a spur, it dominates the Perche region. Two towers from the old defences have been rebuilt. The church of

Saint-Sauveur (16&17C) has an important altarpiece, a *Transfiguration* painted by Oudry père, and Louis XV panelling.

Environs: Sainte-Gauburge (10 km. NW): The *Musée des Arts et Traditions Populaires du Perche* is housed in a former monastic establishment (14,15&16C).

Bellou   (130 inhab.)
14 Calvados   p.410☐G 4

A charming manor house set in a park, Bellou dates from the 16&17C. Once surrounded by moats and flanked by square towers and turrets, its timber-frame walls stand on a stone base and have high, flat-tiled roofs.
The modest 17C *Manoir de Chiffretot* stands nearby.

Bénisson-Dieu (La)   (360 inhab.)
42 Loire   p.420☐K 9/10

Lodged in the valley of the Teysonne below a small Roannais village, the abbey church of La Bénisson-Dieu was part of a Cistercian abbey originally known as 'La Bénédiction de Dieu'. The well is all that remains of this monastery. The shortened church is dominated by a 167 ft. high fortified Gothic belfry (15C), above which rises a pointed spire. The church is roofed with multi-coloured glazed tiles and dates from several periods: the seven-bayed nave is Romanesque (late 12C/early 13C), as is the left aisle, two bays of which have been transformed into the sacristry; the right aisle shows strong Gothic influence as a result of its 15C restoration; the Lady Chapel dates from the 17C (Italian inspired paintings, fine marble statue of the Virgin carved in Genoa in 1637). Note the statue of Saint Anne and the Madonna and Child (late 15C) in the church. The sacristy has several fine religious items in gold.

| **Bergerac** | (28,700 inhab.) |
| 24 Dordogne | p.419□G 12 |

Birthplace of the philosopher Maine de Biran and the tragedian Mounet-Sully. Bergerac's connection with Cyrano de Bergerac is purely legendary (he derived his name from a family estate in the Val d'Oise). On the river Dordogne, at the western edge of Périgord, this crossroads town has lost most of its old monuments and its château, although it still has a quite picturesque old quarter. The narrow Grand-Rue leads to a heavily restored Gothic church, one chapel of which has two interesting 14C paintings. The *Musée du Tabac*, in the Hôtel de Ville, offers a complete history of tobacco (a local crop) from the 15C to the present day. The *Maison du Vin* is housed in a former monastery (12,15&17C).

Environs: Monbazillac (6 km. S.): Occupying both banks of the Dordogne, the vineyards of Bergerac extend up to an elegant square manor house, which, although built about 1550, is medieval in appearance. The *Cave Co-operative* of Bergerac has set up a fascinating *museum* devoted to wine (furniture, books, prints, tools) in the château.

| **Bergues** | (4,850 inhab.) |
| 59 Nord | p.411□J 1 |

Military architecture has shaped Bergues, surrounding it tightly with fortifications. There are towers, some dating from the Middle Ages, bastions, canals acting as moats, and a few monumental, carved gateways (e.g. Porte de Cassel). However, the Revolution and war have left their mark. Only a few remnants of the former abbey church of *Saint-Winoc* (11C) are left: an 18C door, two towers, one square and massive, the other, the Tour Pointue (rebuilt in 1815), more delicate. The belfry, which

Bergerac, museum, Delftware

Monbazillac, château

to 1127. **West-Cappel** (7 km. S.): The 16C church houses magnificent carved panelling (17&18C). **Esquelbecq** (20 km. S.): Spruce, painted houses, a 16C hall church with three gables decorated with multicoloured bricks, a splendid brick château of feudal appearance and a curious hexagonal lantern. Situated on the Yser it is a perfect example of a Flemish village.

Bernay	(11,300 inhab.)
27 Eure	p.410☐G 4

Restored after having been shamefully abandoned, the former abbey church of Bernay dates from the 11C, although it was altered in the 15&17C. The crossing has a bold elevation and the S. transept is very beautiful. The church of the Sainte-Croix, from the 14&15C, received objets d'art and tombstones from the Abbey of Bec-Hellouin. The high altar has a monumental 17C altarpiece. The 15C basilica of Notre-Dame-de-la-Couture was a place of pilgrimage and houses a Virgin of the same date.

Environs: Beaumesnil (13 km. SE): 'Pride of the Ouche region', the Louis XIII château is most elegant and has gardens by Le Nôtre. **Broglie** (19 km. SE): An immense, largely 17C château. Church originally Romanesque.

Besançon	(126,200 inhab.)
25 Doubs	p.417☐N 7

Now a major economic, intellectual and artistic centre, the capital of Franche-Comté occupies an unusual site in a loop of the Doubs with wooded hills all round. The town owes a great debt to geography and an even greater one to history, retaining the treasures of a long, prosperous and presti-

Besançon, Palais Granvelle

was demolished in 1944, was hailed as the most beautiful in France. The brand new replica, in sand-coloured brick, has less ornament but is otherwise a faithful copy (octagonal bell tower on top of a 155 ft. square tower). The quiet streets and canals of this small, typically Flemish town retain the air of another time, a time whose tangible opulence is reflected in the Mont-de-Piété, built 1629–33. Inside, is the *Musée Municipal*, which has several fine paintings of the Flemish and French schools, as well as a good collection of 16&17C drawings.

Environs: Hondschoote (10km. E.): A once flourishing centre of the serge industry, at one time having up to 28,000 inhabitants, but now no more than 3,000. There is a Renaissance-style Hôtel de Ville, a 16C church with a tall tower and the *Nordmoden*, an old mill which may date back

Besançon, Porte Rivotte

gious past. This artistic town preserves the still-vivid memory of famous men who were born here, such as Victor Hugo (1802) and the Lumière brothers (1862 & 1864).

The Citadel: Besançon's strategic importance is underlined by the citadel, which sits on top of a rocky ridge 390 ft. above the Doubs. The surrounding ramparts carry a wall walk with watch-towers, and from here there is an unforgettable view of the old town's brown tiled roofs, the suburbs and the surrounding hills. Anyone interested in military architecture will admire the system of fortifications designed by Vauban. Three rows of extended esplanades form 'fronts' which bar the summit of the hill along the whole of its breadth to hinder the progress of an attacker. Now demilitarized, the citadel buildings cater for other interests and

house the *Musée Populaire Comtois* and the *Musée d'Agriculture Traditionelle*. These provide graphic displays of the daily life in Franche-Comté in the past.

Old Besançon: The old museum-like town is full of charm and its various monuments and fine 16,17&18C houses trace the high points in its history from Roman times. Partially closed to traffic, the Grand-Rue follows the line of an ancient route. In the charming *Square Archéologique A. Castan* a line of ancient columns marks the site of a water reservoir, which supplied an aqueduct whose channels are still visible. Close to the cathedral the 2C *Porte de Mars* known as the *Porte Noire* recalls the pomp of Roman triumphs in its now weathered carvings and double row of columns. Work started on the *Palais Granville* in 1534. A majestic Renaissance building, it is evidence of the irresistible rise of Nicolas Perrenot de Granvelle, Chancellor to Charles the Fifth. Although the façade is severe, the inner courtyard has galleries with basket arches. Inside, the collections of the *Musée d'Histoire et d'Ethnographie de la Franche-Comté* are on display. The tapestry of Charles the Fifth (17C) recalls the fact that Besançon sided with the Holy Roman Empire against Burgundy, which had become French. The superb 16C *Porte Rivotte*, flanked by two round towers, is part of the ramparts surrounding the old town. The projecting part bears the arms of Louis XIV—Besançon became French after being taken in 1674. The former *Palais des Intendants* (Administrators' Palace) now houses the préfecture and is the work of Victor Louis. This princely 18C mansion bears witness to the former prosperity of Besançon. Above its pilastered façade there is a pediment; inside there is a masterly staircase in wrought iron. The *Hôpital Saint-Jacques* retains its magnficent wrought-iron grille and an intact 18C pharmacy.

Cathedral of Saint-Jean: Dating back to the 12C, this building lacks a façade, the nave having an apse at both ends instead. The Romanesque (strong, square pillars) and the Gothic (upper storey and the vaults) blend quite successfully. However, the cathedral's main glory lies in its wealth of artistic works. They include the *Virgin and Saints* (1518), a fine painting on wood by Fra Bartolomeo, and the *Rose of Saint-Jean* (1050), a remarkable, circular Romanesque altar in marble. The belfry has a superb 19C astronomical clock.

The **Musée des Beaux-Arts** was established in the old corn-exchange, which was adapted for the purpose. The public's access to its exceptional collection of paintings by Cranach, Bronzino, Tintoretto, Rubens, Jordaens, Zurbarán, Goya, Courbet, Bonnard and Renoir is assisted by the use of concrete in the form of gently sloping ramps and landings. There is also a remarkable room containing drawings. The municipal library has manuscripts and early printed works of great value, as

Besançon, Porte Noire

Besançon, Préfecture

well as magnificent editions from the 16,17&18C.

Bessans	(250 inhab.)
73 Savoie	p.421☐O 11

Walled in by the mountains, this old village of Saint-Jean-de-Maurienne has been rebuilt since the last war and the tremendous floods of the Arc in 1957. Perched on a knoll and sheltered from the fury of the torrential river, the 17C *church* houses a reed crucifix by Jean Clappier (this local 17C artist, painted and carved numerous votive offerings, charming, naïve pieces found in many chapels in the region). The painted façade of the modest chapel of *Saint-Antoine* bears some strange, realistic allegories of the vices and the virtues, which unfortunately have been damaged. Inside, the Life of Christ unfolds in pictures along the walls. The date of the chapel is uncertain, possibly 14C or 16C.

Besse-en-Chandesse	(1,770 inhab.)
63 Puy-de-Dôme	p.420☐J 11

The former 'capital of the mountains', Besse is situated 3,300 ft. above sea-level, on the S. slope of Mont-Dore. A belfry of black lava towers above the dark stone-roofed houses and the surrounding ramparts. The town retains its medieval character, with the remains of walls, the former castle, the old round tower known as the Prison, the belfry and the town gate, all of which bear witness to its past importance. It is a picturesque old town with its jumble of roofs, the old 15C 'taules', or shops of the Rue de la Boucherie and the house of Reine Margot (Queen Margot).

Saint-André: This squat, partly Romanesque mountain church (nave, aisles, cross-ing are 12C; choir and apse are 16C) contains magnificent foliated, allegorical or historiated capitals with depictions of sheep and monkeys, which were much-loved by the artists of the Auvergne. Guilds are represented on the carved misericords of the beautiful choir stalls.

Béthune	(28,300 inhab.)
62 Pas-de-Calais	p.411☐J 2

Set amidst wet grasslands, this important river port is in the throes of change as it turns away from coal mining and prepares for the future. Béthune does, however, keep up one old tradition. Ever since the terrible plague of 1188 the Brotherhood of the Charitables de Saint-Éloi have carried the dead, of whatever degree, by hand to their last resting place. The narrow houses around the Grand-Place are crammed together so that as many as possible have their fronts on the street. The splendid 14C *Tour Communale* also stands here; to-

Bessans, Chapelle St-Antoine

Beynac-et-Cazenac, general view

day it is free of the clutter of stalls which once surrounded it. Although it is 154 ft. high, this airy, sandstone bell tower presents a restrained appearance.

Environs: Lillers (13 km. W.): Some 17C houses, but the main point of interest is the only Romanesque building (much altered in the 17C) in northern France. The façade of the collegiate church of *Saint-Omer* (1120–50) has suffered greatly with time but the inside is still remarkable. Broad and light, it has an ambulatory, a beautiful three-storeyed nave with a wooden ceiling and a 12C Christ of the 'holy blood of the miracle'. **Olhain** (15 km. S.): An exceptionally well preserved château-fortress rebuilt in 1407. The gateway leads into a lower courtyard, beyond which a drawbridge controls access to the strong castle. The superb, cylindrical keep is surrounded by

water and the whole effect of this rustic, feudal castle is one of real beauty.

Beychevelle (château)
33 Gironde   p.418☐E 11

At the heart of the endless, rolling vineyards of the Médoc, the château of Beychevelle looks down on the Gironde across a broad sweep of grass. A long, low and elegant Louis XV house (rebuilt in 1757), it produces one of the most distinguished of Bordeaux wines.

Beynac-et-Cazenac   (410 inhab.)
24 Dordogne   p.419☐H 12

Protected by a strong fortress perched on top of a cliff, this picturesque Périgord village lies on the banks of the Dordogne and is a stop for barges. The powerful *château* with its stark keep dates mainly from the 13&14C. It is now only an empty shell but the vaulted Salle des États remains grand in appearance and the oratory has 15C frescos. The parapet walk offers an extensive view.

Béziers   (85,700 inhab.)
34 Hérault   p.424☐J 15

A lively and picturesque city, Béziers is a centre of the wine industry and rugby. It shelters beneath its fortified former cathedral, which along with the old town stands on a hill occupied by man since prehistoric times (here too the Romans founded a colony). The Paul-Riquet walks lined with plane trees are named after a local man who was responsible for the digging of the 17C Canal des Deux-Mers. They lead to a garden, the Plateau des

Beychevelle, château

Poètes, which has numerous busts of writers and a panoramic view. The Hôtel de Ville has an 18C bell tower. The Romanesque church of the *Madeleine* was extensively altered during the Gothic period and even more so in the 18C. Now, only the apse and the S. side are original. The basilica of *Saint-Aphrodise* is also partially Romanesque but with a 13C Gothic choir. Beneath it there is a Romanesque crypt containing the tomb of the first Bishop of Béziers. A carved Gallo-Roman sarcophagus serves as a font.

Saint-Nazaire: Standing at the edge of the plateau, the fortified former cathedral dates from the late 13C (choir, transept) and the 15C (nave, façade). It retains parts of an early Romanesque church, particularly at the base of the bell tower. The portal displays the symbols of the Church Triumphant and the Synagogue Overwhelmed (14C). The apse has spectacular 18C decoration; the sacristy occupies a 15C chapel with a fine stellar vault.

Saint-Jacques: Romanesque in origin but altered in classical style, although the 12C apse is unchanged. The *Pont-Vieux* is 13C, the *Pont-Neuf* 19C, as is the *Pont-Canal*, which barges use to cross over the Orb.

Museums: The Hôtel Fabrégat houses the well-stocked *Musée des Beaux-Arts*, which has an interesting collection of Greek vases as well as numerous paintings from the Middle Ages to the Renaissance. Outstanding works include a portrait by Hans Holbein the Younger and works by Domenichino, G.-F. Cipper, Giuseppe Bonito, Goya and Delacroix. The wide-

Béziers, church of St-Nazaire

Billom, Romanesque church grille

ranging *Musée du Vieux Biterrois* occupies a former Dominican church. It is devoted to Béziers, its long history and to St. Aphrodise, the patron saint of the town whose emblem was a camel. There are also exhibits relating to wine and old crafts, a collection of costumes (including coifs and bonnets), and there is also a reconstruction of an old inn. The underwater archaeology collections are based on the finds of divers who have explored the 'ship graveyard' near Cap d'Agde.

Billom	(4,200 inhab.)
63 Puy-de-Dôme	p.420□K 10

Billom is a small, busy town situated between the Limagne plain and the granite plateau of the Livradois. It is full of medi-

eval charm and has had a brilliant past. Known to Charlemagne, it was the seat of Auvergne's first university, which had up to 2,000 students and remained a centre of teaching until the 16C. Buildings from this period include the fine 15C Maison du Chapitre with a triple doorway, the 15C Maison de l'Échevin (magistrate), the 16C Maison du Bailli and a 16C bell tower with a wooden lantern. The *medieval quarter* provides a good impression of cities in the Middle Ages, having narrow, cobbled streets, no pavements and tightly-packed, irregularly arranged houses. The most picturesque of these streets, the *Rue des Boucheries*, has fine timber-framed houses, meat stalls, and old iron hooks from which joints of meat were hung. The church of *Saint-Cerneuf* has a Romanesque choir with a fine grille from the same period but the ambulatory, a crypt, the nave, aisles

Biot, view

and transept are all Gothic, having been rebuilt in the 13C. The apse is possibly the oldest in the Auvergne to have an ambulatory with apsidal chapels.

Biot (2,750 inhab.)
06 Alpes-Maritimes p.426□O 14

Standing high above the Brague valley, this small, picturesque and interesting town clusters around a square with 13&14C arcades and a church which was originally Romanesque (fine altarpieces, including the *Virgin of the Rosary* by Louis Bréa). The chapel of Sainte-Anne (1580) and the 17C Tour de l'Horloge (clock tower) are in the main street.

Environs: Musée National Fernand Léger (2 km.): Opened in 1960, the vast,

museum is devoted to the eclectic career of this great Norman painter (1881–1955). One of the founders of Cubism, he was also involved in typography, the design and decoration of glass, tapestry, etc. and all these different facets of his art are displayed in the plain, light rooms. Built in a functional style, the museum was the idea of Nadia Léger, the painter's widow and is state run. On the façade there is a vast polychrome ceramic work based on a design by Léger for Hanover stadium.

Blanc (Le) (8,450 inhab.)
36 Indre p.419□H 9

Situated on the borders of Brenne and Poitou, the upper town with its 12C château controls a ford across the Creuse. This has now been bridged. *Saint-Cyran* is a simple, Romanesque church which is now deconsecrated. The 17C church of *Saint-Étienne* has a retable with Corinthian columns and a 13C gilded copper reliquary casket with Limoges enamel. The church of *Saint-Génitour*, in the lower town, has a 12C choir ending in a flat wall, a 13C nave and transept and a 12C Romanesque belfry. It also has some fine Romanesque capitals.

Blasimon	(780 inhab.)
33 Gironde	p.418□F 12

Laid out as a bastide, this village is associated with the church of a ruined former abbey, a modest establishment which was once dedicated to St.Maurice. The abbey church, with its single aisle (12&13C) and elegant, late-12C façade (15C or 16C with a low bellcote) stands in a romantic, green valley. It was damaged in 1793 but the vandals spared the fine decoration on the Romanesque portal (carving which is exuberant, gracious and full of spirit).

Blasimon, abbey

Blaye	(4,300 inhab.)
33 Gironde	p.418□F 11

Known as *Blavia* in the Franco-Roman period, Blaye is a former daughter-town of Bordeaux, and stands on the estuary of the Gironde. The estuary is guarded by an important fortified *citadel*, which was completed by Vauban (1685–8). It is a strange military town set on a rocky plateau and its streets, squares and gardens are entirely surrounded by moats, bastions and walls, which gives the town a timeless, slightly melancholy quality. Two fortresses, l'Île Paté and Médoc, stand on the opposite bank. The citadel of Blaye has only once been under siege, in 1814. The church of Blaye is 17C.

Blesle	(860 inhab.)
43 Haute-Loire	p.420□J 11

A striking little village near the Alagon gorge; it has fortifications, a postern gate, towers and an 18C keep. The former abbey church of *Saint-Pierre* stands high above the roofs of the town, and is a complex and unusual building. It has a short raised nave, a long transept with a Carolingian doorway and a vast late-12C choir. The exterior is decorated with interesting sculpture: on a window in the choir there is a carving of a woman with snakes; there is a procession of imaginary animals on the archivolt of the great window in the N. wall of the transept. Fine Romanesque twin windows overlook one of the little streets by the church.

Blois	(52,000 inhab.)
41 Loir-et-Cher	p.414□H 7

At the heart of Blois is the Gabriel bridge

(1717–24) over the Loire. The city clings to the banks of the river, and twisty streets lead to the famous château. Louis XII was born here in 1462, Denis Papin in 1647 and Augustin Thierry in 1795.

Blois, the capital of a powerful region and an important bridgehead, was formerly protected by a keep which has now disappeared. The fief was bought in the 14C by Duke Louis of Orléans, the brother of Charles VI. His illegitimate son Dunois defended the château during the last stages of the Hundred Years' War, until it was liberated by Charles d'Orléans, the heir of Blois. This poet prince, who had for a long time been held prisoner in England, married Marie de Clèves on his return to France, and their son was the future Louis XII. He married Anne of Brittany, by whom he had a daughter; she later married François I and lived at Blois where she entertained kings and princes — including Charles V (the Holy Roman Emperor). In 1536 Henri III opened the States General in the château; the assembly supported the League and issued orders favourable to the Protestants, thus giving the civil and religious wars a new impetus which the King could not sustain. In 1558 there was a second meeting of the States General at Blois, even though Paris was rising against the monarchy. At the risk of his own downfall Henri III had the Duc de Guise (the Balafré, leader of the Catholic party) assassinated, along with his brother, the Cardinal of Lorraine. After his death the château lost favour with kings. Marie de Medici was imprisoned here from 1617–19.

Gaston d'Orléans, the son of the Duc de Guise, was compelled to live in the château and planned to pull it down entirely. However, as he was short of money he had to be content with building a new SW wing. After his death in 1660 the château lay almost forgotten during the 17&18C, and was damaged by vandals at the time of the Revolution. Restored without taste but reasonably faithfully 1843–70, it was then very badly damaged again in June 1940, when a large part of the town was ruined.

Château and museums: The château,

Blois, general view

built on a promontory, consists of four quite separate sections: the oldest of these is 13C and comprises the state rooms; the NE (Louis XII) wing, which includes the main doorway, was built 1498–1503; the NW (François I) wing is Renaissance (1515–24); the SW (Gaston d'Orléans) wing (opposite the entrance on the other side of the main courtyard) was built by François Mansart in the 17C. This notable collection of buildings of different styles is almost entirely unfurnished and the rooms appear empty and cold. The main courtyard is open to the S; a small Louis XII gallery adjoins the Saint-Calais chapel, which was consecrated in 1508; it is cut off at the nave and has modern stained-glass windows. On the other side of the terrace is the Tour du Foix, which is part of the former medieval fortifications and has a 17C oratory.

FRANÇOIS I WING: This exuberant Renaissance wing contains the superb staircase and is the most famous part of the château—the Duc de Guise was assassinated here. The exterior façade overlook-

ing the Place Victor Hugo has two storeys of loggias and above them an elegant gallery. The interior façade, overlooking the courtyard, is splendidly decorated; the cornice has a balustrade with the the arms of François I and Claude of France, and dormer windows with statues of children and salamanders (the king's emblem) inbetween; the windows are framed by pilasters decorated with arabesques. In the centre of the earlier façade, which has been shortened, is the *Grand Escalier* (staircase) in an open octagonal tower; it was used for balcony appearances at royal receptions. A tour of the building begins on the first floor in the queen's appartments, which were restored in a heavy-handed fashion by Duban in the 19C; a dressing-room has carved panelling concealing secret cupboards which can be opened by pressing a lever concealed in the skirting board. On the second floor are Henri III's appartments, where the Duc de Guise was assassinated.

THE HALL OF THE STATES GENERAL: This is between the François I and Louis XII wings. It dates from the 13C, and is the ol-

Blois, château, Louis XII wing   *Blois, château, François I staircase*

Blois, detail of the façade

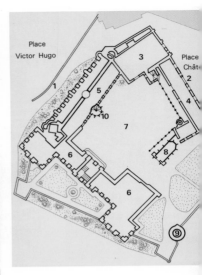

Château of Blois 1 Entrance ramp **2** Entrance **3** Salle des Etats **4** NE wing, Louis XII **5** NW wing, François I **6** SW wing, Gaston d'Orléans **7** main courtyard **8** Chapelle Saint-Calais **9** Tour du Foix **10** main staircase.

dest part of the building, showing traces of the original feudal fortress. It is 98 ft. long and 40 ft. high and has 17C tapestries designed by Rubens. The States General met in this room in 1576 and 1588.

LOUIS XII WING AND MUSEUMS: This wing is late Gothic and consists of a long gallery and two spiral staircases. It houses the *Musée des Beaux-Arts* on the first floor, and the *Musée des Arts Religieux* on the ground floor. The porcupines on the doorways are the emblem of Louis XII. The Musée des Beaux-Arts is housed in attractive rooms built in red brick alternating with light-coloured stone; it has many paintings from various schools (15–19C), as well as various objets d'art, including frescos from the time of Louis XII, 16C painted silk, pictures by Caron, Vignon, Boucher, Ingres, David, Isabey and Diaz de la Peña, tapes-

tries, furniture, crockery and musical instruments. On the ground floor the Musée des Arts Religieux has four rooms and houses collections of statues, crucifixes, reliquaries, chasubles and musical instruments.

GASTON D'ORLÉANS WING: This part of the building was built by François Mansart from 1635 in a classical style which contrasts unhappily with the Fran[ce]ois I wing. Incomplete, today it houses a public library containing some 80,000 volumes. The position of this wing explains the off-centre placing of the Grand Escalier: part of the François I wing was pulled down to make way for the end of the new building. There is a fine dome over the unfinished stair-well.

Musée Robert-Houdin: Jean Eugène

Blois, château, interior of the François I wing

Robert-Houdin was a very famous 18C conjuror and illusionist. His house, which is close to the château, has an interesting collection of souvenirs and personal possessions.

Saint-Nicolas: A former abbey church and the most interesting in Blois, it was built in the 12&13C and is a happy mixture of Romanesque and Gothic. The plain façade has twin towers with 18C openwork spires. The crossing has an unusual circular lantern with rib vaulting supported on pendentives. There is a mixture of unusual historiated and foliate capitals.

Cathedral of Saint-Louis: Only the W. façade and the five-sided apse remain of this 16C building in the E. quarter; the rest is a 17C reconstruction in the Gothic style. The heavy lower 12C part of the tower has

two 16C storeys above it, and a 17C lantern dome. The crypt of Saint-Solenne, which was cleared in 1928, occupies the nave and apse of a church which probably dates from the 10C.

The Hôtel de Ville is behind the cathedral in the former 18C bishop's palace. From here the route into the lower town has many picturesque houses: the 15C Maison de Denis Papin, beneath which the Rue Pierre-de-Blois runs, and Renaissance houses in the Rue des Papegaults, du Puy-Châtel, and Fontaine-des-Élus. Near the Rue Denis-Papin is the Rue Saint-Honoré with the very fine 16C *Hôtel d'Alluye*, which was built around a courtyard with Italianate galleries decorated with medallions of the twelve Caesars and Aristotle. The *basilica of Notre-Dame-de-la-Trinité* is some way from the centre of the town and

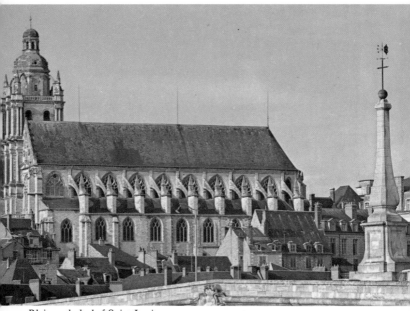

Blois, cathedral of Saint-Louis

was completed in 1939. It has an impressive campanile with a carillon of 48 bells weighing 17 tons.

Bonaguil (château)
47 Lot-et-Garonne   p.423☐H 12

This massive fairytale fortress (also known as the 'mad château') sits on a spur and demonstrates the imagination and will power of a feudal lord born out of his time. Bérenger de Roquefeuil started to build this huge mock-medieval castle at the very end of the 15C, when everyone else was brightening up baronial halls and making them into comfortable residences. This 'burg' looking out over a fine landscape of woods and fields was completed in 1520. 1,148 ft. of walls and thirteen towers and

turrets surround this solitary fortress which no-one could break by siege. It is both a masterpiece of military art—and of futility. At the centre of the complex the main courtyard is surrounded by mid-15C buildings, the remains of the modest château built by Bérenger's father.

Bonifacio: see Corsica

Bonneval   (4,900 inhab.)
28 Eure-et-Loir   p.414☐H 6

Bonneval, a small town on the Loir, has an old bridge and the 13C church of Notre-Dame. Two interesting Gothic houses and parts of both the ruined abbey and the fortifications survive.

| Bonnieux | (1,380 inhab.) |
| 84 Vaucluse | p.425□M 14 |

Bonnieux, formerly part of the Comtat
Venaissin, is still protected by ramparts and
towers. This pleasant market town is set
on the slopes of the Lubéron. The 'old
church' on the top of the hill, is in part
Romanesque and dates from the 12–15C;
there are 16C paintings of the Passion.

Environs: Lacoste (6 km. E.): This terraced village, once populated by Swiss
heretics, belonged to the family of the Marquis de Sade. It is grouped around an unusual tower and dominated by the high
walls of an enormous château, which was
owned by the de Sade family in the 18C.
Ménerbes (8 km. W.): a picturesque
château in a formerly fortified village; it
was the last Calvinist stronghold in the
area. The 14C church has a 17C altarpiece
and two primitive ones. The area has many
crude dry stone huts known as *bories*.

Bonaguil, château

| Bordeaux | (226,300 inhab.) |
| 33 Gironde | p.418□F 12 |

The capital of Aquitaine and an important
port, Bordeaux offers a fine display of 18C
architecture; the 'Grande Façade' stands
commandingly on the curve of the
Garonne which links the town with the Atlantic. Set among vineyards, this 'city of
the Chartrons' (wine merchants) has become a major modern provincial capital
and the centre of an important urban community, while still maintaining the grandeur it achieved under the royal
administrators ('intendants') of Louis XV
and XVI. At the same time as these 18C
buildings are being restored, Bordeaux is
also receiving its share of futuristic architecture and concrete buildings (in the
Mériadeck and du Lac quarters). The

greatest of the pre-Revolutionary architects
was Victor Louis (1731 – c.1802), who
designed the lavish Grand Théâtre and the
houses nearby. The town became richer
under English rule in the period when
Aquitaine was called Guyenne, and it has
many fine medieval monuments. However,
only a faction of old buildings have survived as on the whole the 18C swept away
the past, pulling down the ramparts which
were suffocating the city, and building fine
squares and spacious avenues, the ornate
splendour of the Bourse and the garden (altered in the 19C). The town, which has
been the seat of government on three
sombre occasions (in 1870, 1914 and
1940), will always bear the stamp of the
18C in its general layout and in the details
of its architecture and ornament, e.g. in the
buildings with their rounded corners, the
finely carved mascarons, the balconies

which have convex supports or corbels, the wrought-iron work, door knockers, locks and railings on corridors and landings, etc. Buildings painted a brilliant shade of light blue—which matches the light stone beautifully—dominate the town. This shade, mandatory for classified buildings under restoration, was the colour used by the original architects. Bordeaux, now two thousand years old, is proud of its ancient architecture, its cultural activities and its university. It is a large town which gives away its secrets to those who are prepared to explore it slowly and carefully and to move away from the magnificent central avenues planned by the Intendants. The beauties of 'old Bordeaux'—the Grand Théâtre, the Bourse and the Hôtel de Ville—are striking features for the visitor, but the modern city is interesting too; former marshland has been transformed by an ambitious programme (the *Quartier du Lac* with its remarkable exhibition hall designed by Francisque Perrier, and the *Quartier de Mériadeck* where one of the most important town planning projects of the 1970s is being completed). There is a superb view of the 18C 'Grande Façade' from the *Pont de Pierre* with its seventeen arches, which was completed in 1822. There is a completely different panorama from the daring *Pont d'Aquitaine* which was built 1960–7: some 1,738 yards long, its superstructure is 164 ft. above the river.

Place and Hôtel de la Bourse: The former Place Royal achieved its present dazzling elegance and coherence when it was altered by Jacques Gabriel in 1728; he was succeeded by his son Jacques Ange Gabriel, the architect of the Place de la Concorde and the École Militaire in Paris. Around it stand the Douane, the splendid building which houses the maritime museum, and the Bourse, which was opened in 1749. This enormous building was damaged in World War 2 but has been beautifully restored. It was the centre of

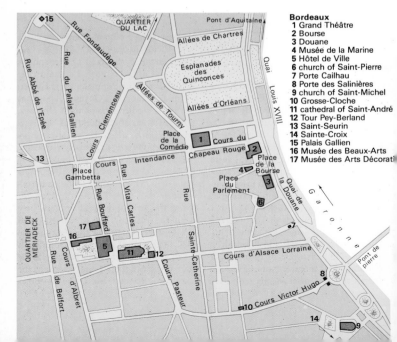

Bordeaux
1 Grand Théâtre
2 Bourse
3 Douane
4 Musée de la Marine
5 Hôtel de Ville
6 church of Saint-Pierre
7 Porte Cailhau
8 Porte des Salinières
9 church of Saint-Michel
10 Grosse-Cloche
11 cathedral of Saint-André
12 Tour Pey-Berland
13 Saint-Seurin
14 Sainte-Croix
15 Palais Gallien
16 Musée des Beaux-Arts
17 Musée des Arts Décorat

trade in the period when Bordeaux was dealing with the 'isles'. The exterior has fine pediments carved by Pierre Vernet and Claude Francin, and inside there is a great hall with ornate wrought-iron grille, a magnificent main staircase and the splendid rooms used by the chamber of commerce. The *Cours du Chapeau-Rouge*, which leads from the Bourse to the Grand Théâtre, following the line of the medieval fortifications is lined with some very fine houses.

Grand Théâtre: Victor Louis' masterpiece was built in 1773–80 on a site where there were Gallo-Roman remains. It has a superb Corinthian colonnade, with huge statues of goddesses and the Muses on the peristyle. The monumental staircase, which was the inspiration for the staircase in the Opéra in Paris, is illuminated by a cupola. The perfectly semicircular auditorium is lit by an enormous crystal chandelier. The ceiling was repainted in 1918 after the original work by Robin. Near the theatre are the elegant and restrained *Allées de Tourny*, which are lined with houses built to a uniform plan. Excavations for a

car park revealed numerous Gallo-Roman remains on the site.

Hôtel de Ville: The former archbishop's palace shares the general 18C elegance of the *Place Gambetta*; it was built 1772–81 for the Prince Archbishop de Rohan. This splendid building, which today houses the Mairie, was built by the architects Étienne and Bonfin: it has a notable main staircase and fine panelling.

Old Bordeaux: This term is used, not very precisely, for the areas of the town around *Saint-Pierre* (14&15C, heavily restored), between the Bourse and the Place de la Monnaie. The layout of this ancient quarter, which has been transformed by restoration, sharply contrasts with the Bordeaux of the Intendants and its intricate web of picturesque streets still has a medieval appearance. The 16C *Porte Cailhau* has Gothic and Renaissance features. The *Porte des Salinières*, opposite the Pont de Pierre, was built in 1750–5 opposite a semicircle of Louis XV buildings. The *Porte de la Monnaie*, which leads to streets from an-

Bordeaux, Hôtel de la Bourse

Bordeaux, Grand Théâtre

Bordeaux, cathedral of Saint-André

other era, was built in the same period. The fine church of *Saint-Michel* (14–16C) is dominated by a tall free-standing 15C *tower* from which there is a fine view of the town. The crypt has Gothic vaulting. On the edge of Old Bordeaux is the *Grosse Cloche*, a gate from the 13&15C, which contains the town bell. The clock dates from 1759; the wrought-iron balustrade is 18C.

Cathedral of Saint-André: The cathedral is almost as large as Notre-Dame in Paris. Romanesque elements survive, but in the main it dates from the 13&14C and has a fine Gothic apse with a plain, almost bare, façade which is often overlooked as it is so close to the town walls. The most striking portal is the 13C Porte Royale, which has good carvings. The detached 15C bell tower, the *Tour Pey-Berland*, is

unfortunately topped by an enormous and incongruous 19C statue of Notre-Dame d'Aquitaine.

Saint-Seurin: The porch and crypt of this former collegiate church date from the 11C. The church was rebuilt in the 12–14C, and then endowed with several chapels; the façade was rebuilt in the 19C. The crypt, a vaulted oratory, houses interesting architectural fragments and sarcophagi. Another 12C church (rebuilt in the 13C) is *Sainte-Croix*, but this was unfortunately spoiled in the last century by Abadie's heavy-handed restoration; fine capitals have survived. Practically nothing remains of the important Gallo-Roman city of *Burdigala* except the *Palais Gallien*, a large, derelict 3C amphitheatre.

Museums: The *Musée des Beaux-Arts*

Bordeaux, Tour de la Grosse Horloge

Bordeaux, Porte Cailhau

overlooking the gardens of the Mairie, has a notable collection of 19&20C masterpieces by Delacroix, Corot, Odilon Redon, Matisse, Vlaminck and Lhote. There are also paintings by Perugino, Veronese, Murillo, Rubens and Frans Hals, as well as works by local painters, including Albert Marquet, who was born in Bordeaux in 1875. The important *Musée d'Aquitaine* is about to move to the Cours Pasteur. It has a fine collection of local history, arts and folklore, with more than 600,000 exhibits; its prehistoric section is one of the most important in France. The *Musée des Arts Décoratifs*, housed in an elegant 18C mansion in the Rue Bouffard, is particularly attractive. It has varied collections of furniture, faience, glass, iron work and copper. It also has a reconstruction of a Bordeaux merchant's room and exhibits on the work of the local architect Victor Louis.

The little *Musée de la Marine* is in a fine house on the corner of the Place de la Bourse. It deals with the maritime tradition of Bordeaux and has an interesting collection of model ships, including one of the *Louis-le-Grand* which is 16 ft. long.

Boulogne-sur-Mer	(49,300 inhab.)
62 Pas-de-Calais	p.410☐I 1

Boulogne, an important fishing port, is a lively, sparkling town. The *Basilica of Notre-Dame* (1827–66) dominates the town, which is terraced almost like an amphitheatre. Notre-Dame stands on the site of the former cathedral, of which only the enormous Romanesque crypt survives. This classical building has remarkable vigour: the campanile on the monumental

Bourbon-l'A., church of St-Georges

dome of the central tower is topped with a cross, and the whole structure is 328 ft. high. The most striking feature of the upper town, which contains the Hôtel de Ville (1734) and an 11&13C grey stone belfry, is the rectangle of 13C fortified walls; they have several gates, and a château and a bastion at one of the corners. The parapet walk has shady gardens and fine views of the harbour and the sea. The *town library* exhibits a collection of manuscripts, some dating from the 9C, and incunabula; the *museum* has a fine geological and prehistoric section and a number of of Greek vases, including a superb amphora showing the suicide of Ajax.

At the gates of Boulogne is the column of the Grande Armée, a memorial to Napoleon's great dream of the conquest of Britain. The critic and essayist Sainte-Beuve was born in Boulogne in 1804.

Boumois (château)

49 Maine-et-Loire   p.413☐F 7

The light tufa of this great manor house stands out clearly against the fields. Boumois dates from the 15&16C, and still has something of a military air, but it is now above all an elegant and refined house whose architecture seems to hover between Flamboyant and Renaissance styles. The large round tower has a 17C dome; the pigeon loft has 1,800 holes, which could be cleaned easily by means of a device of revolving ladders. The château, which was badly damaged in the last war, is surrounded by moats; it was the property of the Dupetit-Thouars family, one of whom died gloriously as a naval officer on board the *Tonnant* in the Egyptian campaign. There are many mementoes of this hero of the battle of Aboukir in the château.

Bourbon-l'Archambault (2,600 inhab.)

03 Allier   p.420☐J 9

The name of this spa, which was known to the Romans, derives from Borvo, the Celtic god of water, and the Archambaults, first of the Bourbon lords. The ruins of the *castle* of the Dukes of Bourbon stand proudly on a cliff above the town; the castle was rebuilt at the beginning of the 14C, but only three towers remain of the 24 which used to protect the fortress. They are very large and are connected by a curtain wall; each tower has a spiral staircase. The surviving Quinquengrogne tower was part of the fortified walls which originally surrounded the courtyard.

Saint-George: The church was built in the 13C and rebuilt in the 15C and the 19C (choir). It has a very plain façade, the doorway has no tympanum and its arches are decorated with carvings of eggs, pearls and palms. The fluted pilasters at the base of the archivolt show Burgundian influence. Inside, however, the capitals are in the style of the Auvergne and some are particularly good, with musicians, a *Last Judgement*, and scenes of debauchery. The church has a fine 14C *Virgin in Majesty* and three magnificent reliquaries which are on view in the church hall. The Logis du Roi, now the tourist office, is the former bath house, and dates from the 17C. It houses the small *Musée d'Archéologie, d'Histoire et d'Ethnographie*. On the first floor the 14C painted wooden *Vernouillet Virgin* is an interesting example of the crude hieratic Virgins common in the Auvergne.

Bourdeilles   (650 inhab.)
24 Dordogne   p.419☐G 11

The château of Bourdeilles stands above the fast-flowing Dronne on the edge of a quiet village. The building consists of two sections: the older one dates from the 13C, while the more recent is a 16C Renaissance construction built by Jacquette de Montbron, sister-in-law of the writer, the Abbé Brantôme. The pale grey fortress is now only an empty shell, but Jacquette's noble and elegant building houses a fine collection of furniture. The splendid Renaissance collections were bequeathed by M. and Mme Santiard-Bulteau, who are buried in a small 15C oratory which now serves as a funerary chapel.

Bourg-en-Bresse   (45,000 inhab.)
01 Ain   p.421☐M 9

The home of the astronomer Lalande and the historian Edgar Quinet is in the heart of Bresse amidst modern roads and buildings. The old town is hemmed in by steel,

concrete and glass, but some older buildings remain, such as the house at the corner of the Rues Gambetta and Basch, and the Maison des Gorrevod, near the Palais de Justice. Bourg was for a short time the seat of a bishop, and building of the former *Cathedral of Notre-Dame* was started in 1505, although work was not completed until the 17C. It is a large Renaissance building; the carillon is a copy of the one in Westminster, and there are fine 16C choir stalls.

Environs: Church and Monastery of Brou (1 km. SE of the centre): The church and monastery of Brou were built by Margaret of Austria in response to a vow by her mother-in-law, Margaret of Bourbon. Margaret of Austria was the granddaughter of Charles the Bold and the governor of Flanders, also the widow of Philibert le Beau, Duke of Savoy, who owned the county of Bresse. In 1506 work on the monastery began; the church was built 1513–32 by the Brussels architect Louis Van Bodeghem (or Loys Van Boghem). The three famous tombs at Brou were commissioned in 1510 from Michel Colombe, but he was already very old and died shortly afterwards, having made only the models. The tombs were built by a team of artists under the supervision of Jean Roome, known as Jean of Brussels. The statues for the princes' tombs were commissioned from Conrad Meyt. The choir stalls were the work of local 'huchiers' under the direction of Pierre Berchod.

Church: The priory church of Brou is a Flamboyant building in the Belgian style. It was rebuilt in the 18C and the only distinctive feature of the exterior is the E. doorway; the presentation of Margaret of Austria and Philibert le Beau to Christ by their patron saints is shown on the tympanum; St. Nicholas of Tolentino, to whom the building is dedicated, is portrayed on the pier. The bright nave is separated from the choir by a lavishly decorated *rood screen*. The *choir stalls* are masterpieces of local craftsmanship decorated with scenes from the Old and New Testaments. There are 74 of them, all executed with unusual virtuosity; they occupy two of the right bays of the choir. *Tombs:* The tomb of Marguerite de Bourbon, which is reminiscent of the tombs in the former Carthusian monastery of Champmol in Dijon, is in a recess on the right. The tomb of Philibert le Beau stands in the centre of the choir; it has two recumbent figures, one representing the prince in state armour and the other showing him as a naked corpse. The tomb is decorated with small statues in a complex arrangement of niches. The much more lavish tomb of Margaret of Austria is beneath an ornate canopy. Here also there are two recumbent figures: one is a formal idealized effigy, and the other is more human and more moving. The tomb is very mannered, and shows German-Flemish influence. *Stained glass:* This is to a large extent in the style of Brussels. One window is based on an engraving of the Assumption by Dürer; above it,

the *Triumph of Christ* is a copy of a Titian engraving. This window lights the chapel of Margaret of Austria (on the left of the choir), which contains an important and unusual altarpiece depicting the Seven Joys of the Virgin.

Priory and Musée de l'Ain: This monastery, built by Bresse masons, is set around three cloisters. Among other things it has been used as a barracks and a lunatic asylum; it now houses the Musée de l'Ain.

Bourges	(80,400 inhab.)
18 Cher	p.419☐I 18

The emblem of the town is the higher of the two massive towers of the cathedral of *Saint-Étienne*, one of the finest in France. This great church, which has fascinated so many writers, is set among the 15&16C houses of the old town. Balzac said, 'All Paris is not worth the cathedral at Bourges', while Stendhal declared, 'This vast ca-

Brou, rood-screen of the church

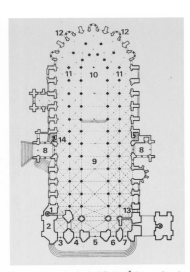

Bourges - cathedral of Saint-Étienne 1 staircase **2** N. tower **3** portal of Saint-Guillaume **4** portal of the Virgin **5** portal of the Last Judgement **6** portal of Saint-Étienne **7** portal of Saint-Ursin **8** side portals **9** nave **10** choir **11** double ambulatory **12** radiating chapels **13** astronomical clock **14** crypt

Brou, detail of a tomb

thedral fulfils its purpose perfectly. The traveller wandering among its immense columns is filled with awe: he senses the nullity of man in the presence of the Divinity'. The town was mentioned by writers before the 19C. Julius Caesar, who visited the town, then known as *Avaricum*, in 52 BC, said that it was 'not far from being the most beautiful city in Gaul'. A 16C chronicler remarked, 'The town rises like a perfectly regular mountain, whose summit, crowned by the cathedral and the great tower, gives it the appearance of a pyramid'. Bourges has made its contribution to art throughout the centuries, and it has always played its part in the history of France, of which it was for a time the capital (1422 –37). It has been besieged on many occasions, and has received popes, kings, St. Thomas à Becket, Charles VII, Joan of Arc, Calvin, Louis XIV and the exiled Don Carlos. It has been a university town since 1463; in the Middle Ages it was a great Christian centre and became rich from the manufacture of cloth. Jacques Coeur, who was born here *c.* 1395 and built a magnificent palace, remains the greatest figure in the history of the town. He was banker to Charles VII, and an imaginative businessman and diplomat, who established commercial links with distant countries, thereby amassing the enormous fortune which was the source of so much envy. The lycée was formerly a Jesuit college; among its pupils were Jules Sandeau, Alain-Fournier, the author of *Le Grand Meaulnes*, and Georges Bernanos. Joseph Lakanal, the creator of the central school in Bourges and a great French educational reformer, taught here at the end of the 18C. The university owes much of its fame to Cujas, the 16C jurist.

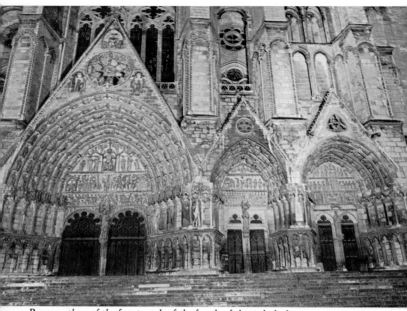

Bourges, three of the five portals of the façade of the cathedral

Cathedral of Saint-Étienne: This enormous building with its flying buttresses was started *c.* 1192 and built in phases from the E. end towards the W.—no doubt the earlier Romanesque cathedral was pulled down as work progressed. Two symmetrical towers topped with spires were planned originally, but could not be built. The cathedral was consecrated in 1324, and the side chapels between the buttresses were built in the 15&16C. A crude spiral staircase with 406 steps leads to the top of the tall left tower, which was rebuilt in the 16C; there is a very fine view of the town roofs with their grey slates or faded red tiles, and of the woods and fields of the countryside.

PORTALS IN THE W. FAÇADE: The W. façade was conceived in the 13C and rebuilt in the 14C, when Duke Jean de Berry put in the windows on the present grand scale. The five highly ornamented doorways are an original feature. A number of sculptures were damaged or totally destroyed by the Protestants in 1662. The two doorways on the left were rebuilt in the 16C: the first depicts the Life of the Virgin, and retains some 13C elements; the second shows the life of St.William, who was Archbishop of Bourges in 1200–6. The fine late-13C central doorway has an excellent *Last Judgement* in the typanum. The doorways on the right, dedicated to St.Stephen, the patron saint of the cathedral, and to St.Ursin, the first bishop of Bourges, date from the mid 13C. The statues on the piers are modern. SIDE PORTALS: Fine late-13C Romanesque with 15C door leaves. The porch is 13C. INTERIOR AND CRYPT: The simple, lofty nave without transepts broadens towards the choir. The stained glass is very fine— the 13C windows in the choir, the ambu-

Bourges, cathedral, the 'Entombment', in the crypt

latory and the apsidal chapels are particularly important. In the second aisle on the right is the tower-like astronomical clock (1423); this was originally sited by the rood-screen, which was destroyed in the 18C. The crypt is reached by a long sloping corridor and has a cunning system of vaulting whereby the pillars are extended upwards into the double ambulatory. This 12C underground church contains the marble *recumbent figure* of Duke Jean de Berry (15C), a large *Entombment* and fragments of the rood-screen. The flagstones have sketches made by the original builders of the cathedral, most notable is that of the rose-window in the façade.

The **Grange des Dîmes,** (tithe barn), Rue des Trois-Maillets, dates from the 13C. Payments in kind to the cathedral chapter were stored here. The ground floor has Gothic vaulting, and the first floor has a 17C roof frame.

Palais Jacques-Coeur: This lavish house was built for the famous financier in 1443–51 on the foundations of the Gallo-Roman town wall. This splendid mansion is one of the best surviving examples of late medieval domestic architecture. It was built at the very beginning of the Renaissance in the form of an irregular quadrilateral set around a central courtyard; the E. section is graceful and elegant; the W. section stocky and somewhat fortress-like. The house was used by Jacques Coeur as a residence and warehouse: the reception rooms, the gallery with its fireplaces decorated with curious friezes, the chapel with its painted vaulting and the bedrooms balance the banker's strongroom, the attics where valuable goods

Bourges, cathedral, stained glass

Bourges, Palais Jacques-Coeur

were stored, and the loft for the pigeons which were the banker's means of communication with his distant counting houses. The house has been restored, and is decorated with the emblems of its first proprietor; it also houses numerous 15&16C works of art. The *Maison de Jacques Coeur* in the Rue d'Auron belonged to his father-in-law.

Hôtel Lallemant: This essentially 16C house is reached from the Rue Bourbonnoux through a door with a semicircular archway. It is in a mixture of styles; the main façade is early Renaissance, although the mullioned windows are Gothic. The house was built on the site of the Gallo-Roman town walls, and houses tapestries, furniture, collections of objets d'art, enamels, faience and glass. This is a very varied museum, which also has collections

of toys, African and Oriental objects and 19C sewing and embroidery.

Hôtel Cujas and the Musée du Berry: This charming Renaissance house was built *c.* 1515 for a Florentine merchant and bought in 1585 by the jurist Jacques Cujas. The museum, which is run on modern lines, shows Berry from pre-Roman times: family life, art and folklore.

Bourges is in many ways an open air museum, there are innumerable interesting houses: the 15C Hôtel Pelvoysin, the 16C Maison de la Reine Blanche, the Palais de Justice which is housed in a 18C convent, the 18C Hôtel de la Préfecture, etc. The *Rue Mirabeau*, which is lined with 15&16C houses with pointed gables, has retained its medieval appearance. The most picturesque thoroughfares in old Bourges lead to a square of wooden houses, some of which are decorated with 15C sculpture. The *Porte Saint-Ursin* dates from the 11C, and is part of a Romanesque collegiate church which was destroyed in 1799. It is decorated with lively sculpture depicting themes from medieval French literature, and the passing of the months. The Maison de la Culture is housed in a very solid building which was started before World War 1, and is the cultural centre of the town. It was one of the first multi-purpose buildings of this kind in France, housing shows, concerts, dances, exhibitions, discothèques and a reading room. There is a fine modern park, the *Jardin des Prés-Fichaux*, designed by the landscape gardener Paul Marguerita, who laid out lawns, pools and rose gardens on the marshy site where the Protestants used to meet in the 16C to escape from the world and sing the psalms of Marot.

Bourgueil   (3,620 inhab.)
37 Indre-et-Loire   p.414□G 7

Bourgueil is surrounded by vines which produce a light, fruity wine, and is dominated by a church with Romanesque walls and an airy Angevin chancel. *Saint-Germain* dates largely from the end of the 12C, but the façade has a pre-Romanesque gable. The 18C prior's residence, part of the 15C cloister, the 17C 'abbot's castle', and the remarkable 13C wine-cellar are the surviving features of the Benedictine abbey, founded in the 10C and mentioned by Rabelais. Nuns occupy the building today. Close to the nearby village of Chevrette is the Cave de la Dive Bouteille; this is reminiscent of the stone quarries of Syracuse, though on a smaller scale. It is a disused quarry with collapsed vaulting, and houses a collection of wine presses and coopers' tools.

Brancion   (170 inhab.)
71 Saône-et-Loire   p.420□L 9

Brancion is sited like an eagle's eyrie; its beautifully restored houses are set beneath a church consecrated in 1150; it has the balance and simplicity which are the hallmark of the Cistercians; the frescos are 14C. The impressive remains of the château date from the 10C (foundations), and the 14&15C.

Brantôme   (2,090 inhab.)
24 Dordogne   p.419□G 11

Brantôme is a charming town in the Périgord Vert set on an island in the Dronne. It has a Renaissance riverside pavilion and several picturesque houses. Its history was for a long time linked to the history of the important and ancient abbey which tradition holds to have been founded in 769 by Charlemagne, who is said to have placed relics of one of the Holy Innocents there. Pierre de Bourdeille, a strange character who died in the early 17C, the author of the famous *Vies des Dames Galantes*, returned from a long period as a soldier to be a less than vigorous abbot of Brantôme.

The long, quite severe abbey buildings gained nothing from restoration in the 19C. They date from the 17&18C, and currently house the Mairie and the school, and also a little *museum* of prehistory and painting, with works by the important local painter Fernand Desmoulin. The Gothic *abbey church*, which has been over-restored, has a chilly, soulless interior. The very fine 17C statue of Notre-Dame-du-Reclus was stolen in 1977, but the thieves ignored the two wooden reliefs dating from the same period in the choir. The complex and unusual 115 ft. high bell tower stands on the cliff which dominates the church. The tower dates from the first half of the 11C, and is in a style which is unusual in the Périgord: it has a lower chamber with a strangely vaulted dome.

Bressuire	(18,000 inhab.)
79 Deux-Sèvres	p.418□F 8

An important farming village, as its large fair-ground shows, Bressuire is the centre of the bocage of the Vendée. In 1794 the bloody battles of the Vendée campaign were fought out here between the 'blues' of the Republic and the royalist Catholic army.

Notre-Dame: This parish church escaped the inferno of March 1794. Basilica-like in dimensions, it displays a variety of styles, the portals and capitals are Romanesque, the single aisle has Angevin vaults, and the rectangular choir is 15C. The elegant bell tower rises above the old roofs of the town to 184 ft. and resembles those of the cathedral in Tours. It was built in the 16C

Brantôme, bell tower of the abbey church

and had a lantern added in the 17C, which gives it its Renaissance appearance.

Château: Standing some way from the village and surrounded by greenery are the remnants of the formidable fortress of the Beaumont-Bressuire. The origins of this fortress go back a thousand years, when it comprised a double curtain wall and 48 semicircular towers.

Brest	(172,200 inhab.)
29 Finistère	p.412□A 5

Situated at the head of its roadstead, on the steep slopes of the Penfeld, the town of Brest commands an outstanding natural harbour. The old town was devastated by the Allies during the last war but the splendid château (12–17C, built on the site of a Roman fort) has survived. It houses the Préfecture Maritime and the interesting *Musée Naval* (Tour Paradis), which exhibits paintings, models and a variety of other items connected with the history of the navy from the 16C to the present day. To the side, the famous *Cours Dajot* laid out on the ramparts in the 18C offers a fine view over the commercial port and also the Laninon naval dockyard. On the other bank, close to the Pont de Recouvrance (the largest lifting bridge in Europe), is the much altered 14C Tour Tanguy, which houses the *Musée du Vieux Brest.*

Briançon	(11,500 inhab.)
05 Hautes-Alpes	p.421□O 12

Situated in Dauphiné on the borders with Provence, Briançon, at 4,350 ft., is the highest town in Europe. It is also one of the most unusual ones in the Alps, completely enclosed by the powerful fortifications built by Vauban at the end of the 17C, fortifications which formed part of a complex defensive system that commanded the valleys. An ancient town, it is also the centre for excursions to several nearby ski resorts. Although the modern town has spilled out beyond its walls the most interesting part still lies within them. *Notre-Dame*, a church which proves that Vauban was not just a great military architect, was built at the top of the town at the beginning of the 18C. Two worn stone lions guard the main doorway; they were taken from the previous building, which was demolished when the ramparts were laid out. Cold, severe, majestic, Notre-Dame houses some interesting 17&18C paintings, painted statues, brightly coloured altars decorated with gold and a fine painted wooden Crucified Christ from the 17C. The Grande-Gargouille, a street laid out in the Middle Ages, takes its name from an open rivulet channelling water to the Durance. The Petite-Gargouille, which runs parallel, has a similar channel. Starting at the top of the Grande-Gargouille, the Grand-Rue runs around the town and leads to the foot of a fort, where it offers an extensive view over the town.

Environs: The neighbouring villages are typical of the region, with old chapels and churches in Villard, Saint-Pancrace, Prelles and Saint-Martin-de-Queyrières in particular. **L'Argentière-la-Bessée** (16 km. W.): This small industrial centre is today devoted to aluminium but it takes its names from the old silver mines. The chapel of Saint-Jean, the only remnant of a 12C commandery, stands on a rock above the Durance. On another height there is a 15C church with a 16C fresco.

Bricquebec	(3,200 inhab.)
50 Manche	p.413 □ E 3

At the heart of the village there stands a ruined *château* with a keep surrounded by a polygonal curtain wall. An interesting example of medieval military architecture, it dates in the main from the 14C. The old main gateway, the Tour de l'Horloge, houses a small museum of regional architecture and history. Growing tired of this severe fortress in the 16C, the d'Estouteville family built a charming Renaissance residence, the Château des Galleries.

Brienne-le-Château	(4,150 inhab.)
10 Aube	p.411 □ L 5

The town lies on the plain below the hill on which stands the *château*. Built at the end of the 18C, on the site of a feudal fortress, it is an imposing, regular and cold building. Restored after the damage of June 1944, *Saint-Pierre-et-Saint-Paul* displays a variety of styles. The successful Flamboyant choir has an ambulatory and radiating chapels (16C) and the apse has 16C stained-glass windows. Brienne still has its old timber market buildings and the young Napoleon was a pupil at its military school.

L'Argentière, Chapelle St-Jean

Brignoles   (10,500 inhab.)
83 Var   p.425☐N 14

An old Roman crossroads and the cradle
of the Parrocel family of painters, the old
town stands on a spur. The church is
15&16C; the 13C former *Palais des Comtes
de Provence* houses a small regional museum which has a remarkable 13C carved
sarcophagus from a nearby chapel.
At *La Celle* (2.5 km.) there are the remains
of a Benedictine convent (of dubious
morality according to local tradition).

Brioude   (8,450 inhab.)
43 Haute-Loire   p.420☐K 11

Dominating the plain of the Allier, this important agricultural market town has been
a centre of pilgrimage for centuries, with
people coming to pray at the tomb of St.
Julian, the 4C martyr.

Basilica of Saint-Julien: Built between

Brioude, basilica of St-Julien

the end of the 11C and the end of the 12C,
it is the largest Romanesque church in the
Auvergne. It is remarkable for its apse, the
tiers of which recall the great churches of
Basse-Auvergne. The five apsidioles of the
ambulatory are pierced by fine windows
framed by small columns. The capitals of
these are very varied and display sirens,
dragons and cocks with human heads—
typical of Romanesque symbolism, in
which the sinner is transformed into a
beast. The upper part of the apse is decorated with magnificent polychrome
masonry. The interior blends breadth,
power and harmony of colour. The beauty
of its polychrome masonry is matched by
the variety of its splendid capitals and the
richness of the frescos, most notably on the
first storey of the narthex. Freshness, poetry, freedom of design, the talents of the
Auvergnat artists are there to be seen. The
basilica contains several works of art, including a gilded wooden Virgin with a bird
(14C) and a leprous Christ (15C), an in-
tensely realistic work from a former leper-
house in the region.

Brissac   (1,760 inhab.)
49 Maine-et-Loire   p.413☐F 7

'A half-built new château in a half-
destroyed old château,' so said the Duc de
Brissac of his fine residence. This tall, imposing and varied building retains certain
medieval elements. It was rebuilt in 1614
–21 by Charles II de Cossé-Brissac, Marshal of France, who joined the League but
who yielded Paris to Henri IV (the property was elevated to a dukedom for him,
and his descendants still own it). One front
overlooks the village of Brissac whilst the
other one faces the fine, large park through
which the Aubance flows. The E. wing has
a slender pavilion with a dome in the style
of Henri IV and is flanked by two large
machicolated towers, remnants of the 15C

building. To the N. a second building ends in a strong pavilion with tall chimneys in the style of Louis XIII. Broad staircases lead to the main appartments, which, with their carved panelling, painted joists and fine furniture, are very 16C in appearance. Amidst the family portraits there is an unexpected one of Mme. Clicquot, the famous 'Veuve' (widow) of the champagne house. An important figure in Reims in the 19C, she was indirectly related to the Brissacs. The chapel is in the S. tower and contains a bas-relief in white marble by David d'Angers, who was a native of the region and one of the most prolific sculptors of the first half of the 19C.

Brive-la-Gaillarde (54,800 inhab.)
19 Corrèze p.419☐H 11

The gateway to Périgord and Quercy, it is a city of busy streets lined with fine houses built of dressed stone and dominated by Saint-Martin. The suburbs, however, are rather dreary. It was the birthplace of Cardinal Dubois, the Regent during Louis XV's minority. Brive earned the sobriquet 'la Gaillarde' from the boldness of its inhabitants during the sieges which it has undergone. *Saint-Martin* has been much altered (19C spire) but it dates back to the 12C. A number of historiated Romanesque capitals survive from this period in the transept, in the side aisles of the choir and, on the outside, the curious brackets of the cornice. The Gothic nave is outstanding for the height of its twelve pillars. The sacristy houses several reliquaries, one of which is known as 'the eleven thousand virgins' and is in embossed, carved and gilded copper from the 14C. The town has some old houses with turrets and carvings from the 15&16C (Rue des Échevins); the Collège des Pères Doctrinaires (17C). The charming *Hôtel Labenche* (16C) houses the town library, the warm colour of the stone

emphasizes the ornament of the inner courtyard, with its large arches bearing a series of projecting busts appearing to lean out of false windows. The *Musée Ernest-Rupin* is in an elegant 16C house and has important collections devoted to prehistory, medieval sculpture and painting. One room deals with local history.

Brou (church): see **Bourg-en-Bresse**

Brouage (440 inhab. formerly)
17 Charente-Maritime p.418☐E 10

A dead town in the heart of the marsh, Brouage is a strange citadel. Once on the coast, the ramparts, which the sea no longer beats against, have for centuries looked down on quiet pastures. From the Middle Ages onwards the town's fortune depended on salt and the canal connecting it to the sea was then navigable. In about 1555, Jacques de Pons fortified Brouage, surrounding it with a turfed slope. It was fought over by the Catholics

Brive-la-Gaillarde, Hôtel Labenche

and Protestants during the Wars of Religion and it remained a Catholic and Royalist base, being used by Richelieu whilst preparing for the siege of La Rochelle (1628). With its defences strengthened, it became the most important fortified position on the Atlantic coast. After sheltering the Comte de Daugnon, who declared himself King during the Fronde, Brouage rapidly declined. As the areas of mud expanded, the salt marshes were drained and Rochefort superseded it in military importance.

The **fortifications** (1630–40) are a fine example of 17C military architecture of a type intermediate between the Renaissance and Vauban. The curtain wall forms a square whose sides are 437 yards long. The walls were strengthened at the corners and half-way along the sides by bastions with domed watch-towers. The fine gateways, such as the Porte Royale, with the arms of France and Navarre, had pilasters and pediments. Inside the perimeter, several military buildings of Richelieu's period survive: forges, underground harbours, food stores.

Brouage was the place of exile of Marie Mancini, Cardinal Mazarin's niece. Her uncle had sent away after the young Louis XIV had fallen in love with her, since, for reasons of state, the Cardinal wanted the future Sun King to marry the Infanta of Spain. Samuel Champlain, the founder of Quebec, was born in Brouage in 1570.

Bussy-Rabutin (château)
21 Côte-d'Or   p.416☐L 7

This elegant château, standing on a green hillside, is the product of the dreams and caprice of an extraordinary 17C figure, Roger de Bussy-Rabutin. Exiled to his estate as a result of the scandal following the circulation of his highly indiscreet *Histoire Amoureuse des Gaules*, this soldier-writer contented himself in his banishment with decorating in a most idiosyncratic way the château he had inherited (a rather grim medieval fortress which had been altered and embellished in the 16&17C). Bussy-Rabutin inspired artists to paint the extraordinary paintings on wood of the Cabinet des Devises, sometimes enigmatic works that are based on his life or denounce the frivolity of his ex-mistresses. He had the panelling of this room decorated with views of great châteaux, which are of considerable interest, since they depict the past appearance of these buildings. On the piano nobile, the Salle des Grands Hommes de Guerre contains the portraits of 65 famous commanders, amongst whom Rabutin shamelessly included himself. The sumptuous bedroom of the count is decorated with portraits of the ladies of the Court and the countess. Bussy-Rabutin appears again in the Salle de la Tour Dorée, in the company of Louis XIII and Louis XIV, along with other great figures and beauties of the period. In addition to the paintings, there are inscriptions that are somewhat two-edged with respect to the ladies: 'the most agreeable and the most unfaithful', 'lighter than the wind'. On the edge of the plateau and commanding a splendid view, the nearby village of *Bussy-le-Grand* has a Romanesque church which appears to date from the mid 12C, although the apse was rebuilt in the 18C. The future Marshal Junot was born in Bussy in 1771.

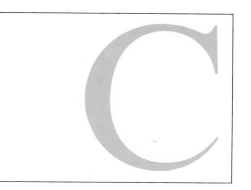

C

Cadillac
33 Gironde

(3,350 inhab.)
p.422☐F 12

Surrounded by vineyards, this former bastide (founded in 1280) rises in tiers above the river Garonne. Much of the 14C fortifications still survive, e.g. the Porte de la Mer and the Tour de l'Horloge (Sea Gate and the Clock Tower). In the centre there is an arcaded square—'à cornières' (meaning angles)—as they say in SW France. A *former collegiate church* of the late 15&16C stands on the square; the façade and tower were rebuilt in 1866. Inside there is a fine 17C altarpiece, the gift of the Duke of Epernon. The church is flanked by the funerary chapel of the ducal family (1606). The remarkable mausoleum which it housed was destroyed during the Revolution, but a few fragments were salvaged and taken to the château, while the bronze *La Renommée* is to be found in the Louvre. *Château*: This splendid building dates from the beginning of the 17C. It was built by Jean Louis de Nogaret de la Valette, Duke of Épernon, who was one of the followers of the 'roi-femme', Henri III. The Duke was instrumental in setting up the Regency of Catherine de Medici, and he fell foul of Richelieu (who, like Louis XIII, Louis XIV and Mazarin, had once been a guest at the château). Extensively damaged during the Revolution, the château, which has monumental fireplaces, has recently undergone major restoration.

Cadouin (Abbey of)
24 Dordogne

p.419☐G/H 12

The many pilgrims to the Saint Suaire in

Cadouin, cloister

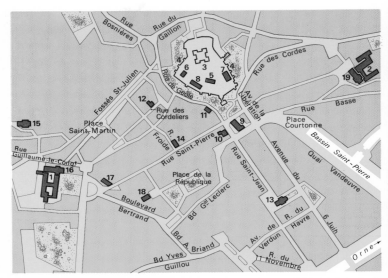

Caen 1 Abbaye aux Hommes **2** Abbaye aux Dames **3** château **4** ramparts **5** chapel of Saint-Georges **6** Salle de l'Echiquier **7** Musée des Beaux-Arts **8** Musée Ethnographique et Régionaliste **9** church of Saint-Pierre **10** Hôtel d'Escoville **11** Maison des Quatrans **12** Hôtel de Colomby **13** Saint-Jean **14** Saint-Sauveur **15** Saint-Nicolas **16** Saint-Étienne **17** Vieux-Saint-Étienne **18** Notre-Dame de la Gloriette **19** La Trinité

Cadouin included Eleanor of Aquitaine, Blanche of Castile and St.Louis. Built in the 12C, this abbey attracted pious visitors, until in 1933 scientific analysis proved that its 'Shroud of Christ' had been woven in the 11C and, incidentally, had a faint inscription calling upon Allah! Thus pilgrims no longer come to this lovely Cistercian abbey church. The church was consecrated in 1154 and the abbey itself is a mixture of dates and styles. The chapterhouse is 12C, while the 15&16C cloister is Flamboyant Gothic and Renaissance. The architects and decorators of the splendid Romanesque *church* made free with the strict rules of the Cistercian order. Indeed, although St. Bernard condemned every kind of decorative carving, some fragments survive on the exterior together with a score of capitals. The façade is wide and imposing and with buttresses and arcades

shows a distinct Saintonge influence. The church is dominated by a distinctive wooden tower. In the little square of Buisson-de-Cadouin there are some old market buildings and a 13C gate.

Caen	(122,800 inhab.)
14 Calvados	p.413□F 4

Caen is a modern town, which abounds in old bell towers and boasts of a magnificent architectural heritage. The capital of Basse-Normandie, it was tragically damaged in the battles of June and July 1944. The city dates back to the 11C when its strategic position found favour with William the Conqueror, who built the Abbaye aux Hommes here, while his wife had the Abbaye aux Dames built. Villages subse-

Caen, Vieux-Saint-Étienne

quently grew up around these and then merged into one. As the favourite residence of the ruling dukes, Caen was naturally much patronized by their successors. It was captured by the French King Philippe Auguste and occupied by the English, who improved and extended the château—one of the largest of the Middle Ages — and founded the University (1432).

Château and museums: The château itself, between the two abbey churches, was at one time masked by later additions. However, bombing caused such damage that it was heavily restored after the war. A fortress founded by William the Conqueror, it is surrounded by ramparts of the 12,14&15C. The Porte de la Ville (Town Gate) dates from 1440. These walls enclose a number of buildings of different styles: the chapel of Saint-Georges (Romanesque

nave), the Hall of the Échiquier (Exchequer) and the 17C Governor's House.

The *Musée des Beaux-Arts*, a dull modern building from the 1960s, houses an outstanding collection of paintings (Roger van der Weyden, Perugino, Tintoretto, Rubens, Courbet and Boudin in particular). The *Musée Ethnographique et Régionaliste* in the Governor's House shows Normandy before industrialisation.

Saint-Pierre: A Gothic-Renaissance church begun in the 13C and completed in the mid 15C. It has an extravagantly decorated apse and countless pinnacles and gargoyles. The much-copied 14C bell tower was destroyed by a shell in 1944. However, an exact replica has been built. The interior of the church is in various styles, becoming more and more ornate as one approaches the choir and ending in a

Caen, Abbye aux Dames

Caen, Saint-Pierre, the apse

profusely decorated apse and delicately worked ambulatory chapels.

The post-war façade of the nearby *Hôtel d'Escoville* hardly prepares one for the very attractive 16C Italianate courtyard. Damaged in part, this mansion, like the 16C *Maison des Quatrans* (Rue de la Geôle) and the Louis XIII *Hôtel des Colomby* (Rue des Cordeliers), is one of the most interesting of those still standing.

Saint-Jean: A 14&15C building, also greatly damaged at the end of the war; now seems slightly crooked. Subsidence has made the façade tilt and rendered the completion of the central tower impossible.

Saint-Sauveur: This rather curious church lacks unity and has two dissimilar naves, one 14C and the other 15C. The staircase visible from the Rue Froide leads

nowhere—it must once have led to a gallery that is no longer there. The bell tower is reminiscent of that of Saint-Pierre.

Saint-Nicolas: Built by the monks from the Abbaye aux Hommes at the end of the 11C, this unusual church makes a romantic impression with its graveyard. The tower at the side of the façade is 15C.

Saint-Étienne: This was the church of the Abbaye aux Hommes, and owes its existence to William the Conqueror and Abbot Lanfranc, Prior of Bec-Hellouin and later Archbishop of Canterbury. It has been very well restored and is a harmonious blend of its original Romanesque (11C) and Gothic. It was considerably enlarged in the 13C by the talented 'Maître Guil-

Caen, towers of Saint-Étienne ▷

laume', who replaced the original choir with a much grander one without spoiling the overall harmony. Saint-Étienne has one of the finest of Romanesque façades: it is in a typical Norman style—heavy central section flanked by towers — and has inspired many architects over the centuries. The 13C apse is in direct contrast with its fine rounded-off edges and pinnacle turrets. The high 11C nave is simple and very pure; the Romanesque part extending as far as the transept. The oldest Gothic choir in Normandy has 17C choir stalls and a high altar of 1772.

The Abbaye aux Hommes: This former abbey is next to Saint-Étienne and nowadays houses the Town Hall. It was rebuilt in the 18C under the supervision of the monk and architect Guillaume de La Tremblaye and still has several panelled rooms (locutory, refectory, chapterhouse). The guardroom, which is Gothic, is a remnant of the 13C abbey.

Little now remains of *Vieux-Saint-Étienne* behind the abbey, except the choir (13C) and the lantern-tower (15C). Nearby is *Notre-Dame-de-la-Gloriette*, built 1684–9; it is a rather theatrical-looking church, an imitation of the *Gesù* in Rome.

La Trinité: Built 1060–1130, this is less impressive and more elaborate than Saint-Étienne. It is nearly all Romanesque, and was the chapel of the Abbaye aux Dames, founded by Queen Matilda. The crypt, which is partly underground, beneath the choir, is a perfect example of the Romanesque, with its short pillars and carved capitals.

Cagnes-sur-Mer	(29,530 inhab.)
06 Alpes-Maritimes	p.426☐P 14

Cagnes is a rather ordinary and scattered seaside resort, but the older part situated higher up on a crag is picturesque. The history of *Haut-de-Cagnes* is really that of the fortress built at the beginning of the 14C by Rainier de Grimaldi. Added to in the 17C it has frequently been restored. In 1939 was acquired by the town and two

Cagnes-sur-Mer, château museum

museums were established here (there is a festival of painting in the summer). The old town has a medieval atmosphere with its labyrinth of tiny streets.

Château-musée: This is built around a fine Renaissance patio. The *Musée de l'Olivier* is in the vaulted medieval rooms on the ground floor. On the first floor there is a succession of 17C rooms—the ceiling of the Salle des Fêtes is immediately striking. It was painted about 1620 by a member of a great family of Italian artists Giovanni Battista Carlone. The *Musée d'Art Moderne Méditerranéen* on the second floor, is in the former appartments of the Grimaldis (works by Kisling, Carzou and Chagall). The chapel of *Notre-Dame-des-Protections*, below the level of the château, has some fine 16C frescos on the vaulting and the walls of the apse. The church of *Saint-Pierre* is partly Gothic.

Musée Renoir: In 1907, in his sixties, Pierre Auguste Renoir bought a property called Les Collettes and built a simple house among the olive trees, where he lived

Cagnes-sur-Mer, château portal

until his death in 1919. Here some of his works of art and personal possessions are exhibited. One bronze, *La Baigneuse*, is in the garden.

Environs: Villeneuve-Loubet: (4 km. W.): The house where the great cook and writer Auguste Escoffier was born in 1847 now contains the *Musée de l'Art Culinaire*. On view are memorabilia of the great chef and a large archive on gastronomy prior to the 'nouvelle cuisine'.

Cahors	(22,000 inhab.)
46 Lot	p.423□H 13

Cahors, the capital of Quercy, is caught in a loop of the river Lot. This was once navigable and improvements carried out from the 13C onwards enabled the local wines to be carried down to Bordeaux. The town is overlooked on the other side of the loop by a semicircle of small hills. It has preserved its historic quarters, squeezed in between the main thoroughfare and the docks behind the cathedral. In Gallo-Roman times it was called *Divona Cadurcorum*, then *Cadurca*, finally becoming Cahors. Pope John XXII (1245), the poet Clément Marot (1496) and the politician Léon Gambetta (1838) were all born here. There is nothing of great interest in the town from the last couple of centuries, but at least it has not been ruined by modern concrete; only the administrative centre, which is too high and rather ugly, stands out.

Pont Valentré: This bridge, with its famous silhouette, was built across the Lot in 1308, and is protected by three towers, once closed by gates and portcullises, the central one having a lookout post. This central tower is known as the *Tour du Diable* (Devil's Tower): it is said that the Devil helped the master-builder, who yet managed to keep his soul. Cross the Valentre Bridge to reach the unusual Fontaine des Chartreux — a natural spring whose workings were not fully understood until 1969.

Cathedral: The domes of this large cathedral dedicated to Saint-Étienne can be seen in the centre of old Cahors. A disconcerting mixture of styles it was begun at the end of the 11C; the splendid portal, now in the N. side (see below), was carved in 1130. It was altered in the 13&14C, when the heavy, fortified façade was completed, and a Flamboyant cloister was added at the beginning of the 16C. There were also several changes in the 17C (the raising of the ground level, gallery opposite the pulpit, new high altar, rose-windows).

THE ROMANESQUE PORTAL: This remarkable door was probably moved from the W. to the N. side of the cathedral in the 13C. The carving and the position of the tympanum under a deep arch are reminiscent of Moissac. The highly decorated façade has slender blind arcades around the porch and a cornice with grimacing heads. There are some odd little figures enacting battle-scenes on the archivolt. The compartmentalized *tympanum* is a famous piece of Quercy sculpture. The central panel shows the Ascension, flanked by two angels turning to call the Apostles and the Virgin. Above the figure of Christ, some small angels emerge from the clouds to welcome Him. There are further carved scenes all around, which show the life and martyrdom of St. Stephen.

INTERIOR: The plain nave, crowned by two domes on pendentives, contrasts with the choir, which is decorated with paintings and lit by stained-glass windows. In the 19C, the frescos on the W. cupola (about 1320) were uncovered after being hidden for years by coats of whitewash. They show the stoning of St. Stephen, with his executioners and eight prophets.

CLOISTER: This restored cloister is a fine

Cahors, cathedral tympanum

example of Flamboyant architecture. There is a very attractive statue of the Virgin with long plaited hair on a pillar in the NW corner.

Maison de Roaldès: This house stands on the Quai Champollion near the Cathedral. It dates from the late 15C and has two contrasting façades, one with timber-framing and a balcony under the roof and turret, and the other, N. one, in the typical decorative style of Quercy from about 1500. The part of old Cahors between here, the cathedral, the Cours Gambetta and the Lot is especially pretty.

Church of Saint-Barthélemy: This predominantly 16C church is in the upper part of the old town. The exterior is harmonious and there is a fine bell tower, but the nave, with ribbed vaulting, has been disfigured by inane decoration. In the first chapel to the right the enamelling on the modern font depicts Pope John XXII, who was born in 1249 near the church and baptized here.

Near the church you can see the ruins of a 14C house, known as the *Palais de Jean XXII*, built by the Pope's brother. It has a lovely crenellated tower, some 100 ft. high.

Barbacane: This tiny barbicaan is a former guardhouse and forms part of the 14C fortifications. These close off the town, where it is not protected by the river Lot. The nearby *Tour Saint-Jean* or 'des pendus' (The Hanging Tower) is unusual in that it is open along its entire height.

The former Bishop's Palace houses a small and very varied *museum*, dealing with the town's history and that of its great men, together with archaeological collections and paintings.

Environs: Château de Mercuès: (8 km. W.): This fine 15C building perched high up, has been transformed into a hotel. **Luzech**: (21 km. W.) This large village has retained its medieval character. It is dominated by a square 12C keep; 14C church of *Saint-Pierre*. There have been archaeo-

Calais, Rodin's the Burghers of Calais, detail

Cambrai, cathedral of Notre-Dame

St.Gregory), local historical papers on the subject of Calais' constant struggle with the English, and also exhibits relating to the tulle and machine-made lace industries, which were so vital to the town's prosperity. The bronze sculpture *The Burghers of Calais* by Rodin (completed in 1886 and erected in 1895) is the town's great pride and attraction. It is highly realistic and shows six men resigned to delivering up the keys of their city to King Edward III of England to avoid a massacre of the townspeople in 1347. This monument in the heart of the city, which was recaptured by France in 1558, seems to express the burghers' staunch pride in the face of their forced submission.

Calvi: See **Corsica**

Cambo-les-Bains	(5,130 inhab.)
64 Pyrénées-Atlantiques	p.422☐D/E 14

Cambo is a charming Basque health resort, shaded by large trees. The memory of Edmond Rostand, author of *Cyrano de Bergerac* and *L'Aiglon*, pervades the place. Rostand fell in love with the 'mauve mountains and the blue Nive', and built the vast *Villa Arnaga*, here in 1903–6. Set amidst a French park and garden, it is a pastiche of Labourdin architecture (Labour being one of the Basque regions) and its interior is an odd combination of styles. Memorabilia of the writer and his celebrated circle.

logical digs on the ancient setttlement (oppidum) of l'Impernal above the village.

Calais	(79.400 inhab.)
62 Pas-de-Calais	p.410☐I 1

Calais is the foremost French port for travellers and claims to be the 'key to France'. Much successful rebuilding has been undertaken since 1944. The Hôtel de Ville, with its 240 ft. belfry, has been rebuilt in the 15C Flemish style and is once again very attractive. Of historical interest are the 13C Tour du Guet (watchtower), which served as a lighthouse until 1848, and the circular apsidal chapel of the church of *Notre-Dame* (1631). The modern *museum* (1965) contains a very fine Flemish Primitive painting (*The Mass of*

Cambrai	(41,000 inhab.)
59 Nord	p.411☐J 2

Cambrai, in the heart of a rich agricultural region, is one of the oldest towns in France. The fabric Cambric takes its name from here. Things of interest include a Spanish house of carved wood (1595), lovely 17&18C houses, and the Porte Notre Dame (gateway) with its diamond-shaped stones. Fénelon was Archbishop of Cambrai in 1695.

The town has some fine pieces of religious architecture. The former abbey church of Saint-Sépulcre, the Cathedral of *Notre-Dame*, has been restored frequently, but always in keeping with its neoclassical style (early 18C). There is a monument to Fénelon inside, which was carved by David d'Angers (1826) and also eight large trompe-l'oeil grisailles. The chapel of the *Collège des Jesuites* (1692) has an ornate baroque façade with a remarkable *Musée Provincial d'Art Sacré* inside. Finally there is the church of *Saint-Géry*, which is sober and classical but notable for its dome over the crossing, the red and black marble rood screen (1635) and the superb *Entombment* by Rubens.

Musée Municipal: There is a very varied collection of works of arts here—from local faience to paintings of the great Dutch, Flemish, Spanish, Italian and French schools. There is also a large local archaeological collection, sculptures, including the 12C *Woman Against a Column*, and an interesting series of modern French paintings.

Environs: Abbaye de Vaucelles (11 km. S.): This monastery was founded in 1131. Today, only ruins remain of one of the largest of Cistercian churches (early 13C).

Cannes	(71,100 inhab.)
06 Alpes-Maritimes	p.426 □ O 14

Cannes lies on the Côte d'Azur and is world-famous for its finely curved Croisette, the casinos, luxury hotels, two harbours full of yachts, the Festival and the show-business figures that gather here (the

Cannes, château of Saint-Honorat

Midem). However, it still has an old part. Once just a simple fishing village, it became a great resort in the 19C, thanks to an English politician, Lord Brougham. In 1834 he decided that he liked the 'finest sky in the world' (Prosper Merimée) and built himself a villa here. A natural leader of fashion, he drew in his friends and as a result the new La Bocca quarter was soon renamed the *Quartier Anglais*.

Old Cannes is full of narrow, sloping streets, steps and alleyways, and is built on the side of the Suquet hill. On the top of the hill is a square *keep*, 66 ft. high (begun in 1070, not finished until 1385). Beside this tower is the *Musée de la Castre* with a collection of Mediterranean archaeology. The old port at the foot of the Suquet, where Guy de Maupassant kept his boat, and the bay were the inspiration for parts of *Sur l'Eau*.

Environs: Iles de Lérins (20–30 mins. by boat): The **Ile Sainte-Marguerite** has a fort altered by Vauban, where the mysterious 'man in the iron mask' was imprisoned (17C), as was Marshal Bazaine, defeated in 1870. The smaller **Ile Saint-Honorat**, with its pine trees, eucalyptus, and cypresses, has preserved its famous abbey, a successor to the monastery founded by St. Honoratus at the end of the 4C (it now belongs to the Cistercians of Sénanque). Some of the old fabric has remained and is surrounded by 19C buildings (the small *Musée Lapidaire*). The old fortified monastery 'le château' is on a headland. It goes back to the 10C, but was altered at various times. Its cloister is partly 14C.

Carcassonne	(46,350 inhab.)
11 Aude	p.423☐| 15

This formidable strongpoint, with its crenellated ramparts and towers, protects the wine-growing Aude region . Carcassonne is a medieval military masterpiece

Carcassonne, church of Saint-Nazaire

Carcassonne old town 1 Double wall **2** Porte Narbonnaise **3** Château Comtal **4** barbican **5** Porte d'Aude **6** church of Saint-Nazaire **7** Grand Théâtre

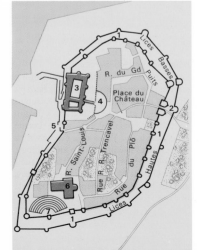

—somewhat 'modified' by Viollet-le-Duc in the 19C. Unmarked by time, the town's heart, the ancient and proud *Cité*, with its double wall, overlooks the new quarters, laid out in the form of a bastide, and the rolling acres of vines. The defences seem, from a distance, almost too medieval to be true. At first sight they could be mistaken for the film set of a historical epic. By car, the *Cité* can only be entered through the *Porte Narbonnaise*, in itself a complicated and impressive defensive work. The builders of the Cité in medieval times had only to refurbish and reinforce the 3&4C Gallo-Roman walls. Carcassonne controlled the trade-routes between the Toulouse region and the Mediterranean and was threatened, besieged or captured on many occasions, in particular by the Visigoths, the Saracens and the ruthless crusaders of Simon de Montfort, who

Carcassonne, the old town

came to crush the Cathar heretics. It was fortified mainly in the 13C, but lost its strategic importance in the 17C when Roussillon was annexed to France (1659). Carcassonne is an important centre of the wine trade.

Château Comtal: The castle of the counts was built in the 12C in the form of a stronghold within a citdel, separate from the other defences. Since St.Louis' time it has been protected by a strong barbican, a wide moat and large towers. It was restored by Viollet-le-Duc, who replaced the hoarding on top of the walls.

Church of St.Nazaire: The W. façade of this basilica was altered rather freely by Viollet-le-Duc. It has a simple Romanesque nave of characteristic southern style (11&12C), and a Gothic transept and choir (late 13C and early 14C). The sanctuary is lit by high 13&14C blue windows, which are amongst the most remarkable stained glass in the Midi.

Ville Basse: The towered Cité, with its old houses piled haphazardly along winding streets, is very different from the Ville Basse, which is laid out on a regular plan and whose nucleus was a bastide set up by St.Louis on the other bank of the Aude. The *Musée des Beaux-Arts* is in this part of Carcassonne and it offers a fine display of paintings by, amongst others, Jordaens, Van Goyen, Chardin, Rigaud, Marquet, Max Ernst and Dali; as well as a collection of ceramics. The *Cathedral of Saint-Michel* (13C), much restored, contains a wealth of ecclesiastical gold, and several paintings by Jacques Gamelin, born in Carcassonne in 1738.

Carnac, lines of standing stones

Carennac (390 inhab.)
46 Lot p.419□I 12

This pretty village on the banks of the Dordogne retains its ramparts and fortified gate. The characteristic brown-tiled houses surround the former *prieuré-doyenné* (priory), where Bishop Fénelon lived (1681 – 5; we owe the lovely decoration of the State Room to him). The porch of the little Romanesque church of *Saint-Pierre* has a carved decoration (12C) over the door representing Christ in Majesty, which is similar to those at Beaulieu and Moissac, and is framed by the symbols of the four Evangelists. Inside the church is a 16C Entombment; the cloister has a Romanesque gallery and three others, which are Flamboyant.

Cargese: See **Corsica**

Carnac (3,730 inhab.)
56 Morbihan p.412□C 7

At low tide there is a wide beach in front of the old village of Carnac. In the village itself the sober bell tower of the church of *Saint-Cornély* (17C) stands out. Its northern-style porch with Doric columns is crowned by a splendid canopy of carved stone. Inside, the panelled vault depicts the life of the saint, patron of horned beasts, whose day is the second Sunday in September.
Not far away, on la Trinité, is the *Musée Miln-Le Rouzic*, where you can see a fine collection of prehistoric finds from the area

Carnac, megaliths

(pottery, polished axes, necklaces, jewellery).

Megaliths: The megaliths, or standing stones, of Carnac are famous, and make it an open-air museum in itself, surrounded by gorse and heather. There are thousands of stones, standing separately or in parallel lines (alignments) or in circles (cromlechs); there are also dolmens and barrows. Relatively little is known about these monuments and the Neolithic civilization which produced them. It has been widely accepted that the barrows, the dolmens (these would once have been covered with earth and stones) and the passage graves were for burial purposes, but the standing stones (menhirs) are still a mystery. There is, of course, a wealth of legend and much speculation as to their meaning—particu-

larly as to the number in this one place: 'We may simply conclude that they are religious monuments. By using this vague, easy term, we can try to hide our ignorance. The upright stones are part of a religious cult, and above all relate to the main symbol of godhead among primitive and half civilized peoples—the sun, which dies each day and rises again.' (R.-P. Giot).

Alignments: These alignments are arranged according to the stars, and would seem to be for predicting eclipses—the Mané-er-Grah at Locmariaquer is a universal lunar reference point. Of the local alignments, including the magnificent Kerzerho group (in the Erdeven Commune), the ones at Carnac are the most important. Now divided into three distinct groups between the two hamlets of Kerlescan and Ménec (4 km.), they were possibly all originally part of one alignment. The Kerlescan group is made up of 555 small standing stones and a cromlech of 39 stones. The Kermario group has 1,029 standing stones arranged in 10 parallel rows, and some of the stones at the W. end are 18 ft. high. The Ménec alignments nearer Carnac include 1,099 standing stones aranged in 11 lines. There is a semicircle of 70 standing stones which is now partly hidden by the houses of the village.

Barrow of Saint-Michel: There is a chapel dedicated to St.Michael and a small wayside cross perched on the mound. It is 360 ft. long and 197 ft. wide, and has several stone chambers. The jewellery and weapons found here are in the Musée Miln-Le Rouzic.

Environs: Locmariaquer (13 km. E.): This little commune, facing the Gulf of Morbihan, also has some remarkable megaliths. In a nearby field is the largest known monolith, the Mané-Er-Grah or Men-Er-Hroëch, split up into four sec-

tions, the whole measuring over 66 ft. Behind this looms the Table des Marchands, a long dolmen half buried under the remains of a barrow. On the inside there are some drawings cut into the stone; these look like an axe, ears of corn and the sun. The Mané-Lud dolmen is in the form of a low table with the supports decorated with stylised motifs. On one there is what appears to be an attempt to draw a face, or it could be birds in flight. On another are drawings like boats with oarsmen.

Carpentras (25,500 inhab.)
84 Vaucluse p.425□M 13

Formerly the capital of the wealthy Comtat Venaissin, Carpentras is known today for its confectionery, especially humbugs. It was a Papal State until the Revolution and it prospered under the Popes, expanding beyond its first wall. A second one was built in the 14C.

Cathedral of Saint-Siffrein: This was

Carpentras, cathedral of St-Siffrein, detail of the Porte Juive (Jew's Door)

begun in 1404 by the Archbishops of Arles on the site of the old Romanesque cathedral (remains visible in the apse) said to have been founded by St.Siffrein. The S. door, known as the *Porte Juive* (Jewish door), dates from the end of the 15C. Above it is the curious 'Boule aux rats' (a globe gnawed by rats). The inside of the cathedral is a remarkable example of S. Gothic style; the one large nave is flanked by side chapels and there is a smaller polygonal apse. The choir was decorated by the peasant Jacques Bernus, an artist of the Provençal school, in the late 17C/early 18C.

The Palais de Justice is in the former *Bishops' Palace* (mid-17C), the work of an architect from Avignon. Much of the lavish original decoration remains: paintings, panelling, and the carved ceiling in the Bishops' State Room. The *Synagogue* is one of the oldest in France. It was built at the end of the 14C, rebuilt in the 18C and then restored. The ritual baths are on the ground floor; on the first floor the room given over to public worship still has its Louis XV decoration.

The *Hôtel-Dieu* (fine 18C façade) still has its unusual pharmacy. Cupboards, which have painted apothecary-monkeys, now hold a lovely collection of Moustiers faience. The much-damaged 1C *Arc de Triomphe* was the entrance to the Gallo-Roman town. The *Porte d'Orange* is a remnant of the 14C fortifications and has a high tower. There are several interesting museums in Carpentras. The *Musée des Beaux-Arts* incorporates the *Musée Comtadin* (local works of art and crafts, votive offerings) and the *Musée de Peinture* (picture gallery) and also the *Musée Sobirats* (decorative arts) and the *Musée Lapidaire* (sculpture, inscriptions), which is in the former Chapelle des Visitandines (also known as Pénitents-Gris), a baroque building.

Carrouges (château)
61 Orne   p.414□F 5

This massive brick and granite château encircled by a moat stands guard over the old border between Normandy and Maine, near the forests of Écouves and Andaine. Altered and redecorated, it still retains its warlike appearance (mainly 15C), emphasized by the machicolated late-14C keep. Inside, however, the château is full of luxurious Renaissance and neoclassical rooms. The elegant gatehouse is 16C. Nowadays, the former Canons' Residence is occupied by the reception room and offices of the *Parc Naturel Régional Normandie-Maine*.

Cassel
59 Nord   (2,500 inhab.)   p.411□J 1

The green, valleyed slopes on which Cassel is situated rise out of the plain of Flanders and dominate the extensive 'low

Carrouges, the gatehouse

Castres, the bishop's palace

country'. The highest point in Nord (574 ft.), it has always been at a crossroads and the routes converging on it follow the 7 Roman roads which led to it. The town was built on the plateau on the summit, and faces south. The *Grand-Place* is a vast paved and slightly sloping area with a few buildings remaining from old Cassel. To the E. is the collegiate church of *Notre-Dame* (1298), a massive Gothic structure with old brick walls, nave and aisles, three gables on the façade and a huge square central tower. Behind this is the stone and brick façade of the former Jesuit church (1687), quite different with its lively baroque lines. To the S., the 16&17C former *Hôtel de la Noble Cour* has a stone façade, casement windows with alternate triangular and rounded pediments, a high roof with dormer windows, crow-stepped gables at the sides and a Renaissance doorway with grey marble columns. Inside, the archive room, with Louis XV panelling, is also very attractive. There is a *Musée d'Histoire et de Folklore* here (parchments, faience and Flemish furniture). On leaving the Grand-Place, climb to the top of the hill, where the feudal château is situated. On the esplanade is the *Castel Meulen*, an 18C windmill. Beyond this, the view over Flanders is well worth seeing. General Foch followed the progress of the battle of Yser (October 1914 to June 1915) from here.

Environs: Hazebrouck (13 km. S.): This town on the plain was once the administrative capital of Flandre Maritime. The church of *Saint-Éloi*, with a beautiful brick bell tower (1532), has a wealth of sober panelling and a pretty 18C grille inside. Also note the side façade on the right wing of the former Augustinian convent (1616). This huge Flemish style building now houses the *Musée d'Art et de Folklore Régional*: there are some interesting 16,17&19C paintings, together with processional figures.

Castellane	(1,230 inhab.)
04 Alpes de Haute-Provence	p.426☐O 14

Hidden by a circle of small mountains, Castellane is dominated by the chapel of *Notre-Dame du Roc* (1703). Its old quarter is concentrated around the Rue du Mitan. The 12C church of *Saint-Victor* is rather unusual; a tower and gate remain of the huge wall which surrounded the town in the 17C.

Castres	(47,500 inhab.)
81 Tarn	p.423☐I 14

This is an industrial town spread over both banks of the river Agout. It has a long textile tradition (it is an important wool centre). The original city was on the right bank of the river, where the Romans made a camp. It gained considerable autonomy in the 11C, suffered in the Wars of Religion and became a Huguenot centre. Today, its centre is the Place Jean-Jaurès, which has a statue of the local politician. Jaurès was born in Castres in 1859, and he features in the *Musée Goya* in the Old Bishops' Palace (which also houses the Hôtel de Ville) The impressive collection of Goyas was bequeathed to the town by a local painter in the 19C. It includes the vast and famous *Junta of the Philippines* (about 1814), and a set of etchings, the *Caprices* (1790s). The former cathedral of *Saint-Benoît*, on the site of a 9C abbey church, was built in the 17C and early 18C and left unfinished. It contains some marble statues (late 17C)

Castres, Musée Goya, self-portrait

and several 18C paintings from a Carthusian monastery. The church of *Notre-Dame-de-la-Platé* was completely rebuilt in the middle of the 18C.

Cateau (Le)	(8,900 inhab.)
59 Nord	p.411☐K 2

This is a charming little town on the border of Cambrésis and Thiérache, lining the banks of the Selle. Henri Matisse was born here in 1869. The *museum* has some of his drawings and engravings, as well as works by his contemporaries (Gromaire, Dunoyer de Segonzac and Herbin). A *belfry* (1705) on the Grande-Place blends well with the Renaissance *Hôtel de Ville*. The former *Palace of the Archbishops* of Cambrai, with its classical lines and garden, is of interest.

Caudebec-en-Caux, church organ

The abbey church of *Saint-André*, now the church of Saint-Martin, displays a curious mixture of styles but is still a pleasing baroque building.

Caudebec-en-Caux	(2,730 inhab.)
76 Seine-Maritime	p.410☐H 3

The Pont de Brotonne spans the Seine just outside this small, charmingly situated town, which lies in a broad part of the Seine valley. The name Caudebec comes from the Norse words meaning 'cold' and 'stream', while Caux is a throwback to the ancient Calète population.

The church of **Notre-Dame** is surrounded by dull houses, which were rebuilt after the war. It has a stone open-work balustrade and is a good example of Flam-

boyant art, indeed Henri IV called it 'the most beautiful chapel in the Kingdom'. It was begun in 1426 and building continued throughout François I's reign. Between 1490 and 1539 the 160 ft. tiered spire, the large portal and the last two bays of the nave were finished. The church has no transept and is irregular in structure, but has an elegant triforium. Note in particular the oddly placed pillar in the axis of the nave behind the high altar; the carved stone organ loft—the organ itself is splendid too and the astonishing Chapelle du Sépulcre, where famous men are shown with the recumbent figure of Christ under a carved canopy (16C).

To the N. of the church is a lovely old house and remains of two towers from the old town wall. In the Place Thomas-Basin (named after the Caudebec-born bishop who tried to rehabilitate Joan of Arc) is the fine medieval Maison des Templiers with a little *museum* of local history.

Environs: Pont de Brotonne (1 km. upstream): This cable-stayed bridge was opened in 1977. It measures 4,193 ft. including the side spans (2,287 ft. for the main span, which runs 164 ft. above the Seine). **Church of Sainte-Gertrude** (3 km. NW): Consecrated in 1519, Flamboyant style, with a fine stone tabernacle inside. **Villequier** (4 km. downstream): The Domaine de Villequier, in marvellous countryside, has a splendid view over the Seine valley. The château has been turned into a hotel. This is the place where Léopoldine Vacquerie, Victor Hugo's daughter, drowned on 4 September 1843. The tragedy inspired the most moving poems in the collection *Les Contemplations* (*Pauca Meae*). The large family house of Charles Vacquerie, who died with his young wife, is now a museum. Fully furnished, it displays exhibits on the private, literary and political life of Hugo. A

Cavaillon, triumphal arch ▷

Cavaillon, cathedral of Notre-Dame

Cellefrouin, abbey of Saint-Pierre

12,14&15C church with a panelled vault and fine 16C stained-glass windows dominates the young couple's tomb.

Cavaillon	(21,530 inhab.)
84 Vaucluse	p.425□M 14

Cavaillon, the former capital of the Cavares and then the Roman colony of *Cabellio*, has an important archaeological monument — the 1C double Roman arch, which was moved in 1880 to the foot of the hill of Saint-Jacques. Cavaillon is in a farming area, primarily melon-growing. It is built around the large Cours Gambetta, at the end of which is an 18C gate, once part of the ramparts. In the charming chapel of an old hospital (1755) is the *Musée Archéologique Régional* — prehistoric, Gallic and Gallo-Roman periods.

The *Synagogue*, built 1770–4, is decorated with stucco, Louis XV panelling and rococo wrought-iron work. It is one of the most beautiful synagogues in France. In the basement you will find the *Musée Israélite Comtadin* with exhibits from the large local Jewish community.

The Cathedral of Notre-Dame and Saint-Véran: Legend has it that this Cathedral is built on a site dedicated to religious worship in the 6C by St. Véran, Bishop of Cavaillon. It seems to have been built in 1115–25, but was not consecrated until 1251, by Pope Innocent IV. It has been altered and restored, but is still one of the most interesting Romanesque monuments in Provence. Take time before entering to admire the lovely frieze on the N. and S. sides with its variety of subjects. Inside, the Romanesque structure is appar-

Châalis, former abbey church

ent despite the additions; there are some rich 16–18C furnishings. The adjacent small *cloister* is charmingly simple. The chapel of *Saint-Jacques* is also Romanesque and dominates Cavaillon from the top of Mont Caveau, an old Gallic oppidum.

Cellefrouin	(590 inhab.)
16 Charente	p.419☐G 10

The abbey church of *Saint-Pierre* was built on land bequeathed in the 11C by a local nobleman, Frouin, after whom the monastery was named. The raising of the ground level in the 18C (the pillars in the nave go down nearly 4 ft. into the ground) mars the fine proportions of the façade, with its narrow arcades and buttresses. The interior is austere, with a barrel-vaulted

nave flanked by side aisles. Either the artists were lacking in imagination or the monastery was too poor. The capitals in the nave are completely plain, but there is a very striking consecration cross at the base of the wall of the right transept. A little way off from the church the graveyard lantern in the village cemetery is in the form of a cluster of eight columns with a conical, scalloped roof.

Céret	(5,990 inhab.)
66 Pyrénées-Orientales	p.424☐J 16

This is a little Catalan town with remnants of the old fortifications, an 18C church and the distinction of having commissioned Aristide Maillol to design its 1914–18 *Monument aux Morts* (War Memorial). It is a quiet little place, amid orchards, and attracted Fauvist and Cubist painters, many of whom stayed here early this century. In the *Musée d'Art Moderne* established by the painter Pierre Brune, are works by Matisse, Braque, Picasso, Juan Gris, Dufy, Chagall and other contemporary artists. There is a whole room devoted to the Catalan sculptor Manolo.

| **Cerisy-La-Forêt** | (920 inhab.) |
| 50 Manche | p.413□F 4 |

The broken silhouette of the *former abbey church* of Cerisy-La-Forêt stands out against the nearby forest. Shortened by several bays in the 19C, this 11C Church is in the tradition of the great Romanesque buildings of the Golden Age of Norman architecture (Caen, Boscherville, Lessay). The apse, with its three rows of windows, is striking and is beautifully articulated. The choir stalls were made in 1400 by local craftsmen.

Ermenonville, tomb of J-J Rouseau

| **Châalis (Abbey of)** | |
| 60 Oise | p.429□J 4 |

This abbey was sold off as national property during the Revolution, and then ransacked and divided up. However, the remains still give an idea of the former grandeur of this 12C Cistercian establishment, to which the forest of Ermenonville belonged. One arm of the transept remains (13C) and also the 13C chapel with mid-16C frescos by Primaticcio, and the large Residence built for the extravagant Abbot by Jean Aubert, the architect of the Chantilly stables (1740s). It now houses a *museum* displaying the varied collections bequeathed to the Institut de France by Madame Jacquemart-André: Egyptian and Gallo-Roman antiquities, paintings of various schools (panels by Giotto), sculptures, furniture from the Renaissance to the 18C, tapestries and memorabilia of Jean-Jacques Rousseau.

Environs: Ermenonville (3 km. S.). Surrounded by forest, this village has a 16C

La Chaise-Dieu, fresco

church with a 13C choir, and the charming Louis XV château dates from the 1760s. Ermenonville cultivates the memory of Jean-Jacques Rousseau, who was a guest of the Marquis de Girardin, owner of the property. When old and ailing, the writer lived in a pavilion, which no longer exists. He died in 1778 and was buried in the marvellous park on the *Ile des Peupliers*, at the end of a lake. The garden is in 18C style and has a number of follies. Near the Mer de Sable, where the actor Jean Richard set up an amusement park, is the *Désert*, where the Marquis de Girardin had some of Rousseau's writings inscribed in stone.

Chaise-Dieu (La)	(1,050 inhab.)
43 Haute-Loire	p.420□K 11

From *Casa Dei* (House of God), the name finally became La Chaise-Dieu. This, with Notre-Dame du Puy, is the most famous religious building in the Auvergne and it stands out, gaunt and powerful, on the bleak plateau. It was founded back in the 11C by Canon Robert de Turlande of Brioude, who chose this bleak spot 3,300 ft. above sea level. When he died, there was a community of 300 monks and the monastery governed numerous French, Spanish and Italian priories.

The present-day church, rebuilt in the 14C by Pope Clement VI, a former monk of La Chaise-Dieu, was designed by an architect from Languedoc, in typical southern style. It has a severe façade flanked by two four-cornered towers, joined by an arcade. The perspective of the interior with its nave and two aisles, all the same height, is broken by a large, Flamboyant rood-screen. The church has the original furniture and decoration. The choir has fine, soberly carved oak stalls (14&15C) and a series of lovely 16C Flemish tapestries. The church's most famous feature, however, is in the N. aisle —three 15C tempera panels extending over 85 ft. and depicting the Dance of Death: Pope, King, knights, citizens and craftsmen and, preceding them, a skeleton.
Two sides of the late-14C cloister survive. Behind the apse is the Tour Clémentine

Chalais, church of Saint-Martial, detail of side arch

5C), a rectangular keep with ...icolations, which was designed to ...istand sieges.

Chalais
16 Charente
(2,540 inhab.)
p.418□F 11

On the edge of Charente, Chalais has some of the atmosphere of Périgord and is known for its important agricultural shows. The château is a powerful, rather austere building with a pointed, slate-covered roof. It is 14C, altered in the 16&18C, and dominates the old town. It used to belong to the Talleyrand-Périgord family, and has retained a high, square tower with machicolations and a working drawbridge. The church of *Saint-Martial*, which was damaged in the Wars of Religion and then partly rebuilt in 1629, has a richly carved Romanesque façade. In the façade there is a portal with four arches covered in Moorish-style decoration, and side arches with, to the right, the Holy Women at the Sepulchre.

Châlons-sur-Marne
51 Marne
(55,700 inhab.)
p.415□L 4

Châlons stands on a crossroads in the middle of a vast, chalky plain devoted to cereal-production and related industries. It combines the liveliness of a big provincial city with the quiet atmosphere of an old bourgeois town. The shady avenues of the Jard have been there since the Middle Ages— St. Bernard preached the Crusade here. The old houses, with their overhanging upper storeys, have retained their charm, and the 17&18C building reflects the best of a rich and ostentatious period. The former *Hôtel des Gouverneurs de Châlons*, with its elegant 17C façade, houses the Municipal Library (many illuminated manuscripts and precious bindings). The old *Hôtel de l'Intendance de Champagne* is almost Louis XV in style with its sober architecture and decoration of carved garlands, and is used as offices for the *Préfecture*. On leaving the town, notice the Porte Sainte-Croix, a triumphal arch built in honour of Marie Antoinette's arrival in

Châlons-sur-Marne, church of Notre-Dame-en-Vaux

France to marry the Dauphin. The *Musée Municipal* has a remarkable collection of Hindu divinities; the *Musée Goethe-Schiller* has numerous personal souvenirs of the two great poets.

The Cathedral of Saint-Etienne: There is an obvious clash of styles here, and the whole effect is at first disharmonious. The lovely Romanesque tower (12C) is a remnant of the previous cathedral; the high, narrow nave (13C) is pure Gothic. Above the triforium, the clerestory is virtually a wall of glass, which floods the nave (9 bays, 89 ft. high) with light. The stained glass in the N. arm of the transept is outstanding (13C), although all the 13–16C glass is superb. The cathedral is lavishly furnished.

The church of Notre-Dame-en-Vaux: This is still one of the finest 12C buildings in Champagne, in spite of the ravages of the Revolution. It is situated on the bank of the Mau canal, and has a fairly austere Romanesque façade and two elegantly pointed lead spires. The galleries are supported by Romanesque pillars with capitals, but the structure of the nave with its ribbed vaulting and the apse with three radiating chapels are early Gothic. As is common in the Champagne school, the apsidal chapels of the ambulatory are separated by a colonnade. There are some magnificent early-16C stained-glass windows. The *Musée du Cloître de Notre-Dame-en-Vaux* was opened in 1978, and you can see the 12C remains which were unearthed after a series of long and thorough excavations. It opens on to the old cloister (destroyed in 1759 and turned into a garden) and contains the statues, capitals and columns which had been cut up to serve as the foundations for a new cloister. Archaeologists painstakingly collected the fragments—some statues had been broken into 7 or 8 shapeless blocks.

The church of Saint-Alpin: This dates from 1136 and has been altered and restored over the years. Note the splendid 16C stained glass and a series of grisailles (about 1530); also some lovely paintings on wood.

Châlons-sur-Marne, cathedral of St-Étienne, rose-window in the S. transept

The church of Saint-Jean: This is the oldest church in Châlons, with an 11C Romanesque nave. The chapel of the Arbalétriers (cross-bowmen), which projects outwards at one of the corners, has a Flamboyant balustrade.

Environs: Notre-Dame-de-l'Épine (10 km. E.): Standing in the plain, this church, with its open stone-work was begun about 1410. Obviously inspired by Reims, it boasts a wealth of Flamboyant decoration, a fine 15C rood-screen and also some Renaissance furniture.

Chalon-sur-Saône	(60,450 inhab.)
71 Saône-et-Loire	p.421 □ L/M 8

Chalon stands on the Saône, which here divides around two islands. It is surrounded by residential and industrial areas and is a lively bustling town with a long history. In Gallic times it was the busiest port of the Aedui, who ruled the Morvan area. It became part of France along with Burgundy in 1477, and the building of the Canal du Centre (1783–92) by the Chalonnais engineer Gauthey encouraged its expansion. The pioneer of photography, Nicéphore Niepce, was born here in 1765 in the Rue de l'Oratoire. The exhibition in the *Musée de la Photographie* includes some of his early cameras (in the old Hôtel des Messageries Royales by the river).

Old Chalon: This part of the town is dotted about with half-timbered houses (lovely old houses in the Rue du Châtelet and the Rue and Place Saint-Vincent). The creation of a pedestrian precinct has given it back a lot of its medieval charm. This quarter extends as far as the church of *Saint-Vincent*, a former cathedral with a dreadful neo-Gothic façade from the last century. The church itself is in a variety of styles: 11&12C in its oldest parts, but en-

larged and altered in the 14–16C. The chapels in the right aisle are enclosed by remarkable stone screens; at the entrance to the cloister, one chapel has a very pretty early-16C tapestry.

Musée Denon: Named after Vivant-Denon, a local man and protégé of Bonaparte, who pioneered Egyptology and organized the Louvre. This well-stocked and interesting museum contains a large collection of archaeological finds, paintings (including the *Altarpiece of St.Blaise* about 1500, the *Triumph of Amphitrite* by Luca Giordano and *Portrait of a Negro* by Théodore Géricault), and countless objets d'art. The museum is housed in a former 17C convent, to which a neoclassical façade was added in the last century.

Chamalières-sur-Loire	(480 inhab.)
43 Haute-Loire	p.420 □ K 11

The village comprises just a few houses on the bank of the river and one of the purest Romanesque churches in Haute-Loire. The main point of interest in this plain, solid building is the choir: the huge half-dome vaulting has most unusual proportions. The carving is sparse, what there is being on the doorway of the N. aisle (battles of monsters and heroes), and on the magnificent 'bénitier des prophètes' (holy-water stoup)— an extraordinary Romanesque piece, supported by four statues. A door in the N. wall leads out to a garden, where there are remains of the early cloister.

Chambéry	(56,800 inhab.)
73 Savoie	p.421 □ N 10

This former capital of the Dukes of Savoy

Chambéry, church of Lémenc, crypt ▸

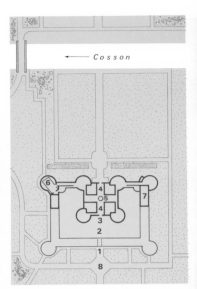

Château de Chambord 1 Porte Royale (entrance) **2** main courtyard **3** keep **4** guardrooms **5** main staircase **6** chapel in NW tower **7** François I's apartment **8** Place d'Armes

Chambéry, Jesuit chapel

was devastated in World War 2 and then again by a fierce fire in 1946. However, the pretty and unusual old quarter has survived, half-hidden by dull modern buildings. Mysterious alleys, secret passages and a whole medieval-looking labyrinth lead to the arcades in the Rue Boigne (19C) and to the château. (These 'allées' or 'trajets' were covered walkways running underneath the houses so that the defenders of the town could reach the places under attack in safety). Rue Boigne, a prostitutes' haunt in the Middle Ages, is a short and narrow street opening into the Rue Basse-du-Château, which led to the château and was the principal street in the town.

The 15C church of **Saint-François** was once the chapel of a convent, but in 1779 it was raised to the status of a cathedral. It has a fine Flamboyant portal, and the interior was entirely painted in trompe-l'oeil by Vicario (19C). Its contains fine pieces of religious art and a Byzantine diptych. The former Archbishop's Palace next to it houses the *Musée Savoisien* (a large and varied regional collection). In the Place du Palais-de-Justice, an old grain market has been turned into the *Musée des Beaux-Arts* — primitive paintings from Savoy, a fine portrait by Paolo Uccello, a series of children's games by Titian, a *Madonna and Child* by Guercino and mythological scenes by Watteau.

Château of the Dukes of Savoy: This castle was bought from the first Lords of Chambéry by a Count of Savoy in 1295. It has a tower with a small turret and has been greatly enlarged, altered and restored over the years. The oldest parts of it are 13–15C. The *Sainte-Chapelle* stands apart

Chambord, aerial view of the château

amidst this variety of styles, with its pleasing 18C Jesuit façade and Gothic nave and choir (early-15C). The apse is lit by some beautiful 16C windows and the chapel was decorated with trompe-l'oeil by Vicario (1831). A famous relic is missing, however, for the *Saint-Suaire* (Holy Shroud) is now in Milan.

Saint-Pierre du Lémenc: A winding avenue leads up to this church, whose crypt has a pre-Romanesque rotunda (the upper part dates from the 15&16C). This building is on the site of the old *Lemencum*. Madame de Warens was buried in its cemetery in 1762.

Environs: Les Charmettes (2 km. along the Avenue de la Grande-Chartreuse). This plain country house is in a small valley and is full of memories of Jean-Jacques Rous-

seau and Madame de Warens, who stayed here in 1735–41. The oratory is exactly as designed by the writer's devout and sensual mistress; the rest was rebuilt later.

Chambord (château)
41 Loir-et-Cher   p.414□H 7

This breathtaking, fantastic edifice, alone in its wooded setting, is the largest of the châteaux in the Loire valley. It is in an immense private forest, teeming with wild boar and deer, kept for Presidential hunting. Chambord ranks with Versailles and Mont Saint-Michel as one of France's greatest architectural attractions and is a magnet for tourists. It rises in a huge clearing as a mass of terraces, gables, turrets, pinnacle-turrets and ornamented chim-

Chambord, lantern

Henri II, Charles IX and Henri III. Visiting Chambord, one can't help being struck by the awkward arrangement and the general lack of comfort. This did not deter Emperor Charles V in 1539—this stone colossus was built to be seen and marvelled at rather than lived in comfortably. Even though the masons were still at work, François I often stayed here in his later years to hunt the Sologne game.

Louis XIV sometimes left his beloved Versailles for Chambord, where Molière performed *Monsieur de Pourceaugnac* and *Le Bourgeois Gentilhomme* in the Salle des Gardes, which was transformed into a theatre. King Stanislas of Poland and Marshal de Saxe lived here shortly before the arrival of the vandals of the Revolution. Napoleon gave it to Marshal Berthier, who nonetheless rallied to Louis XVIII in 1814. The soldier's widow could not afford the upkeep and put it up for sale. As the result of a subscription, it became the property of the Duc de Bordeaux, the last survivor of the older branch of the Bourbon family, who took the title Comte de Chambord. He left the much-dilapidated château to the Bourbon-Parma family. Then, after a long legal battle, the State invoked its right of pre-emption and acquired it. Since 1950 there have been major restoration works; the old moats have been re-dug and a *Musée de la Chasse* set up in several of the plainer rooms.

The spirals of the *Grand Escalier* begin in the middle of the *Salle des Gardes* and cross and recross as they climb to a 100 ft. lantern, which crowns the terrace. 'Like our churches it is supported and protected by the arcades of its wings, so slender and delicate that they seem made of light.' (Alfred de Vigny). It leads to the fairy-tale *terrasse*, which is a world apart from the rest of the château. These terraces were used as a belvedere and promenade when the Court was staying at Chambord. There is a superb view of the forest.

On the ground floor of the donjon (mainly

neys. 'From a distance, the building is an arabesque. It is like a woman with her hair blowing in the wind,' said Chateaubriand. Victor Hugo went even further, 'Magic, poetry, even madness are here in the wonderful strangeness of this palace of fairies and knights'. The pale colour of the stone is accentuated by the green background, and its dimensions are truly astonishing. It measures 505 ft. by 384 ft., has 440 rooms, a famous staircase with two spirals which do not meet, 14 main staircases, and 70 lesser staircases; all this crowned by the fantastic roof with its 800 capitals and 365 chimneys. François I decided to build Chambord in 1519: he was fond of hunting and wanted somewhere for his guests to stay, and he also liked the idea of leaving behind an original monument he considered worthy of himself. 1,800 workmen began the project, which continued under

Champ-de-Bataille, château (aerial view)

1533) are what were the old Salles des Gardes, which display all the state coaches pointlessly ordered by the Comte de Chambord, and the *Salle des Chasses de François I* (16C tapestries and trophies). On the first floor there are various apartments, and on the second is a collection of weapons and engraving. Although the château has very little furniture, it does have tapestries, paintings and *objets* which belonged to the Comte de Chambord, the last legitimate Pretender to the French throne.

The chapel in the NW tower was begun under Henri II and finished by Mansart under Louis XIV. Its interior dates from Louis XV's time.

In the forest of Chambord (13,417 acres), 330 yards from the château, there is a small village. The forest itself is a national hunting reserve surrounded by 20 miles of walls. Its 1000 wild boar and 500 hinds and stags are used to repopulate other French forests.

Champ-de-Bataille (château)
27 Eure   p.410☐H 4

This harmonious château of pale stone and rose-coloured brick is situated on the edge of a forest. Its name comes from a battle fought between Cotentin rebels and Guillaume Longue-Epée (William Long-Sword), Duke of Normandy. Built 1680–1701 and pillaged in the Revolution, it is once again owned by the Harcourt family, one of the oldest in Normandy. It has been tastefully re-furnished and is full of objets d'art. The two almost identical wings face each other across a huge courtyard, which opens on to the park through a very fine gate.

Environs: Le Neubourg (4 km. SE): The 15C church of *Saint-Paul* has lovely furnishings and 17&18C statues. There are also the remains of a château where various Kings of France and Dukes of Normandy stayed: it was here that the first French opera *Toison d'Or* was performed with the signature Pierre Corneille on the libretto.

Champ-sur-Marne	(6,450 inhab.)
77 Seine-et-Marne	p.429☐J 5

This elegant house, built at the begining of the 18C by the architect Jean-Baptiste Bullet, was nicknamed 'the enchanted palace' by the guests of the wealthy army contractor who financed its completion. (The first owner, bankrupt, died of a seizure on the steps when he was about to be arrested.) In 1757 it was rented by Madame de Pompadour, and the gardens were re-arranged in the French style at the same time. Ma-

dame de Pompadour spent a fortune on improvements to her luxurious home. Champs now belongs to the State and is near to the new town of Marne-la-Vallée. The park, which surrounds it, has retained its lovely 18C decoration, splendid furniture and numerous works of art.

Chancelade	(2,420 inhab.)
24 Dordogne	p.419☐G 11

The monastery buildings of Chancelade are hidden away in the greenery by the winding Beauronne river in Périgord Vert. They comprise the deconsecrated Romanesque chapel of Saint-Jean, a beautiful Romanesque abbey church (12C, altered in the 16C) resembling Charence churches to some extent, various monastic buildings and the attractive Abbot's House (16C). In a *Musée d'Art Diocésain* you can see holy vessels, reliquaries, statues and several paintings, including *The Mocking of Christ* by Georges de la Tour.

Nearby, in the *Abri Préhistorique de Ray-*

Chantilly, château, W. façade

monden, the skeleton of the *Homme de Chancelade* (Chancelade Man) and also various Magdalenian objects were found; these are now in the Musée de Périgueux.

Chantilly   (10,680 inhab.)
60 Oise   p.411 □ J 4

The château of Chantilly is an extraordinary gem in the Ile-de-France. Its setting of water and greenery was planned by Le Nôtre (Louis XIV's favourite landscape-gardener), who laid out the park for the Grand Condé. The famous races held on the race-course every year are run in the shadow of the magnificent *Grandes Écuries* (stables begun by the architect Jean Aubert in 1719), which Gérard de Nerval compared to a basilica. The château itself, standing on an islet in a lake formed by the Nonette, is really two buildings, one plain and 'authentic', the other spectacular but completely rebuilt.

PETIT CHÂTEAU: Also known as the *Capitainerie*, the Petit Château is the work of the architect Jean Bullant, an admirer of the Italian style, though his work is in the French tradition (Écouen is his work). It was built in the middle of the 16C for the Constable Anne de Montmorency, companion and marshal of François I, and a wealthy art-lover. Although it is now joined to the Grand Château, this small palace has remained almost untouched.

GRAND CHÂTEAU: Rebuilt in about 1880 by the architect Daumet (the first building having been destroyed in the Revolution), the Grand Château is a rather 'overdone' building. The rebuilding was financed by the Duc d'Aumale, a son of Louis-Philippe, to whom Chantilly was left by the last of the Condé family. (The original Grand Château was built by Louis II de Condé, a brilliant general under Louis XIV, known as the Grand Condé).

Musée Condé: The Duc d'Aumale, as well as being a fanatical art-lover, had also defeated Abd el-Kader in Algeria, had opposed Napoleon III, and been exiled for a long period in England. The treasures he

Chantilly, Crucifixion by Memling

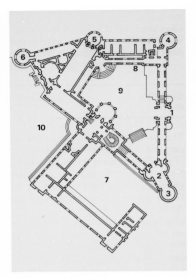

Château de Chantilly, Musée Condé 1 Entrance **2** chapel **3** chapel tower **4** Tour du Connétable **5** Tour Senlis **6** Tour du Trésor **7** Petit Château **8** Grand Château **9** main courtyard **10** Parterre de la Volière

collected at Chantilly were varied and idiosyncratic, and were donated to the Institut de France, to which he belonged. They form the basis of the vast *Musée Condé*, which is housed in the two linked châteaux. It is difficult to catalogue these treasures; they are so heterogeneous and unique. The celebrated *Rose Diamond* in the Cabinet des Gemmes, paintings and miniatures in the Santuario (Raphael, Filippino Lippi), the incredible miniatures by Jean Fouquet, *c.* 1455), works by Memling, Piero di Cosimo, Botticelli, Nattier, Mignard, Greuze, Ingres, superb panelling, marvellous manuscripts, etc. The Rose Diamond is now rarely exhibited and then with strict security. It was stolen in 1926, and then found by accident in an apple, where the thieves had hidden it.

Parks, Maison de Sylvie, 'Hameau',

Jeu de Paume: The extensive, formal park of Chantilly is crossed by the river Nonette. Le Nôtre took the opportunity to transform it into the *Grand Canal*, from which a branch, the *Manche*, runs at right angles through the geometric, French-style parterres. In stark contrast are the fantastic cascades of the *Jardin Anglais*. There is a gracious garden by Le Nôtre in front of the pretty *Maison de Sylvie*, rebuilt by the Grand Condé, with a rotunda added by the Duc d'Aumale. It is named after the beautiful Marie-Félice Orsini, the wife of Henri II de Montmorency, who was beheaded at Toulouse in 1632. When in hiding at Chantilly, because of some licentious verses, the poet Théophile de Viau named her Sylvie and dedicated some odes to her. The 'Hameau', a Louis XVI style hamlet, was to be copied at Versailles (Trianon) and consists of some pretty little houses. The

Jeu de Paume, dating from the mid 18C, forms an interesting annex to the museum.

Chaource

(970 inhab.)
10 Aube   p.415□L 6

Built on the site of a Carolingian town, it is still possible to trace the circular outline of the fortified wall. There remain a number of old houses built on wooden piles. The church of *Saint-Jean-Baptiste* unites Gothic (13C choir) and Renaissance (S. door). It constitutes what amounts to an art museum from the Troyes region, including a moving Entombment. This painting, with its eight expressive figures, is attributed to the Troyes studio of the 'Master of Sainte-Marthe', or 'Master of Chaource'. There are also some outstanding funerary frescos, which show the family tree of Marie de Vauldrey, benefactress of the parish.

Chaource, S. portal of church

Chapaize

(130 inhab.)
71 Saône-et-Loire   p.420□L 9

The beautiful former priory church dates from the early 11C. The apse was successfully rebuilt in the 12C. A remarkable tall clock tower over the crossing, decorated with Lombard bands, rises above an octagonal dome on pendentives.

Charité-sur-Loire (La)

(6,470 inhab.)
58 Nièvre   p.420□J 8

La Charité-sur-Loire, Notre-Dame, choir

Standing near the Loire, you will find the strange and fascinating shadow of an old abbey church, where houses have grown up in the side aisle of a vanished nave. The abbey of La Charité-sur-Loire, founded by Cluny in the 11C, comprised 200 monks and controlled 50 daughter houses. It became one of the great staging-posts on one of the pilgrimage routes to Santiago de Compostella. It was badly damaged during the Hundred Yers War and again in the Wars of Religion. It declined when its revenues were held in commendam and was abandoned during the Revolution. The church appears extensive despite its mutilation, but has long been deserted. Victor Hugo wrote: 'At Charité-sur-Loire, near Bourges, there is a Romanesque church which in its size and the richness of its architecture ranks with the foremost in Europe. But it is half ruined. It is crumbling, stone by stone, as lost as eastern pagodas in their desert of sand.'

Notre-Dame de la Charité was once the largest church in France after Cluny, and was built in several stages—at the end of the 11C and in the first decades of the 12C. It was ravaged by fires in the 13&16C. The ruined nave was not restored when work was carried out in the 17C. Instead a truncated church with four bays, transept and choir was put together. So Notre-Dame seems as if cut in two—the Romanesque tower and the main portal of the old façade are separated from the present church by a pretty little square where the nave used to be. At the foot of the tower, the remarkable *tympanum* of a bricked-up doorway survives: the scene depicted is perhaps that of Christ receiving the Order of Cluny presented by the Virgin Mary (this pure Romanesque work has been interpreted in many different ways). The church as it stands has an impressive transept, a majestic triumphal arch and a magnificent Romanesque choir. The rich decoration on the capitals is extremely varied in its motifs. Excavations in the apse have revealed remains of a simple 11C church.

Charleville-Mézières (63,350 inhab.)
08 Ardennes   p.415□L 3

These two towns on the river Meuse have each kept their own personality.

La Charité-sur-Loire, church of Notre-Dame

Charleville is the birthplace of the poet Arthur Rimbaud (b.1854) and remains faithful to his memory, although he left at the age of 17. There is a bust of him in the square which he mocked, and the quai where he lived and wrote *Le Bateau Ivre* bears his name. The huge Old Watermill, the *Vieux Moulin*, houses the *Musée de l'Ardenne* and the *Musée Rimbaud*. The stone and brick of its façade is repeated in the *Place Ducale*, with its high slate roofs. This focal point of the town founded by Charles de Gonzague (1580–1637) has a rather fine group of 23 houses with rose-pink bricks and chains of stone in the Louis XIII style remains. At their base an arcade encircles most of the square.

Mézières is an old stronghold which stood on an invasion route. The Chevalier de Bayard won a great victory here in 1521, and a citadel was built in 1590. These 16C fortifications have seen many assaults and shellings — you can still see the signs of them on the W. side. There are still a few towers and the powerful Tour du Roi stands out. The sober and classical Hôtel

de la Préfecture contrasts strongly with the basilica of *Notre-Dame-de-l'Espérance*, which has Flamboyant decoration and a beautiful Renaissance tower.

Charlieu	(5,070 inhab.)
42 Loire	p.420□L 9

Charlieu is a pretty little town on the edge of the industrial districts of Roanne and Brionne in Burgundy, which are dotted with Romanesque churches. This commercial town, known for its large cattle shows, grew up around a monastery, which became Cluniac in the 10C; its name derives from *carus locus* 'cher lieu' (dear place). Some buildings remain from the Benedictine abbey, as well as a cloister where exhibitions and concerts are held. There is also the famous *narthex* of an abbey church which no longer exists, although the foundations are visible. This 12C narthex has a fine doorway, which led into what was the nave (built during the second half of the 11C) and has some splendid carving on

Charleville-Mézières, Place Ducale

the N. side (1130–40). A skilful unknown artist decorated the tympanums with scenes full of life (*Marriage at Cana, Ascension*, in two rows).

On the edge of Charlieu is the *Couvent des Cordeliers*, dating from the end of the 13C. The state declared the great 14&15C cloister a listed building at the eleventh hour, even as the roof was being taken down. (Bought by Americans, it was being dismantled.) The monastery church is single-aisled and in the main dates from the end of the 14C.

Charroux, abbey tower

Charroux, church museum

Charroux	(1,640 inhab.)
86 Vienne	p.419☐G 10/11

You can get an impression of the splendour and size of the former abbey of *Saint-Sauveur* from the tall and mighty tower which looms above the roofs of Charroux. The abbey was founded at the end of the 7C and later enjoyed the protection of Charlemagne. These ruins have an important history—a Council of 989 established 'la paix de Dieu' (the peace of God) and in 1096 the high altar of the new church was consecrated by Pope Urban II (who was in France preaching the First Crusade). There are some remarkable relics—a piece of the True Cross drew thousands of pilgrims to the place. It has been possible, from engravings and excavations, to piece together the plan of the immense abbey church, 413 ft. long. It brilliantly solved the problem of incorporating a circular structure, that of the Holy Sepulchre in Jerusalem, into the traditional Latin cross form; the whole building was arranged around the circular sanctuary dominated by the tower. The church consists of a nave with nine bays preceded by a narthex, a transept with chapels and an apse with radiating apsidal chapels. There is a museum in the chapterhouse containing

Chartres, cathedral of Notre-Dame

valuable Romanesque ivory croziers and Gothic goldsmith's works; also some lovely 13C sculpture taken from the great W. portal. There remain some old markets and houses in Charroux itself.

Chartres (41,250 inhab.)
28 Eure-et-Loir p.410□H 5

Visible from miles away across the fertile plain of La Beauce, this celebrated cathedral, with its dissimilar spires and high nave, towers above the rooftops of Chartres. Charles Péguy, the poet, wrote about it and twice walked from Paris to Chartres in 1912. It is the central 'character' of Huysmans' novel *La Cathédrale*, and has become a symbol of faith and of France itself. Renowned for its architecture, statuary and stained glass, 3 million tourists a year visit the 'Acropolis of France' (as Rodin called the plateau on which it is built). It stands on the plateau with its apse above the valley of the Eure. This great work of art is an admirable expression of medieval thought and spirit. Émile Mâle wrote, 'It is at Chartres that the encyclopaedic nature of medieval art is best seen… The cathedral is the visible expression of medieval thought: nothing important has been left out. Its 10,000 painted or sculpted figures form an assemblage that is unique in Europe'. This admirable building has miraculously escaped the ravages of time and of man.

The History of Notre-Dame: Chartres is at a crossroads in the rich, agricultural Beauce area, and is the successor of *Autricum*, an important town of the Carnute

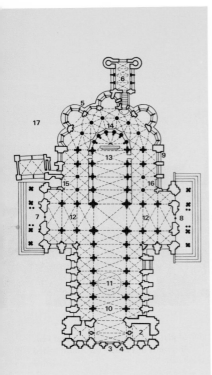

Chartres, cathedral of Notre-Dame
1 new bell tower
2 old bell tower
3 Portail Royal
4 King's Gallery
5 apse
6 chapel of Saint-Piat (treasury)
7 N. porch
8 S. porch
9 entrance to crypt
10 nave
11 labyrinth
12 transept
13 choir
14 choir screen
15 Notre-Dame du Pilier
16 Notre-Dame de la Belle-Verrière
17 garden of the bishop's palace

Gauls. It expanded in the Gallo-Roman period, was held by several powerful lords, and then re-annexed to the Crown by Philip the Fair in 1286. The town grew prosperous in the Middle Ages, and was left unscathed by the Wars of Religion, although it had been besieged by the Huguenots in 1568 and captured by Henri of Navarre in 1591. There have been several buildings on this spot since the 4C. The 9C building, destroyed by fire in 1020, was rebuilt by Abbot Fulbert on a much grander scale and his successor consecrated it on 17 October 1037. Work continued in the 12C, with the Clocher Neuf (the lower part), then the Clocher Vieux and the Portail Royal. However, another fire in 1194 left only the façade and the towers standing. Work on reconstruction was begun again very quickly, under an unknown master-builder, and the new Cathedral was consecrated in October 1260. Some alterations in the 14,15&16C did not really change the appearance of the building (only the Flamboyant spire changed its shape). In the 18C several stained-glass windows were destroyed and the choir badly damaged. In 1836, fire wrecked the roof and so a metal framework was installed. Recently restoration work has had to be done on the famous stained-glass windows, which were becoming distorted and suffered from a strange 'maladie du verre' (glass disease).

EXTERIOR: Notre-Dame is dominated by the *Clocher Neuf*, the N. tower, which was begun in 1134 and gained a Flamboyant spire in the early 16C, and by the *Clocher Vieux*, started about 1145, along with the magnificent *Portail Royal*, and finished in 1170. This triple portal is a splendid example of the best in Gothic statuary. Its statue-columns and tympanums glorify Christ. On the right-hand doorway: *Virgin and Childhood of Christ*, on the central one *Christ in Glory, Evangelists and Apostles,* and on the left-hand doorway the *Ascension*. The bays above this portal date

Chartres, cathedral, stained glass

from the 12C and the rose-window and the upper part are 13C. The Gallery of Kings (of Judah) linking the two bell towers was begun in 1250. The gable, with its large statue of Christ, shelters a figure of the Virgin. The porches in the S. and N. façades, at each end of the transept and preceded by flights of steps, were added in the 13C. They are decorated with lovely statues, those of the S. porch being earlier and more sober in style. The flying buttresses of the apse fan out over the garden of the Bishop's Palace; the 14C chapel of *Saint-Piat* extends beyond the apse.

INTERIOR: The inside of the cathedral is rather dark despite the blue light from the stained-glass windows. The layout takes the classical Latin cross form with a nave, aisles, a broad transept with aisles, and a wide choir with a double ambulatory and radiating chapels. The building is over 426 ft. long, some 121 ft. high (the bell towers are 338 and 367 ft. high) and the transept, including the porch, is 252 ft. across.

STAINED-GLASS WINDOWS: These cover more than 21,500 sq. ft. The windows are a unique masterpiece of the 12&13C and the blue tint of the glass is beautiful when in direct sunlight. The three W. windows, installed about 1150, were part of the previous cathedral and were miraculously unharmed in the fire of 1194. The large rose-window on the W. façade depicts the Last Judgement. The one in the N. arm of the transept, a gift from St. Louis and Blanche of Castile, is known as the *Rose de France* and glorifies the Virgin, while the window in the S. arm exalts Christ. A really superb window, the second one in the S. ambulatory, with red tints as well as blue, shows a beautiful representation of the Virgin and is known as *Notre-Dame-*

Chartres, cathedral, choir screen

de-la-Belle Verrière (mid 12C, the frame being later, about 1200). The artists who created the windows at Chartres are not known.

CHOIR: Work was started on the richly decorated choir screen in 1514 when Flamboyant was still the predominant style and it was finished after the advent of the Renaissance (some parts are later still). It was designed by Jehan de Beauce, and depicts 40 scenes extending over more than 270 ft. There are 200 statues in all, in an astonishing decoration of carved soft stone. The rather strange extension, the chapel of *Saint-Piat*, houses the cathedral's treasures: pieces of the old rood screen, ecclesiastical gold items and the 'Sainte Chemise' of Notre-Dame (which is in fact a veil). The 340 ft. *crypt* is the largest in France and dates from the beginning of the 11C.

Near the Cathedral: René Heron de Villefosse wrote, 'Chartres would not be Chartres without its cathedral. But the town does have its curiosities: from the strangely-named narrow streets to the wooden and gabled houses.' The mainly Renaissance church of *Saint-Aignan* backs on to the old ramparts. The church of *Saint-Pierre* in the lower town dates from the 12&13C, but its massive tower is early 11C. It has some remarkable stained glass (14C) and was formerly the chapel of a Benedictine abbey. The church of *Saint-André*, very much rebuilt, is 12C. There are also some medieval houses which are worth visiting, and the fine *Hôtel Montescot* (early-17C) and an old 13C tithe-barn called the *Cellier de Loëns*.

In part of the *Bishop's Palace* (17&18C) is the *Musée de Chartres*, which has a large number of paintings, including a portrait

La Chapelle-Glain, Château de la Motte-Glain

of Molière, and also some pieces from Chartres churches. The Flemish series of *Moses* tapestries formerly hung in the choir of the cathedral.

Châteaubriant	(13,800 inhab.)
44 Loire-Atlantique	p.413□E 7

Châteaubriant guards the Brittany border and dominates a vast area—the Mée district—with its forests and lakes. Its feudal château, built partly in the 11C, belonged to the Châteaubriant, Dinan and Laval families in succession. It was dismantled by French forces in 1488 and only a few ramparts, the fortified gate, a powerful keep and the chapel (recently restored) were left. In 1533, the Governor of Brittany, Jean de Laval, had an elegant Renaissance house built with ornamented dormer windows in the roof. The gallery is a different style again—a Doric colonnade with semicircular arches. The first floor is brick enriched with green schist.

Saint-Jean-de-Béré: This church was founded by the Benedictines at the end of the 11C and now stands in a suburb. It is of reddish sandstone. On its S. façade is a rustic throne with a porch-roof, which shelters two bas-reliefs of the *Annunciation* and the *Visitation*. The porch has a saddleback roof (15C). Inside there are three 17C highly worked stone altarpieces, which add a touch of the baroque.

Environs: The Château de la Motte-Glain: (18 km. SE): This semi-fortified house, a little distance from the village of La Chapelle-Glain, was built at the end of the 15C by Pierre de Rohan, and has numbered the Duchess Anne and Charles VIII amongst its guests. The château is classical in plan, with a main section and two wings projecting at right angles. To the S. there is an imposing gate-house with a two-storey central part protected by two pepperpot towers. **Abbaye de La Meilleraye-de Bretagne:** (21 km. S.): This abbey stands on the edge of the forest of Ancenis, in a peaceful spot beside a lake. The 18&19C abbey buildings are built of pale Loire tufa, whereas the Romanesque porch is red sandstone. It was founded by the Cistercians in the 12C, and is today occupied by Trappists. The abbey chapel was altered in the 14&15C, but still shows the severity dictated by St. Bernard.

Châteaudun	(16,000 inhab.)
28 Eure-et-Loir	p.414 □ H 6

Châteaudun is spread out on a plateau above the Loir, laid out in regular 18C style. It was largely rebuilt after the ac-

cidental fire of 1723. In 1870 the Prussians set fire to it again, and many houses were destroyed, in revenge for the staunch defence mounted by the Dunois National Guard. In 1940 yet another fire damaged the oldest church in Châteaudun and the Sous-Préfecture. Châteaudun has belonged in its time to the Counts of Blois, Louis d'Orléans (brother of Charles VI and father of Jean Dunois, Joan of Arc's companion), and to the poet-prince Charles d'Orléans. An unscrupulous local businessman, Dodun, became a wealthy Controller of Finance in the 18C and was involved in the rebuilding of the city by Jules Hardouin after the fire. (This architect was the nephew of the great Jules Hardouin-Mansart.)

Château: This remarkably restored château rises above the Loir. Now furnished and decorated with tapestries, it dates from various periods, but notably the 15&16C. The lofty building is dominated by a massive and imposing round keep (12C), which was given a remarkable conical roof in the 15C. This tower overlooks

Châteaudun, château

a *Sainte-Chapelle*, 15C Flamboyant, which houses 15 lovely statues. The chapel backs on to a 15C building, the Dunois wing, which is a severe Gothic edifice, but with a certain air of comfort about it. The N. *Longueville* wing dates from the beginning of the 16C, and on the valley side it is supported by an impressive substructure. Flamboyant and Renaissance in its decoration, this wing was never completed.

La Madeleine: This 12C church, which backs on to the ramparts, is the oldest Dunois church (fine Romanesque portal and crypt). The old town lies in between this church, damaged in 1940, and the château. *Saint-Valérien*: This is a late 12C/early 13C church with a 15C bell tower and tall crocheted spire. In the semicircular S. portal there is a three-cusped tympanum. The enormous chapel of Tous-les-Saints was built in the mid 16C. The chapel of *Notre-Dame-du-Champdé*: Situated on the edge of the town, it was demolished at the end of the last century and only its delicate Flamboyant façade (about 1520) remains, now the entrance to the cemetery. The *museum* has a very varied collection (prehistory, ethnography, mineralogy and medieval sculpture), as well as thousands of stuffed birds, eggs and nests.

On the right bank of the Loir is the church of *Saint-Jean-de-la-Chaîne*. It is Romanesque in origin, but was altered in the 15C and a strong tower was added in 1506. Upstream from the Saint-Médard bridge is the 13C chapel of *Notre-Dame-de-la-Boissière* and the remnant of an ancient commandery.

Château-Gaillard
27 Eure   p.414□H 4

The strong walls of Château-Gaillard overlook a bend in the Seine and dominate the site of Andelys, where the painter Nicolas Poussin was born in 1594. This enormous citadel was erected in just two years (1196 –8) by Richard the Lionheart to protect Rouen from the advance of Philippe Au-

Château-Gaillard, ruins and the Seine

Château-Gontier, the bocage

guste. Château gaillard means strong castle and it was reputed to be impregnable, but the English were unable to hold it in October 1203, when the French laid siege to it and took it by surprise. The castle was demolished in 1603 except for the keep, which was pulled down later. Now it is in ruins, but even the remains give an idea of this masterpiece of military architecture.

The Gothic church of Petit-Andely *Saint-Sauveur*, dates from the end of the 12C (the choir) and the beginning of the 13C. In Grand-Andely the church of *Notre-Dame* has some superb 16C glass, and the church itself is 13C (the façade, nave and choir), 15&16C. It was badly damaged in 1940. The *Musée Nicolas Poussin* in the Rue Sainte-Clotilde contains a famous painting by him, *Coriolanus Moved by the Tears of his Mother*. Remains of a Roman theatre

have been uncovered in the nearby hamlet of Noyers.

| **Château-Gontier** | (8,650 inhab.) |
| 53 Mayenne | p.413 ☐ F 6 |

The old town of Château-Gontier straddles the Mayenne. It has an important cattle-market with modern market buildings and the vast area of cattle pens, where the livestock is kept in thousands. The old town is spread out on the steep right bank, dominated by the 11C church of *Saint-Jean*. It was, however, very heavily restored after being severely damaged in the war and is an austere building with modern stained-glass windows. It contains some 11C frescos in the transept and has a marvellous crypt, in which the groin vaulting is supported by strong columns. The little *museum* of Château-Gontier exhibits antiques, sculptures and paintings. On the left bank is the church of *La Trinité* (17C), once the chapel of an Ursuline convent. The deconsecrated chapel of Notre-Dame-du-Genneteil is Romanesque.

Châteaumeillant (2,430 inhab.)
18 Cher p.419☐I 9

Saint-Genès is a fine Romanesque building on the edge of a large village which originates from a Gallic settlement. It is named after the saint who converted the area, and dates mainly from the first half of the 12C (with a modern bell tower). It has an interesting apse with a ring of apsidal chapels, but it is unfortunately difficult to get a good view of the outside from a sufficient distance. It has some fine statues and a number of historiated capitals.

Châteauneuf (70 inhab.)
21 Côte-d'Or p.420☐L 8

Châteauneuf now overlooks the intersection of the autoroute and the poplar-lined Canal de Bourgogne, but it once commanded the route from Dijon to Autun. The fortress and the village have an astonishing view and seen from the plain they are impressive. The château was 'neuf' (new) in the 12C, and underwent major alterations in 1460–94. The attractive Gothic residence is still surrounded by moats, thick walls and massive towers. The village itself has few inhabitants and is quiet and pretty with old houses, market buildings and narrow streets.

Environs: Château de Commarin (6 km. N.): The two squat towers protecting the wings of this lovely 17&18C country

Châteauroux, Château Raoul

château are 14C. The building, with its high roofs and broad moat, is a happy mixture of different periods, but the 1702 rebuilding is very noticeable.

Châteauroux (55,600 inhab.)
36 Indre p.419☐I 8

The 15C *Château Raoul* stands on the site of a 10C fortress in the heart of this the main town of Indre. It is now occupied by the Préfecture, and dominates the old quarter. The 16C Porte de la Vieille Prison (Old Prison), once a gate in the wall, still exists. The *Musée Bertrand* is housed in the fine 18C house which belonged to General Bertrand, the faithful follower of Napoleon. It displays Imperial memorabilia — weapons, objets d'art, documents etc.

Château-Thierry, ramparts, detail

town with ancient origins, marking the eastern edge of the Ile-de-France. The main square and one of the streets are named after the great writer of fables, and his life and works are represented in a *Musée Municipal* in the house where he was born. This museum does, however, have other exhibits as well. There are still two gates and a tower remaining from the ancient town wall, and some old houses. Where the *Vieux Château* once perched on a hill, there is now a pleasant park. This former fortress was once one of the most formidable strongholds in the region but now only a few walls and towers remain.

Châtellerault	(37,700 inhab.)
86 Vienne	p.419□G 8

The roofs of this town are a mixture of Touraine slate and Poitou tiles. On the border of Poitou, it is typical of the Loire valley. Descartes was born not far away. The town was founded in the high Middle Ages — in the 10C Airaud, Vicomte de Poitou, built himself a castle and the place was then known as *Castellum Airaldi*, later becoming Chatellerault.

Henri IV Bridge: (end of 16C, beginning of 17C): This sizeable bridge was commissioned by Catherine de Medici, and built by Charles Androuet du Cerceau, one of a famous family of architects (his uncle built the Pont-Neuf in Paris). The seven stone arches of this bridge span a total of 472 ft. It is 69 ft. wide and flanked by strong towers with conical slate roofs. There used to be a central pavilion linking them and protecting the entrance to the bridge. In the middle, there is a sailors' cross, decorated with anchors, which is a throwback to the old Vienne fleet.

There are also ceramics and a series of paintings and drawings (15–19C). The church of *Saint-Martial* is a mixture of styles from different centuries — a 15C panelled nave ending in a 13C bay, a fine Renaissance belfry and porch.

Environs: former abbey of Déols (4 km.): The tall spire of a Romanesque bell tower soars above this suburb of Châteauroux, which in the Middle Ages was the seat of one of the most powerful abbeys in the kingdom.

Château-Thierry	(13,850 inhab.)
02 Aisne	p.411□K 4

Jean de La Fontaine was born here in 1621 into a wealthy merchant family. It is a small

The church of Saint-Jacques: From the

Châtellerault, church of Saint-Jacques, capitals

12&13C. This has a 19C neo-Romanesque tower and façade. The choir and two transepts still have the original barrel-vaulting and in the 13C the nave was given Gothic Angevin vaults. The S. side chapel has a fine lierne vault with historiated bosses. The choir and chancel still have two interesting Romanesque capitals (showing the Journey to Emmaus and the Sacrifice of Abraham). In the left transept there is a wooden statue of St. James (17C) to remind one that the church is on the pilgrimage route to Galicia. The N. tower has a set of 52 bells, among the best in France.

Hôtel Sully: Better known as the *Maison des Sibylles*, this house was built for the humanist Gaspard d'Auvergne, one of the first translators of *The Prince*, by Machiavelli. The decoration of the façade and inner courtyard consists of medallions alternating between prophets and sibyls, hence its name. The attractive *Maison Descartes* (Renaissance) was lived in by the grandfather and then the father of the philosopher, who himself lived there in early infancy. There is an old well in the courtyard and two rooms in the house are devoted to Descartes and his family. The *Musée Municipal* is now in the remaining wing of the château built by Jean d'Harcourt in the 15C. François I lived there and his niece Jeanne d'Albret was married from there. In the museum are a number of souvenirs from Châtellerault's past: paintings, iconography, wood carvings, weapons, cutlery and countless pieces of faience. The *Musée de l'Automobile* is in a former arms manufactory. Amongst the production cars and prototypes you can see an 1882 steam-powered car, cycles, motorcycles and a fine collection of posters.

Châtel-Montagne (500 inhab.)
03 Allier p.420□K 10

The 12C church of Notre-Dame commands a broad view over the area. Its austere lines seem to blend perfectly with the rough materials used. The façade of this granite building is indeed rather severe and has buttressed arches. Its nave and two aisles are narrow and tall and the apse has an ambulatory and radiating chapels, a typical feature of the Auvergne school. The somewhat primitive capitals inside match the overall simplicity of the building

Châtillon-sur-Seine (7,930 inhab.)
21 Côte-d'Or p.415□L 6

Châtillon combines what were two separate towns. It is a Burgundian town, facing Champagne, and criss-crossed by branches of the Seine. The church of *Saint-Vorles* watches over it, an early-11C Romanesque

building which is well worth visiting, although it has been altered several times. Perched on a rocky escarpment with a 'resurgence' of the Seine below it, the building unites a Carolingian plan with the innovations of the early Romanesque style. The church of *Saint-Nicolas*, mostly 12C, follows the plan of the Cistercian abbey at Fontenay, but was enlarged in the 16C.

Museum and Vix Treasure: The remarkable museum of Châtillon, housed in an elegant Renaissance house which was left unscathed by the last war, has a fascinating Gallo-Roman collection (statues, numerous everyday objects). But outshining them all is the magnificent 'Trésor de Vix', found in 1953 on Mont Lassois above the village of Vix (7 km. NW of Châtillon). A slight rise suggested the presence of a razed barrow and excavations revealed a funeral chamber with a collapsed roof but otherwise untouched. It dates from 500 BC and in it the skeleton of a princess was found, buried with all her jewellery, the remains of a chariot, and the superb 'Vase de Vix'. Over 5 ft. high and weighing 440

Châtel-Montagne, church

lb., this wonderfully decorated masterpiece in bronze was probably the work of a Greek sculptor from the colonies in S. Italy. This giant vase, which points to trading at a particularly early date, dominates one room of the museum, and is surrounded by other artefacts found in the royal tomb.

| **Chaumont** | (29,000 inhab.) |
| 52 Haute-Marne | p.416☐M 6 |

Chaumont stands on a plateau with steep sides and overlooks gently undulating countryside, with a superb viaduct to emphasize the uneven relief of the site (171 ft. high and spanning the deep valley of the Suize). A fortified town, it was a seat of the Counts of Champagne until 1329, and still has the *Hautefeuille* tower, an impressive 11&12C keep. There are also some original old houses with flat-tiled roofs and staircase turrets projecting in front of the façades. The basilica of *Saint-Jean-Baptiste* is an interesting combination of Gothic

and Renaissance. It houses sculptures by Bouchardon and a very striking 15C polychrome stone Entombment.

Environs: Vignory (20 km. N.): The church of *Saint-Étienne* has a very fine nave, which is still in the Carolingian tradition, and a Romanesque choir. The whole effect is of grandeur in simplicity.

| **Chaumont-sur-Loire** | (800 inhab.) |
| 41 Loir-et-Cher | p.414☐H 7 |

Grim and fortress-like on a dull day, this château is transformed when the sun shines on its slate roofs and white stone. Chaumont, like Amboise, directly guards the broad valley of the Loire. It was built by Charles d'Amboise and his sons and grandsons from about 1466 on the site of an old demolished fortress. Queen Catherine de Medici bought it and then made her ex-rival Diane de Poitiers take it in exchange for Chenonceau. Henri II's former mis-

Chaumont, 'Entombment' (15C)

tress didn't like it, and only went there rarely, but she did carve her initial—D—under the parapet walk. It was very much restored in the 19C and lavish stables were added by the Broglie family. The State purchased it in 1938.

The building, in thick foliage, has three wings and an inner courtyard, which opens on to a terrace overlooking the Loire. Several of the rooms are empty, and only part of the house is open to visitors: the dining-room (16C Flemish tapestries, Renaissance furniture), the guard room, Diane de Poitiers' bedroom, the Council Room (very fine Italian tiled floor, late-16C Flemish tapestries), and Catherine de Medici's bedroom. The chapel, which can be seen from a gallery, is 15&16C, except for the 17C vault. In the adjoining tower there is a room where the Florentine astrologer, Ruggieri, may have worked. In the stables, which provide superb accommodation for horses, there are some English engravings, crops and harnesses. The old dovecote became a riding-school. It had been used as a kiln, since in the 18C there was a pottery at Chaumont for a while.

Chauvigny (6,690 inhab.)
86 Vienne p.419□G 9

Chauvigny is on a spur above the Vienne and commands a broad view over the surrounding region. Its strategic position explains why there are four feudal châteaux side by side. The vast 11C *Château Baronnial* rises above the E. escarpment. It belonged to the Bishops of Poitiers, who held Chauvigny—the town was important to them since it guarded the approach to Poitiers itself. The keep still exists, as well as the ramparts with traces of the new castle; a residence was added in the 14C. The *Château d'Harcourt* was built on the E.

precipice in the 13&15C by the Viscounts of Châtellerault. Of this castle there are only some ramparts and the gate-house still standing. There are only a few ruins of the third castle, the *Château de Mauléon*, around the church. To the NE, the fourth, the *Château de Beaumont*, has an enormous square keep—the Tour de Gouzon. The Tour de Flins, slightly lower down, controlled the route from Angles and Bonneuil.

The church of Saint-Pierre: This 11&12C Romanesque former collegiate church, founded by the Bishops of Poitiers, is built of lovely grey stone and has a bell tower with two rows of high arcades. The crocket capitals of the middle storey are already Gothic in style and the building of the church, spread over more than a century, finished with this tower. It is interesting to note the beautifully balanced and superbly carved apse and apsidal chapels. The arches are decorated with geometric designs and the corbels of the cornice have carved masks, etc. The nave has a broken barrel vault and is flanked by narrow, high side-aisles, which provide the only light. The columns have capitals with palm-leaf moulding. Most interesting of all, however, is the choir. The extraordinary capitals with their mixture of crudeness and oddity, depict a fantastic world of dragons, monsters, sphinxes with woman's heads, sirens and an oriental atmosphere which permeated Romanesque art through ivories and imported fabrics. One of the capitals bears a rare signature from the Romanesque period: *Gofridus me fecit*.

The church of Notre-Dame (11&12C): This church is in the lower town. It is a rather modest Romanesque bulding with an octagonal dome on pendentives, resting on arches with prettily carved capitals. It contains an allegorical fresco dating from

Chaumont-sur-Loire, château

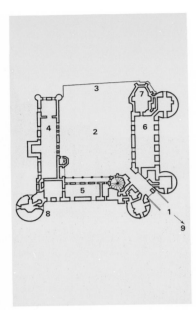

Château of Chaumont-sur-Loire 1 Entrance **2** main courtyard **3** terrace **4** W. wing **5** S. wing **6** E. wing **7** chapel **8** Tour d'Amboise **9** stables

Chauvigny, church of Saint-Pierre, capital

the 15C showing Humanity carrying its Cross.

Environs: In the middle of the Merovingian cemetery of **Saint-Pierre-les-Eglises** (2 km. S.) there is the simple pre-Romanesque church of Saint-Pierre. Its small apse (9/10C) has some frescos which are considered to be the oldest in Poitou.

Chenonceau (château)
37 Indre-et-Loire   p.414☐H 7

The supremely elegant Château of Chenonceau, on the Cher, combines the grace of the Renaissance with the nobility of newly emerging classicism. It rests on its arches built across the river, between woods and fields, and is always beautifully maintained. It has been well restored and today is a big tourist attraction, which has revitalized the adjoining village, Chenonceaux (with an 'x'). Thomas Bohier, a collector of taxes in Normandy, bought the property in 1513 and left the supervising

of the building work to his wife Katherine Briçonnet. His son, being bankrupt, gave the château to François I, who used it for hunting. Henri II inherited it, and gave it to his mistress Diane de Poitiers, who was nineteen years his senior and from whom he was inseparable. She loved the place and commissioned Philibert Delorme (who also built the Châteu d'Anet) to build an arched bridge over the Cher as an extension to the main building. She spent a fortune in improvements to her home. When Henri II died, his wife Catherine de Medici took revenge on her rival and made her exchange her beloved Chenonceau for Chaumont. She had a gallery built along the arches by Philibert Delorme, and he also built magnificent stables and re-styled the park. At this time there were some extravagant fêtes at the château; this was later followed by a quiet period (until 1601) during which Queen Louise de Vaudémont, Henri III's widow, lived in mourning here. Then Chenonceau changed hands many times. Jean-Jacques Rousseau stayed here as the cosseted guest of Mme. Dupin, wife of a rich tax-farmer. He refers to his stay in *Les Confessions*: 'We enjoyed ourselves greatly in this beautiful place and we lived luxuriously. I grew as fat as a monk.' The château escaped damage in the Revolution, was bought in 1813 by the Menier family (chocolate makers), and was converted into a military hospital in World War 1.

The approach to the château is along a lovely avenue of plane trees. On the right, the outbuildings built according to Philibert Delorme's specifications contain a *Musée de Cire* (wax museum). To the right of the terrace, which runs around the gardens of Diane de Poitiers and Catherine de Medici, there is a keep with the initials and the motto of the first owner—'S'il vient a point, me souviendra.' Built on the foundations of an ancient mill, the *Château Bohier* is a large square pavilion in early Renaissance style. The *Grande Galerie*, 260 ft. long and two-storeyed, spans the Cher on five arches. Like many of the Loire châteaux, Chenonceau was originally very sparsely furnished. The Court carried with it its tapestries, coffers, silver and sometimes even its furniture. Of particular interest here are: the portrait of Diane

Chauvigny, church of Saint-Pierre, details of capitals

Chenonceau, aerial view

Cherbourg, Château de Tourlaville

de Poitiers by Primaticcio, the *Three Graces* by Van Loo, and works by Jordaens, Veronese, Rubens, Rigaud and Mignard. The Chambre de François I is the most richly furnished and decorated room.

Cherbourg	(34,650 inhab.)
50 Manche	p.413☐E 3

Cherbourg lies in a broad bay on the N. coast of the Cotentin peninsula. Its view of the sea is obscured by an enormous breakwater, which protects the harbour from the buffetings of the Channel. A masterpiece of marine construction, it was not finished until the mid 19C, although work had been started in the presence of Louis XVI! There is a fort on the Mon-

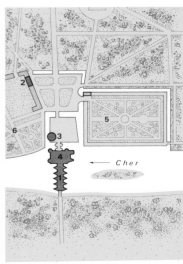

Château of Chenonceau 1 Grande Galerie **2** waxwork museum **3** keep **4** Château Bohier **5** garden of Diane de Poitiers **6** garden of Catherine de Medici

tagne du Roule, dominating the town, where the Germans fought off fierce attacks from the Allies in 1944. It now houses the *Musée de la Guerre et de la Libération*, which is devoted to exhibits connected with the occupation of the area and the progress of operations.

The church of *La Trinité* managed to escape the damage Cherbourg suffered in the war. It is mostly 15C. In the *Musée des Beaux-Arts* you will find a collection of paintings, including a unique series of works by Millet, who was born in a nearby village. The Parc Emmanuel Liais, established by a naturalist, astronomer and former mayor of the town, is famous for its exotic plants. Emmanuel Liais's house now contains the *Musée de Sciences Naturelles, de Préhistoire et d'Ethnographie*.

Cheverny (720 inhab.)
41 Loir-et-Cher p.414□H 7

This distinguished château on the edge of the Sologne dates from the early 1630's. It consists of a high and narrow central section flanked by two square pavilions with rounded roofs and lanterns. The outbuildings to the left of the main entrance are said to be part of an old 1510 manor house. They now contain the *Musée de Vénerie*, full of hunting trophies. In the nearby kennels there is a pack of hounds which is still used for hunting each winter with the famous *Trompes de Cheverny* sounding the cry. The château has belonged to the Marquis de Vibraye since 1825, and is still lived in. Unlike the royal residences of Blois and Chambord, which are almost empty inside, the interior decoration and furnishing of Cheverny is magnificent. The dining-room on the ground floor has the same curiously decorated panelling by Jean Mosnier, a local 17C painter, that can be found at Beauregard. The large drawing-room contains some 17&18C paintings and some outstanding furniture including Louis XV chairs. The small drawing-room has five Flemish tapestries, inspired by Teniers, as well as some very pretty furniture. There is a large and impressive carved staircase in the centre of the house leading to the upper apartments, where you can see paintings by Mosnier, tapestries and the luxurious royal bedroom.

Cheverny, aerial view of the château

Chinon	(8,300 inhab.)
37 Indre-et-Loir	p.419☐G 8

High up on a spur where the regions of Touraine, Anjou and Poitou meet is a ruined château, overlooking on the one side the vines which produce the 'vin de taffetas', so beloved of Rabelais, and on the other the Vienne and an astonishing medieval-looking town. 'Chinon, a small town with a great name' as one saying goes. Armand Lanoux waxed lyrical: 'The feeling of history is so intense in Chinon that at any moment you expect to see a squire encased in metal leaping out of a side street, or a madman dressed in apple green, a leper with his bell or a whistling page.' This town, with its medieval atmosphere, has exploited its past well, thanks to some very good restoration. The town can trace its origins to a Gallic town and a Gallo-Roman camp, and it was once a fief of the Plantagenets; Henry II of England died here in 1189, and Richard the Lionheart may have done so too (1199).
Joan of Arc came here in 1429 to try to persuade Charles VII to fight for his kingdom. François Rabelais came from here—he was born at La Devinière in about 1494, the

son of a lawyer, and spent his childhood here. The region and its people were the inspiration for his prolific writings: Gargantua, Pantagruel, Gargamelle and Frère Jean des Entommeures, so measured in their excess, are all drawn from the region.

Old Chinon: The old town on the right bank of the Vienne is reached by a bridge, the piers of which are 12C. Although it is only 11 km. from the atomic power station at Avoine, this town seems quite untouched by modern life, with its narrow cobbled streets and fascinating medieval houses. In the *Rue Voltaire* and the *Grande Carroi* (crossroads) you will find gables, turrets, corbels and mullions. The *Maison des États Généraux* is a large 15C house with a corner turret, whose name comes from the Assembly called in 1427 and 1428 by Charles VII. It is claimed that Richard the

Lionheart died here. Today it is a museum displaying the collections of furniture and objets d'art of the Société du Vieux Chinon, and also a full-length portrait of Rabelais, as Delacroix pictured him. The former collegiate church of *Saint-Mexme*, mutilated and deconsecrated, is 15C; the church of *Saint-Étienne* dates from the end of the 15C; the church of *Saint-Maurice* is 12&16C (nave and Angevin choir).

Château: Standing on a narrow spur, with cliffs on three sides, the castle consists of three distinct parts. There is the dismantled *Fort Saint-Georges*, the *Château du Milieu* with its lovely 12–15C *Pavillon de l'Horloge* and the *Château du Coudray*, whose towers are 12C (Tour du Moulin) and 13C.

Dominating the town, however, are the ruins of the *Vieux Logis*, the royal residence where Henry II Plantagenet died, and Charles VII received Joan of Arc. The little museum in the tall, slender Tour de l'Horloge has many exhibits concerning the Maid of Orléans. On the top of the tower there is a wooden lantern with an old bell (1399) inside—the 'Marie Javelle'.

Cîteaux
21 Côte d'Or   p.421 □ M 8

The mostly modern buildings of the famous abbey where St. Bernard arrived in 1112 are situated among oaks, hornbeams and beeches. Citeaux takes its name from the reeds by the banks of a lake (Cistels), and it was once the head of a large order, rivalling even Cluny. Its severe reform was

Chinon, château

disseminated throughout Europe, and more than 1000 abbeys were founded. Clairvaux was one of its daughter houses, along with Fontenay and Pontigny.

| **Civray** | (3,110 inhab.) |
| 86 Vienne | p.419☐G 9 |

This little commercial town lies on the border of Haut-Poitou and Angoumois on the banks of the Charente.

Saint-Nicolas (12C, restored in the 19C): This church stands out among the Romanesque monuments of Poitou. Harmoniously proportioned, it has an octagonal bell tower and lantern lighting the sanctuary. But its reputation stems from its historiated façade. Rectangular in plan, it has six semicircular arches in two rows, separated by a cornice with corbels. An impressive narrative unfolds on this façade. The archivolts of the central portal bear the traditional Poitou themes: Christ in Majesty, Wise and Foolish Virgins, the Assumption, the signs of the zodiac and the labours of the months. On the upper row there used to be a Poitevan horseman in the left arch, decorated with angels and musicians, but now there is only the mutilated horse. Under the right row, there are nine statues which have been variously identified; apart from a seated bishop, referred to as St. Nicholas, the other figures, both male and female, could either be saints or apostles.

Hôtel de la Prévôté: (end of the 15C): This house, with its pretty Gothic door and Renaissance windows, is also called the Maison Louis XIII, because Louis

Civray, church of Saint-Nicolas, statues in tympanum

XIII and Anne of Austria stayed here just after they were married. In the Place d'Armes there is a 15C house.

Clamecy	(6,150 inhab.)
58 Nièvre	p.416□K 7

Clamecy was an important 'wood port' when Paris was supplied from the Morvan woods. It is also the birthplace of the writer Romain Rolland, who won the Nobel Prize in 1916. He was born in 1866 in this interesting old town with its carved tower of Saint-Martin, and all his life he remembered the 'town of beautiful reflections and plain hills'. It is a pretty place with lots of old houses. The church of *Saint-Martin* dates mainly from the 13&14C, but its exterior is Flamboyant—the early-16C façade

and square tower are elaborately decorated. The apse is square-ended, there is no transept, and the church is divided by a roodscreen installed by Viollet-le-Duc to stabilize two pillars which were moving apart. The museum in the elegant 16C hôtel of the Duc de Bellegarde has a lovely collection of faience and exhibits relating to the timber trade and the floating of logs down the river.

Clères	(1,090 inhab.)
76 Seine-Maritime	p.410□H 3

The large, typically Norman, fairy-tale manor at Clères is much restored, but there are still original parts (medieval and 16C). It stands in the middle of a wildlife park with hundreds of birds and animals in

Civray, angel musician on the church

natural surroundings. Colette called it a veritable Eden and wrote warmly of it. Nearby is the *Musée de l'Automobile des Moteurs et des Motos*, where armoured vehicles from the last war are displayed side by side with veteran cars. There are about 60 models altogether, from the Belle Époque to the present day.

Clermont-Ferrand   (161,200 inhab.)
63 Puy-de-Dôme   p.420☐J 10

Backing on to the volcanic mountains of the Puys and overlooked by the oldest and the most famous, the Puy-de-Dôme, Clermont-Ferrand, the capital of Auvergne, is a university town and an industrial centre and was once the rival of Riom. It has expanded to the E. and N. continu-ously over the years, swallowing up neigh-bouring villages and suburbs, and finally incorporating Montferrand, to which it has long been united. Clermont, formerly *Nemetum* and then *Augustonemetum* (in honour of Augustus) was a flourishing city in Roman times. Saints and scholars have visited it (St. Austremoine, who founded the first church in Auvergne; Gregory of Tours, the first medieval chronicler). It has seen many struggles between the ruling counts and the bishops. In 1095 a Coun-cil was held at which Urban II preached the First Crusade. Right on its doorstep was its rival Montferrand, which was favoured by the monarchy in order to curb the power of the bishops of Clermont, and it was not until 1731 that the two were joined. Blaise Pascal was born here in 1623, and an invention of his is on show in one of the museums.

Old Clermont: Although often passed over in favour of Montferrand, the old streets here in the heart of old Clermont still have their 'old-world' look. It is worth-while exploring behind the rather austere façades of the houses to discover the richly-decorated inner courtyards of an unjustly neglected Clermont. The *Rue Pascal* (the old 'Rue des Nobles') the *Rue du Port* and the *Rue des Chaussetiers* can offer façades, carved doorways, and balustraded win-dows dating from the 15,16&17C.
Note the *Hôtel Vachier-Fontfreyde* (No. 17) in the Rue du Port, which has lovely wrought-iron balconies (18C) and a Gothic door with the Vachier coat-of-arms in the courtyard. At No. 19, the *Hôtel Ribbeyre*, built under Louis XV, has a second court-yard reached through a vaulted passage. The door has a finely carved basket arch built of lava. No. 23 has a 16C façade with a projecting bay-window. The *Hôtel de la Vilatelle* (No. 38) has a very fine portal. In the Rue Pascale, above the vents of the cel-lars, several levels of which run under the old town, are some more sombre façades

hiding courtyards and gardens (note the Renaissance staircase of the *Hôtel de Champflour,* No. 21). In the Rue des Chaussetiers, the courtyard of the *Hôtel Savaron* is 16C but is Gothic in construction. The staircase turret has a beautiful carved door 'des hommes sauvages'.

Fontaine d'Amboise (Place de la Poterne). This is a charming Renaissance fountain in Volvic stone with three basins and a lantern with small naked figures pouring water; on the top is a hairy Hercules carrying the coat-of-arms of the House of Amboise.

Basilica of Notre-Dame-du-Port: This is one of the finest examples of Auvergne Romanesque, dating from the 11&12C. There are houses all around it so that it is difficult to appreciate fully the admirable arrangement of the apse, which comes as a surprise. It is not in the sombre Volvic stone which makes Clermont rather gloomy, but in a warm-coloured stone, which has mellowed over the years. *Apse:* This has an overall feeling of balance and harmony, becoming progressively less heavy to the radiating chapels to the octagonal tower. On the gables above the windows, against which the roofs of the chapels lean, is the Mozarabic-influenced polychrome masonry so dear to builders from Basse-Auvergne and Velay. *S. side:* Like the nave this is divided into bays, and the buttresses and wide semicircular arches reflect the rhythm of the pillars inside. In the fourth bay there is a lovely door of an original Auvergne design—a huge rectangular opening with fish-bone design, saddle-back lintel and semicircular tympanum. From left to right the lintel has: the *Adoration of the Magi,* the *Presentation in the Temple,* the *Baptism of Christ.* In the tympanum there is a Christ in Majesty between two seraphim. The fullness of the relief of these late-12C sculptures suggests the Gothic.

Clermont-Fd., Fontaine d'Amboise

INTERIOR: You can see the pillars of the nave beyond the low, rather archaic vaulted narthex, with the carved bases of their capitals. The barrel-vaulted nave has no clerestory. As is the custom in Auvergne, the tribunes or galleries supporting the central barrel are built above the narrow, high, groin-vaulted side aisles and they open on to the nave by way of triple bays. Note a strange honeycombed course made of shingle on the upper parts of the walls. The crossing, framed by three dividing arches, each relieved by a triple bay, is crowned by a dome on pendentives. The marvellously arranged choir is flooded with light and separated from the ambulatory by eight slender columns with the oldest and finest capitals in the church (about 1150–60). The four historiated capitals of the apse are obviously by the same sculptor, Robertus, who signed one of them. Seemingly crude

Clermont Fd., Notre-Dame-du-Port, part of choir

(rather overcrowded with figures), they still show a great sense of order and symmetry. You can pick out the struggle of the Vices and the Virtues, the Annunciation, Original Sin and the Assumption. *Crypt:* This lies beneath the choir and repeats its arrangement. It houses a black Virgin which is fact a reproduction of the vanished original, Byzantine in style, which was venerated by crowds of pilgrims in the 13C.

Cathedral: This is in complete contrast to Notre-Dame-du-Port both in its form and materials. Rather unjustly called 'The coalmen's cathedral' by the Goncourt brothers, it is built of Volvic stone which does give it a rather sombre appearance. A 5C basilica and a Carolingian church (the crypt remains beneath the choir) previously stood on the site. The first stone of the present cathedral was laid in 1248 and work continued for centuries, finally being completed in the 19C with the portal and the spires by Viollet-le-Duc. *Exterior:* The most interesting parts are the façades of the transepts, flanked by unfinished 14C towers: the only complete one is by the N. transept but it has no spire. Known as 'La Bayette', it does have an octagonal watchtower. *Interior:* It was possible with the very strong Volvic stone to make the pillars thinner and to build the vault at a height of 98 ft., above an almost unbroken line of glass. At the end of the transepts, there are two beautiful rose-windows (14C), based on those in Notre-Dame in Paris. The radiating apsidal chapels are lit by splendid late-13C stained-glass windows, with medallions and panels said to come in part from the workshops of the Sainte-Chapelle in Paris. These depict the life of Christ, the Virgin and the saints to

Clermont-Fd., basilica, black Virgin

Clermont, cathedral, Pietà

whom the chapels were once dedicated. In the ambulatory there is a very fine 14C door, framed by vine-leaf motifs, leading to the sacristy. There are traces of 13&14C frescos to be seen in several chapels. Behind the high altar there is a magnificent and surprisingly large gilt copper 18C Easter candlestick. The crypt has a lovely 4C Christian sarcophagus in white marble, with various episodes from the life of Christ on it.

There are other relics of a rich Christian heritage in the town itself. The chapel of *Beaurepaire,* built by the Franciscans, is part Romanesque, part Gothic (semicircular bays and Gothic decoration). The 13C chapel of the *Visitation* has some 13&14C tombs. The 13C church of the *Cordeliers* (Franciscans) now houses the Departmental archives. The church of *Saint-Genès-des-*

Carmes (14&15C) is the only Flamboyant chuch in Clermont and is single-aisled with a beautiful apse. In the 18C chapel of the *Carmes-Déchaux* (Discalced Carmelites) there is a fine carved 4C sarcophagus which is used as an altar.

Museums: As well as its open-air museum, the Parc des Volcans, the town has several more conventional ones. The Musée Lecoq has local zoological, mineral and botanical collections. The *Musée du Ranquet* is in the old *Hôtel Fontfreyde,* known as the 'House of the Architects', which is a fine Renaissance building.

There are interesting enamels to see, and one very rare 14C letter-case, some lovely medieval sculptues, 18C paintings and furniture. The Pascal Room contains an example of the famous calculating machine that the author of the *Pensées* invented to help his father (see **Rouen**). The *Musée du Bargoin* is devoted to prehistory and to Celtic and Gallo-Roman archaeology (Cheix skeleton, pre-dating the last volcanic eruptions). It also has a department of paintings (from the 14C to the present-day), which is worth visiting.

Old Montferrand: This fallen rival of Clermont, built on a slight rise, has retained its medieval appearance. The Gothic and Renaissance houses have been very well restored. It was rebuilt at the end of the 12C and laid out on the regular bastide plan of southern France (two main streets at right angles cutting the town into four). From the 15C onwards numerous houses were built for nobles or wealthy citizens. An outstanding example is the *Hôtel Fontfreyde* (16C), also known as the 'Maison de Lucrèce', which has a remarkable inner courtyard with a beautiful door to the staircase turret and medallions with figures on the gallery balustrade.

Also visit the 16C *Hôtel de Lignat*, known

as the 'Maison du Notaire' with its fine doorway, inspired by the Italian Renaissance; and the *Maison de l'Apothicaire*, with its timber framing and statuettes on consoles depicting the apothecary, syringe in hand, and his patient. Also interesting is the *Hôtel d'Albiat* (superb 'Porte des Centaures' in the courtyard). The church of *Notre-Dame de-la-Prospérité*, begun at the end of the 13C, enlarged in the 15&16C, has a lavish Flamboyant door in the W. façade with a beautiful rose-window above it.

Cléry-Saint-André	(2,020 inhab.)
45 Loiret	p.414☐I 6/7

This large village on the Loire châteaux route is dominated by the cold, pale Flamboyant basilica of *Notre-Dame*, which houses the famous tomb of Louis XI. On the left side there is a square 14C tower, which is the only vestige of the previous church, destroyed by the English during

Clermont-Ferrand, frescos in the cathedral

the Hundred Years War. Inside, the church is elegant, but severe, and there is no triforium between the arcades and clerestory, which makes it seem bare. The royal burial-vault was opened up in 1889 and the skulls of Louis XI and his second wife, Charlotte of Savoy, sawn open for embalming, are preserved there, together with their bones. The king died in 1483, his last words being of Notre-Dame-de-Cléry—he had always been devoted to the Virgin and to Cléry, where he tried out his tomb while still living. He had not wanted to be buried with his ancestors at Saint-Denis: Paul Murray Kendall wrote, 'He was different, and wanted to lie in his own church of Notre-Dame-de-Cléry [...] his statue in copper with purple and blue enamel awaited him on his tomb there'. The tomb was destroyed in the Revolution and rebuilt in 1896 and is now beneath the last arch of the nave. Raised on four columns, a marble slab carries the statue of the king praying to the Madonna—sculpted in 1622 by Michel Bourdin from Orléans (the original statue had been destroyed by Huguenots). At the side of this there is a vault which is the burial place of Tanguy du Châtel, who was killed in battle in 1477 at the king's side. On the right a flagstone covers the urn containing Charles VIII's heart. The chapel of *Saint-Jacques* in the S. aisle has rich Renaissance decoration with a wooden statues of St. James (16C) and St. Sebastian (17C) and a stone Virgin (17C). The decoration here reminds one that Cléry was a staging-post on the pilgrimage route to Santiago de Compostella. In the neighbouring 15C chapel lies the gallant Dunois, companion-in-arms of Joan of Arc, with his family. In the middle of the choir above the modern high altar is a much-venerated oak statue of Notre-Dame-de-Cléry. This 16C statue was modelled on the first one, which was burned by the Huguenots. The sacristy with its fine Flamboyant door houses the church's 'treasure'.

Clermont-Fd., rose-window in the cathedral

Clermont-Fd., old Montferrand

Cléry, basilica, tomb of Louis XI

Cluny (4,680 inhab.)
71 Saône-et-Loire p.420 □ L 9

The Romanesque belfry of the 'Eau Bénite' was once a beacon of Christianity and stands as a memorial to the art and faith of the Middle Ages—it also bears witness against the crime of vandalism, for it looms above a mere carcass of a truly great church, which has been systematically taken to pieces. The abbey church was sold off as national property after the Revolution, and then calmly used as a stone quarry until 1823. These outrages continued methodically, even with explosives, despite protests from the Municipality and from Chaptal, Minister of the Interior under the Consulat. In 1944 shelling failed to wipe out the remains of this vanished marvel, although about thirty houses were destroyed in the little village of Cluny which grew up around the abbey.

The great abbots of this monastery—'The mother of western civilisation' according to Viollet-le-Duc—were canonized. Cluny was founded in 910. The wooded land was given to a handful of Benedictine monks (led from the Jura by Berno) by Guillaume d'Aquitaine, Count of Auvergne, Velay and Mâcon. Conditions to this gift stipulated that Cluny should be exempt from all servitude, apart from the Holy See, and that the monks should have the right to elect their own abbots without outside interference. Cluny owed its power and the spread of its influence to these freely elected abbots. The abbey's glory and renown grew from the 10C onwards. St.Odo, a diplomatic and ascetic man, was abbot after St.Berno and he was followed by St. Aymard, St.Mayeul, St.Odilo, St.Hugh of Cluny and Peter the Venerable. Under them Cluny became almost the centre of the Church in the 11&12C. The abbey church combined both temporal power and spiritual authority ('From wherever the wind blows, Cluny collects rent'). Its abbots were advisers to kings and popes and Cluniac monks became popes themselves. It began to decline, however, at the end of the 12C and this decline was accelerated by the commendam system until in the 16-18C the worldly, ostentatious abbots only came to Cluny for the religious festivals.

Abbey church: It is rather disconcerting to visit Cluny because the abbey church is no more than a ghost in stone. However, even the remains convey a certain grandeur. They are the ruins of the third church—the one built by St.Hugh—which was begun in 1088 and completed in 1135 when Peter the Venerable was abbot. This was the largest church in Christendom before St.Peter's in Rome was built, and it succeeded Cluny I, pulled down and replaced by Cluny II at the end of the 10C.

Cluny II itself survived in part until the 18C. This third church was a wonder of the Christian world because of its sheer size and elaborate decoration. It had enormous influence—a Cluniac school of architecture grew up, in which the master builders adopted the Latin cross ground plan, an elevation with large arcades, a false triforium and clerestory windows and a dome over the crossing on pendentives. The churches which followed on from Cluny III include Paray-le-Monial (also built by St.Hugh), Saint-Lazare d'Autun, Semur-en-Brionnais, Notre-Dame de Beaune, La Charité-sur-Loire and many other small churches.

This truly outstanding church was 614 ft. long and its vaulting was some 100 ft. above the ground. Only about one-tenth of it is left today. But these ruins, dominated by the powerful tower of Eau Bénite, clearly show the Cluniac structure, particularly in regard to elevation.

Abbey: Several parts of this powerful abbey, which was largely rebuilt in the 18C, remain. The 13C monks' granary and storehouse abuts on to the massive *Tour du Moulin* (12C) and consists of a low vaulted room used as a cellar and another room with a beautiful Gothic timber ceiling. Here you will find two large models showing what the façade and apse of Cluny II looked like. Ten large, historiated capitals from the destroyed abbey church, well-lit and borne by columns, display a rather confusing iconography and superbly illustrate the sculpture which emerged from the Cluniac school.

Musée Ochier: This museum in a 15C former Abbots' Palace has a very interesting collection of Romanesque remains, some documents providing information about the former appearance of the abbey and convent, and other objects which belonged to the community at Cluny. The library has some 4,000 volumes, most of which came from the monastery.

Cluny, bell tower of the Eau-Bénite

Town of Cluny: Here too there are some relics from the abbey (16C abbot's residence known as the *Palais d'Amboise* in the public park; 14C *Tour Fabry* dominating the stud farm; 11&12C *Tour des Fromages*). Because it shared in the abbey's prosperity, the town has some lovely Romanesque houses. The church of *Notre Dame*, mutilated and austere, goes back to the 13C. The church of *Saint-Marcel*, with a 17C nave, has an octagonal belfry and Romanesque choir and apse. The chapel of the *Hôtel-Dieu* contains the remains of an unfinished early-18C mausoleum.

Environs: Berzé-le-Chatel (7 km. SE): The feudal château here overlooks the houses of vine growers and was the seat of the old barony of the Mâconnais. **Berzé-le-Ville** (11 km. SE): This was the favourite retreat of St.Hugh and was a rural dependence of Cluny. The old *priory chapel* is on raised ground and its walls have numerous early-12C arches. The rather humble oratory houses some breathtaking paintings by Cluniac artists: they were protected by the distemper which covered them until the 19C and have an extraordinary intensity and freshness. You can see what the painted decoration of Cluny III was like from the frescos in the apse, which show Christ blessing. He is shown in a mandorla and is surrounded by saints, apostles and martyrs, together with the the the martyrdom of St.Lawrence and the legend of St.Blaise.

Cognac	(22,600 inhab.)
16 Charente	p.418□F 10

This 'brandy capital' on the banks of the Charente had its heyday under the Valois. François I was born in 1494 at the château of Cognac and lived here for part of his childhood with his sister Marguerite d'Angoulême. Of the ramparts, only the *Porte*

Saint-Jacques (15C) survives (its lovely twin, machicolated towers used to comand a bridge that has now disappeared). The château is unfortunately rather damaged, but it still has an air of the golden age of the Valois about it. The 'balcon du roi' on the façade facing the Charente has François I's emblem, two salamanders, decorating its base. The Governor's House with its octagonal staircase turret is from the time of Jean de Valois; the guard room was added by Louise of Savoy and has ribbed vaulting.

The church of Saint-Léger: This building bears the imprint of many different periods. It was built in the 12C and its nave is reminiscent of the one in the cathedral of Angoulême. 15C ribbed vaulting replaces the domes here, and only the transept still has a Romanesque dome on pendentives. Above the doorway of the Romanesque façade there is a Flamboyant rose-window. The beautifully made capitals by sculptors trained at Saint-Pierre in Angoulême are decorated with monsters, leaves and various scenes.

Berzé-le-Châtel, castle

Old Quarter: The old houses here are blackened by the fungus which produces the alcohol fumes. In the Grand-Rue there are half-timbered houses. In the Rue Madeleine are the Hôtel de Javrezac (16C) and the Hôtel de la Madeleine, which has a fine doorway with salamander motif. In the Rue Saunier (Cognac was originally an important port for the salt trade) there are Renaissance and classical houses — the Hôtel de la Gabelle, and the Hôtel Brunet du Bocage. The *Musée Municipal* has some interesting old paintings (*Lot and his Daughters* by Jan Massys, Adam et Eve by Frans Floris), some lovely 17C French furniture, and a collection of Gallé glass. There are also collections devoted to local iconography and local souvenirs.

Environs: The church of Chatre (5 km.): This charming Romanesque building, lying in a valley, belonged to the Augustinians, who improved it in the 12C. The nave has a line of domes on pendentives and the elegant and sober façade, in Saintonge Romanesque style, has a multilobed arch over the central doorway.

Cognac, Porte Saint-Jacques

Collioure	(2,700 inhab.)
66 Pyrénées Orientales	p.424☐J 16

This old Mediterranean harbour was 'discovered' in 1905 by Matisse and Derain and then frequented by Dufy, Marquet, Juan Gris and a number of other modern painters. Prettily situated at the foot of the Albères, it was protected by a medieval castle (greatly altered in the 17C) at a point which cuts the port into two bays. The old place has a great deal of charm, with its sloping, flowery little streets. The late-17C church has an old lighthouse with a pink dome as its bell tower; the church has nine interesting altarpieces.

Colmar	(67,400 inhab.)
68 Haut-Rhin	p.417☐O 6

Voltaire, always prone to ill temper, saw it as an ugly little town: 'half German, half French, and altogether bizarre'. On the other hand, the writer Georges Duhamel called it simply: 'the most beautiful town

Cognac, barrels in a cellar

Cognac, half-timbered house

in the world'. Colmar is certainly not bizarre, nor would it claim to outshine, Paris, Rome or Venice (although one of its quarters is known as 'Little Venice'). It does, however, have one of the most interesting museums in France, some lovely half-timbered houses, streets straight out of an operetta, and the foothills of the Vosges with several picturesque vine-growing villages nearby. It is, in short, a most attractive town—friendly, pleasant and full of medieval, Renaissance and 18C houses, which have not been spoilt by modern buildings. One can see from the excellent restoration in the style of Alsace, which has been carried out in the Quartiers des Tanneurs (Tanners), de la Poissonerie (Fishmongers) and de la Herse (Portcullis) how much importance is attached to tradition. At one time the council was thinking of pulling down some of the more dilapidated buildings to make way for modern ones, but good sense prevailed and new building is restricted to the edges of the old town. Colmar proudly preserves its appearance and there is no question of resurrecting the misconceived 19C attempts to realign its streets. There is an ugly sports complex on the edge of the Quartier des Tanneurs but otherwise the restoration of Colmar has even been taken to such lengths as disguising the television aerials which rather spoil the old parts of other towns. The town dominates the valley of Munster and to a lesser degree that of Kayserberg. The Ill was once navigable up to here, and in the past Colmar's citizens used to boast that they could travel as far as Amsterdam via the Rhine from the town's Customs House. Because of its position—it is on the site of and takes its name from the Gallo-Roman *Villa*

Collioure, general view

Columbaria — Colmar has always been sought-after, particularly by the bishops of Strasbourg in the late 12C. Emperor Frederick II came here and claimed sovereignty over it in the early 13C. A rich, free imperial city, in 1354 Colmar joined the Decapolis, the confederation of Alsatian cities. When the Empire foundered, Colmar turned to France and was treated on equal terms with the Crown in 1635. Subsequently it suffered the general fate of Alsace, becoming German on two separate occasions. In 1945 it was part of a 'pocket' of resistance and though the vineyards and villages suffered badly, it was miraculously spared. Colmar is the birthplace of Frédéric Auguste Bartholdi and in the house where he was born in 1834 there is a little museum devoted to the sculptor of the *Lion* of Belfort and the *Statue of Liberty* in New York.

Old Town: The list of houses seems endless. Strolling around the town, look for the *Maison des Têtes* (1609), with its carved oriel and gabel with volutes. The former *Corps de Garde* has a light Renaissance balcony; the *Maison Pfister* (1537) has a remarkable, angular oriel; the *Maison zum Kragen* ('with a ruff'), so-called because there is a figure wearing a ruff set into the corner post; and there are also some fine houses in the Rue Mercière. The fine *Ancienne Douane* (Old Customs House) is 15&16C. The *Quartier des Tanneurs*, which is lapped by the waters of the Lauch, although very much restored, is a mass of marvellous houses. Even though the flat-bottomed barges of the market gardeners no longer draw up at the steps of the 19C market buildings, the restored quarters of *La Poissonnerie* and *Petite Venise* have retained all their old charm.

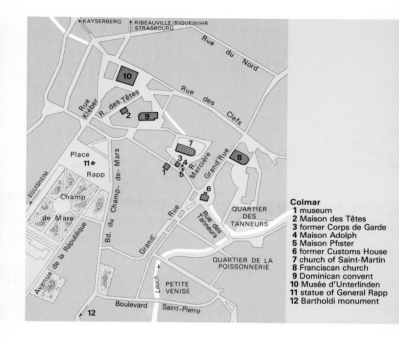

Colmar
1 museum
2 Maison des Têtes
3 former Corps de Garde
4 Maison Adolph
5 Maison Pfister
6 former Customs House
7 church of Saint-Martin
8 Franciscan church
9 Dominican convent
10 Musée d'Unterlinden
11 statue of General Rapp
12 Bartholdi monument

Saint-Martin: There is still a rather bedraggled stork's nest on the apse at Saint-Martin — now rare, storks seem to have migrated and forgotten the most important religious monument in Haute-Alsace. Formerly a collegiate church, Saint-Martin blends traditional local architecture with the new ideas coming from the Ile-de-France, and shows the transition from Romanesque to Gothic. It was begun in about 1250 on the site of earlier buildings, and was largely complete by about 1375. The spire of the bell tower was burnt and replaced at the end of the 16C by a lantern. With its tinges of pinkish-beige and faded red, Saint-Martin has some interesting portals (the best carvings are on the St. Nicholas doorway). It is lit by countless 15&16C stained-glass windows and has an 18C organ, recently renovated, a *Pietà* from the same period with candles always burning in front of it, and a large 14C Crucifixion.

The 14C former church of the Franciscans was at one time cut in two so that one half was Protestant and the other Catholic. The 14&15C Rhenish Gothic church of the *Couvent des Dominicains* (Dominican Monastery) is lit by beautiful 14C stained glass. This slender, much restored church contains the exceptional *Virgin in a Bower of Roses* (1473) by Martin Schongauer, a 'Virgin in the Garden' of the type so favoured by Rhenish painters. Vandals have stripped the church of many of its possessions and in 1972 this painting was stolen. However, it was found in Lyon the following year, 500 years after it was painted. This painting is only temporarily on display here and it will eventually be returned to Saint-Martin.

Colmar, Petite Venise

Musée d'Unterlinden: This enthralling museum, whose name means 'under the lime trees', is housed in the old Dominican monastery and is one of the richest and finest museums in France. It houses a collection of well-displayed masterpieces. Arranged around a cloister with twin arches, the museum has a very diverse set of collections, ranging from Palaeolithic objects to works by Picasso, Vasarely and Georges Mathieu, taking in Romanesque and Gothic sculptures, fine medieval paintings, popular art, furniture, ironwork, children's toys, dolls, automatons and so on. The former *chapel* is mainly devoted to Martin Schongauer (born in Colmar in about 1450) and Mathis Grünewald, who was possibly the former's pupil. Schongauer was a painter and engraver, and was responsible for the engravings in the cabinets and for the breathtaking panels of the *Dominican altarpiece*. The intense *Isenheim altarpiece* is by Grünewald; it is the work of a master of colour, both inspired and tormented. The three panels of this huge altarpiece, which used to be closed during Holy Week as a sign of mourning, are now kept open, so that it may be appreciated in all its splendour.

Environs: See **Éguisheim, Kaysersberg, Ribeauvillé, Riquewihr.**

Colmars	(310 inhab.)
04 Alpes de Haute-Provence	p.426□O 13

This old strongpoint standing out against the thick winter snow guards the high valley of Verdon. It still looks very 17C, with its belt of walls flanked by towers and the

Colmar, cloister of the Musée d'Unterlinden

fortresses of Savoy upstream and of France downstream. The side aisle and sacristy of the Gothic church form part of the defensive system.

Combourg (4,720 inhab.)
35 Ille-et-Vilaine p.413☐E 5

This château, the setting for the childhood terrors of François René de Chateaubriand, rises above the peaceful town of Combourg and its lake. It was built in the 11C, altered in the 14&15C and became the property of the writer's family in the 18C. Simple in plan, the buildings are arranged in a rectangle with four corner towers, high walls, machicolations, battlements and parapet walks. The most attractive of the towers are the Tour du More (11C) and the Tour du

Croisé (15C). The interior, which was transformed in the 19C, has recently been restored to its original arrangement. The old archive room and the writer's room— 'a sort of garret at the top of the staircase tower' (or Tour du Chat) have been turned into a museum (various souvenirs). The most vivid record is still the pages of the *Memoires d'Outre-Tombe* describing family life in the château and that of the village in the years 1784-6.

Environs: Château de Lanrigan (5 km. E.): This granite château is in complete contrast to the military severity of the château of Combourg. It was built at the beginning of the 16C and successfully combines the Flamboyant and Renaissance styles. An elegant stone-roofed gallery joins the octagonal staircase tower to the main building. There are two four-centred

Combourg, château

arches decorated with kale motifs. Above the façade, with its arched doorways, there is a high slate roof broken by gabled dormer-windows.

Commercy (8,180 inhab.)
55 Meuse p.416□M 5

This small industrial town on the left bank of the Meuse lies close to a forest. The church of *Saint-Pantaléon*, built in the 16C and extensively altered in the 19C, has two paintings by Girardet. The museum in the *Hôtel de Ville* has an interesting collection of ceramics and ivory, some of which are 16C. However, the 18C château and the town itself did not escape damage in the war—the château, where Stanislas I, the deposed king of Poland liked to stay, was burnt down in 1944. It has risen again from its ruins: the columns and the pediment of its façade, the arcades of its outbuildings and the semicircular place in front of it form a superb, geometrically rigorous whole.

Compiègne (40,720 inhab.)
60 Oise p.411□J 4

Compiègne is on the edge of a huge, open forest on the banks of the Seine, close to its junction with the Aisne. It has been a favourite residence of kings since Charles the Bald built a palace and founded an abbey in the 9C. The early Capetians loved to hunt here and it became a stopping-off point for kings on their way back from their coronation at Reims—Charles VII ac-

Compiègne, aerial view

companied by Joan of Arc did this in 1429. The Maid of Orléans was captured the following year by the English and the Burgundians as she tried to come to aid of the garrison of Compiègne. She was later to experience prison, trial and burning at the stake. There were several royal châteaux on this site. Louis XV, wanting to get away from the pomp and formality of Versailles, asked Jacques Gabriel and then Jacques Ange Gabriel, his son, to replace the old, much altered and enlarged château of Charles V with a modern one. The old building, which was in a variety of styles, was demolished in the mid 18C. Louis XIV had said of it, 'At Versailles I am housed like a king, at Fontainebleau like a gentleman, at Compiègne like a peasant.' The new château on the other hand, completed by Louis XVI and sumptuously refurbished by Napoleon, gave no grounds

for such a complaint. Napoleon III and the Empress Eugénie were particularly fond of it and it enjoyed a brilliant period. The Armistice of 11 November 1918 was signed in a forest clearing nearby and, symbolically, the one of 22 June 1940 was signed on the same spot, this time marking the collapse of France. Compiègne suffered in both World Wars.

Features of interest: The royal château rather overshadows what is in fact an interesting town. The *Hôtel de Ville*, Flamboyant in appearance, has been so much restored that one can hardly call it ancient. It was in fact built under Louis XII and has a modern equestrian statue of him in a niche. It is dominated by a tall belfry whose slate spire has four pinnacle turrets. At the foot of the spire are the 'Picantins', three jack-o'the-clocks which strike the hours and quarters. The *Musée de la Figurine Historique* is housed here. It is a fascinating museum with a collection of 90,000 toy soldiers from all periods—and enjoyed by all ages. Nearby is the former *Abbaye Sainte-Corneille*, which is badly dilapidated, and the church of *Saint Jacques*, which is 13C (choir and transept), 14&15C. Further into town, the church of *Saint-Antoine* is 13–15C. Near the Oise, in the Hôtel Songeon, a Directoire residence, is the *Musée Vivenel*, named after the 19C architect who donated some major collections. It is devoted to Antiquity and all periods from the Middle Ages on (sculptures, ivories, enamels, porcelain, paintings and drawings). The gutted *Tour de Beauregard* is a 12C keep.

Château: This large, regularly laid out palace forms a triangle and has the long façade of the *Grands Appartements* (State Apartments) facing the garden and park. Sober, even severe on the outside, the lavishly furnished and decorated interior is quite different, with its wood panelling, mythological themes painted by Girodet, paintings by Natoire, tapestries, sculptures, silks, carved bronzes, porcelain and chandeliers. Marie Antoinette's *Salon de Jeu* (Games Room) has been restored to its pre-Revolution appearance and has some pretty, almost transparent curtains and silk hangings from Lyon with a hollyhock design. The vast *Galerie de Bal*, which was prepared for the marriage of Napoleon to Marie-Louise, has paintings on its barrel vault depicting Imperial victories. The Aile des Maréchaux (Marshals' Wing), where the wedding guests stayed, houses the *Musée du Second Empire*, which is devoted to Napoleon III, the Empress Eugénie and their court. There are numerous paintings.

Musée de la Voiture: This was established in 1927 in the kitchen courtyard, which was covered over by glass. The mu-

Compiègne, belfry, the 'Picantins'

'The Empress Eugénie and her Maids of Honour' (detail) by Winterhalter

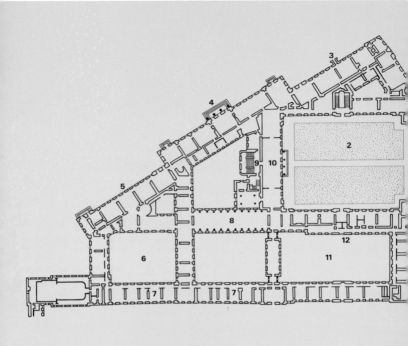

Château of Compiègne 1 Entrance **2** main courtyard **3** Marie-Antoinette's apartment **4** apartment of the king and the emperors **5** apartment of the empress **6** Cour de l'Orangerie **7** car museum **8** Galerie de Bal **9** Escalier d'Honneur 1 Salle des Gardes **11** Cour de la Régie **12** museur of the Second Empire **13** museum of the empres

seum has since expanded and displays vehicles from the time of Louis XV on: state carriages from the 18C, the *Jamais Contente* (which reached over 60 miles an hour in 1899), a carriage of the Kings of Spain, the 1924 Citroën half-track which was the first car to cross Africa, the Madeleine-Bastille omnibus and a steam coach. In addition to the four-wheelers (and a Dion-Bouton three-wheeler) there is an important collection of bicycles—the 1817 hobbyhorse, the 'grand bi' (penny-farthing) with an enormous front wheel, the first pedal cycle.

Park: The Petit Parc is surrounded by the Grand Parc, which is part of the forest. The 18C Petit Parc was altered by Napoleon who is said to have had the long, broad prospect of the *Berceau de l'Impératrice* laid out to remind Marie-Louise, the daughter of Francis I of Austria, of the Schönbrunn gardens.

Concarneau   (19,050 inhab.)
29 Finistère   p.412 □ B (

Concarneau is the third largest fishing por

in France after Boulogne and Lorient. There is a walled citadel, the *Ville Close*, built on a rocky islet at the mouth of the Moros. It is surrounded by strong 14C ramparts, completed by Vauban in the 17C, and it is linked to the mainland by two bridges which were once draw-bridges. One of the gates, flanked by an elegant clock tower, leads into the main street, the Rue Vauban. This is lined by houses which have recently had shop windows opened in them. The *Musée de la Pêche* deals with the history of the port and of the different types of fishing carried on there. It has numerous tanks in which one can see some of the better known forms of marine life. A 17C house in the small Place Saint-Guénolé was used as the Governor's Residence. From the *Porte au Vin*, through which the boats passed to deliver their cargoes of wine, you can see the inner harbour, where fish are auctioned.

Environs: La Forêt-Fouesnant (9 km. W.): In the centre of the village dominating the Anse de la Forêt there is a small 16C churchyard set amidst hydrangeas. The church, with its bell tower and spire, has a porch decorated with old statues of St.Roch and of the saint-king Mélar. The carved wooden baptistery (1628) has a piscina and basin hewn from a single block of granite. Nearby, the 16C *Manoir du Stang* is now a hotel. The buildings, with their many turrets, form a right angle and have numerous windows set in their granite façades and gables. One of the harvest wagons bears Renaissance decoration. **Fouesnant** (13 km. W.): Famous for its cider, Fouesnant also boasts one of the best Brittany costumes—to be seen on the War Memorial near the church. Originally Romanesque, the church was built in the 12C and altered in the 18C, and has a nave of five bays lit by loophole windows. There are geometric and fantastic motifs on the capitals in the transept (monsters, masks, etc.). A little way away from the village is the *Chapelle Sainte-Anne* (1685), which is the site of the annual local procession on 26 July. Prettily situated, this chapel shares the naïve grace of the numerous chapels scattered through the Brittany countryside. The perforated bell tower is flanked by two domed turrets. The façade has a pediment and a statue of St.Anne in a niche.

Conches-en-Ouche   (3,780 inhab.)
27 Eure   p.410☐H 4

Perched on a spur beside the fast flowing Rouloir, Conches was once called Chastillon, but changed its name at the beginning of the 11C when Norman soldiers returned from Spain bringing with them a relic of St.Foy, which they had acquired at Conques in the Rouergue. The town grew up around the church dedicated to the saint and a Benedictine abbey. The Flamboyant church of *Sainte-Foy* has a carved and rebuilt spire. It dates from the 15&16C and is lit by a remarkable collection of Renaissance glass. The choir windows are 30 ft. high and have some very fine stained glass, probably the work of Romain Buron. There are still a lot of half-timbered 15&16C houses here (particularly in the Rue Sainte-Foy, an old street on a hillside). A garden with a panoramic view has been laid out within the old feudal walls, dominated by a dilapidated 12C keep and round towers. Only a few Romanesque arches and the remains of a Gothic church survive from the old abbey.

Condom   (8,080 inhab.)
32 Gers   p.423☐G 10

The Condom countryside, in the heart of Armagnac, is a land of liqueurs, broad horizons, châteaux, pretty churches and well-situated villages. The seat of a bishop until the Revolution, this pretty little town

Concarneau, the Ville Close

consists of houses from different periods grouped around a 16C *cathedral* and the Flamboyant *cloister* with remarkable ribbed vault. On the road to Fleurance you will see the church of Pradau has a 12C Romanesque gate. The former *Chapelle des Cordeliers* (14C), a ruin in the late 1960s, has now been restored and houses a restaurant—restoration in both senses of the word!

Environs: Larressingle (6 km. W.): The small 'Carcassonne of Gers' clusters around its ruined château. Formerly held by the bishops of Condom, the village has an almost intact fortified wall.

La Romieu (11 km. NE): This simple village, with its arcaded square, has some old houses and a spectacular church and cloister. The powerful and somewhat severe

Gothic church dominated by heavy towers is elegant in its simplicity. The adjacent 14C cloister has lost its upper storey. The nearby *Château de Madirac* dates from the 1580s.

Confolens   (3,200 inhab.)
16 Charente   p.419□G 10

The capital of Charente, Confolens is in a granite region covered by oaks and chestnuts. It takes its name from its site at the confluence of the Vienne and a picturesque river, the Goire. The granite *Pont Vieux*, 560 ft. long, is 15C—it is slightly humpbacked and it once had a drawbridge defended by three towers, now destroyed. Also in granite, and rather severe, is the church of *Saint-Barthélemy* with a sombre façade and an interesting portal. It is semi-circular and framed by little columns with archaic capitals and crowned by a carved band on which is a depiction of the Paschal Lamb and the symbols of the Evangelists.

Old Quarters: A large, square keep is all that remains from the old fortifications. This dominates a group of half-timbered houses dating from the 15&16C. The streets sloping down from the *Porte du Four* lead to the church of *Sainte-Maxime*, which is a former priory church. It has two rib-vaulted naves and is mainly 15C. At the end of the narrow Rue du Soleil is the *Manoir des Seigneurs de Confolens*, a pleasant 15C house with two gables flanked by a heavy staircase tower with Renaissance door. The courtyard of the old *Hôtel d'Assier des Brosses* (18C), which houses the Hôtel de Ville, opens on to the street through a very fine emblazoned door.

Environs: Lesterps (8.5 km.): The abbey church of *Saint-Pierre* (11C, vaults of nave 17C) is remarkable for its bell tower and porch, which is Carolingian in style. It is 130 ft. high and has four storeys with column-buttresses, pilasters and elegant arches.

Conches, church of Ste-Foy, window

Conques	(430 inhab.)
12 Aveyron	p.423☐I 12

Standing on a steep slope on the side of a narrow valley some old houses are grouped around the apse of one of the most famous of pilgrimage churches. In the Middle Ages, the passion for relics turned this solitary place into a religious centre whose repute spread as far as Spain and Italy. Ever since the 11C, Conques has been a stage on one of the four main French routes to Santiago de Compostela.

Abbey church of Sainte-Foy: 11&12C, central bell tower 14C, towers of façade 19C. The polychrome *tympanum of the Last Judgement* on the W. doorway is set in a bare façade, but still preserves its colouring. There are 124 figures, with strange and fixed expressions, grouped around the central figure of Christ, whose right hand is raised towards the Elect and his left points downwards towards the Damned. There are numerous inscriptions describing the realistic and anecdotal scenes shown with all the vigour of the Romanesque sculptors. The interior is typical of the large pilgrimage churches; the ambulatory allowed pilgrims to file past the choir where St.Foy's relics were on display. The N. arm of the huge transept has a very fine sculpted group of the *Annunciation*, identical in style to the work on the portal. On the sacristy walls are the remains of 15C frescos of the life of St.Foy.

Laressingle, fortified village

the Albigeois and the Rouergue, it is one of the sights of the Midi and known as 'La Dame de Pierre' (the lady of stone), while Albi is the 'Dame de Brique' (the lady of brick), it is really a remarkable example of Gothic domestic architecture. The *Porte de l'Horloge* is 16C, whilst the Town Hall occupies one of the most beautiful houses, the *Maison du Grand Fauconnier*, restored by Viollet-le-Duc, and so named because of the falcons decorating its façade. In the stone-pillared hall (1352) there is a 300-ft. well. The church of *Saint-Michel*, built from 1460 onwards, incorporates the square apse and small transept from a former church (17C altarpieces). The 14C *Maison du Grand Écuyer* houses the *Musée Yves Brayer*. The *Chapelle du Saint-Crucifix* on the road to Bournazel dates mainly from the 16C (panelling, stuccoes, 18C paintings).

Treasure: This amazing hoard of stones, enamels and precious metals is the finest of all the great French medieval treasures. The famous *Majesté de Sainte Foy* (10C) in wood and gold-leaf can be seen amongst other splendid reliquaries. It is covered with many precious stones, cloisonné enamels, pearls and cabochons.

Cordes (1,070 inhab.)
81 Tarn p.423☐I 13

Cordes was a bastide founded in 1222 by Count Raymond VII of Toulouse. Still largely surrounded by its four concentric walls, it basks in the sun on a high spur, and seems to merge into the landscape with its barbicans, towers and sumptuous 14&15C houses. Lying on the borders of

Cormatin (580 inhab.)
71 Saône et Loire p. 420☐L 9

In the 19C church there is a magnificent 15C *Vierge de Pitié*, a Burgundian work in solid gold. The sumptuous Renaissance château, built from 1600 onwards in a huge park by the Grosne, is wonderfully decorated inside (one wing has been demolished). There are French-style ceilings, painted wood-carvings, fine furniture and paintings by Nattier and Mignard. Lamartine stayed here on several occasions.

Cormery (1,110 inhab.)
37 Indre-et-Loire p. 414☐H 7

There are still traces of the fortifications that once surrounded this small town. It grew up around an abbey founded by a priest from Saint-Martin in Tours in 791,

Confolens, general view

and was originally completely isolated in the woods and meadows around the Indre. The *Tour Saint-Jean* (15C) has survived from this abbey, as has the massive *Tour Saint-Paul*, the bell tower of the large 11C abbey church, which was destroyed in the Revolution. This tower has a porch, a tall chapel and a belfry, and there are some unusual decorations, rather worn, on its W. façade (bee's nest, rose motifs, bas-reliefs). An old 13C refectory adjoins it. The nearby prior's residence with its elegant staircase turret dates from the 15C.

Church of Notre-Dame-du-Fougeray: This church is a little apart, dominating the village; it dates from about 1150. The form of its apse is rather unusual for the area. Its bell tower, rather too squat and too low, seems out of proportion, and was partly destroyed by the English in 1358.

The interior of the church has a balanced and austere look about it. There are four mysterious figures, whose heads have been re-modelled, in the arches of the apse.

Corsica	(293,300 inhab.)
20	p.427☐Q/R 17/18/19

The 'mountain in the sea', Corsica, is not a large island, but its varied landscape and great individuality make it a most attractive place. In 1975 it was divided into two Départements. The sea eats into its 500 miles of coastline, making deep gulfs and fjords reminiscent of Scandinavia. Mount Cinto is 8,865 ft. high. It is an island of fragrant scrubland ('I would recognize it just from the smell,' said Napoleon). It has some lovely country and views, and also

Conques, abbey church of Ste-Foy

Cordes, the village

the relics of a long history. It was inhabited from Neolithic times, and had a megalithic civilization before being taken by the Phocaeans, who founded *Alalia* which was to become Aleria in the 6C. The Romans gradually established themselves between 260 and 162 BC before facing fierce resistance from the mountain tribes. It was retaken by Byzantium in 552 and was then held by the Pope, Pisa and Genoa. France took possession intermittently in 1553, 1737 and 1747. In the 18C the famous Pasquale Paoli rose to prominence and founded a university. He bravely resisted the French troops but was defeated at Ponte Nuovo in 1769. In the same year the future Emperor of the French, Napoleon Bonaparte, was born at Ajaccio. It is an island with a strong personality, and has kept its own language, which is similar to Italian.

Ajaccio (51,770 inhab.) W. coast: At the end of a superb gulf, the birthplace of Napoleon has been nicknamed 'la Blanche' (the White), although its old houses and façades by the harbour are more grey, yellow, ochre and pink. The old town is rather austere, and virtually rectangular in plan. The *cathedral*, with its fine proportions, where Napoleon was baptized, dates from the 2nd half of the 16C and has a *Vierge du Sacre-Coeur* by Delacroix, 17C frescos and 18C Genoese sculptures. The citadel is 16C.

Museums: A Second Empire palace houses the remarkable *Musée Fesch*. This was established thanks to a legacy from an art-loving prelate, Cardinal Joseph Fresch (Napoleon I's uncle), who was Bishop of Lyon at the beginning of the 19C and Ambassador to the Holy-See before being disgraced for disapproving of his nephew's

Ajaccio, the citadel

behaviour towards the Pope. The museum is particularly rich in 14–18C Italian paintings. Its best works incude the *Mystic Marriage of Catherine* by the Umbrian Allegretto Nuzy (14C), the *Virgin of the Garland* by Botticelli (1470), the *Madonna and two Saints* by Cosmè Tura, also 15C, as well as the *Man with a Glove* by Titian and *Leda* by Veronese — two marvellous 16C works; there are also some 18C views of Venice. The Chapelle Impériale contains the tombs of several members of the Bonaparte family. The *Musée Napoléonien* is in the Hôtel de Ville. Here there are many mementoes of the Emperor and his family (portraits, coins and medals). The *Maison Bonaparte* has a simple façade on the Place Letizia (Christian name of Napoleon's mother). It was left to the State in 1923 by Prince Victor-Napoleon, and has been turned into a museum. There are

Ajaccio, portrait of Napoleon

plenty of objects and documents concerning the Emperor and his family. You can visit the 'chambre natale' (the room where he was born) and the one which was his as a child. The Bonapartes' genealogy is explained on the second floor.

Environs: Château de la Punta : (13 km. NW): The Pozzo di Borgo family, the descendants of a diplomat who opposed Napoleon, built this château. The stones used in the building came from the Tuileries Palace in Paris, burnt down by rioters in 1871. The château is actually a copy of one of the pavilions of this palace, and is richly furnished inside, with tapestries and portraits.

Aléria (2,730 inhab.) E. coast: The name of Aléria calls to mind both Corsica's present troubles and also those of its distant past. It is on a plateau 4 km. from the sea, and excavations have revealed the remains of quite a large Roman city on the site of a Greek colony. The *Musée Jerome Carcopino*, in an old Genoese fort, deals with Corsica's history and has ceramics, winebowls, cups and bronzes.

Aregno (530 inhab.) NW: The strange and beautiful church of the *Trinità* is a 12C Romanesque church in Pisan style, with coloured stones forming an irregular chequered pattern. The façade is decorated with blind arcades and strange figures. Inside, there are two frescos—*The Four Doctors of the Latin Church* (1458) and *St. Michael Weighing Souls and Slaying the Dragon* (1449).

Bastia (52,000 inhab.) E. coast: The largest town in Corsica, with more than 50,000 inhabitants. Bastia by the island's standards is a busy little town which is growing and building all the time, although it still has its old port and centre. There is a ring of council houses and es-

Ajaccio, Place Maréchal-Foch

tates around the old part, but it hasn't lost its charm. The small port is for fishing and sport, leaving all the heavy vessels to the large new one. There are tall grey houses and arcaded buildings which were well restored in 1958 by one of the best of modern architects, Fernand Pouillon. A little way back from the waterfront is the church of *Saint-Jean-Baptiste* with its two towers, dating from the 17&18C. Inside it is ornately decorated. Nearby, the chapels of the *Immaculée Conception* and *Saint-Roch* are worth visiting for their 17C interior decoration.

The old port area is called *Terra Vecchia*, while the area around the citadel is known as the *Terra Nova*, and is reached through the Place du Donjon. This fortified site, established by the Genoese in the 14&15C, contains plenty of old houses, the church

Bastia, the harbour and church of St-Jean-Baptiste

of *Sainte-Marie*, formerly the cathedral, and the old Governors' House. *Sainte-Marie*, dating from the end of the 15C, was greatly altered in the 17C. It houses the superb silver statue of the *Assumption of the Virgin*, an 18C work by a Sienese artist (it is taken out of its case every 15 August to lead a procession around the town). Hidden behind the former cathedral is the *Chapelle Sainte-Croix*, 16C, and sumptuously decorated in Louis XV style. Housed in a niche, the venerated figure of the *Christ des Miracles* was found in the sea in 1428 by fishermen. The *Musée d'Ethnographie Corse* in the old Governors' House is devoted to the geology, history and traditions of the island. In the courtyard, the conning tower of the *Casabianca* reminds one of the role of that submarine on the eve of Corsica's liberation by its own people.

Bonifacio (3,020 inhab.) S. Coast: On an extraordinary site atop a sheer cliff, Bonifacio also has a long and busy waterfront. The historic upper town is enclosed within strong walls and linked to the citadel, which is still occupied by the army. Strange, picturesque, Bonifacio was once an important Genoese colony, and there are lots of old narrow houses several storeys high lining the winding streets, often with flying buttresses (in fact they are water pipes collecting rainwater from the roofs). The extensively altered church of *Sainte-Marie Majeure* dates from *c* 1200. Above a deep cistern, the porch or *loggia* housed the notaries who drew up the laws, and the Elders who debated local matters. The church's interior has been decorated in classical-baroque style which all but hides its Romanesque elements; it is crowned by an elegant bell tower.

Bonifacio

Cargèse, the church

Calvi (3,690 inhab.) NW coast: Calvi, the capital of the hilly and fertile Balagne area, has been an important port for a long time. There is a powerful citadel overlooking the charming and busy marina, and its walls and bastions surround a half-ruined quarter (the fortifications were built by the Genoese in the 16C). The citadel, which stands on a ridge, is occupied by the army. The church of *Saint-Jean-Baptiste* was rebuilt and raised to cathedral status in the 16C. There is a font (1568), an interesting 15C polyptych with a missing central panel, and also a *Christ des Miracles* from the same period, in ebony. The throne, dating from 1757, is extremely prettily decorated. The ancient *Virgin of the Rosary*, which comes from Seville, is sumptuously dressed and has a whole wardrobe—it is differently dressed for feast-days. The oratory of *Saint Antoine* (15C) belonged to a

brotherhood, but now houses various religious works of art, including a remarkable 16C ivory Christ (this 'treasure' is made up of pieces once scattered around Balagne). The church of *Sainte-Marie Majeure* is partly 18C.

Environs: Algajola (15 km. NE): This port, said to have been founded by the Phoenicians, is protected by a 17C citadel. The church of *Saint-Georges*, partly fortified, contains a 17C *Descent from the Cross* possibly by Guercino.

Cargèse (910 inhab.) W. coast: Overlooking the sea and its small port, Cargèse has two 19C churches facing each other, one Roman Catholic, and the other Orthodox (many Greek families came here in the 18C).

Corte (6,070 inhab.) inland: This town

Corte, the citadel

was beloved of Pasquale Paoli, who established a constitution for a sovereign Corsican nation here in 1755. Ancient and rather austere, it is the historical capital of the island. It is on an important crossroads, and is dominated by a 15C *citadel*, which is one of the bases of the Foreign Legion in Corsica. A sloping, cobbled street leads to the old quarter around on the Place Gaffori (named after a Corsican general whose house was besieged in vain by the Genoese in 1750). The church of the *Annonciation* has a 17C façade and some interesting furnishings.

Filitosa, W. coast: Filitosa lies a little way inland from the Gulf of Propriano in the gentle countryside of the Valinco valley. The prehistoric site stands on a spur between a river and a stream. The worn, enigmatic statue-menhirs here date from the second millennium BC. Alongside these are some powerful monuments from the Toréenne period (1500–1000 BC). A museum displays objects found in the excavations.

Mariana, E. Coast: Two remarkable Romanesque chuches stand on an ancient, deserted Roman site just to the S. of Bastia. The simple but beautifully harmonious *cathedral church*, known as *La Canonica* is an outstanding 12C Pisan building. Its exterior is astonishing because of the different sizes of the slabs of stone covering it, with the light shining on the unfilled holes in which the scaffolding was fitted during construction. The sober church, bare inside, is divided into a nave and two aisles by rectangular pillars and lit by arrow-slit windows. The church of *San Parteo* 330 yards away was built in the 11&12C.

Murato, church of St-Michel

La Porta, the church and village

Morosaglia (1,020 inhab.) inland: Near this village in the region of La Castagniccia and close to Bastia is the house where Paoli was born in 1725. There is also a Romanesque church.

Murato (650 inhab.) N.: In the Nebbio region, 1 km. from the village, is an astonishingly original 12C Romanesque church with walls of alternating white and green stone (a sort of serpentine) and strange porch and bell tower. There are some bizarre carvings which experts have not been able to understand.

Porta (La) (450 inhab.) inland: Lost amidst a sea of chestnut trees (hence the region is called La Castagniccia) the tiny village of La Porta is dominated by the high golden bell tower (1720) of a baroque church built in the mid 17C. It has some

small organs (1780) with exceptional tonal quality.

Porto-Vecchio (7,800 inhab.) E. coast: Full of sturdy houses, Porto Vecchio is now a resort. Some of the Genoese fortifications have survived, and the church with its square bell tower is 19C.

Saint-Florent (1,360 inhab.) N. coast: A pleasant little port and resort which grew up on the site of a Roman town—a few broken relics of which remain. 1 km. from the centre, the *ex-Cathédrale du Nebbio* is one of Corsica's most important Romanesque monuments, along with *La Canonica* in Mariana. It is built of white limestone, and seems to date from 1125–40. An elongated church, the façade and apse are relieved by blind arcades and have interesting historiated capitals.

Cos d'Estournel, château and vineyard

Sartène (6,050 inhab.) inland: Prosper Mérimée set his *Mateo Falcone* in Corsica, but only discovered the island personally about ten years after he wrote the novel! All the tourist brochures will tell you that Sartène is 'the most Corsican of all Corsican towns'. It has no great architecture, but it is quite typical, with its sunken cobbled streets, vaults and flights of steps. The *Procession du Catenacciu* on Good Friday is one of the most interesting of the traditional Corsican ceremonies.

Cos d'Estournel
33 Gironde   p.418☐E 11

Among the wine-growing châteaux of the Médoc, there are some truly 'historic' buildings, such as the elegant Beychevelle.

However, most of the region's attraction and charm is due to the large 19C houses dominating the vines which produce the famous vintages. Near *Saint-Estèphe*, a large village with not much character and an 18C church, stands the strange house of *Cos d'Estournel*, with its oriental pagoda and palace. It was built in the last century by a landowner who decided to abandon wine-growing and breed Arab horses instead—local tradition has it that he was inspired by the Sultan's Palace at Zanzibar. Cos d'Estournel is still one of the best 'grand crus classés' of Bordeaux.

Couches   (1,570 inhab.)
71 Saône-et-Loire   p.420☐L 8

The vines grow right up to this picturesque

market village in a valley of the Vielle, which still has many interesting historic sights (much altered church, medieval tower, 17C buildings). The château, which dominated the road from Autun to Chalon, is heterogeneous in style and has a strong, square keep, walls, machicolated towers, and a 15C chapel. Badly decayed with the passage of time, it has been carefully restored as far as possible.

of the size of the defensive system, as are the ruins of the castle. This stands on a spur and forms an irregular rectangle, with a round tower the size of a keep at each corner. It is well worth visiting: the rib-vaulted Salle de Gardes and the lower rooms of the towers are still intact; the cellar is remarkably preserved. The remains of the Salle des Neuf Preux and the Salle des Neuf Preuses are also most impressive.

Coucy-Le-Château-Auffrique
(1,120 inhab.)
02 Aisne   p.411 ☐ K 3

The proud lord of Coucy, Enguerrand III, chose this good defensive position for the stone symbol of his power. In 1230–42 he built a colossal fortress, which for a long time was famed for having the most beautiful cylindrical keep in Europe (destroyed during World War 1). At the same time, the village was fortified by the addition of a wall flanked by towers. The magnificent *Porte de Laon*, a true gatehouse, is evidence

Coulommiers
(12,000 inhab.)
77 Seine-et-Marne   p.411 ☐ K 5

Coulommiers was once an important market and gave its name to the cheese which was sold there (a kind of Brie, which has been modified in order to travel well). It is now an expanding industrial town, but the remains of a 17C château and its chapel stand in a pleasant, flowery park. The chapel houses a small *Musée d'Archéologie et d'Histoire Locale*. Nearby, among a group of modern buildings, there is a *Templar Commandery* with an early Gothic chapel.

Coulommiers, Templar Commandery

Coupesarte (60 inhab.)
14 Calvados p.410 □ G 4

This charming manor is not spectacular but it is typical of the Auge region. Half-timbered, it dates from the 16C and has been well restored, the lower part being of stone and brick. The corbelled roofs can be seen reflected in the water of the moat.

Environs: Château de Grandchamp-le-Château: (3.5 km. via Saint-Julien): This rather strange 16&17C building is a mixture of Louis XIV (main building) and the half-timbered regional style (the corner wing—one of the tallest half-timbered buildings in Normandy).

Courances (château)
91 Essonne p.429 □ J 5

Much of this 16&17C château's charm lies in its wooded setting with canals and pools — a pleasing mixture of water and greenery. The sober brick and sandstone château was altered for the worse in the 19C, but is now more or less as before, except for the staircase, which was copied from Fontainebleau and stuck on to the main façade. The park behind the house was designed by Le Nôtre.

Coutances (11,950 inhab.)
50 Manche p.413 □ E 4

Coutances, the 'religious capital' of the Cotentin, stretches out on high ground: the spires and lantern-tower of its Gothic Cathedral visible from afar. The town was fortified by the Roman Emperor Constantius Chlorus (the pale)—hence Cotentin. Coutances was badly damaged by shelling in June 1944 but its churches escaped more or less unharmed.

Cathedral: The cathedral was begun in 1218 and the main body finished in the mid 13C. It stands on the site of a Romanesque building, parts of which it incor-

Courances, aerial view of the château

porates. The side and apsidal chapels date from the 14C. This large church is quite plain, perfectly balanced and has grown as the result of adapting and enlarging the Romanesque church—the master builders were very adept at this. Its lantern, known as *Le Plomb*, is one of the most beautiful in Normandy. Two of its large supporting pillars are Romanesque, although they show subsequent Gothic alterations. The nave was restricted to the lay-out of the original church, but the choir was freshly designed: its lines are pure and it is wider. The central chapel opens on to the ambulatory and contains the venerated 14C statue of Notre-Dame-de-Countances (14C).

Saint-Pierre: This gracious 15&16C church is late Gothic with early Renaissance features (main portal, top of the Flamboyant tower). *Saint-Nicolas:* This secularized church is late Gothic in style, apart from the 18C central tower.

Crépy-en-Valois (10,920 inhab.)
60 Oise p.411 □ J 4

The former capital of the Valois region stands on high ground surrounded by its old defences. The church of *Saint-Thomas*, which suffered badly in the last century, still has its tall 15C spire. Very little of the château remains, and what there is houses the *Musée du Valois et de l'Archerie* (everything you could wish to know about bows, and crossbows). The Romanesque church of *Saint-Denis*, which has been greatly altered, stands in front of the ruins of an ancient abbey.

Creusot (Le) (35,500 inhab.)
71 Saône-et-Loire p.420 □ L 8

A large industrial town in a wooded and

mountainous region, Le Creusot grew up around a metal works, founded in 1836 by the Schneider brothers. The *Écomusée de la Communauté Urbaine Le Creusot/Montceau-les-Mines* is a museum of the past and the present, concerned with people, work and the environment; it is also a research and conference centre. There are several associated institutions in the region, for example at Montceau-les-Mines, Blanzy (*Musée de la Mine*) and Perrecy-les-Forges, where the narthex of a priory houses an exhibition on the Romanesque period and on the forges of the past.

Crèvecoeur-en-Auge (600 inhab.)
14 Calvados p.410 □ G 4

A large moat surrounds this pretty, fortified house, which consists of a 15&16C gatehouse, a half-timbered farm, a remarkable 15C dovecote and a chapel, probably dating from the 12C. The château was very well restored by Conrad and Marcel Schlumberger. These brothers perfected a

Coutances, vaulting of the lantern

system of electric prospecting used by oil engineers when drilling, and the manor is inescapably linked with oil—the museum has a prospectors' truck/laboratory, drilling equipment and various related items of equipment. There is an audio-visual display to help explain the techniques of the oil industry.

Environs: Cambremer (4.5 km.) 11&12C church, largely Romanesque.

Culan
18 Cher

(1,160 inhab.)

p.419□I 9

The strong fortress of Culan stands on the steep bank of the Arnon, above a medieval bridge. The château was mostly rebuilt in the 15C by a companion-in-arms of Joan of Arc, whose guest she was here after the siege of Orléans. It still has its three towers, crowned with their wood and slate hoarding. The façade giving on to the courtyard is flanked by three square staircase towers, decorated with dormer windows. Inside

there are Gothic fireplaces, beautiful tapestries (Flanders, Aubusson) and sumptuous 15–18C furniture.

Cunault
49 Maine-et-Loire

p.413□F 7

The old priory church of *Notre-Dame-de-Cunault* (or Cunaud), with its strong, elegant bell tower in the N. wall, well-proportioned apse, exceptional interior arrangement and remarkable capitals, is one of the most beautiful churches in the Loire valley. Built in calcareous tufa (the pale local stone) by monks from Tournus and once the destination of pilgrimage, the church was abandoned in the Revolution. In 1838 Prosper Mérimée recognized its worth and was instrumental in getting it restored. Notre-Dame incorporates the huge bell tower from an earlier church, and dates mainly from the second half of the 12C. Building may have continued until the beginning of the 13C (the three W. bays). The W. vaults of the nave would

Crèvecoeur-en-Auge, the château

seem to be from the mid 13C. On the tympanum of the W. portal there is a fine carved group (Madonna and Child with angels), dating from about 1200–10.

The long, tall body of the church, which is similar to Poitevin churches, has three equal aisles and over 200 astonishing historiated capitals, with devils, chimeras, men fighting or riding monsters, and religious scenes. There are a few traces of the old painted decoration here and there. There is also a Pietà and a lovely 16C piece of oak furniture, a 13C carved polychrome wooden reliquary and a statue of St. Catherine (15C). The oldest part of the church, the apse, has lost its central apsidal chapel. There is a pretty François I residence in front of the church.

Environs: Gennes (3 km. NW): The church of *Saint-Vétérin*, largely rebuilt in the 13&14C on a slope full of Merovingian tombs, still retains traces of the 11&12C. The church of *Saint-Eusèbe* has pre-Romanesque sections of wall. It dates from the 11C (choir and transept), 12C (bell tower) and the 15C (spire, ruined nave). At **Trèves** (1 km.), there is a 12&15C church and the tall tower of a strong, ruined château.

Cunault, priory church of Notre-Dame, tympanum of the W. portal

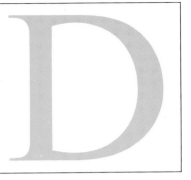

Dabo (3,020 inhab.)
57 Moselle p.417□O 5

This collection of scattered hamlets set in forest and pasture-land was badly damaged by war in the 19C. It is dominated by a neo-Romanesque chapel (19C) perched on a high rock and dedicated to St.Leo. He was born at Éguisheim into the powerful Dabo family (who were Alsatian counts) and became Pope Leo IX.

Dampierre-sur-Boutonne (390 inhab.)
17 Charente-Maritime p.418□F 10

The *château* was built in the first half of the 16C on an island in the Boutonne, and

Dampierre-sur-Boutonne, the château

consists of a rectangular main block flanked by two massive towers with battlements and machicolations. The courtyard façade has two pleasing Renaissance galleries separated by a delicately carved frieze with foliated scrolls and leaf motifs. Their stone ceilings are divided into rectangular coffers with different pendent keystones (the one on the first floor is the main feature of the château). Each one of the 93 coffers has a different motif and motto: there are the monograms of Henri II, Catherine de Medici and Diane de Poitiers. Inside there are two fine chimney-pieces, and a 16C room with a ceiling with painted beams.

Dax	(20,300 inhab.)
40 Landes	p.422□E 14

The keynote here is water: the name comes from the Latin *aquae*, and the town is still the second most important spa in France. On the border of the forests of the Landes and the rich Chalosse, it has exploited the hot water from its springs and silt from the Adour (the sticky 'Dax mud' is especially effective for rheumatism). The *Fontaine Chaude*, steaming away in the historic centre of the town, is also known as *The Fontaine de la Néhé*, in memory of a tutelary deity; it always has a halo of steam. There is a Tuscan portico.

The Romans came to take the waters of Dax and there are remains of the 4C fortifications on the promenade. The Gallo-Roman town wall was almost intact until the 19C, when a 'modern-minded' Council decided to pull it down.

The *cathedral*, rebuilt in the 17C with some later alterations, retains the Apostles' doorway (13C) from the earlier church. Another Dax church, *Saint-Vincent-de-Xaintes*, dates from the 19C—in the choir there is a magnificent Gallo-Roman mosaic which must have come from a temple. The *Musée de Borda* is in the Hôtel Saint-Martin d'Agès, one of the few old houses here. There are exhibits of ancient objects, as well as popular art and folk art, and also exhibits concerning the adored regional

Dax, church of St-Paul-lès-Dax, frieze on apse

pastime of bullfighting (there is a bullring in Dax).

There is a 15C tower on the church of *Saint-Paul-lès-Dax*, a small village on the other side of the Adour. It has a remarkable 12C Romanesque apse with a frieze of religious scenes and a fantastic bestiary. These bas-reliefs show marked differences, some being very crude and others exquisitely executed.

Die   (4,200 inhab.)
26 Drôme   p.421 □ M 12

This ancient, small town owes much of its reputation to its sparkling wine—'clairette de Die'. The *Dea Augusta* of Antiquity, it has a number of Gallo-Roman remains: the NE ramparts (built of stones from monuments destroyed in an early barbarian invasion), the *Porte Saint-Marcel* (a broken arch) and stone fragments collected in the *Musée Municipal*. The cathedral was Romanesque, as one can see from the S.

wall and one portal, but it was altered in appearance when restored in the 17C, after the Huguenots had sacked it. The Hôtel de Ville contains a 12C mosaic.

Dieppe   (26,120 inhab.)
76 Seine-Maritime   p.410 □ H 3

This important passenger, fishing and commercial port is overlooked by a château on the cliffs, which is now a museum with some wonderful ivories. Dieppe is also the main seaside resort in Normandy. It grew up at the mouth of the Arques, where the Vikings ran their long boats aground, and was made rich by enterprising shipbuilders like Jean Ango, a supporter of François I. Its navigators travelled to the four corners of the world. In 1610, the future Admiral of Louis XIV, Abraham Duquesne, was born here. Although it did suffer in the last war, Dieppe still has two beautiful churches and numerous old houses; near the casino there is a gate from the old town wall. The old town mainly lies between the

Dieppe, the fishing harbour

château and the railway station, which serves the port; The Grande-Rue, a busy shopping area (closed to cars), runs through the middle. In the centre is the triangular Place Puits-Salé, dominated by a lovely Norman façade (modern well).

Church of Saint-Jacques: A few stones of this church are from the earlier Romanesque building, which was burnt down during the fighting between Philippe Auguste and Richard the Lionheart. The latter was subsequently replaced in the late 13C/14C by the present building, which is rich, pure Gothic. The 15C saw a touch of Flamboyant; Renaissance elements were added to the choir in the 16C. The lower part is simple, while the upper parts are more elaborate. The 15C tower beside the W. façade has a large and very fine rose-window. On the side bordering the Rue Sainte-Catherine the rather worn S. doorway is primitive Gothic in style (buttreses from the former Romanesque church). *Interior:* Nave and choir date from the 13&14C; the delicate screens in the side aisles are successful 19C pastiches of Flam-

boyant art. The *Chapelle du Sacré-Coeur* has a very pretty vault and Renaissance decoration; the central chapel is a happy mixture of Flamboyant and Renaissance styles. The wall dividing the treasury from the ambulatory is extravagantly carved with tales of early navigators.

Saint-Rémy: This imposing church has been restored but there are original parts. It was built in the 16&17C in two stages, as the Wars of Religion interrupted the work. The façade is Louis XIII in style and the bell tower over the crossing dates from the 18C.

Old Château and Museum: Rebuilt in the 15C in flint and sandstone, the 'old château' was built to defend the town against the English, who captured it in 1420, allowing the Governor to remain in his post. The château presents a coherent appearance, despite the many alterations, which include the incorporation of a ruined bell tower and the porch from a destroyed Gothic church. An informative and pleasant museum houses items concerned

Dieppe, church of St-Jacques

Arques-la-Bataille, church of St-Pierre

with Dieppe's past, the era of the great navigators, the Belle Époque of seaside resorts, etc. There are also canvases by painters who loved the Normandy coastline (Isabey, Boudin, Pissarro, Blanche, and many other 19C artists). There are lovely model boats, furniture and religious silverware. The museum further recalls the composer Camille Saint-Saëns' connection with the town. The *Dieppe Ivories* are carved with amazing skill; they are as light as lace and are either practical (such as incense-boxes, tobacco shredders or compasses) or purely decorative. The museum has dozens of remarkable pieces by local craftsmen, dating from the 17,18&19C.

Environs: Arques-la-Bataille (6 km. SE): Arques, with its old houses clustering in a green valley, has a very elegant Flamboyant church, *Saint-Pierre et Saint-Paul*. It was started in about 1515 and not finished until the 17C (fine rood screen, 1540). The powerful château, which was built in the 11C and then rebuilt and altered, now consists of ruins lying around the foot of a still impressive keep. Henri

IV made his headquarters here in 1589 while fighting the army of La Ligue (the Catholic League). There is an obelisk (1877) on the edge of the forest of Arques commemorating his victory.

Offranville (7.5 km. SW): The 1914–18 Memorial in the Gothic church was decorated by the painter and critic Jacques-Émile Blanche, who lived in the 18C manor of Tôt.

Château de Miromesnil: (8 km. S.): This lovely 16&17C château, with its pink brickwork and contrasting pale stone tiles, is situated in a large beech wood.

Digne	(16,580 inhab.)
04 Alpes-de-Hte-Provence	p.425☐N 13

Digne is at the centre of several radiating valleys of the Alpine foreland and is an important lavender market and stopping-off point on the tourist *Route Napoléon*. Its origins are very old indeed. It is a quiet

Dieppe, Musée des Beaux-Arts, ivory model

Courbons, hamlet

Dijon, Burgundian roof

departmental capital and the seat of a bishop. The town was badly hit by fierce air raids in 1944, but most of the damage has been repaired. It is divided quite sharply into the *Ville Basse* by the fast-flowing Bléone, and the *Ville Haute* with its streets hugging the hill of Saint-Jérôme, on which there is a church, begun at the end of the 15C, finished in the 19C. It is said locally that the former cathedral of *Notre-Dame-du-Bourg* was founded by Charlemagne (the stump of one of the towers seems to be Carolingian), but this is not proven. Work on the building began before 1200 and finished in 1330; the body of the church is almost Cistercian in its severity. There are medieval wall paintings in the Romanesque nave, which has a broken barrel vault.

Environs: Courbons (6 km. NW): This hamlet, perched high up and half ruined, is overlooked by a 14C church combining the Gothic and the Romanesque.

Dijon	(156,800 inhab.)
21 Côte-d'Or	p.416□M 7

When François I first saw Dijon, bristling with bell towers, he exclaimed 'Oh, what a beautiful town'. The capital of Burgundy, Dijon is a town with a strong personality; forward-looking, but respecting its past too. There are now new growth industries as well as the traditional food industry, the number of green spaces has increased, old streets have been converted into pedestrian precincts and many old building have been renovated. Dijon is close to the famous Côte de Nuits wine-growing area and has

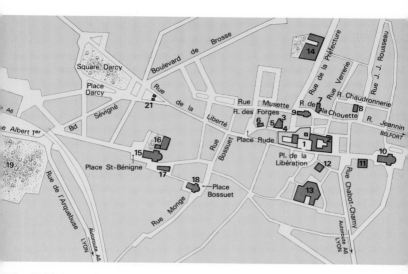

Dijon 1 Palais des Ducs **2** Musée des Beaux-Arts **3** Hôtel Chambellan **4** Hôtel de Jean Maillard **5** Hôtel Aubriot **6** Hôtel Morel-Sauvegrain **7** Hôtel de la Vogüé **8** Maison des Cariatides **9** church of Notre-Dame **10** church of Saint-Michel **11** Bourse-Musée Rude **12** Musée Magnin **13** Palais de Justice **14** Hôtel Bouhier de Lantenay **15** cathedral of Saint-Bénigne **16** Musée Archéologique **17** church of Saint-Philibert **18** church of Saint-Jean **19** Jardins de l'Arquebuse **20** charterhouse of Champmol (psychiatric hospital) **21** Porte Guillaume

an incredible wealth of interesting buildings and museums in its historic centre. Before the 10C, the town was unexceptional; it owes its growth to the Dukes of Burgundy, especially the second, Valois line (Philip the Bold, John the Fearless, Philip the Good and Charles the Bold). After the death of Charles the Bold it reverted to France along with the rest of Burgundy. The ambitious Charles had ruled over a huge area stretching as far as the North Sea, but was no match for the patient, politically shrewd King Louis XI, one of the prime architects of France. Dijon blends the picturesque Middle Ages, the noble 17C and the sumptuous 18C. Fortunately the historic old quarters were left untouched by broad boulevards and systematic 'planning' in the last century and have been spared the instrusive modern buildings of the concrete age. The vast and rather severe *Palais des Ducs* (King's Residence after the annexation by the Crown) dominates the centre—a composite building which today houses the Town Hall and the splended Musée des Beaux-Arts. This is one of the twin attractions of Dijon, the other being the cathedral of Saint-Bénigne. Each has its attendant museum, churches, large old houses and fine hôtels.

Palais des Ducs: The Ducal Palace, incorporating one of the largest museums in France, owes its unity and majesty to the 17&18C. It originates from a château built from the 1360s onwards and includes the tall *Tour Philippe le Bon* (tower of Philip the Good) completed in the 15C, and some medieval Rabelaisigne kitchens. Many architects worked on the remodelling and enlarging of the Palace at the end of the 17C and first half of the 18C, including Jules

Hardouin-Mansart, who can really be considered its designer. It is very extensive and is arranged around three courtyards, the largest of which faces the harmonious Place de la Libération and its semicircle of arcardes. The main courtyard leads to the *Cour de Flore*, which is flanked by the *Salle des États* and the *Salle de Flore*. There is a lavish staircase built about 1735 by Jacques Gabriel and leading to the vestibule of the *Salle des États*, which was redecorated at the end of the 19C. It is linked to the *Salle de Flore* with its decoration glorifying the Princes of Condé who governed Burgundy on behalf of the King. The *Chapelle des Élus* is Louis XV in style. On the other side of the main courtyard lies the Cour de Bar with its staircase and gallery (*Galerie de Bellegarde*) built at the beginning of the 17C.

Musée des Beaux-Arts: This is a rich, varied and exciting museum which will not disappoint the visitor. It is housed in a 19C wing of the Palace and extends into the older part. It is extremely well laid out, despite its great size, and with its vast collections it acts as both a Louvre and a museum of modern art. There is a wealth of 'great' works here, covering all periods and all genres (painting, sculpture, furniture, tapestries, silverware). Note in particular the works of the Dijon sculptor Rude and the Burgundian Pompon (one of the greatest animal sculptors), some exceptional Swiss and Rhenish paintings, some masterly Flemish and Italian pieces (Rubens, Veronese, Titian, and Reni) and some very interesting 19C paintings. There is also a very well presented series of contemporary works, a museum within a museum. In the course of the tour you can visit the ducal kitchens, with their vast fireplaces, and the huge *Salle des Gardes*. This last is very beautiful with its Flamboyant chimney-piece and Renaissance gallery, added in the 16C, superb 'booty' from the Charterhouse of Champmol (scan-

dalously destroyed in 1792)—the tombs of Philip the Bold and John the Fearless and some wonderful altarpieces.

The Palace is surrounded by medieval houses and hôtels, and elegant residences of parliamentarians. It is worth strolling slowly around this area, noticing the façades in particular. In the *Rue des Forges* look out for the courtyard of the *Hôtel Chambellan*, late-15C; the highly ornamented *Hôtel de Jean Maillard*, 17C; the *Hôtel Aubriot*, 13C, but much restored; the *Hôtel Morel-Sauvegrain*, 15C, also restored. The *Rue de la Chouette* has the harmonious *Hôtel de Voguë*, early-17C, a medieval house with shops in its arcades. The *Rue Verrerie* is thoroughly medieval and the *Rue Chaudronnerie* has the Renaissance *Maison des Cariatides*.

Notre-Dame: This strange and beautiful church near the Palace dates from the 13C. Its light, monumental façade overlooks the pedestrian Rue Musette. At the top is the 'Jaquemart family', mechanical figures which strike the hours and the quarters (father Jaquemart was taken from Courtrai, a rebel town, in 1383 by Philip the Bold; the people of Dijon later gave him a wife and children). The façade is Italianate and covered with gargoyles, which were reworked in the 19C from old documents; its doorways were savagely defaced in the Revolution. The pleasing, skilfully designed interior is lit by some very fine stained-glass windows, which are mainly 13C. A 12C *Vierge Noire* (Black Virgin) is venerated as the Protectress of Dijon.

Saint-Michel: The spectacular and very ornate Renaissance façade of this church is deceptive, since it precedes a Gothic nave in restrained Flamboyant style—the result of changing architectural taste during building, which occupied the last years of the 15C and the first half of the 16C. There is a most unusual central portal in the highly rhythmic, mannered façade (the

Dijon, façade of St-Michel

Dijon, Place François-Rude

vault too is unusual). The central tympanum was carved from 1551 by Nicolas de Lacour.

Musée Rude: The secularized and defaced former cathedral of *Saint-Étienne* houses the stock-exchange and the *Musée Rude*. François Rude was born in Dijon in 1784 and there are reproductions of all his works which are not on show in the *Musée des Beaux-Arts*. Particularly well known is his *Le Départ des Volontaires*, a huge high relief from the Arc de Triomphe in Paris.

Musée Magnin: This museum is housed in a sober 17C hôtel, which was remodelled by the town planner Auguste Perret. It reflects the varied taste of Maurice Magnin, a great collector who was interested in unknown artists of the past and in meretricious pieces. The house,

with its fine, staircase, also has works by famous artists, including Tiepolo, Vouet, Le Sueur and Poussin; additionally there are some interesting panels, more important for their quality than for the fame of the artist.

Palais de Justice: This is in the large Hôtel du Parlement (16C) and has preserved a great deal of its sumptuous decoration (ornate ceilings, cornices and panelling). The large hall with panelled barrel vaulting, known as the Salle des Pas-Perdus, was once lined with stalls and refreshment bars. Fashionable Dijon met here to parade and to gossip.

In the old part of Dijon there are lots of buildings worth seeing: in particular, the *Hôtel Bouhier de Lantenay*, a splendid 18C residence which now houses the Prefec-

Dijon, Puits de Moîse

was built from 1280 onwards. In the apse there is a shadowy and subterranean complex which was filled in during the Revolution but cleared in the middle of the last century. The crypt is essentially the base of the large circular church which was grafted on to the apse of the earlier *Saint-Bénigne* at the beginning of the Romanesque era.

Abbey and Archaeological Museum: The abbey of Saint-Bénigne which grew up on the edge of the ancient castrum was very prosperous and a large suburb developed around it. The remains of the monastery beside the Cathedral house a most interesting archaeological museum. In the huge Gothic dormitory there are Romanesque, Gothic and Renaissance sculptures. The Romanesque basement (a vaulted room which became a cellar as soil was piled up) is a strange and poetical place— a rough stone structure, it houses a fascinating collection of Gallo-Roman votive offerings found at the source of the Seine (the river *Sequana* was worshipped by the ancients).

ture. The cathedral, like the *Palais des Ducs*, stands in an architecturally interesting area, near the lively Place Darcy.

Cathedral of Saint-Bénigne: Bénigne was a legendary figure who was endowed with all the virtues by locals in the high Middle Ages. He was possibly modelled on one of the first apostles of Burgundy. His supposed tomb became the object of pilgrimage, in spite of the initial suspicion of the Church authorities, and a monastery was set up nearby. Bénigne was given a crypt and then a succession of larger and larger churches. At the beginning of the 11C, a very fine Romanesque edifice was built by Abbot Guillaume de Volpiano, one of the most influential figures in medieval Burgundy. Part of the rotunda still survives. The present church of *Saint-Bénigne*, a vast, severe Gothic building,

Saint-Philibert: A stone's throw from Saint-Bénigne is this former Romanesque church with its delicate 15C spire. The main portal dates from the 13C; the S. portal is late Romanesque. The very sober interior is used for large, temporary exhibitions.

Nearby, the church of *Saint-Jean*, where Bossuet was baptized in 1627, has been mutilated and stripped of its decoration. The Place Bossuet (near the church's apse) has a half-timbered house and also some corbelled houses owned by parliamentarians. At the corner of the Rue Bossuet and the Rue de la Liberté a Renaissance hôtel and a 15C house with picturesque gables face each other.

'Puits de Moîse: On the edge of the town near the lovely Arquebuse gardens there is a huge psychiatric hospital, which occupies the site of the old *Chartreuse de Champmol*, founded by Duke Philip the Bold. The 'Puits de Moîse', which is really a calvary, stands in the middle of a basin in the cloisters of the old charterhouse. The surviving base, minus its upper parts, is decorated with the powerful, severe figures of Moses, David, Jeremiah, Zacchariah, Daniel and Isaiah. These statues (1395–1404) are the work of Claus Sluter, a Dutch artist trained in Flanders who settled in Dijon and was one of the pioneers of the realist movement.

Dinan	(16,370 inhab.)
22 Côtes-du-Nord	p.413☐ D 5

Dinan is built on a rocky crag high above the peaceful river Rance, near the estuary. It is a land and maritime crossroads. The old town is surrounded by ramparts, and the streets are full of character with pretty half-timbered 15&16C houses, which have porches and, sometimes, overhangs (the famous *Rue de Jerzual* leading to the old port, the Rue du Petit-Fort and the Rue de la Cordonnerie, in particular). The Rue de l'Horloge has a 15C belfry, 280 ft. high, with four bells, the largest called after the Christian name of its donor, Anne de Bretagne; the clock is by the German Hamzer. The 16C *Hôtel de Kératry*, originally built in the commune of Lanvollon in the W. of the département, was moved to Dinan when it was in danger of ruin, and then restored; today it houses the Tourist Office. The *Hôtel Beaumanoir* (early 16C) opens on to the Rue Haute-Voie through a superb doorway, which is the same period as the house, with a staircase turret alongside it. On the Place des Merciers is a house known as 'Mère Pourcel' which has an interesting 16C wooden spiral staircase. The Benedictine convent from the 18C is now the Roger-Vercel College of

Dinan, basilica, capital

Secondary Education (Rue de Léhon). It was made a college before the Revolution; its most famous pupil, François René de Chateaubriand, curtailed his studies rather abruptly by running away. Apart from the chapel, which now contains the gymnasium, part of the cloister and the old nun's choir with its decorated ceiling are all that remain of the convent.

Château: Near the Porte Saint-Louis (17C) which, with the Porte du Guichet, guarded the S. access to the town. It is really a group of fortresses linked by a curtain wall. The highest part—105 ft.—is the *Donjon de la Duchesse Anne*(14C) consisting of two linked towers with a parapet walk supported by trefoil machicolations. This old garrison houses the *Musée Historique* with collections of old weights and measures, local head-dresses and a reconstruction of a local interior, as well as some charming woodcuts for popular prints. Next to it is the massive *Tour de Coëtquen* (15C), which was mainly used as a firing point—its walls are pierced by round loopholes. The city ramparts run across moats and amusement parks and link fifteen towers. The Tour de Sainte-Catherine has a lovely view over the port and the English garden.

Basilica of Saint-Sauveur: Romanesque in origin, this church was rebuilt in Flamboyant style in the 15&16C. The façade's side arches (12C) are decorated with statues under canopies, which were unfortunately rather mutilated in the Wars of Religion. The portal, crowned by two projecting sculptures (a winged lion and horse) has a 19C tympanum. The capitals are decorated with lively motifs which reflect a strange world of monsters and sirens. To the right of the central arch there is a figure of a woman suckling a toad. The inside is heterogeneous in style and has rich furnishings: the high altar is 18C; finely-carved credence-tables in the apsidal chapels; 12C font with caryatids and, in the left aisle there is a 15C stained-glass window depicting the four Evangelists. A 15C cenotaph, which was restored in the last century, contains the heart of Du Guesclin, a former Constable of France.

Former Convent of the Cordeliers (Franciscans): Just behind the square of the same name, which is lined with 16C houses with porches. The convent has a pointed doorway. Today the 15C buildings are occupied by a college and enclose a main courtyard flanked by small watch turrets. The Gothic cloister and the chapterhouse are also worth visiting.

Saint-Malo: Although work on this church began in the 15C, it was not completed until the 19C. The strange pyramidal bell tower over the crossing rather

clashes with the harmony of the rest of the building, which is Flamboyant. On the S. side there is a rather elegant Renaissance doorway leading to the right transept. The gallery has a balustrade with trefoil arches. At the end of the nave a modern holy-water stoup is supported by a grimacing demon.

Environs: Léhon (1.5 km. S.): The village of Léhon, huddled beside the Rance just upstream from Dinan, has a 9C priory founded in honour of Saint Magloire, the Bishop of Dol-de-Bretagne. Only the Gothic refectory and the 12C abbey church remain of the old monastery, but the latter has some very old choir stalls, interesting paintings on wood and a very fine holy-water basin. The cloister is 17C. Nearby on a hillock are the ruined towers of the *Château de Léhon*, built in the 12C by the lords of Dinan. **Château de la Conninais** (1.5 km. N.): This Renaissance house, guarded by a rough 15C keep with dormer windows, is part of a pleasant group of buildings along with the dovecote, a decorated well and a chapel. **Château de la Bourbansais** (15 km. E.):

Dissay, château

A splendid avenue of beech trees leads to this château, which lies just outside Pleugueneuc. Behind a low curtain wall, there are two main wings at right angles; these are flanked by round towers, which show signs of a series of alterations (16–18C). Beside these, there are 18C pavilions; other buildings have high roofs and house the outbuildings and the chapel. The approach with its lawns and the French garden with its sphinx and large urns (18C) are surrounded by acres of land, in which the owner has established a zoo.

Dissay	(1,750 inhab.)
86 Vienne	p.419☐G 8

The 15C château built by Pierre d'Amboise, Bishop of Poitiers, is a fortress on the right bank of the Clain. Rectangular in plan, it has towers at the four corners, a gatehouse and a drawbridge. At the top of the staircase in the NW tower there is a magnificent ribbed vault whose ribs spread out in a palm shape. The chapel is in the NE tower; its ornate floor tiles are matched by exquisite murals of the fountain of mercy (with inscriptions): the Cross of Redemption is opposed by the idea of evil represented by the arch-sinners Adam, David, Manasseh, and Nebuchadnezzar.

Dives-sur-Mer	(5,870 inhab.)
14 Calvados	p.410☐G 4

This port, where William the Bastard (soon to become William the Conqueror) assembled his fleet in 1066 to attack England, is now silted up. Known as *Portus Divae* in Roman times, it is now a small industrial town and, to highlight this, there is a huge industrial complex right on the coast which somewhat spoils the view (visible even from Cabourg, the seaside resort which Proust turned into his famous Balbec). The church of Notre-Dame was founded by William the Conqueror; it still has some fine Romanesque elements, although it was altered and enlarged in the 14&15C. The *market*, a sea of brown roof

Dives-sur-Mer, the church

Dol-de-Bretagne, choir stalls

tiles and extraordinary timber work, dates from the 15&16C.

Dol-de-Bretagne	(5,050 inhab.)
35 Ille-et-Vilaine	p.413☐E 5

The little town of Dol grew from a monastery founded in the 6C by St.Samson. It huddles around the majestic cathedral and old fortifications, which were built on the edge of a huge area of marsh recently invaded by the sea. This ancient religious capital, first a bishop's and then an archbishop's seat (9–12C) has been part of the diocese of Rennes since the Revolution.

Cathedral of Saint-Samson: The cathedral was built in the 13C on the site of a Romanesque building destroyed by the

English. It has three towers, one of which is incomplete. The sanctuary, to the N., has a military look with crenellated parapet with arrow slits. The S. façade has two rib-vaulted porches, the Porte de l'Évêque and the Grand Porche built in the 14C before the right transept. Its wide arches support a delicate balustrade flanked by pinnacles. The tall nave (65 ft. high) has three storeys: clerestory with a gallery, elegant triforium and large arcades with pillars strengthened by columns. The choir, which ends in a flat apse enhanced by a fine historiated 13C stained-glass window (including in particular St.Margaret, Abraham, Christ and the first bishops of Dol) has 80 carved oak choir stalls dating from the 14C. The N. transept has the tomb of Bishop Thomas James, one of the first Italian Renaissance monuments in Brittany.

Grande-Rue des Stuarts: This, the principal street in the town, is 'a large, old Gothic Street lined right and left with pillared houses which jut in and out' (Victor Hugo). There are a few houses which are especially interesting. The *Maison des Plaids* (or *des Palets*) built in the 12C of bonded granite, is one of the oldest houses in France. Its façade with a bay decorated with quatrefoils and sawteeth rests on a Romanesque arch with carved archivolts. Further on, the *Maison de la Guillotière* (15C) houses the *Musée Historique de Dol* with some interesting old Breton statues of saints. The Cour des Chartiers (15C) has a charming polygonal staircase turret.

Environs: Château des Ormes (6 km. S.): This former palace of the bishops of Dol, standing in pleasant surroundings outside Épiniac, has a rather austere appearance. It has a beautiful Flamboyant door (15C) and two pavilions (16&18C) which frame the plain main section of the building. **Château de Landal** (14 km. SE): This was built in the Middle Ages and partly rebuilt in the 19C. It consists of a residence with four towers with conical roofs (two are 15C); the fortified outer wall has a parapet walk. The chapel in the neighbouring village is supposed to have been built following a vow made by a lady of Landal. A carved door leads to a single aisle lit by five mullioned windows. At the intersection of choir and nave there is a bellcote with three arches.

| **Dole** | (30,230 inhab.) |
| 39 Jura | p.421 □ M 8 |

Dole, the gateway to the Jura and the former capital of the Franche-Comté, is full of reminders of its past glory. The old town around Notre-Dame is very pretty with its labyrinth of narrow winding streets, fountains and balconies. The brown tiles of the old 15–18C houses make a splash of colour along the banks of the Doubs. The town is proud of its son Louis Pasteur, who was born here in 1822; his birthplace is now a museum.

Basilica of Notre-Dame: Its imposing outline dominates the centre of old Dole. The high bell tower (230 ft.) used to serve as the belfry. Inside this splendid 16C Flamboyant building note the carved polychrome marble throne (17C) and a splendid organ gallery with Renaissance arches framed by red marble columns. In the choir and on the triumphal arch of the Sainte-Chapelle there are some beautiful statues of Apostles (15C).

The Chapel of the Collège de l'Arc (1582): A very fine Renaissance porch with Italianate loggia is richly ornamented with caryatids and balustrades. Inside there is a picture gallery and an archaeology museum.

The Hôtel-Dieu (17C): This fine com-

Dole, Collège de l'Arc, detail

posite building has a balustraded balcony, which runs all along the main façades and ends, unusually, in a corner-turret (1686). Dole is noted for the *Palais de Justice* (fine cloister and 18C well), the *Hôtel Froissard* (window grilles and inner courtyard) and the quiet Place aux Fleurs.

| **Domfront** | (4,520 inhab.) |
| 61 Orne | p.413 □ F 5 |

Domfront is situated on a narrow ridge. Some houses in the village include the the remains of the fortifications. There is a garden with a panoramic view where the old castle used to be; the sides of the 11C keep alone remain. The church of *Notre Dame-sur-l'Eau* with its delightful apse is on the Varenne. Built about 1020 it was altered in the 12C and several bays were removed in the 19C when a road was built. However, it is still a beautiful Norman building in pale granite; inside there are tombstones and a simple Romanesque altar. Some 12C frescos were uncovered in the course of restoration. It was built by Benedictines from Lonlay (9 km. NW)—their abbey is ruined now and only the Romanesque transept and Gothic choir of the abbey church have survived.

Domme	(890 inhab.)
24 Dordogne	p.419☐H 12

A 13C hilltop bastide fortified by Philip the Bold. It has a broad outlook over the valley of the Dordogne and the peaks of Périgord Noir. Irregular in plan, it is unlike a typical bastide. There are many old houses and the town walls still survive, although they have lost their upper parts; their towers and fortified gateways (the most interesting of which is the Porte du Tours, probably a guard post) have also survived. Opposite the *Maison du Gouverneur* (16C), the old Halle (market), with its strong stone pillars, lies on top of the entrance to a cave with passages running underneath the town. The simple church was destroyed by Protestants and rebuilt in the 17C to the original plan. The small museum contains a reconstruction of an ancient Périgord kitchen, complete with a wax couple.

Environs: Castelnaud (8 km. W.): The château of Castelnaud, overlooking a bend in the Dordogne downstream from Domme, kept watch on the strong fortress of Beynac on the opposite bank. Perched high above the old village, this stronghold was much fought over in the Revolution and has been heavily restored.

Les Milandes (6 km. W. of Castelnaud): The heavily restored Gothic and Renaissance château has a charming chapel and extensive lands around it. The music-hall star Josephine Baker planned to live here with her numerous adopted children, but the project collapsed and ruined her.

Domme, the old market

Domrémy-la-Pucelle (270 inhab.)
88 Vosges p.416☐M 5

This little village owes its place in history to Joan of Arc, who was born here in 1412. However, the old Domrémy she knew has changed drastically over the years: the church has been altered from top to bottom and the area around Joan of Arc's house completely transformed. The humble house itself is still there with its thick walls, tiled floor and the small, dark, low-ceilinged rooms—a typical peasant's house of the time. Now Joan's coat-of-arms grace the tympanum over the door. Beside the house is a museum which recalls the epic of 'La Bonne Lorraine'. The modest church still has the polygonal stone font where she was baptized. 1.5 km. S. is the basilica of *Bois-Chenu* built on the side of a hill and dedicated to Joan. It was begun in 1881 in a rather over-elaborate style. The crypt contains the 15C polychrome wooden statue of the *Vierge de Bermont*, which the Maid herself may have prayed before. Opposite the basilica is Joan's na-tive district, with the Meuse running through the meadows.

Douai (47,570 inhab.)
59 Nord p.411☐J 2

In the heart of the industrial Nord, Douai nevertheless has a certain bourgeois charm. It is the capital of the coal country and was also a university town and parliamentary seat. In the *Palais de Justice*, the former *Salle de Révision* of the Flanders Parliament has some splendid panelling. The old stronghold is still surrounded by ramparts with the *Porte d'Arras* and its two large 14C towers and drawbridge, and the *Porte de Valenciennes* (15&16C) with rib-vaulted guard rooms. There are some lovely 18C houses such as the *Maison du Dauphin* with its wrought-iron balcony and the *Hôtel d'Aoust*, whose inner façade is decorated with statues. There is also some very fine church architecture. *Notre-Dame*, for example, is an elegant sandstone Gothic church with a 13C nave. The imposing col-

Domrémy, Joan of Arc's house

Douai, the belfry

legiate church of *Saint-Pierre* was rebuilt 1735–50 but has kept the huge tower which was begun in the 16C (the interior is richly ornamented and furnished).

Hôtel de Ville and Belfry: This is a really splendid building, immortalized in the famous painting by Corot. Part of the façade is Gothic (1463) and part modern, but true to the original style. 130 ft. up rises one of the finest examples of a Gothic belfry—all the finer for being wholly original; built in 1380 it has not been altered since 1475. 'So amusing, so mad, so alive,' said Victor Hugo. Indeed, the tracery at the top and the carillon inside do give it an air of gaiety.

Museum: The museum's collections are housed in a magnificent old charterhouse —a gracious Renaissance edifice of brick and stone which, together with the convent buildings, surrounds a small cloister (1633). There is a fine carved bronze *Tripod of Bacchus*, the *Polyptych of the Trinity* (1510) attributed to Jean Bellegambe, born in Douai about 1470, works by Veronese and Carracci, as well as a polyptych by Jan Van Scorel.

Archaeological finds: Excavations in 1976 near the Place Saint-Amé on the site of an old cannon-foundry have revealed links with the distant Merovingian era. Part of a wooden building was found in one layer — this was probably a Count's residence.

Dourdan (7,500 inhab.)
91 Essone p.428☐I 5

Formerly a fortified place and a grain market since the Middles Ages, Dourdan is now a commercial and industrial centre. It was once the capital of Hurepoix and has seen many a siege and attack. Hugues

Capet, the founder of the Capetian dynasty, was born here and the town was scarred by almost every war until the 17C. The church of *Saint-Germain*, altered and much restored, is 12&13C. Its 14&15C façade, like the one at Chartres, is flanked by unequal towers with steep slate roofs. The tombstone of the poet Jean-François Regnard is behind the altar (he lived an adventurous life and died in 1709 at Dourdan). The château, built in the 1220s by Philippe Auguste, is now without its upper part. There is a wide-ranging *Musée d'Art et Traditions Populaires* in the buildings next to the walls.

Dournazac (1,010 inhab.)
87 Haute-Vienne p.419☐H 10

The towers and massive keep of the magnificent granite feudal *Château de Montbrun* are reflected in a lake. An important fortress, which was often besieged, it has retained its moats. Built in the 12C the tall, square keep with semicircular arches and projecting machicolations has survived from the same period. The main residence and the curtain wall are 15C. The elegant Renaissance *Château de Lambertie* with its mass of pointed roofs has been successfully restored; nowadays it is a children's holiday camp.

Draguignan (22,410 inhab.)
83 Var p.426☐O 14

Once fortified, old Draguignan is still medieval-looking and lies on the side of a chalk hill. It has a bartizan and wrought-iron campanile (late-17C); the latter replaced the belfry which Louis XIV had had razed to punish the town after the

Douai, 'the belfry' by Corot (Louvre)

Fronde. The former Summer Palace of the Bishops of Fréjus (18C) houses a rich library of manuscripts and incunabula, as well as a museum with paintings by David Téniers, Gigoux and Parrocel, Gallo-Roman antiquities, Moustiers faience and other collections. A short street leads from the charming Place du Marché, with its fountains, to the Place aux Herbes, where there is a medieval 'Roman Gate'.

Environs: Hermitage of Saint-Hermentaire (5 km. SW): Originally Romanesque, the chapel has a Gothic doorway and is opposite the remains of Gallo-Roman public baths.

Dreux	(34,050 inhab.)
28 Eure-et-Loir	p.410□H 5

Dreux is located on the numerous streams of the little river Blaise and nestles beneath the hill on which the chapel of *Saint-Louis* stands. This was built at the beginning of the 19C to serve as a mausoleum for the Orléans family and was finished in Louis-Philippe's time; some of the stained-glass windows are by Ingres. Inside there are numerous tombs. Dreux, originally Gallic, has had a rather turbulent past, enduring both sieges and battles.

The 13C church of **Saint-Pierre** has often been damaged and then rebuilt. It dates mainly from the late 15C/early 17C. One of the two strong towers flanking the W. front has barely been started, while the N. tower has a splendid Renaissance upper part. The large doorway has been badly defaced but is still a fine example of Flamboyant art. Inside the church there is an organ-chest from 1644, interesting statues and fine stained-glass windows from the 16&17C.

The square *belfry* on the Grande Rue dates from the 16C and has a 17C campanile.

The *Musée Municipal* is in a nearby chapel and has varied collections devoted to local history — it also has a fine painting by Claude Monet, *Les Glycines*.

Dreux, Chapelle St-Louis

Dunkerque/Dunkirk   (83,800 inhab.)
59 Nord   p.411☐I 1

Before the war, Dunkirk—'church on the dunes' — was essentially a Flemish city from the 17&18C. 1944 left it in ruins with very little of the old town left. However, it recovered and started looking to the future—new town-planning took over, factories were built and an ultra-modern port has developed to rival the largest in France. Now it is more dynamic than ever with cranes and tall furnaces dominating the skyline.

The museum has some interesting Flemish and Dutch paintings. In the old port near the Minck (a fish market) just one of the 28 towers of the old 14C fortifications is left—the octagonal *Tour de Leughenaer*. In the centre of the town the restored church of *Saint-Éloi* is interesting. It is late Gothic and has a nave and four aisles, an old free-standing bell tower and a large square brick tower dating from the 15C, which has long been used as a belfry. In the very heart of the town the statue of Jean Bart by David d'Angers has miraculously escaped damage and commemorates the brave French corsair, who was born in Dunkirk in 1650.

Durtal   (3,250 inhab.)
49 Maine-et-Loire   p.413☐F 7

Durtal is a little town by the Loir; there is a large forest nearby. The château which dominates the town can be reached via the street running along the old ramparts and through the *Porte Verron* (15C). The château has two fine 15C machicolated towers and some buildings from the old fortress. The S. wing is in the style of the second Renaissance and the W. pavilion dates from Henri IV's reign. There is an old people's home there today and its appearance has changed greatly.

Dunkirk, the port

E

Écouen (4,490 inhab.)
95 Val-d'Oise p.428□I 4

The architect Jean Bullant died here in 1578. He was influenced by Philibert Delorme but felt more affinity with the Italian style. The *château* is one of his most important works. (Jean Goujon was one of the decorators.) The château was built in the mid 16C on the site of an old Mont- morency fortress. 'Inspired by antiquity', it houses the *Musée de la Renaissance*, which was assembled from the resources of the vast Musée de Cluny in Paris (tapes- tries, sculptures, paintings, furniture, sil- verware, enamels). Laid out around a square courtyard with a low 19C wing, it is a most beautiful example of the French Renaissance during Henri II's reign; not only is it well-proportioned but it also presents a majesty appearance without be-

Écouen, the château

ing austere. Écouen was a girls' college of the Legion of Honour before it became a museum. A great deal of restoration had to be done before the collections could be opened to the public in 1977 but, despite its former dilapidation, there are still many of the original features, in particular a polychrome marble chimney-piece in the main hall and several other painted ones.

The 16&17C church, flanked by a strong tower, has a modern façade and some very fine Renaissance stained glass windows; those in the choir date from 1545.

Environs: Luzarches (11 km. N.): This large village is the birthplace of Robert de Luzarches, who in the 13C designed the cathedral of Amiens. It has a composite church dedicated to Saint Côme and Saint Damien, patrons of doctors. The façade is pure Renaissance; part of the choir and apse are Romanesque. The **Château de Champlâtreux**, nearby, is a fine 18C house.

Écouis	(710 inhab.)
27 Eure	p.410□H 4

Écouis is famous for its former *collegiate church*—a sober early 14C building built by a local nobleman who was Superintendent of Finance under Philip the Fair. (He ended up on the scaffold in Montfaucon in 1315, only two years after the church was completed). The large nave, revaulted in the 18C, contains a number of works of art, mostly from the same period as the church, some later. The beautiful statue of *Notre-Dame d'Écouis* is 14C, as is the ravishing statue of St. Agnes, which has long wavy hair. Near the latter, in the left transept, is a 15C *Ecce Homo*; the *Annunciation* to the left of the nave is also 15C. There are some remarkable choir stalls of Renaissance design, which are the work of a Norman artist who was influenced by Italian art.

Éguisheim	(1,460 inhab.)
68 Haut-Rhin	p.417□O 6

One of the most charming villages in the Alsace wine-growing region, Éguisheim is overlooked by three ruins which were a great inspiration to Romantic engravers. The village is picturesque indeed with its old, sometimes very bowed, houses. The 'Three Châteaux' are a reminder of the families who enjoyed power in the early Middle Ages.

Clustered around the ruins of yet another château, the village is completely round and follows the lines of the old ramparts. Pope Leo IX, who was related to the local counts, was born here in 1002.

Embrun	(5,000 inhab.)
05 Hautes-Alpes	p.426□O 12

The old town, perched on the Le Roc escarpment, was once ruled by powerful bishops. Now it is a resort thanks to Elec-

Écouis, collegiate church, the nave

Embrun, St-Étienne, le Réal

tricité de France, who are responsible for the vast expanse of water, which connects with the Serre-Ponçon reservoir. In ancient times called *Ebrodunum*, it has been the seat of a bishop since the 4C; it was also the fiefdom of archbishop princes of the Holy Roman Empire. The town, which still has a Franciscan convent and old houses, is dominated by a 12C keep, the *Tour Brune* and the church of *Saint-Étienne*, which was formerly a cathedral. Built early in the 12C it nevertheless incorporated Gothic elements and has a superb porch, with rather unusual decoration, known as *Le Réal* (the Royal). The two pink columns supporting it rest on lions, one holding a child, the other a dog; behind, two crouching male figures serve as bases for two clusters of small columns; on the tympanum is a figure of Christ with the symbols of the Evangelists.

There is a fine rose-window in the façade of the original black and white stone church. Inside there are two renovated 15C organs which are among the oldest in France; there is also a mosaic of the miraculous image of the Virgin (Louis XI wore a miniature copy of this on his hat), which was formerly exhibited to pilgrims in the porch. *Notre-Dame's* treasure includes some very beautiful religious works.

Épernay	(31,110 inhab.)
51 Marne	p.411□K 4

Only a few modest traces remain of Épernay's historic and often violent past. In the church of *Notre-Dame*, which was rebuilt in the 19C, there is some 16C stained-glass in the arcade windows. The portal of the old church and the façade of Louise of Savoy's house are both Renaissance. But the finest monuments in Épernay are undoubtedly the caves hollowed out of the chalk and used for storing champagne!
The surrounding vine-covered hillsides account for the town's fame and indeed wealth — as you can see from the smart houses of the citizens. The museum, which is very modern and has archaeological and ceramic collections, is primarily a museum of champagne.

Épinal	(42,810 inhab.)
88 Vosges	p.417□N 6

Épinal, situated as it is on a strategic crossroads surrounded by forest and near to the still wild Moselle, was from very early days a stronghold. The château, which once dominated the town, is now just a pile of ruins in a forested park. However, the heart of the town, which was founded in the 10C, is still the area around the basilica of *Saint-Maurice*. This is much restored but

Épinal, basilica of Saint-Maurice, Entombment

full of character for all that, with its massive 12&13C Germanic bell tower, 13C three-storeyed Burgundian nave and wide 14C Gothic choir, inspired by the style of Champagne. It contains a Rhenish Deposition dating from the 16C and a splendid and very feminine Virgin (15C). To the W. of the sanctuary is the astonishing *Portail des Bourgeois*, a deep, vaulted porch with intersecting ribs—unfortunately the lavish decoration was badly damaged in the Revolution. Beyond this church you come to the *Place des Vosges* with its arcaded houses (there is a beautiful Renaissance loggia on the façade of one of them).

On the left bank of the Moselle is the church of **Notre-Dame au Cierge** (1958), a functional, concrete building, fortunately relieved by the huge iridescent stained-glass window at the end of the choir, and the Porte d'Honneur, which is decorated with *cloisonné* enamel on red copper.

Musée Départmental des Vosges and Musée International de l'Imagerie: The Departmental Museum is devoted to regional archaeology and the art and tradition of the Vosges. There is a rich collection of drawings, a moving *Virgin Mary* by Rembrandt (1661) and a splendid *Job Scolded by his Wife* by Georges de la Tour. Épinal remains a centre of popular colour prints; the *Musée de l'Imagerie* traces the long history of popular pictures distributed by pedlars for the protection, information and education of the masses. The *Imagerie Pellerin* has carried on the tradition of the 'images d'Épinal' since 1740; in their workshops you can see the machines and techniques used. The Bibliothèque Municipale (town library) on the other hand, is

Espalion, the Pont-Vieux

quite different. Its historic rooms (18C wood panelling) house precious manuscripts and early printed works.

Époisses (château)
21 Côte-d'Or   p.415□L 7

This enormous château, near the pleasant village of Auxois, has a moat—now dry—and a strong double wall. Indeed, it is almost a town itself, with a church, old outbuildings and a large dovecote. In the main it is 16C but some parts e much older. The château, which was damaged during the Revolution, still has its 17C decoration and furniture. In particular visitors can see the room in which the young Henri IV slept after the battle of Arnay-le-Duc and also the room kept for Madame de Sévigné

when she stayed there. There are many mementoes of these guests and some good paintings (Philippe de Champaigne, Largillière, Mignard and Oudry).

Espalion   (4,810 inhab.)
12 Aveyron   p.424□J 12

This charming small town is in the Espalion basin, a broad part of the valley of the Lot. Both the town and its surroundings are extremely attractive. The 13C *Pont Vieux*, with three arches on massive piers, links the historic Quartier des Tanneurs with some solidly built old houses. The Renaissance château now houses the *Musée Folklorique Joseph-Vaylet* (old local pieces, fine collection of holy-water stoups). The 11C church of *Saint-Hilarian de Perse*, 1

Itxassou, galleries in the nave

Étampes, the Tour Guinette

km. from the town centre, is a small Romanesque building in red sandstone; its tympanum shows the influence of Conques.

| **Espelette** | (1,190 inhab.) |
| 64 Pyrénées-Atlantiques | p.422□D 14 |

Basque ponies, the pottokaks, run free on the hillsides above this attractive town. The old château is now the Town Hall and a monastery. Espelette—the name comes from *espeleta eta*, meaning place planted with box—has a few houses in typical local style. The *church*, with its cemetery containing discoidal stele has a huge bell tower and porch and dates from the first half of the 17C; this style with three storeys of carved wooden galleries, is very common in the Basque country.

Environs: Itxassou (4 km. W.): This is a little village of white houses divided into two distinct groups, a layout very common in this area. It has a particularly Basque single-aisled 17C church with carved galleries and painted ceiling. The future abbé of Saint-Cyr, a Bayonne priest who became a Jansenist theorist, was the parish priest here when young. The nearby 'Pas de Roland', a rock overhanging the Nive, is supposed to have been cleft by the gallant follower of Charlemagne.

| **Étampes** | (19,760 inhab.) |
| 91 Essonne | p.410□I 5 |

Étampes was annexed to the crown by Hugues Capet and the early Capetians were fond of this valley with its little branching rivers. The town, spread out at the foot of an old 12C keep, the *Tour Guinette*, has retained Gothic buildings and luxurious Renaissance houses (those of Diane de Poitiers and Anne de Pisseleu and the Hôtel de Ville, which has a local history museum). The Danish Queen Ingeborg was forced to live here by her husband Philippe Auguste; he had tried to divorce her but was forbidden to do so by the Pope. Étampes was besieged on numerous occasions.

Ravaillac was here in 1610, when it is said that his decision to assassinate Henri IV was revived in front of a cross at the entrance to the town. (The Angoulême schoolmaster believed that Christ had reminded him of his duty to kill the King, who was too close to the Protestants.)

Notre-Dame-du-Fort: This fortified 12&13C church stands over the crypt of a Romanesque church. Note the rather daring Romanesque bell tower and the remarkable S. portal (mid 12C and similar to that at Chartres but rather mutilated). Notre-Dame is irregular in plan and has

Étampes, Notre-Dame-du-Fort

been altered. The choir is lit by some 16C stained-glass windows, the best of which shows the twelve Sibyls.

Saint-Basile: This church was much altered in the 15&16C. However, the semicircular Romanesque doorway remains in the W. façade and there are still some 12C elements (the bell tower over the crossing in particular). The church of *Saint-Gilles*, founded by Louis VI in 1123, was also rebuilt in the 15&16C. The church of *Saint-Martin* from the 12&13C is dominated by a 16C tower which has tilted as a result of subsidence. The choir is rather remarkable and has an ambulatory and radiating chapels and numerous tombstones.

Environs: Morigny (3 km. N.): The truncated church of an old Benedictine abbey, it is now a parish church. The square tower is 13C, though some parts are 11C. The *Palais des Abbés* contains important collections, particularly relating to prehistory. **Chamarande** (10 km. N.): The rather sober mid-17C château by François Mansart stands in a vast park, through which the cascading Juine and canals run. **Farcheville** (11 km. E.): This château dates from the 13C and is surrounded by moats and a fortified wall. It looks very medieval; one wing is late 17C. **Méréville** (16 km. S.): The château, built by a rich financier at the end of the Ancien Régime, was once surrounded by a famous park, full of whimsical monuments. However, this area of greenery has now been eaten away by developments.

Étretat	(1,530 inhab.)
76 Seine-Maritime	p.410☐G 3

Étretat has a few pretty old houses, a Romanesque-Gothic church, which is a dependency of the abbey of Fécamp, and some pleasant market buildings which have been rebuilt as they were originally. From an architectural point of view there is not a great deal to see. However, it is worth visiting the natural arches and needles cut by the sea in the soft Caux cliffs. Erosion has created a fantastic landscape in Étretat; this was mentioned by Guy de Maupassant and inspired paintings by Eugène Delacroix, Eugène Boudin, Isabey, Johan Jongkind, Gustave Courbet, Claude Monet, Félix Vallotton, Henri Matisse and many others. The first painter to come here was Isabey (1840–50). The great Courbet captured his *Vague* (wave) at Étretat; this painting is now in the Louvre.

| Eu | (8,900 inhab.) |
| 76 Seine-Maritime | p.410 □ H 2 |

Girt by forest, Eu was an ancient Gallo-Roman river port and a residence of the Dukes of Normandy. It has belonged to several great French families and was ruled by the Orléans family.

Château: This building of brick and stone with high dormer windows and slate roofs was begun in 1578 by Henri de Guise (the 'Balafré'), who was murdered at Blois on the orders of Henri III. It was improved by Mlle. de Montpensier and then sacked in the Revolution. The Duke of Orléans, soon to become King Louis Philippe, restored it in the 19C and it had to be partly rebuilt after a fire in 1902. It now houses the Town Hall and the *Musée Louis Philippe* (history of the château's past owners, history of Eu, trophies won by the Prince of Orléans). On the first floor is Mlle. de Montpensier's room with its original 17C decoration.

Collegiate church of Saint-Laurent: This pure, beautifully proportioned 12&13C church is dedicated to the Irish Archbishop St. Lawrence O'Toole, who died at Eu in 1181. Apart from alterations which spoiled the 15C apse, the church has kept its original, bare, pleasing form and has remained a very fine example of Norman Gothic. *Interior:* The choir and transepts have galleries; the nave does not,

Eu, collegiate church of St-Laurent, Entombment (15C)

although they were planned by the master builders when work started. In the right arm, there is a slender column with a torso in front of the 15C font. Marble columns were added to the pillars of the crossing in the 18&19C and these bear urns embossed with the Orléans motto or epitaphs (one contains the heart of Catherine of Clèves, Duchess of Guise). In the reliquary on the high altar are the relics of St. Lawrence O'Toole. Passing through a little carved door at the entrance to the ambulatory, you come to a chapel which contains a fine 15C Entombment. *Crypt:* Here there are the tombs of the Counts of Eu (the House of Artois) from the time of Louis Philippe and also some beautiful Gothic statues (late 13C).

Évreux	(50,360 inhab.)
27 Eure	p.410☐H 4

Originally a Gallo-Roman city, Évreux was devastated by Norman pirates in 892 and thereafter has been repeatedly burnt, sacked and ravaged. The city was most recently damaged by German bombs in June 1940 and American ones in July 1944. Unfortunately, the rebuilding has not been a success and the town has lost much of its charm. One pleasant part is the walk along the ramparts by the Iton, from the belfry (1490) to the cathedral — a remarkable and well restored monument.

The Cathedral of Notre-Dame: Although the cathedral was damaged in the last war, the successful blend of 12–17C styles is still apparent: the spectacular façade is an inspired Renaissance addition; the unusual tower, the *Gros-Pierre*, is Louis XIII style. There is a wealth of stained glass inside. The apse is surrounded by glass and there are also fine stained-glass windows in the chapels (windows, or pieces of glass dating from the 11–16C).

Évreux, the belfry

The woodwork is equally impressive: note the chapels' screens, the ornate carved wooden door to the ambulatory (16C), and the carved 18C choir stalls, which have lovely grilles from the same period.

Old Bishop's Palace and Museum: This 15C Flamboyant Bishop's Palace today houses a very pleasant archaeological museum. In addition to an archaeology section, there are paintings, furniture and pottery. In one room on the second floor there is an exhibition of 19C paintings, pre-Impressionists and Impressionists, a small canvas by Goya, a fine Guillaumin and a very pretty view of the *Bassin de l'Eure au Havre* by Boudin.

The Church of Saint-Taurin: Taurinus

Évreux, the cathedral

was a local saint who founded the diocese of Évreux at the end of the 4C or beginning of the 5C. He seems to have been a fearless opponent of the Devil, even taking one of his horns! The church which is dedicated to him was formerly the abbey church of a prosperous Benedictine community and dates from the 11,12&14C with later alterations (Louis XV façade). The S. transept is pure Romanesque. The reliquary of St.Taurinus is kept in the sacristy or presbytery and is a 13C masterpiece in silver-gilt.

Excideuil
24 Dordogne

(1,660 inhab.)
p.419☐H 11

The impressive ruins of the château of Excideuil are situated on a spur overlooking the town and the surrounding countryside. This strongpoint, the residence of powerful feudal lords, was enlarged and altered by six different dynasties of viscounts in the 11–16C. When the Talleyrand family became owners they were unable to carry out the restoration that had been needed since the beginning of the 18C. As a result the château was already very dilapidated at the time of the Revolution. What remains is 14C and Renaissance. The church of Excideuil, founded by the Benedictines in the 12C, was burnt several times and then largely rebuilt in the 16C. There is a wonderfully ornamented Flamboyant S. portal. Inside is a 16–17C polychrome *Pietà* and an elaborate 17C altarpiece.

Eyzies-de-Tayac (Les)
24 Dordogne

(780 inhab.)
p.419☐H 12

The valley of the Vézère in the heart of Périgord Noir is one of the cradles of mankind. Prehistoric man lived here beneath the limestone cliffs and numerous caves have wall-paintings showing Quaternary animals (see also **Montignac**). On the museum's terrace a statue of 'Cro-Magnon Man' stares at the horizon beyond this well-named 'Capital of Prehistory'. The *Musée National de Préhistoire*, housed in the re-

Évreux, the church of St-Taurin, shrine of St. Taurin (16C)

stored 10&11C fortress of the Lords of Beynac, features various local finds, all with a very clear commentary. It is the best possible introduction to prehistoric Périgord for there are plenty of illustrated explanations of the various prehistoric periods and descriptions of the development of stone tools and cave art. One of the outstanding works from these Dark Ages is the famous bas-relief of *Vénus de Laussel*, which dates from what is known as the Gravettian age (about 24,000 BC) and the wild ox of Fourneau du Diable, from the upper Solutrian (about 15,000 BC).

Grotte de Font-de-Gaume: Discovered in 1901 this long cave lies some 60 ft. above the valley and is actually a passage with a series of chambers. To reach it you must climb up a steep path. Inside there are countless stunning wall paintings and engravings of animals in black and ochre. There are bison, goats and mammoths, reindeer and many other animals, all from the Magdalenian period, although the exact date is unclear (the Magdalenian period is the last part of the upper Palaeolithic and ended about 9,000 BC).

Grotte des Combarelles: Discovered three days before Font-de-Gaume, this narrow tunnel is decorated with over three hundred animal drawings, all Magdalenian. *Abri du Cap-Blanc:* This small shelter beneath the rock has carved animals in high relief (life-size horses, deerheads, bison).

Roc de Tayac: Accessible only by flights of steps, the caverns in this steep cliff contain a small *Musée de Spéléologie* (cave museum). The excavations were fortified and used as shelters in the Hundred Years War. *Gorge d'Enfer:* Here, in a pleasant green valley, there is an open-air zoo—the animals are descended from those roaming the area in prehistoric times. *Gisement de Laugerie-Basse:* Near the fairy-like *Grotte Grand-Roc* with natural stalactites and stalagmites, this site is protected by a large overhang. An exposed cross-section shows the different layers corresponding to the civilizations which followed on from the middle of the Magdalenian period to the dawn of history. A little museum here displays finds from excavations.

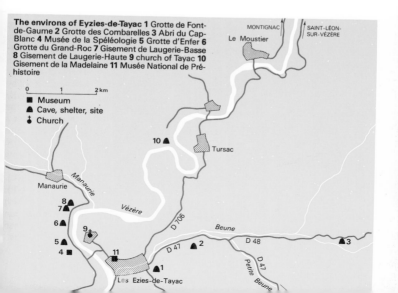

The environs of Eyzies-de-Tayac 1 Grotte de Font-de-Gaume 2 Grotte des Combarelles 3 Abri du Cap-Blanc 4 Musée de la Spéléologie 5 Grotte d'Enfer 6 Grotte du Grand-Roc 7 Gisement de Laugerie-Basse 8 Gisement de Laugerie-Haute 9 church of Tayac 10 Gisement de la Madelaine 11 Musée National de Préhistoire

St-Léon-sur-Vézère, the church

Les Eyzies, the church of Tayac

Gisement de Laugerie-Haute: Near to Laugerie-Basse and also the subject of investigation since 1863, this site was settled by early man for about 20,000 years.

The church of Tayac: This beige-coloured fortress, lit by loophole windows, protects the straggling nearby village of Eyzies. 12C, it has a certain sober elegance, a fortified façade and apse. There are numerous fortified churches in the SW; these were used as sanctuaries for the local people in the Hundred Years War, when the area was in a constant state of turmoil.

Environs: Tursac (5.5 km. NE): The Romanesque fortified church here is dominated by a bell tower-keep and has a line of domes. On the other side of the Vézère, the *Gisement de la Madeleine* gave its name to the Magdalenian period of the Palaeolithic. **La Roque-Saint-Christophe** (9 km. NE): The cliffs here are naturally hollow and have subsequently been extensively excavated and adapted by man, particularly by cave dwellers in the Middle Ages. On the other side of the river, the hamlet of **Le Moustier** has a modest but charming Romanesque church. There is an important prehistoric site nearby to which Le Moustier owes its fame—it gave its name to the Mousterian period (about 75,000 to 80,000 BC). **Saint-Léon-sur-Vézère** (14 km. NE): The 11&12C Romanesque church, which has been wonderfully restored, has a plain Romanesque bell tower. Gallo-Roman remains were found in the foundations.

Èze, the village

Èze (1,860 inhab.)
06 Alpes-Maritimes p.426□P 14

This little village clings to a pyramidal rock high above the sea and offers splendid views over the whole of the Riviera. At the summit there are the ruins of the 14C castle of the Riquiers, lords of Èze. The old, restored houses and the network of little streets and covered passageways still have a certain character. The 18C church has a lovely statue of the *Assumption* and some 15C fonts. The *Chapelle des Pénitents-Blancs* dates from the 14C. A botanical garden at the top of the village has succulents and cacti.

The old part of the village lies on the Middle Corniche, a road with splendid views ascending Mont Boron.

Èze, view of the Riviera

F

Falaise   (8,610 inhab.)
14 Calvados   p.413☐F 4

William the Conqueror's birthplace was badly damaged in 1944. The château visible today stands on a sandstone promontory and, restored and altered, it is essentially the work of one of William's sons (12C). Partially dismantled when Henri IV captured it, and then sacked, it

Falaise, the château

is nevertheSS still very attractive. A 13C wall with towers surrounds the keep where legend has it William was born in 1027. The damaged church of *La Trinité* from the 13,16&17C, is predominantly Flamboyant. The church of *Saint-Gervais* is late 12C (part of the nave and lantern tower are Romanesque). Its appearance was greatly changed in the 13,15&16C. The church of *Notre-Dame-de-Guibray* is Romanesque in origin; it too has been altered, especially inside.

Faou (Le)   (1,610 inhab.)
29 Finistère   p.412☐B 5

This village on a crossroads halfway between Brest and Quimper was a once-prosperous port. A few 16C corbelled houses, whose fronts have been hung with slates, remain. The 16C church has a high bell tower with a balcony, and a dome with four lantern-lights. The S. porch with its stone benches contains statues of the Apostles.

Environs: Abbey of Landévennec (18 km. W.): The Landévennec peninsula at the mouth of the Aulne has the remains of

Le Faou, old house

Le Faouët, Chapelle St-Fiacre, detail

the oldest abbey in Brittany, which was founded by St. Guénolé (or Winwaloe). The buildings were restored in 1950 and are now occupied by Benedictines. The original 5C church was destroyed many times and in the the 10&11C it was replaced by the abbey church, which is itself now in ruins. It has some interesting examples of pre-Romanesque and Romanesque art. The periphery of the apse with its three apsidal chapels is rather well preserved. A porch with five arches is Carolingian. Note especially the fine capitals with their geometric patterns (palm leaves, wheels, knot-work, leaf motifs, chevrons). One of the chapels in the transept has a tomb thought to be that of King Gradlon, the famous king of Cornwall who figures in the legends of the town of Ys. It has been possible through excavations to work out the exact plan of this building.

Faouët (Le)	(3,150 inhab.)
56 Morbihan	p.412☐B 6

Situated in the hilly country of Argoat, in the interior of Brittany, Le Faouët is grouped around a large square, dominated by the huge 16C market building, which has fine woodwork and small octagonal bell tower. However, the church, which dates from the same period, is no more interesting than the nearby chapels, which are charming examples of Breton architecture.

Environs: Chapelle Saint-Fiacre (3 km. S.): The sober façade of this 15C church, which overlooks the esplanade, has a gabled bellcote with turrets on either side. Inside, there is a richly traceried wooden rood screen (1480), which has both

Le Faouët, Chapelle St-Fiacre, polychrome statues

sacred and profane images. Scenes from the Bible alternate with rather bold depictions of the cardinal sins: a man vomiting a fox represents drunkenness, a peasant gathering apples represents theft, and lasciviousness is represented by a love-scene. The pendent keystones of the vault supporting the gallery end in carved angels (on the nave side) and a fawn or faun (on the choir side). In the apse and the transepts, the stained-glass windows date from the 16C.

Chapelle Sainte-Barbe (2.5 km. NE): An impressive Renaissance staircase with balustrade leads to the 16C sanctuary perched on a rock by the Ellé. On the first level a stone arch leads to the oratory of *Saint-Michel;* it is flanked by iron rings which were probably used as hand grips by pilgrims. The chapel is supported by pinnacled buttresses and has a Flamboyant choir and bay with Renaissance glass.

There are carved panels and statues inside. **Chapelle Saint-Nicolas** (6 km. NE): Rather more modest. It has a small granite bell tower with a gable flanked by a turret and contains a rustic Renaissance rood screen in painted wood which comically illustrates the story of St. Nicholas. **Chapelle Saint-Sébastien** (4 km. N.): The apse of this chapel is three-sided with pointed gables on buttresses decorated with gargoyles. Inside, the beams have carvings (hunting scenes, and scenes from daily life, episodes from the *Roman de Renart*). The main beam running across the nave is 16C. **Kernascléden** (14.5 km. E.): This church, completed in 1453, is one of the jewels of Breton art. It is very varied in style; its S. façade has a lovely rose-window and two porches, the larger of which, decorated with leaves and vine-branches, contains statues of the Apostles. There are

Fécamp, Trinité, the lantern

Fécamp, Trinité, Death of the Virgin

some remarkable frescos in the choir on the stone vault and upper walls; these are 15C and depict scenes from the life of the Virgin and Christ (there is a fresco of the Resurrection on the triumphal arch). In the right transept there is a huge panel which is in rather bad condition but represents a Dance of Death and Hell with the damned being boiled, roasted or impaled on the branches of a tree.

Fécamp	(22,230 inhab.)
76 Seine Maritime	p.410☐G 3

Fécamp, formerly the home port of the daring Newfoundlanders with their fleets of trawlers, lies cradled between two cliffs at the end of a valley in the Caux region. The birthplace of the writer Jean Lorrain and very probably of Guy de Maupassant too, it was also the native town of two Dukes of Normandy. Today it is an important port and seaside resort. It is dominated by the church of a once-important abbey, which was founded in about 660 and was very prosperous until the end of the Ancien Régime (Guillaume de Volpiano was one of its abbots). There are only scant remains of the castle and palace which was begun by the Dukes of Normandy in the 10C, but some abbey buildings survived the Revolution (the monks' old windmill, Louis XVI buildings which now house the Town Hall).

La Trinité: This imposing and majestic old abbey church dominates the town. It is very large—a little longer than Notre-Dame in Paris—and was built 1175–1220 on the site of a church which had been

Fécamp, la Bénédictine

struck by lightning. It is early Norman Gothic with an elegant Louis XV façade. The sober nave is high and has side aisles and galleries; the lantern of the tower above the crossing is 130 ft. high. In the right transept, the *Chapelle de la Dormition* contains an expressive group of statues, the *Death of the Virgin*: dating from 1495, this includes carved fragments of the old rood screen and a tabernacle (1420). The stone called 'du pas de l'ange' is said to bear the imprint of a heavenly messenger who appeared to Guillaume Longue-Épée in 943. The choir is superb, with 18C choir stalls and high altar as well as a lovely Renaissance altar. The axial *Chapelle de la Vierge* is late 15C and seems to be distinct from the rest of the church. It has a 16C white marble tabernacle and a modern reliquary containing some of the Precious Blood. The Chapelle du *Sacré-Coeur* on the left of the choir has the 17C tomb of Guillaume de Volpiano, who died in 1031.

The Church of Saint-Étienne: This is near the port; Flamboyant, it was largely rebuilt in the 19C.

The **Musée Municipal** occupies an 18C house, and features some remarkable 16C portraits, together with various paintings and sketches by Delacroix and Monet. There are also archaeological and faience collections, and documents on old Fécamp, seafaring and Caux folklore.

The Bénédictine: This extraordinary 19C château, with its carved pediments, pinnacle turrets and pointed roofs, is a memorial to the famous liqueur developed here by the monks of Fécamp (it is now made in modern factories at Tourville-les-

Fécamp, Musée de la Bénédictine

Valmont, ruins of the abbey

Ilfs). Its 'Gothic' and 'Renaissance' rooms house a rich and varied collection of works of art. The unusual museum exhibits a mixture of works, and includes some fine pieces e.g. a polyptych from the Cologne school, about 1500, and a triptych from the workshop of the Master of Frankfurt, from the late 15C/early 16C. There are some fine pieces of furniture, Roman lamps, old ironwork, silverware and old forceps, not to mention exhibits connected with the liqueur invented by the monks in the 16C, which is still made with 27 herbs and spices.

Environs: Abbey of Valmont (11 km. E.): This abbey, where Delacroix loved to stay, was founded in the 12C and altered in the 17C. The ruined abbey church is still very attractive and looks lovely against its green background. The *Chapelle de la Vierge*, which is still intact, is a Renaissance masterpiece, and contains tombs with recumbent figures and a 16C *Annunciation* attributed to Germain Pilon. There are some 16C windows in the bays. The nearby **Château des Sires d'Estouteville** still has its square keep, which was built in William the Conqueror's time, and also a Renaissance residence.

Fénelon (château)
24 Dordogne   p.419☐H 12

This castle, where the author of the *Aventures de Télémaque* was born, is near the Dordogne and almost on the edge of Quercy. Standing on a hilltop and surrounded by a double wall, it still looks very feudal, with its mullions, machicolations

La Ferté-Alais, bell tower

was turned into a country house and so lost its military appearance. There are some remains of a Renaissance gallery on the impressive viaduct over the ravine.

Ferté-Alais (La) (1,950 inhab.)
91 Essone p.410☐I 5

The village is situated on the edge of a wooded plateau which has long been quarried for sandstone and silica. Clinging to the memory of a former châtelaine—its name means 'Adelaide's fortress'—the 'fort' has long since disappeared, but the 11&12C Romanesque-Gothic church is still here, with its lovely bell tower and a spire which was rebuilt in the 17C. Inside there are some decorated capitals and also furnishings (the latter coming from a former abbey).

Ferté-Bernard (La) (9,800 inhab.)
72 Sarthe p.414☐G 6

This little town in the valley of the Huisne was the birthplace of Jehan de Beauce, one of the builders of Chartres Cathedral, and also of Robert Garnier, a 16C author. It owes its name to an ancient fortress and its feudal lords. The church of *Notre-Dame-de-Marais* is the town's outstanding building. Flamboyant and Renaissance it dates from the 15&16C. The choir is remarkable, being lit by superb glass (late 15C/early 16C); the organ-chest is supported by a very ornate corbel (16C). The 15C *Porte Saint-Julien* by the Huisne was once part of the old town wall and has withstood various sieges. The 16C market still has its original timber but it now houses the *Salle des Fêtes*. There are a few old houses in the town; a 15C aqueduct still carries water from a spring near the fountain in the Place Carnot. The *Tour des*

and stone roofing tiles. François de Salignac de La Mothe-Fénelon, the future 'Bishop of Cambrai' was born here in 1651 and it still has numerous mementoes of this liberal Bishop.

Fère-en-Tardenois (3,070 inhab.)
02 Aisne p.411☐K 4

There are some splendid 16C market buildings in the centre of the town and these have large tiled roofs and impressive timber-work supported by stone pillars. The 15&16C church contains a remarkable collection of carved wooden furniture dating from the 17C. On a hillock to the N. there are the ruins of a 13C fortress with seven towers resting solidly on their serrated foundations. In the 16C the château

Ferté-Milon, ruins of the château

Moulins, a remnant of the old fortifications, forms part of an old house at the corner of the Rue Viet.

Ferté-Milon (La)   (1,690 inhab.)
02 Aisne   p.411☐J 4

The birthplace of Jean Racine in 1639. The village is overlooked by the ruins of the fortress, which was rebuilt in the 14C (a man called Milon was one of its first lords). The tall, broad façade of the château looks out on to countryside. It is an impressive structure. Two strong towers in the centre protect the entrance, above which there is a 15C bas-relief of the *Coronation of the Virgin*. The church of *Notre-Dame*, combining a 12C Romanesque nave and a Renaissance choir, was financed by Catherine de Medici. The *Chapelle de la Vierge* is lit by a fine 16C stained-glass window above the altar. The church of *Saint-Nicolas* from the 15&16C has some heavily restored 16C windows. The statue of Jean Racine is by David d'Angers.

Figeac   (10,860 inhab.)
46 Lot   p.423☐I 12

Figeac rises in terraces up the hillside above the river Célé. It has a medieval centre with old houses, many of which have projecting turrets and typical Quercy open-fronted attics, known as 'soleilho'. The town grew up around an abbey and was an important Protestant stronghold at the end of the 16C and the beginning of the 17C. The only part of Figeac that is of archaeo-

Figeac, church of St-Sauveur

La Flèche, Chapelle St-Louis

logical interest is on the right bank of the river, where there are some picturesque sloping streets.

Saint-Saveur was once a dependency of the Cluniac abbey and dates from the 11C, although it was much altered in the 13,14,17&19C. It combines Romanesque and Gothic styles. The chapterhouse dates from the 14&15C and is now a chapel.

The 12C church of **Notre-Dame-du-Puy**, at the top of Mont-Viguier (the site of the damaged house of the King's provost, or viguier), overlooks the brown rooftops of the old town. It was altered in the 14&17C and the Gothic nave is joined to a Romanesque apse. The choir has a large 17C altarpiece with paintings of the *Assumption* and the *Coronation of the Virgin* in a carved walnut frame.

The 13C **Hôtel de la Monnaie**, crowned by a soleilho, now houses the little *Musée Lapidaire et Historique*. One room is devoted to the Egyptologist, Jean-François Champollion, who was born in Figeac in 1790.

Filitosa, see **Corsica**

Flavigny-sur-Ozerain, see **Alise-Sainte-Reine**

Flèche (La)	(16,350 inhab.)
72 Sarthe	p.414☐F/G 7

Henri IV spent his youth in this Angevin town on the Loir. For a long time a commercial centre it is now an industrial centre too. Henri founded an important Jesuit

Fleury-en-Bière, the château

college here which counted René Descartes among its pupils. Now the huge 17&18C buildings contain the famous *Prytanée Militaire*, a military college for over 1,000 pupils. The chapel of *Saint-Louis* (early 17C) is sober outside, and Jesuit baroque inside. It contains an urn with the ashes of the hearts of Henri IV and Marie de Medici. The pretty chapel of *Notre-Dame-des-Vertus* on the edge of La Flèche, is Romanesque in origin and is decorated with Renaissance carving.

Flers　(21,250 inhab.)
61 Orne　p.413□F 5

Flers, a small Bocage town, was rebuilt after the last war and subsequently enlarged by new building. The 16&18C château is surrounded by water and has a long history. It contains a museum dealing with the Chouan uprising, the 'Bocage Normand' region, and the local textile industry. The church of *Saint-Germain* is a heavy modern building with some fine stained-glass windows by contemporary artists.

Fleury-en-Bière　(330 inhab.)
77 Seine-et-Marne　p.429□J 5

The pretty, flowery village is separated from the 16&18C château by a strong wall. The château itself has a regular stone and red brick façade at the end of a large main courtyard surrounded by vast outbuildings. The 12C chapel, which dates from the fortress preceding the present château, is now a parish church.

Foix	(10,250 inhab.)
09 Ariège	p.423 □ H 15

This was a stronghold of the Albigensian heretics, who were victims of a cruel crusade at the beginning of the 13C. It belonged to Béarn and was not subject to the Crown until the Béarnais Henri IV came to the throne. The town, dominated by the fortified outline of its château, is surrounded by mountains. Of the old fortress only scant ruins and three towers remain. The tall, cylindrical keep houses the *Musée Départmental de l'Ariège*, which deals with local prehistory and history, art and tradition. The former abbey church of *Saint-Volusien*, (14&17C), is endowed with a fortified choir; it contains 15C choir stalls. (The crypt is reputed to have been an oratory founded by Charlemagne.) Foix has numerous old houses.

Folgoët (Le)	(2,220 inhab.)
29 Finistère	p.412 □ A 5

Two things have made this little town in the windswept heart of the Léon region well known. The first is a legend: in the 14C, there was a pious 'innocent' called Salaün, known as the madman of the woods (fou du bois—Folgoët). When he died, his savage piety was rewarded—a magnificent lily grew on his tomb with a Hail Mary in gold letters on the petals. The other factor contributing to its fame was the patronage of the Dukes of Brittany, who were instrumental in building its fine church.

Notre-Dame: This church was built in the 14C on the site of the miracle of the lily (there is an annual Pardon on 8 September). Standing on a vast esplanade, the imposing façade has two towers, one of which is unfinished. The N. tower has an openwork gallery and a stone spire with four pinnacle turrets. On the S. side there is a very ornate portal. The porch of the *Chapelle de la Croix* to the W. has some lovely statues. The panelled choir and the nave with its intersecting ribs are lit by a large stained-glass window in the square ended apse. A splendid 15C rood-loft is set in the arch separating them. Built of Kersanton stone, which is very fine-grained, it is regarded as one of the great masterpieces of Breton art. At the rear of the church is the spring of Salaün, dominated by a statue of the Virgin. The little *Musée Lapidaire* contains statues and fragments from the 1543 calvary.

Environs: Château de Kerjean (14 km. NE): This semi-fortified 16C house stands a little outside the village of Saint-Vougay. It has belonged to the State since 1911 and is one of the finest houses of its kind in the area. The main residence, protected by a thick wall, consists of two wings at right angles around a courtyard. The gateway is flanked by two square pavilions; there is an elegant well beneath a stone canopy in one corner. To the E. the chapel combines Gothic and Renaissance; its wooden vault is supported by lovely beams with carved dragons. Some of the rooms are used as a museum and have old furniture and statues.

Fontainebleau	(19,600 inhab.)
77 Seine-et-Marne	p.411 □ J 5

This huge palace was called 'the house of the centuries' by Napoleon and, indeed, it does have elements of all styles from the 16–19C. Set in parkland and a seemingly endless forest, where the Capetian kings used to hunt (they made it one of their principal residences and the last of the line, Philip the Fair, was born and died here), the buildings are rather haphazardly arranged around six courtyards. Legend has it that the name Fontainebleau comes from one of the royal hounds who was lost in the forest. However, it is more likely that it comes from Fontaine-Belle-Eau. The present palace goes back to François I's time. He pulled down the medieval palace and commissioned the best architects and artists of the day to build him a splendid new one. The painter and decorator Fiorentino Rosso and, above all, the eclectic Primaticcio, a native of Bologna, were among them. Thus the Fontainebleau School, with its twofold French and Italian influence, grew up from the bevy of artists working here. Henri II and Catherine de Medici carried on the work and architects such as Philibert Delorme and Jean Bullant drew up new plans. Then Henri IV took over and greatly enlarged the château (adding the *Cour des Offices*, the *Cour des Princes*, the *Jeu de Paume*, and landscaping the gardens). There developed a second Fontainebleau School during his reign, influenced, this time, by Flemish art. Louis XIII was born at Fontainebleau and he finished the work begun by his father.

Louis XIV preferred Versailles to this 'new Rome', where in 1685 he signed the Revocation of the Edict of Nantes. However, he did have the gardens improved by Le Nôtre; he also decorated appartments here for his favourite, Madame de Maintenon. After this, Louis XV, Louis XVI, Napoleon and Louis-Philippe all left their mark here — the château was almost the capital of France at times. Louis XV and Marie Leszczyńska were married here, Jean-Jacques Rousseau was a guest here and organized the first performance of the *Devin du Village* in 1754. Pope Pius VII, who dared to excommunicate Napoleon, (1812–14) was imprisoned here. The Emperor retired to Fontainebleau after his defeat, signed his abdication here and bade farewell to his Old Guard. In the 1960s the château underwent major restoration.

Exterior: The château faces the *Place du Général-de-Gaulle*. The first of the palace's courtyrds is the *Cour du Cheval Blanc* or *des Adieux*, which had a plaster statue of a horse for a long time; it also witnessed the scene of Napoleon's departure for Elba. On the right is the Louis XV wing,

Foix, the château

Fontainebleau, château, the Cour du Cheval Blanc

on the left the François I wing and at the end there is a composite building with the famous *horseshoe staircase* by Jean Androuet du Cerceau (*c.* 1630). The *Cour de la Fontaine* is dominated by the François I gallery and framed by the *Reines Mères* (Queen Mothers') wing and the *Belle Cheminée* wing. It opens on the 'Carp Lake', which still contains voracious carp (it is said that some of them are over 100 years old). The *Porte Dorée* is set in a large pavilion (1528), which has restored paintings and François I's salamander emblem on the tympanum. It leads to the *Cour Ovale* with the Royal Appartments (on the left) and the wing with the sumptuous *Salle de Bal*. The last courtyard, the *Cour des Offices*, is framed by buildings from Henri IV's time.

The secluded *Jardin de Diane* lies to the N. in front of the windows of the *Grands Appartements* of Napoleon I.

On the other side of the château lie the *Jardin Anglais* (redesigned in the 19C) and the vast *parterre* with canals and the *Bassin du Tibre*. The huge park is laid out around a grand canal more than a kilometre long, which was commissioned by Henri IV. To the N. of it is the *Treille du Roi*, planted in the 18C.

Interior: This extraordinarily sumptuous palace has been built in a variety of styles and is a veritable museum of panelling, wall paintings, tapestries and furniture. The *Grands Appartements* on the first floor and the *Petits Appartements* on the ground floor are open to visitors. The *Galerie François I* is one of the features of the palace, with its marvellous Italian decoration by

Rosso Fiorentino. Note also the *Salle de Bal*, decorated by Primaticcio and the *Grands* and *Petits Appartements* of Napoleon I with Empire style furniture and 18C decoration. Through the lovely *Salle du Conseil*, before Marie Antoinette's apartments, is the Kings' bedroom, which became the *Salle du Trône* (Throne Room) under Napoleon (Louis XIII ceiling, Louis XIV and Louis XV decoration on the walls). In the *Salle des Tapisseries* there is a series of Gobelin tapestries woven in Louis XIV's reign. There are several museums in the palace, in particular the *Musée Chinios* founded by the Empress Eugénie. It has mostly oriental pieces brought back after the Anglo-French expedition to China under the Second Empire.

The town: This quiet, residential town grew with the château and today some noblemen's hôtels remain. In the Rue Royale there is a museum with Napoleonic exhibits. **Avon** is almost twinned with Fontainebleau; only the park separates them. It was here that the writer Katherine Mansfield lived until she died in 1923. The church of *Saint-Pierre* is 16C and contains royal officers' tombs in the ambulatory.

Fontaine-Henry	(360 inhab.)
14 Calvados	p.413☐F 4

This château in an English park is in part medieval, although its most beautiful parts date from the late 15C/early 16C, when it was decorated with carvings and lace-like stonework. This graceful building contains some fine furniture and a collection of paintings. The 13C chapel was altered in Renaissance style.

Environs: The former church of Thaon (1 km.): This is a masterpiece of 11&12C rustic architecture. In Romanesque style it merges perfectly with its peaceful surroundings. The side aisles were removed in the 18C.

Fontenay (abbey)
21 Côte-d'Or   p.415☐L 7

Nowadays the site of the old abbey on the edge of a beech-grove and in a valley with a large stream running through it is green and pleasant. But when the Cistercians led by St.Bernard arrived here it was like the end of the world. In 1118 they founded a daughter abbey of Clairvaux and Cîteaux here. It was very prosperous until the 15C, but then declined. During the Revolution it was sold off and turned into a paper mill. In 1906, the land was bought by an art-lover from Lyons, who got rid of the industrial buildings and began a painstaking restoration of the historic monuments. The gatehouse is flanked by the hostel in which the Cistercians accommodated pilgrims and visitors. The lovely 13C bakery has a cylindrical chimney; the dovecote is 17C. The *abbey church* was begun in 1139 and consecrated in 1147. It is joined on to the abbey buildings and is very bare, for St.Bernard rejected luxury and the grandeur of Cluny. The building's beauty lies in the pure outlines of the broken arches and the overall perfection of its bareness. Inside there are stained-glass windows without lustre—as they were originally. A smiling statue of *Notre-Dame-de-Fontenay* is probably late 13C. The huge dormitory dates from the 14C and was given an impressive chestnut timber roof in the 15C. The austere Romanesque cloister leads to an elegant chapterhouse with vaults which spring from clustered columns. The scriptorium, the calefactory, the prison where local petty criminals were kept and a forge (the monks used the poor quality local iron ore) all survive from the old abbey.

Fontainebleau, château, Galerie François I

Fontenay-le-Comte (16,770 inhab.)
85 Vendée p.418☐E/F 9

Fontenay is on the river Vendée between the 'damp marshes' and the forest of Vouvant. It is the capital of Bas-Poitou and a market town which was at its height during the Renaissance—'Fontaine et source de beaux esprits' (fountain and source of bright spirits) is inscribed on the fountain which gave it its name. Rabelais came here in 1520 to learn Greek from the Franciscans.

Notre-Dame: Notre-Dame-de-Fontenay has a spire very like the one at Luçon Cathedral. It is essentially Flamboyant (15C, with major restoration in the 16C). The Flamboyant main portal, set back beneath its enormous pointed arch, has a glazed tympanum. The lower part is divided by a central post on which there is a finely carved 19C Madonna. The archivolts bear the wise and foolish virgins. Inside, the *Chapelle de la Vierge*, with its pendent keystones and small columns, is one of the most beautiful products of the Renaissance in Vendée. The church's decoration is es-

Château de Fontainebleau 1 Entrance **2** Cour du Cheval Blanc **3** Louis XV wing **4** François I wing **5** horseshoe staircase **6** Galerie François I **7** Queen Mothers' wing **8** wing of the Belle Cheminée (chimney-piece) **9** Cour de la Fontaine **10** Porte Dorée **11** Cour Ovale **12** Salle de Bal **13** Cour des Offices **14** Cour des Princes **15** Jardin de Diane **16** Jardin Anglais **17** parterre **18** Bassin du Tibre **19** park, canal **20** Treille du Roi **21** Grands Appartements de Napoléon I **22** Salle du Conseil **23** Salle du Trône **24** Marie-Antoinette's apartments **25** Salle des Tapisseries f2)26 Chinese museum **27** Jeu de Paume (tennis court) **28** Chapelle de la Trinité **29** Étang des Carpes

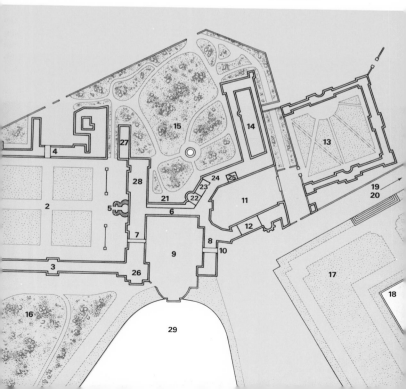

sentially 18C; around the throne there is an allegorical group representing Religion crushing Heresy.

Fontaine des Quatre-Tias (tuyaux): This dates from 1542. The master builder incorporated coats-of-arms with the salamander emblem, a gift from François I. The town's motto also appears here and a list of its principal magistrates.

Old houses: Around the Cathedral and along the quiet streets there are old houses. In the Rue du Pont-aux-Chèvres stand the hôtel of the Bishops of Maillezais (16&17C), a Renaissance house with turrets (15C), and the *Hôtel de Villeneuve-Escaplon*, which has a fine Louis XIII doorway decorated with the figure of Laocoön, with Hercules and Diana on either side. The Place Belliard has the house of General Belliard (Napoleon's saviour at Arcole), opposite which there are five houses with triangular pediments, which were built under Henri IV (two have arcades and are similar to ones in La Rochelle).

Château de Terre-Neuve: The double façade of this charming Renaissance house appears at the end of a long avenue of chestnut trees. It was built for the poet Nicolas Rapin at the end of the 16C and embellished and altered in subsequent centuries. There are statues of the nine Muses decorating the façades and a porch which came from the Château de Coulonges, as well as inscriptions of lines written by Rapin. One of the chimney-pieces is remarkably decorated with a griffin supporting the canopy. There are also ornate coffered ceilings, fine 16C panelling and Louis XV and Louis XVI furniture.

Fontevraud	(1,870 inhab.)
49 Maine-et-Loire	p.419☐G 8

Fontevraud (spelt Fontevrault for many years) is at the meeting point of Anjou, Touraine and Poitou. The little village in its wooded setting seems a somewhat humble companion for the great royal abbey

Fontenay, the abbey

with its extensive Romanesque remains, which was almost a town in itself (it was unfortunately used as a prison from 1804 to the early 1960s). Quite a few buildings had to be cleared away to accommodate this, but the main ones have survived and have since been restored. This powerful and extraordinary abbey was founded at the beginning of the 12C by the theologian and preacher Robert d'Arbrissel on land belonging at that time to the diocese of Poitiers. Building began in 1101 using donations from the Counts of Anjou and other noblemen. The community of Fontevrault was unusual in that men and women were not segregated and were ruled over by an Abbess (the monks acted as chaplains and were responsible for the daily running of the abbey). The vast monastery was largely rebuilt in the 16&17C. It was much favoured by the Plantagenets and also owed a great deal to the 'queen of abbesses', Marie-Madeleine Gabrielle de Rochechouart de Mortemar, the sister of Madame de Montespan.

Notre-Dame-de-Fontevraud: This light, majestic abbey church has great purity of line and was built in two distinct phases: in the 12C—the choir, ambulatory, transept and bell tower over the crossing were built and could have been consecrated in 1119 by Pope Callistus II; the nave (there are no aisles) with its four domes and reminiscent of that of Angoulême Cathedral, was added in 1110–28. The church has some magnificent capitals, some of which have quite incomprehensible motifs. Notre-Dame contains the tombs of many Plantaganet princes and princesses (the Angevin family which ruled England). There are funerary statues of Henry II and Eleanor of Aquitaine, their son Richard the Lionheart and their daughter Isabel of Angoulême. *Cloister:* The huge cloister was rebuilt in the 16C as was the lovely chapterhouse. The S. walk varies between Flamboyant and Renaissance in style; the other walks date from a time when the style was changing from Renaissance to classicism. *Kitchens:* The unusual and extensive kitchens dating from the early 12C look very strange from the outside, partly because of the rather outlandish restoration.

Fontenay-le-Comte, château de Terre-Neuve

The building is octagonal with semicircular projections; in the upper part it changes in plan as a result of a clever system of arches. There is a high central chimney and also numerous lesser fireplaces. Legend has it that this odd building had been the den of a robber, but it has never really done anything more sinister than supply the monastery refectory.

Saint-Michel: The parish church, it is surrounded by a wooden gallery with strong stone pillars. It has a 13C nave with Angevin vaulting, a fine 17C high altar and several works of art which belonged to the abbey.

Fontgombault	(310 inhab.)
36 Indre	p.419□H 9

This little village is set in a lovely spot on the right bank of the river Creuse. It is noted for its Romanesque abbey, which was founded in the 11C and which has

been occupied once again by Benedictines since 1945. *Abbey church:* This church was ruined by the English, the Protestants and the Revolutionaries in turn, and was then restored at the end of the 19C. There is a richly carved doorway in the façade. The eight-bayed nave ends in a large and well-proportioned apse, the choir is flanked by double side aisles and the ambulatory has five radiating chapels. In the nave there is a Romanesque recumbent figure of Pierre de l'Étoile, the founder of the abbey.

Forcalquier	(3,450 inhab.)
04 Alpes-de-Haute-Prov.	p.425□N 13

Forcalquier has been an important regional centre since the high Middle Ages. It was ravaged in the 14C by bands of marauders and by Huguenots in the 16C. The old city, spread out like an amphitheatre on the side of a crag, with the ruined citadel and a late-19C chapel on the summit, commands a marvellous view. An old convent in the Place du Bourguet now houses the

Fontevraud, aerial view of the abbey

Town Hall and an interesting *Musée Archéologique et d'Histoire Locale*. The former cathedral of *Notre-Dame* was begun at the end of the 12C and consecrated in 1372. The side aisles were added in the 17C and the fine Provençal nave is Romanesque; Gothic choir. The 13&14C Franciscan convent has been very well restored and refurnished. There is an unusual cemetery to one side with cleverly clipped yews and topiary.

Environs: Mane (3.5 km.): This large village surrounded by small hills and 'pointed huts' is dominated by a hill on which a medieval fortress stood. There is a 16C church, old houses, fountains and a 17C convent. Nearby is the old priory of **Notre-Dame-de-Salagon** with its beautiful Romanesque church and the **Château de Sauvan**, an elegant 18C building which is well furnished.

Fougères	(27,650 inhab.)
35 Ille-et-Vilaine	p.413□E 5

Fougères, on the W. edge of Brittany, is one of the best preserved fortified towns. Its situation is exceptional—in an enclosed ravine on a loop of the river Nançon; it was once encircled by marshes and bracken. The town's sloping streets contain several historic houses where Chateaubriand, Alfred de Musset, Gustave Flaubert, Victor Hugo (*Quatre-Vingt-Treize*) and Balzac (*Les Chouans*) stayed and drew inspiration.

Château: Looking at the Château from the Place aux Arbres it appears as a series of fortified walls flanked by 13 towers. It was built in the 11–15C. The entrance is to the E. under the square 13C Tour de La Haye-Saint-Hilaire, which is set into an outer wall known as the Avancée. The large inner courtyard, which is today an open-

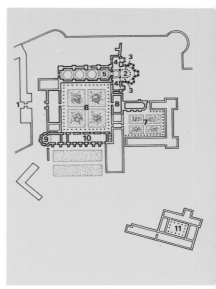

The abbey of Fontevraud 1 Entrance **2** choir **3** ambulatory **4** transept **5** funerary statues of Henry II and Eleanor **6** great cloister **7** cloister of Saint-Benoît **8** chapterhouse **9** kitchen **10** refectory **11** Chapelle Saint-Lazaire

Fontevraud, the kitchen roof

air theatre, held the main part of the building. On the highest part of the site there is a citadel which included the keep (demolished in the 12C). It is defended by two towers, the Tour Mélusine (14C) and the *Tour du Gobelin* (12&14C), which are linked by a wall. The Surienne and Raoul towers, built in the 15C to strengthen the S. side, are horseshoe-shaped. Some of the town's fortifications remain, including the Porte Notre-Dame, which is linked to the château by a wall and framed by two immense 14&16C towers. Under the machicolations, there is a statue of the Madonna in a niche with a broken arch.

Saint-Sulpice (15 – 18C); This church with its elegant slate bell tower stands next to the château. A short nave with panelled vaulting leads to the choir with its 18C woodwork and paintings of the Assumption and the Sacrifice of Abraham from the same period. The chapels in the side aisles contain fine stone Flamboyant altarpieces. The date of the 'miraculous' *Notre-Dame-des-Marais*, a statue of the Virgin suckling the infant Christ, is unknown.

Forcalquier, church of Notre-Dame

Saint-Léonard: Built in the upper town in the 15&16C on the site of an old Romanesque church. It was completely transformed in the last century and its present façade dates from that time. Only the base of the bell tower remains from the original building. The most interesting parts are the richly decorated Flamboyant side façades. The exterior of the N. side aisle has a pretty gallery with balustrades and some extraordinary gargoyles. Inside, the baptistery chapel still has fragments of its 16C stained glass. There are some 19C paintings by Eugène and Achille Devéria.

Belfry: These secular replicas of bell towers are very common in the N. of France. In Brittany the only examples are in Fougères and Dinan. This tall 14C tower is built of bonded granite. It is square at the base and octagonal at the top. It has a rather fine balustrade with Flamboyant decoration and gargoyles.

Forêt de Fougères: This famous Chouan haunt is full of megalithic monuments, including the dolmen *de la Pierre-Courcoulée*, the dolmen *de la Pierre-du-Trésor* and the alignment *du Cordon-des-Druides*. The *Celliers de Landéan*, a vast underground 12C chamber, were probably used as a hideout by noblemen from Fougères.

Fougères-sur-Bièvre   (600 inhab.)
41 Loir-et-Cher   p.414☐H 7

The château is a powerful, rather rough medieval castle which was rebuilt in about 1470 by one of Louis XI's Treasurers. Flanked by cylindrical towers, it has a pretty courtyard and the keep from an earlier fortress. The windows were opened up in the 16C. Inside it has no furniture but there are enormous chimney-pieces and a fine keel roof. The village church is partly Romanesque.

Fréjus (30,800 inhab.)
83 Var p.426□O 14

Julius Caesar founded the *Forum Julii* (Caesar's market) 50 years before Christ, and it became a stage on the Aurelian Way. The Emperor Augustus built a naval base here, but it began to decline in the 2C and the port gradually silted up. The Saracens partly destroyed the town in the 10C; it was made into a bishop's seat and then began to prosper again in the 14C under Henri II's patronage. The port was unusable by the time of the Revolution and was demolished and levelled.

Roman city: It is obvious from the visible ruins that this was an important port in Roman times, with its immense arena —the first amphitheatre of its kind built in Gaul—capable of seating 10,000 people. It had to be heavily restored, but part of the old vaulted galleries are almost intact. Some of the outstanding remains include a gate from the vanished ramparts,

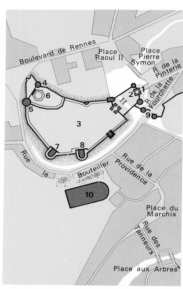

The Château of Fougères 1 Entrance **2** Tour La Haye-Saint-Hilaire **3** walled area **4** Tour du Gobelin **5** Tour Mélusine **6** keep **7** Tour Surienne **8** Tour Raoul **9** Porte Notre-Dame **10** church of Saint-Sulpice

Fougères, the château and ramparts

Fréjus, cathedral, the baptistery

Fréjus, cathedral, door leaf

the ruins of a theatre and an aqueduct, an archway from the public baths known as the Porte d'Orée and traces of fullers' workshops (the Roman arsenal's laundry). Augustus' Light, slightly apart from the rest, has nothing to do with the Emperor; it was built on a ruined tower in the Middle Ages to act as a beacon at the entrance to the port.

The Episcopal City: This is fortified and clustered around the cathedral, the cloister, the bapistery and the bishop's palace, which are all laid out around the Place Formigé, the heart of the historic town. The *cathedral* was built at the end of the 10C. It has been much altered and shows elements of local early Gothic — note the vaults, bell tower and 13C porch, the 16C outer door, the 15C choir stalls and a fine altarpiece of 1450 by Jacques Durandi

above the sacristy door. The 11C left aisle could have been the nave of an earlier fortified church. The 12&13C cloister originally had two complete storeys. In the 14C the original vaults of the galleries were hidden by a fine painted wooden ceiling with unusual motifs. The adjoining rooms house the *Musée de l'Archéologie*, where you can see Gallo-Roman antiquities found in local excavations. The baptistery at the side is one of the oldest of its kind in France (end of the 4C or beginning of the 5C); The former bishop's palace now houses the Town Hall and is only partly medieval.

Environs: Saint Raphaël (2 km.): A former resort for the Romans of Fréjus, it is now a seaside resort. It has a 12C Romanesque church and the *Musée d'Archéologie Sous-Marine* with a remarkable collection of amphorae.

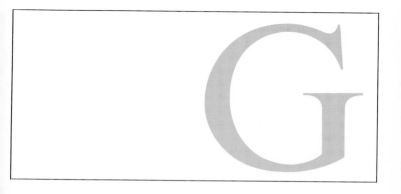

Ganagobie
04 Alpes-de-Haute-Prov.   p.425☐N 13

The monastery here is built right on the edge of a plateau and has a breathtaking view over the Durance valley. It was a Cluniac house until the Revolution, when it was destroyed. Today it has been restored and is occupied by Benedictines. The 12C church of Notre-Dame is Provençal Romanesque in style and has a spectacular decorated portal with the figure of Christ surrounded by the symbols of the four Evangelists and angels. The lintel has the Apostles. In the apse and some of the apsidal chapels there are fine 12C mosaics which are of oriental inspiration. The cloister, with its Cistercian-like severity, has been much altered and resembles the one at Montmajour; it was restored in the 12C along with the refectory. There are traces of the chapterhouse and of a calefactory which was turned into a kiln. Opposite the priory there is a dry stone hut.

Gannat
03 Allier   (6,600 inhab.)
    p.420☐J 10

Gannat straddles the border between the Langue d'Oc and the Langue d'Oil (regions of N. France). Parts of the old fortifications and the château, with its four corner towers remain. The château now houses a museum with numerous parchments and valuable Gospel books. The church of *Sainte-Croix* was rebuilt in Gothic style (nave) and then altered at various times up until the 17C (apse, ambulatory, bell tower). It also has some interesting Romanesque elements (N. part of the apse). Some curious capitals on the outside of the apse depict the Nativity. The 11&12C church of *Saint-Étienne* has a barrel-vaulted porch and a 15C bell tower. Inside there are 17C carved wooden altars.

Gap
05 Hautes-Alpes   (28,950 inhab.)
    p.425☐N 12

This half Alpine, half Provençal town is on the *Route Napoléon*. Historically it belongs to Dauphiné, but there is a definite feeling of the Midi about it. The neo-Gothic cathedral dates from the last century. The *Musée Départemental* stands on the edge of a fine park and displays a wide range of collections (in particular of Moustier pottery). It also contains the mausoleum of Lesdiguières, a High Constable and fearless Protestant leader who became a Catholic shortly before his death in 1626.

Gerberoy   (110 inhab.)
60 Oise   p.410☐I 3

This former strongpoint stands on a hill between the Ile-de-France and Normandy. It is a lovely place, full of flowers, spotlessly clean and possessing a former collegiate church, which was rebuilt in the 15C. There are a number of half-timbered houses in the sloping, cobbled streets and the village is still surrounded by moats. Unfortunately, only one tower remains from the old château.

Gien   (15,250 inhab.)
45 Loiret   p.415☐J 7

This flower-bedecked town in the Loire valley is at the start of the *Route Jacques-*

Château of La Bussière

Coeur—a route lined with châteaux and manor-houses leading to Bourges. The town was badly damaged in June 1940 when the Germans arrived. But it has been skilfully rebuilt in brick, pale stone and slate. There is a large château with a sombre but attractive modern church facing it; the concrete fabric is covered with thousands of local bricks. It is dedicated to Joan of Arc, who passed through Gien in 1429, and it is lit by contemporary stained glass by Max Ingrand. It also contains a Stations of the Cross made in the large local pottery works. There is a splendid view over the town from the restored stone bridge (16C).

Château and Musée International de la Chasse: The château was badly damaged in 1940 but has been beautifully restored. It was built at the end of the 15C by Anne de Beaujeu, a daughter of Louis XI. An elegant building with patterned brickwork, it houses a remarkable *Musée International de la Chasse* which is full of works of art, as well as weaponry from all periods and trophies. Everything is connected with hunting—the impressive 37-calibre duck-gun, the animal sculptures, ceramics, paintings by François Desportes and Jean-Baptiste Oudry, engravings, collections of hunting buttons. The strange room exhibiting some 500 trophies contains a veritable forest of horns and antlers. Indeed this unusual museum, opened in 1952, is as interesting for its presentation as for the items themselves.

Environs: Château de la Bussière (12 km. NE): This elegant château is reflected in a large lake dug in Louis XIV's time, and it is the first stop on the *Route Jacques-Coeur*. In front of the fine house, largely rebuilt after the Wars of Religion, there is a Louis XIII tithe barn and extensive outbuildings in a park designed by Le Nôtre. In the house there is a marvellous *Musée International de la Pêche* devoted to the art and technique of fishing. The château is well furnished and has portraits, prints and lithographs. Most of the contents are connected with water (beautiful Iranian glazed pottery, Chinese dishes decorated with carp, fish made out of silver, outstanding 16&17C engravings). Note in particular the remarkable 16C brick kitchens, with a huge 19C charcoal range, where you can see fish kettles, dishes and cake moulds shaped like fishes.

Gimont (2,870 inhab.)
32 Gers p.423□G 14

This former bastide is on the main road from Toulouse to Auch—the road in fact runs beneath the immense 16C market buildings. The *Musée Cantonal*, standing next to the market, contains fossils and prehistoric, Gallo-Roman and medieval exhibits. The church of *Notre-Dame*, S. Gothic in style, dates from the 15&16C but has been much altered. In one chapel there is a small 16C triptych.

On the other bank of the river Gimone, at the foot of Gimont, **Cahuzac** has a 16C church which was a place of pilgrimage dedicated to the Virgin.

Gisors (8,260 inhab.)
27 Eure p.410□I 4

Gisors, devastated in the last war, has been very successfully and tastefully rebuilt. It is dominated by the impressive ruins of a strong fortress. Situated on the edge of the old Duchy of Normandy and the capital of Vexin, the town has always been of great strategic importance. The château, on higher ground with a commanding view of the town, is built around a keep, which stands on a mound. There are lawns planted with flowers where the old royal residence used to be, but the 12C wall, with round and triangular towers, is still standing. The other keep, the *Tour du Prisonnier*, was built by Philippe Auguste and guards the main entrance. It derives its name from the unusual bas-reliefs in a

Gien, museum of hunting, trophy room

dark room, which was formerly a cell; the figures of saints, religious scenes and many other themes were probably carved by a couple of bored prisoners.

Saint-Gervais et Saint-Protais: This splendid church, tragically damaged in June 1940, was almost beyond repair. However, after a long process of careful and devoted work it has been restored. It was begun in the 13C but most of the building dates from the late 15C up to the late 16C and it combines Gothic with Renaissance. The large 16C façade has two towers, one incomplete. True to Renaissance tradition, the main portal and the smaller one on the right are decorated with interesting sculptures. The N. tower has a plain lower section and a highly ornate upper part—from a distance it looks like late Gothic, but closer inspection reveals some medallions in which the influence of the Renaissance is apparent. The highly ornate portal on the N. side dates from the 1520s. The 16C nave with its pillars minus capitals is in contrast to the choir, which dates from the first phase of construction. In the S. aisle there are some remarkable carved pillars; the chapels have numerous works of art.

Gordes	(1,570 inhab.
84 Vaucluse	p.425□M 1

Gordes was half-ruined by the Germans in 1944 and the population left. It owes its revival to Vasarely, the pioneer of kinetic and op art, who fell in love with the area, as did André Lhote and Chagall before him.

Château, Fondation Vasarely: The château was built in the 16C on the site of an earlier fortress. It is a sober and elegant building, one of the few intact examples of the Renaissance in the area. Vasarely restored it in order to house a museum in which he could exhibit his work (from the 'graphic period' to the 'universal structures'). The old village clinging to the side of the Vaucluse plateau has some 16C houses and its huge classical church contains some 17C altarpieces.

Gisors, the keep

Gordes, overall view

Environs: Musée du Vitrail (Moulin des Bouillons, 3 km.): The museum has a fine collection of old documents concerning the techniques and history of stained-glass window making. **Abbaye de Sénanque** (4 km. W.): This austerely beautiful abbey, built on Cistercian lines, merges perfectly with the surrounding countryside. It was founded in 1147–8 and its name is a distortion of *sana aqua*. The church, which does not face E. because the valley is too narrow, was built from 1160 on; the nave with its broken barrel vaulting was added in 1180. The cloister in the centre of the monastery was built in several stages—hence the variety of the capitals. The chapterhouse, which once had a wooden ceiling, was not vaulted until the 15C. Only one of the two fireplaces remain in the monks' room; they used to sit beside them to copy their manuscripts. In 1544 the abbey was pillaged and burnt by the Valois. It declined until the Revolution, when it was dissolved; it was not occupied again until 1854. In the 19C the refectory was used as a chapel—you can see the family-tree of the daughter-houses of Cîteaux, and

Gordes, abbey of Sénanque

various sculptures. There is a permanent exhibition on the Sahara in the old farm building, which also houses the ticket office and bookshop.

Gourdon	(5,110 inhab.)
46 Lot	p.423□H 12

This little hilltop town with its large fawn-coloured church has boulevards running around it where once there were ramparts —the 'Tour de Ville'. Gourdon remained loyal to France in the Hundred Years War and was defended by a fortress with very ancient origins; it was burnt by the English, rebuilt and then demolished in the 17C. It occupied the hilltop where there is now a terrace and commanded a wide all-round view of the Bouriane countryside. The Rue de Majou is very medieval in appearance and has 14,15&16C houses on either side. It leads to the Hôtel de Ville, rebuilt in the 17C, and the church of *Saint-Pierre*. This church was built at the beginning of the 14C and then altered; its lovely façade with tall towers faces an attractive arcaded square. The *Chapelle Notre-Dame,* near the 14C *Porte de Majou,* used to back on to the ramparts. Just outside the town is the *Chapelle Notre-Dame-des-Neiges,* which is essentially 16C but has an older apse. Inside this little church is a 'miraculous' fountain and a late-17C altarpiece.

The Grottes de Cougnac, 2 km. from Gourdon, are noted for their prehistoric cave paintings (ibex, elephants, human figures), stalactites and natural 'columns'.

Gournay-en-Bray	(6,610 inhab.)
76 Seine-Maritime	p.410□I 3

This little town S. of Bray was very badly damaged in World War 2. A commercial town, it is the centre of the Petit Suisse industry—the white cheese invented in the 19C. It is of no great interest, except for one building, the former collegiate church of *Saint-Hildebert* which, though much altered, dates from the 12&13C and retains various features, including several Romanesque capitals.

Environs: Saint-Germer-de-Fly (7 km. SW): A little village with a huge church which belonged to a former abbey. Although altered in part, the vast, plain nave is early Gothic and gives the impression of having the *Sainte-Chapelle,* built during St.Louis's reign, in tow. Airy and with perfect lines, it has a fine rose-window and fifteen other large windows (only part of the 13C glass remains).

Grand	(590 inhab.)
88 Vosges	p.416□M 5

This little village on the border of Champagne contains one of the most important

Gourdon, church of St-Pierre

archaeological sites in France. As well as the church and the chapel of *Sainte-Libaire* (15C), Grand has many reminders of the fact that it was built on the site of an extensive Gallo-Roman town, with public baths, a drainage system, basilica, temple and theatre (where first Grannus, the Gauls' god of war, and then Apollo were honoured). Excavations began in the 19C and have been stepped up in recent years. They have revealed a splendid 3C Roman mosaic which is the largest ever found in France, and also the spectacular ruins of one of the largest amphitheatres in the Roman world.

Grande-Chartreuse	
38 Isère	p.421□N 11

The focal point of this mountain stronghold with its forests and pasture is the large monastery established here in 1084 by Saint Bruno, the founder of the Carthusian order. It was destroyed by an avalanche in the 12C and has been burnt down and successively rebuilt maany times. It was abandoned during the Revolution and again from the beginning of this century until 1941. The Carthusians are a closed, contemplative order, shutting themselves off completely from the outside world. Visitors are only allowed into the *Musée de la Correrie,* which is in the refurbished 16&17C buildings where the lay brothers, who were responsible to the 'père courrier' (hence 'correrie'), lived. As you pass from room to room in the museum the history, daily life and liturgy of the Carthusians is clearly explained and illustrated (photographs, a large model of the charterhouse, and a reconstruction of a hermitage). The 12C church has works by Le Sueur and his studio depicting Saint Bruno, and a late-14C triptych. Outside the museum, the *Chapelle Saint-Sauveur* is an exact copy of the *Chapelle de la Grande-Chartreuse.*

Grande-Pressigny (Le)   (1,260 inhab.)
37 Indre-et-Loire   p.419☐G/H 8

This village in an attractive setting in the Claise valley is overlooked by the impressive ruins of its château, consisting of a powerful rectangular keep (12C), an octagonal tower (16C) and a Renaissance main wing with a remarkable *Musée Préhistorique*. This extremely well-presented and labelled collection of palaeolithic tools is among the best in the world.

Environs: Descartes (11 km. NW): This little town could well be the birthplace of the famous philosopher. It is not known for a fact that René Descartes was born here but he was certainly baptized in the church of *Saint-Georges*, (a fine Romanesque building dating from the 11&12C) in 1596. His grandmother's house is now a small museum.

Granville   (15,170 inhab.)
50 Manche   p.413☐E 4/5

This old haven of privateers is built on a rocky promontory; the upper town is surrounded by ramparts—the Grande Porte to the town still has a drawbridge. The interesting history of the town, its privateers and its fishermen is retold in the *Musée du Vieux Granville*, which also contains furniture, pottery, copper, pewter, headdresses and costumes. The church of *Notre-Dame*, a rather squat building, dates from the 15,17&18C; the central tower was built in 1593. It is built in a lovely red granite from the nearby Îles Chausey and contains an old and much venerated statue of Notre-Dame. The great couturier, Christian Dior, was born in Granville in 1905, hence the Christian Dior garden on the edge of the lower town.

Grasse   (35,330 inhab.)
06 Alpes-Maritimes   p.426☐O 14

Grasse has been the 'perfume capital' since the 13C. It is rather a sleepy place at the start of the *Route Napoléon* and its network of little streets with passages and flights of steps lead to the *Place aux Aires*, which has 18C houses, arcades and fountain. The Place aux Herbes contains the market and the Place du Petit-Puy is dominated by a square 12C tower and the former cathedral.

Notre-Dame: This former cathedral was built at the end of the 12C and altered in the 17&18C. In the building you can see the beginning of Provençal Gothic and also Lombard influence. Inside there is one of the rare religious paintings by Jean-Honoré Fragonard, *Christ Washing the Disciples' Feet*, which hangs above the sacristy door. There are also a fine 15C triptych on wood attributed to Bréa, a 17C *Mystic Marriage of St. Catherine* and three paintings by Rubens (1601).

Grande-Chartreuse, the abbey

The Musée d'Art et d'Histoire de Provence: (More commonly known as the *Musée Fragonard*.) Housed in the old *Hôtel Cabris*, which was built in the 18C by Mirabeau's sister. You will find works by Fragonard (1732–1806; born locally), valuable documents on local history, and objets d'art from Basse-Provence. There is an archaeological room and an extensive library, as well as collections of ceramics, ironwork and furniture.

Grenoble	(169,750 inhab.)
38 Isère	p.421 □N 11

Grenoble is spread out on the plain at the confluence of the fast-flowing Drac and the Isère. It is overlooked by the last spur of the Grande-Chartreuse massif, by the powerful limestone bastion of Vercors and by the peaks of the Belledonne range. It is a university town and industrial centre which has grown rapidly in recent years and with its neighbouring communes it forms a large urban concentration. It was

Grasse, church of Notre-Dame

also the birthplace of Henri Beyle, better known as Stendhal (1783). There is a historic centre and an old quarter, Saint-Laurent, which are in strong contrast to the ultra-modern buildings in the town: the Hôtel de Ville, designed by Maurice Novarina, containing various contemporary works, the boldly conceived *Stade de Glace* by the architects Junillon and Demartini, the speed skating ring, with one of Vasarely's works, the huge *Maison de la Culture* built in 1967–8 to plans by André Wogenscki, the Olympic Village, the *Cité Nouvelle de la Villeneuve*, the Conference Centre, and the University complex. Grenoble is descended from the Roman *Gratianopolis* and has been capital of the Dauphiné since the 12C. Recently it has been one of the fastest growing of French towns and it took advantage of hosting the 1968 Winter Olympics by adopting a concerted policy of development. However, this forward-looking modernity is not just a recent phenomenon for in 1838 Stendhal wrote, 'It is as though all the houses in Grenoble have been rebuilt in the last twenty years...the mayor works a twelve-hour day'.

The Place Grenette is a lively pedestrian precinct and forms the centre of Grenoble. It takes its name from the old grain market. The Grand-Rue, lined with old houses, is also closed to traffic. The philosopher Condillac was born here in 1715, as was the politician Casimir Perier (1777) and the painter Ernest Hebert (1817); No. 20 was Stendhal's grandfather's house—the courtyards with loggias are 17C. Henri Beyle's birthplace is in the Rue Jean-Jacques-Rousseau.

Saint-André: This stands on a paved square with a bronze statue of Bayard (19C). It dates from the 13C but was enlarged in the 15C. It was once a dependency of the Dauphin's Palace and contains Bayard's mausoleum, for this famous 'fearless knight beyond reproach' was born near Grenoble in 1475.

Palais de Justice: One side of this building is in white stone and the other in bluish-grey. It is the former Dauphinois Parliament building and dates from the 15&16C; it was enlarged in the last century. There is some beautiful carved woodwork by the 16C German artist Paul Jude inside; the ceiling of the courtroom was carved in 1668 by a local carpenter from drawings by Antoine Le Pautre.

The Town Gardens: These are dominated by a trellised vine beloved of Stendhal, which shades the terrace behind his grandfather's house. There are also the remains of a Roman wall.

The Cathedral of Notre-Dame: This 12&13C building has been spoilt over the years and is wedged in between houses. It has an uninteresting modern façade. Inside there is a 15C ciborium. The fountain of the Trois Ordres is a memorial to the events of 7 June 1788 when Grenoble rose in revolt on the famous *Journée des Tuiles* (Day of Tiles), which can be seen as the start of the Revolution.

'Saint-Laurent, the Bastille (fortress): This old quarter lies along the right bank of the Isère on the site of an Gallic township. Picturesque and much restored, it has a concentration of old houses.

The Church of Saint-Laurent: A Romanesque church, rebuilt in the 16&17C. The crypt, a Merovingian chapel, was built using Gallo-Roman materials. Beyond this building there is a gate built by Vauban in the 17C and also some 19C military buildings, which have since been converted into houses.

The convent of Sainte-Marie d'En-Haut was founded in 1619 by St.Francis of Sales and St.Jane Frances de Chantal; it now houses the *Musée Dauphinois* (see below under principal museums). You can reach the old fort of the Bastille from the left bank by means of a funicular railway, the téléphérique. The front faces Grenoble and

Grenoble, Palais de Justice

Grenoble, crypt of the church of Saint-Laurent

the mountains and its 'casemates' house a *Musée des Voitures Anciennes* featuring some splendid vintage cars.

Principal Museums: The important *Musée des Beaux-Arts* was established in the *Place de Verdun* in 1870. It contains paintings, sculptures and drawings, including *Christ Healing an Invalid* by Veronese, *View of Venice* by Canaletto, *The Doge Crossing St.Mark's Square* by Guardi, *Intérieur Blanc* by Bonnard, *Portrait of Paul Poiret* by Derain. It also contains many late-19C, modern and contemporary works by Monet, Sisley, Renoir, Signac, Vlaminck, Matisse (a particularly fine collection), Mirò, Ernst, Tanguy, Mathieu and Raysse. *The Musée Dauphinois:* The restored convent of *Saint-Marie d'En-Haut*. It is a pleasant modern museum devoted to all aspects of the Dauphinois cultural heritage. The *Musée Stendhal* is in the *Hôtel Lesdiguières* (19C) and features documents on the childhood and youth of the writer. The *Musée Hébert* is in the Tronche in the painter's house, and is devoted to his work.

Gros Bois (château)
94 Val-de-Marne   p.429☐J 5

This elegant Louis XIII style château belongs to the Société d'Encouragement à l'Élevage du Cheval Français (the Society for the Promotion of Horse Breeding). It has undergone major restoration. Built at the end of the 16C and successfully altered at the beginning of the 17C by Charles de Valois, it has belonged to various people, including Barras under the Directoire and Marshal Berthier, Prince of Wagram. Berthier was a great soldier under the Empire, although he turned against Napoleon on his return from Elba. He lavishly furnished and decorated Gros Bois and filled it with portraits, sculptures, books, maps and battle plans; he left only the dining room with its original Louis XIII decor. The château is like a museum of the Empire and contains, amongst other items, Jacob furniture and paintings by Gros.

Environs: Brie-Comte-Robert (8 km. SE): This important Brie market has very little of its feudal château left. The church of *Saint-Étienne* is 13C but has been altered, and has an original rose-window in the apse.

Guebwiller	(11,360 inhab.)
68 Haut-Rhin	p.417☐O 6

This old Alsatian town in the Vosges is at the mouth of a valley which has long rejoiced in the pretty name of Florival. It is an attractive, straggling industrial and wine-growing town with several surviving old houses; the Town Hall is in a lovely 16C mansion. The warm tones of the 12&13C church of *Saint-Léger* are due to the red sandstone so commonly used in Alsace. Although it has been much altered, the façade is very fine indeed with two towers and stone spires, an elongated open-sided porch and gable covered with diamond-shaped motifs. The church of the *Couvent des Dominicains,* founded in the 13C, is used for artistic performances—music festivals are held in the nave and the *Musée du Florival* is in the choir. The red sandstone church of *Notre-Dame* is 18C and dominates the lower town.

Environs: Murbach (4.5 km. NE): In a pleasant wooded valley there is a group of houses clustered around the tall stump of a church. In spite of its mutilation, this abbey church — or rather the transept and apse, which are all that remain—is one of the most beautiful Romanesque monuments in Alsace. It once served the old Benedictine community which founded the town of Guebwiller. The 12C sanctuary was sacked by the Duke of Weimar's army in the 17C and then more or less abandoned well before the Revolution. The tall silhouette of the truncated abbey church against the greenery is immensely striking by virtue of its size and bulk. It is dominated by two strong towers and there are some carvings on the upper portions of the façade (imaginary people, lively little scenes). There are two mausoleums inside. **Lautenbach** (6 km. NE): The former collegiate church in the middle of this quiet village dates from the end of the 11C and the 12C. It is also built of sandstone and possesses a remarkable Romanesque porch (there is a curious scene on the impost of the doorway, thought to represent adultery).

Guérande	(8,000 inhab.)
44 Loire-Atlantique	p.413☐D 7

A very well-preserved medieval fortified town overlooking the salt marshes (the 'pays blancs', white country), which once brought it great prosperity. The ramparts have ten towers and four massive postern-gates, the largest being the *Porte Saint-Michel* (15C), framed by two huge machicolated keeps. These house the *Musée du Vieux Guérande* devoted to regional art and tradition.

The 12–15C church of **Saint-Aubin** in the town centre has a Flamboyant double portal. There are a few surviving Romanesque pillars in the nave with variously carved circular capitals; three of these depict the horrors of Hell. Transept and choir are 13C; the latter have some fine stained-glass windows illustrating the life of the saint.

Guérande, church of St-Aubin

Temps Perdu, Basin and Oriane de Guermantes, have no connection at all with the early-17C château here, which was later altered and endowed with a park by Le Nôtre. Proust did not know Guermantes at all at the time when he described the Duke and Duchess's 'salon'; he simply liked the name. The château, which was decorated by Robert de Cotte and Mansart, was badly restored in the 19C, but preserves its luxurious interior decoration. It was Robert de Cotte who designed the decoration of the charmingly named gallery 'la belle inutile'.

Environs: Ferrières-en-Brie (3.5 km. S.): This château with its vast park was completely rebuilt in the 19C by Baron Rothschild. During the siege of 1870 Bismarck met the French negotiators here. The church is 13C. **Jossigny** (6.5 km. E.): This Louis XV château set in a park was built in the mid 18C and combines classical and rococo styles; its roofs are like Chinese pagodas.

Guéret	(16,150 inhab.)
23 Creuse	p.419□I 9

This former capital of La Marche stands on a plateau to the N. of Limoges. The 15&16C *Hôtel des Moneyroux* is an elegant Renaissance building with two wings and a pretty corner staircase turret. The *Musée Municipal*, in an 18C hôtel, contains Aubusson tapestries, Gallo-Roman remains, local exhibits and, in the extraordinary silver room, a superb collection of Limoges enamel, ceramics and faience.

Guermantes	(240 inhab.)
77 Seine-et-Marne	p.429□J 5

The characters from *A la Recherche du*

Guillestre	(1,580 inhab.)
05 Hautes-Alpes	p.426□O 12

This is a tourist stop on the *Route des Alpes* on the edge of the Queyras. Its slate roofs are huddled at the foot of the *Tête du Cugulet*. The early-16C church has a porch with pink columns supported by crouching deer, like the one at Embrun.

Environs: Mont-Dauphin (4 km. NW): This deserted village, a late-17C Vauban citadel, is enclosed by bleak fortifications.

Guimiliau	(700 inhab.)
29 Finistère	p.412□B 5

This peaceful market town near the Arrée

Guillestre, church porch

Lampaul-Guimiliau, church of N.-D.

hills possesses a Breton 'parish close'. These enclosures have statues and are a common expression of Christian art in Basse-Bretagne, varying little from village to village. They are built around a cemetery and have a triumphal gateway which symbolizes the soul's passage to eternity. The old ossuary was first attached to the church and then made into a separate building which was used to store exhumed bodies, thus obviating the need for a churchyard; it later became the funerary chapel. The marvellous granite Calvary has its origins in Christian standing stones and the crude, sometimes ugly wayside crosses, but they were refined and improved over the centuries.

The Guimiliau Calvary (1581): This has an octagonal base flanked by four buttresses and displays an extraordinary wealth of Old and New Testament characters — 180 in all. The frieze consists of scenes from the life of Christ with deliberately anachronistic clothes and the figures of the Evangelists at the four corners. The carving on the platform represents the Passion, the Resurrection taking up the main side. A single cross dominates the whole, the thieves' crosses having disappeared. There is an altar with Doric columns crowned by a statue of the founder of the Léon diocese, St. Pol.

The façade of the funerary chapel (1648) is decorated with Ionic columns and small semicircular bays with a pulpit.

Saint-Miliau: This is 16&17C and has a doorway on the S. side with arches bearing statuettes. Over the triangular pediment there is a statue of the saint to whom

Guimiliau, detail of calvary (16C)

the church is dedicated. In the porch are statues of the Apostles and one of Christ framed by two caryatids and a holy-water stoup with a finely carved dais. There are some fine furnishings in the church. In the right aisle the font has a carved oak canopy (1675) with a dome and two lantern lights supported by twisted columns. The 17C organ-gallery and throne are both equally ornate.

Environs: Lampaul-Guimiliau (3.5 km. W.): The 'parish close' here is another of the monuments on the edge of the Élorn valley from Saint-Thégonnec to Daoulas. It has a sober 17C Calvary with a crucifix flanked by the thieves. Its semicircular monumental gate (1669) supports a balustrade with three crosses on it. The ossuary (1667) contains an altar of the Trinity and statues of St.Roch and St.Sebastian. In the

church of *Notre-Dame*, with a projecting 16C bell tower, a 16C rood-beam divides the nave from the 17C square-ended apse. There is a figure of Christ with the Virgin and St.John and beneath this are polychrome scenes of the Passion on the nave side, and the Annunciation on the choir side. As well as a baptistery with a canopy and a 17C organ-chest, there are six fine altarpieces from the same period. There are also a startlingly realistic Descent from the Cross (1530), with six figures carved from a single piece of oak, and a painted stone Entombment (1676).

Guingamp	(10,750 inhab.)
22 Côtes-du-Nord	p.412☐C 5

Guingamp stands on the Trieux. Its ramparts and château have been demolished but its old quarter, with its winding streets, has kept all its charm. In the main square, lined with lovely old houses, there is a Renaissance fountain with three stone and lead basins on top of one another; these are decorated with an attractive variety of animals with the Virgin — known as 'La Plomée'—in the centre.

The Basilica of Notre-Dame-du-Bon-Secours: As a result of rebuilding, this church is Gothic on the N. side and Renaissance on the S. It was built in the 14&15C on the site of an old chapel—the large Romanesque arches of the crossing survive. It is dominated by a 13C central bell tower with a recently restored spire. The W. portal has finely carved archivolts and is one of the first examples of Renaissance architecture in Brittany. The statue Notre-Dame-du-Bon-Secours is on show in a chapel in the N. porch: she is a Black Virgin who is venerated on the occasion of an annual candle-lit procession on the eve of the first Sunday in July.

Guingamp, N.-D.-du-Bon-Secours

Environs: Abbaye de Sainte-Croix (1.5 km. S.): Only the capitals of the transept and the choir remain of this 12C church. The *Manoir Priorial* (16C) faces these ruins with its hexagonal turret and second, smaller, projecting turret. **Chapelle Notre-Dame** (2 km. W.): This pretty Gothic chapel built in 1507–21 is in the centre of the village of **Grâces**. The beams running lengthwise are carved with satirical (scenes of drunkenness) and fantastic motifs.

The Chapelle d'Avaugour (10 km. SE): 16C, it has some interesting carved wooden

furniture and some statues of the Apostles.

The Chapelle Notre-Dame-du-Tertre (14 km. E.): This chapel dominates the village of Châteaulaudren and is chiefly remarkable for its interior decoration. Apart from the 15C alabaster Virgin and the fine 16C altarpiece on the high altar, there are 96 paintings, all 15C, on a red and gold background on the panelling of the choir. These are in the style of medieval miniatures and illustrate scenes from the Old and New Testaments. In an adjoining chapel there are some other panels depicting the lives of St.Margaret and St.Fiacre.

Haguenau

(26,870 inhab.)
67 Bas-Rhin   p.417☐P 4

Haguenau, one of the first medieval cities
in Alsace, was founded close to a castle by
Frederick Barbarossa's father. Nowadays
the overall impression is of a forward-
looking city surrounded by forest, but its
churches, old houses and museums are
reminders of its past. The church of *Saint-
Georges* was built in the 12&13C; subsequently altered, it was damaged in 1945
and finally restored. It combines Romanesque and Gothic (the transept, tower over
the crossing, polygonal apses and side
chapels are 12–16C). It contains the two
oldest bells in Alsace. The church of *Saint-
Nicolas* was founded at the end of the 12C
but dates in the main from the 13C. It contains some outstanding 18C panelling
which came from the old abbey at
Neubourg.

Musée Historique: The collections cover
prehistory, Roman civilization and the history of the Imperial town; the wide variety
of exhibits includes articles from local digs,
ecclesiastical silver, locally printed books
from 1489 onwards, coins, etc.

Musée Alsacien: In the former Chancery
(15C). It is a pleasant little museum with
some tastefully presented exhibits on popular art and tradition, furniture, old trades,
devotional items ('canivets', painted images
delicately cut out), costumes and head-
dresses, pewter, pottery and popular
pictures.

Hambye

(1,320 inhab)
50 Manche   p.413☐E 4

Abbaye d'Hambye: These proud ruins
in a green valley form a most romantic
scene. The abbey was founded by a small
number of monks in the 12C; it declined
in the 17C and was sold and broken up in
the Revolution. The splendid 12&13C abbey church is in ruins but astonishingly tall
none the less. There are guided visits
which include the various abbey buildings,
among them the 12C locutory and a
Gothic chapterhouse.

Harcourt

(930 inhab.)
27 Eure   p.410☐H 4

Château: The name Harcourt is that of
a great French family and derives from a

certain Harulf (court comes from the Latin *curtis*—domain). It was ruined in the Revolution, but it has now been restored as a result of a major programme of work. It was built at the end of the 14C on the site of several earlier fortresses; the E. side was altered in about 1700. The medieval curtain wall, still with its towers, only half surrounds it now. Louis Gervais Delamare, the forestry pioneer, established a superb forested park around the château after the Revolution. Several trees which were planted in the last century have grown to an enormous size. The French Academy of Agriculture now owns the fine building and lands.

Hautecombe (abbey)
73 Savoie   p.421 □N 10

This important religious monument is reflected in the steely grey waters of the Lac du Bourget about which Lamartine wrote. It was founded in the 12C by monks who had adopted the Cluniac reforms, and was

Haguenau, church of St-Georges

Harcourt, the château

Hautecombe, the abbey

re-occupied from about 1922 by the Solesmes Benedictines. It was heavily restored in the 18&19C. After the Revolution the abbey was turned into a pottery, but then Charles Félix, the King of Sardinia, bought it. In 1860 it was the subject of a special protocol in the treaty ceding Savoy to France.

ABBEY CHURCH: Its appearance was greatly altered by 19C restoration. The decoration is extravagant and, indeed, there is nothing Cistercian about it except the basic plan. St.Bernard, who founded Cîteaux, would undoubtedly have disapproved of this profuse decoration of stucco and marble which was prevalent at the time—the 'Gothic troubadour' fashion. An outstanding Carrara marble group of *Queen Marie-Christine Protecting the Arts and the Poor* dates from the 19C. The *Pietà* in the right transept is also remarkable; there is a delicate 16C *Annunciation* on a predella in the transept. The adjoining, altered cloister is mainly 15C. The restrained *Grange Batelière* near the small harbour of the abbey still survives from the 12C; it defended the monks' boats and was also used as a warehouse.

Hautefort	(1,140 inhab.)
24 Dordogne	p.419□H 11

This spectacular château, surrounded by an immaculate park and gardens, broods over the peaceful town. It has undergone major reconstruction since its destruction in 1968 (there was a fire caused by a cigarette stub tossed into some sawdust). The Périgord romantic novelist Eugène Le Roy

Haut-Koenigsbourg, the château

was born here in 1836 (he wrote 'Jacqou le Croquant' and was the son of the steward and the sewing maid at the château). The château dates mainly from the 17C but still retains older elements; the foundations of the two round towers and the vaults (10&11C), the 16C gatehouse and the parapet walk. The fine dome, made of chestnut timber added in the late 16C or early 17C to the tower of the W. wing so that it matched that of the E., was untouched by the fire. The latter tower contains the chapel with the altar used in Charles X's Coronation at Reims.

Hauterives   (1,080 inhab.)
26 Drôme   p.421 □ M 11

Hauterives is situated in a quiet valley and

has a bizarre 'palace' which enraptured the Surrealists and was made a listed building by André Malraux. Ferdinand Cheval (1836–1934), a country postman, spent 30 years realizing his dream; tirelessly collecting unusual pebbles on his rounds to incorporate in this extraordinary creation of cement, crenellations and pinnacle turrets.

Haut-Koenigsbourg (château)
67 Bas-Rhin   p.417 □ 06

This colossal, stunning fortress looming out of the trees cost the Germans millions of marks—they wanted to make it a symbol of their occupation of Alsace. Its rebuilding, ordered by William II, was rather a travesty—'too medieval to be true' with its towers and thick walls, but the château still impresses by its vast size. Lower down are the ruins of the *Château de Kintzheim*.

Havre (Le)   (216,650 inhab.)
76 Seine-Maritime   p.410☐G 3

This industrial town is an important port for ocean-going ships, the second largest in France after Marseilles. Its industrial areas have also expanded inland for quite a distance. François I ordered Admiral Guillaume de Bonnivet to build a port here in 1517, in a 'safe and convenient place'. Richelieu ordered its enlargement and Colbert commisssioned Vauban to alter it. It was the birthplace of the writer Bernardin de Saint-Pierre (1737), the poet and playwright Casimir Delavigne (1793), the composer Arthur Honegger (1892), the painters Othon Friesz (1879) and Raoul Dufy (1877) and President René Coty (1882). The painter Eugène Boudin had a stationery and picture-framing shop here and it was he who discovered a very young adopted citizen of Le Havre, Claude Monet.

The visitor to Le Havre has to use his imaginaton to picture what the town was like before the war, with little bistros and old and dilapidated houses. The bombing completely flattened the town and when the architect Auguste Perret rebuilt most of it he did so in a modern but not exactly appealing style. Taking the 16C grid pattern as a base, he rebuilt on a grander scale; he thought big and, remembering the requirements of traffic flow, he made a rather soul-less town. He was concerned with balance and rhythm in modern buildings, but there is not much warmth in them. However, he did give the town its superb church, *Saint-Joseph*. From the outside, this square concrete building with its seemingly endless octagonal bell-tower (340 ft. high) is only relatively attractive. Inside it is very original, impressive and rather moving, mostly because of its height and the changing effects of the light through its stained-glass windows. The vaulting of *Saint-Joseph* is some 260 ft. high and the church is undoubtedly a great success in terms of contemporary religious art. Auguste Perret was also responsible for the huge Place de l'Hôtel de Ville with its straight perspectives. The *Hôtel de Ville*, some 350 ft. long, is dominated by a 17-storey concrete tower. Behind it is a rather unexpected bell tower belonging to an interesting modern church by Henri Colbosc (1964). In the 18C the Rue de Paris was an attractive thoroughfare; today it is a major road, completely rebuilt after the war. The huge *Palais de la Bourse* is a modern building of grey granite which contains the Salle des Pas Perdus decorated by Untersteller.

Musée des Beaux-Arts: A monument erected by the outer harbour in 1964 marks the square in front of the museum, which is built of glass, aluminium and steel. The museum is functional, plain and very well-lit, and was opened in 1961 by André Malraux. It has a very extensive collection, from the 16C to the present day. The greater part of it is devoted to the Impressionists and pre-Impressionists—the drawings, paintings and gouaches by Eugène Boudin are almost a museum within a museum (works from 1853–93). There are also a number of Fauvist paintings, works by Dufy, and other well-chosen contemporary works.

Musée de l'Ancien Havre: Completely different, this museum is housed in a 17C timber-framed house which escaped damage in the last war. It deals with the long and glorious past of the town and the surrounding region. There are models of boats, watercolours, engravings and china. Of particular interest is a letter from François I ordering the building of Le Havre.

The church of *Saint-François* is a relic of what was once a picturesque quarter, and dates from the 16&17C. The Gothic and Renaissance cathedral of *Notre-Dame* (late 16/early 17C) was partly destroyed and then restored. Nearby is the former *Palais de Justice* (18C), which was rebuilt exactly as it had been and houses the *Musée d'Histoire Naturelle*. The old *Abbaye de Graville*, outside the town centre, is early 12C but very much altered. The abbey church is a sizeable Romanesque building which suffered in the war. It has a Romanesque tower over the crossing and a damaged façade. Inside there are some historiated capitals. The *Musée du Prieuré* traces the history of the religious community and displays fragments of masonry, statues and also many models of old houses.

Sainte-Adresse is situated close to Le Havre and almost merges into it. In the last century many painters stayed here—Jongkind, Monet, Bazille, Dufy and Marquet.

Environs: Harfleur (6 km. E.): A large sea and river port until it silted up in the 16C. The spire of its lovely Flamboyant church, *Saint-Martin* (15&16C), is visible from afar. The Town Hall occupies a 17C stone and brick château. **Montivilliers** (13 km. NE): This town is clustered around a monastery which is now part of the suburbs of Le Havre. It is dominated by the two towers of the old abbey church (second half of the 11C and beginning of the 12C). It is dedicated to Notre-Dame and was enlarged in the 15C with the addition of a Gothic church on its left side.

Herbault   (980 inhab.)
41 Loir-et-Cher   p.414☐H 7

This Renaissance manor nestling in the small valley of the Bonne Heure is sur-

rounded by a magnificent forest. Altered in the 19C, it has been well restored by the present owners and stands at the end of an avenue of plane trees. Built of brick and tufa, it is roofed with slates. The outbuildings are 17C.

Hesdin   (3,340 inhab.)
62 Pas-de-Calais   p.410☐I 2

Hesdin, on the river Canche, has a 16C Gothic church with a Renaissance portal and 18C furnishings. The Hôtel-de-Ville faces the Place d'Armes, and has a late-16C, highly ornamented 'folly'.

Honfleur   (9,050 inhab.)
14 Calvados   p.410☐G 4

This town was a favourite with the Impressionists, who loved the ever-changing Normandy sky. Eugène Boudin was born here in 1824 and the town figures in countless

Le Havre, church of St-Joseph

paintings from Richard Bonington's time (early 19C) up until the Twenties. Honfleur is very different from the large, sprawling conglomeration of Le Havre, from which it is separated by the broad Seine estuary, and it has preserved its historic charm — the Vieux Bassin, its wooden church, historic houses, and sloping streets. In fact, it has hardly changed since Alphonse Allais (born in Honfleur in 1855) as a child met Baudelaire here.

Vieux Bassin: This is the essence of Honfleur; where it was once painted, it is now photographed. It was built by the sailor Abraham Duquesne and is full of tall houses with bluish grey slates. It also has the *Lieutenance*, a turretted building which was once the King's Lieutenant's residence (it incorporates a gate from the old fortifications). The church of *Saint-Étienne* is a modest Gothic building from the 14&15C, which houses the *Musée du Vieux Honfleur*. The museum also occupies some wooden houses and an old manor, and it features some good works of popular art, faience and reconstructions of Normandy work-

shops and interiors. Nearby two 17C salt warehouses solidly built in timber, house temporary exhibitions. The church of *Saint-Léonard* was rebuilt in the 17C and has a Louis XV style octagonal bell tower.

Sainte-Catherine: An unusual wooden church, built in the 15C with two parallel naves (the two choirs were altered in the 19C). The vaulting is like the hull of a ship. At the back of the church there is an 18C organ with a 16C balustrade. The choir on the right has an 18C altar and the one on the left a *Christ on the Mount of Olives* attributed to Jordaens (1654). The strange, detached bell tower, also in wood, was painted by Monet and is covered with weatherboarding. The neighbouring streets have preserved their old-world charm.

Musée Eugène-Boudin: This most interesting museum has overflowed from an old convent into modern premises. It was created on the initiative of Alexandre Dubourg, the Honfleur painter. It has several old works, but more especially a

Honfleur, interior of the church of Ste-Catherine

rich collection of watercolours and other pictures by artists who painted Honfleur, the surrounding countryside and the estuary in the last century and the beginning of this one (the first painters who fell in love with Honfleur stayed at the *Ferme Saint-Siméon* which was a country inn, now replaced by a luxury hotel). Eugène Boudin, who came from the Saint-Léonard district, is the main artist, and this museum, together with the one in Le Havre, provide a complete picture of him. Jongkind, Isabey, Daubigny, Monet and many other lesser known artists who worked in and around Honfleur are also featured.

Côte de Grâce: This green hill has a wonderful view. In June 1940 Othon Friesz painted the fire blazing in the petrol refineries at Le Havre from here. The chapel of *Notre-Dame-de-Grâce*, the object of a pilgrimage at Whitsuntide, is 17C.

Houdan	(2,870 inhab.)
78 Yvelines	p.414□I 5

Now full of second homes, Houdan was formerly an active farming centre, with many poultry farms in the neighbourhood. Standing on a cross-roads, it was a strong point, as you can see from the enormous 12C keep, which is now a water-tower, and the three 16C towers. The 15&16C church is Flamboyant (façade, nave) and Renaissance (apse). Inside, the vaulting is adorned with large pendent keystones.

Hyères	(39,600 inhab.)
83 Var	p.425□N 15

Hyères is a resort with endless beaches, a

Houdan, 12C keep

marina and fine gardens—'a town of palmgroves'. It is also interesting historically. The church of *Saint-Louis* is a simple 13C building where Louis IX prayed when he returned from his first Crusade in 1254. The church of *Saint-Paul* was built in the 16C and includes some remains of an earlier Romanesque church, as well as numerous painted votive offerings. Adjoining it is a pretty Renaissance house.

Environs: Chapelle Notre-Dame-de-Consolation (3 km.): This has a magnificent view over the Giens peninsula and the Hyères islands (Porquerolles, Port Cros and Le Levant). Modern, it contains a very old statue of the Virgin, which is venerated (in particular on the 15 and 16 August).

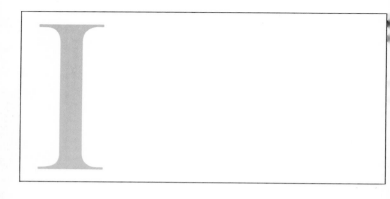

Ile-Bouchard (L')
37 Indre-et-Loire   (1,730 inhab.)
p.419☐G 8

Once a cargo port on the Vienne, this town is surrounded by orchards. It takes its name from the founder of a fortress (destroyed long ago) on an island nearby. The Romanesque parts of the church of *Saint-Gilles* go back to the late 11/early 12C. The ruins of the priory of *Saint-Léonard* are on a hillock on the left bank of the Vienne. Only the apse and ambulatory with apsidioles remain of the 11C priory church. However, the carving on the foliated capitals—showing scenes from the life of Christ — are remarkable.

Environs: Tavant (3 km. W.): The church of *Saint-Nicolas*, probably early 12C, is interesting both architecturally and for its carving, but its main claim to fame are the paintings in the crypt and the choir above it. The figure of Christ with the symbols of the Evangelists and angels are painted in the half-dome; while in the vault there are paintings of the angels appearing to the shepherds, the Annunciation and the Nativity. The crypt with its heavy cylindrical pillars was once poorly lit by a small window, but it was none the less decorated with strange and expressive frescos—a rich and sometimes incomprehensible iconography. The figures of Christ, the Virgin, St.Peter, Adam and Eve, and the serpents representing lust are easy enough to recognize, but there are other characters whose significance is unclear. Perhaps one is David piercing a lion with his sword? And who are the figures carrying a beam? These passionate frescos obviously show an early Christian or even antique influence but they remain, in part, an enigma.

Issoire
63 Puy-de-Dôme   (15,700 inhab.)
p.420☐J/K 11

This old town near the Cévennes, with its narrow streets, has the second largest Romanesque church in the Auvergne (after that at Brioude). *Saint-Austremoine* (12C) is in the heart of the town in a huge square where the breadth of its splendid apse can be admired. It is a perfect example of Auvergnat style. Harmoniously arranged in three tiers, it is enhanced by a polychrome pattern of stones. On the outside of the apsidioles there is an unusual set of signs of the Zodiac. Although covered with gaudy distemper in the 19C the interior retains its majesty. The capitals in the choir, which take the Passion as their

ssoire, capital in the church

Issoudun, Chapelle St-Roch

ubject, are the most remarkable of the historiated capitals. The crypt follows the orm of the apse and is the largest and most beautiful in Auvergne.

ssoudun	(16,550 inhab.)
6 Indre	p.419☐I 8

Because of its position in the centre of Berry, Issoudun was involved in the bitter struggle between Philippe Auguste and Richard the Lionheart. The *Tour Blanche*, a 12C keep built by Richard the Lionheart,

and a 12&16C belfry—an old gateway into the town—are all that is left of the old fortress. The church of *Saint-Cyr* dates from the 15&16C and has a sizeable nave without a transept and some outstanding 16C stained glass in the square-ended apse. The 12&16C Hôtel-Dieu, now housing the *Musée de l'Hospice Saint-Roch*, is composed of buildings of various dates grouped around a huge courtyard. In the chapel there are elements of the original decoration, in particular two magnificent Trees of Jesse. The museum has a very fine collection of Nevers faience (in the pharmacy).

JK

Joigny　　　　　　　(11,930 inhab.)
89 Yonne　　　　　　　　p.415☐K 6

This sleepy old town rises on the bank of the meandering river Yonne and has some picturesque parts. The region is part of Champagne but seems to have more in common with Burgundy geologically and historically. It is a gastronomic centre thanks to the restaurant of La Côte Saint-

Joigny, church of St-Jean

Jacques. The name Joigny comes from *Jauniacus* or *Joviniacum* but, despite these Latin names, the Romans were not particularly interested in the site and the town grew up later around a monastery and a fortress. The townspeople are officially called 'Joviniens' but often refer to themselves as 'maillotins', recalling the mallets which the 15C rebels carried when they laid siege to the château and killed the count. In 1530 the town was almost completely burnt down but luckily a few fine houses escaped.

Saint-André: This 'double' church is rather disconcerting; it was enlarged and altered in the 16C and preserves the mutilated nave of an old monastery chapel. It has two 15C windows and a polychrome Notre-Dame of the same date, a 13C tomb and a 15C Pietà. There is a fragment of an English ladder on one wall which is a reminder of the siege in 1429.

Saint-Jean: A 16C church which towers above the rooftops. The main body of the church, unfortunately separated from the apse by a wall, has fine coffer-vaulting, the work of a local artist at the end of the 16C. The right aisle contains a 16C Entombment and a tomb with a recumbent figure of a countess who died in 1187. The buildng of a new château after the great fire was never finished; near the church a single pavilion survives from this abandoned project. The 11C or 12C *Porte Saint-Jean* is a remnant of the old fortress; opposite it there is an imposing 16C wooden house.

Saint-Thibault: Built 1490–1529, at the end of the Gothic period, it was severely damaged in the fire and partly rebuilt; the square tower is 18C. It is a mixture of Flamboyant and Renaissance with the merest touch of classical. The choir is strangely out of line with the nave. The church contains several works of art, among them a really charming, smiling 14C Virgin. The Place du Pilori in front of the church has an unusual 16C house which has been restored to its original form. The medieval town wall has disappeared and only the *Porte du Bois* (13C) survives.

Environs: Saint-Cydroine (4 km. E.): This elegant and simple former priory church with its octagonal tower is on the presumed site of the martyrdom of St. Cydroine or Cydoine, who was beheaded in the 3C. The attractive Canal de Bourgogne which was dug in 1775–1834 starts near here. It is 150 miles long and links the Seine with the Rhône). **Saint-Aubin-sur-Yonne** (4 km. NW): This 12C church has been altered and thereby has lost much of its character.

Josselin	(3,000 inhab.)
56 Morbihan	p.413 □ D 6

This little town on the side of a hill overlooking the quiet river Oust is grouped around the important château which has been owned by the Rohan family since the 15C. The feudal external appearance of the château—with its tall towers and peppperpot turrets linked by machicolated walls

— has been preserved despite its many restorations. The residence, in the main courtyard, was built in the 15C and is a masterpiece of Flamboyant architecture, having ogee arches, colonettes, crockets and finials in abundance; the roof has ten magnificent double-storey dormer windows with pointed gables and crocket pinnacles. The base of the roof is masked by a delicate traceried balustrade.

Basilica of Notre-Dame-du-Roncier: This church is Flamboyant apart from a few remains of the 12C sanctuary. It is dedicated to Notre-Dame-du-Roncier, a black wooden statue of the Virgin which was found among brambles in the 9C. (There is only a mounted fragment of this left). The W. portal has double doors with a pretty 15C Virgin under a canopy on the pier. The wrought-iron throne in the nave is an 18C work by a local blacksmith. The Chapelle Sainte-Marguerite contains a majestic black marble mausoleum which is damaged but bears recumbent figures of the High Constable Olivier de Clisson, count of Josselin, and his wife.

Josselin, the château

Jouarre, the abbey

Jumièges, ruins of the abbey

Environs: Guéhenno (10 km. SW): This little town has the only large Calvary in Morbihan. Erected in 1550, it was destroyed during the Revoluton and restored in the 19C. It consists of a double, projecting entablature with bas-reliefs, which are framed by statues of the four prophets, added when it was being restored. On the platform there are scenes of the Passion, and the central cross has statues of the Virgin and St. John on one arm. Below, the figure coiled around the shaft is Jesse; the thieves have bent arms and legs. The nearby modern column with the symbols of the Passion is crowned by a cock which symbolizes Peter's denial of Christ. The ossuary takes the form of Christ's tomb and consists of three rooms. There are two guards at the entrance and two holy women are about to enter; an angel waiting for Jesus to appear carries a rather laconic Latin inscription announcing the forthcoming Resurrection. The scene is completed by a figure of the risen Christ. It shows how the craftsmen of the time wanted to convince the faithful of the reality of eternal life which would prolong the short earthly existence.

Jouarre   (2,670 inhab.)
77 Seine-et-Marne   p.411 ☐ J 4/5

This ancient market town by the peaceful *Ferté sous Jouarre* (fortress) lies on the edge of a plateau and dominates the Morin region. The abbey has survived and Benedictines still occupy it, although one of the buildings dating from the 18C is now the town hall. A squat 12C tower with

Jumièges, aerial view of the village and the abbey

Renaissance vaults, once the belfry of a Romanesque church, houses the small *Musée des Religieuses*, which has temporary exhibitions. Behind the parish church is a nondescript building housing the *Musée Briard* which stands above a 7C crypt— really two half-buried chapels: *Saint-Paul/Saint-Ébrégisile* and *Saint-Adon*. Here the capitals of Gallo-Roman columns have been used and inside there are some interesting sarcophagi. The *parish church* was built in the 15C but major alterations have marred the 16C nave. There are old and new stained-glass windows, some remarkable reliquaries (the oldest two are 12C) and a stone statue of Notre-Dame-de-Jouarre. The church of La Ferté-sous-Jouarre has been altered but still has its 14C tower. The town hall of this little town is also worth a visit—it is in a rather strange 'Modern Style'.

Jumièges (abbey)
76 Seine-Maritime   p.410□H 3/4

These ruins are exceptionally striking; collapsed vaults, truncated towers, gaping bays reflect the greatness of Romanesque art in Normandy. The former abbey church of *Notre-Dame* is a glorious ghost from the past, rising out of the greenery and perfectly at one with the landscape. Built in the mid 11C, a large part of it has crumbled, but its style and purity are still impressive. (Its tragic state is not the result of time, but unfortunately of man; it was broken up after it was sold off as national property in the Revolution). A few buildings of various dates have survived from the great abbey founded in the 7C by Saint Philibert e.g. the church of *Saint-Pierre*, also ruined (pre-Romanesque parts, the

Kaysersberg, the church

rest 13&15C), the chapterhouse minus its vaults, the Romanesque-Gothic 'Grand Cellier' and the abbey residence dating from the 17C, which now houses a Musée Lapidaire (stone sculpture and inscriptions). The church of *Saint Valentin* on a hillock has a Romanesque nave and Renaissance choir.

Jumilhac-le-Grand   (1,540 inhab.)
24 Dordogne   p.419 □ H 11

This village on the borders of Limousin and Périgord-Vert is overlooked by an astonishing château dating mainly from the 14C and altered during the Renaissance and the 17&18C. It is large, romantic and feudal, irregular in plan and covered with tall and intricate roofing, peppered with slate turrets and finials along the ridges. It was originally owned by the Templars, it then passed from hand to hand. Legend says that a frivolous châtelaine was shut up here on three occasions by her husband and she consoled herself by spinning and decorating the room in which she was imprisoned. The Romanesque former chapel has been much altered; its fine octagonal bell tower over the crossing can be seen close to the fortress.

Kaysersberg   (2,960 inhab.)
68 Haut-Rhin   p.417 □ O 6

This town was a stronghold of the SS resisting the French and American troops. It guards the entrance to the Weiss valley and luckily escaped the destruction of December 1944. Overlooked by a ruined château, its substantial old houses straggle out along either side of a very long main street. Doctor Albert Schweitzer (1875–1965) was born here and Kaysersberg has dedicated a little museum to the doctor, missionary and musician who won the Nobel Peace Prize in 1952. The *church* goes back to the 12C but major work in the 15C greatly altered its original structure. However, there are Romanesque capitals, a carved portal, an important 15C Crucifixion, a very fine 16C retable by a Colmar artist and a Holy Sepulchre of the same date. The town has retained its 15&16C fortified bridge and its Town Hall is now in a charming Renaissance house. Another museum boasts a 14C 'Vierge Ouvrante' (the Virgin is depicted on two leaves with angels painted on the reverse); it also has many pieces of religious and popular art.

Labastide-D'Armagnac
40 Landes   (810 inhab.)
         p.422☐F 13

A former English royal bastide (late-13C) it is grouped around a typical square with a variety of arcades. It is said that King Henry IV got the idea for this from the Place des Vosges in Paris. The Gothic church with its strong 15C tower contains a 16C Pietà and a gilded altar in the 18C fashion with a trompe-l'oeil retable behind it. The small *Chapelle du Géou* is dedicated to *Notre-Dame-des-Cyclistes* and many Tour de France competitors visit it each year. It is built on the foundations of a Roman temple.

Labrède
33 Gironde   (1,770 inhab.)
         p.422☐F 12

Château: This medieval fortress on the edge of the extensive Landes forest and the Graves wine-growing area is reflected in the wide moat by which it is surrounded. Originally Gothic it has been altered, but retains its 13C keep. It was owned by Montesquieu, the author of *L'Esprit des Lois*, who was baptized in the nearby parish church in 1689. He spent his childhood here and always liked coming back, dividing his time between writing, tending his vines and working as a member of the Bordeaux Parliament. Visitors to the château can see his study, bedroom, and his large, vaulted library (most of Montesquieu's manuscripts were sold before the last war, but there are a few valuable documents among the thousands of books collected by him and his descendants).

Lagny-sur-Marne
77 Seine-et-Marne   (16,900 inhab.)
         p.411☐J 5

Formerly a strongpoint and the site of a major fair, Lagny is nowadays linked to the new town of Marne-la-Vallée. It spreads out along the banks of the Marne and rises in tiers up the side of the hill. *Notre-Dame-des-Ardents-et-Saint-Pierre* is a former abbey church begun in the 13C on the site of much earlier sanctuaries. It has a modern façade and bell tower which are uninteresting. Inside, the single, superb choir is practically all there is, as the work was stopped due to lack of funds. Joan of Arc is supposed to have brought a child back to life in the chapel behind the altar. The name Notre-Dame-des-Ardents comes from the 'mal des ardents', a painful illness,

Lamballe, collegiate church of Notre-Dame, S. portal

probably caused by using poor-quality flour contaminated with ergot. The Place de la Fontaine has a very pretty 12C basin (with 16C bronzes) and some old houses. The secularized church of Saint-Furcy has a Flamboyant façade.

Lagrasse (610 inhab.)
11 Aude p.424☐J 15

Lagrasse grew up around a Carolingian abbey in a basin of the Orbieu valley with bare hills all around. Various buildings of different periods have survived from this religious community. These are dominated by a 16C keep or bell tower; the large cloister dates from the 18C and the small cloister from the 11&13C, although it has been rather outlandishly altered. The village has

a 14C church and a few old houses and was linked to the abbey by a medieval hump-backed bridge.

Lamballe (5,550 inhab.)
22 Côtes-du-Nord p.413☐D 5

This little town is the old capital of the counts of Penthièvre and is renowned for its fairs and its stud-farm. Standing on a spur is the impressive *collegiate church of Notre-Dame* from the 12–15C, which was once the chapel of a château razed to the ground by order of Richelieu. This church has a N. portal framed by twenty columns with fine capitals. Inside there is a pretty carved wooden rood screen (15C), which closes off the S. part of the choir. The church of *Saint-Martin* was the church of an 11C priory. It has a 17C spire and a little wooden roof on its side porch (16C). There are a few Romanesque elements in the nave. The 15C church of *Saint-Jean* is crowned by a tall octagonal tower and contains an interesting 18C bas-relief in white marble.

Environs:Château de la Hunaudaye (14 km. E.): This château is surrounded by a vast forested area. It is 14C and although it was ruined in 1793, it is obvious that it was once important. The ivy-covered ramparts are flanked by moats and towers, and here and there a semicircular bay, a tall chimney, a fragment of staircase and a row of machicolations give it a rather strange appearance.

Landerneau, the church

| **Landerneau** | (15,660 inhab.) |
| 29 Finistère | p.412☐B 5 |

This little estuarine harbour on the borders of Cornouaille and Léon owes its fame to the ancient and strange custom of tin-kettle music: when a widow gets married here such raucous public celebration follows that the phrase 'It will make a noise in Landerneau' has become proverbial. The town lies on both sides of the Élorn with the picturesque *Pont de Rohan* linking the two halves. There are two churches. On the right bank is *Saint-Houardon* with its domed tower and fine Renaissance porch of 1604. On the left is *Saint-Thomas de Cantorbéry* which has a fine bell tower with three balconies one above the other, and inside beams decorated with charming rustic scenes.

Environs: Pencran (3 km. SE): This little commune has a very interesting 16C parish close. A monumental gateway with three lantern lights and a staircase leads to it. The Calvary erected in 1521 has the three traditional crosses with figures. On

the central one, Roman soldiers, St.John and a holy woman are depicted on the arms; at the intersection of the shaft there is a moving Pietà above a kneeling, weeping Magdalene. The ossuary (1594) is not far away and has an ornate façade with arcades and niches, which are now empty. The church of *Notre-Dame* (16&17C) is flanked by a magnificent S. porch whose tympanum has a Nativity. At the sides are statues of the Apostles crowned by finely tooled canopies. Inside, the beams are carved and there is a Descent from the Cross painted on wood, which dates from 1517. **La Roche-Maurice** (5 km. NE): The former village cemetery dominates the Élorn valley and is especially remarkable for its ossuary built in 1639. There is a fine row of semicircular arches on columns and pilasters with carved panels on the stylobate depicting the various classes in society. Above the holy-water stoup, Death (Ankou) armed with an arrow cynically observes: 'I kill you all'. In the 16C church the choir is shut off by an elegant rood screen and has the original stained-glass window. **La Martyre** (10 km. E.): This parish close is dedicated to the martyrdom of Salomon (Salaün), a King of Brittany who was murdered in 874, and also to Notre-Dame. It is a very fine enclosure which is reached through a triumphal gateway with a small 16C Calvary on top. The ossuary was built in 1619 and has a semi-naked female caryatid; 'Death, Judgement, Hell...when man thinks of these he should tremble' is written in Breton on a phylactery. There are some 15C sculptures in the church's porch, and on the tympanum a rather mutilated Nativity shows the Virgin lying down suckling the Infant Christ while Joseph watches over. The somewhat composite interior has 16C panelling and stained glass. **Ploudiry** (11 km. E.): Because of the parochial rivalry between the towns in this region there is a proliferaton of parish closes. This one is less well known than the others and includes a fine

ossuary decorated with medallions, which show a Dance of Death. The church was built in 1665 and it contains Renaissance choir stalls, two 17C altarpieces and a holy-water stoup of the same period. The stained-glass window in the apse depicts the Crucifixion.

Langeais	(3,900 inhab.)
37 Indre-et-Loire	p.414 □ G 7

This historic town where Rabelais may have stayed is dominated by one of the finest châteaux in the Loire Valley. It was built in the 1460s and from the outside looks like a strong and severe medieval fortress. Inside, it is sober but very elegant and full of signs of the coming Renaissance. It was built by order of Louis XI; Charles VII married the very young Anne of Brittany here. It is admirably furnished and full of valuable Flemish and Aubusson tapestries. It now belongs to the Institut de France, and its present appearance is entirely due to the good taste of its

Langeais, the château, courtyard façade

previous owner, Jacques Siegfried. He restored the rooms to their 15C appearance and called in the best craftsmen to make what was lacking. In the Guard Room there is a monumental chimney-piece carved with a depiction of the chateau's parapet walk.

The parish church of *Saint-Jean-Baptiste* has preserved Romanesque sections, although it was very much disfigured in the last century. The old and dilapidated church of *Saint-Laurent*, the site of several digs, seems to be 11C.

Environs: Cinq-Mars-la-Pile (5 km. E.): Two large towers, a moat and a fine stone bridge survive from the château of the Marquis de Cinq-Mars. He was beheaded at the age of 22 for having plotted against Richelieu. The village is partly troglodytic and retains a church with Romanesque origins (late 11C, with an early-12C apse).

Langres	(12,280 inhab.)
52 Haute-Marne	p.416 □ M 6

This was once a strongpoint and the seat of an ancient diocese. Today it is the seat of the *Sous-Préfecture* of the Haute-Marne and the descendant of the antique *Andematunum* (only a disfigured Gallo-Roman gateway survives). On the very edge of a plateau the renovated ramparts command a broad view. Diderot was born here in 1713, . The austere cathedral of *Saint-Mammès* was begun in 1141 and continued during the second half of the 12C, when the Gothic style was beginning to make its mark. In the 18C a classically inspired façade and towers were added to this Burgundian Romanesque and Gothic building. The chapel of Amoncourt dates from 1549. The church of *Saint-Martin* is 13C and is dominated by an 18C bell tower (it has a fine 16C Christ on the high altar).

The *Musée Saint-Didier* features a collection of Gallo-Roman antiquities, medieval sculptures and paintings. There is another museum in the *Hôtel du Breuil de Saint-Germain* (in part late 16C), which has a very varied collection and is also devoted to Diderot.

Lannion	(18,300 inhab.)
22 Côtes-du-Nord	p.412 □ C 5

The little town of Lannion is built on the steep banks of the Léguer, near its estuary. It has a historic quarter and some picturesque houses. There is an impressive stairway of some 140 steps up the side of the hill leading to the church of *Brélévenez*, which was built in the 12C by the Templars, and then altered in Gothic style. There are some fine 17C altarpieces inside and an 18C Entombment in the crypt.

Environs: Chapelle de Kerfons (7 km. SE): There is a 15C Calvary in the village square next to the T-shaped chapel, which

Lannion, old front

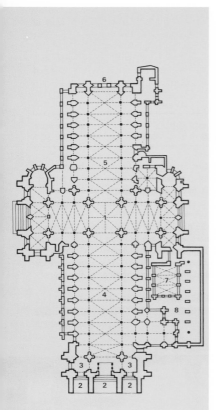

Laon - cathedral of Notre-Dame
1 lantern tower
2 porches
3 towers
4 nave
5 choir
6 apse
7 chapterhouse
8 cloister

dates from the 15&16C. An elegant painted and carved wooden rood screen (late 15C) separates off the choir, which has pieces of 16C stained glass. **Château de Tonquédec** (10 km. SE): This 15&16C fortress perched on a rocky spur dominates the deep, wooded Léguer valley. Richelieu ordered it to be demolished in 1622, nevertheless, what remains today is still imposing—walls, towers and a thick-walled keep in which some chimney-pieces have survived.

Laon	(30,170 inhab.)
02 Aisne	p.411 ☐K 3

Perched on a ridge overlooking the plain, the five tall towers of the cathedral soar skywards, making Laon a kind of beacon. St. Remi and the Le Nain brothers were born in this ancient town with a glorious past. Victor Hugo said, 'Everything is beautiful in Laon — the churches, the houses, the countryside, everything'.

Cathedral of Notre-Dame: Built 1155 –1235, this vast and varied cathedral is like a town within a town. Its style is transitional between Romanesque and Gothic. Masters of the Romanesque, its builders had discovered Gothic, the new building style, which strove after space, height and light. The result is that Notre-Dame is a great Gothic achievement, although it does include some Romanesque features, such as the lantern-tower (140 ft. high) over the crossing. The main façade, with its interplay of light and shade, is striking in its splendour. It is a marvellous blend of stones, semicircular curves and strictly arranged levels. Three deep porches with pointed roofs and carved gables lead to the doorways with fine dramatic carvings (these have, in large part, been reworked during the successive restorations). Above this is a rose-window, flanked by two large

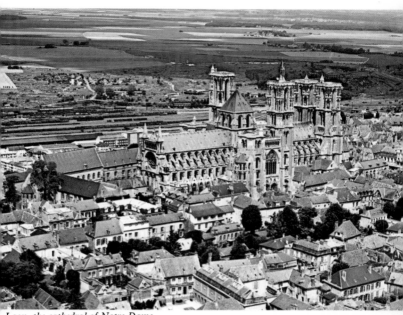

Laon, the cathedral of Notre-Dame

windows and crowned by an arcaded gallery with a statue of Notre-Dame watching over the city. The two flanking towers, which are considered to be among the most beautiful in the world, rise to 170 ft. Pierced and turretted, they are a wonderful piece of architecture gloryifying God; an element of fantasy is added in the form of enormous oxen at the corners. These are said to be in memory of a hard-working animal that used to pull carts during the Cathedral's construction.

INTERIOR This lives up to the promise of the W. front. The choir is only slightly shorter than the nave; the perfectly balanced elevation is arranged in four tiers: large arches on heavy cylindrical pillars, a tribune, a blind triforium and a clerestory; above it there is some splendid sexpartite vaulting. The square-ended apse has a rose-window and three lanceolate bays with 13C glass. The treasure includes a 12C icon of the *Sainte Face*, and some 17C tapestries. The chapterhouse leads to an elegant cloister.

Saint-Martin: In the early 12C, a Premonstratensian abbey was founded in the Quartier du Bourg and *Saint-Martin* was its church. This abbey church was restored shortly after the last war and has a long nave and two large towers above its attractive transept. The main façade was altered at the end of the 13C. It is tall, with three doorways and a huge bay; a high relief on the main gable depicts St. Martin dividing his cloak. The interior appears bare—the square choir with its flat apse lacks side aisles and the nave has neither tribune nor triforium. Apart from the recumbent figures of Jeanne de Flandre and a lord of Coucy on their tombs, there

Laon, the cathedral of Notre-Dame

now the Palais de Justice (unusual 12C chapel on two floors). In the Quartier du Bourg, the Hôtel du Petit-Saint-Vincent is an early 16C building with turrets.

Museum: Mainly archaeological—with extremely interesting collections of Greek vases, amphorae and figurines. There is a diptych by the Master of the Hours of Rohan, a rather bold work of contrasting colours and one of the masterpieces of 15C European art. In the museum garden there is an octagonal building with a dome and Romanesque windows, which is probably a 12C funerary chapel on the site of an old Templar cemetery. Inside there is a striking recumbent effigy by Guillaume de Harcigny.

Library: This collection of illuminated manuscripts, some of which date from the 8&9C, is world famous. You can also see a Gallo-Roman mosaic of Orpheus found in local excavations.

is a striking *Dieu de Pitié* in one chapel behind its stone Renaissance screen. The 17&18C abbey buildings, the abbot's house and the cloister and gardens still adjoin the church.

Old Laon: The upper town is protected by its citadel and its thick stone walls with towers and rampart walks. Three fortified 13C gates lead in to it, the *Portes d'Ardon, de Soissons* and *des Chenizelles*. There are houses of all periods along the winding streets and around the picturesque squares, with here and there a strange pinnacle-turret, an ornate gable or a charming watch-tower, and elsewhere cylindrical chimneys or a monumental carriage-entrance. In the quarter around the Cathedral, there is a pleasant group of medieval houses, among them the Hôtel-Dieu with its Gothic hall and Bishop's Palace,

Lapalisse	(3,780 inhab.)
03 Allier	p.420□K 9

The brave Marshal La Palice became famous in Italy before making his name in the celebrated 'lapalissades'. These originated from a song written by his soldiers who saw him die heroically at Pavia in 1525. 'A quarter of an hour before he died he was very much alive' (i.e. he fought bravely to the very last breath). The château dominating the town still belongs to his descendants. Only the towers from the outer wall are left of the original château (12&13C). The present one was built in Italian Renaissance style by Florentine builders, and the main wing (15&16C) contains some fine furniture. The *Salon Doré* (Gold Room) has a gold coffered ceiling and was decorated with a set of 15C Flemish tapestries, unfortunately stolen.

Lassay-les-Châteaux, the château

statues and a 15C altarpiece inside and pilgrims still come here to pray to St. Mathurin, who was once regarded as a healer of madness.

Lascaux: see Montignac

Lassay-les-Châteaux	(2,600 inhab.)
53 Mayenne	p.413☐F 5

The château of Lassay, flanked by round or semicircular towers, is situated on a granite spur. It replaces a fortress which was demolished by order of Charles VII. The rebuilding was carried out by Jehan de Vendôme from 1458 onwards and it withstood most attacks. A drawbridge precedes the main entrance, there are machicolated towers and the outer walls are 6 ft. thick.

Now there are only two remarkable ones left from the series of the *Neuf Preux* (Nine Champions). In the chapel there are some fine statues on the tombs.

Larchant	(510 inhab.)
77 Seine-et-Marne	p.415☐J 6

Today Larchant is a sizeable village and was once an important fortified town. Possibly the birthplace of St.Mathurin in the middle of the 3C, who was buried here in a chapel which became the object of an important pilgrimage. The church of *Saint-Mathurin* occupies virtually the same site as this funerary chapel. It is dominated by a tall bell tower whose spire collapsed in the 17C. The church dates from the 12C (choir) and the 13&14C. There are some

---

Lautenbach: see Guebwiller

Lauzun	(940 inhab.)
Lot-et-Garonne	p.423☐G 12

The château here dates from the 15C; it was enlarged in the 16&17C and completed in the last century. It possesses some remarkable Renaissance chimney-pieces, but the most interesting thing about it is its connection with one of the outstanding figures of Louis XIV's time, the Duc de Lauzun. Born here in 1633, he was an ambitous and unscrupulous courtier who found favour with the Sun King for a time, was imprisoned for some impertinence and seduced the 'frondeuse' (i.e. a member of the Fronde, a party opposed to Louis XIV) Grande Mademoiselle. He built the domed

Laval, the Pont Vieux

Laval, Notre-Dame-d'Avénières

pavilion between the old château and the Renaissance house, but his involvement in court intrigues and his struggles with authority left him precious little time to spend here. The church in the large village has furniture from a former Recollect chapel.

Environs: Eymet (6.5 km. NW): This is a 13C bastide with an arcaded square and the remains of a medieval château.

Laval	(54,550 inhab.)
53 Mayenne	p.413 □ F 6

This attractive town in the Bas-Maine was a Royalist enclave in the Revolution. It is proud of its châteaux and historic quarters, as well as of the extraordinary people who

came from the town. In the old stronghold near to which the Chouans (Royalist insurgents) gave their rallying cry sounding like the hooting of a tawny-owl (hence their name), Ambroise Paré was born in about 1509. Henri Rousseau, the future 'Douanier' was born here in 1844, Alfred Jarry in 1873 and Alain Gerbault, the lone sailor, in 1893. Laval is nowadays the Préfecture of the Mayenne region and the seat of a bishop. It straddles the river Mayenne and from the *Pont-Neuf* there is a good view of the Gothic humpbacked bridge, the quays (with old wash-house boats), the tiered old town and châteaux. The medieval quarters are full of old overhanging houses, Renaissance houses (such as the *Maison du Grand Veneur*) and 18C hôtels. The *Grand-Rue* slopes down to the Quais de la Mayenne, and still looks very medieval— it was the main thoroughfare at the time

Laval, the Vieux Château, detail

painter, although there are numerous paintings by other primitives. The huge Salle d'Honneur on the first floor is nearly 100 ft. long with wooden vaulting. It contains some interesting medieval carvings and tombs with effigies; there are also some 15C wall paintings. Two other rooms are devoted to ironwork and a *Musée Lapidaire* occupies the chapel. The keep is more or less a museum too, displaying items concerning the château's history, 19C paintings by a local artist etc.; it too is crowned by a superb wooden roof.

Cathedral: Romanesque in origin, but very much altered, especially in the 15C when it was greatly enlarged. (Work has continued on and off since this time.) It was the church of the Trinity until becoming a cathedral in the last century. The single aisle and the transept have Angevin vaulting. Some features from the late 11C have survived. There is a monumental 17C altarpiece glorifying the Trinity and a lovely 16C triptych from Antwerp.

Basilica of Notre-Dame-d'Avénières: Downstream from the Pont Vieux, this church is a lovely sight reflected in the river Mayenne. It dates mainly from the 11&12C and has a Romanesque apse (the bell tower was rebuilt in the 19C). At the entrance to the nave there are two very striking painted wooden statues (the Ascension, St. Christopher). In the N. part of the crossing there is a 15C Pietà and a wooden triptych, a gift from Jeanne de Laval, the wife of the 'Bon Roi René'.

Notre-Dame-des-Cordeliers: Altered, but dating from the late 14C. The church of *Saint-Martin* dates from the late 11C. On the left bank, the church of *Saint-Vénéran* has a fine Flamboyant portal. 2 km. N. of the town centre is the old, pre-Romanesque church of *Notre-Dame* at Pritz. It has been altered and enlarged (11&12C), and the apse was damaged. The church was aban-

when Laval was fighting the English, who ruled almost the whole of Maine at the beginning of the 15C.

Châteaux: The *Nouveau Château* or Galerie des Comtes de Laval houses the *Palais de Justice* and has a Renaissance façade. It was built in the mid 16C and a pavilion added in the last century. The *Vieux Château*, protected by a powerful cylindrical keep, 160 ft. high topped by rough masonry, is 12&16C. The oldest part, a room jutting out in the E., is known as the 'crypte du donjon'. It consists of two wings at right-angles; the side facing the Mayenne is severe, whereas that giving on to the courtyard has delicate and rich Renaissance decoration. On the ground floor of the main residence there is the *Musée Henri-Rousseau* which has only a single work by the famous primitive

doned for a long time and was in need of major restoration. There are wall paintings inside, particularly on the E. wall (11C) and on the triumphal arch (13C); the choir contains several carvings.

Environs: Abbaye de Clermont (16 km. W.): This was founded by St.Bernard in about 1150 and is a daughter house of Clairvaux. The bare, light abbey church survives from the second half of the 12C. One original abbey building, used for lay brothers, also still stands.

Lavardin   (490 inhab.)
41 Loir-et-Cher   p.414☐H 7

This picturesque old village on the Loir was at one time protected by a powerful château, of which a rough, half ruined keep remains among the other ruins (the fortress was demolished under Henri IV). The church of *Saint-Genest* is 11C and was built when the Romanesque style was dying out. Some remarkable 12&16C wall paintings inside show the Tree of Jesse and the Baptism of Christ—the oldest ones are on the N. aisle of the choir.

Environs: Montoire (2.5 km. W.): This quiet little village, also on the Loir, is where Hitler met Marshal Pétain in October 1940. The remains of the château are still visible and there are other old buildings, as well as the 11C chapel, which was part of a monastic community whose abbot was the poet Ronsard. There are some 12&13C frescos in this half-ruined chapel.

Lavaudieu   (230 inhab.)
43 Haute-Loire   p.420☐K 11

Here are the remains of a fine Romanesque Benedictine abbey founded in the 12C. It was later occupied by noble canonesses.

The simple church is crowned by a two storey bell tower of red sandstone. There is a charming little cloister with wooden galleries. The refectory beside it has a fine 13C fresco.

Lavaur   (8,300 inhab.)
81 Tarn   p.423☐I 14

This little town stands on a crossroads on the route from Toulouse to Castres, and still has plenty of charm. It once had a castle and was the seat of a bishop until the Revolution. Its beautiful southern Gothic church has retained Romanesque elements from the original building. Dedicated to St.Alain, it dates from the 13,15&16C. On one small Romanesque tower there is a painted wooden Jack o' the clock with a mechanism dating from 1523. The Flamboyant portal beneath an octagonal bell tower is watched over by the figure of the saint on the pier; on the lintel is the Adoration of the Magi. There is an 18C Pietà in a Flamboyant tomb recess in one of the chapels.

Layrac   (2,510 inhab.)
47 Lot-et-Garonne   p.423☐G 13

This little Gascon town grew up around a monastery visited by Pope Urban II in 1096. He consecrated the then unfinished church, which was completed in the 12C. You can still see the house where Jeanne d'Albret, Queen of Navarre stayed in 1572.

Lectoure   (4,400 inhab.)
32 Gers   p.423☐G 13

This surprising little town developed from

Lavaur, Pietà in the church ▷

a former Gallo-Roman settlement and much of the old ramparts still remain. The impressive cathedral of *Saint-Gervais-et-Saint-Protais* with its powerful bell tower is a complex church dating from the 12&13C. (It was a Romanesque domed church). It seems that it was partly demolished in 1472 and soon rebuilt by a master builder from Touraine; in the 16&18C there were some major enlargements and improvements. The superb 15C bell tower is 160 ft. high and had a tall spire which fell before the Revolution. The tall, broad nave is separated from the incomplete choir by a large triumphal arch. Inside this former cathedral you can see some splendid furniture and a marble *Assumption*, a fine 18C work in an ambulatory chapel. The Hôtel de Ville is now in the former Bishop's Palace, which dates from the second half of the 17C. This is a majestic building with a delicate staircase leading off the main hall. The town's streets, with towers, old houses and a fountain, are redolent of its past; the museum documents the town's history and also houses many Gallo-Roman remains.

Environs: Fleurance (11 km. S.): This was laid out as a bastide in the 13C. It has a 15C Gothic church with a 14C façade, which was altered and had a parapet walk added in the 16C. There are three windows by the Gascon master Arnaud de Moles in the choir; one of them is signed and dated 1500. **Château de Gramont** (14 km. E.): This medieval château governs the Arrats valley, and has a fine Renaissance wing (twin Portes d'Honneur, carved façade); it has been tastefully re-furnished.

Lessay   (1,340 inhab.)
50 Manche   p.413□E 4

This large agricultural market town has a famous fair. It owes its origin to an abbey

founded in the 11C by the monks from the far-off Bec-Hellouin. The admirable abbey church dates mainly from the end of the 11C and was mined by the Germans in the last war; the lantern-tower and vaults have collapsed, and the whole church was tragically ruined before the decision to restore it — no mean feat — was made. The pale church of Cerisy-la-Forêt was rebuilt using old stones, and as far as possible the masons used medieval methods. It is light and sober, and although it does not have the patina of time, it has recaptured the spirit of the original building. The tracery of the modern stained-glass windows was inspired by old Irish illuminated manuscripts. An 18C building with intricate detail has survived from the convent rebuilt by Marist monks.

Lille   (177,220 inhab.)
59 Nord   p.411□J 1

A traveller said of Lille in the early 18C, 'Lille is the Paris of the Low Country'. L'Isle, as it was then, first became known in about the 11C and quickly prospered under the aegis of enterprising merchants. The town has been successively marked by countless sieges, by the Revolution, and by the ruthless industrialization of the 19C. Nowadays Lille has come into its own as a regional metropolis of NW Europe; the town is receptive to innovation, overflows with activity and is moving towards prosperity again. In Lille-Est, the new part of the town, there are many experiments in urban architecture. The homogeneous old quarters, which were largely the work of skilled local craftsmen, have been renovated and restored.

Religious buildings: Even though Lille is a commercial town and does not boast any real gems of religious architecture, there are a few interesting churches. For ex-

Lille, Porte de Paris

Lille, the Grand Théâtre

imple, *Saint-Maurice*, begun in the 14C and finished in the 19C, has a façade with five gables and a lacework spire. It is a good example of a hall church typical of the Nord. The whole effect is very successful with the five equal aisles, the mass of tall columns and the finely ribbed vaulting. In the chapel of *Dieu de Pitié* there is a very realistic 16C wooden statue of Christ being scourged. The church of *La Madeleine* is a splendid circular building with chapels on the periphery and a lovely wrought-iron grille in the choir. The silver tabernacle door is a masterpiece of the Lille goldsmith Baudoux. The dome of La Madeleine, some 150 ft. high, may not survive much longer. The church (now deconsecrated) was built 1675–1713, and is now in need of urgent repairs. The church of *Saint-André* was built in the first half of the 18C in the Jesuit style and has a splendid throne

(1763), a chased silver tabernacle door and 17C marble busts of St.Peter and St.Paul, which are a fine addition to the baroque interior.

Military buildings: Lille, on a strategic European crossroads, has had a turbulent history. It was owned by the Counts of Flanders, and then the Dukes of Burgundy, becoming a Spanish possession before being re-annexed to France. Many bitter struggles have been fought over it, and thus the city learnt early on of the need to protect itself. The *Noble Tour* (1459), a truncated keep and now a Resistance Memorial, survives from the oldest ramparts. The *Roubaix* and *de Gand* gates were built 1610–22 and were also part of the defences. The *Citadelle* was built on Louis XIV's initiative when he took the town in 1667, and it became the 'most beautiful

Lille, Musée des Beaux-Arts, 'The Concert in the Egg' by Bosch (detail)

and most complete in the Kingdom'. A masterpiece of military architecture by Vauban, it takes the form of a regular pentagon, with bastions and ravelins. The buildings each have a special function, and are arranged so as to form an impregnable town within a town. The whole is strangely beautiful: brick walls are dressed with stone, the monumental *Porte Royal* is decorated with brackets and volutes, and the entire complex is harmoniously balanced. Since the ring of ramparts has been broken, the *Porte de Paris*—a triumphal arch erected to the glory of Louis XIV by Simon Vollant in the late 17C—is no longer one of the only entrances to the city. The monument has a large carved group (showing Victory about to crown Louis XIV) on the top of its tall semicircular arch; it is also decorated with figures of Mars, Hercules and others from mythology.

Civil buildings: The streets of Lille have an elegant assortment of houses, which reinforce its artistic image. There is a definite Lille style of architecture which has been controlled by the administration in order to maintain a balanced urban landscape. Even the monumental buildings of the early 20C — the Grand Théâtre, the new Palais de la Bourse, the Hôtel de Ville — merge perfectly in with the town centre. Only the chapel and a superb spiral staircase turret in brick remain of the *Palais Rihour*, where the Dukes of Burgundy lived. This huge residence goes back to the end of the Middle Ages. The *Hospice Comtesse*, justly considered to be one of the finest monuments in Lille, has the splendid Salle des Malades in which there are wooden vaults and 15C windows with broken arches. The community buildings are still resplendent with their original deco-

Lillebonne, theatre/amphitheatre

Beauregard (1687). The old *Hospice Saint-Saveur* with arcaded galleries, windows framed by pilasters and garlands still belongs to the generation of 'pictorial stone-cutters'. Then came the French influence and with it order. The *Hôtel d'Avelin* (1777) and the old *Hôtel de Wambrechies* are examples of this new-found rigour. The *Palais de Justice*, a concrete and glass tower finished in 1969, is part of this asceticism. The carved wall of the *Salle des Pas Perdus* and splendid contemporary tapestries create a radiance of shimmering colour.

Musée des Beaux Arts: This is housed in a 19C palace and is one of the richest museums in the province. From Flanders (Jean Bellegambe, Bruegel the Elder, Hieronymus Bosch) to Italy (Titian, Tintoretto, Veronese), from Rubens to Goya, from Watteau to the Impressionists, this collection brings together the work of many schools. There is a drawings cabinet (superb works by Raphael), sculptures, silverware, ivory, ceramics, pieces of brass and copperware, and Flemish coins.

Environs: Hem (10 km. NE): This little town possesses a fine modern building which blends perfectly with its surroundings. The *Chapelle de Sainte-Thérèse-de-l'Enfant-Jésus* (1958) is a perfect example of sobriety adapted to today's liturgy. The wall of stained glass is by Manessier.

ration (kitchen with 17C Lille tiles, Abbess's apartment with original furniture), but they are now occupied by the *Musée d'Arts et Traditions Populaires* with its Flemish interiors. A few houses have survived from the first half of the 17C, such as the *Maison des Vieux Hommes* (1624) with its sandstone base and brick and stone fabric. The *Maison de Gilles de la Boe* (1636) is covered with carving. This tendency to ornamentation was at its height with the building of the Ancienne Bourse, which consists of 28 houses side by side (with an arcaded gallery) in a square around a courtyard. The carved decoration is sumptuous: caryatids, garlands and medallions enliven the walls with a riot of colour which is characteristic of Flemish baroque art. A few houses have whole façades which were treated as sculpture, either on their own or in a row like the

Lillebonne	(10,310 inhab.)
76 Seine-Maritime	p.410 □ G 3

Lillebonne was once the capital of a Gallic nation, the Calètes. It was then the prosperous *Juliobona* of Gallo-Roman times, a river and sea-going port which declined after it silted up. The *Hôtel de Ville* houses a small *Musée d'Antiquities*, and nearby some impressive remains of an amphitheatre have been uncovered, which would seem to go back to the 1C (altered in the 2C and used as a bastion during barbarian invasions, then as a quarry). The church of *Notre-Dame* with its tall 16C spire was somewhat altered in the last century. There is an interesting 16C alabaster relief inside and choir stalls said to be 17C. The château, founded by William the Conqueror, was rebuilt in the 12C.

Environs: Tancarville (13 km. W.): Since its opening in 1969, the *Pont de Tancarville* has been considered a masterpiece of modern engineering. Bold and spectacular, it spans the broad Seine estuary, nearly one kilometre across at one point. The extensive ruins of the château which guarded the river from the top of a chalky cliff are a reminder of the past. There are medieval parts (ruined 12C keep) and the 'château neuf' built in the 18C.

Limoges	(147,450 inhab.)
87 Haute-Vienne	p.419☐H 10

Strategically placed in an open valley of the Vienne on the W. side of the Massif Central between Auvergne, the Loire and the Garonne, Limoges faces Aquitaine, with which its past and economy is very much linked. The capital of Limousin, an administrative and cultural centre and university town, it has been expanding since the 19C. The town's rich past is very evident in the old quarters with their steep streets, bell towers and museums. Also, the remains of a large Roman town are gradually being discovered in local excavations. When the city was threatened by barbarian invasions, it took refuge behind its ramparts at 'Puy Saint Etienne', where the Cathedral was built. St. Martial brought Christianity to Limoges and, near the site of his burial in an early Christian cemetery on the edge of the town, a second town

Limoges, St-Étienne, portal of St-Jean

grew up called Château de Limoges. The two communities were joined together at the end of the 18C to form Limoges as it is today. Limoges is renowned for its enamel-work, which was at its height in the Middle Ages, and also for porcelain, which is still very important. Two humpbacked medieval bridges cross the Vienne, the *Pont Saint-Étienne* (13C) — a fine example of Gothic civic architecture, and the *Pont Saint-Martial* (late 12C) built on the remains of a Roman bridge and leading to the picturesque Rue de la Boucherie.

Cathedral of Saint-Étienne: The crypt and the base of the bell tower are from the Romanesque church built in about 1013. Work on the Gothic cathedral began in 1273 and continued until the mid 16C; then started up again at the end of the 19C (last three bays of the nave and narthex).

Limoges, Musée National

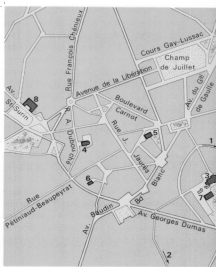

Limoges **1** Pont Saint-Étienne **2** Pont Saint-Martial **3** cathedral of Saint-Étienne **4** church of Saint-Michel des Lions **5** church of Saint-Pierre du Queyroix **6** Chapelle Saint-Aurélian **7** Musée Municipal **8** Musée National Adrien-Dubouché

Exterior: The moderation and elegance of northern art was beginning to influence the Midi in the mid 13C, and although Saint-Étienne does not have the grandeur of the northern cathedrals, it does have very fine proportions. The 200 ft. bell tower has a Romanesque porch and two lower storeys, which were hidden during strengthening work in the 14C. The upper storeys, which are visible, were built in 1242, 30 years before work on the Gothic church began. The portal of *Saint-Jean* was built 1515–30 and features all the wealth of Flamboyant decoration. The Renaissance door leaves bear scenes from the lives of St. Stephen and St. Martial. There is a beautiful Flamboyant rose-window between the two galleries; the gable has windows.

Interior: There is a great feeling of unity here, despite the various different stages of building. The cathedral is cruciform, built of lovely granite, with a three-bay choir, ambulatory and radiating chapels. The five bays of the nave have side aisles and chapels. The pillars with their bundles of small columns give the building life and light. The limestone rood screen at the end of the nave is one of the most beautiful Renaissance works in Limousin. There are large pieces of 15C glass in the apse. The ambulatory has three fine funeral monuments—the tomb of Raynaud de la Porte (first third of the 14C), that of Bishop Bernard Brun (interesting example of 14C sculpture) and the mausoleum of Jean de Langeac (16C), which is decorated with scenes of the Apocalypse inspired by Albrecht Dürer's engravings.

Saint-Michel-des-Lions: This church takes its name from the two Gallo-Roman stone lions on either side of the entrance. Building began in 1364 and went on until the 16C. The elegant bell tower is over 200 ft. high, has three octagonal sections above a square storey and is crowned by a tall stone spire. The base of the N. portal is Flamboyant. Inside the furnishings are very old, and include a 13C silver-gilt reliquary, a really extraordinary work.

Saint-Pierre du Queyroix: This church dates from the 14,15&16C. The façade is flanked by a lovely Limousin-style tower rather like those on the cathedral and Saint-Michel-des-Lions. It has solid ribbed vaults on massive pillars and a stained-glass window signed by Pénicaud (15C)—he was a master enameller and also a painter and glassmaker. The furnishings are interesting; they include a 13C Christ, a Pietà and a 17C altarpiece.

Chapelle Saint-Aurélian: This dates from the 15C and has a 17C façade and bell tower. Outside there is a lovely Gothic cross with three orders, each featuring a group of Apostles under a canopy. Inside,

the gilt and ornaments make the church very attractive (altarpieces, 17&18C gilded wooden statues, the principal reliquary of St. Aurelian).

Musée Municipal: In the former Bishop's Palace (18C). Several rooms are devoted to a major collection of Limoges enamel of 300 items; there are also medieval champlevé enamels, Renaissance painted enamels and more recent pieces. The Limoges workshops, outstanding since the 12C, have perfected their ancient art, specializing in champlevé enamels (the enamel is made by pouring a richly coloured vitreous substance over a grooved copper plate). There are paintings and exhibits from ancient Egypt and a collection of pieces of masonry which are entirely from the Limousin region.

Musée National Adrien-Dubouché: This museum has one of the best ceramic collections in France, after the *Musée National* in Sèvres. It covers every aspect of the technique of ceramics (antique pottery, Chinese vases, hard-paste porcelain from

Limoges, museum, enamel chest   *Limoges, 16C Limoges enamel*

France and abroad). The museum is named after its founder and was opened in the 19C. It contains some 10,000 items. The history of porcelain is interestingly described. The industry came to be centred at Limoges at the end of the 18C when the makers used the kaolin found in Saint Yrieux, about 40 km. from the town.

Lisieux	(26,680 inhab.)
14 Calvados	p.410☐G 4

Lisieux is the capital of the green Auge region, which is renowned for fine manor houses. It is also a centre for the crowds of pilgrims who come to venerate Thérèse Martin—'little Saint Thérèse', who lived at the local Carmelite convent and died there in 1897 before she was 25. An ancient town (it was the capital of the Gallic Lexovii), its historical appearance changed little until the last war, when it was repeatedly bombed and burnt.

Cathedral of Saint-Pierre: This vast

former cathedral escaped damage. It stands near the Louis XIII-style Bishop's Palace, which is now occupied by the Palais de Justice. It has dissimilar towers on the façade and a central tower with a lantern and powerful buttresses. It was largely built 1170, although work went on until the 15C. The façade and N. tower date from the 13C, while the S. tower is a Romanesque pastiche of 1579. The fine portal known as 'du Paradis' on the S. side and the large, severe interior are robust examples of early Gothic art. The choir with 14C stalls on either side is Norman Gothic and very similar to the choir of Canterbury Cathedral. One chapel is dedicated to St. Thérèse who received her vocation in this cathedral in 1887.

Saint-Jacques: This restored and deconsecrated church in the picturesque heart of Lisieux is now used for exhibitions. A Flamboyant building, it was damaged in the war—indeed very few old houses remain in its vicinity.

Carmelite Convent: This is the convent

Lisieux, the basilica of Saint-Thérèse

Lisieux - basilica of Saint-Thérèse 1 Parvis 2 campanile 3 nave 4 choir 5 Way of the Cross

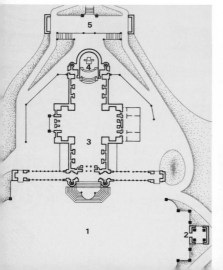

where Thérèse of Lisieux took the veil in 1890, lived as a humble Carmelite and died after dreadful suffering. She lies in a shrine in a 19C chapel which is full of votive offerings. The *Salle de Reliques* is devoted to her childhood and life.

Basilica of Sainte-Thérèse: This large church (with a heavy, unfinished bell tower in front of it) is an object of pilgrimage and stands on the side of a hill dominating Lisieux. It was begun in 1929 but the war interrupted when work was well advanced and it was not finally finished until the 1960s. A huge basilica on two levels, it is full of marble and mosaics. The large nave and spectacular choir stand above a huge crypt with three aisles. The N. cloister houses an exhibition on the Carmelite convent.

Museums: The *Musée du Vieux Lisieux* is in an old half-timbered house, and its collections are devoted to the distant past of the town and the Auge region. The little *Musée des Merveilles de la Mer* displays

thousands of extraordinary shells collected by a former sacristan of the convent.

Environs: Saint-Germain-de-Livet (6.5 km. S.): This enchanting manor from the 15&16C is partly timber-framed and lies hidden in a valley. 'A little jewel for a young princess', said the Normandy writer La Varende. It contains lithographs, fine old furniture, porcelain and paintings.

Lisores	(250 inhab.)
14 Calvados	p.410□G 4

The village of Lisores lies in the Auge, the region of Livarots and Camemberts. It retains the memory of the great contemporary painter Fernand Léger, whose family owned property here. The open-air museum—a barn which has been turned into an exhibition hall—documents the stages of his career, as well as exhibiting a number of his works. On the gable there is a large mosaic, the *Fermière et la Vache*, which was based on one of his gouaches.

Saint-Germain-de-Livet, the château

Loches, Porte Royale

Loches, the church of St-Ours

A nearby chapel has several stained-glass windows by Léger.

Loches	6,820 inhab.)
37 Indre-et-Loir	p.419☐H 8

Alfred de Vigny wrote, 'I was born at Loches, a little town in Touraine, thought to be pretty'. But the poet left his birthplace in 1797, too young to remember its medieval charm, the alleys and monuments, the château and the curious church. It was a major medieval stronghold, taken and retaken by the English and the French in the course of the Hundred Years War. In 1429 Joan of Arc came to the place; Charles VII and Agnès Sorel were lovers here; Louis XI's enemies were imprisoned here and Louis XII visited it. Bathed by

the gently flowing branches of the Indre, it is a town of art and history, and now seems to sit back in its forest setting, well pleased with having managed to preserve its charm. Near the 15C feudal *Porte des Cordeliers* (which protects the entrance to the town from the Beaulieu side) and just before the old town, is the 16C bell tower, the *Tour Saint-Antoine*. The Grand-Rue has old houses and leads to the Renaissance Hôtel de Ville by the 15C Porte Picoys. Along the sloping Rue du Château you will find the Chancellerie and the Maison du Centaure, the former dating from Henri II's reign and the latter from that of his father, François I.

Town walls, château, keep: The powerful 13&15C machicolated *Porte Royale* opens into the fortified area, which is encircled by over a mile of walls. It has the

Loches, St-Ours, portal

cited the King's brother to rebel against him. In Louis XII's reign, Duke Lodovico Sforza of Milan was imprisoned at Loches — he was captured at Novara in 1500 and died in 1508 just as he was about to be set free.

Saint-Ours: (Near the Logis Royal.) Formerly a collegiate church dedicated to Notre-Dame, since the Revolution this church has been named after the founder of the first monastery at Loches. The church has an unusual outline with its conical spires, and it caught the imagination of Viollet-le-Duc, who said that it had 'a strange, wild beauty which was quite unique'.

PORCH AND DOORWAY: The doorway is mainly 11&12C, altered in the 14&15C and restored in the last century; the porch is vast and dates from the second half of the 12C. The portal is Romanesque in appearance, although it was built when the Gothic style was beginning to make its mark in Touraine. It has no tympanum and is carved arch-stone by arch-stone in the manner of Aquitaine; decoration consists of palm motifs, animals, imaginary monsters and many figures. There is an Adoration of the Magi above the arch-stones, and this was was damaged in the Revolution (large Virgin in Majesty, with the infant Christ in the centre). On either side of the doorway there are figures forming columns, and these were obviously intended for another position. The porch, with its Angevin ribbed vaulting, contains a strange round holy-water stoup, which was formerly a Gallo-Roman altar.

entrance to the little *Musée du Terroir et du Folklore* and the *Musée Emmanuel-Lansyer* (a 19C painter whose works are on show, as well as sketches by Delacroix, engravings and etchings and various objets d'art). The *Logis Royale,* at the N. end of the citadel, consists of two contrasting parts: one, very feudal in appearance with a tall tower, probably dates from Charles VII's time, the other was built under Louis XII and is more elegant and ornate. Agnès Sorel's restored tomb is in this château (it was mutilated in 1793) and so is the highly elaborate oratory of Anne of Brittany. At the other end of the citadel there is a huge 11C keep, a Romanesque building with Louis XI's *Tour Neuve* and the *Martelet* next to it — infamous prisons in which Louis incarcerated his enemies. Cardinal Jean Balue, the Bishop of Évreux, was imprisoned here for 10 years for having in-

INTERIOR: The oldest part of the church (11C) lies behind the above-mentioned doorway. It forms the ground-floor of a bell-tower-porch and serves as a vestibule (semicircular vaulting and archaic capitals). Arcades separate the nave from the aisles, which were added after the Romanesque period. Its rather unusual vaulting consists of octagonal cones, a form which developed from the domes used in Aquitaine (these 12C cones, known as 'dubes', have been rebuilt). The crossing is crowned by an octagonal dome on squinches and this in turn bears a square tower with a spire and pinnacle turrets. The left aisle is 14&15C, whereas the right one dates from the end of the 12C and was rebuilt in the last century.

CRYPT: This little vaulted nave beneath the S. apsidal chapel contains a fresco of St. Brice dating from the second half of the 12C.

Environs: Beaulieu-lès-Loches (1 km. away, on the right bank of the Indre): Foulques Nerra, Count of Anjou, founded an important abbey here in 1004. The abbey church was seriously damaged by a tornado and rebuilt in the mid 11C; its central bell tower collapsed during the Revolution and the S. wall of the nave disappeared during the enlargement of a square. Now the church is but a shadow of what it once was, although, dominated by its fine 12C Romanesque bell tower, it is still impressive. It abuts on to a wall whose size gives one an idea just how large the abbey church was (the present-day church is the result of 15C alterations made to the end bays of the Romanesque nave). Near this church is the former *Logis des Abbés* (abbots' residence), with an exterior pulpit. *Saint-Laurent* is a late-12C church (Romanesque bell tower, Angevin vaulting).

Locronan, church of Saint-Ronan

is surrounded by some lovely houses with carved and moulded doorways; its broad bell tower is now without its spire. It is linked to the 16C Chapelle du Pénity via the highly ornate porch. Inside, the recumbent figure of St.Ronan is supported by six angels; there are also a remarkable polychrome Descent from the Cross and a 16C Entombment. The 17C pulpit has medallions showing the life of St.Ronan. The treasure includes a Louis XIII monstrance, a 16C reliquary and a Gothic chalice.

Locronan	(690 inhab.)
29 Finistère	p.412□B 6

Locronan lies on the edge of a small granite outcrop and its houses are clustered around the Grand-Place, a marvellously preserved 16&17C masterpiece of civil architecture. The 15C church of *Saint-Ronan*

Environs: Manoir de Moëllien (2 km. NW): This charming manor, built in the 17C, has a monumental portal. The Renaissance façade is partly incomplete and is flanked by a heavy, square three-storey tower. **Kerlaz** (6 km. SW): This little village has a parish close with a Renaissance portal of 1558, a calvary of

Lons-le-Saulnier, church of St-Désiré, 15C Entombment

1645, an ossuary with basket-handle bays, and a 16&17C church containing some very old statues.

Lons-le-Saunier	(23,300 inhab.)
39 Jura	p.421☐M 8/9

Rouget de l'Isle was born in this pleasant town in 1760. Two churches here are worth a visit: *Saint-Désiré*, partly built in the 11C, has an elongated Romanesque nave and a Gothic choir (17C), and contains a fine 15C Entombment. The 13C church of the *Cordeliers* (Franciscans) has been much altered and has some remarkable 18C woodwork. The Rue du Commerce has 16&17C arcades and there is a fine 18C hospital with a lovely wrought-iron grille enclosing the main courtyard. Inside there is a really

remarkable collection of pharmaceutical vases. The museum is mainly devoted to prehistory, with an amazing 30 ft. Neolithic pirogue (dug-out canoe) which was found on the banks of the Lac du Chalain.

Lorient	(71,930 inhab.)
56 Morbihan	p.412☐B/C 6

Tucked away in its roadstead, where the rivers Blavet, Scorff and Ter join together and flow into the sea, Lorient has never been anything other than a new town. It was founded in the 17C by the French East India Company on waste ground on the edge of Port Louis, which was granted by the King; in the present century it was almost completely destroyed by bombing in the last war. Two Louis XV pavilions at the entrance to the Arsenal survive from the old town, the Tour de la Découverte being flanked by two 17C powder mills. One of these houses the Musée Naval which has an interesting collection of porcelain from the East India Company. Also, along the Quai des Indes there are several old houses, and not far away Notre-Dame-de-Victoire (or Saint-Louis), a modern granite and concrete church with a tall bell tower. It has a square nave with a dome and the bare fabric is decorated with multi-coloured glass, frescos and a most original Stations of the Cross.

Environs:Hennebont (10 km. NE): This town on the steep banks of the Blavet is built around a fortified centre, the Ville Close, which was badly damaged in allied air raids; it is reached via the 15C Porte Bro'Erec'h. There are only a few 16&17C houses left inside the ramparts. The 16C church of *Notre-Dame-du-Paradis* in a nearby square has an imposing square tower with a Flamboyant spire. The tall porch, in the same style, is decorated with elegant niches. The upper storeys and buttresses have galleries, pinnacles and lantern lights with brackets. The interior has contemporary glass by Max Ingrand and an interesting 17C organ. **Port-Louis** (17 km. S.): This was built on a peninsula in the late 16C. The *citadel* of Port-Louis commands the Lorient roadsteads. The *Naval Museum* covers naval history from the 16C to the present day.

Loudun	(8,250 inhab.)
86 Vienne	p.419☐G 8

Loudun is set on a hillside and surrounded by boulevards, which follow the line of the old ramparts. The town has twisty streets and fine 17&18C hôtels; it was prosperous in the Middle Ages, but declined during the Reformation and in the 17C was disturbed by the mysterious affair of Urbain Grandier, the brilliant young priest who was accused of bewitching nuns and burnt at the stake. Théophraste Renaudot, an inventive spirit who founded the first printed newspaper in 1631, was born in Loudun.

Loudun, the square tower

Loudun, St-Hilaire, window

The *Tour Carrée* is 11C and the top was removed by order of Richelieu at the time of the demolition of the château. *Saint-Hilaire-du-Martray* is 14C and has on its S. side a beautiful late-15C chapel with some Flamboyant features. There is a fine 15C painting on wood on the altar and this is perhaps by Gérard de Bruges. The church was attached to a Carmelite convent of which an 18C chapterhouse survives. *Saint-Pierre-du-Marché* has a fine Renaissance doorway. The *Charbonnneau-Lessay Museum* shows Loudun's past in Gallic and Gallo-Roman exhibits, weapons and helmets, head-dresses, clogmakers' tools, numerous religious objects and a model of the old town.

Lourdes	(18,100 inhab.)
65 Hautes-Pyrénées	p.422☐F 15

Lourdes, the gateway to the Pyrenees, was formerly a much disputed fortress and is now a busy centre of pilgrimage where religion and commerce live uneasily side by side—the shop windows are a bewildering mixture of souvenirs and pious objects. The town owes its fame to Bernadette Soubirous, to whom the Virgin Mary appeared on numerous occasions in 1858. When the ingenuous daughter of a poor miller confided her experience to her parents crowds gathered at the grotto where the apparitions had taken place and a previously unknown spring began to flow. The bishop investigated the affair, proclaimed the visions authentic, and authorized devotion to Notre-Dame de Lourdes. Today it is the largest centre of pilgrimage in the world.

The *Basilique du Rosaire*, the *crypt* and the *Basilique Supérieure* are all late-19C, showing the contemporary taste for the Romano-Byzantine and Neo-Gothic styles. The vast underground *Basilique Saint-Pie X*, consecrated in 1958 by the future pope (John XXIII) can hold 20,000 pilgrims under its daring pre-stressed concrete vaulting. There is a *museum* devoted to Bernadette (1844–79), who was canonized in 1933. The former feudal *château*, perched on a rocky outcrop, was enlarged and altered before becoming a prison in the 17C, after which it became a barracks. It houses the large *Musée Pyrénéen*, which covers various aspects of the Pyrenees and the Béarn (popular art and tradition, folklore, costume, furniture, fauna etc).

Environs: Saint-Savin (16 km. S.): Formerly an important religious centre in the Bigorre region, it looks down on a sizeable valley 3 km. from the attractive summer resort of **Argeleès-Gazost**, a spa with a charming historic quarter. The *church*, formerly the abbey church of a Benedictine community, dates from the 10&11C and acquired its fortress-like appearance in the 14C. The tympanum of the Romanesque doorway in the main façade has a Christ in Glory with priestly vestments (such representations are extremely rare).

Lourdes, the basilica

Louviers, the church of Notre-Dame, Entombment

The church contains a stoup with caryatids known as 'cageots' (medieval outcasts assumed to be lepers) and a 15C organ chest decorated with three movable masks: the mouth and eyes opened and closed when the organist played. The former chapterhouse has a little *Museum of Religious Art*.

Lourmarin   (690 inhab.)
84 Vaucluse   p.425☐M 14

The château of Lourmarin stands firmly on a mound near the hillside village where the inventor Philippe de Girard was born in 1775; there is a small museum in his family house. Albert Camus stayed here and was buried in the cemetery in 1960. The fine château, deserted for a time and inhabited by tramps, was restored before the war by an industrialist from Lyons who bequeathed it to the Academy of Aix. 'As various in its style as were the epochs which made it glorious', it consists roughly speaking of two parts: the 'old' château, rebuilt at the end of the 16C with a spiral staircase dating from 1542 and very fine fireplaces, and the W. Renaissance building, which has been very tastefully redecorated with faience, paintings, and old Spanish and Provençal furniture.

Environs: Cucuron (7 km. NE) This large village, perched between two Lubéron peaks, has a tightly packed old quarter below the ruins of its little medieval château. Parts of the old defences survive and there are beautiful early-17C houses which still have Renaissance features. The Romano-Gothic church contains a monumental altarpiece ordered by Mazarin's niece in 1661 for a convent in Aix.

Louviers, church, Virgin on portal

Louviers (18,880 inhab.)
27 Eure p.410☐H 4

This former centre of the cloth industry was seriously damaged in the war. Some old buildings do remain, in particular *Notre-Dame* with its imposing bell tower. It dates mainly from the late 15/early 16C but incorporates some 13C elements. The S. side is highly ornate, and the side aisles of the large church have 15&16C stained-glass windows. There are also numerous works of art, including 15C statues and a 15C mausoleum, a rustic 16C Pietà and a *Nativity* and *Adoration of the Magi* painted in the 17C by the local artist Jean Nicolle. The *Municipal Museum* has a varied collection of Rouen faience; it also deals with the history and techniques of cloth manufacture. On the banks of the Eure there are remains of a 17C convent.

Ansouis (5 km. SE of Cucuron): There are medieval ruins near the splendid early-17C residence of the Sabran family, which looks down on the terraced village. Its N. aspect is somewhat fortress-like but otherwise the buildings are quite welcoming. The Chambre des Saints is a memorial to El-zéar de Sabran and Delphine de Signes, who were married here in 1299 but lived in complete chastity. **La Tour-d'Aigues** (5 km. S. of Ansouis): The château was rebuilt 1555–71, burnt down in the 18C and ruined in the Revolution. All that remains is a door decorated in antique style (probably the work of the Piedmontese engineer/architect, Ercole Nigra), two pavilions and a 13C keep which had been altered and has now partly collapsed. The barrel-vaulted nave of *Notre-Dame* is partly Romanesque, the choir dates from the early 13C.

Luçon (9,580 inhab.)
85 Vendée p.418☐E 9

The spirit of Richelieu haunts this pleasant cathedral town. It is no longer the 'muddy' bishopric which that contemptuous young cleric found at his installation, but an important commercial and historic centre of the Marais region.

Cathedral of Notre-Dame: Only the N.transept gable with its fine Poitevin façade remains from the Romanesque period. This former abbey church, consecrated in 1121, underwent a period of rebuilding after it became a cathedral in 1317 and has been much altered; the three-storeyed nave dates from the 14C, and the four bays of the choir in early Flamboyant style were completed in the 15C. The fine cloister is 16C. The cathedral was sacked in the Wars of Religion and restoration work went on throughout the 17C; the final phase was the building of a classical façade by Leduc (known as Toscane). The Duchesse de Berry laid the foundation stone of the 280 ft. spire in 1828 but it was blown down by a storm in a single night and had to be entirely rebuilt in the following year. The chapel of the Ursuline Convent is 17C and has fine painted wooden vaulting and an altarpiece with white marble columns.

Environs:Saint-Michel-en-l'Herm (15 km. S.): This abbey has a fine 11&15C chapterhouse separated from the calefactory by a vaulted corridor. The abbot's house, the monks' wing and the refectory were designed by Toscane in the 17C. There is also a fine collection of Vendée head-dresses in the abbey.

Lude (Le)	(4,120 inhab.)
72 Sarthe	p.414☐G 7

This small town on the banks of the Loir is famous for the 'Son et Lumière' at its château, which occupies the site of a fortress and has a marvellous terrace and a park with four large round towers (of dubious military value). It is 15,16&18C (the fine Renaissance façade was built in 1529 –30). It has an oratory with 16C wall paintings and also contains tapestries and luxurious furniture. The town iself has narrow streets and one very pretty Renaissance house; Saint-Vincent with its 12C choir has elegant Angevin vaulting.

Lunéville	(24,700 inhab.)
54 Meurthe-et-Moselle	p.417☐N 5

This town owes a great deal to the dukes of Lorraine, who enjoyed staying here. It has remained much as they made it in the 18C when, thanks to their interest, it acquired its château and park both of which

Luçon, cathedral cloister

are built on a grand scale; Diderot and Voltaire often added lustre to the life of the court.

Château-Musée The vast main courtyard and broad central building are unmistakeably reminiscent of Versailles in their layout and grandeur. Boffrand, a pupil of Hardouin-Mansart, was in charge of the operation from about 1702. There is a splendid 18C park with a fine combination of shrubberies, flower beds and pools. Inside the château there is an unusual museum of decorated pharmaceutical jars (18C) in brilliant white, made in the faience factories of Lunéville.

Saint-Jacques: The façade with its two cylindrical towers, each topped with a dome and statue, has startling rococo decoration; the baroque excess is emphasized

Lunéville, church of St-Jacques, clock

Lusignan, church bell tower

by the monumental clock on the pediment. The church was built from 1730–47 by the architects Heré and Boffrand and contains fine rococo furnishings and remarkable 18C woodwork.

Lusignan	(2,780 inhab.)
86 Vienne	p.419☐G 9

Lusignan's old houses and ruined ramparts rise in terraces on a hillside overlooking the Vonne. The little town abounds in memories of the Poitevin family who ruled Jerusalem and Cyprus for four centuries, and by the legend of the sprite Mélusine, who is said to have built the château in one night. The château is now ruined; the Promenade de Blossac was laid out in the 18C to give access to the remains.

Notre-Dame-et-St. Junien: This dates from the 11&12C. The squat bell tower with multiple colonnettes is set above a dome on pendentives. The interior capitals are decorated with vegetable motifs, knot patterns and rearing animals. In the sacristy is a doorway with an entire bestiary carved on its mouldings.

Luxeuil-les-Bains	(10,710 inhab.)
70 Haute-Saône	p.417☐N 6

This little spa town has some fine historical monuments and is known for its association with St.Columban, who founded the celebrated abbey here in the 6C. The *Basilica of Saint-Pierre* is a Gothic building begun in the 13C with fine furnishings in its three aisles, including Renaissance

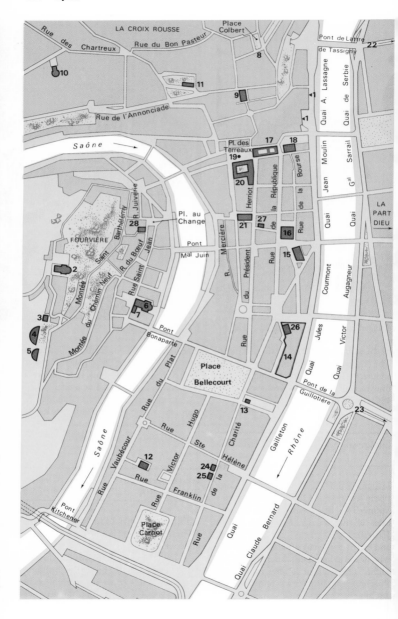

choir stalls (1545) and an elaborate organ chest (1617). Adjacent to the church is a fine 14&15C red sandstone cloister. Luxeuil has a striking number of old and curious houses like the *Maison de François I* with Renaissance arches, the *Hôtel du Cardinal Jouffroy*, a 15C house with a fine carved balcony and the *Hôtel des Échevins*, whose pepper-pot turrets and crenellated tower contrast with the delicacy and purity of the Flamboyant loggia. The house is occupied by a *museum*, which has paintings by Courbet and Vuillard and tombstones.

Luynes	(2,620 inhab.)
37 Indre-et-Loir	p.414☐G 7

This attractive village, which has interesting houses built into the rock of the river banks, was once an important feudal centre. Above the little cluster of historic houses and market buildings is a château, rebuilt in the 13C and frequently altered and enlarged. There are impressive remains of a Gallo-Roman aqueduct nearby.

Lyon	(462,900 inhab.)
69 Rhône	p.421☐L/M 10

Two thousand years of history separate the

Lyon 1 Entrance to the Traboules 2 basilica of Notre-Dame 3 Gallo-Roman museum 4 theatre 5 Odéon 6 cathedral of Saint-Jean 7 Manécanterie (choir school) 8 Cour des Voraces (Traboule) 9 church of Saint-Polycarpe 10 church of Saint-Bruno-les-Chartreux 11 amphitheatre of the Trois-Gaules 12 church of Saint-Martin d'Ainay 13 bell tower 14 Hôtel-Dieu 15 church of Saint-Bonaventure 16 Palais du Commerce et de la Bourse 17 Hôtel de Ville 18 Grand Théâtre 19 Bartholdi fountain 20 Palais Saint-Pierre (Musée des Beaux-Arts) 21 church of Saint-Nizier 22 Parc de la Tête d'Or 23 Musée de la Photographie 24 Musée des Arts Décoratifs 25 Musée Historique des Tissus 26 Musée des Hospices Civils 27 Musée de l'Imprimerie et de la Banque 28 Musée Historique de Lyon et Musée de la Marionnette

first boatmen on the Saône and the Rhône and the latest high speed train. Lyon is a major European city and the second largest urban centre in France; it has two contrasting focal points, the historic 'holy hill' of Fourvière and the high tower above the ultra-modern buildings of La Part-Dieu. This great city has a definite character of its own: it is industrial and intellectual, inward-looking and international. It has a remarkable concert hall, named after Maurice Ravel, an impressive operatic and theatrical season and the Théâtre National Populaire in Villeurbanne, an ultra-modern municipal library and numerous museums. The city is also famed for gastronomical delights: Rabelais remembered its soups and fricassées, Chateaubriand its *tête de veau*, Stendhal its 'divinely cooked vegetables', fish, game and wines. Not only does Lyon's gastronomy owe a great deal to the cooks of the past, the famous 'mères', but it also as a fine reputation today, with the international star Paul Bocuse and the 'dynasties' of Vettard, Lacombe, Brazier, Nandron and Bourillot.

History: Lucius Muniatus Plancus, a former lieutenant of Julius Caesar, was ordered by the Roman Senate to found a colony at the confluence of the Saône and the Rhône in 43 BC. The city expanded rapidly on the Fourvière hill, became the effective capital of Gaul and was soon converted to Christianity. *Lugdunum* then suffered total decline as a result of barbarian invasions and recovered only after several bleak centuries. It was annexed to the French crown in 1312. In the 16C it was richer and more densely populated than Paris and became one of the principal centres of banking and commerce; it produced great scholars, booksellers and doctors; the latter category included Rabelais, who worked at the Hôtel-Dieu from 1532. He published *Pantagruel* and *Gargantua* in Lyon, met the poet Maurice Scève and the free-thinking, talented and

Lyon, Hôtel de Ville

Lyon, Notre-Dame-de-Fourvière

ardent Louise Labé, known as 'the beautiful Cordière', and saw the Calvinist Clément Marot make due apology outside Saint-Jean. Over the centuries Lyon spread along the right bank of the Saône, on to the *Presqu'île* (peninsula) and finally to the other side of the Rhône. There was a great deal of building in the 18C under Michel Perrache and Jean-Antoine Morand, and the town was partially rebuilt in the 1960s & 70s when quarters such as La Part-Dieu were completely transformed. Lyon has an underground railway, is near Satolas international airport and has excellent road and rail links. The city has two thousand years of history behind it and is the centre of a major urban and industrial community and the capital of the Rhône-Alpes region.

Districts and 'Traboules': The centre of Lyon between the Saône and the Rhône

is commonly known as the *Presqu'île* (peninsula). The picturesque old quarter of Lyon is on the Fourvière hill on the right bank of the Saône. The strange, tall houses of *la Croix-Rousse*, once the stronghold of the canuts (silk weavers), huddle above the lavish residences on the Presqu'île. The town has spilled over on to the left bank of the Rhône where the straightforward de Brotteaux quarter rubs shoulders with the ultra-modern *La Part-Dieu* complex. The *traboules* are typical of the Croix-Rousse and Vieux Lyon areas; they are mazes of passageways, courtyards and stairways which can be followed for long distances away from the main streets (the word comes from the Latin *transambulare*).

Fourvière: Fourvière is a hill with an end-

Lyon, Bartholdi fountain

less road tunnel running beneath it. It is a Roman Catholic area and contains the important basilica of Notre-Dame. There is an outstanding Gallo-Roman museum (see under *museums*) exhibiting a spectacular group of classical buildings: the ruins of a theatre founded some time before Christ, parts of an odeum which almost certainly dates from the 2C, and numerous other remains. The somewhat disconcerting *Basilica of Notre-Dame*, begun in 1872 by the Lyonnais architect Pierre Bossan and largely completed by 1896, is a mixture of the Romanesque and Byzantine styles, and is profusely decorated with marble, mosaic, bronze and gold. Huysmans called it 'Asiatic and barbaric'. This massive church almost smothers a simple 18C chapel, which incorporates two Romanesque capitals from an earlier building. **Vieux Lyon:** This wonderful area at the foot of the Fourvière was very nearly flattened by bulldozers. Neither local people nor visitors knew of this fine Renaissance complex which had fallen into disrepair. It fortunately underwent major restoration and is now an attractive collection of pretty narrow streets, doorways, turrets, astonishing courtyards, fine staircases and 'traboules'. The main thoroughfare is the Rue Saint-Jean and particularly interesting are the Gothic *Hôtel du Chamerrier* (No. 37, 16C) and the lavish *Demeure des Vistes* (No. 29, 15C). In the courtyard of No. 16, which has a superb 17C doorway, is the *Tour Rose*, which gives access to the splendid *Rue Boeuf*. In the Rue de Gadagne is the impressive *Hôtel de Gadagne*, which houses the Musée Historique and the Musée de la Marionnette (see under *museums*). At 2 Place au Change is the 14C façade of the *Maison Thomassin* with its 16C courtyard, spiral staircase and galleries. The Rue Juiverie was a wealthy street; note No. 4, the 16C *Hôtel Paterin* or *Maison Henri IV* and No. 8, the *Hôtel Bullioud* with its gallery on pendentives, built in 1536 by Philibert Delorme.

Cathedral of Saint-Jean: The cathedral is a mixture of styles from Romanesque to Flamboyant. It was started in the mid 12C, finished in the 15C and improved and refurbished in the 16C before being damaged during the Wars of Religion and the Revolution. The doorways are decorated with surprising reliefs, reminiscent of those on the side doorways of Rouen cathedral: alongside the usual religious or seasonal representations there are hares joined together by the ears or sirens playing the harp.

INTERIOR: Although work on the nave went on for nearly a century it is a coherent whole. The chapels in the side aisles include the late-15C Chapelle des Bourbons, which is Gothic and Renaissance. The oldest parts of the church, the choir and the apse, are mainly 13C and show Provençal influence but are essentially Burgundian Romanesque. In the apse is the archbishop's *cathedra*, a white marble frieze overlaid with red cement, as well as some remarkable 13C stained glass. *Astronomical clock:* This probably dates from the 14C and has been repaired many times. It is 30 ft. high and a row of figures move in a circle at noon and then at 1,2&3 p.m. *Manécanterie and treasure:* The building known as the Manécanterie (choir school) with its severe medieval façade stands beside Saint-Jean facing the square, and has been much altered since the late 11C or early 12C. The treasure is a fine collection of ecclesiastical objects in gold.

The Croix-Rousse: If the Fourvière hill is the 'hill of prayer', then the Croix-Rousse is the 'hill of work'. The *Maison des Canuts* was founded by a textile workers' co-operative and is devoted to the silk manufacturers who worked in this quarter in the 19C; it is both shop and small museum combined. The Croix-Rousse, partly occupying the plateau and partly the steep

Lyon, Musée des Tissus ▷

slope down to the Presqu'île, has some spectacularly severe and gloomy *traboules*. The most striking of these is that which begins in the Place Colbert with the famous *Cour des Voraces*. *St.Polycarpe* is 17C, the façade 18C. *St.Bruno-les-Chartreux* was once part of a convent and is also 17&18C; the dome was built by Soufflot. The ruins of the *Trois-Gaules amphitheatre* are not particularly interesting except to the specialist; they were uncovered in 1968 (Rue des Tables-Claudiennes, Square du Jardin-des-Plantes).

La Presqu'île: The area of the Presqu'île, bounded by the motorway intersection and the railway station and the confluence of the Rhône and the Saône is of no particular interest, but the area between the concrete labyrinth of the Centre d'Échange and the Croix-Rousse is really the heart of Lyon. There is a large pedestrian precinct, a majestic square, the Bellecour, and also churches, museums and numerous shops. *Saint-Martin-d'Ainay* is in a quiet district which was once cut off from the Presqu'île by a stretch of water. A former abbey

Lyon, Gallo-Roman museum

church and now a minor basilica, it was consecrated in 1107 by Pope Pascal II and is a fine Romanesque edifice whose appearance was somewhat altered in the 19C. In the crossing it has four large monoliths from the altar of the Gauls in the Croix-Rousse. *Place Bellecour:* This is the most important square in Lyon and measures 340 by 220 yards. Henri IV advised the town council to lay out this splendid esplanade and Louis XIV forbade building on it. It has Louis XVI houses all around it; the W. and E. sides were rebuilt about 1800, but the square still has the stamp of the 18C. The equestrian statue of Louis XIV was melted down in the Revolution and remade in 1825 by Martin Desjardins. In front of the enormous Hôtel des Postes is a solitary tower which is all that remains of a 17C hospital. The *Hôtel-Dieu* is near the Place Bellecour and has a section known as the Petit-Dôme which is 17C, but it is mainly the work of Soufflot, who started to rebuild it in 1741. The Grand Dôme designed by the architect of the Panthéon in Paris was burnt down in 1944 but rebuilt in concrete in a style very close to that of the original.

Saint-Bonaventure: This church in the Place des Cordeliers is a rather cold but beautifully proportioned building commissioned by the Franciscans (Cordeliers) between 1330–1471. At the entrance tapestries show the life of St. Bonaventure (Cardinal Jean Fidanza) who died in Lyon in 1274. The chapels were built in the 15&17C by the tradesmen's fraternity. Opposite the church is the majestic Palais du Commerce et de la Bourse, a very ornate 19C building.

Hôtel de Ville: Hardouin-Mansart was commissioned with the restoration of municipal buildings in 1702, which he transformed and considerably improved by his work. The Hôtel de Ville is approached from the Place de la Comédie through two attractive courtyards separated by a row of columns; at either end of this peristyle are towers capped with domes and lantern lights. At the entrance to the audaciously vaulted entrance hall, which gives on to the Place des Terraux, there are old sealed standard weights and measures and two plaques commemorating the inception of the Resistance under Jean Moulin and the Liberation of Lyon. The Town Hall has some 17C painted ceilings by Thomas Blanchet and a little *Musée Édouard Herriot* (an important politician and former mayor of Lyon and who died in 1957). Behind the Town Hall is the *Grand-Théâtre* or Opéra, rebuilt in the 19C after Soufflot's original theatre burnt down. In the Place des Terreaux the façade and belfry of the Town Hall face the monumental *Fontaine de Barthold*, an allegory of 'rivers flowing to the sea' presented at the Exposition Universelle of 1889. The *Palais Saint-Pierre*, a former 16C abbey, is on one side of the square and houses the Musée des Beaux-Arts.

Saint-Nizier: This is a fine Gothic church with Flamboyant elements (13C, the greater part 15C). It occupies the site of a 2C oratory built by St.Pothin, who was martyred at the same time as St.Blandine. The central doorway of the façade is Renaissance, the left tower 15C and the other 19C; both have spires. The right transept contains a statue of Notre-Dame-des-Grâces by Antoine Coysevox. The Place des Jacobins was called the Place de Confort at the time when Rabelais was writing; it has a marble fountain (1880) with statues of four Lyonnais artists: the architect Philibert Delorme, the engraver Gérard Audran, the sculptor Guillaume Coustou and the painter Hippolyte Flandrin. The originally medieval *Rue Mercière* has retained its Renaissance character.

The Part-Dieu: This remarkable town within a town on the left bank of the Rhône was conceived by Louis Pradel, the Lyonnais mayor and entrepreneur who died in 1976. He was fond of concrete; the Part-Dieu and the Gallo-Roman museum make up for his other mistakes, which were sometimes on a grand scale. This huge modern complex is on various levels, with a maze of terraces and galleries. It contains administrative offices, the headquarters of the town council, a concert hall, a major library and an up-to-date shopping centre decorated with marble and fountains.

Parc de la Tête-d'Or: A golden head of Christ is said to have been hidden here and never again recovered. The elegant iron railings with rose designs were forged in the Belle Époque by Joseph Bernard.

Principal Museums: Lyon has many fine museums and is in the process of setting up still more: the most recent are the remarkable Musée Gallo-Romaine de Fourvière and the *Musée de la Photographie* in the former residence of the Lumière brothers in the Rue Premier-Film. Auguste and Louis Lumière were born in Besançon

Lyon, Musée des Tissus

but settled in Lyon; they perfected the art of photography and were the fathers of the modern cinema.

MUSEUMS ON THE PRESQU'ÎLE. *Musée des Arts Décoratifs* (30 Rue de la Charité): This extremely varied collection is housed in an 18C hôtel designed by Soufflot; it includes fine furniture, tapestries, faïence, weapons and silver. *Musée Historique des Tissus:* This is next to the above-mentioned museum and is also housed in an 18C building. It is devoted to the history of fabrics and explains techniques of their manufacture; it also features countless masterpieces in every imaginable thread and colour. Lyon was the centre of the silk industry before it turned to artificial fabrics. It was also the home town of the *canuts* and of Joseph-Marie Jacquard, who invented a method of automatic weaving at the beginning of the 19C. *Musée des Hospices Civils* (Hôtel-Dieu): This is in the Petit Dôme and deals with Lyon's ancient medical tradition. It also contains a number of objets d'art. *Musée de l'Imprimerie et de la Banque* (13 Rue de la Poulaillerie): This is a dual-purpose museum in a 16C hôtel; it is very tastefully laid out and features two of the city's most famous activities. There is a superb collection of wood engravings and prints. *Musée des Beaux-Arts* (Palais Saint-Pierre, Place des Terreaux): The cloister of the former monastery has a permanent exhibition of sculpture (Rodin, Bourdelle). The body of the museum houses a varied collection in some 80 rooms, particularly 19&20C paintings (Géricault, Delacroix, Ingres, Courbet, Manet, Daubigny, Corot, Van Gogh, Renoir, Gauguin, Marquet, Derain, Vlaminck, Dufy, Ernst, Masson, Man Ray etc.) There are also many works by Lyonnais artists, including the strange paintings of Louis Janot (1814–92).

MUSÉES DU VIEUX-LYON ET DE FOURVIÈRE: *Musée de la Civilisation Gallo-Romaine* (17 Rue Cléberg): This museum, which looks out over the Fourvière archaeological site, occupies a modern concrete building, which blends well with its background (the architect was Bernard Zehrfuss). It is original in layout and has a collection of statues, sarcophagi, mosaics, inscriptions and domestic objects. There are two famous pieces: the *Calendrier Gaulois de Coligny* and the *Tables Claudiennes*, which are the text of one of the Emperor Claudius' speeches in Lyon. *Musée Historique de Lyon et de la Marionnette:* This dual-purpose museum occupies one of the most beautiful houses in Vieux-Lyon (16C). The Musée Historique, covering the period from Middle Ages to the present day, shows fragments from churches and abbeys, furniture, china, old views of the city and memorabilia concerning the Revolution and the Empire. The first floor is devoted to Guignol, the puppet created at the beginning of the 19C by the Lyonnais Laurent Mourget; there is also a large collection of other puppets.

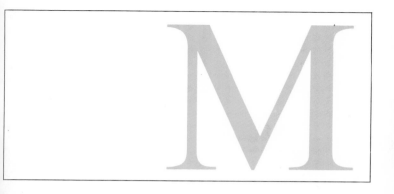

Mâcon

71 Saône-et-Loire

(39,600 inhab.)

p.421 □ L/M 9

Historically Mâcon is part of Burgundy, but it has an independent spirit and is proud of having been the capital of an important county. It stands on the Saône, at the point where the Éduen Gauls established a river-port, and has closer links with Lyon, with which it has good communications by river, road and railway, than with Dijon. The Mâconnais is pleasant and hilly, with many Romanesque churches and manors. Alphonse de Lamartine was born here in 1790. The town is full of character, in spite of having very few historic buildings (many old houses and the ancient Carmelite convent were rashly pulled down). The Hôtel de Ville is housed in a lavish 18C house and the Hospice de la Charité has a fine oval chapel designed by Soufflot. *Vieux Saint-Vincent* is the remains of a cathedral destroyed in the Revolution (Romanesque narthex with Last Judgement in the tympanum, which is a foretaste of the Gothic). A tall *Renaissance house* in the Place aux Herbes is decorated with countless figures of medieval appearance.

Hôtel Sénecé and Musée Lamartine (Rue Sigorne): This lovely 18C house contains a dual-purpose museum; one section concerns the decorative arts, while the other is a veritable Lamartine sanctuary, full of information on this writer and politician who was devoted to the Mâconnais all his life. (He was born near here at 3 Rue de la Barre.)

Musée Municipal des Ursulines (Rue des Ursulines): The museum is housed in a late-17C convent and covers the period from the finds in Solutré to the present day. It is a pleasant, well-organized collection, and offers thorough coverage of Burgundian prehistory, local excavations including the famous site at Solutré and the Gallo-Roman past of Mâcon.

Environs: Saint-André-de-Bâgé (8.5 km. E.): This isolated former priory church dates from the beginning of the 12C and shows Cluniac influence. The nearby village of Bâgé-le-Châtel has ruins of its defences and a château. **'Circuit Lamartine':** Lamartine loved the Mâconnais region where his family lived and where he spent his childhood. He owned property in the area and wanted to be buried here. The district is featured in his *Harmonies*. **Château de Monceau** (7.5 km. NE): This 17C building stands among

Magny-en-Vexin, the church

vineyards which the writer inherited. He loved the arbour and spent a long time in the summerhouse writing his *Histoire des Girondins*. **Bussières** (11 km. W.): As a child Lamartine was taught by the village priest and his curate, and based the hero of *Jocelyn* on the latter. **Milly-Lamartine** (12 km. W.): Although he was born in Mâcon, Lamartine claimed to have seen the the light of day for the first time in this charming village, which he often visited as a child and where the house built by his grandfather still stands. Lamartine was devastated at having to sell this house, 'whose very walls breathed like a living thing'. **Saint-Point** (25 km. W.): Lamartine and his wife and daughter are buried in a neo-Gothic crypt near the modest church here. The old manor was 'medievalized' by the writer according to Romantic taste. It stands in extensive park-

land and contains memorabilia of Lamartine. The local countryside is described in *Le Tailleur de Pierre de Saint-Point*, which was inspired by a local artisan-sculptor.

Magny-en-Vexin	(4,560 inhab.)
95 Val-d'Oise	p.410 □ I 4

Magny was formerly a stopping-point on the Paris-Rouen road and is now an agricultural centre. Some old houses remain, and one of them, a harmonious Louis XVI building, houses the Mairie. The 15C *church* was radically rebuilt in the 16C and has marked Renaissance features. It contains some interesting baptismal fonts (one in the right side aisle dates from 1534), three beautiful statues on the mausoleum of the former seigneurs (17C.

in the right transept) and an attractive alabaster Virgin (14C, above the altar).

Environs: Château d'Alincourt (4 km. N.): This attractive mixture of 15–17C buildings is set in a rather isolated position in the countryside and is only rarely open to visitors. .

Villarceaux (10 km. SW): There are two châteaux in the large park here: the more important is a charming Louis XV building, privately owned and visible from the road; the other is 15C, the so-called 'Ninon de Laclos' manor house, which has 16C outbuildings housing a restaurant. Its rooms seem to have remained much as they were when the frivolous Ninon, beloved of a Marquis de Villarceaux, knew them.

Ambleville (7 km. W.): This partly Renaissance château stands in fine gardens opposite a modern church which has a painting attributed to Ribera.

Maillezais, church portal

Maillezais	(850 inhab.)
85 Vendée	p.418 □ F 9

In the 10C Maillezais was a full-scale town in the heart of impenetrable marshland. Now the limestone cliff overlooks only meadows; on it stand the imposing remains of the 11&14C former Abbey of Saint-Pierre, where Rabelais stayed. Inside the fortified walls are the ruins of the abbey church. The W. entrance has been walled up, but the 11C narthex, the N. wall of the nave and one arm of the 14C transept survive.

Excavations have brought to light the ground plans of the monastery and the convent, showing the dormitory, refectory and octagonal kitchen. The parish church is an impressive Romanesque building whose doorway has capitals decorated with imaginary beasts.

Maintenon	(3,310 inhab.)
28 Eure-et-Loir	p.410 □ H/I 5

This pleasant little town enlarged by modern estates occupies a site at the confluence of the Eure and the Voise. The château was given by Louis XIV to his beautiful but prudish favourite, Françoise d'Aubigné, Marquise de Maintenon, the poor widow of the poet Scarron and granddaughter of the Protestant poet Agrippa d'Aubigné. She supplanted Mme de Montespan and married the Roi Soleil after the death of Queen Marie-Thérèse.

Château: The château, which replaced a medieval fortress (of which only one tower remained) was much restored by a rich treasury official during the Renaissance. It was given to Mme de Maintenon in

1674, and she enlarged it. It then became the property of the Nouailles family and was excessively renovated in the 19C and badly bombed in the last war, after which the exterior was restored by the Department of Historic Monuments while the owners worked on the interior. The Renaissance façade faces the main courtyard, and is joined to a Flamboyant chapel by a long building instigated by Mme de Maintenon. The main courtyard is connected to the second courtyard by a vault which passes under the château; this route was formerly protected by a drawbridge. *Mme de Maintenon's apartments* are open to visitors. Of particular interest is the portrait of her by Mignard (that of her rival Mme de Montespan was painted by Largillière). The château is set in an extensive park on the Eure and the Voise.

Aqueduct: Héron de Villefosse wrote, 'If the château makes one think of a swashbuckling film, then the aqueduct which is its backdrop could certainly sustain the role of the Pont du Gard'. The aqueduct is unfinished. It was damaged by bombing in 1944, and is covered with wild vines. It was commissioned by Louis XIV to bring water from the Eure to the gardens of Versailles, but work on it was abandoned in 1688.

Environs: Gallardon (12 km. SE): This old village between Jurepoix and la Beauce is overlooked by a ruined tower known as the 'épaule de Gallardon' because of its shape. The former priory *church of Saint-Pierre* stands on a typical small provincial square. Dating from the 12&13C, it was refurbished in the 15&16C; Romanesque elements remain (particularly the doorway), but the church is mainly Gothic. It has a magnificent choir with ambulatory, which shows the influence of Chartres.

Maisons-Laffitte	23,810 inhab.
Yvelines	p.428☐I 4

This residential town, famous among racegoers, is the most important horse-training centre in France. In the last century its

Maintenon, aerial view of the château and the town

park was split up; one part was reserved for walking and riding, the other was divided into building plots (the residents still have to conform to the table of charges laid down in 1834). The park belonged to the banker and failed politician Jacques Lafitte and was formerly part of the château, which now has only very small gardens.

Château: The work of François Mansart, it is a superb classical building in pale gold stone built 1642–51 for the influential René de Longueil, the president of the Parisian Parliament. It was intended to be used by the King, who had the 'right to lodge' here, and Louis XIV, Louis XV Louis XVI and their queens and favourites stayed here, as did Voltaire. The future Charles X, the Count of Artois (Louis XVI's brother), bought the château before the Revolution and established the racecourse. The château was sold to Maréchal Lannes, who entertained Napoleon here. It was then acquired by Lafitte in 1818. He was extremely wealthy at the time and received La Fayette, Benjamin Constant, Thiers and Arago as guests. The château commands a wide view and has a fine gate which came from a château in Picardy. The building has a magnificent staircase with a dome and remarkable interior decoration. The *king's apartment* on the first floor is a huge state room with a musicians' gallery. The *king's bedroom* was completely altered in the 18C (as were the Count d'Artois' apartments and the summer dining-room), but it has now been almost completely restored in the original style.

Malesherbes (3,860 inhab.)
45 Loiret p.415□I/J 6

This peaceful little town in the Gâtinais is surrounded by woods and has a 12&13C church, which was later altered. The château was rebuilt in the 18C and replaced the one where the young and beautiful Henriette d'Entraygues, Henri IV's mistress, lived. It was rebuilt by the chancellor, Guillaume de Lamoignon, the father of Malesherbes, one of Louis XVI's ministers, who protected the Encyclopaedists, defended the king before the Convention and was executed in the Terror. The chapel contains the tomb of Admiral d'Entraygues and his wife. The two recumbent tomb figures have their backs to each other; legend has it that even beyond the grave the Admiral was angry with his wife for being unfaithful to him. The *church of Saint-Martin* (12,13&15C) contains an interesting 15C Entombment.

Malle (château)
32 Gironde p.422□F 12

This harmonious château is on the edge of the *Sauternes* and *Graves* vine-growing regions. It was built by a parliamentarian from Bordeaux in the 17C. It is outstandingly decorated and furnished, and the

Malmaison, the bed of Josephine

Italian influence is particularly marked in the fine gardens.

Malmaison (château)
92 Hauts-de-Seine   p.428☐I 5

This château, which has retained its medieval name: *mala mansio* (mauvaise maison), is a characterless 17C building, with wings and a veranda added under the Consulate. The architecture is rather plain, but the château is enlivened by the memories it holds of Napoleon, the Empress Josephine and their intimates. Lively parties were held here when the future emperor was first consul, and it remained the property of Josephine after their divorce; she died here in 1814. Napoleon himself spent a few days here in 1815, just before his final exile. It was then sold, bought by Napoleon III, sold again, and saved from ruin during the Belle Époque by a banker, who presented it to the state. It has been restored since the last war, and now houses an important *Napoleon Museum* devoted to the Emperor and Josephine (furniture, portraits and other paintings, musical instruments, including the Empress's own harp, aiguière and bassin du sacre, some fine porcelain, and the Austerlitz table with portraits of the crowned Emperor surrounded by his marshals). In the *Osiris pavilion* there are items connected with Saint Helena (clothes, iron bedstead, account book and the death mask of the exiled Emperor). The *Pavillon des Voitures*, formerly the stables, contains a carriage which Marie-Antoinette brought from Austria and also the *Opale* in which Josephine returned to Malmaison after signing her divorce papers. (The Emperor was separated from her because she had not given him an heir, and he was about to marry Marie-Louise, the daughter of the Emperor of Austria.)

The **Château de Bois-Préau** was part of Josephine's property and was given to the state by its American owners in 1929. It is an annexe of the Malmaison Museum and contains items on the King of Rome, paintings, sculpture and numerous articles connected with the Emperor and his family.

Manosque, Porte Saunerie

Manosque   (19,550 inhab.)
04 Alpes-de-Haute-Provence   p.425☐N 14

The birthplace of Jean Giono (1895–1970) is ringed by boulevards following the line of the former ramparts. Two gateways survive: the 14C Porte Saunerie and the Porte Soubeyran, which has a wrought-iron bell tower.The Rue Grande leads to the Romanesque *church of Saint-Sauveur* (16C bell tower, 17C side-aisles), and then to the Hôtel de Ville, which is in an 18C house. The Gothic apse of the *church of Notre-Dame* appears to date from the 13C; the ribbed vaulting in the nave and side aisles was not added until the 16 or 17C. One chapel with an altar made from a tomb has a Virgin and Child in black wood.

Mans (Le)

Sarthe

155,250 inhab.
p.414☐ G 6

In the middle of June every year this lively, growing town is invaded for the '24 hours', one of the most famous of the Grand Prix races. The older parts of Le Mans rise in tiers around the majestic Gothic and Romanesque cathedral. Along the river Sarthe you can see the remains of the Gallo-Roman town wall (3&4C), which are a reminder that the former capital of Maine is on the site of an important Celtic town. There have been many rebellions and sieges in the town, and there was much bloodshed in 1793 when the Vendéens were fighting the Republicans. The town was handed over to the Germans in 1871 after the French lost a battle in the area. Le Mans was badly damaged in the last war and today it is surrounded by modern buildings and industrial areas—although around the Place de la République and the *Church of the Visitation* there are numerous historic houses including: the Renaissance building where the poet Paul Scarron (husband of the future Mme de Maintenon) lived; the house known as the *Maison de la Reine Bérengère* (15&16C); the *Maison des Deux-Amis*; the *Maison d'Adam et Ève* and the *Hôtel de Vignoles*. The 18C *Palais des Comtes du Maine* now houses the *Hôtel de Ville*.

Cathedral of Saint-Julien: This superb cathedral is dedicated to the evangelist who became the first bishop of Le Mans in the 3C. The upper parts of the building have an astonishing quality of lightness and appear to be lifted by the flying buttresses. This audacious medieval building is in a variety of styles. The façade, the fine doorway with sculpted columns and carved

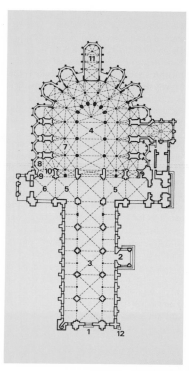

Le Mans - cathedral of Saint-Julien 1 Entrance **2** portal **3** nave **4** choir **5** transept **6** left transept **7** ambulatory **8** Chapelle des Fonts **9** tomb of a count of Maine **10** memorial to Guillaume du Bellay **11** Lady Chapel **12** menhir

tympanum in the S. porch as well as the rather modest nave are Romanesque. The marvellous choir (1217–54) and the light and spacious transept with its many windows are Gothic. Alongside the shimmering 12–15C glass is the deeper blue and red of the 13C windows above the triforium. The baptismal chapel in the left transept at the edge of the ambulatory has some fine Renaissance works: the tomb of a count of Maine—the brother of 'good' king René; and a memorial to Guillaume du Bellay—diplomat, writer of memoirs and cousin to the poet du Bellay, who was a member of the Pléiade. There is 13C stained glass in the axial chapel of Notre-Dame-du-Chevet, which has a 17C grille. Near Saint-Julien there is a red sandstone menhir about 15 ft. high; opposite is the heavily restored Hôtel du Grabatoire which is the bishop's residence. There is a fine view of the apse of the cathedral from the Place des Jacobins.

Notre-Dame-de-la-Couture: This composite building was once the abbey church of a convent, which stood in the midst of cultivated land (hence 'couture' = culture of land; however its meaning has since changed and it is now associated with the word 'culte' = worship). The church was built in the 11C (choir columns and crypt) and the 16C, and has Angevin ribbed vaulting. The 13C façade has a very fine doorway. In front of the pulpit there is a pretty Virgin carved by Germain Pilon in 1571. The shroud of one of the seven saints known as Bernard is on show (the saint in question was bishop of Le Mans in the 6&7C). The préfecture is housed in the former monastery, which was rebuilt in the 18C.

Sainte-Jeanne d'Arc: A large, elegant hall with Angevin vaulting, which was formerly part of a late-12C hospital. It was turned into a church; patients' beds were formerly placed in the side aisles.

Tessé Museum: The museum is named after the marshal who once lived here; his house was replaced by the former bishop's residence, which was then altered to house the museum. It has numerous paintings, particularly of the Italian and classical French schools (Vouet, Poussin, Le Sueur, Philippe de Champaigne). There is also a superb chased enamel plaque from a 12C tomb.

Museum of History and Ethnography: The museum occupies the *Maison de la Reine Bérengère*, which has a carved façade. It is a local history museum exhibiting Sarthe pottery, woodcut blocks, engravings of old Le Mans and objets d'art and handicrafts.

Le Mans, Maison d'Adam et Ève

Le Mans, cathedral S. portal

Environs: Abbaye Notre-Dame-de-l'Épau (4 km. SE): Founded in the 13C by Berengeria, the widow of Richard the Lionheart, this Cistercian abbey was rebuilt after being destroyed by fire in the 14C. The tomb with a recumbent figure of Berengeria is in the church.

Mantes-La-Jolie

78 Yvelines

(42,570 inhab.)
p.410☐ 4

On the edge of undulating countryside full of second homes, Mantes is today almost suburb of Paris thanks to the motorway and railway. The town, greatly damaged in the war, is now quite industrialized. William the Conqueror, who captured the town, was fatally wounded the day after his victory. The French and English went on fighting over it until the mid 15C. Henri IV met his mistress Gabrielle d'Estrée here and it was here that he decided on his second renunciation of the Protestant faith, thus securing the French throne.

Collegiate Church of Notre Dame: This large and beautiful late-12/early-13C church is contemporary with Notre-Dame in Paris and was the subject of paintings by Corot, along with many other Mantes scenes. The building has cathedral proportions and was once surrounded by a fortified wall; it was restored and partly rebuilt in the last century. Although it was repeatedly bombed in 1944, its three remarkable doorways have survived. The central one, the finest, though not the tallest, was built in the last third of the 12C. It is dedicated to the Virgin—her death and resurrection are shown on the lintel underneath the coronation in the tympanum. The doorway on the right is very different and is topped by an ornate pointed gable (about 1300). The doorway on the left was built first and is rather archaic.

INTERIOR: The nave is tall and light because of the pretty 12C rose-window in the façade and also because of the other stained glass (both restored and modern). To the right of the choir the Chapelle de Navarre is rectangular, vaulted from a central pil-

Mantes-la-Jolie, 'Château de Rosny-sur-Seine' by Corot (Louvre)

Mantes, collegiate church of N.-D., the nave

Marmoutier, the church

lar and lit by high windows. Dating from the mid 14C, it is guarded by four charming statues of queens which are what remains of a screen destroyed in the Revolution.

The Tour Saint Maclou: This dates from the beginning of the 16C and was formerly the bell ower of a church destroyed in the Revolution. Outside the town is the *church of Gassicourt*, dating from the 12&13C. A former Cluniac priory church it is dominated by a Romanesque saddle-back bell tower over the crossing.

Environs: Château de Rosny sur Seine (6 km. W.): Rebuilt by Sully *c.*1600, work on this stone and brick château was never completed. The Duchesse de Berry wanted to finish it in the 19C but the parts which had been added were so badly done that they were mostly removed to aid further renovation. An attractive park was planted with thousands of mulberry bushes by Olivier de Serre, the agriculturalist. The Louis XII château, well furnished by Jacob, contains some beautiful tapestries, tableaux and engravings. The Duchesse de Berry's grand salon has Renaissance decoration.

Mariana: see **Corsica**

Marmoutier	(1,970 inhab.)
67 Bas-Rhin	p.417☐O 5

The W. façade of this massive, austere, fortress-like *church* in Marmoutier is one of the masterpieces of Alsatian Romanesque. This former abbey church dominates the large well-sited village and is striking primarily for its balance and solidity. The monumental façade would seem to have been built 1150–60; the choir and nave are Gothic, rebuilt in the 13C. The façade is very sparsely decorated and could even be called severe; there are three towers, with arches and string courses separating the different storeys; there are also a few rather curious carved motifs: kneeling figures meditating on the tops of the gables, a lion with its tongue out near a small carved picture featuring a wild hotchpotch of heads. The porch has finely carved capitals and the doorway a plain tympanum with elegant little columns. Behind this there is a narthex. The church contains a fine 18C organ-chest.

Marseille	(914,400 inhab.)
13 Bouches du Rhone	p.425□M 15

The new 'Centre Directionnel' of Marseille was built on virtual wasteland near the Old Port. Now, the heart of the ultramodern town stands side by side with the ancient remains which are the evidence of a history going back to about 600 BC. This former gateway to the E. is now a large metropolis which takes pride in being the Europort of the S. The city is also proud of its underground train system and its artificial beaches, but above all the city is proud of its long past. The history of Marseille began with the Phocaeans who landed in a vast sheltered creek—the Vieux Port of today. They founded an important port and commercial centre as a base for their conquest of Gaul. *Massalia*, as it was then, became prosperous and in the 2C BC it was encircled by ramparts to defend it against Celtic-Ligurian tribes. Even Julius Caesar was unable to attack the city head on and starved the inhabitants out in order to capture it. It became Christian and remained independent of central Merovingian and Carolingian government, being ruled instead by bishops and counts. It only reverted to France at the end of the

Marseille 1 Notre-Dame-de-la-Garde **2** cathedral of Notre-Dame-de-la-Major **3** old cathedral **4** Vieille Charité **5** Hôtel de Ville **6** basilica of Saint-Victor **7** Fort Saint-Jean **8** Fort Saint-Nicolas **9** Musée des Beaux-Arts **10** Muséum d'Histoire Naturelle **11** Musée Grobet-Labadié **12** Château Borély, Musée Archéologique, Musée Lapidaire **13** Musée Cantini **14** Musée des Docks Romains **15** Musée du Vieux Marseille **16** Musée de la Marine (Bourse) **17** Château d'If

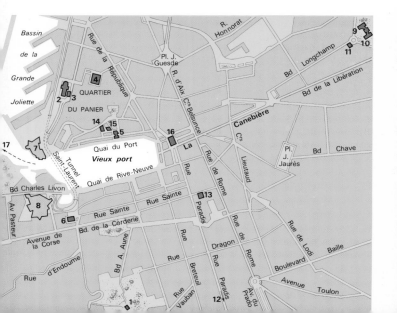

15C after King René died. Louis XIV built forts to protect the town which expanded its naval activity. The Great Plague in 1720 checked this expansion. During the Revolution, the city's extremists sang a propaganda hymn written by Rouget de l'Isle—the *Chant de Guerre aux Armées de Frontière*, which was later rechristened the *Marseillaise*. Marseille, almost ruined when the Empire collapsed, recovered and revived with colonization and the advent of the Suez Canal. In the last war it suffered a great deal of bombing and one of its old quarters was completely flattened by the Germans. The town of Marius and of the tellers of tall stories has preserved its picturesque Mediterranean charm, but has had to fight for survival. When decolonization occurred and the city lost its markets, it became the S. counterpart of Rotterdam and as an industrialized town had to struggle to survive the economic crises of the 70s.

The city is well situated around the colourful old port and famous *Canebière*, whose name comes from 'chénevière' (hemp-field), and recalls a former hemp-rope industry. The town, which is quite extensive, stretches along the cliffs and the corniche above the sparkling Mediterranean. Vieux Marseille, greatly damaged in the war, huddles above the port around the Cathedral and the Major and the Vieille Charité. A golden statue of the 'Bonne Mère' overlooks the town—a Madonna on the bell tower of the large church of *Notre-Dame-de-la-Garde*. This 19C Romanesque-Byzantine building is clad in marble and commands a wide view of Marseille, whose symbol it has become.

Cathedral and Major: The vast, cold Cathedral, built in the last century, dominates the old Major, which was partly knocked down to make way for it. (In fact, only vigorous protests prevented its total destruction.) Dating from the 11C, rebuilt in the 12C and subsequently modified, Notre-Dame-de-la-Major is much more interesting inside than out. It has a large nave and ample octagonal dome on pendentives, a lofty transept, and an apse with blind arcades. In spite of extensive damage this former Cathedral is still a fine example of Provençal Romanesque art.

Vieille Charité and the Quartier du Panier: Near the Cathedral above the docks of the Joliette and the Vieux Port is the picturesque and rather dilapidated quarter known as Panier, which recalls old Marseille with its little streets lined with tall houses and its passageways. The **Vieille Charité**, a 17C masterpiece by Pierre Puget, has been restored. At the centre of the building there is an elliptical chapel.

The baroque *Hôtel de Ville* is a remnant of historic Marseille and faces the Vieux Port. It has been partly rebuilt, but dates from the mid 17C, the work of Gaspard Puget, the brother of the architect who built the Charité.

Basilica of Saint Victor: This former church of a once-powerful abbey dominates the Vieux Port with its forts of Saint-Jean and Saint-Nicolas. The abbey became Benedictine in the 9C and had possessions as far away as Spain and Syria. It is dedicated to a Roman officer martyred in the 3C for his faith. The basilica consists of a tall bare 13C and 14C church and a maze of deep crypts, a dark and mysterious world, parts of which go back to the 5C. The striking 'catacombs' date from various periods and were altered in the Middle Ages, thus making it difficult for archaeologists to be exact about them. They are very complicated in conception and include a vast atrium (formerly in the open air) and various chapels. A passage joins them to the little cave of Saint Vic-

Marseille, Notre-Dame-de-la-Garde

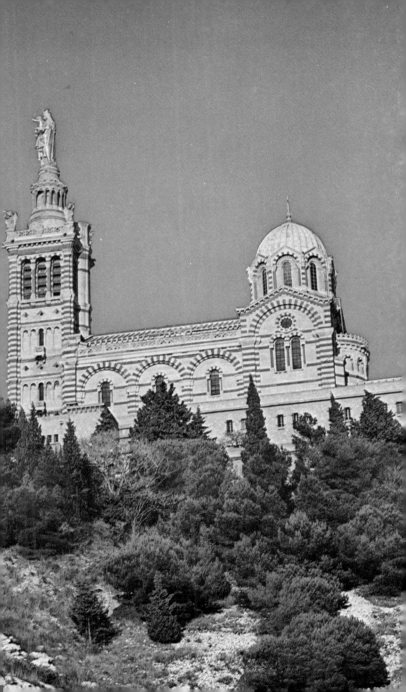

Marseille, 'The Port in 1754' by Joseph Vernet (Musée de la Marine, Paris)

tor, where the martyr is said to be buried. There are several sarcophagi in the crypts (2C or 3–5C), the remains of a mosaic and wall painting, many pieces of masonry, and a painted walnut Black Virgin dating from the 13C or 14C. The church was fortified in the 14C but retained the sober 12C porch containing a carved sarcophagus and some reliquaries.

Museums: Marseille has some of the most important musuems in France. They are rich and varied, with exhibits ranging from pre-history to more modern periods.

Musée des Beaux Arts: This was re-opened in 1980 after major alterations. It occupies one wing of the 19C Palais de Longchamp and contains Flemish works (Rubens), Italian (Perugino, Bassano) and French (Philippe de Champaigne, Vouet,

Largillière, Chardin) as well as works by Provençal artists. There are original works by the Marseille architect, sculptor and painter Pierre Puget (1620–1694) and some copies. There are also two compositions by Puvis de Chavannes, which were inspired by Marseille, as well as 19C and early 20C paintings and a beautiful series by Daumier.

Muséum d'Histoire Naturelle: This museum occupies the other wing of the Palais de Longchamp and specializes in Provençal flora and fauna. There is an aquarium in the basement and an interesting zoo near the Palais.

Musée Grobet-Labadié (140 Blvd. de Longchamp): This house was furnished and decorated by an art lover in the early 20C. There are medieval paintings and

Marseille, the Fort Saint-Jean

sculpture, Renaissance works, tapestries from the 16–18C, iron-work and paintings by Murillo, Daubigny and Greuze.

Château Borély, Musée Archéologique, Musée Lapidaire (Parc Borély): This château is a large luxurious 18C house which retains the name of its first owners. It contains important Mediterranean antiquities (particularly from Egypt), hundreds of classical ceramics and a superb gift from Feuillet de Borsat, consisting mainly of French 18C drawings. The Musée Lapidaire, in the outbuildings, has objects found in land and marine archaeological investigations.

Musée Cantini (19 Rue de Grignan): This pleasant museum, accommodated in a 17C house, features Marseille and Provence faience (rare 17&18C pieces).

However, it is also as up to date as the Pompidou Centre in its collection of contemporary works by Vieira da Silva, Arman, Raysse and César.

Musée des Docks Romains (28 Place Vivaux): Remains of Roman docks were found on the site of a modern block of flats before the quarter was rebuilt. They include enormous earthenware jars (*dolia*) which were used as silos, pottery, and remains of ancient boats.

Musée du Vieux Marseille (Rue de la Prison): This museum occupies a 16C house whose façade is decorated with diamond shapes. On display are fine Provençal furniture, old cribs and carved wooden figures, paintings, engravings and exhibits concerned with the making of playing cards.

Musée de la Marine (Bourse): This pleasant modern museum is devoted to the city's long maritime tradition, covering the development of navigation from the Phocaean period. There are numerous models.

Off Marseille on an arid little island lies the 16C fort/prison which Alexandre Dumas used for the imprisonment of his famous character, the Count of Monte Cristo.

Martainville (château)
76 Seine-Maritime   p.410☐H 3/4

The stone and brick château makes an attractive group with its outbuildings and pigeon loft and reflects the wealth of the rich merchant who built it (1485–1510). Modified and restored in the 17C, its kitchen with a Gothic fireplace, halls and bedrooms have now been turned into the *Musée Folklorique de Haute Normandie*, which shows pottery, household utensils,

objects from daily life, glassware and old furniture.

Environs: Ry (9 km. NW): This peaceful village in the Crevon valley is dominated by a *church* from the 12&16C, which has a surprising carved wooden Renaissance porch with Italianate decoration and superb woodcarving. However, the fame of Ry is largely literary and Flaubert specialists agree that it was the model for Yonville l'Abbaye in *Madame Bovary* and that it was here that the author met the models for Emma and M. Homais.

Château de Vascoeuil (3 km. SE of Ry): The historian Jules Michelet lived and wrote in this sturdy manor house, which dates from the 14–16C and has a park and gardens in the French style; today the house is full of his memorabilia. A large dovecot stands in front of the house.

Martel   (1,560 inhab.)
46 Lot   p.419☐H 12

Martel, the church of St-Maur

This medieval-looking village is said to have been founded on the causse (limestone plateau) by Charles Martel in the 8C and, indeed, his emblem—three hammers (martels)—appears on the village's coat-of-arms. However, the village seems to be unconnected with the Frankish conqueror of the Saracens for it appears only to have existed since the 11C. The *church of Saint Maur*, dominated by the tall bell tower with a 16C upper part, was itself only built in the early 14C. In the porch there is the tympanum from an earlier Romanesque sanctuary. The glass in the trefoil bays of the choir dates from the 16C. Martel is set around the 18C market buildings and the large *Hôtel de Raymondie*, dominated by a belfry-tower was built *c.* 1280–1330. There are towers overlooking the many historic houses in the village.

Maubeuge (35,480 inhab.)
59 Nord p.411 □ K 2

This industrial town in the Sambre valley
was burnt down in 1940, but has been
tastefully rebuilt since. The modern buildings are harmonious and welcoming. The
modern façade of the church of *Saints-
Pierre-et-Paul* is decorated with a mosaic inspired by Lurçat. The majestic *Porte de
Mons* has survived—three arches beneath
a decorated façade (1685)—and also the baroque Jesuit College chapel (17C).There is
a zoological garden beside Vauban's fortified town wall. The brick and stone buildings of the 18C Chapitre des Chanoinesses
house a *museum*. Original works by Jan
Gossaert, popularly known as Mabuse and
one of the masters of the Flemish school
who was born at Maubeuge in the 15C, are
unfortunately not on show here, but there
are some paintings by Van Dyck and Coypel. There are also interesting local historical documents.

Environs: To the N. of Maubeuge is the
Avesnois, a park-like landscape of water,
woods and valleys.

Avesnes sur Helpe (18 km. S.): The capital of the 'Little Switzerland of the North'.
It is a picturesque old town with steep
streets and tall slate roofs. Among the
town's outstanding features are the 18C
classical Hôtel de Ville in blue stone, the
collegiate church of Saint- Nicolas (1535), a
lovely piece of Gothic work topped by a
sturdy bell-tower-porch. **Solre le
Château** (18 km. SE): The square in this
quiet village is remarkable architecturally.
The pretty brick former market buildings
with arches (1574) now house the town
hall. The early-16C *church*, which is set
back a little, has a very strange bell-tower-
porch which is solid and square with a
beautiful leaning spire of mauve slate and
an amusing onion dome. Inside, the

church has interesting furnishings and
there is some 16C stained glass. **Sars-
Poteries** (17 km. E): The exciting *Musée
de Verre* features 'bousillés' or multi-
coloured glass objects in baroque shapes
(lamps, glasses, etc.) which the old glass-
makers made in their spare time.
Ramousies (28 km. SE): The church is
extraordinarily rich and contains a splendid 16C altarpiece.

Mauléon-Licharre (4,490 inhab.)
64 Pyrénées-Atlantiques p.422 □ E 15

This Basque town near Béarn, the capital
of the Soule area (a small region in the Sai-
son valley), has a few old houses and the
ruins of a château. The Hôtel d'Andurain
on the left bank of the Gave is almost lost
under its large Béarnais-style roof. This sober early-17C house has mullioned windows, four corner towers and grimacing
masks on the façade. The cemetery by the
river has a hexagonal chapel which was formerly the choir of a 15C church.

Gotein, the church

Environs: L'Hôpital Saint-Blaise (13 km. NE): This hospital dedicated to Saint Blaise lies on the edge of the Basque country, and was intended for pilgrims on their way to Compostela. A curious and elegant church dating from the 12C, strong Mudejar influence is still apparent. **Gotein** (3.5 km. S.): This 16C church with a canopied porch is dominated by a three-gabled bell tower, symbolizing the Trinity and typical of the region. **Church of Sainte-Engrâce** (33 km. SE): This isolated building is situated at the bottom of a valley, which ends in a cul-de-sac beneath a barely accessible Pyrenean pass. Romanesque, it has three vaulted aisles, interesting capitals and a fine 17C altarpiece.

Mauriac	(4,570 inhab.)
15 Cantal	p.419 □ I 11

Mauriac's black lava houses are grouped around one of the most important Romanesque monuments in the Haute Auvergene, the 12C *Basilica of Notre-Dame-des-*

Mauriac, porch of the basilica

Miracles. Two towers flank the W. façade with its fine portal; the tympanum depicting the Ascension is unfortunately damaged: it shows Christ in a mandorla flanked by two lively angels. The archivolt is decorated with signs of the zodiac and seasonal motifs. The carvings are uncharacteristic of the Auvergne and are probably the work of Languedoc sculptors. In the plain interior there are a few carved capitals. There is a fine 12C baptistery at the end of the S. side-aisle.

Mayenne	(13,500 inhab.)
53 Mayenne	p.413 □ F 6

Mayenne, built on the banks of the river of the same name, owes its existence to a medieval château which was the subject of many battles. Only the ramparts, towers and a residential building remain of this once-powerful fortress, which was rebuilt in the 15C. The town was badly damaged by bombing in 1944, but still has some 17&18C buildings; the Town Hall was built 1660–90. The *Church of Notre Dame*, which has a partly Romanesque façade, a Gothic nave and transept, 17C side-aisles and tower, was altered in the 19C. It has also been restored since the war. It contains a graceful 16C wooden statue of Notre Dame des Miracles.

Meaux	(43,110 inhab.)
77 Seine et Marne	p.411 □ J 4

Meaux came into being as an oppidum of the Meldois (Meaux) Gauls, and has retained the name. It is proud of having had the great Bossuet as bishop. Today the city is expanding, although it has retained its historic charm in the quarter around the cathedral, and in its ancient trees, canals, and quays, which follow the tight loop of the Marne. It has become industrialized and at the same time has remained an important agricultural centre; the Brie from here has been famous for centuries, and is one of the best cheeses in France.

Cathedral of Saint-Étienne: This was begun in the 12C and was essentially completed by the late 12/early 13C, although the finishing touches were not added until the 16C. It upholds the memory of the 'Eagle of Meaux', and its architecture shows the evolution of the Gothic style. Built in fragile limestone, the Flamboyant façade has had to be restored. There are two towers on either side of the façade, one, the slate-clad 'Tour Noire' is still incomplete. The left doorway (late 14C) features the life of Saint John the Baptist and the central one (13C) the Last Judgement; that on the right, which is also 13C, is dedicated to the Virgin. The Saint Étienne door on the right of the cathedral is an imitation of the doorway on the S. side of Notre Dame in Paris. Inside, the building is light and lofty (about 95 ft. to the vaulting). It contains

a 17C organ on a Flamboyant arch and also Bossuet's tomb, with a black marble plaque, in front of the choir stalls. The Porte Maugarni (15C) to the left of the choir is named after a bandit hanged there in 1372; this execution on consecrated ground caused a great scandal. The remains of an earlier building on this site were discovered underneath the choir.

Vieux Chapitre, former Bishop's Palace: The Vieux Chapitre (chapterhouse) is a pretty 12C house where the canons lived. One of its rooms communicating with the Cathedral by means of a charming passageway, is used as a sacristy. The former Bishop's Palace also has ancient origins but was greatly altered in the 17C. It contains the *Musée Bossuet*, which houses a varied collection (prehistory, local history, paintings and 17C pharmaceutical jars). The garden where Bossuet liked to walk was designed by Le Nôtre and overlooks the former ramparts which incorporate fragments of the Gallo-Roman wall. Bossuet's 'study' is hidden away at the back.

Meaux, tympanum of the left portal of the cathedral's W. front

Meillant (660 inhab.)
18 Cher p.420☐J 8

The present château, which is elegant, light and sumptuous, dates from the end of the 15C and the beginning of the 16C. It was built by Charles I and Charles II d'Amboise and Cardinal Georges d'Amboise supervized the building work. To the W. it looks medieval, while the façade and the Tour du Lion are Flamboyant with a strong early Renaissance influence. The château, a mass of turrets and tall rooftops, has a vast arms room called the Salle des Cerfs and also luxuriously furnished state rooms. A lovely chapel in the courtyard has an early-16C Rhenish altarpiece.

Environs: Saint-Amand-Montrond (9 km. S.): The *church of Saint-Amand* is a 12C Romanesque building, whose side chapels were added from the mid 15C. It has interesting capitals, some of which are decorated. The former Hôtel Saint-Vic contains a small museum. See **Noirlac.**

Melle (4,730 inhab.)
79 Deux-Sèvres p.418☐F 9

Melle, the Roman town of *Metullum*, was chosen as the location of the Carolingian mint because of its proximity to argentiferous lead mines. It also has a wealth of Roman remains. In the Middle Ages it was the second most important stage after Poitiers on the pilgrimage route to Santiago de Compostela, which perhaps explains the presence of so many admirable buildings in a limited area.

Church of Saint-Hilaire: This 12C church has a fine apse of several storeys and is dominated by a tall square bell tower with little columns. The N. doorway is beautifully designed and above it in an arched recess there is one of the 'Poitiers horsemen' which appear on some churches in the area and cause so much argument. (Today it is thought that they show the Emperor Constantine riding rough-shod over paganism.) The massive, sober main fa-

Meillant, the château

çade is one of the finest designs in Haut-Poitou. The nave is barrel vaulted and has fine columns with decorated capitals (a particularly interesting capital shows a boar hunt). The inner doorway in the right side-aisle is of interest for the decoration of Christ surrounded by apostles and saints on the archivolts.

Saint-Pierre: This 12C church is beautifully proportioned and is situated on a tree-lined terrace at the northernmost point of the town. Built in the local yellow limestone, it has an imposing but sober interior with an interesting series of capitals and very ornate exterior decoration. As with Saint-Hilaire the greatest effort has been made with the side doorway, which is the one most clearly visible.

Saint-Savinien: This is the simplest church in Melle. It is 12C and was first the chapel of the château and then a collegiate church; 1801-1926 it was used as a prison. The church has a single aisle and a fine E. doorway of a type unusual in

Poitu and reminiscent of Limousin architecture—columns support a moulded tympanum and a saddle-back lintel with a depiction of Christ in Majesty framed by two lions.

Environs: Celles-sur-Belle (7km NW): The *Church of Notre-Dame* was destroyed by Protestants in the 16C, and rebuilt in 15C style. The interesting and curious Romanesque doorway, which opens into the narthex, was part of the first abbey-church; it has a series of many-lobed archivolts which show an oriental influence.

Melun	(39,800 inhab.)
77 Seine-et-Marne	p.411 □ J 5

Melun is one of the two capitals of Brie —the other is Meaux—and an important commercial centre. Like Paris the town grew from a settlement on an island in the Seine and the old but rapidly expanding town has Gallo-Roman origins. The Cape-

Melle, capital in the church of St-Pierre

tian kings had a residence here. The *Church of Saint-Aspais* dates from the first half of the 16C but still has Gothic elements. A medallion in the apse recalls Melun's liberation by Joan of Arc in 1430. The Hôtel de Ville nearby is housed in a Renaissance residence which was extended on the left side in the 19C. There is a statue of the Humanist Bishop Amyot (born in Melun in 1513) in the courtyard. The *Church of Notre-Dame* was built on the island in the Seine in the first third of the 11C and has been very much altered since (the vaulted nave is Gothic, the façade Renaissance). It contains *Descent from the Cross* by Jordaens and *Moses Saved from the Waters* attributed to Primaticcio. The suburb of **Dammarie-les-Lys** has the ruins of the Abbey of Lys, a Cistercian establishment founded in the 13C.

Menars	(470 inhab.)
41 Loir et Cher	p.414☐H 7

In 1760 Madame de Pompadour, Louis XV's famous mistress, bought the domaine of Menars and asked Jacques Ange Gabriel to finish the château begun more than a century earlier. The Marquise died in April 1764 just when the ground-floor decoration had been finished. Menars passed to her brother the Marquis de Marigny and he called on Soufflot, the architect of the Panthéon. He finished the building to Gabriel's plans and placed some charming little edifices in the fine gardens overlooking the Loire. The château was damaged in the Revolution but has been well restored and the interior decoration in 18C style is very fine.

Mende	(11,980 inhab.)
48 Lozère	p.424☐K 12

This town is caught between the bleak moors of Mende and the Lot, and has old granite houses, which indicate the circular line of its medieval town wall. The Tour des Pénitents is all that is remains of the former ramparts. The 14C Notre-Dame bridge spans the Lot with wide arches.

Cathedral: This surprisingly large church is one of the biggest Gothic buildings in the S. The porch was rebuilt in 1900 and the façade has two towers, of which the more ornate is called the bishops' bell tower; it is 16C and about 270 ft. high. The fine 17C rose window in the façade was created by an architect who worked at both Auch and Albi. The furnishings are almost all 17C and extraordinarily lavish. They include carved choir stalls, a series of Aubusson tapestries, and a remarkable organ-chest. The apsidal chapel has a 12C Black Virgin probably brought back from the Holy Land after the Crusades. The Cathedral once had a huge bell weighing 20 tons which was removed and melted down by the Protestants, and now only the clapper is left; this is more

Melun, church of Notre-Dame

than 6 ft. high and can be seen on the left of the entrance.

The *Musée Ignon-Fabre* deals with prehistory, the Gallo-Roman period and Lozère folklore.

Menton	(25,320 inhab.)
06 Alpes-Maritimes	p.426☐P 14

Menton, standing on the steep cliffs and flowered hills of the Côte d'Azur, overlooks an attractive bay near the Italian border. The picturesque old town on several levels clusters around the narrow *Rue Longue*, which is lined with 16&17C houses. The charming little *Place Saint-Michel* has two churches facing each other; *Saint-Michel* is 17C and has lavish decoration and a fine baroque façade. The *Chapelle des Pénitents-Blancs* contains a wealth of 18C statuary. The *Musée Jean Cocteau* was arranged as the poet and painter wished it to be in an old harbour bastion and contains many of his works. The *Jardin des Colombières* is

an aesthete's park; it was designed by Ferdinand Bac, an imaginative landscape painter who was very fond of the area.

Environs: The cliff villages of **Saint Agnes, Gorbio** and **Castellar** have very pretty streets, covered passageways and remains of châteaux.

Méry-Sur-Oise	(4,710 inhab.)
95 Val-d'Oise	p.410☐I 4

Méry is very close to the new town of Cergy-Pontoise. It has a 15&16C church and a sumptuous château, which was rebuilt in the 18C and is surrounded by a large park; Buffon advised on the design of the park.

Environs: Abbaye du Val (4km SE): the ruins of this large Cistercian abbey are on the edge of the forest of l'Isle Adam, in private property. It was partly pulled down in the last century (12,13&17C buildings). Near the convent is a 15C wash-house.

Mende, stalls in the cathedral

Mesnières-en-Bray	(630 inhab.)
76 Seine-Maritime	p.410☐H 3

The spacious Renaissance château of Mesnières is similar to the one at Écouen. It has massive towers with purely ornamental machicolation for it is a house, not a fortress. Built in the 15C, it was originally arranged around a square, but the gallery which closed the square was demolished in the 18C.

Environs: Neufchâtel-en-Bray (6 km. SE): This little town suffered heavily in the last war when its picturesque wooden houses were completely destroyed. Now it looks quite modern; the theatre is a modern building by Paul Auzelle, and the Hôtel de Ville is decorated with a huge female head sculpted by Calka in 1954. The church was damaged in 1940 and partly rebuilt, but the 13C choir and 16C nave have survived. There is a polychrome stone Saint Sépulcre dating from 1491.

Metz	(117,200 inhab.)
57 Moselle	p.417☐N 4

Metz has a pleasant setting at the confluence of the Seille and the Moselle. The city has a very long past, many reminders of which survive. The old city, a seat of civilization from the 6C onwards, has been a capital city for a long time. Its location near the Franco-German border has meant much hardship: sieges and battles have caused great destruction. Now, as one of the major towns in Lorraine, which is in the heart of a depressed industrial area, it is faced with the problems of industrial redevelopment. Verlaine was born here in 1844

Cathedral of Saint Étienne: This strange church came into being in the 13C when two adjacent churches, facing in different directions but sharing a vault, were joined together. The present chapel of Notre-Dame is the former choir of Notre-Dame-de-la-Ronde, whose doorway on the left is distinguished by its carved draperies and fantastic little figures. Despite its mixed origins and the additions over the centuries (the nave is 13&14C, the transept 15C and the choir early 16C) and despite the ravages of the Revolution, the building presents an appearance of overall harmony.

EXTERIOR: This beautiful piece of architecture is impressive for the quality and balance of its side façades, each flanked by a tower. The chapterhouse tower on the left, and the parish belfry, called the Tour de Mutte, are arranged in perfect symmetry.

INTERIOR: The interior is astonishingly bright. The choir is raised and the transept has many windows and beautiful stellar vaulting. The nave is a gem of Gothic art, whose vaulting is up to 130 ft. high, making this one of the tallest naves in France —the height is emphasised by the low side-aisles and the strikingly large windows. Above the triforium a carved frieze of drapery and leaves runs right round the building, and everywhere the stone gleams in the light from the windows (which cover a total area of about 23,000 square ft.). Master glassmakers from the 13 – 20C created this 'Lanterne du Bon Dieu'; some of these are anonymous, some are known: Herman von Munster (14C), Valentin Bousch (16C), and nearer to our time, Villon, Bissière and Chagall. The furnishings are not lavish, but there are a few remarkable pieces: an ancient porphyry vat, a marble bishop's throne from the Merovingian period and a little 16C organ. The crypt has a fine 16C polychrome *Entombment* and in the sacristy there is Saint Arnulf's gold ring and a 12C purple cope

Metz, cathedral, glass by Chagall ▷

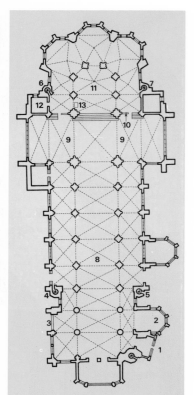

Metz - cathedral of Saint-Étienne 1 Entrance
(portal of the Virgin) **2** Chapelle Notre-Dame **3**
portal of Notre-Dame de la Ronde **4** tower of the
chapter **5** city belfry known as the Tour de Mutte
6 Tourelle de la Boule d'Or **7** Tourelle de
Charlemagne **8** nave **9** transept **10** crypt **11** choir
12 sacristy **13** bishop's throne

with gold embroidery which belonged to
Charlemagne.

Other religious buildings: Metz has
been a major bishopric since the 9C and
a number of churches remain. *Saint-Pierre-
aux-Nonnains,* the most famous, is supposed to be the oldest in France. A Roman
basilica in the 4C, it was rebuilt in the 7C

and has deteriorated since then. Only the
nave with its high arches remains. Nearby
are the ruins of a building thought to have
contained the baths. The unusual late-
12/early-13C *Chapelle des Templiers* has an
octagonal nave opening on to a square choir
with a half-domed apse. The former abbey
church of *Saint Vincent* was begun in the
13C and finished in the 18C, when a particularly massive façade was added. The
Gothic nave with three aisles is beautifully
proportioned. The elegant Gothic church
of *Saint Martin*, built in the 13C on a
Gallo-Roman wall, is a building of contrasts: the narthex is low and dark but the
nave is tall and slender with an extremely
light 16C choir. *Saint Eucaire* is an attractive and unusual mixture of styles dating
from the 12&15C; it is half Romanesque
(superb square bell tower) and half Gothic
(rib-vaulted side chapels). *Saint Maximin*
is 12&18C and has a vigorous baroque
doorway. *Saint Clément* from the 17&18C
has a nave with three aisles. The church
of *Saint Thérèse de l'Enfant Jésus* has some
lovely stained-glass windows which lighten
its post-war concrete.

Military architecture: The Tour
Camoufle (15C) is a relic of the old fortifications. The famous *Porte des Allemands*
dates from the 13&15C and is like a little
fortified château: the two openings are each
flanked by two towers and joined by an
arched gallery over the Seille.

Civil architecture: The façade of the
magnificent *Hôtel de Saint-Livier*, part of
which is 12C, has two watch towers at either end of a crenellated wall. Its inner
courtyard has a Renaissance loggia and a
well. The strange *Grenier de Chevremont*
was built in 1457 to store the town's grain.
It is a high building with merlons, battlements and a heavy timber roof on massive
cylindrical columns. The large doorway in
the façade of the *Palais de Justice* (1778) has
trophies around it, and there is a fine

Metz, cathedral, portal of N.-D.

Metz, Musée Archéologique

wrought-iron stairwell. The old houses around the *Place Saint Louis*, some of which are 14C, were money-changers' shops. Opposite the cathedral is the *Place d'Armes* containing the Hôtel de Ville and the Corps de Garde. These are the work of Jacques François Blondel (1705–74), who favoured classical restraint and designed the square bearing in mind the rigour demanded by military architecture.

Musée: The former Petits-Carmes monastery houses the *Natural History Museum*, the *Beaux-Arts Museum* and the *Museum of Gallo-Roman Archaeology*. The latter occupies the remains of the Roman baths, an unusual setting which is well suited to the presentation of antique civilization in all its aspects: daily life, medicine navigation, etc. The Beaux-Arts museum has pictures from the great European schools of the 15–20C, including works by Rembrandt, Dürer, Van Dyck, Titian, Delacroix and Corot.

| **Millau** | (22,580 inhab.) |
| 12 Aveyron | p.424☐J 13 |

Millau, a busy town on the limestone plateau not far from Larzac, is situated in an area of gorges and caves at the point where the Tarn and the Dourbie converge. Since the Middle Ages it has been the capital of the leather glove industry. Despite the ups and downs of fashion and the economic climate, Millau is still a tawing and glove-making town; it has also added furniture making to these industries. In the past, as the ancient town of *Condatomag*, and in medieval times, its speciality was ceramics.

present-day Millau; its products were exported far and wide in the 1C.

Milly, Chapelle Saint-Blaise

Milly-la-Forêt (3,490 inhab.)
91 Essonne p.415☐J 5

Jean Cocteau lived in this ancient little town, which is right on the edge of the Forest of Fontainebleau, and died here in 1963. Its Gothic church is essentially 15C but retains some 12C elements. To the S. is the *chapel of Saint-Blaise-des-Simples*, which was originally Romanesque, but was decorated by Cocteau and now contains his tomb. Its name derives from the fact that many medicinal herbs ('simples') are grown in and around Milly.

The Gothic **belfry**, some 160 ft. high is a relic of the former Hôtel de Ville. Its square base is 12C and the octagonal upper part 17C. The pretty Place du Maréchal Foch with an empire-style fountain has retained its old arcades. On the W. side, locally known as 'le couvert', there is a barely legible inscription on one of the capitals, which reads: 'Be careful what you do'. All around the square there is a network of historic streets and courtyards.

The church of **Notre Dame** has Romanesque origins, was badly damaged in the Wars of Religion and rebuilt in the 17C.

In 1939 the apse was decorated with frescos by Jean Bernard. A 15C mill on two arches over the Tarn now houses a museum. You can see pottery made in the Gallo-Roman workshop of Graufesenque, which is near

Mirepoix (3,860 inhab.)
09 Ariège p.423☐I 15

This 13C bastide, a bishopric until the Revolution, is arranged in classical style around a central square with arcades, surrounded by timber-framed houses. The *former Cathedral*, begun in the 14C, was not finished until the last century when the rib vaults were added. The fine bell tower and Gothic nave date from the beginning of the 16C.

Moissac (12,140 inhab.)
82 Tarn-et-Garonne p.423☐H 13

This quiet Gascon town among vines and orchards is an important centre of Romanesque art. It has a surprisingly beautiful abbey church with a glorious carved doorway, and cloisters.

Abbey church: This important church

Moissac, cloister of the abbey church

Moissac, detail of the S. portal

dates from the very early 11C but was partly rebuilt in the 15C after the domes in the nave collapsed. The bell-tower-porch remained standing, and seems to have been built *c.*1120. The massive carved doorway shows some Byzantine influence, but principally it demonstrates the great originality of the workshop of 'ymagiers', whose style was subsequently much copied. A timeless, majestic figure of Christ dominates the tympanum; he is surrounded by symbols of the Apocalypse. On the lintel are rosettes, and on the pier interlaced lions, St. Paul (to the left) and St. Jeremiah. St. Peter and Isaiah appear as statues on the jambs, and the entire doorway is decorated with a wide range of sculpture (braids, palm leaves, beasts and scenes of the chase). The central section undoubtedly dates from before 1115 and the carving on the side (the Virgin and the

Childhood of Christ) was added later, some time before 1130. On the left are depictions of the sins of the flesh and of the spirit. The two statues on the tops of the columns at the edge of the porch are of the Abbé Roger (superior of the abbey when the decoration was finished) and on the left either Saint Benoît or another abbot of Moissac. The massive narthex was finished in the 11C and is decorated with carved capitals (leaves, wild beasts), and a scene of the taming of a lion. After this amazing architectural ensemble the rest of the church in its plain southern style is a slight anticlimax. However, it contains a 15C Pietà and Flight from Egypt, an Entombment in painted wood (from the funerary monument of an abbot who died in 1485) and above the altar a wonderful 12C Christ on the Cross. The choir grille is 16C and the choir stalls 17C.

Moissac, arcaded walk of the abbey church's cloister

Cloisters: One of the most beautiful products of the Romanesque period; it was consecrated in 1100. The spacious close is framed by long walks with wooden ceilings. There are statues of the apostles on the corner pillars. The restored capitals are Romanesque (flowers, beasts, scenes from the Old and New Testaments); the Gothic arches were rebuilt in the 13C. There are fragments of sculpture in the cloister chapels and a history of the influence of Moissac, particularly in Quercy.

Abbot's Palace and Musée Moissageais: The former Abbot's Palace is a huge, originally medieval, building. Two chapels survive; one is Romanesque and the other Gothic with a Louis XIII stairwell. The palace houses a museum of art and folklore (ceramics, costume, everyday objects, tools, ironwork).

Vieux Moissac: Even though it is outshone by its abbey church the town of Moissac is none the less quite interesting. There are some old houses (17&18C) near the former monastery. The *church of Saint Martin*, on the site of a Gallo-Roman villa, goes back to the 7C, but has been altered and restored. It contains some 15C murals.

Monaco	(24,600 inhab.)
Principauté de Monaco	p.426□P 14

The little sovereign state on the Côte d'Azur is completely independent of France. Its tall modern buildings are perched rather perilously above the port and strips of land reclaimed from the sea. The enclave, once under the sovereignty

Monaco, the rock and Monte-Carlo

of the Republic of Genoa, was fought over by the Guelphs (supporting the Pope) and the Ghibellines (supporting the Emperor). In the end the Grimaldi family gained possession of the citadel and of the 'Rocher', and managed to maintain its autonomy, except for a brief period from 1793–1814 when it was attached to France. However, the Grimaldis surrendered Menton and Roquebrune to France as their inhabitants voted for this by a very large majority. At the end of the 19C Monaco became the world capital of gambling.

Vieux Monaco: This is on the 'Rocher', a large promontory, and has a mass of narrow streets with brightly coloured façades. The Prince's Palace is a huge building incorporating some 13&14C remains of the Grimaldi fortress. There are also 15,16&17C buildings. The large state rooms are full of paintings: Holbein, Breughel the Elder, Philippe de Champaigne, Jean-Baptiste Van Loo and Bonnat. The 19C cathedral contains a lovely altarpiece painted in 1500 by Louis Bréa of Nice.

Musée Océanographique: In the Avenue Saint-Martin, this vast building has a cold and monumental majesty. The oceanographer-prince Albert built it at the beginning of the century, and apart from its famous aquarium it also has wide-ranging oceanographic collections.

Monte-Carlo: This is the modern part of Monaco, on the Spélugues plateau. The lavish Grand Casino was built in 1878–9 by Charles Garnier, the architect of the Paris Opéra.

Monastier-Sur-Gazeille (1,970 inhab.)
43 Haute-Loire p.420□K 12

A plaque here commemorates the visit in
the 19C of the English romantic writer
R.L. Stevenson, who chose Monastier as
the starting point for his 'Travels with a
Donkey'. However, the village is known
mainly for its Benedictine monastery. This
is 11C, altered in the 15C, and its massive
abbey church is very striking for the variety of colours of its fabric, especially in the
main bay. Inside the Flamboyant choir,
rib-vaulted nave and Romanesque transept
blend very well. The treasures include a
very valuable reliquary bust.

Moncontour (1,150 inhab.)
22 Côtes-du-Nord p.412□C 5

This little town, perched on a spur of land
where two valleys meet, figures large in
Brittany's military history. Its defences
were largely dismantled under Louis XIII,
but parts survive. The *church of Saint
Mathurin* near some half-timbered and
18C houses is especially interesting for its
interior decoration. Six 16C stained-glass
windows in the nave and choir depict the
lives of Jesus, Saint Mathurin and Saint
Yves. There are several altars, 17&18C
paintings and woodwork, and a silver reliquary of Saint Mathurin in the sanctuary
(he was famed for curing the mentally ill.)

**Environs: Chapel of Notre-Dame-du-
Haut** (3 km. SE): Just outside the village
of Trédaniel, this little chapel contains an
astonishing number of polychrome
wooden statues of healing saints. For many
years these played the part of doctors. Saint
Lubin was prayed to for rheumatism, Saint
Mamert (with his entrails showing) for
colic, Saint Yvertin for migraine and so on.
Château de la Toche-Tréby (5km E.):

This was built in the 16C but looks medieval. It is arranged around a square in the
classical manner (main wing with two
wings at right-angles and domed turrets).
Two towers protect the entrance with its
double doors—one for pedestrians, one for
carriages. The main courtyard has an elegant well.
Abbaye de Boquen: Founded by Cistercians in 1137, this abbey prospered until
the 15C. There are still a few fine capitals
from this period in the cloisters; the chapterhouse with its twin bays is 13C and the
choir and transept of the abbey church are
12C. In a restored chapel there is a pretty
13C wooden Virgin.

Mondoubleau (1,820 inhab.)
41 Loir-et-Cher p.414□H 7

This large hillside village has some old
houses. The fortress established at the end
of the 10C is in ruins, but it is still impressive. Its round keep, nicknamed the 'butter pot' is 115 ft. high and leans
dangerously.

Environs: Château de Saint-Agil:
(7.5km NE): This château, in a vast park,
is surrounded by moats. It was extensively
altered in the 18C; the entrance pavilion
dates from the 16C. There are some 16C
stained-glass windows in a chapel of the
church of the same period.

Monpazier (560 inhab.)
24 Dordogne p.423□G/H 12

The fortress here is typical of those established by the English at the end of the 13C.
It centres on a large harmonious square and
is regular in design, although the arches are
all different. The straight streets cross each
other at right angles. The grey and ochre

church, built at the same time as the fortress itself, was altered in the 15&16C.

Environs: Château de Biron (7 km. S.): The château dominates the village and commands a fine view of the region. Built from the 12–17C, it is now in need of restoration. It was once the fortress of an important family, the Biron-Gontauts, and has a fine 16C Renaissance chapel.

Montaigne (château)
24 Dordogne   p.418☐F 12

This château on the edge of the Périgord was the refuge of Michel de Montaigne. He was born here in 1553, lived here between two journeys and spent the last years of his life here (dying in 1592). In the last century the place was ravaged by fire, but the isolated tower by the entrance escaped; the author of the *Essais* had his bedroom, private chapel and library in this tower.

Montargis
45 Loiret   (19,870 inhab.)   p.415☐J 6

Rather exaggeratedly called 'The Venice of the Gâtinais', the town's flower-covered façades extend along the branches of the Loing. It is the sous-préfecture of the Loiret and very picturesque in places, with a few old houses and a mixture of lively and quiet streets around the *church of la Madeleine*. This church was badly damaged by fire in 1525 and has been much restored. The 12C nave survives and a fine choir by Jacques Androuet du Cerceau was added in the late 16/early 17C. The spire of the bell tower is by Viollet-le-Duc. Imposing walls and some 15C Romanesque elements remain from the former château. In the garden of the Hôtel de Ville the fine Gothic façade of an old house has been rebuilt.

Montargis, the church of the Madeleine

Environs: Ferrières-en-Gâtinais (13 km. NE): This little town by a peaceful river is full of steep, winding streets. The church of *Saint-Pierre et Saint-Paul* dates from the second half of the 12C and the 13C (the transept with dome is unusual). The old chapel of Notre Dame de Bethléem is hidden behind a screen of chestnut trees and contains a Grand Siècle altarpiece.

Montauban
82 Tarn-et-Garonne   (50,420 inhab.)   p.423☐H 13

This lively town on a loop of the Tarn is dominated by the pink of its brick buildings. The *Pont Vieux* is 13C and was once fortified; from it there is a fine view of the town, a former fortress and Protestant

Montauban, the Pont-Vieux (13C)

stronghold, whose defences were dismantled after it resisted Louis XIII's troops. It has some industry and commerce, and many fairs and 'braderies' (annual street markets involving the whole town). There are several 17&18C houses, especially in the Rue de la République and the Rue de la Résistance.

Place Nationale: This is isolated in the heart of the town, and rather enclosed, opening on to the narrow streets around it at the corners alone. In pink brick, it has an Italian look about it. On market days it is very lively, but as a general rule it is spoiled by parked cars. It is remarkable none the less, with its double-vaulted galleries and harmonious three-storeyed brick houses. Its severity is due to the fact that it was rebuilt after a fire, the work was completed at the beginning of the 18C.

Cathedral: This dominates the upper town. It is a cold, majestic, rather soulless classical building dating from the late 17/early 18C. In contrast to the brick everywhere else, it is white, and is the work of Robert de Cotte and François d'Orbay. It contains *Le Voeu de Louis XIII*, a painting by Ingres.

Palais Épiscopal et Musée Ingres: The former Bishop's Palace is a large 17C building dominating the Pont Vieux and the Tarn, and inside is the well-designed Musée Ingres (the painter was born in Montauban in 1780). In the basement rooms, which include the Salle du Prince Noir (14C, a relic of an English château), there are collections on local archaeology and medieval works: mosaics, bronzes and Gallo-Roman objects, funerary stones, capitals and sculpture. The first floor is devoted to Ingres and has paintings and numerous drawings. The museum also contains about 40 sculptures, drawings and watercolours by Antoine Bourdelle (born in Montauban in 1861), old masters (some of which came from Ingres' private collection) and modern works. Near the museum, at the end of the Pont Vieux, is the *Monument aux Morts de 1870*, a bronze by Bourdelle. The nearby *church of Saint Jacques* has a Toulouse-style brick bell tower (18C spire); the church itself is 13C, but has had major alterations over the years.

Montauban, works by Bourdelle

Montbard (7,750 inhab.)
21 Côte-d'Or p.415□L 7

This busy little industrial town was the birthplace of the Count of Buffon, the king's superintendent of gardens, and the author of the authoritative *Histoire Naturelle*. He was born in 1707, spent part of his life here and was buried here. He inherited the fief of Montbard and pulled down the old ducal château to make way for a park and trees. Of this building only a 13C watch tower and the tower where the naturalist installed his library remain.

Montbéliard (31,600 inhab.)
25 Doubs p.417□O 7

The enormous *château*, with two massive round towers (15&16C) with lanterns, dominates the prosperous industrial town. Inside there are archaeological and zoological collections, the latter in memory of Cuvier, who was born at Montbéliard in 1769. Until 1793 the town belonged to the House of Würtemberg, and there are some buildings by Schickhardt which look German. The Pavillon de l'Horloge is 17C and has a high roof with dormer windows and a typical scrolled gable. The Maison des Princes has a Renaissance façade on four floors. The *Temple Saint Martin*, early 17C, is one of the oldest Protestant churches in France and has a remarkable carved wooden coffered ceiling. The 16C market buildings are very attractive and the Hôtel de Ville, built in red sandstone, has an attractive balcony. The Hôtel Beurnier has interesting *Musée Historique* dealing with local art and tradition.

Montbenoit (180 inhab.)
25 Doubs p.421□N 8

An unpretentious village in an isolated picturesque valley with the ruins of an interesting abbey. The nave of the *church* is 12C; the choir and apse are 16C. Inside it is richly furnished and has a beautiful

Montbenoît, stalls in the church

marble recess and carved stalls. The carvings are remarkable, being highly symbolic and wonderfully imaginative. The 15C *cloister* has archaic sculpture.

Montbrison	(11,200 inhab.)
42 Loire	p.420□L 10/11

Old Montbrison, built on a volcanic outcrop at the foot of the Forez mountains, has numerous 15C houses with lovely Renaissance façades; there are also some 17&18C hôtels inside the ring of boulevards (which have replaced the old town walls). The *Hôtel de Ville* and the *Palais de Justice* occupy 18C hôtels.

Notre-Dame-d'Espérance: This is the most impressive monument in Montbri-

son. A former collegiate church founded in 1226 and only completed in the 15C, the building presents a unified appearance. Apart from one highly ornate doorway the 15C façade is extremely simple; it has a square bell tower at each side (the right one is unfinished). In form it is a primitive basilica (no transept or ambulatory) and its elegant choir (13C) is a fine example of Rayonnant Gothic. The church contains the tomb of Guy IV of Forez who founded the church.

Diana: Opposite the apse of *Notre Dame d'Espérance* is the lovely hall called the 'Diana', which was rebuilt in 1226 for the marriage of the Count of Forez. It is much restored and has a coffered wooden ceiling with 1,700 painted sections. Beside it is a little museum of sculpture (prehistory to the Renaissance). The *Musée de la Poupée* contains a magnificent collection of French and foreign dolls, complete with doll's clothes, furniture, etc.

Montbrun-les-Bains	(480 inhab.)
26 Drôme	p.425□M 13

This old village in the lavender growing region of Provence is situated on a sunny hillside; its modern part (the Bourgade) spreads down into the valley. The village has a medieval belfry and the remains of a 14C castle. Montbrun-les-Bains was well known in the past for its therapeutic spa waters.

Mont-de-Marsan	(30,170 inhab.)
40 Landes	p.422□F 13/14

This town in the Landes is situated at the point where the Douze and the Midou converge to form the larger river Midouze. It is a lively place with its Fêtes de la Madeleine, bullfights and Courses Landaises (a local form of corrida with young cows, which takes place in mid-July). On either side of the picturesque Rue des Arceaux there are 18C houses. All that remains of the 14C castle built by Gaston Phoebus is the *Donjon Lacataye*, which houses a *museum* devoted to two Montois sculptors, Charles Despiau (1874–1946) and Robert Wlérick (1882–1944).

Montélimar	(29,150 inhab.)
26 Drôme	p.425□L 12

Montélimar, the gateway to Provence and to the Tricastin region, is famous for its nougat. Known in Gallo-Roman times as *Accusium*, it then became *Montillium Adhemari* because of the Grignan noblemen,

Montbrison, the church of Notre-Dame

the Adhémars, who split the town in half and sold it to the Count of Valentinois and the Avignon Popes. This strange situation continued until the two 'quarters' both reverted to the French Crown and Montélimar became one town again. In August 1944 both the town and the surrounding area suffered severe damage.

Château: The fortress and mound date from the 12C (the great Tour de Narbonne) and the 14&15C. The S. part, or citadel, consists of a strong rectangular keep with Roman windows; the chapel contains 12C frescos.

In the Place Émile-Loubet stands the lovely early-16C house known as Diane de Poitiers' house (it belonged to her uncle). The church of *Sainte-Croix* in the town centre has a much restored apse, which is

Montford-l'Amaury, window in church

almost lost among the late-15C houses, and a 16C bell tower.

Environs: Rochemaure (5 km. W.): This Ardèche village is dominated by a remarkable ruined castle (13–16C) and the remains of a medieval hamlet. Stendhal adored the place. **Abbaye d'Aiguebelle** (17 km. SE): This heavily restored abbey on the Provence–Dauphiné border is a fine example of Cistercian architecture. St. Bernard visited it when it was just finished in 1147.

Montfort-l'Amaury   (2,500 inhab.)
78 Yvelines   p.410☐I 5

This appealing little town, dominated by the ruins of a demolished fortress, now finds itself in the middle of an area of 'résidence secondaire' (second homes). It was once ruled by powerful feudal lords. Victor Hugo and Ravel (who has a small museum devoted to him) are both associated with the place. The church of *Saint-Pierre* dating from the time of Louis XII, is Gothic and Renaissance in style and has some lovely 16C stained glass. The Flamboyant cemetery entrance leads to a late-16/early-17C charnel-house. There are a number of timber-framed houses in the town.

Environs: Pontchartrain (10 km. NE): The château, built in the 17C by François Mansart, is reflected in the waters of the river Mauldre and surounded by a lovely park.

Montgeoffroy (château)
49 Maine-et-Loire   p.413☐F 7

This graceful 18C château with twin towers and 16C chapel still has Ancien Régime furniture and décor inside. There are interesting works by Rigaud, Pourbus, Le Jeune and Van Loo in particular. In the saddlery there is a collection of whips and harnesses; old carriages are exhibited in the stables.

Montier-en-Der   (2,140 inhab.)
52 Haute-Marne   p.416☐L 5

Set amid forest and lakes, this large village has the remains of a Benedictine abbey founded in the 7C. Badly damaged in 1940, the former *abbey church* (with 10C nave) has now been restored to its original condition. The choir was finished in about 1220 and is a remarkable example of Champenois Gothic (the apse has four tiers). The rib vaulting in the apsidal chapel is particularly beautiful.

Montignac, wall painting in the cave of Lascaux

Montignac	(3,200 inhab.
25 Dordogne	p.419☐H 11

Montignac, at the start of the so-called 'Prehistoric Valley' of the Vézère, is a small town of considerable charm. The *quais* (streets along the river) are lined with old houses and in the past saw bustling activity. The famous *Grotte de Lascaux*, discovered in 1940 2 km. from the town, is a veritable museum of cave painting—219 yards of incredibly fresh and lively painting, some of which could be as old as 25,000 BC. These hundreds of brilliantly executed animal pictures were protected by a naturally deposited transparent film of calcite and by the pervading dryness of the atmosphere. When the cave was opened up and visitors poured in, there was a near-catastrophe for the fragile paintings began

mysteriously to deteriorate; thus Lascaux had to be closed to the public. The *Gisement de Régourdon*, a prehistoric burial place (now with a small museum) was discovered in 1950 on the side of a hill; a large number of bones of brown bears were also found — probably used for religious purposes.

Environs: Le Thot (7 km. SW): The *Centre d'Art Préhistorique du Thot* gives an introduction to prehistoric art (numerous explanatory notes, photographs and audio-visual material). It is built on a small hill about 2 km. from Thonac, where there also stands a modest church with a bellcote. The church has a Romanesque Madonna. Looking out over the Vézère, the 16C château of Thonac combines Renaissance elegance with medieval robustness. **Saint-Amand-de-Coly** (9 km. E.): This, the most unusual church in Périgord (12C with 13C alterations) is a magnificent, rather curious fortified building. Legend has it that the abbey was founded in the 7C by St. Amand. The church stands in lush, romantic countryside. In 1575 the Huguenots entrenched themselves here, and it took two thousand men with artillery nearly a week to dislodge them, during which time their attacks badly damaged the monastic buildings around the church. The W. front is untypical of the region, having a remarkably wide pointed arch framing the doorway, and a tall stained-glass window. (Beneath the window there is a place of refuge.) Inside the ground slopes sharply upwards to the choir. The church is sparsely decorated. It once had a cloister and other buildings, but now nothing remains of these.

Montlhéry	(4,240 inhab.)
91 Essonne	p.410□I 5

Montlhéry was once the fief of powerful

Montlhéry, the tower

lords. Now it is a centre of market gardening and tomato-growing and is the main place of interest in an area which, as one of the Parisian outer suburbs, has lost much of its character. The famous 13&14C *tower* was the keep of a heavily fortified castle (now completely ruined).

Environs: Longpont (2.5 km. NE): The church of *Notre-Dame* dates from the 12C (Romanesque nave) and the early 13C (the damaged doorway). Inside there are funeral slabs. **Linas:** (1 km. SE): The *church* is 13–16C and attracts fewer Parisians than the Linas-Montlhéry motor-racing track.

Mont-Louis	(440 inhab.)
66 Pyrénées-Orientales	p.423□I 16

Close to Font-Romeu, the Megève of the Pyrenees, Mont-Louis is above all known for its solar furnace, which was built well before the era of energy saving. A stronghold in a commanding position overlooking the small region of the Cerdagne close to Spain, it was designed by Vauban and its walls and citadel still give it a military air.

Montluçon	(58,830 inhab.)
03 Allier	p.420□J 9

Although Montluçon is now engulfed within a huge industrial zone, the old part is medieval and very fine.

Vieux-Château: Dating from The 15&16C, it is situated on an esplanade with an extensive view over the town. The Dukes of Bourbon lived here. The rectangular main wing has a large crenellated tower which is joined to the belfry by a gallery. Inside is the *Musée Municipal* (history, folklore, art, industry, regional fauna and flora), and also the *Musée International de la Vielle*.(The vielle was a popular medieval musical instrument.) Some of the instruments in this museum bear the signatures of the great Parisian instrument-makers.

Notre-Dame: Rebuilt on the site of an earlier Romanesque church in the 14&15C, it was finished in the 16C. Works of art inside include a 15C wooden polyptych, two fine 16C windows, an altarpiece and a 17C gilded wooden statue.

Saint-Pierre: Dating from the 12C and surrounded by old houses, this church has a wide nave without side aisles and ends in a very pronounced transept. Separating the nave from the transept arms there is a triumphal arch flanked by 'passages berrichons'. Behind the high altar there is a 16C stone cross which formerly stood at one of the entrances to the town. One of the apsidal chapels has a 15C stone statue of Mary Magdalene dressed in the style of Louis XII. The cast of this masterpiece can be seen in the *Musée des Monuments Français* in Paris.

Montmaurin	(190 inhab.)
31 Haute-Garonne	p.423☐G 15

This village is situated on a limestone massif, which was formerly heavily wooded. The surrounding area has yielded signs of very early human habitation (neolithic remains in the caves hereabouts). 19&20C excavations have shown that the site was very important in Gallo-Roman times, the most notable discovery being a huge villa with numerous annexes—a veritable palace with about two hundred rooms. Dating from the 1C and embellished in the 3&4C, it must have been most luxurious. Several of the rooms had hot-air heating, the windows were glazed, and there was an ice box for preserving food (piles of shells were found in the kitchens).

Montmédy	(2,720 inhab.)
55 Meuse	p.416☐M 3

The upper part of this town was a stronghold on a steep-sided promontary (over 1,000 ft. high). Vauban fortified it in the 17C and made it a walled citadel with two gates and drawbridges and a long passageway. The defences are very ingenious with bastions and underground passages. In the 18C church there is an interesting 16C black marble tombstone.

Montmirail	(3,440 inhab.)
51 Marne	p.415☐K 5

This formerly fortified little town perches on a hill above Petit-Morin. Cardinal de Retz was born here in 1613; Napoleon fought one of his last battles here in 1814. The 14&16C church, in a square planted with fine trees, has a great deal of charm. The brick and stone *château*, begun in the 16C and finished in the 17C in accordance with Louvois' taste and requirements, is pure Louis XIII. It is a fine sight—there is a double staircase and the main courtyard is harmoniously framed by two pavilions.

Montmoreau-Saint-Cybard	
	(1, 180 inhab.)
16 Charente	p.419☐G 11

This large village on the Charentais border has steep streets leading up to the 15C *château*. This solidly built structure is roofed with brown tiles, has two towers and a Romanesque porch with some fine capitals. It is linked to the Romanesque chapel by a passageway. The circular chapel is surrounded by an arcaded wall; the capitals here are decorated with lively vignettes, bizarre animals and palm leaves.

Saint-Denis: Dating from the 12C, it has a 15C Chapel of the Virgin and was restored in the 19C. The façade with its fine doorway is the most interesting part; five arches are decorated with palm motifs and geometric patterns, and the multifoil intrados betrays an Eastern influence.

Environs: Puypéroux (8 km. N.): The abbey church of Saint-Gilles is 12C. The exterior is sober; the apse has plain radiating chapels. The most interesting part inside is the octagonal dome surrounded by narrow passages. The columns have fine capitals.

Montmorillon (7,420 inhab.)
86 Vienne p.419□H 9

This little capital of the Brandes region overlooks the tranquil river Gartempe. I has three Romanesque buildings. The church of **Notre-Dame** was built in two distinct phases; transept and choir first, followed by the nave. Beneath the 11C choir the crypt has some of the most famous wall paintings in Poitou. Depicting the life of St. Catherine, to whom the crypt is dedicated, they are technically accomplished and cannot be earlier than 13C. The apse of the upper church, built in beautiful white limestone with elegant arches, is very attractive; the square bell tower is modern The single nave was revaulted in the 15C with Plantagenet rib vaulting. The façade wall was completely rebuilt in the 14C.

Saint-Laurent de la Maison-Dieu: The Montmorillon hospital was founded in the early 12C. Of the late Romanesque church the side bell tower and façade gable (altered in the 17C) survive. The delicately carved limestone upper frieze shows various scenes from the childhood of Christ. *Octogone:* A funerary chapel in the courtyard of the old Maison-Dieu. An unusual monument dating from the late 12C, i

Puypéroux, abbey church, capital

Montmorillon, church crypt

complements another 17C octagonal edifice which was probably a calefactory.

Montpellier (195,600 inhab.)
34 Hérault p.424☐K 14

Montpellier has a rich past and today is a lively city. Predominantly 17&18C, it is the administrative capital of the Languedoc-Roussillon region, and one of the most beautiful cities in southern France. Only rarely are skies clouded and it is well known for its local wines. A university city, its bustling streets, fine gardens and good buildings are beautifully cared for. The city reverted to the French Crown in the 14C, having belonged first to Aragon and then to the Kingdom of Majorca. Much of its reputation is due to its university, where Rabelais completed his medical studies. In the 16C the city experienced bitter fighting between Catholics and Protestants and there was bloodshed inside the cathedral. It opposed Louis XIII, and under Louis XIV became the capital of Languedoc.

Old hôtels: In the 17&18C many elegant hôtels were built; these were sometimes somewhat severe little classical palaces and sometimes deliciously refined domestic residences. The best include the *Hôtel de Ganges* (préfecture), the *Hôtel de Castries* (Rue Saint- Guilhem), the superb *Hôtel de Saint-Côme* (Chambre de Commerce), the *Hôtel Bonnier-de-la- Mosson* (Rue des Trésoriers-de-la-Bourse), the *Hôtel de Manse* (Rue Embouque-d'Or) and the *Hôtel de Lunaret* (Rue des Trésoriers-de-France, housing the collections of the Société Archéologique), the *Hôtel de Sarret* (Place de la Canourgue), the *Hôtel Richer-de-Belleval* (Hôtel de Ville). A guide book is needed for these beautiful houses alone.

Promenade du Peyrou: This wonderful walk — in fact a series of terraces above

Montpellier 1 Hôtel de Ganges (Préfecture) **2** Hôtel de Castries **3** Hôtel de Saint-Côme **4** Hôtel Bonnier de la Mosson **5** Hôtel de la Manse **6** Hôtel de Lunaret **7** Hôtel de Sarret **8** Place de la Canourge **9** Promenade du Peyrou **10** Porte du Peyrou **11** Jardin des Plantes **12** cathedral of Saint-Pierre **13** Fontaine des Trois-Grâces **14** Esplanade **15** Musée Fabre **16** Musée Atger

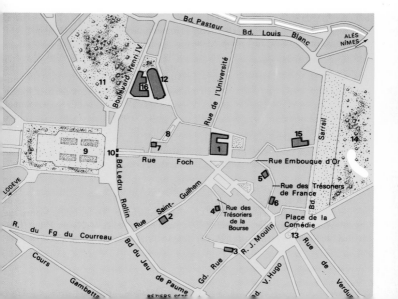

Montpellier, Promenade du Peyrou

Montpellier with splendid views — was created 1689–1776. The equestrian statue of Louis XIV dates from 1838. The graceful octagonal water tower, a charming building fed by an aqueduct some 2,800 ft. long, was inspired by the 18C *Pont du Gard*. The *Porte du Peyrou* (1691) is the provincial cousin of the Porte Saint-Martin in Paris.

Near the promenade is the *Jardin des Plantes*, created by order of Henri IV (1593), by Richer de Belleval. Enlarged in the 19C, it was then redesigned in the 1950s. The Orangerie is late 18C.

Cathedral of Saint-Pierre: A 14C monastic church and the only religious building not to have been totally ruined by the Protestants. It became a cathedral in the 16C and was restored in the 17C; the present transept and apse date from the 19C. The towers make it look like a fortress; there is a 14C porch. The bare, sombre nave is S. Gothic in style.

Place de la Comédie and the Esplanade: A lively area at the edge of the old town. The Place de la Comédie consists of a marble-flagged open space, locally known as 'l'Oeuf' (the Egg) on account of its shape. The 18C fountain of the Three Graces is by the sculptor Étienne Antoine. Leading at an angle off this square is the Esplanade—a promenade of the same date as the Peyrou.

Musée Fabre: Rue Montpelliéret. This museum houses numerous fine works of art. It is named after one of its donors, the local painter François-Xavier Fabre (1766 –1837), who adapted the Hôtel de Mas-

Maguelone, former Romanesque cathedral

silian to accommodate these exhibits (a gallery was added later). Recently reorganized, it contains a large number of paintings, sculptures, objets d'art and furniture. Among the best exhibits there are some very fine marbles by Houdon (*Winter* and *Summer*, and a seated figure of *Voltaire*), Flemish and Dutch paintings (Teniers the Younger, Gabriel Metsu, Jan Steen, etc.), some good Italian paintings, works by Greuze, as well as several paintings by Courbet and Delacroix. The pre-Impressionist Bazille (a native of Montpellier) is represented by several works, which were painted shortly before his death (he was killed in the Franco-Prussian War). The museum also contains contemporary works and, in the annexe in the Hôtel Cabrières-Sabatier-d'Espeyran, there are pieces of furniture, tapestries and objets d'art.

Musée Atger: Rue de l'École de Médecine. This museum contains some remarkable S. French and Italian drawings. It occupies the first floor of the Faculty of Medicine in the former college of Saint-Benoît (founded in the 14C).

Environs: Maguelone (16 km. S.): A quiet once fortified town on what was an island but is now joined to the mainland. The former Romanesque cathedral has a lovely carved doorway (delicately sculpted lintel, 1178). It contains tombs and fragments of tombstones.

Montréal (220 inhab.)
89 Yonne p.415☐K 7

This charming, picturesque old village still

Montréal, detail of a stall in the former collegiate church

has part of its fortifications and was once an important military position. The former collegiate church restored by Viollet-le-Duc occupies a commanding position on a mound and dates essentially from the late 12C. Inside there is a magnificent 15C alabaster altarpiece, various sculptures and some splendid stalls made in 1522 by the Rigolley brothers (Burgundian craftsmen). They depict with great skill scenes from the Old and New Testaments.

Montrésor	(470 inhab.)
37 Indre-et-Loir	p.419 □ H 8

This charming village on a small river was once a seat of an important lord. The fortress was first rebuilt in the 10C by Foulques Nerra the Count of Anjou, and again at the end of the 14C. The *château* proper was not built until the early 16C. In 1849 a Polish family acquired it and restored it, leaving their mark with objets d'art, documents about Poland and bas-reliefs of Sobieski's battles. The château contains some fine 19C furniture and many paintings. The former collegiate church is Gothic and Renaissance, and dates from the first half of the 16C. It contains the Bastarnay family tomb (they were the former Lords of Montrésor). The wooden market buildings are 17C.

Environs: Chartreuse du Liget (5 km. W.): On the Montrésor side of the charterhouse you can see the fortified house with its chapel (called the *Couroirie* or *Corroirie*) which was once an annexe. The charterhouse itself, hidden among the greenery on the edge of the Forest of Loches, was founded by Henry II of England and unfortunately time has taken its toll on the building. The monumental doorway and the cloister date from the 18C, and the chapel from the 12C (interesting wall paintings).

Montreuil-Bellay	(4,240 inhab.)
49 Maine-et-Loire	p.418□F 8

This characterful little town overlooks the slow-moving river Thouët. The *château*, on the site of a Roman entrenchment, dates mainly from the 15C. There is a gatehouse, an oddly arranged Petit Château (kitchen, four separate houses, former canons' residences) and a fine Château Neuf (New Château) flanked by towers and with a chapel; the Château Neuf contains some fine furniture and Flamboyant fireplaces. Adjoining the château is the church of *Notre-Dame* dating from the second half of the 15C; its single elegant aisle has Angevin vaulting.

Environs: Le Puy-Notre-Dame (7 km. SW): Once a fortified village, it has a beautiful Angevin church (13C). **Abbaye d'Asnières** (7 km. NW): The remains of an abbey which was sacked by the Huguenots. Note the abbey church, which has a very fine 13C choir.

Montreuil-sur-Mer	(2,840 inhab.)
62 Pas-de-Calais	p.410□I 2

The sea receded long ago from this little town, and now its pleasant atmosphere is enhanced by the distant murmur of fresh water. It was once a stronghold, and its pink brick and white stone ramparts flanked by 16&17C towers are most attractive. The walls of the citadel (begun 1567) incorporate the remains of the former

château (two round 13C towers mark the old entrance). To the side of these is the Tour Berthe (14C) which used to be one of the town gates. It contains the chapel of the Hôtel-Dieu, which has largely been rebuilt but is still full of splendid furnishings (lovely panelling, baroque altar embellished with gilding and mirrors). The church of *Saint-Saulve* has been constantly re-modelled since it was built in the 11C; it is a composite building but its magnificent nave is predominantly Flamboyant. In addition to statues and 18C paintings, it houses the treasure from the Abbey of Saint-Austreberthe, including a wooden cross covered with silver strips (7–8C), a splendid example of silverwork.

Montrichard	(3,860 inhab.)
41 Loir-et-Cher	p.414□H 7

This peaceful town on the Cher, with lush countryside all around it, retains a quasi-medieval appeal in its old quarters (the *Maison du Prêche*—11C, the *Maison de l'Ave Maria*—16C, the *Hôtel-Jacques-de-Beaune*—16C). It is overlooked by a 12C keep and its associated defences which are remnants of a fortress dismantled by order of Henri IV. The *church of Nanteuil* dates from the 12C (Romanesque apse and choir) and the 13&15C. The church of *Sainte-Croix*, once a lord's chapel, retains Romanesque parts.

Environs: Château de Gué-Péan (11 km. W.): This is a former 14&15C hunting lodge, where many kings stayed, as well as Fénelon, La Fayette and Balzac. It contains a fireplace by Germain Pilon and some fine pieces of furniture and works of art. **Château de Montpoupon** (11 km. SW): This has now been restored but dates originally from the 15&16C. It houses the *Musée de la Vénerie* (a museum of hunting, which contains many interesting objects and trophies). **Pontlevoy** (7.5 km. NE): This large village grew up around an abbey, whose former abbey church survives. It is 13,14&15C with 17C altarpieces. In addition to other remains, there are some old houses and a church with 11C features.

Montreuil-Bellay, the château

The Château de Gué-Péan

Mont Saint-Michel	(110 inhab.)
50 Manche	p.413□ E 5

This granite island off the Normandy coast has an unreal, fairy-tale appearance. Both monastery and fortress, it rises in tiers and is watched over by a statue of the Archangel Michael. Only at exceptionally high tides does the sea, which comes in 'with the speed of a galloping horse', cut it off from the mainlaind. (In fact the sea has been receding since the Middle Ages.) The mount presents a dream-like appearance, with its wonderful conglomeration of cleverly tiered stone perched on a huge high rock. Its origins too are dreamlike, for legend has it that the Archangel Michael appeared in a dream to Aubert, Bishop of Avranches, and ordered him to build an oratory on a deserted island (then called Mont Tombe). The prelate hesitated, the leader of the heavenly hosts insisted, and the first humble church was consecrated by 706. Soon another chapel was added and it became a place of pilgrimage; then a handful of monks moved on to the windswept rock. In 960 an important Benedictine abbey was founded by Richard I, Duke of Normandy. Work continued over the centuries, piling building upon building; some fell down, but they were rebuilt stronger than ever.

Notre-Dame-sous-Terre, a late 10C pre-Romanesque building (its stone vault was very daring for its time), became the crypt beneath the final bays of a larger Romanesque church. Other crypts were built to

Mont-St-Michel

Mont-St-Michel, Porte du Roi

Mont-St-Michel, abbey church

serve as bases for the large Romanesque abbey church of 1017–1144, which stands on the narrow summit of what was Mont Tombe. The abbey buildings cling perilously to the rock all around. In the second half of the 12C a great abbot, Guillaume de Thorigny, acted as host to Louis VII and Henry II of England, who came to negotiate peace. Thereafter nothing was too fine or too vast: Gothic buildings were raised in the 13C and work went on until the 16C (the church's choir fell down and was completely rebuilt in the 15C). The gatehouse and the fortifications around the entrance were added in the 14C and the ramparts were strengthened 1425 – 40, which made the abbey a great maritime fortress, and enabled it to remain French during the Hundred Years War. Despite attempts at reform, Mont-Saint-Michel declined in the 17C and it was finally suppressed during the Revolution. It had been used as a 'bastille' from time to time under the Ancien Régime and after the Revolution it was officially turned into a prison—like the abbey of Fontevraud in the Loire valley. In spite of protests by Chateaubriand, Victor Hugo, Alfred de Vigny and Viollet-le-Duc, it was not until 1863 that the prison was closed down. Then major restoration work ensued and the present bell tower was built, the spire of which carries the acrobatic St.Michael by Emmanuel Frémiet, a nephew of Rude, who was a popular establishment artist at the end of the last century.

Complexe Univers: This strange town, with only one street but numerous stairways, passageways and different levels, is a veritable labyrinth in which you pass from one century to another, visiting it

Mont-St-Michel, the Merveille and the cloister

level by level and not according to period or architecture. It has changed little since Gustave Flaubert observed, 'It is totally absorbing! One visit is not enough to understand the layout of all these buildings'.

Defences and town: A single gate, the *Porte de l'Avancée*, opens in the circle of walls which protects the accessible parts of the rock. It leads into a 16C fortified courtyard with a 1530 guardhouse on the left and two mortars captured from the English in 1434 on the right. The second courtyard and the Porte du Roi lead into the staight, steep *Grande Rue*, which is lined with 15&16C houses and displays of souvenirs for tourists. There are two *museums*, the *Historial* and the *Historique*; these tell the history of the Mount with the help of wax figures and dioramas. The parish church of *Saint Pierre*, paved with 17C funeral slabs, dates mainly from the 15&16C. The *Grand Degré* leads to the abbey: this was the main stairway and had the advantage of being easy to defend.

Abbey church: Originally this was entirely Romanesque, but much of the church collapsed in 1103 and 1420 and later three of its bays were removed. The neoclassical façade was added in 1780. The severe, balanced Romanesque nave contrasts with the lightness of the choir, which was rebuilt at the end of the 15C in Flamboyant style. The external design of the choir is dazzlingly light and bold. An open staircase on one of the massive flying buttresses leads to a gallery with a superb view. There are crypts under the abbey church, one being the pre-Romanesque Notre-Dame-sous-Terre which has already been mentioned.

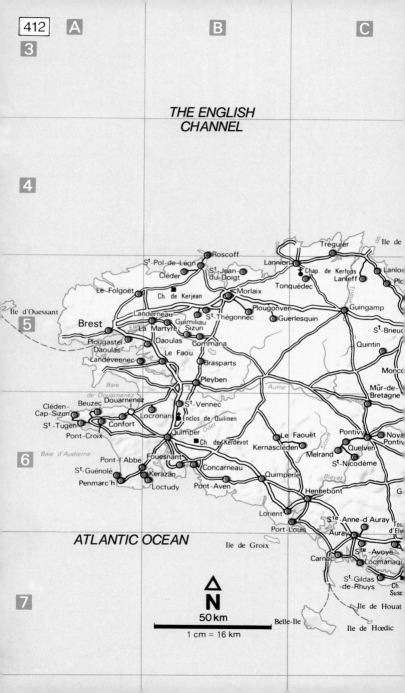

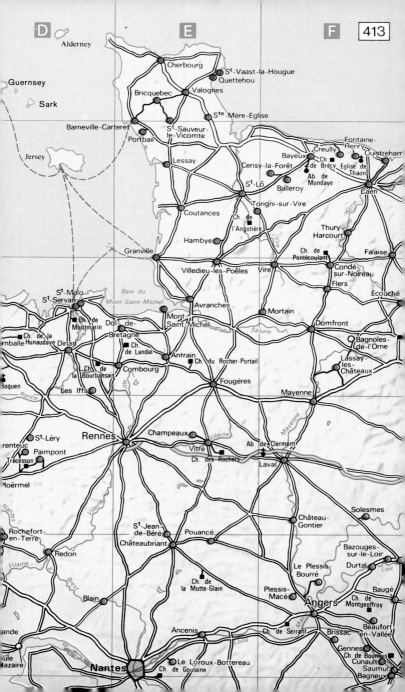

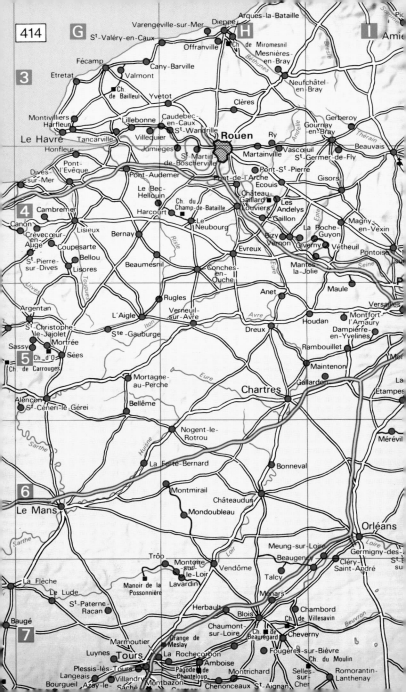

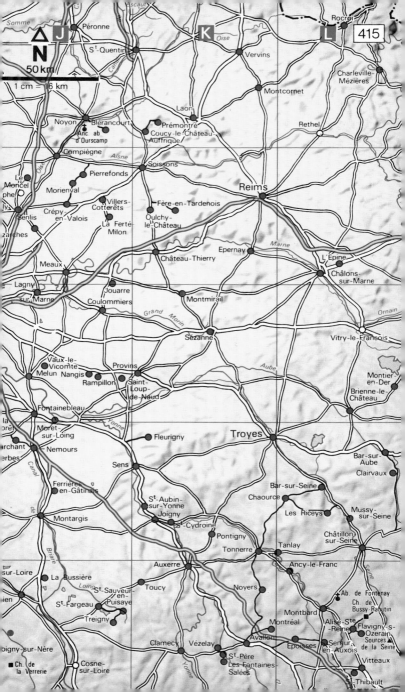

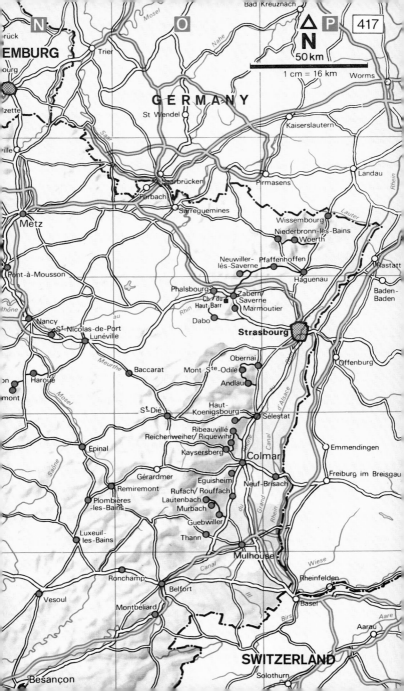

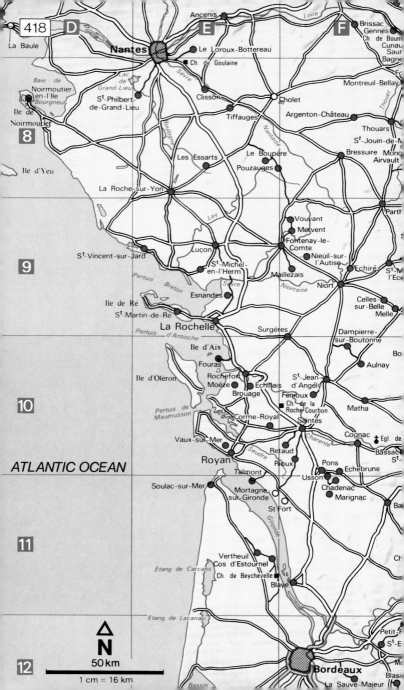

D **E** **F**

La Baule

Ancenis
Loire

Nantes
Le Loroux-Bottereau
Ch. de Goulaine

Brissac
Gennes
Ch de Boum
Cunau
Saur
Bagne

Montreuil-Bellay

Baie de
Noirmoutier-
en-l'Ile
Bourgneuf
Lac de
Grand-Lieu
St-Philbert-
de-Grand-Lieu
Sèvre
Clisson
Cholet

8
Ile de
Noirmoutier
Argenton-Château

Fo
Thouars
St-Jouin-de-M

Tiffauges
Nantaise

Ile d'Yeu
Les Essarts
Le Boupère
Pouzauges
Bressuire Mon
Airvault

La Roche-sur-Yon
Lay
Vouvant
Mervent
Fontenay-le-
Comte
Parth

9
St-Vincent-sur-Jard
Luçon
St-Michel-
en-l'Herm
Maillezais
Nieuil-sur-
l'Autise
Echiré
S^t-M
l'Ec
Niort

Pertuis
Breton
Esnandes
Sèvre
Niortaise
Celles
sur-Belle
Melle

Ile de Ré
St-Martin-de-Ré
La Rochelle
Surgères
Dampierre-
sur-Boutonne
Pertuis
d'Antioche
Bo

10
Ile d'Aix
Fouras
Rochefort
Moëze
Echillais
Brouage
St-Jean-
d'Angély
Fenioux
Ch. de la
Roche Courbon
Aulnay

Ile d'Oléron
Pertuis de
Maumusson
Corme-Royal
Saintes
Matha

Vaux-sur-Mer
Cognac
Egl. de
Bassac
S^t.

ATLANTIC OCEAN
Royan
Seudre
Retaud
Rioux
Pons
Echebrune

Talmont
Usson

Soulac-sur-Mer
Mortagne-
sur-Gironde
St Fort
Chadenac
Marignac
Ba

11
Vertheuil
Cos d'Estournel
Ch. de Beychevelle
Blaye

Etang de Carcans
Gironde
Ch

Etang de Lacanau
Petit-P
S^t-E

12
△
N
50 km
1 cm = 16 km
Bordeaux
La Sauve-Majeur
Me
Blasi
Bassin

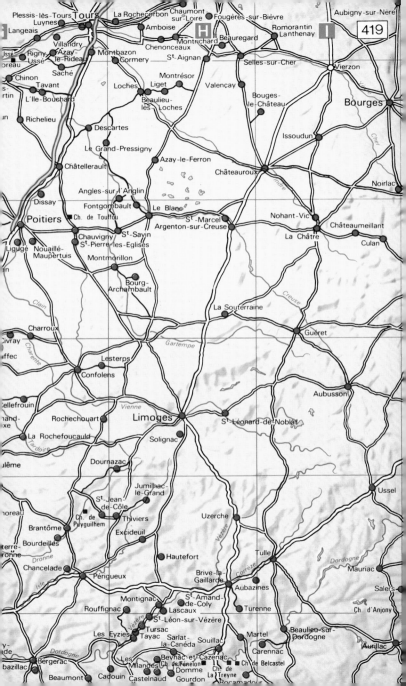

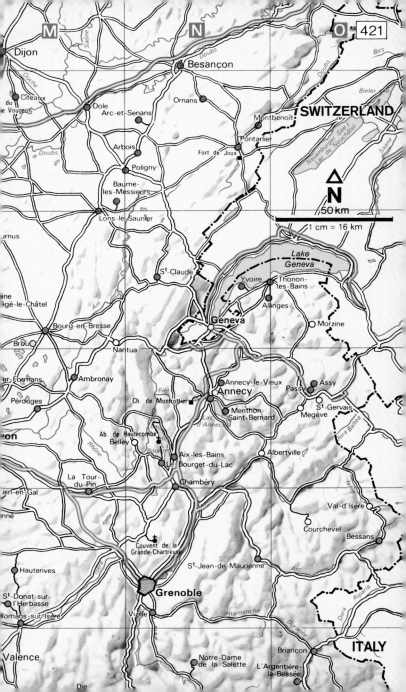

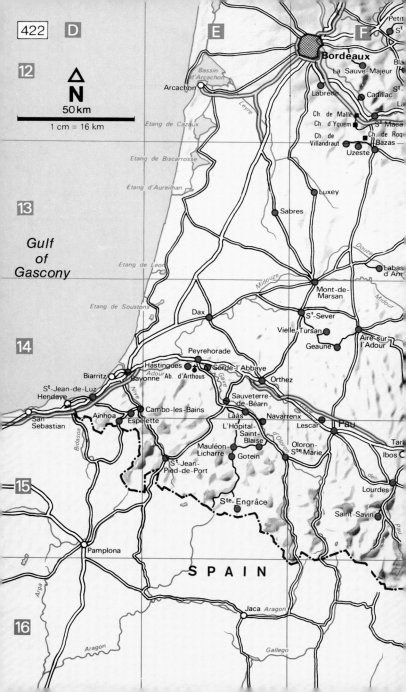

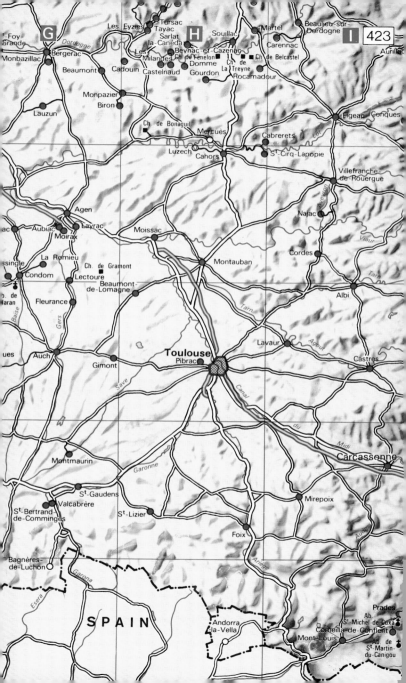

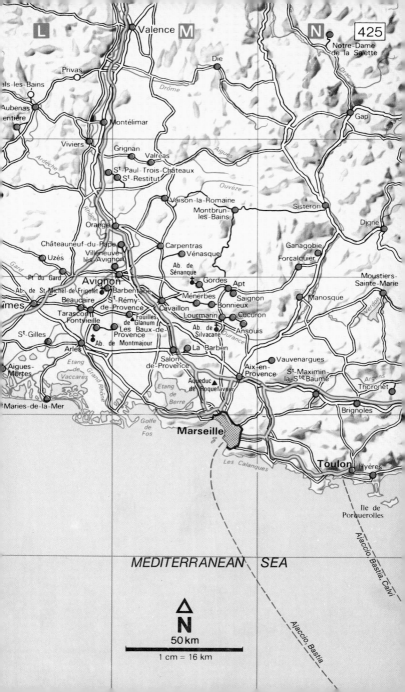

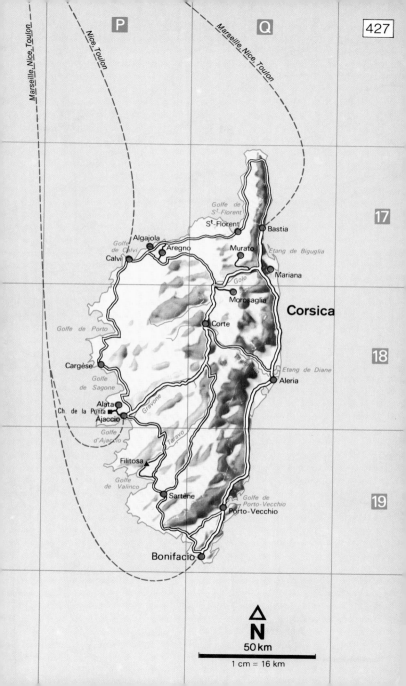

Marseille Nice Toulon

Nice Toulon

Nice Toulon

Marseille Nice Toulon

Golfe de
St-Florent

St-Florent

Bastia

Algajola

Aregno

Murato

Golfe
de Calvi

Calvi

Etang de Biguglia

Mariana

Golo

Morosaglia

Corsica

Golfe de Porto

Corte

Cargèse

Etang de Diane

Golfe
de Sagone

Aleria

Alata

Gravone

Ch. de la Punta

Ajaccio

Golfe
d'Ajaccio

Tavaro

Filitosa

Golfe
de Valinco

Golfe de
Porto-Vecchio

Sartène

Porto-Vecchio

Bonifacio

△
N
50 km

1 cm = 16 km

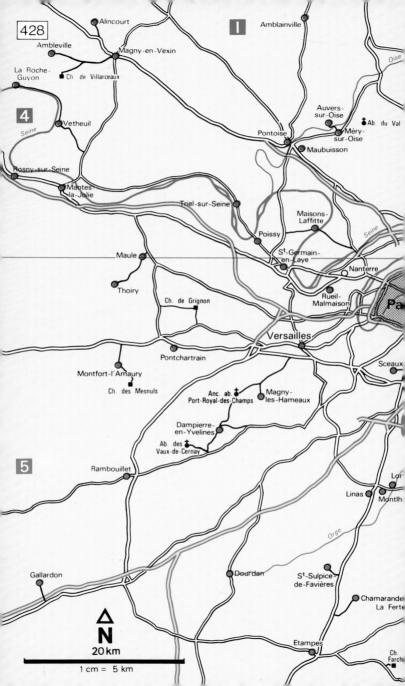

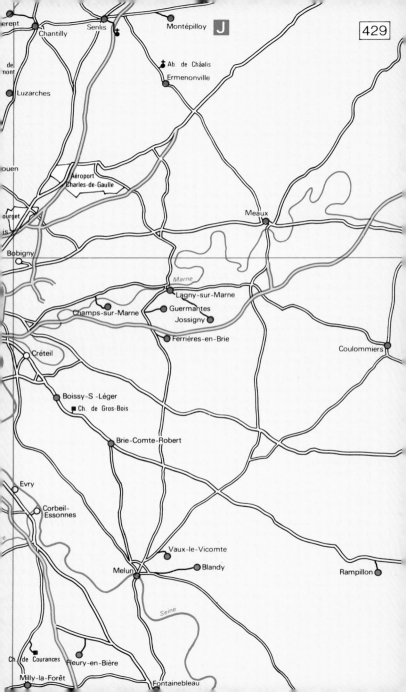

Merveille: The 'Merveille' is a group of early-13C monastery buildings resembling a fortress on three levels. At the top there is a hanging garden surrounded by galleries, the *cloister*, which was finished in 1228 and is very prettily decorated. On the same level is the *refectory*, a vast hall cleverly lit by narrow windows, which is roughly contemporary with the cloister. Underneath the refectory and contemporary with it there is the large *Salle des Hôtes*, divided into two naves. The *Salle des Chevaliers*, under the cloister, is made up of four naves. On the lower level of the 'Merveille' are the cellar and the almonry. The austere, cold Salle de l'Aquilon is 12C.

Montsoreau (500 inhab.)
49 Maine-et-Loire p.419 □ G 8

The château of Montsoreau is reflected in the Loire, which once reached as far as its walls. Solid and elegant, it is fortress-like, although it was originally built to be pleasant and comfortable. In 1520 a pretty turret was added along with the main staircase inside. The *Musée des Goums* moved from Rabat to the château in 1956. It deals with the cavalry recruited by Lyautey and the Conquest of Morocco. Alexandre Dumas based his *Dame de Montsoreau* on a dramatic incident in the life of one of the châtelaines.

Environs: Candes-Saint-Martin (1.5 km. E.): This town is almost the twin of Montsoreau. Traces of its former defences and a little 15C house used as a residence by the Bishops of Tours have survived. St.Martin died here in 397. The very beautiful, sober church of *Saint Martin* dates from the 11C and was fortified in the 15C. The St.Michel porch is light and beautifully proportioned with Angevin vaulting supported on a central column. There are several statues inside. The three aisles are

Montsoreau, the château

of equal height and are decorated with statuettes and figurines at the points from which the ribs spring.

Moret-sur-Loing (3,150 inhab.)
77 Seine-et-Marne p.415 □ J 5/6

This picturesque little town on the banks of the Loing is protected by two fortified gates which survive from the medieval town wall. It was the subject of several paintings by Alfred Sisley, who lived here in the years just before his death in 1899. There are several historic houses, e.g. the *Maison de François I* which is attributed to Jean Goujon and Pierre Lescot. This lovely, very ornate house was dismantled and rebuilt in Paris but returned 'home' in 1958; it is now in the courtyard of the

Moret s/Loing, Maison de François I

Morlaix, Maison de la Duchesse Anne

Mairie. The *church* has a 13C choir but otherwise dates from the 14&15C and contains two fine 16C organs.

Morlaix (20,530 inhab.)
29 Finistère p.412□B 5

This town is situated on the slopes of a deep valley where the Jarlot and the Queffleuth merge to form the Dossen estuary. It is dominated by the striking outline of a two-storeyed viaduct, which was built in 1861 for the Paris-Brest railway. The lower part of the town has tiny streets and alleys lined with pretty half-timbered houses with overhanging upper storeys and a few shops which resemble medieval stalls. The most beautiful house, known as the 'Maison de la Duchesse Anne', has

a three storey timber-framed façade decorated with saints and gargoyles and dates from the 15C. Inside, in a little courtyard with a roof and lantern-light, there is a magnificent carved wooden staircase.

Musée Municipal: Housed in the church of the old Dominican convent in the Place des Jacobins, the museum has a variety of very interesting exhibits. As well as rooms dealing with the art and ethnography of Léon and with religious statuary, it has rooms exhibiting old paintings (Flemish, Dutch, Italian and French schools), and some modern ones (Courbet, Boudin, Monet, Bonnard, Rafaëlli).

Church of Saint Mathieu (1824): Only the square tower of 1548 remains of the original building. The altar in the left side aisle has a statue of *Notre Dame du Mur* which opens to reveal a Trinity—this very original work dates from the late 15C. The pulpit and organ-chest are 17C.

Church of Sainte Mélaine: Rebuilt in the 15C in Flamboyant style. It has some very fine furnishings — old altarpieces, carved oak baptismal fonts (1660) and a 1680 organ-chest.

Environs: Plougonven (11 km. SE): A town near the Arrée hills with a remarkable 1554 *wayside cross* in the parish close. The octagonal base has two carved surfaces and the traditional three crosses on top. On the lower surface Saint Yves, the patron of the parish and of lawyers, appears surrounded by the poor and wealthy. The 15&16C *church* has an elegant bell tower with a spire and staircase tower built on to it. Nearby the fine Renaissance *ossuary* of 1532 has bays with clover-leaf arches. **Guerlesquin** (21 km. SE): This agricultural town, a few km. away from Plougonven, has an enormous square surrounded on all sides by old houses. In the middle there is a square 17C house with turrets,

which was formerly a courtroom. **Saint Jean du Doigt** (16 km. N.): This pretty village is named after the finger relic of St.Jean, which has been kept in the church since the 15C. A Flamboyant triumphal arch leads into the parish close. Apart from a Renaissance fountain with three basins, there are also two ossuaries (16&17C) and a church (recently damaged by fire). Its *treasure* includes three reliquaries, a wonderful silver-gilt chalice (16C) with an enamel of the Nativity and a medallion of François I, a 16C silver chalice with eight enamel figures depicting contemporaries of the silversmith (including Ronsard and Michel de l'Hospital).

Morosaglia: see **Corsica**

Mortagne-au-Perche (5,110 inhab.)
61 Orne p.410☐G 5

In the past the citizens of this town boasted, 'Mortagne on the mountains, the

Plougonven, 16C calvary

most beautiful town in France'. This former capital of Perche is very high up, with a panoramic view. There are many relics of its past, including arcaded market buildings and old houses. The church of *Notre-Dame* in the heart of the town has a massive façade tower. Built in the late 15/early 16C, it was enlarged in the 19C. The N. doorway is very ornate and has a disfigured gable and fine doors. One chapel in the left aisle has a stained-glass window representing the departure of the Percherons for Canada (numerous local families went there before the Revolution). The *Porte Saint-Denis* (in the apse), a remnant of the vanished fortifications from the 12C or 13C, supports a 16C building. A simple 15C cloister remains from a convent of the order of Saint Clare which later became a hospital. The philosopher Alain was born here.

Mortain	(3,130 inhab.)
50 Manche	p.413☐E/F 5

This flower-bedecked little town lies in a very fertile part of Normandy. Because of the damage it suffered in the last war it is quite modern. However, the former collegiate church of *Saint-Évroult* is essentially 13C — a remarkable Romanesque doorway with geometrical decoration survives in the S. aisle. The *Abbaye Blanche*, founded in the 12C, was linked with Citeaux and is Romanesque in parts. Its church, consecrated in the early 13C, is Cistercian in type. The former monastery is now a lively cultural and missionary centre and has an exhibition of African ethnography.

Moulins	(26,910 inhab.)
03 Allier	p.420☐K 9

This former capital of the Bourbonnais

derives its name from the many windmills which have stood along the Allier since the Middle Ages. It was the residence of the Dukes of Bourbon in the 14C and became the capital of the Duchy at the end of the 15C, when a glittering court developed and many artists were attracted to it. The oldest part is relatively small and includes a few beautiful medieval houses around the Cathedral, the belfry and the remains of the old château; its 15C keep is called 'la mal coiffée', probably because of the flat roof which makes it look ugly in silhouette.

Cathedral of Notre Dame: This former collegiate church consists of two distinct parts. The remarkable choir, built 1474–1507 in Flamboyant style, was extended in the 19C by the addition of the nave and mock 13C Gothic towers. The chapels and the apse have 15&16C stained glass. Around the ambulatory there is a series of depictions of the court of the Bourbons. At the foot of the Crucifixion window there is a 16C Entombment and in one of the chapels a 12C Black Virgin (a replica of the one at Le Puy, recalling the fact that

Moulins, jack o' the clock

Moustiers, faïence

Moulins was on the pilgrimage route to Santiago de Compostela via Le Puy). The sacristy has the famous *Triptyque du Maître de Moulins* painted at the end of the 15C for Pierre II of Bourbon and his wife Anne de Beaujeu. The outer surface is in grisaille and represents the Annunciation and the open shutters show the wise men presented to Christ and the Virgin. At its side is the 16C Flemish triptych called *de Bethléem*.

Jaquemart: This belfry, over 60 ft. high, stands on the *Place de l'Hôtel de Ville*. The covered gallery and the bell tower date from the mid 17C. The remarkable set of chimes is a faithful copy of the 17C original and consists of an amusing family of four mechanical figures.

Mausoleum of the Duke of Montmorency: Dating from the 17C, it can be found in the chapel of the Lycée Banville, which is housed in the former convent of the Visitation. This classical and rather pompous work is attributed to Michel Anguier. Around the figures of the Duke and Duchess are Strength, Generosity, Courage and Faith.

Palais de Justice: The former Royal Jesuit College, built in pink and black brickwork, is characteristic of 17C Bourbon architecture.

Musée d'Art et d'Archéologie: Housed in part of the former château (Renaissance pavilion), its exhibits include some lovely 16C tapestries, weapons, important Gallo-Roman and prehistoric finds, faïence and remarkable German paintings.

Musée du Folklore: This charming 15C house has reconstructions of Bourbon interiors, documents and costumes, etc.

Bibliothèque Municipale: The library houses a great number of incunabula and books of hours from the 13&15C, as well as the *Bible de Souvigny*, a 12C illuminated manuscript with magnificent miniatures.

Moustiers-Ste-Marie	(600 inhab.)
04 Alpes de Haute Provence	p.425☐N 14

Moustiers, famous for faïence, occupies a pretty and unusual site at the end of the Verdon gorge; buildings cluster around the bottom of a cliff and up both sides of a deep crevasse. It grew up around a 5C monastery and achieved prosperity through the production of faïence which was at its height in the 17&18C. A little *museum* has examples of this work, although the most outstanding pieces are in the Musée Cantini (see *Marseille*). The *church* in the pretty old town has a Lombard-style bell tower with a Romanesque nave and Gothic choir. The church is dominated by the chapel of Notre-Dame-de-Beauvoir which, according to legend, was founded by Charlemagne. Rebuilt in the 12C and altered in the Gothic style, it retains a modest Romanesque porch.

Mulhouse	(119,330 inhab.)
68 Haut-Rhin	p.417☐0 6

This large town, a crossroads in S. Alsace, is dominated by a tall modern tower. An industrial town traditionally linked with Switzerland, it was largely rebuilt after the last war. It has nothing to match the allure of Colmar or old Strasbourg, but there are none the less a few historic monuments and houses and some superb buildings around the *Place de la Réunion*. There are also some unusual museums. An independent-minded town, it voluntarily opted to become French in 1798. Its prosperity is largely due to the manufacture of printed calico, or 'indiennes'. This industry developed in the mid 18C, when the town became a small-scale continental version of Manchester. The potash industry, once important, is now in decline and the town has grave pollution problems.

Place de la Réunion: A square of historic appearance in the heart of the modern town. The *Temple Saint-Étienne*, rebuilt in the 19C, has some very fine 14C stained glass. In front of it is the 15C Maison Mieg and there are some old houses at the corner of the Rue des Boulangers and the Place Lambert. Mulhouse has a marvellous *Hôtel de Ville* (see *Musée Historique*) but otherwise there are very few relics of the past. These include the *Chapel of Saint Jean* (14&15C) in the Grand-Rue, two towers from the former château of the bishops of Strasbourg and the Tour de Bollwerk (14C, a remnant of the fortified town wall).

Musée Historique (Place de la Réunion): The former Mulhouse Hôtel de Ville was built in 1431 and rebuilt in the mid 16C after a fire; it was described by Montaigne as a 'magnificent gilded palace'. One façade has a replica of the old 'pierre des bavards' (gossips' stone) which was formerly hung around the necks of slanderers and gossips. The Hôtel de Ville has been very carefully restored and sittings of the Municipal Council are still held here in the beautiful Salle du Conseil de la République de Mulhouse (1552). However, today the building is first and foremost the setting for the very attractive Musée Historique. This is a museum of great variety, which includes finds from prehistoric S. Alsace, Gallo-Roman times, examples of medieval art and exhibits concerned with the history of Mulhouse from the 16C to 1830. There are also some of the best examples of popular art, as well as touching and charming collections of toys, dolls, etc. The magnificent beamed attic has weathercocks and shop signs, silverware, pewter, stoves and fireplaces.

Musée des Beaux Arts (4 Place Guillaume-Tel): This museum occupies a bourgeois house and has some interesting paintings, in particular one by Pieter Breughel the Younger; there are also works by Alsatian artists (Jean-Jacques Henner, Charles Walch and Léon Lehmann among others).

Musée de l'Impression sur Étoffe (Rue des Bonnes Gens): This enchanting museum is most informative on the techniques of fabric printing and it has some exceptional examples of fine and primitive art from the 18–20C. Most of the material is local, but there are exhibits from Jouy, Nantes, Bordeaux and elsewhere. Exhibits range from flowered handkerchiefs to a cloak said to have belonged to Marie Antoinette, from the dress printed from a copper plate to beautiful cashmere shawls and pastoral wall-hangings, all of which show that the printing of cloth is one of the most attractive of the decorative arts and should perhaps even count as one of the fine arts. The collection of 'illustrated' handkerchiefs classified according to theme is extremely unusual. In the Salle de Documentation there are piles of enormous and fascinating books, which contain hundreds of thousands of sample designs collected and catalogued since 1833.

Musée Français du Chemin de Fer (2 Avenue A.-de-Glehn): This fascinating museum outside the town is a kind of huge station full of locomotives which were once famous for their speed records. There are also historic pullman cars, restaurant cars, and wagons lits. Among the veterans are locomotive number 33 'Saint Pierre' (1844, 40 mph), locomotive number 5 'Suzanne' (1847, 40 mph), and also the saloon car used as an office by General Joffre in 1914–15. The *Musée des Sapeurs-Pompiers* (part of the above museum) describes the history of fire-fighting and has some 18C hand pumps.

Musée, Hôtel de Ville, detail

Murato see **Corsica**

Mûr de Bretagne	(2,260 inhab.)
22 Côtes-du-Nord	p.412□C 6

The little town of Mûr de Bretagne lies on the edge of Lac de Guerlédan in a wooded valley. It has a modern church (1878) in which there is a beautiful smiling Virgin. On a neighbouring hillside the 17C *chapel of Sainte-Suzanne* has some interesting painted woodwork illustrating scenes from the Passion; there are also some very old statues. The left transept has the remains of a carved wooden rood screen (scenes of the Passion). The building is surrounded by huge oak trees and has a pretty bell tower with balconies and a stone spire.
Environs: Le Quillio (9 km. NE): The

16C church has an elegant S. porch. The woodwork in the 17C choir came from the Cistercian abbey of Bon Repos, which is now in ruins. A simple calvary in the cemetery is decorated with a pretty Pietà.

Mussy-Sur-Seine	(1,680 inhab.)
10 Aube	p.415□L 6

This little town on the Seine has a few 15&16C houses to remind one of its past; there are also the remains of the château of the Bishops of Langres. The lovely 13C Gothic *church* is full of fine examples of sculpture; a 15C Saint John the Baptist which is typically champenois, a very expressive 16C Pietà, Saint Michael subduing the devil, also 16C, and the 13C monolithic tomb of Guillaume de Mussy and his wife.

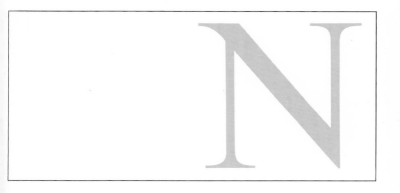

Najac (930 inhab.)
12 Aveyron p.423☐I 13

This village is perched on a granite spur overlooking a narrow bend in the Aveyron. It has a 13C church and a number of rather crude Gothic houses made of stone, some of which were built for the King's officers in the 13C. To the E. lie the ruins of the château built by Alphonse de Poitiers, the brother of St. Louis. Belonging to the Crown, it symbolized Royal authority in the distant Rouergue region.

Nancy (111,500 inhab.)
54 Meurthe-et-Moselle p.417☐N 5

This former capital of the Duchy of Lorraine is an expression of a deeply creative and original civilization. Despite the grave problems stemming from the decline of the region's iron and steel industry, the people of Nancy have shown themselves ready to adapt and fight for survival if necessary. The town appears to be a busy modern metropolis and a cultural centre in spite of its present difficulties. Originally a fortified 11C village, in the 16C the Dukes laid out a new town on a regular grid pattern

and this now forms the old town. In the middle of the 18C, Stanislas Leszczynski, the deposed King of Poland and father-in-law of Louis XV, arrived in Nancy. This enlightened philosopher king gathered around him the cream of Lorraine's talent: the architect Emmanuel Heré (1705–63), the iron-worker Jean Lamour (1698–1771) and the sculptor Nicolas Adam (1705-78). (Adam's family house is open to visitors.) With this group Stanislas was able to fully indulge his obsession for building. Because of his genius for combining town planning with art, he created a town and monument in one, beautiful and yet structured.

Stanislas's buildings: These buildings —constituting a masterpiece of baroque town planning, which is rather rare in France—employ interesting perspectives and embody good taste in their terraces, balconies and decorative art. A series of squares combine the grace of the 18C with the majesty of the 17C. The purpose behind the buildings is not purely decorative, however; they also had a political purpose (to confer prestige on the Prince) and a practical one (to aid the efficiency of public functions). The *Place Stanislas* is the focal point (it was formerly the Place Royal dedicated to Louis XV) and it was altered from 1752 under Heré's direction. There

Nancy 1 Hôtel de Ville **2** statue of Stanislas **3** Arc de Triomphe **4** Palais du Gouvernement **5** Pépinière **6** Porte de la Craffe **7** Hôtel d'Haussonville **8** Hôtel de Ferrari **9** cathedral **10** Notre-Dame de Bon-Secours **11** Musée Historique Lorrain (Palais Ducal) **12** Eglise des Cordeliers (Franciscan church) **13** Musée des Beaux-Arts **14** Musée de l'École de Nancy

are five pavilions (the largest S. of the Hôtel de Ville has Stanislas's coat-of-arms on it), and two monumental arcades, which together form a rectangular area with cut off corners. Some splendid railings by Lamour close the square; to the N. they form a portico and frame the fountains of Neptune and Amphitrite, by the sculptor Guibal. Even though it has been somewhat whittled away, the square is still vast (400 ft. by 340 ft.) and is the epitome of harmony and good taste. The railings, which have pilasters and acanthus and shell motifs, and are embellished by gilding, form a marvellous tracery of wrought iron, perfectly balanced and in keeping with the architecture. Lamour was also responsible for 56 balconies on the pavilions and for the *Hotel de Ville's* ramp, all of which are highly successful pieces of monumental

ironwork. The master iron-worker managed to restrain the rococo style from deteriorating into an orgy of the baroque. A triumphal arch in the purest Roman tradition leads into the long **Place de la Carrière**. This, a 16C tournament ground, was again altered by Heré and it is now lined by 18C houses. Beyond this, facing the triumphal arch, the *Palais du Gouvernement* closes the prospect, its elongated, curved colonnade almost completely enclosing the main courtyard. The nearby **Place d'Alliance** is surrounded by 18C hôtels. It was designed by Heré in 1753 in order to balance the town which was expanding to the E. The *Pépinière* adjoining the Palais du Gouvernement is a splendid town park, created in 1765. It is enhanced by one of Rodin's works, which is dedicated to the painter Claude Gellée (better known as Claude Lorrain).

Hôtels in Old Nancy: There are a few historic houses in the very heart of the old town, whch still has the relics of its 14C defences, the Porte de la Craffe with two cylindrical towers. Time has not been exactly kind to these old parts but here and there in a courtyard one comes across a well or an open staircase. Some, such as the *Hôtel d'Haussonville*, are Renaissance, and others are 18C like the *Hotel de Ferrari*.

Religious buildings: The town, lacking in old churches, is proud of its remarkable 18C ones. In 1742 Boffrand completed the impressive, vast yet well proportioned cathedral begun by Hardouin-Mansart in 1703. The façade has a strong vertical emphasis because of the two tall towers and the three projecting orders of columns. Inside it is restrained and rather pompous, the monumental aspect being emphasized by the wrought-iron grilles of the side chapels (some by Lamour). The treasure includes magnificent work by 10C silversmiths—one of the most precious pieces is the *Evangeliary of St. Gauzelin*, whose

Nancy, Place Stanislas, the railings by Lamour

engraved silver plate is decorated with fine translucent enamel medallions.

Notre-Dame de Bonsecours was built by Heré in 1738 at the request of Sanislas who wished to be buried here. Heré was inspired by the Italian Renaissance in building the façade and by German baroque for the interior design. He created an admirably balanced building with an overall simplicity of structure. The church is full of marble, stucco and paintings on the vaulting, and the furnishings are superb. Stanislas's tomb, carved by Vasse, is coldly classical and contrasts with the mausoleum of Catherine Opalinska, his wife, which is by Nicolas Adam and is lyrical and full of hope. At the rear of the church there is a rather curious early-16C statue of Notre-Dame-de-Bonsecours, to whom the church is dedicated.

Musée Historique Lorrain: This highly original museum brings to life the history of Lorraine, and highlights the artistic heritage of a province which has been rich in talent. The first outstanding feature of the museum, which is housed in two very interesting buildings, is its architecture. The Ducal Palace was built in the 13C, rebuilt from about 1502 and then restored very carefully in the early 19C. It is contemporary with the Loire châteaux and still has its fortifications. Architecturally it is all purely functional, apart from the doorway with its superb Flamboyant gable, all the more striking against the very sober façade. The museum collections are devoted to the ethnography and arts of Lorraine through the ages. There are collections of Gallo-Roman archaeology, medieval sculpture, 15&16C tapestries, as well as domestic objects, which reveal popular art and tradition. But there is also a veritable treasure here in the shape of a series of works by 17C Lorraine artists, including almost all of Jacques Callot's engravings, some by Jacques de Bellange and fine paintings like the *Servante à la Puce* by Georges de la Tour. The deconsecrated *église des Cordeliers* (Franciscan church) is now an annexe of this museum. This is a unique example of Gothic architecture in Nancy, the nave is late 15C and the church was the burial place of the Dukes of Lorraine. The octagonal ducal chapel built above the burial vault has a dome with trompe-l'oeil panels and a central lantern-light (1607). The tomb of Philippe de Gueldre is one of the remarkable works in this church-museum and it is an example of the mastery of Ligier Richier, who was deeply inspired by medieval Christianity.

Musée des Beaux-Arts: On the Place Stanislas, it contains the whole spectrum of European painting from the Middle Ages to the present day. There are several outstanding works here from the 17,18&19C, including the *Death of Charles the Bold at the Battle of Nancy*, by Eugène Delacroix. There is also a selection of contemporary works (Dufy, Utrillo and Modigliani).

Musée de l'École de Nancy: In the late 19C the 'modern style' began to challenge the prevailing cult of the past, which resulted in the main in the production of pastiches. Some of the masters of this style were from Nancy e.g. Émile Gallé (1846 –1904) and Louis Majorelle (1859–1926), who were both actively involved in the rebirth of the decorative arts in France and created works (furniture, glassware, ceramics, faience) whose forms were inspired by plants and the insect world. 'My garden is my library' as one of the exponents of this style said.

Nant　　　　　　　　　　　(960 inhab.)
12 Aveyron　　　　　　　　　　p.424 □ K 13

This charming little town on the borders of Causse Noir and Causse de Larzac is full

Nancy, Musée des Beaux-Arts, the 'Death of Charles the Bold' by Delacroix

of narrow streets with vaulted passageways around the old market building (14C). The 14C Pont de la Prade crosses the Dourbie at this point.

Abbey church of Saint Pierre: Pope Innocent II elevated the old priory of Nant to an abbey in 1135. The monks then set about building the present church, whose W. doorway has a polygonal bell tower. The central door was replaced in the 14C with a Gothic portal. Inside, the first floor is in the form of a gallery with a ribbed dome. The twin pillars and columns in the nave are decorated with very fine capitals which incorporate strap-work, shells and chequer patterns.

Nantes	(263,700 inhab.)
44 Loire-Atlantique	p.413□E 7

The ancient city of Nantes, at the narrowing of the Loire where the Erdre and the Sèvre-Nantaise converge, owes its prosperity to its exceptionally favourable geographical location. It is an estuary town but out of reach of naval attack, and it was one of the safest harbours when the Atlantic trade began to develop. It was the rival of Rennes, the historic cultural and administrative capital of Brittany, and became an industrial and commercial centre. The Dukes of Brittany made their residence in the famous château built in 1466 by François II. It is enclosed within daunting fortifications and contains a lovely palace with a courtyard which once rang with the sound of jousts and tournaments, pantomimes and mystery plays. Nantes' influence continued and in the 18C it was at its height with the trade to the Indies and the slave trade.

The town began to develop as a result of its wealth. Merchants and ship-owners moved into the area around the Quai de la Fosse near the huge warehouses full of sugar, tobacco, cotton, rare woods and spices, abandoning the narrow streets in the historic medieval part of the town. Some of them were even more daring and, with the example of Venice in mind, they built astonishing palaces on piers on the

Nancy, the tomb of Stanislas

Nantes, Grand-Logis of the château

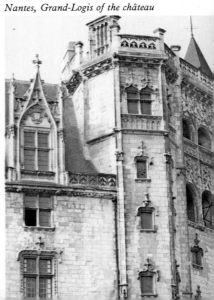

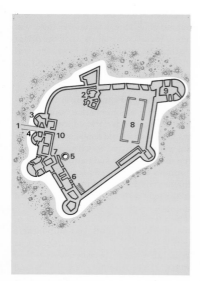

Château of Nantes 1 Entrance **2** old keep **3** Tour du Pied-de-Biche **4** Tour de la Boulangerie **5** well **6** residence **7** Tour de la Couronne d'Or **8** Bâtiment du Harnachement **9** Tour du Fer à Cheval **10** Bâtiment du Grand-Gouvernement

Nantes, Château-des-Ducs

Saulzaie sandbank which became the Île Feydeau. Nowadays, although the arm of the Loire has disappeared, the houses in the Rue Kervégan with their wonderful balconies supported by corbels with pagan and exotic carvings still bear the mark of these merchants with their love of spectacle and of the bizarre. The new quarters have luxurious houses on the Cours Cambronne and the Place Graslin, which were inspired by the Carrefour de l'Odéon in Paris. There are also some interesting ones in the Rue Crébillon (which has an shopping arcade from 1883 beside it, the Passage Pommeraye), and also on the Place Royale where there is a fountain (1865) decorated with statues symbolizing Nantes, the Loire and its tributaries.

Château and museums: Today the château contains three museums. It is,

however, an imposing Gothic and Renaissance fortress built by the Dukes of Brittany, mostly in the 15C, and occupies the site of an earlier 13C château (the old keep survives). On either side of the entrance are two towers, the Tour du Pied-de-Biche and the Tour de la Boulangerie; the entrance itself has a 15C drawbridge and a 18C stone bridge. The inner courtyard is enhanced by a superb well, whose carved surround is crowned by a superb piece of wrought iron depicting the ducal crown. Beside it is the *Grand Logis* with highly ornate Flamboyant dormer windows, and this is flanked by the *Tour de la Couronne d'Or* with its beautiful loggias by Mathelin Rodier, who was the cathedral architect. François II and Anne of Brittany's successors added buildings but these are of lesser interest, for example the Bâtiment du Harnachement (1784). The *Musée des*

Arts Décoratifs in the Tour du Fer à Cheval contains period furniture, ceramics and other objets d'art. The *Musée des Arts Populaires et Régionaux* in the Bâtiment du Grand Gouvernement is devoted to Breton folklore, and contains costumes, faience, pottery and popular pictures. There are also reconstructions of traditional interiors. The *Musée des Salorges* in the Bâtiment Harnachement is all about Nantes' naval history and the regional industries which made the town prosper.

Cathedral of Saint-Pierre: Though it was begun in 1434, Nantes cathedral was not finished until 1893, when the apse and radiating chapels were added. Its unity is striking, even though it had to be restored after a fire. The façade, with its tall towers (about 200 ft.) is interesting mainly for its three portals, with arches finely carved with characters and scenes from the Bible. Inside, the organ loft is above a porch, and a spiral staircase with columns leads up to it. It is followed by the well balanced nave. The pillars, without capitals, rise straight up to the high vault. Above the arcades runs an elegant triforium. *Transept:* In the right arm is the tomb of François II and of Marguerite de Foix; a Renaissance masterpiece by Michel Colombe (*c.* 1430 – 1512). Statues representing Justice, Strength and Moderation and Prudence support the black marble slab with the recumbent figures in white marble, their heads supported by three angels. At their feet lie a lion and a hare, symbols of loyalty, and in the niches are figures of the Apostles, patron saints and mourners. On the other side, in the left transept, is the cenotaph of General de Lamoricière (1806–65), with its four bronze statues in the corners representing martial valour, charity, history and faith. The *Psalette* beside the cathedral is today the *Musée d'Art Religieux*, but was once the seat of the archdeaconry. It is a lovely 15C house with a staircase turret and cut off corners; the

Nantes, 'Mme de Senonnes' by Ingres

basket-arch doorway has carved coats-of-arms and a trellis.

Sainte-Croix: Built in the 17C and altered in the 19C, it is situated in the oldest part of the town. Its bell tower is very tall and has a belfry on the top containing the old bell (1663) of Nantes. The Romanesque style doorway (1685) leads to a nave with Gothic windows. The church contains a 19C pulpit and an altar and altarpiece with paintings of the same period.

Hôtel-de-Ville: Most of the building, including the annexes are 17C. They consist of three old hôtels: the Hôtel de Derval, which has a Renaissance façade with five arches facing the main courtyard, the Hôtel de Rosmadec, which is Louis XIII with a fine stone staircase and balustrades inside, and the Hôtel de Monti de Rezé.

Préfecture: Housed in the former Chambre des Comtes de Bretagne (1763), it has a projecting central section with four Ionic columns crowned by a triangular pediment. Inside, there is a spiral staircase leading to the Salle des Procureurs.

Musée des Beaux Arts: 10 Rue Georges-Clemenceau. The museum of fine arts is housed in a 19C building and its 2,000 paintings make it one of the great French museums. Among the works from the Italian School there are two parts of a predella of St.Benedict by Borgognone, several works by Perugino and Tintoretto, an outstanding group of pieces by the school of Caravaggio, two works by Guardi from the Carnaval series and one by Canaletto. The Flemish School is represented by Breughel, de Velours and there are some landscapes by Rubens. There are also three masterpieces by Georges de la Tour: *Hurdy-Gurdy Player, Angel Appearing to Joseph* and the *Denial of Peter*, as well as the *Young Prince* by Le Nain, and paintings by Watteau, Lancret, Greuze, Géricault, Delacroix and the famous *Portrait of Madame de Senonnes* by Ingres as well as one of Courbet's best works, *Winnowing*. Other rooms are devoted to the Impressionists (Monet, Sisley, Maufra), and more recent painters (Dufy, Van Dongen, Valadon, Vlaminck, Rouault, Manessier, Kandinsky and Vasarely).

Musée Dobrée: Place Jean-V. Archaeological collections devoted to pre-history and antiquity have been assembled in the Manoir de la Touche (15C). The nearby Palais Dobrée, built in the 19C by a well-known collector from Nantes, houses medieval collections (ivories, enamels, illuminated manuscripts, tapestries, sculpture and religious paintings). It also has some 16&17C furniture, a print room with original engravings by Rembrandt and Dürer, 18C silver and a few other interesting paintings. The new building has a historical section.

Muséum d'Histoire Naturelle: Place de la Monnaie. This scientific museum was founded at the end of the 18C and moved to the former Hôtel de la Monnaie in 1868.

Nantes, Musée des Beaux-Arts, 'Winnowing' by Courbet

It has a large regional and general collection, a vivarium, herbaria and an impressive library. Many of the exhibits belonged to 18C ship-owners.

Musée Compagnonnique: Rue Cl. Guillon-Verne. Only recently opened in the elegant Manoir de la Hautière, this small museum contains outstanding examples of craftwork and also old tools.

Musée Jules Verne: Rue de l'Hermitage. This is devoted to the novelist Jules Verne (1828–1905), who was born in Nantes.

Environs: Château de Goulaine: (14 km. SE): The château just outside the village of Haute-Goulaine still has its fortified wall and moat. It was built at the end of the 15C by Goulaine noblemen, and is a pleasant mixture of Flamboyant—pinnacled dormer windows, lancet decoration —and the early Renaissance of the façades. The residence faces the large courtyard and has two very fine staircase towers, one on either side. The chapel and stables (17C) complete the group. The other façade opens on to a French parterre. **Le Loroux-Bottereau** (20 km. E.): The village church dominating the Goulaine marshes contains some priceless late-12C Romanesque frescos, which came from a nearby chapel. The frescos depict the legends of St.Giles and Charlemagne. On the lower panel you can see the kneeling Emperor repenting of the incest he committed with his sister, Gisèle, who appears on the left. **Clisson** (28 km. SE): The château here was owned by the Clisson family and then by the Dukes of Brittany. Now ruined, it is none the less very attractive. A bridge over the moat leads to a 15C entrance erected by Duke François II when he built the W. section of the building. Only the chapel, the residence and the kitchens remain of the 13C medieval fortress. *Garenne Lemot and Garenne Valentin:* When the sculptor Lemot and the Cacault brothers returned from Italy at the beginning of the 19C, they undertook the task of rebuilding the town of Clisson after the ravages of the Vendée wars. Thus the town acquired a rather surprising Mediterranean look. They designed parks, grottoes, statues and tem-

Nantes, Musée des Beaux-Arts, 'Le Cargo Noir' by Dufy

ples dedicated to classical deities for their property, which lay between the Sèvre-Nantaise and the Moine. **Blain** (37 km. N.): The château of Blain, near the forest of Gavre, is now occupied by a school. It has an imposing machicolated wall and squat towers with arrow slits. The castle has been frequently altered since it was built in the 12C. To the S. is the Tour du Pont Levis (16C) and some elegant buildings which contrast with the crudeness of the fortified parts and with the Tour du Connétable (1380).

Narbonne	(40,550 inhab.)
11 Aude	p.424☐J 15

This town, surrounded by vines, is a sous-préfecture and an important crossroads for tourists. It has a very an old centre, but the present-day town shows no trace of the ancient Narbonne (*Colonia Narbo Martius*) which was an important port rivalling Marseilles in Roman times. However, the sea has receded a long way since Cicero

Narbonne, cathedral of St-Just

called the Narbonnaise region the 'Boulevard of Latinity'. The town was once divided up, one part, the 'Bourg', held by a viscount and the other, the 'Cité', by the bishop. It finally fell to the French Crown in the 16C. Charles Trenet, the great French music-hall singer, was born here in 1913.

Palais des Archevêques: This large fortified building was built by architects who were inspired by the Palace of the Popes at Avignon. It is protected by three square 13&14C towers (the strong keep of Gilles Aycelin bears the name of the prelate who had it built). The group of buildings has more of the fortress about it than the ecclesiastical residence, and it includes the Hôtel-de-Ville built by Viollet-le-Duc in the 19C. The Passage de l'Ancre is an impressive fortified street between the Tour Saint-Martial and the Tour de la Madeleine (1273, the oldest of the towers) and it separates the largely Romanesque Palais Vieux from the 14C Palais Neuf. The *Musée d'Art et d'Histoire*, in the archbishops' apartments, has ceramics, Limoges enamels, paintings and illuminated manuscripts. The 14&15C cloister occupies the site of a pre-Romanesque cathedral of which only a bell tower remains.

Former cathedral of Saint-Just: Built 1272–1354, it is now reduced to no more than a tall, cold choir inspired by the great cathedrals of N. France; it has lovely 14&15C stained glass. The nave could not be built because the ramparts ran across the site and the town Consuls refused to allow these to be demolished. The chapel of the Annonciade next to the sacristy is 15C and in fact occupies the old chapterhouse. The treasure includes tapestries, fine pieces of silver and ivories.

Basilica of Saint-Paul-Serge: This church on the other side of the narrow Canal de la Robine bears the name of the first

Bishop of Narbonne, who was buried on the site. It has 12C elements and a tall choir built in the first half of the 13C. The porch forms the base of a 16C bell tower. The N. portal leads to a 4C early Christian cemetery with sarcophagi in the crypt.

Musée Lapidaire: This museum is housed in a deconsecrated church, Notre-Dame de Lamourguier, and displays exhibits from the Narbonne of antiquity and the Middle Ages: inscriptions, sarcophagi, stele and capitals. The church itself is still attractive and was once a dependency of the famous Marseilles abbey of Saint-Victor.

Environs: Abbaye de Fontfroide (14 km. SW): This isolated abbey standing at the mouth of one of the gorges of the Corbières, is far removed from the bustle of modern life. It dates from the late 11C, adopted the Cistercian reform and became very prosperous in the 12&13C. However, it declined under the commendam system and was suppressed in the Revolution. It is a cousin of the 'three Provençal sisters'

—the abbeys of Sénanque, Silvacane and Thoronet—and has been very well restored. The bare abbey church dates from the second half of the 12C and is a fine example of Cistercian architecture, its beauty stemming from its elegant simplicity and purity of line. The S. chapels were added in the 14&15C. In one 13C room there is a 15C stone calvary. The abbey buildings are arranged around a cloister with Gothic walks, and the oldest of these, against the church, dates from about 1250. The chapterhouse has nine ribbed vaults and was built in the early 13C.

Navarrenx	(1,150 inhab.)
64 Pyrénées-Atlantiques	p.422☐E 14/15

Navarrenx is a quiet village sheltering behind an impressive wall with a series of bastions. The wall extends for some 1,650 yards and was built in the mid 16C after plans by the Italian architect Fabrice Siciliano. These were very much ahead of their time; they were later improved by

Narbonne, cathedral of St-Just, tapestry 'The Creation of the World'

Vauban. On the left bank of the torrent is the Tour Herrère, which dates from the 15C. It marks the original location of the cité, which was moved when Henri II d'Albret decided to fortify it.

Nemours
77 Seine-et-Marne

(11,240 inhab.)
p.415☐ J 6

This ancient town has a Gothic and Renaissance church and a medieval château with strong round towers and a separate keep, which was altered in the 15&16C. This fortress houses the wide-ranging *Musée Municipal*.

Nérac
47 Lot-et-Garonne

(7,650 inhab.)
p.423☐ G 13

This is the capital of the little Albret region, and was the seat of the brilliant court of Marguerite d'Angoulême. It was also a Protestant stronghold when the future King Henri IV waged war against the Catholics. The Renaissance château was used as a citadel by the Béarnais and now houses a small museum. The church of *Saint-Nicolas* dates from 1780 and is the work of Victor Louis, the architect of the Grand Théâtre in Bordeaux. The hump-backed Pont-Vieux over the Baîse is Gothic and leads to the old quarter of Petit-Nérac.

Neuf-Brisach
68 Haut-Rhin

(2,580 inhab.)
p.417☐ P 6

This town by the Rhine belongs to another age with its ramparts, irregular streets and squares, 17C houses and the Place d'Armes. A severe yet beautiful stronghold built by Vauban, it is a fine example of 17C fortification.

Nevers
58 Nièvre

(47,730 inhab.)
p.420☐ J 8

Nevers is descended from a Gallic city mentioned in Caesar's Commentaries.

Fontfroide, the abbey

Historically and administratively it belongs to Burgundy but the town seems to have more in common with the Sancerre and Bourbon regions. Standing on the Loire, it was once dependent on river trade. It also owes a great deal to one of its Dukes, Louis de Gonzague. In about 1570 he sent for Italian glass and enamel workers and they set up a very successful industry which continued until the Revolution. The barges used to be loaded with glass and faience and some fine examples of these can be seen in the *Musée Municipal*. Nevers, rising in tiers above the Loire, has a lot of modern building all around it but has preserved its old centre. The strong 14C *Porte du Croux* leads to the old town. It also houses the *Musée Archéologique du Nivernais*.

Cathedral of Saint-Cyr-et-Sainte-Juliette: This strange, beautiful cathedral was cruelly damaged at the end of the last war. It is a mixture of styles and has had a lot of restoration. The building combines the remains of a Romanesque cathedral (mid-12C) with the Gothic cathedral built after a fire in 1211, and is unusual in France in that it has two apses. Above a crypt containing a 16C Entombment, the W. end of the Romanesque apse has a wide semicircular arch and a 12C figure of Christ in majesty painted on the vault. At the other end of the church there are the remains of the threshold of the Romanesque cathedral beneath the Gothic choir. The new cathedral was built in several stages; work began at a good pace in the mid 13C but it then slowed down and continued until the 15C. In the S. transept there is a lovely, open Renaissance staircase with St.Michael slaying the dragon at the top.

Palais Ducal: Begun in the second half of the 15C by Jean de Clamecy and finished in the 16C. It is an elegant building, flanked by round or polygonal towers.

Nevers, the church of St-Étienne

On the slim central turret of the façade there appear bas-reliefs depicting the legend of the 'Knight of the Swan' (this German ancestor of the Clèves family, related by marriage to the Gonzagues, was the inspiration for Lohengrin). There are remains of the 16C Château de Gloriette to the E. of the palace.

Saint-Étienne: This is a homogenous building of pure lines. A former Cistercian priory church dating from the second half of the 11C, it has a sober façade and a fine apse with radiating chapels, minus its old towers; the choir has some capitals with carved leaf and palm motifs. A fine example of Romanesque architecture, it is a successful blend of Burgundian and Auvergne styles.

The convent of Saint-Gildard: This is

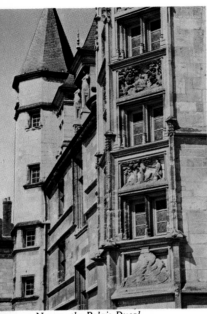

Nevers, the Palais Ducal

the mother house of the Soeurs de la Charité de Nevers. Bernadette Soubirous (St.Bernadette of Lourdes) came here, took the veil in 1867 and died here in 1879. In one chapel, much visited by pilgrims, her embalmed body is kept in a shrine.

Nice	(346,620 inhab.)
06 Alpes-Maritimes	p.426☐P 14

Nice is a great tourist centre and regional metropolis; its famous Promenade des Anglais runs all along the spectacular Baie des Anges. Nice has spread far and wide, to the mouth of the Var and the foot of the hills, and the most modern houses are being built. However, its medieval heart is still intact. It is the pivotal point of the Côte d'Azur, and a port for communication with Corsica, a large seaside resort, a city of cul-

ture and an industrial centre. Its long history goes back to the time when the Phocaeans, who were already established at Marseilles, founded a trading post, possibly called Nikaia. The Romans then developed an administrative and military town on the Cimiez hill, which still yields their traces. It was ruined by barbarian attacks and then expanded seawards, developing on the 'Château Rock' above the port. A part of Savoy, it did not become French until 1860 after a plebiscite. It has been a tourist attraction since the 18C when the English liked to winter here, and it was an Englishman, the Reverend Lewis Way, who laid out the 'camin dei Angles' which became the Promenade des Anglais. Garibaldi was born here in 1807 and Thé odore de Banville, Alexandre Dumas and Berlioz spent a great deal of time here, the later working on his *King Lear*. Nice wa famous in the Belle Époque and since th last war there has been much new building.

Old Town: That part of Nice by the se and between the Cours Saleya and th 'Rocher du Château' is full of winding streets, passageways and staircases. Ther are also tall 17&18C houses. In the Ru Droite, the *Palais Lascaris* is a very elegan Genoese style building which was built i the 17C. It has a lovely staircase an painted ceilings and it is used for exh bitions and chamber music concert *Saint-Jacques*: This is nearby and was bui in the Jesuit style of the *Gesù* in Rome (fir half of the 17C). The *Cathedral of Sain Réparate* is also in old Nice. It is a fin classical building dating from the mi 17C. In the Rue de la Poissonnerie is th *Chapelle de l'Annonciation* with its late-17 baroque decor. In the large church of *Sai Augustin*, also 17C and baroque, there a Pietà by the local artist Louis Bréa. O the edge of the old town, the mid-18C *Pla Garibaldi*, which is surrounded by large a caded houses, is worth a visit.

Nice, Palais Lascaris, the staircase

The Château: Traditionally called the Château, the site is actually occupied by ruins of the citadel which was razed to the ground in 1706. The Tour Bellanda (see *Musée Naval*) is 16C. The hill on which the château stood was extensively excavated when the huge War Memorial was built. It was dedicated in 1928 by Marshal Foch.

Cimiez and the arena: Cimiez, a hill covered by beautiful villas, has some important Roman remains — a 1&3C amphitheatre (this has been cleared and open-air performances are now held here), 2&3C baths, and a baptistery built at the dawn of Christianity. In the middle of the archaeological site is a twin museum in the Villa des Arènes (see under museums). At the top of the hill there is a 19C Gothic church which has retained a 17C porch and contains a *Crucifixion* by Louis Bréa.

There is a 15C cross in front of this church.

Musée Masséna: 35 Promenade des Anglais. This is in a sumptuous Belle Époque house surrounded by gardens, and it contains large and varied collections of books, works by primitive painters from Nice, items associated with the history of the region, views and plans of Nice, furniture, ceramics, folklore, jewellery, etc. The State donated several Impressionist works to the museum and it also has some paintings by Dufy.

Musée des Beaux-Arts-Jules-Chéret: 33 Avenue des Baumettes. This museum, in a quiet residential quarter, is relatively unknown. It is dedicated to the painter Jules Chéret who died in Nice in 1932. There are also Italian and Flemish primitives, works by Fragonard, Hubert Robert and Van Loo (Van Loo was from Nice), Impressionist works (Monet, Sisley, Renoir, in particular), works by Signac, Dufy and Van Dongen, some ceramics by Picasso, works by Carpeaux and collections of Oriental art.

Musée National du Message Biblique Marc Chagall: Avenue du Docteur-Ménard. This ultra-modern, air-conditioned museum dominates the town. Built in 1972, it contains 17 great compositions from the *Message Biblique* by Marc Chagall, as well as 200 preparatory sketches, gouaches, lithographs and sculptures by the great Russian-born artist. There is a concert hall with blue stained glass, a libary, a projection room and a basin reflecting a mosaic inspired by a drawing of Chagall's called *Elijah Ascending to Heaven*.

Villa des Arènes, Musée Matisse, Musée Archéologique, Cimiez: Like Raoul Dufy, Henri Matisse is buried at Nice. He was very fond of the town and died here in 1954 — his studio was at Cimiez. On the first floor of the villa there are about 30 paintings showing the main phases of his career. In the Musée Matisse there are also ceramics, designs for stained glass, engravings, drawings, a bronze as well as personal possessions of the artist. The Musée Archéologique displays the finds from the digs at Cimiez. There are remains of Roman baths within the wall of the Villa des Arènes.

Musée Naval: Tour Bellanda. Here, at the top of the tower where Berlioz lived when he came to compose at Nice, you can see models of ships, of the port and displays of weapons. **Musée du Vieux-Logis:** 59 Avenue Saint-Barthélemy. A reconstruction of a Gothic and Renaissance bourgeois house has been set up in a disused oil crusher. There are paintings, stained glass, sculptures, furniture and 15&16C objects. **Musée de Malacologie**: 3 Cours Saleya. Devoted to the molluscs of the Mediterranean and other seas. **Muséum d'Histoire Naturelle:** 60 bis Boulevard Risso. An unusual collection of thousands of casts of mushrooms, and Mediterranean fish.

Nice, Musée Marc Chagall, 'Le Message Biblique' (detail) by Marc Chagall

Musée de Terra-Amata: Impasse de Tera-Amata. This museum, set up on the site of an elephant-hunters' camp (some 390,000 years old), explains the way of life of the prehistoric inhabitants of the area. On show is the print of a right foot of early man—most probably Pithecanthropus—and a reconstruction of a cabin made of branches; there are also stone tools.

Environs: Sanctuaire de Laghet (14 km. NE): This 17C sanctuary is dedicated to the Madonna of Laghet and has an unusual collection of ex-voto offerings. Guillaume Apollinaire admired its 'naïve and painstaking clumsiness'. The baroque church also contains a statue of the Madonna, dressed in white satin with gold embroidery.

man, the other Celtic. The *Musée Municipal* deals especially with the Gallo-Roman period, displaying the results of local digs. There is also a reconstruction of a hypocaust heating system. The ruined château of Wasenbourg which Goethe so admired was rebuilt in the 13C.

Environs: Woerth (10 km. E.): Here there are monuments which recall the disastrous French defeats of August 1870 and the famous but vain charge of the Reichshoffen cuirassiers which took place nearby.
Château de Fleckenstein (7 km. NW of Woerth): The ruins of a half underground château destroyed in 1680 by the French rise up on a large red sandstone promontory.

Niederbronn-les-Bains (4,460 inhab.)
67 Bas-Rhin   p.417☐P 4

This is a spa which has always exploited its waters. One spring is supposed to be Ro-

Nieuil-sur-l'Autise (870 inhab.)
85 Vendée   p.418☐F 9

The former abbey of Saint-Vincent dates from the 11C and was restored in the 19C. The church was built on the edge of

Nice, Place Masséna

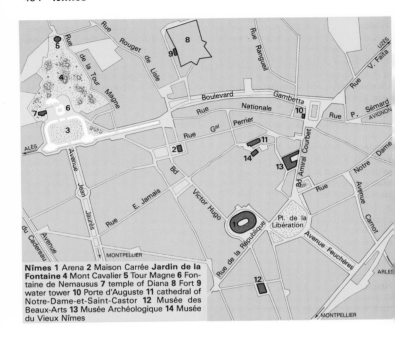

Nîmes 1 Arena **2** Maison Carrée **Jardin de la Fontaine 4** Mont Cavalier **5** Tour Magne **6** Fontaine de Nemausus **7** temple of Diana **8** Fort **9** water tower **10** Porte d'Auguste **11** cathedral of Notre-Dame-et-Saint-Castor **12** Musée des Beaux-Arts **13** Musée Archéologique **14** Musée du Vieux Nîmes

Nîmes, the arena

marshland and only the façade and nave with side aisles remain of the Romanesque parts. The elegant Poitevin façade has some outstanding decorative masonry between the two storeys. Inside, there is a dome with annular ribbing. To the S. of the church, the only cloister in the Vendée which is virtually intact still has its four groin-vaulted walks. It leads to the chapterhouse, monks' lavabo and the cellars.

| **Nîmes** | (133,950 inhab.) |
| 30 Gard | p.425☐L 14 |

This Languedoc town, close to Provence and surrounded by garrigues, still bears the mark of Rome. It takes its name from the tutelary god of a spring, *Nemausus*.
It was a little Gallic town when the Romans decided to establish a major colony here—*Colonia Augusta Nemausis*. This became one of the most beautiful towns in all the Empire and was greatly in favour with those in power. Within its strong town wall, built just at the beginning of our era, it sparkled and prospered, especially in the 2C, but it was then subsequently ruined by invasions. It was reunited with Languedoc and then both were joined to the French Crown in 1271. Nîmes has known a great many religious troubles—it was on the side of the Albigensians and suffered the dreadful crusades of Simon de Montfort (see Albi), its Jews were expelled in 1389, and it sided with the Reformation in the 16C, thereafter going through a very turbulent time. Nîmes is proud of having an academy with the same privileges as the Académie Française (conferred by Louis XIV). The town is undoubtedly best known for its Roman remains but there are also some very picturesque old streets near the Cathedral and some interesting old houses.

Roman monuments: Arena: Very similar to the one at Arles, it could hold over 20,000 spectators. The amphitheatre, built just before the Christian era, was turned into a fortress in the 5C and then cluttered with buildings—some 2,000 people lived here. It was cleared in the 19C and it now stages bullfights. **Maison Carée:** This 1C temple shows Greek influence on Roman art. It was built by Augustus's son-in-law, Agrippa, and is rectangular rather than square. Used as a town hall, it was lived in and was very nearly pulled down to adorn the park at Versailles. It has now been restored and houses the *Musée des Antiques*, which contains a colossal head and statue of Apollo, the reconstructed 'Venus of Nîmes' (which was found broken), friezes and funerary columns. **Jardin de la Fontaine:** A beautiful 18C garden full of Roman remains, it lies just beneath the cedar and pine-covered Mont Cavalier and is dominated by the Tour Magne (1C BC). It contains the Fontaine de Nemausus and nearby there are remains of a building called the Temple of Diana (an 18C nymph has replaced the statue of Augustus which once overlooked the waters). The ruins of a Roman water tower were found at the foot of a bastion known as the Fort (17C). Water was brought to it via the famous Pont du Gard (see under that name). The *Porte d'Auguste* or the *Porte d'Arles* was part of the Roman town wall.

Cathedral of Notre-Dame-et-Saint-Castor: This is 11C but it has been greatly altered over the years. It was almost entirely rebuilt in the 19C. It has a few Romanesque elements and a 4C sarcophagus.

Musée des Beaux-Arts: Rue Cité-Foulc. This has a large antique mosaic on the ground floor and contains a number of paintings from all the major schools from the 16–19C, including some very interesting 16&17C Italian works (a superb *Susanna and the Elders* by Jacopo Bassano);

there are also sculptures by Rodin and Bourdelle.

Musée Archéologique: Boulevard Amiral-Courbet. This occupies an old Jesuit monastery and contains extensive collections, mainly of the art and connected with the day-to-day life of the Gallo-Roman period. There are Greek, Roman, Gallo-Roman and medieval coins.

Musée du Vieux Nîmes: This is near the Cathedral in the 17C Bishop's Palce. It is devoted to the popular art and traditions of the region, and has old furniture, embroidered 18C shawls and waistcoats, and exhibits on weaving, bullfighting and Provençal horse-racing.

Niort	(63,970 inhab.)
79 Deux Sevres	p.418□F 9

Seen from the N. of the Loire, Niort looks like a Mediterranean town with its pale houses, roofs with round tiles and its large sunny square. The capital of Deux Sevres, on the edge of the Poitevin Marais district, the town lies on a gentle slope of the left bank of the Sèvre Niortaise. It dates from the Roman period and was a busy river port until the beginning of this century; it is still an important commercial centre. Now a developing town, there are many new industries, as well as the two traditional ones of leather work and the preparation of the herb angelica.

Keep: This late-12/early-13C keep dominates the Quai de la Sèvre and was part of an English fortress. It suffered many sieges, and was fought over during the Wars of Religion by the Catholics and Huguenots; then under the Bourbons it was used as a State prison. It consists of two enormous square towers which have round corner turrets and which are linked by a 15C building. These buildings house a *Musée d'Ethnographie Régionale* whose exhibits include local head-dresses and a reconstruction of the interior of a peasant's house.

Nîmes, the Maison Carrée

Niort, keep

Niort, former Hôtel de Ville

Notre-Dame: This is 15&16C, altered in the 18C. It is notable for the elegance of its bell tower (1500) whose spire is about 240 ft. high. The corner buttresses have pinnacles with crockets and niches. In the N. façade there is a finely carved Flamboyant doorway. Inside, the church contains some lovely Aubusson tapestries, and the strange 17C red marble mausoleums of a former Governor of Niort, his son and his wife (their busts decorate their tombs). Also note an early-16C Flamboyant font with bas-reliefs and the lovely carved stalls.

Former Hôtel-de-Ville and Musée du Pilori: This fortified house, triangular in plan, dates from the 16&17C and houses the *Musée du Pilori,* which has lapidary and coin collections, regional documents, and objects found in local digs (prehistoric and Gallo-Roman period).

Musée des Beaux-Arts: This is in the former Collège de l'Oratoire. Its exhibits are very varied: 17C tapestries, sets of enamels, ivories and silverware (12–17C). There are portraits by lesser masters of the 17&18C. The *Musée Taire* is devoted to the history of shoes through the ages.

Old Town: The old houses here are mainly in and around the Rue Saint Jean. The most interesting are the *Maison du Gouverneur,* with its Gothic arcade (15C), and the *Hôtel d'Estissac,* an elegant Renaissance house in the Rue du Petit-Saint-Jean.

Environs: Échiré (10 km. N.): *Château de Coudray-Salbart:* Dominating the right bank of the Sèvres, this enormous 13C fortress is very well preserved. It is trapezoidal in plan and it has six towers. There is a corridor inside the walls and the arrow slits face both inside and out.

Nogent-le-Rotrou
28 Eure-et-Loir

(13,590 inhab.)
p.414☐H 6

The château of *Saint-Jean* overlooks the Huisne and the town which has some historic houses. It is feudal in appearance and its walls have 12&13C towers, the strong keep is 11C, and the residence 15C (containing a Musée du Perche). The church of *Notre-Dame* is mainly 13C, while Saint-Laurent and Saint-Hilaire are 15&16C. The latter preserves a 13C choir. In the Hôtel-Dieu, behind Notre-Dame, is the 17C tomb of the Duke and Duchess of Sully.

Nohant-Vic
36 Indre

(520 inhab.)
p.419☐I 9

The dark green Berry countryside around the twin villages of the 'Vallée Noire' (Black valley) figured in George Sand's writings. The area appears in particular in *La Mare au Diable* and *La Petite Fadette*.

The 'château' of Nohant opposite the church with its rustic porch is the large family house where George Sand grew up with her grandmother, and where she died in 1876. Inside, it is much as her many guests knew it—among these were Franz Liszt, and his mistress Marie d'Agoult, Balzac, Chopin, Arago, Delacroix, Flaubert and Dumas fils. 2 km. N. is the 12C *church of Vic*, which has some remarkable 'Romanesque frescos' on biblical subjects; these were greatly admired by George Sand and Prosper Mérimée.

Environs: Le Châtre (6 km. S.): There is a statue of George Sand in this little town which appears in her *Histoire de ma Vie*. A museum in the old 15C château has a wealth of exhibits on George Sand, her friends and the places she immortalized.

Noirlac (former abbey)
18 Cher

p.419☐I 8

The former abbey has been carefully re-

Nogent-le-Rotrou, Château St-Jean

Noirlac, cloister of the abbey

stored—it is a perfect example of Cistercian architecture since there have been few additions to-it over the years. It was founded in the Cher valley in 1150 and shows the importance that St.Bernard and the Cistercian architects attached to simplicity. The plain, peaceful church is intact and flanked by a 13&14C arcaded cloister surrounded by the abbey buildings—the chapterhouse, monks' room with dormitories above it, refectory, cellar and lay brothers' quarters. The large dormitory was turned into attractive apartments in the 17C.

Noirmoutier-en-l'Île
85 Vendée   (4,180 inhab.)   p.418☐D 8

During the Vendée uprising, Maurice Gigost d'Elbée was executed in the Place d'Armes of this small town, the capital of the I le de Noirmoutier. He was the leader of the Catholic Royalist army and had been captured by the Republicans. The château overlooks the square, which has 18C hôtels

Noirmoutier, church

all around. Within the rectangle of the walls is a 15C keep flanked by four round towers and this houses the *Musée Municipal* (local history and ethnography). The church of *Saint Philibert* has a Romanesque choir and Gothic nave and contains two fine 18C altarpieces. The Merovingian crypt, altered in the 11C, was the oratory of the monastery founded by St.Philibert in the 7C. The former Abbaye de la Blanche is to the NW.

Notre-Dame-de-la-Salette
38 Isère   p.425☐N 12

A large cross dominates a neo-Romanesque basilica built in 1861–79 on top of Mont Planeau. The sanctuary is full of the ex-voto offerings of pilgrims venerating the Virgin—the Belle Dame appeared to two local shepherds in 1846.

Noyers
89 Yonne   (840 inhab.   p.415☐K 7

This charming, picturesque town on the Serein seems as if protected from the passing of time by its walls, round towers and fortified gates. It is full of history with 15,16&17C houses along its paved streets. The 15C Hôtel de Ville has 11C foundations and an 18C façade. The church of Notre-Dame was built in 1491–1515 and has Flamboyant elements.

Noyon
60 Oise   (14,040 inhab.)   p.411☐J 3

Calvin was born in Noyon in 1509 and Charlemagne was crowned King of Neustria here in 768. The bishopric was founded in the 6C. The cathedral, **Notre-Dame**, is a fine example of the emergent Gothic. Strong and sober (Romanesque influence), it was begun during the 12C and more or less complete by the 13C. The strong W. façade faces the pretty *Place du Parvis*, with its 16C hôtels. There is a vast porch with three bays, which is dominated by two heavy square 13&14C towers. The partially intact canons' buildings are built on to the cathedral. The chapterhouse is 13C, the cloister too is 13C and has some fine arcades. The chapter 'library' (early 16C) is a pleasant half-timbered building containing some 3,000 volumes, including the *Évangéliaire de Morienval* (9C) with its marvellous illuminations. The cathedral is bathed in light and is a superb blend of Gothic and Romanesque It has a splendid narthex. There are a few mansions in the heart of the town, including a fine Renaissance pavilion.

Environs: Former Abbaye d'Ourscamp: (6 km. S.): The remarkable ruins of the abbey church, built in the 12&13C, are worth visiting. The infirmary, miraculously intact, dates from 1260 and is a Gothic masterpiece. **Blérancourt** (14 km. SE): Here there is an interesting 16C church with a Renaissance façade and remains of a 17C château housing the *Musée National de la Coopération Franco-Américaine*.

Noyers, the walls

Noyon, cathedral of Notre-Dame

Obernai

| **Obernai** | (8,400 inhab.) |
| 67 Bas-Rhin | p.417☐O/P 5 |

The 16&17C, in particular, have left their mark on Obernai, a small Alsace town with an appealing, rather theatrical prettiness. St.Odile was born here according to tradition. The town is clustered around the lovely *Place du Marché* dominated by the old corn market building and a pretty foun-

Obernai, Alsace houses

tain (1904). Its streets and squares are haphazardly arranged and there are some very fine carved and half-timbered houses. Some of the fortifications have survived. The Hôtel de Ville was built in the 15C and altered in the 16&17C. The 13C belfry was once the bell tower of a vanished church, hence its name, kappelturm. *Saint-Pierre-et-Saint-Paul* is a neo-Gothic 19C building.

Environs: Ottrott (4 km. W.): The impressive ruins of two medieval fortresses stand on a spur. One of them, the Rathsamhausen, retains a large early-13C keep.

| **Oloron-Ste-Marie** | (13,140 inhab.) |
| 64 Pyrénées-Atlantiques | p.422☐E/F 15 |

This lively sub-préfecture is split by the deep beds of the rivers Aspe and Ossau which join to form the Oloron. In fact, Oloron was once two towns and traces its history back to the *Iluro* of antiquity. The town was praised by the poet Jules Supervielle and another writer, a young captain who liked writing more than the army—Alfred de Vigny, wrote *Le Déluge* while stationed at Oloron in 1823.

Oloron-Sainte-Marie, church of Ste-Marie, triptych of the Nativity

Sainte-Marie: This former cathedral dates from the 12C and Oloron was a bishopric until the Revolution. The church has been greatly altered and its choir rebuilt in the 14C after a fire. The massive bell tower (which contains the porch) is a relic of the church begun in 1102, and it protects the remarkable Romanesque carved doorway of Pyrenean marble. The tympanum has a touching Descent from the Cross and two secondary tympana beneath this have depictions of the Church persecuted (left) and triumphant (right). The Elders of the Apocalypse appear on the archivolts, together with scenes from daily life. The Saracens in chains on the pier and the equestrian statue of Gaston IV on the base of the arches on the right recall that the Viscount of Béarn was involved in the reconquest of Spain and the First Crusade.

Sainte-Croix: Massive, crude and badly restored in the last century, Sainte-Croix towers above the roofs of Oloron. It dates from the end of the 11C; the 13C dome over the crossing displays Moorish-Spanish influence. There are historiated capitals in the central apse and a large, gilded 18C retable in the left transept. Old Oloron stands on the slope to the N. of the church. The Tour de Grède from the 14C is all that remains of the château around which the Sainte-Croix quarter developed.

Orange
84 Vaucluse

(26,470 inhab.
p.425☐L/M 13

This historic town and agricultural centre is situated on the *Via Agrippa*, a Roman road leading to Lyons. It was the Celtic-

Orange, Roman theatre

Ligurian oppidum of *Arausio* and the site of a Roman legionnaire colony founded at the dawn of our era; it developed during the Pax Romana. The surviving monuments show just how prosperous the colony of *Julia Firma Secundanorum* was. From the 4C onwards, Orange was the seat of a bishop, and the capital of a principality from the 13–18C. The principality passed to the house of Nassau, to which William III of England belonged. It then reverted to France and the title stayed in Holland. The name was given to a Dutch province and a river and province in South Africa.

Roman Theatre: 'The most beautiful wall in the kingdom,' Louis XIV said of the theatre. It is 125 ft. high and 340 ft. across. The tiers in front of the stage, which was once roofed over and closed by a curtain between acts, are on the side of a hill and have been partly restored. It can seat up to about 8,000 spectators for the famous Chorégies (performances with a Greek chorus), which have been held here since 1869. In 1622 the theatre was buried beneath a fortress, but it was cleared in the 19C. It has a tall and much restored statue of the Emperor Augustus.

The Triumphal Arch: This most interesting monument commemorates the founding of the town (1C BC) and is 62 ft. high. Its W. face has been heavily restored and the three other faces still have their beautiful carved decoration.

Cathedral of Notre-Dame: This is Provençal Romanesque in style and was rebuilt in the 12&16C — it was badly damaged during the Wars of Religion. Be-

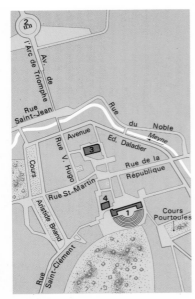

Orange 1 Roman theatre **2** Arc de Triomphe **3** cathedral of Notre-Dame **4** Musée Lapidaire

Orange, Arc de Triomphe

side it is the 18C town hall, which has a belfry of 1671 with a wrought-iron bell-tower.

Musée Lapidaire: This museum has a unique exhibit in the form of the remains of a Roman property register of 77 BC, with the plan for the occupation of plots; there are also public records inscribed on marble.

Environs: Châteauneuf du Pape (13 km. S.): This is surrounded by vines producing one of the finest of the Côtes du Rhône wines. It is dominated by a ruined 14C château, a former summer residence for the Avignon Popes, which was burnt down by the soldiers of the Baron des Adrets in the Wars of Religion. The Germans blew up the keep in 1944.

Orcival	(370 inhab.)
63 Puy-de-Dôme	p.420☐J 10

This old village in a dip between the Dôme and the Dore mountains clusters around the magnificent Romanesque **church of Notre-Dame**. It was built in the 12C, almost certainly along the same plans as Notre-Dame-du-Port. It is grey, sober and modelled on the classical Auvergnat style: the tiers of its apse and the solid oblong mass above the choir. Above it is a two-storied octagonal bell tower with twin bays. Inside, the central nave has a semicircular vault which ends in a broad, light choir, with eight elegant columns. The capitals are simple and mostly foliate. The 12C statue of Notre-Dame d'Orcival is much venerated and is the only Auvergnat Virgin to still have its gold ornamentation. The crypt underneath the choir is identical with it in its plan. The **Château de Cordès**, some way to the N., was built in the 15C and assumed its present appearance in the 17C when the façades were given tall windows. The French parterres were designed by Le Nôtre and the chapel contains a very fine 16C marble altarpiece.

| **Orléans** | (109,960 inhab.) |
| 45 Loiret | p.414☐I 6 |

This city on the Loire is the region's préfecture, the principal town of Loiret and the seat of a bishop. It was dreadfully damaged in the last war but has recovered and expanded to include the neighbouring town of La Source. It originated as the Gallic *Genabum*; became *Aurelianis* under the Romans (hence its present name); and was the site for the coronation of Charles le Chauve in 842; and virtually became the French capital under the first Capetians. In 1305 the university was founded and it soon achieved fame. It was besieged by the English in 1428 and relieved by Joan of Arc the following year. This was a turning point in the Hundred Years War. Each May since 1430 major celebrations have been held to pay tribute to the Liberator, Joan of Arc—the Fête de Jeanne d'Arc is almost a national holiday.

Place du Martroi: The 19C equestrian statue of Joan of Arc has pride of place in this square in the heart of the town. This area was worst hit in the bombing and the 18C former Chancellery was badly damaged in 1944 and restored. It and its 19C replica, the pavilion of the Chamber of Commerce, are on either side of the junction with the Rue Royale, the remarkably rebuilt thoroughfare which forms the axis of city and which leads to the 18C *Pont George V*. The W. part of the square was flattened but has been rebuilt to match the old buildings perfectly. The nearby 16C church of Sainte-Pierre du Martroi suffered in 1944. The adjacent quarter, also ravaged in the war, was remodelled around the Place Charles-de-Gaulle. Here the only surviving old buildings are the façades of the two linked houses of the Porte Renard (16C). Also close by is the house where Joan of Arc stayed; this has been destroyed, rebuilt, destroyed again in the war in 1940,

Orcival, Château de Cordès

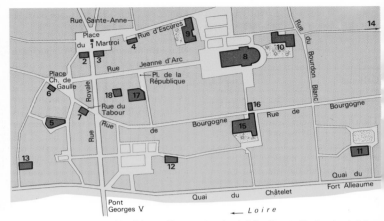

Orléans 1 Statue of Joan of Arc **2** former Chancellery **3** Chambre de Commerce **4** church of Saint-Pierre du Martroi **5** church of Saint-Paul **6** house where Joan of Arc stayed **7** Centre Charles-Péguy **8** cathedral **9** Hôtel Groslot (Hôtel de Ville) **10** former Bishop's Palace (library) **11** church of Saint-Aignan **12** church of Saint-Donatien **13** church of Notre-Dame-de-Recouvrance **14** church of Saint-Euverte **15** Préfecture **16** Salle des Thesès **17** Musée des Beaux-Arts **18** Musée Historique

and now rebuilt yet again, using old materials. Nearby, in the Rue du Tabour, a 16C hôtel houses the *Centre Charles-Péguy* and has a small museum devoted to the writer, who was born in Orléans in 1873. In the Rue d'Escure there are a few elegant citizens' houses (17C) and in the Rue Sainte-Anne there is the late-16C Maison des Oves, so called because of the rounded stones in its façade.

Cathedral: This is a curious church built in Gothic style in the 17&18C. It was 'started and finished too late' and to Marcel Proust was the ugliest in France. It occupies the site of earlier Gallo-Roman, Carolingian, Romanesque and Gothic churches, the last of these being ruined by the followers of the Prince de Condé in 1568. Rebuilding, in a style more or less in keeping with the old one, began from about 1601 when the panache and technique of the Middle Ages had been lost. Jacques Gabriel designed the tall, majestic W. front which is a pastiche, but still

very attractive. The towers, with their strange circular crowns, are by the architect Trouard. The present spire dates from Napoleon III's time. Inside, this last of the Gothic cathedrals (the one at Auch being the penultimate) does not lack grandeur. The choir has carved stalls of 1702–6 after drawings by Gabriel. In the apsidal chapel there is a marble Pietà by Michel Bourdin (1623). The large 17C organ comes from Saint-Benoît-sur-Loire. CRYPT: Here several digs have revealed the remains of earlier churches, one on top of another; these include a little Gallo-Roman basilica embedded in the ruins of the Romanesque choir. Beneath the choir of the cathedral there are some 12&14C sarcophagi. These were bishops' tombs and the prelates were buried with all their priestly paraphernalia including some episcopal croziers, which are now part of the *treasure*.

Near the Cathedral is the old *Hôtel Groslot*, a Renaissance building containing the

Orléans, aerial view

Hôtel de Ville. It was built in the mid 16C and enlarged in the 19C. The statue of Joan of Arc praying on the main steps is by Marie d'Orléans, Louis-Philippe's daughter. In the garden of the old Bishop's Palace is a fragment of the old Gallo-Roman wall; the library is in the former 17C Bishop's Palace. The Campo-Santo, one of the last great medieval cemeteries, was turned over to bulldozers in 1978 to make way for that 20C monument, the car park. This was in spite of protests from eminent historians. To the S. of the cathedral further work has revealed traces of the ancient city, and the archaeologists have had time to act.

Other churches: *Saint-Aignan:* Destroyed in 1428 and rebuilt under Louis XI, it has been mutilated and truncated. It contains a large altarpiece, which was donated by Louis XIII and also a vast Romanesque crypt (interesting capitals). *Saint-Donatien:* Has four 13C pillars, although it was in the main rebuilt in the 17C (it is surrounded by very pretty old streets). *Notre-Dame-de-Recouvrance:* This Renaissance church was restored and redecorated in the last century. *Saint-Paul:* Destroyed in 1940, a free-standing 17C bell tower remains and also a chapel in which Joan of Arc prayed. *Saint-Euverte:* This is 12C and has been greatly altered.

Préfecture and Salle des Thèses: The préfecture, which occupies a former 17C convent, was enlarged in the 19C. Opposite it is the former university library (15C) which is known as the Salle des Thèses. Calvin studied law here.

Musée des Beaux-Arts: Place de la République. The museum occupies the *Hôtel des Créneaux*, which is 15&16C and has a belfry of 1448. It was used as the town hall until the Revolution. The important Musée des Beaux-Arts is famous for its portraits (oils and pastels), French 17&18C works, notably by Jean Valade, Charles Antoine Coypel, J.-B. Perronneau, Thomas Desfriches (a merchant/artist who was the host of many notables in the 18C) and Nicolas de Largillière. The museum also has various Italian, Flemish and

Orléans, Hôtel de Ville

Dutch works (*Skating Scene* by Van Goyen), French 19C works (fine Corot, Boudin and Gauguin) and busts by Houdon.

Musée Historique: Place Abbé-Desnoyers. This was established in a restored Renaissance house, the *Hôtel Cabu* (16C), and it is rich in Gallo-Roman antiquities and objects from the Middle Ages. The remarkable *Gallo-Roman Treasure*, found at Neuvy-en-Sullias, is also on show.

Ornans	(4,400 inhab.)
25 Doubs	p.421 □ N 8

This extremely picturesque town has houses which project out over the river Loue. It has a few fine buildings, including the Hôtel de Grospain (15C) and the Hôtel Panderet de Valonne (17C). The church of *Saint-Laurent* was rebuilt in the 16C and still has the base of the bell tower from an earlier Romanesque building. Since the 17C this has been crowned by a dome and lantern. It contains 18C woodwork and statues, and a silver reliquary bust of St.Lawrence. Gustave Courbet was born at Ornans in 1819 and he was very attached to it all his life, drawing a great deal of inspiration from the area. His birthplace is now a Courbet museum.

Orthez	(10,700 inhab.)
4 Pyrénées-Atlantiques	p.422 □ E 14

Orthez was the capital of Béarn from 1194–1464, after which Pau assumed the role. It is dominated by the *Tour Moncade*, the former keep of a 13C château. The town stands on the Pau at the point where the picturesque *Pont-Vieux*, fortified in the 13&14C, crosses the ravine. There are several old houses, in particular the Maison de Jeanne d'Albret (about 1500) and

the remains of the Hôtel de la Lune, where the chronicler Froissart stayed. The church of *Saint Pierre*, rebuilt in the 15C, once backed on to the ramparts, which is why the N. wall is so bare. It contains a very cold painting by Bonnat, *The Martyrdom of St.Denis*, which is a preparatory sketch for the Pantheon fresco.

Ouistreham	(6,140 inhab.)
14 Calvados	p.413 □ F 4

Ouistreham merges with the seaside resort of Riva Bella and is a major boating centre—indeed one of its features is the forest of masts. Another is the bell tower of a lovely 12&13C Romanesque and Gothic church. The region has been scarred by the airborne operations and landings in June 1944. To the S. of Ouistreham, near **Bénouville** with its 18C château, is the small *Musée de Pegasus Bridge*. This deals with the surprise attack by the British, who captured the double bridge across the canal and the river Orne before the Germans had time to destroy it.

Ornans, the village and the Loue

Paimpont (1,560 inhab.)
35 Ille-et-Vilaine p.413☐D 6

On the banks of a lake, in the heart of a vast
forested region, the village of Paimpont
originated from a 7C monastic foundation.
The abbey buildings, which were restored
in the 18C, now house the municipal
offices and the presbytery. The single aisle
of the 13C church contains a polychrome
statue, Notre-Dame-de-Paimpont, which,
like the panelling, pulpit and choir stalls,
is 17C.

Environs: Paimpont Forest: This is the
largest remnant of the legendary Forest of
Brocéliande, which today consists of only
a few scattered fragments. The Val-sans-
Retour is full of memories of the witch
Morgana; it is here that knights who had
betrayed their lady were kept prisoner.
Near the village of Marette, Merlin the ma-
gician is buried beneath a massive stone.
The Château de Comper, to the N., was
demolished in the 16C (although the main
part of the building was restored in the
19C) and this was supposed to have been
the residence of the witch Viviane.
Château de Trécesson (10 km. SW):
This elegant 15C château, bathed by the
waters of a lake, lies on the southernmost
edge of the forest in the Département of
Morbihan. The château is preceded by a
gateway with a pepper-pot turret on either
side. Reddish stone buildings are grouped
in a square around an inner courtyard
which is closed to the public. **Saint-Léry**
(14 km. NW): The church in this charming village has one of the most beautiful
porches in the region, with little dormer
windows at the top. Next to the portals
with their carved door leaves there is a bas-
relief of a man being devoured by the seven
cardinal sins. Inside is the tomb of the saint
to whom the church is dedicated, and also
a wooden panel depicting his death. **Tré-
horenteuc** (18 km. W.): This Morbihan
village is near the gorge of Val-sans-Retour
on the edge of the Forest of Paimpont, and
it possesses a recently-restored, rather sober church which used to contain the tomb
of St.Onenne (7C), King Judikaël's sister.
But the building is mainly of interest because of its decoration, a combination of
sacred and profane subjects. Morgana appears here too, in the Stations of the Cross
beside figures from the Gospels. In the
nave and the sacristy there are various
paintings illustrating aspects of the Arthu-
rian legend. The glass in the choir depicts
the Quest for the Holy Grail (a holy ves-
sel supposedly used by Jesus at the Last
Supper and used to collect his blood at the

Paray-le-Monial, basilica of the Sacré-Coeur

Crucifixion). The area has numerous megaliths, and one of the many lakes is called the Miroir des Fées (Witches' Mirror).

Paray-le-Monial	(12,130 inhab.)
71 Saône-et-Loire	p.420☐L 9

Paray-le-Monial, on the right bank of the Bourbince, is a major place of pilgrimage and an artistic and historical centre. It started as a small rural parish in 971 when the first monastery was founded here. Its church was considered too small by St. Hugh, the great abbot of Cluny, and so the admirable basilica was built. In the Middle Ages it was very prosperous and became a stronghold in which many monks lived—hence the name. It was in decline when, in 1671, Heaven took a hand. In that year, Marguerite-Marie Alacoque entered the Convent of the Visitation, had a vision of Jesus and, with the support of the Jesuit, Father Claude de la Colombière, began the cult of the Sacred Heart, The cult grew considerably in the 19C and the little town received tens of thousands of pilgrims. (The visionary nun was beatified in 1864 and canonized in 1920.) From May to October there are still large pilgrimages.

Basilica of the Sacré-Coeur: With the destruction of Cluny III (see under Cluny), the former priory church is the most perfect example of Cluniac architecture. This Romanesque gem bathed in light replaces the original church—the narrow narthex could well be a remnant of it, but this is the subject of much controversy. For a long time archaeologists thought that the building dated from the mid 12C, but it seems the present building was built in its entirety 1090–1110. Wholly Romanesque, except for one chapel, it has survived the Wars of Religion, the Revolution and the effects of time, all without too much damage.

EXTERIOR: The basilica is built of pale stone and is superbly proportioned. Its old narthex, reflected in the Bourbince, is splendid, having groin vaulting and two tall, square towers, one crudely rustic and the other more sophisticated and complex. The large, perfectly balanced, apse is reminiscent of those in Auvergne; it has several tiers and is dominated by an elegant bell tower over the crossing, whose spire is about 180 ft. high.

INTERIOR: The height of the interior is surprising, as is its sparseness and the marvellous effect of light, which comes in from cleverly positioned windows. It has a Cluniac elevation—three storeys in the nave, transept and right bay of the choir. The fine ambulatory is known as the

'Promenoir des Anges' (angels' walk). Th interplay of volume and light is more strik ing than the carved decoration which onl serves to emphasize the architecture by it unobtrusiveness. The only really impor tant sculpture is on the outside of the S and N. transept doorways. The Roman esque apsidiole of the right transept wa replaced in the 15C by a Flamboyan chapel. Behind the basilica the *Maison de Pages* is all that remains of the 'château' o the abbots of Cluny. Inside is the *Chambr des Reliques*, a reconstruction of a Visitan dine cell where there are various pieces o memorabilia of Marguerite Marie Ala coque. In the park there is a diorama (193⁵ which tells the history of the town and th life story of the saint.

Chapelle de la Visitation: Rue de I Visitation. Built in the 17C and very muc restored, this is the chapel where Jesus ap peared to the nun and she had the revela tion of the 'heart so full of love'. The sair lies in a gilded silver shrine.

Hôtel de Ville and the Tour Saint

Paray-le-Monial, Hôtel de Ville, detail of the façade

Nicolas: The town hall is in an unusual and splendid Renaissance house whose façade of gold-coloured stone is as highly ornate and carved as an altarpiece. It was built for a rich textile manufacturer in 1525 – 8. Opposite this is the massive, domed *Tour Saint-Nicolas* (16C), which is the bell tower from a former church.

Musée Eucharistique du Hiéron: At the corner of the Rue de la Paix and the Rue Pasteur. This museum, founded in 1890, is devoted to the glory of God and the Eucharist, but, thankfully it is devoid of plaster saints and the like. It contains a number of fine works of art and others of considerable archaeological interest: liturgical objects, paintings and sculptures, altars, tabernacles and a superb tympanum which came from the old priory of Anzy-le-Duc. Opposite the Hiéron a chapel contains the shrine of the blessed Claude de la Colombière; this modern building is in Romanesque-Byzantine style.

Environs: Brionnais: Between Paray-le-Monial and Charlieu (see under that head-

Paray-le-M., bell tower of the basilica

ing), this is one of the most attractive areas in W. Burgundy. A region of green, hilly countryside, it offers some marvellous views and has a great number of very fine and totally original Romanesque churches. This proliferation is almost certainly due to the fine, soft local limestone, and to the influence of Cluny, the Auvergne, and the Loire. However, experts still marvel at the inspiration behind the concentration of these lovely churches in this region. **Montceaux-l'Étoile** (7.5 km. SE): This humble 12C church has a fine carved portal, dating from about 1120. There is an 18C chapel nearby. **Anzy-le-Duc** (11 km. via Montceaux): This large Brionnais church resembled the destroyed abbey church of Charlieu. It dates mainly from the 11C. Groin-vaulted, it is dominated by a lovely octagonal crossing tower, and has some remarkable carvings (portals, cornice brackets and capitals in the choir and nave). **Marcigny** (24 km. SE): Here there is a much altered Romanesque church and some old houses. Also note a large 15C house, the *Tour du Moulin* with the *Musée d'Art Régional et d'Histoire Locale* inside. **Semur-en-Brionnais** (5 km. E. of Marcigny): An old town perched on a hill covered with vines and fruit trees, it is dominated by the château with its heavy rectangular keep in which St. Hugh was born. Note the former collegiate church in front of the charming Hôtel de Ville and the lovely church of *Saint-Hilaire* (transept with dome over the crossing, choir and apses about 1125; the nave with its cluniac elevation is later). The upper part of the bell tower is Gothic. There are some fine carved doorways. **Iguerande** (9 km. S. of Semur): The strong church of *Saint-André* is perched on a hill and dates mainly from about 1100, although the dome over the crossing and the choir are earlier. Also among the most beautiful Romanesque churches in the area are *Bois-Sainte-Marie* (rebuilt in the last century), *Châteauneuf* (12C) and *Saint-Germain-en-Brionnais*.

Paris	(2,317,230 inhab.)
75	p.410/411 □ I 4/5

The capital of France and a département in its own right, Paris is encircled by the ring road called the Périphérique, a modern road system which follows the oval shape of the Île de la Cité, the original nucleus of the city. In 53 BC the Romans found only a small fishing village in constant danger of flooding, but they made *Lutetia* into a flourishing town which spilled over on to the left bank of the river and took in Mount Sainte-Geneviève, on which the Panthéon now stands. Later the town acquired the Gallic name *Parisii* and St.Denis converted it to Christianity at the end of the first century. St. Geneviève resisted the threat of the Huns and in 508 Paris became the capital of the Kingdom of the Franks. From that time its history was linked to that of France, which was emerging as a nation as its kings strove for centralized government. Paris owes a lot to Philippe Auguste. He built its walls from 1180–1210, and the town became prosperous in the 13C (Sainte Chapelle, Notre Dame and the founding of the Sorbonne). The new ramparts, built by Charles V, and the fortress of the Bastille could not withstand attacks by the English, who took the city in 1420 and held it for 40 years. François I and Henri IV added to the beauty of the town and extended its defences. In the 17&18C Paris expanded very rapidly into the surrounding countryside (Marais, Palais-Royal, creation of the Île Saint-Louis, the Place Vendôme, Invalides, Observatoire, Gobelins and Salpêtrière). A city wall 23 km. long was built under Louis XIV; this was known as *des Fermiers Généraux*, and was broken by toll gates. The town suffered much bloodshed in the Revolution, but developed considerably in the 19C. New building ate into the countryside; one of Napoleon III's Préfets, Baron Haussmann, caused much destruction by driving great thoroughfares through the older quarters to give the town the appearance which it has today. At the end of the last century, the suburbs which had been protected by the Thiers fortifications were joined to Paris: Auteuil, Passy, Montmartre, Belleville, La Villette, Grenelle and Vaugirard in particular. The town grew still more between the wars, and was much modernized. After the Liberation in August 1944, there was further expansion and the vast urban and suburban centre acquired peripheral 'new towns'. During the 1960s and 1970s the town was transformed by large-scale building of blocks of flats (Maine-Montparnasse, Porte Maillot, Front de Seine, and the quarter known as La Défense), and by the creation of the Périphérique, the Centre Pompidou and the new Les Halles quarter. At the same time as these developments, which have now been checked, Paris was restoring the former light colour of the stone of its ancient monuments, renovating the Marais district and establishing pedestrian precincts. Paris has a very active cultural life, with innumerable museums, art galleries, theatres and cinemas. Music, somewhat neglected for a time, has now come into its own again. The Opéra has been revived, the *Orchestre de Paris* and the *Ensemble Orchestral de Paris* give numerous concerts, and there are major exhibitions of contemporary art at the thriving Centre Pompidou.

MAIN CHURCHES

Ile de la Cité

Notre-Dame: Cathedral church of Paris and 'parish church of the history of France', the majestic Gothic building built by Bishop Maurice de Sully dominates the heart of the capital. It was built from 1163 on a site which had been a place of worship from ancient times. It is mainly 12C (choir and transept) and 13C, but was modified in the 17&18C. In the Revolution it was brutally sacked, Napoleon I was crowned here in 1804, and it was nearly ruined in 1831 when the Parisians' interest in the building was rekindled by Victor Hugo with his book *Notre-Dame de Paris*; Viollet-le-Duc was commissioned to undertake major restoration which went on for 17 years.

EXTERIOR: Two towers, 220 ft. high, frame the main façade opposite the square, which has been recently restored and an archaeological crypt provided. In the centre of the façade the *Judgement Doorway* is a magnificent work of 1220 – 30 (restored by Viollet-le-Duc). Christ in Judgement escorted by angels, appears on the tympanum with the Virgin and St. John. The archivolts have scenes from the Last Judgement, showing Heaven and Hell. The statues on the pier and at the sides were put there by Viollet-le-Duc. The *Virgin Doorway*, on the left, dates from 1210–20 but again, the statues are largely 19C. The *St.Anne Doorway*, on the right, is the older of the two, and has been modified. The majority of the sculptures date from *c.* 1170, though some of them, particularly St. Marcellus on the pier, are copies; as with the Portail de la Vierge the wrought-iron door hinges are 13C. The statues of the Kings of Judah and Israel on the gallery, like those on the balustrade (which is known as the Galerie de la Vierge) are modern. The large rose-window dates from 1220. The two towers are very slightly different. The N. tower has a staircase inside it giving access to a panoramic terrace and the S. tower contains a 13 ton bell (1400, recast under Louis XIV).
North Doorway: This is known as the cloister doorway. It opens on to the Rue du-Cloître-Notre-Dame and dates from the 13C. There is a very fine *Virgin and Child* on the pier (the Child is damaged). On one side is the charming *Porte Rouge*, designed by Pierre de Montreuil.
South Doorway: This is on the Seine side and is known as the Saint-Étienne door-

way. It was begun in 1257 by Jean de Chelles and finished by Pierre de Montreuil. On the tympanum is the prophecy and martyrdom of Saint-Étienne. The apse is decorated with extremely light 14C flying buttresses.

INTERIOR: The nave has five aisles and spacious galleries. It is 430 ft. long and 154 ft. wide and its vaults are 110 ft high. On the side aisles and around the ambulatory there are 29 chapels with paintings called *mays*, which were donated 1630–1707 by goldsmiths on the 1 May. In the nave (1182–1210) on the inside of the façade is the massive Cliquot organ (1830). The building is lit by three large *rose-windows* (W., N. and S.), with some 13C stained-glass panes remaining (transept), and some modern glass. The choir was altered by Louis XIV and then modified again in the 19C. It has very beautiful 18C stalls and woodwork and contains some remarkable *sculptures*; the Pietà by Nicolas Coustou in the centre and statues of Louis XIII and Louis XIV, and a 14C funerary statue. The bas-reliefs from the former screen (14C) were restored by Viollet-le-Duc. The axial chapel has the kneeling statues of Albert de Gondi, Duke of Retz and of Cardinal de Gondi, which are 17C works; there is also a 14C fresco. To the right of the choir, the chapel of St.Guillaume contains a 15C funeral monument and an 18C mausoleum by Pigalle.

TREASURE: Notre Dame has magnificent treasure in the 19C sacristy, in spite of the fact it was pillaged in the Revolution. The *Croix Palatine*, supposedly containing a piece of the True Cross, belonged to an Emperor of Byzantium in the 12C. There are also pieces of ecclesiastical gold and silverware, manuscripts, and cameos of the popes.

Sainte-Chapelle: Today this is lost among the buildings of the Palais de Jus-

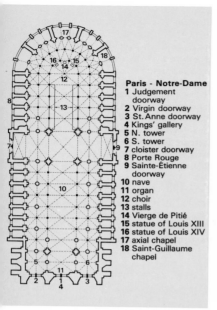

Paris - Notre-Dame
1 Judgement doorway
2 Virgin doorway
3 St. Anne doorway
4 Kings' gallery
5 N. tower
6 S. tower
7 cloister doorway
8 Porte Rouge
9 Sainte-Étienne doorway
10 nave
11 organ
12 choir
13 stalls
14 Vierge de Pitié
15 statue of Louis XIII
16 statue of Louis XIV
17 axial chapel
18 Saint-Guillaume chapel

Basilica of the Sacré-Coeur

tice. It is a Gothic gem with magical *stained-glass windows*, commissioned by St.Louis and probably built from 1243 - 8 by Pierre de Montreuil. It consists of a lower chapel with 13C murals and a light upper chapel; it was restored in the 19C. Its splendid 13C glass, which has mainly survived intact, depicts scenes from the Old and New Testaments in vibrant blues and reds (there were originally 720 in all). The rose window in the façade, which illustrates the Apocalypse, is 15C.

Ile Saint-Louis
Saint Louis-en-Ile (21 Rue-Saint-Louis-en-Ile): Started by Le Vau in 1664 and finished in 1726, this sober, classical church acquired numerous sculptures, paintings and enamels in the second half of the 19C from a priest who collected works of art.

Right Bank (in alphabetical order):

Basilique du Sacré-Coeur: Montmartre is dominated by the unusual silhouette of the Sacré-Coeur, accused by its detractors of appearing to be made of icing sugar. This Romano-Byzantine pastiche was begun in 1876 and consecrated in 1919 and has a high dome and a 300 ft. bell tower. From the dome there is a wonderful view over Paris.

Church of Saint-Augustin: A stone-clad metal structure built in the 1860s by Baltard, the architect of the original Halles.

Saint-Eustache: This Gothic and Renaissance building overlooks Les Halles. It has no tower but a large and dignified interior; the nave is about 300 ft. long and

Church of the Madeleine

the vaulting is as high as that of Notre-Dame. In the apse there is some fine 17C stained glass and there are a number of works of art in the chapels, particularly a painting by Rubens, *Les Disciples d'Emmaüs*. There is also a painting by Simon Vouet, the *Martyre de St.Eustache*, which hangs above a façade doorway. This church is beloved of musicians: Berlioz conducted the première of his *Te Deum* here in 1855 and Franz Liszt played the organ; organ recitals and choral concerts can still be heard today.

Saint-Germain-l'Auxerrois: Opposite the famous colonnade, the former Church of the Louvre has been much altered and has had some unfortunate additions. A fine 15C Flamboyant porch was somewhat spoiled in the 18C. The church is dominated by a Romanesque bell tower to the S. of the choir, and contains a pretty 14C *statue of the Virgin*, the 13C statue of St. Germain which was once on the pier of the main door, a 15C St.Mary of Egypt (which also came from the porch), a 15C *altarpiece* and a 16C *triptych*.

Saint-Germain-Saint-Protais: This church with its admirably harmonious classical façade lies behind the Hôtel de Ville. It has a fine Flamboyant nave with stellar vaulting. The juxtaposition of styles shows how slowly the church was built; work began in 1494 but the façade was not started until 1616, by Louis XIII. There are lovely 16C stalls, candelabra designed by Soufflot on the high altar, 17C wooden statues of the two patron saints, and the restored effigy of Notre-Dame-de-Souffrance (14C). The axial Lady Chapel contains a remarkable *pendant keystone* (1517).

Church of Saint-Germain-l'Auxerrois

the high altar and the *Adoration of the Shepherds* by Coypel in the side chapel.

Saint-Paul-Saint-Louis: Bossuet and Bourdaloue preached in this church, with its scarcely visible dome and baroque façade. It was built in the 17C in imitation of the *Gesù* in Rome. Among other works it contains an allegorical painting by Simon Vouet, *Louis XIII offering St.Louis the Model of the Church* (right transept), *Christ in the Garden of Olives* by Delacroix (left transept) and a marble by Germain Pilon, *Vierge de Pitié* (1586) in a chapel on the left.

Saint Pierre-de-Montmartre (near the Place du Tertre): This early Gothic church is rather overshadowed by the Sacré-Coeur. A Romanesque section survives and there are several 12C decorated capitals and four columns which probably came from a 7C church.

Saint-Roch (296 Rue Saint-Honoré): This classical church designed by Jacques Lemercier was built 1642–1740; Robert de Cotte and his son supervised the work. It does not face E. and is strangely elongated by a line of three chapels; there are numerous works of art, including the *Baptême du Christ* in marble by Lemoyne the Elder and Younger, a bust of Mignard by Lemoyne the Younger, a bust of Le Nôtre by Coysevox, and a *Nativity* group by Michel Anguier from Val-de-Grâce in the circular chapel of Hardouin-Mansart.

Church of the Trinity: This 19C building in Italian Renaissance style has four exterior sculpted groups; that on the first floor is by Carpeaux (La Tempérance).

Left Bank (in alphabetical order):

Panthéon see **Civil and Military Monuments**

Saint-Merri (78 Rue Saint Martin): In complete contrast to the nearby Pompidou Centre, this church, partly hidden by houses, was built 1515–52 at the height of the Renaissance but in Flamboyant style. It was altered in the 18C when the pillars and arcades were covered with stucco. The organ chest is 17C and the fine pulpit 18C.

Saint-Nicolas-des-Champs (254 Rue Saint-Martin): This Gothic and Renaissance church dates from the 15C and was enlarged in the 16C. The magnificent *side doorway* was inspired by Philibert Delorme and opens on to the Rue Cunin-Gridaine. In the nave the first bays are early 15C and the last ones late 16C: smooth columns with pointed vaults contrast with ribbed columns with semicircular vaults. There is an excellent Cliquot organ (1773), paintings by Simon Vouet on

Saint-Étienne-du-Mont, the porch

Saint-Germain-des-Prés

Saint-Étienne-du-Mont (Place du Panthéon): This church contains the shrine of St. Geneviève, the patron saint of Paris. One can see the evolution of religious architecture in this building, built between 1492 (when the choir was started) and 1626 (consecration). It was restored by Baltard in the 19C and is essentially Gothic, with many Renaissance features. The only surviving *rood screen* in Paris is here; made 1521–45, it is a masterpiece of Flamboyant art. In the apse the ossuary galleries have some very fine 17C *stained-glass windows*.

Saint-Germain-des-Prés: This church, on one of the busiest crossroads in the city, is the former abbey church of a very important Benedictine convent which prospered from the 7C until the Revolution. It is bare and austere and its bell tower, which dominates the Place Saint-

Germain-des-Prés, is 11C (except for its final storey which is 12C, rebuilt in the 19C). A porch was added to the Romanesque doorway at the beginning of the 17C. Only the bases remain of the side bell-towers at the far end of the transept (the façade of the S. arm was altered in the 17C and is visible from the Boulevard Saint-Germain). The emerging Gothic left its mark on the choir, but the nave kept its Romanesque appearance. The work of Hippolyte Flandrin (19C) is somewhat disconcerting, and most of the capitals are copies—the originals are in the Musée de Cluny. In the N. transept is the tomb of a King of Poland, the work of the Marsy brothers (17C) and a statue of St. François-Xavier by Coustou (1723).

Saint-Julien-le-Pauvre (Quai de Montebello): This rather lop-sided church dates

vaulting. The abstract stained glass was added in 1966 and is by Jean Bazaine.

Saint-Sulpice: This vast, cold church is almost as big as Notre-Dame. It was begun in 1646 and completed in the middle of the 18C. Servandoni and Chalgrin collaborated on this severe building, which is unfinished outside. A massive organ dominates the airy nave, which has heavy arcades. At the entrance to the side aisles there are two gigantic holy water stoups in the form of shells on bases by Pigalle. The *Chapelle des Anges* on the right has some pompous frescos (1853–63) by Delacroix: *Héliodor Driven from the Temple, Jacob Wrestling with the Angel* and, on the vaulting, *St. Michael Slaying the Dragon.* The *Lady Chapel* (18C) has a strangely lit *Virgin and Child* by Pigalle, baroque decoration and paintings by Carle Van Loo.

Saint-Denis: see **Environs**

CIVIL AND MILITARY MONUMENTS, MONUMENTAL GROUPS

Church of Saint-Sulpice

from the early Gothic period (1170–1240). Its façade was mutilated in the 17C and it has a marquetry screen decorated with icons dividing the choir, a throwback to the church's connection with eastern orthodoxy. Rib vaulting in the N. aisle is original.

Saint-Séverin (1 Rue des Prêtres-Saint-Séverin): This very attractive Flamboyant church is in a pedestrian precinct in the medieval quarter near Saint-Julien. It dates mainly from the 13C (first bays with cylindrical columns) and the 15C, and was enlarged in the 17C by the addition of an elliptical chapel by Hardouin-Mansart. The *double ambulatory*, light and elegant, was built 1489–94. A marvellous *side pillar*—by a virtuoso architect—has a spiral pattern which rises to become part of the

Ile de la Cité: The Ile de la Cité is like a ship, with the spires and towers of Notre-Dame and the Sainte Chapelle as masts, and the Palais de Justice and Préfecture de Police as ballast. It was spoiled in the last century by relentless modernization by Haussmann, and lost its medieval character. The *Conciergerie* with its neo-Gothic façade and towers facing the Quai de l'Horloge has retained the 14C Salle des Gardes, Salle des Gens d'Armes and kitchens. Originally the residence of the the Royal Concierge, it was used as a prison under the Ancien Régime and in the Revolution. Charlotte Corday, André de Chénier, Queen Marie-Antoinette and Robespierre left for the scaffold from here. The *Tour de l'Horloge*, at the corner of the Boulevard du Palais, is so called because of the 14C clock decorated by Germain

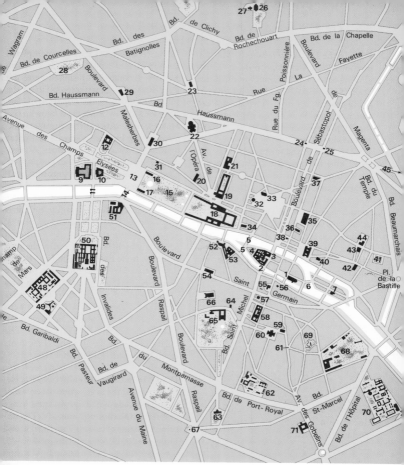

Paris 1 Notre-Dame **2** Sainte-Chapelle **3** Concier-
gerie **4** Place Dauphine **5** Pont-Neuf **6** Pont Saint-
Louis **7** church of Saint-Louis-en-Ile **8** Arc de Tri-
omphe **9** Grand-Palais **10** Petit-Palais **11** Pont
Alexandre III **12** Palais de l'Elysée **13** Place de la
Concorde **14** Pont de la Concorde **15** Jardins des
Tuileries **16** Jeu de Paume **17** Orangerie **18** Palais
du Louvre **19** Palais-Royal **20** church of Saint-
Roch **21** Bibliothèque Nationale **22** Opéra **23**
church of the Trinité **24** Porte Saint-Denis **25**
Porte Saint-Martin **26** basilica of the Sacré-Coeur
27 church of Saint-Pierre de Montmartre **28** Parc
Monceau **29** church of Saint-Augustin **30** church
of the Madeleine **31** church of the Assomption
32 Bourse du Commerce **33** church of Saint-
Eustache **34** church of Saint-Germain-l'Auxerrois
35 Centre Georges-Pompidou **36** church of Saint-
Merri **37** church of Saint-Nicolas-des-Champs **38**
Tour Saint-Jacques **39** Hôtel-de-Ville **40** church
of Saint-Gervais-Saint-Protais **41** Place des
Vosges **42** church of Saint-Paul-Saint-Louis **43**
Hôtel Lamoignon **44** Hôtel Carnavalet (museum
of the history of Paris) **45** Cimitière du Père-
Lachaise **46** Eiffel Tower **47** Palais de Chaillot **48**
Ecole Militaire **49** UNESCO **50** Hôtel des Invalides
51 Palais-Bourbon **52** Institut de France **53** Hôtel
de la Monnaie **54** church of Saint-Germain-des-
Prés **55** church of Saint-Séverin **56** church of
Saint-Julien-le-Pauvre **57** Musée de Cluny **58**
Sorbonne **59** church of Saint-Étienne-du-Mont
60 Panthéon **61** Place de la Contrescarpe **62** Hôpital Militaire du Val-de-Grâce **63** Observatoire **64**
Théâtre de l'Odéon **65** Palais du Luxembourg **66**
church of Saint-Sulpice **67** entrance to the
Catacombes **68** Jardin des Plantes (natural history museum) **69** Arènes de Lutèce **70** Hôpital de
la Salpêtrière **71** the Gobelins factory

Pilon in the 16C (now restored). The harmonious *Place Dauphine*, built at the beginning of the 17C in honour of the future Louis XIII, is still very charming, despite being partly spoiled. The *Pont-Neuf*, which bridges the Seine downstream from the Ile, has been subject to frequent restorations since it was completed in the early 17C. Henri II placed the first stone in 1578 and Henri IV crossed it on horseback in 1607. The present statue of the 'Vert Galant' dates from 1818; the previous one was melted down in the Revolution. The sober and rather fine *Mémorial des Martyrs de la Déportation* is on the downstream tip of the Ile de la Cité; by the contemporary architect Henri Pingusson it is the burial place of a Frenchman deported to German concentration camps during the last war.

Ile Saint-Louis: Moored to the Cité by the Pont Saint-Louis, this island was formed in the 17C by joining two smaller islands, and it is like a world of its own in the heart of Paris. It is quiet, despite the many restaurants, and has some fine 17&18C hôtels (remarkable façades on the Quai de Bourbon). The *Hôtel de Lauzun* (17 Quai d'Anjou) is very elegant. It was built by Le Vau 1650–58 and has magnificent interior decoration. Théophile Gautier and Baudelaire stayed here in the 19C. At the corner of the Quai d'Anjou and the end of the Rue-Saint-Louis-en-Ile is the *Hotel Lambert* (1640), also planned by Le Vau and decorated by Le Brun and Le Sueur.

Right Bank
Arc de Triomphe and Champs-Élysées: The Arc de Triomphe dominates the Place Charles-de-Gaulle or the *Étoile*, as the Parisians call it (twelve radiating avenues). The Arc de Triomphe houses the *Tomb of the Unknown Soldier* of the 1914–18 war. Napoleon was keen to leave a memorial to his glorious armies and commissioned the Arc de Triomphe from Chal-

grin in 1806, but work was not completed until 1836, and even then the arch had no top. It is decorated with some interesting sculptures, the most famous, facing the Champs Elysées, is the *Départ des Volontaires en 1792*, by Rude (also known as *La Marseillaise*). Above the groups commemorating France's victories is a frieze by Rude and a team of sculptors. According to Parisians, the broad and impressive *Champs Élysées* is the most beautiful boulevard in the world; it runs dead straight for 2 km. from the Arc de Triomphe to the Place de la Concorde. Mainly 19C, it is now lined with numerous modern blocks, although further down it runs through gardens which have not really changed since the Belle Époque. The *Petit-Palais*, between parkland and the Seine, and the *Grand-Palais* show the architectural taste of the turn of the century (see under museums). The *Palais de l'Elysées* opens on to the elegant *Rue du Faubourg-Saint-Honoré* which is full of luxury shops. The Palais, the residence of French Presidents since 1873, was built from 1718.

Place de la Concorde: This severe, elegant square at the intersection of two major streets was designed by Jacques Ange Gabriel at the time of Louis XV. The impressive flights of columns on the right and left of the Rue Royale date from 1760–75. The *Chevaux de Marly* group by Coustou was placed at the end of the Champs Élysées in 1795. The *Renomée* and *Mercure* statues by Coysevox at the entrance to the Tuileries gardens also came from Marly. In the middle of the square the *Obélisque de Louqsor* towers almost 70 ft. above two large 19C fountains. The sides of this pink monolith, presented to France by Egypt in 1831, have hieroglyphics to the glory of Rameses II, who built it in the 8C BC. The large statues were added to the *Pont*

The Arc de Triomphe from the Étoile

Place de la Concorde

de la Concorde when it was widened under the Restoration; it was built shortly before the Revolution by Perronet.

Tuileries Gardens, Carrousel: This dignified garden, which contains innumerable statues, was designed in the 17C by Le Nôtre. The *Jeu de Paume* and the *Orangerie* are on a terrace near to the Place de la Concorde (see under museums). The Rue de Rivoli, running the length of these beautifully laid out gardens and on to the Louvre, is lined with early-19C buildings with arcades. The *Arc de Triomphe du Carrousel* is a free imitation of a Roman Monument and dates from the early 19C. It has statues of soldiers of the Empire and also a bronze chariot group (the Restoration of the Bourbons). There are 18 sensuous statues by Maillol on the lawns of the Place du Carrousel.

Palais du Louvre (see also under museums): This enormous Palace with its endless wings housing the Louvre museum dates back to the 12C. In 1190 Philippe Auguste ordered a keep to be built (since pulled down). In 1965 André Malraux had the moats cleared to uncover the *Colonnade* on the Place du Louvre, which was built in the second half of the 17C by François d'Orbay and Claude Perrault in front of buildings by Le Vau; it has 19C statues. The Louvre's ground plan is complicated as the palace has been continually altered and enlarged. The centre of the immense complex, the *Cour Carrée*, is on the site of the original fortress; the outline of the keep is delineated with paving stones. The buildings around the courtyard were built in the Renaissance under the direction of Pierre Lescot and in the 17C by Lemercier, Le Vau and Perrault; they were altered in

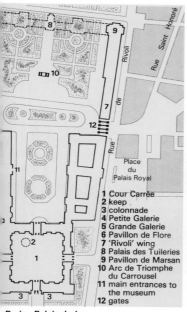

1 Cour Carrée
2 keep
3 colonnade
4 Petite Galerie
5 Grande Galerie
6 Pavillon de Flore
7 'Rivoli' wing
8 Palais des Tuileries
9 Pavillon de Marsan
10 Arc de Triomphe
    du Carrousel
11 main entrances to
    the museum
12 gates

Paris - Palais du Louvre

Obélisque de Louqsor

the 19C. To the left of the W. wing there are fine sculptures by Jean Goujon.

The *Petite Galerie*, built from 1566, and perpendicular to the quai, links the buildings of the Cour Carrée to the long *Grande Galerie* which runs for some 1,800 ft. along the Seine to the *Pavillon de Flore*, rebuilt in the 19C. Also known as the Galerie du Bord de l'Eau, it is a mixture of styles from the 16C–19C. The 'Rivoli' wing is 19C, and the Palais des Tuileries, burnt by rioters in 1871, completes the square of the Louvre.

Near the Louvre the *Palais-Royal* has quiet 18C gardens; the *Théâtre Français* is part of the complex. The palace itself, on the **Place du Palais-Royal**, dates from the 1760s, and the galleries were built by Philippe d'Orléans before the Revolution.

Little remains of Richelieu's sumptuous residence, the Palais-Cardinal.

Bibliothèque Nationale (58 Rue de Richelieu): This includes a 17C complex (galleries by Mansart) and houses a vast collection of books and periodicals (the 1868 Hall du Département des Imprimés is a fine example of ironwork).

Opéra: The Avenue de l'Opéra begins in the Place du Théâtre-Français and is nearly 800 yards long. The majestic Opéra building, built 1862–75 by Charles Garnier, houses the National Academy of Music and Dance; it was commissioned by Napoleon III. The Opéra, devoted to singing and ballet, is the largest theatre in the world, and is richly decorated inside and out. The group on the right of the main façade is the famous *Groupe de la Danse* by

Opéra (Palais Garnier)

Paul Belmondo, a copy of the original by Carpeaux (which is in the Louvre). The gold ceiling of the auditorium is decorated with a work by Chagall (1964).

Main Boulevards: The wide streets which run from the Place de l'Opéra are called the 'Grand Boulevards' by Parisians. To the E. they lead to two 17C triumphal arches erected to the glory of Louis XIV and his armies; these are the *Porte Saint-Denis* and the *Porte Saint-Martin*. The Boulevard Saint Martin ends in the Place de la République, which was built in the last century around the pompous Monument de la République (1883).

Parc Monceau: This is a remnant of a magical 18C garden and still has fairy-tale features: a grotto, a small pyramid, a pool with colonnade. On the Boulevard de Courcelles is the 18C Ledoux *Pavillon* with some fine 19C ironwork.

Montmartre: This is the high ground on which the Sacré-Coeur and the little church of Saint-Pierre stand. It is a very lively and distinctive quarter, a former village, which François Villon called 'moult ancien'. It is crammed with tourists in the high season and consists of narrow streets, stairways and little squares. Its name comes from *Mons Mercurii* (Mont de Mercure or Mount Mercury) or *Mons Martyrum* (Mont des Martyrs, Martyrs' Mount) and it grew up around a Merovingian sanctuary and an abbey. In the 19C and early 20C it was full of artists: Renoir, Suzanne Valadon, Utrillo, Émile Bernard, Gauguin, Dufy, Poulbot (who drew the urchins of Montmartre), Othon Friesz, Juan Gris, Picasso and Van Dongen.

The *Place Blanche* and the *Place Pigalle*, at the foot of Montmartre, are neon-lit at night and are a popular bar and night-club quarter.

New Les Halles Quarter and Beaubourg Plateau: In the past, this area in front of Saint Eustache was full of market stalls and was busy day and night, the 'belly of Paris'. When the market moved to Rungis and the Baltard pavilions were pulled down, it was a building site for eight years; Parisians called it the 'trou des Halles'. Then new businesses appeared, such as the half-underground *Forum* (shops and restaurants), above the huge metro and RER station; gardens were also added. The circular Stock Exchange building is dominated by a slim fluted 16C tower. Near the infamous Rue Saint-Denis, the *Fontaine des Innocents* occupies the site of a charnel-house closed in the 18C. It is a charming Renaissance work by Jean Goujon (1549), modified in 1788. The Rue Saint-Honoré runs along the S. side of les Halles and has old houses, a former chapel (17C), which became the Protestant *Oratory*, the *Fontaine du Trahoir*, and a private chapel dating from François I's time which has been incorporated into a house rebuilt by Soufflot in 1775 (corner of the Rue de l'Arbre-Sec). The *Boulevard de Sébastopol* separates Les Halles from the *Plateau Beaubourg*, where the *Centre Pompidou* is located. The latter is a huge square glass and metal building and contrasts strongly with its surroundings and with the nearby *Church of Saint-Merri*. The old houses around have been renovated and now have art galleries, antique shops and restaurants in them. In front of the Centre and the reconstructed workshops of the sculptor Brancusi at the corner of the Rue Aubry-le-Boucher there is a 'fake classical building', a ventilation shaft painted in trompe l'oeil by Fabio Rieti. The old *Rue Quincampoix* used to be the haunt of prostitutes

Centre Georges-Pompidou

but has now been restored to its former charm.

Place du Châtelet, Tour Saint-Jacques: This square, opposite the Cité, has a 19C fountain in the middle and two theatres facing on to it—the Châtelet and the Théâtre de la Ville. The restored tower, the bell tower of a church destroyed in the Revolution, is 16C.

Hôtel de Ville: The Place de l'Hôtel de Ville was formerly the Place de Grève, and was built in its present form in the 18C and 19C. The square, once used for executions, was a meeting place for workers looking for jobs; the imposing Hôtel de Ville (1882), a Renaissance-style building housing the Paris Mairie, faces it.

Marais: This quarter, cut in two by the

Hôtel-de-Ville

Rue Saint-Antoine, which follows the line of a Roman road, extends almost from the Hôtel de Ville to the Bastille and from the Quais to the Boulevard Beaumarchais. Formerly very dilapidated indeed and saved just in time by major restoration work, it is really an open-air museum of 17C secular architecture (there are also a few houses which are even earlier). Its name comes from the marshy land occupied solely by a few religious establishments at the beginning of the Middle Ages. First the area spread towards the Seine around the H*otel Saint-Paul* (a former royal residence which has been demolished) and then Henri IV began a programme of urbanization in the N. of the area, where there was little more than the Hôtels Carnavalet and Lamoignon. He established the Place Royale (now the Place des Vosges) and planned the building of the hôtels. In the

17C the quarter was aristocratic and upper-class, but in the 18C it lost its appeal and went into decline. It was saved by legislation in 1962 which protected its historical and artistic heritage. The S. of the Marais, with its narrow streets—between the Rue Saint-Antoine and the Seine—is a clear example of the use of small building plots in the Middle Ages. The *Hôtel de Sens*, beside the Seine, is late 15C and has been heavily restored; it contains the Forney library. At the E. end of the quai is the *Hôtel Fieubet*, designed by Hardouin-Mansart in the 17C. There are some very old houses in the little streets and some of these have not been altered at all. Behind here is the Front de Seine with its dull modern Cité des Arts. In the *Rue François-Miron* there are some very old half-timbered houses and the 17C *Hôtel de Beauvais* by Antoine le Pautre. At the corner of the Rue de Jouy

and the Rue Nonains-d'Hyères there is a plain building by Luis le Vau (1648), which was modified by François Mansart. The Rue Saint-Antoine, a lively shopping area, has the *Temple Sainte-Marie* by François Mansart at No. 17, *Saint-Paul-Saint-Louis* and some interesting hôtels. The *Hôtel de Sully* (No. 62) extends up to the Place des Vosges, and dates from 1634. It has been very well restored and contains the office of the Caisse des Monuments Historiques.

Place des Vosges: The centre of the 17C part of the Marais, it is also one of the oldest squares in Paris; in the centre there is now a small garden with railings. The square, set out after the assassination of Henri IV, was the centre of 'précieux' society in the 17C, and feasts and duels were held here. Mme. de Sévigné was born at No. 1 bis, and Victor Hugo lived at No. 6.

Rue des Francs-Bourgeois, Quartier Carnavalet: A very interesting part of the Marais. At the corner of the Rue des Francs-Bourgeois and the Rue Pavée is the *Hôtel Lamoignon,* one of the oldest and most beautiful houses in the quarter (1584-5); it houses the Bibliothèque Historique of Paris. The *Hôtel Carnavalet,* in the Rue de Sévigné, dates from the Renaissance; it was enlarged and decorated in the 17C by François Mansart and houses the *Musée Historique de la Ville de Paris.* At 29 Rue de Sévigné is the *Hôtel de Peletier* which dates from 1686. There are several other 17C hôtels on the short Rue du Parc-Royal. Nearby there is a plain, elegant hôtel built by the architect Libéral Bruant (1 Rue de la Perle).

Archives, Temple: E. of the Marais, in the long Rue des Archives is the *Church des Billettes,* an 18C building with adjoining medieval cloister (No. 22). At the corner of the Rue des Francs-Bourgeois, the *Hôtel de Soubise* has a splendid main courtyard and houses the national archives and a small *Musée d'Histoire de France* (in lovely rooms with 18C decoration). At the corner of the Rue des Quatre-Fils, the *Hôtel Guénégaud,* by François Mansart, is a 17C house containing the *Maison de la Chasse et de la Nature,* a museum showing the history of hunting through displays of works of art and weapons. The peaceful Square du Temple is on the site of a convent which became a prison during the Revolution (the Royal family were imprisoned here).

The Rue *Vieille-du-Temple* once led to the Commanderie du Temple and is full of interesting houses, including the *Hôtel de Rohan* (No. 87) and the *Hôtel Amelot de Bisseuil* or *des Ambassadeurs de Hollande,* a building with a fine doorway built in the late 1650s (No. 47).

Bastille, Nation: The circular Place de la Bastille occupies the site of the famous

Hôtel de Rohan

called it the 'shepherdess of the clouds'. It was built by Gustave Eiffel for the Exposition Universelle of 1889. Some 984 ft. high without its television mast, it is a daring metal construction which greatly offended the intelligentsia in the 19C. Now it is the symbol of Paris and offers a wonderful view of the city. It weighs 7,000 tons and was built in record time (1887–9), dominating the *Champ de Mars*, a parade ground created in the 18C. The vast *Palais de Chaillot* facing it from the other side of the Seine was built for the exhibition of 1937.

École Militaire and UNESCO Building: The École Militaire, designed by Jacques Ange Gabriel (work on it started in 1751), completes the sequence of buildings in the Champ de Mars with its imposing façade (wings finished by Brongniart after Gabriel's death). On the Place de Fontenoy, the courtyard is dominated by the elegant main façade. In contrast to this classical building is the Maison de l'UNESCO, from the 1950s. Built by the American Marcel Breuer, the Frenchman Zehrfuss and the Italian Nervi, this large pre-stressed concrete building was decorated by artists from a variety of countries (mobile by Calder, ceramics by Miró, mosaic by Bazaine).

fortress-prison captured by rioters on the 14 July 1789 and razed to the ground (the ground plan is traced out in paving stones). The square is dominated by the slender *Colonne de la Bastille* with the figure of the Génie de la Liberté (19C). The long Rue Saint-Antoine, home of furniture-makers, leads to the Place de la Nation, which has two tall *columns* and two *pavilions* by Ledoux; these mark the E. entrance to Paris (remains of the Fermiers Généraux town wall).

The Père-Lachaise Cemetery: This park-cemetery with the graves of numerous famous people from Beaumarchais to Colette and Édith Piaf, is an astonishing open-air sculpture museum.

Hôtel des Invalides: See also under Museums (Musée de l'Armée). This complex Grand Siècle masterpiece covers an area of 127,000 square metres. It was built as a 'hospital-palace' which Louis XIV intended to use for soldiers wounded in his service. Building, first under Libéral Bruant and then Hardouin-Mansart (who worked on the churches), continued from 1671 until the end of the 17C. The splendid *doorway* in the central building, decorated with a bas-relief renewed by Coustou,

Left Bank
Eiffel Tower: Guillaume Apollinaire

Eiffel Tower and the Pont d'Iéna

Hôtel des Invalides and the church of Saint-Louis

leads to a large main courtyard surrounded by matching buildings. *Saint-Louis des Invalides* or the *Chapelle des Soldats*, mainly the work of Hadouin-Mansart, is joined to the *Dôme* by the chancel, where there used to be a double altar; the two buildings are now separated by a portico and a glass partition. The Napoleon chapel at the end of the right side-aisle contains the remains of the tomb from St.Helena and the sarcophagus used to carry the Emperor's ashes. The Dôme church, started by Hardouin-Mansart in the 1670s and finished by Robert de Cotte, contains the elaborate *Tomb of Napoleon*, made to designs by Visconti. The famous *dome*, covered with gilded lead, is 340 ft. high.

Faubourg Saint-Germain: The cold and aristocratic Faubourg Saint-Germain was the great 18C residential quarter and the majority of its stately hôtels date from that period; they now house ministries and embassies. The *Hôtel de Biron* (1728–31) is at the corner of the Rue de Varenne and the Boulevard des Invalides, and houses the *Musée Rodin*. The *Hôtel de Matignon* at 57 Rue de Varenne houses the Présidence du Conseil. It was begun in 1721 by the architect Jean Courtonne and is named after of one of its early owners. The interesting *Rue de Grenelle* is enhanced by the pretty 1749 *Fontaine des Quatre Saisons* (No. 57-59). The Ministry of Defence in the *Rue Saint-Dominique* occupies the former convent to which Madame de Montespan retreated. Also interesting is the *Hôtel de Brienne* at No. 14. The Corinthian columns of the *Palais Bourbon* face the Place de la Concorde and the Seine, and its main courtyard opens on to the Rue de l'Université; it includes an hôtel which was much altered in the 18C. The palais is actually a vast group of buildings and houses the Chambre des Députés (19C chamber, library decorated by Delacroix). The *Hôtel de Lassay*, an extension of the Palais Bourbon, was built from 1722. The enormous *Gare d'Orsay*, a fine example of turn of the century ironwork, only just escaped demolition. It will soon house a *Museum of the 19C*. Next to it the *Hôtel de Salm* contains a little *Musée de la Légion d'Honneur* (history of great orders and decorations).

Saint Germain-des-Prés, Montparnasse: This quarter, grouped around the former abbey church of Saint-Germain, occupies land once belonging to a powerful abbey, some buildings of which survive behind the church. It was spoiled in the 19C by the building of large roads and realignment, but has some picturesque streets (*Rue de Fürstenberg* broadening to form a charming square which contains the former *studio of Delacroix*; the narrow *Rues de l'Échaudé, Bernard Palissy, du Sabot, du Dragon*, and *Visconti*). There are some fine 17 & 18C hôtels along the *Rue Jacob* and the *Rue des Saint-Pères*. This quarter was for a long time a quiet bourgeois area, but since the Liberation 'the Parish' has been famous, especially in the jazz age and the existentialist period. Restaurants and discothèques proliferated and smart shop windows transformed the ground floors of lavish apartment buildings. The rather ordinary Rue de Rennes runs from the Romanesque bell tower to the slender tower of the massive Maine-Montparnasse buildings (1960s) and leads on into *Montparnasse*. This area, also known for its night-life, was the great meeting place of artists and intellectuals in the Belle Époque and the Twenties: Modigliani, Kandinsky, Picasso, Klee, Matisse, Chagall, Rouault, Miller and Hemingway were well-known figures in the cafès around here. The Rodin *statue of Balzac* can be seen at the junction of the

Place de Fürstenberg

Boulevard du Montparnasse and the Boulevard Raspail.

Institut de France, Hôtel de la Monnaie (Quai de Conti): The elegant Institut de France building with its dome (academicians are admitted 'under the dome') is the work of Le Vau, who designed it and then died before the building was finished (1688). The institute was founded with funds from a legacy of Mazarin, and now includes five academies, one being the Académie Française, founded in 1634 by Richelieu and recognized by Louis XIII in 1635. The neoclassical *Hôtel de la Monnaie*, built by Jacques-Denis Antoine (1771-7), contains workshops and exhibition rooms connected with the Monnaie, which is responsible for coin and medals.

Quartier Saint-Séverin and Quartier

The Panthéon

Latin: The area beween the Seine and the Boulevard Saint-Germain has been made into a pedestrian precinct. It is still medieval in layout and its narrow streets run around *Saint-Séverin*. Many 17&18C houses have restaurants on the ground floor. The nearby *Maubert* quarter is also very old, but less lively (in the Rue de Poissy there is the medieval *storeroom* of the convent of the Bernardines). The 19C *Boulevard Saint-Michel* is the main thoroughfare of the Quartier Latin, which has for centuries been the student district. At the junction with the Boulevard Saint-Germain remains of *Gallo-Roman baths* (late 2C or early 3C) can be seen through the railings. These are next to the *Hôtel de Cluny*, a religious residence built at the end of the Gothic period, 1485–98. It is a superb medieval house and contains the *Musée de Cluny*. The immense *Sorbonne*, still the symbol of the University of Paris in spite of decentralization, was altered and enlarged in the 19C and bears the name of Robert de Sorbon, who taught nearby at the time of St.Louis. Originally a medieval college, it incorporates a church built in 1635 by Jacques Lemercier (tomb of Cardinal de Richelieu by Girardon, paintings by Philippe de Champaigne).

Panthéon, Contrescarpe: The enormous Panthéon was built by Soufflot from 1755 and stands at the very end of the Left Bank; it contains the tombs of great men. This cold and majestically domed former church has interior frescos by Gros (on the dome) and by Puvis de Chavannes; there are also paintings by L.J. Laurens and de Bonnat. The *crypt* galleries house the cenotaph of Rousseau and the tombs of Voltaire, Hugo, Zola, Jaurès and many other figures

The Palais du Luxembourg

f French history. Near the Panthéon, the *St. Geneviève Library* is an interesting iron building (1844–50). The Lycée Henri IV has remnants of an abbey. The *Montagne Sainte Geneviève* and *Contrescarpe* quarters are picturesque and lively, attracting tourists, students and fringe figures. The charming Place de la Contrescarpe was opened in the 19C in the heart of this ancient area. The crowded and bustling *Rue Mouffetard* (17C fountain at the corner of the Rue du Pot-de-Fer) leads to the heterogeneous *Saint-Médard*, whose oldest parts are 17C.

Val-de-Grâce, Observatoire: The Val-de-Grace is a military hospital with a little *Musée du Service de Santé* housed in monastery buildings founded by Anne of Austria. The complex is dominated by the tallest dome in Paris, on the church built from 1645 to François Mansart's design. Inside the dome is decorated by Mignard (*La Gloire des Bienheureux*); there are also numerous sculptures by Michel Anguier and a high altar with a monumental baldacchino. The severe Observatoire building was built by Claude Perrault (1668–92) and has 19C observation domes. Neither iron nor wood was used in the building to avoid magnetic deviation and the risk of fire. The cellars, 70 ft. below, contain the famous 'talking clock'.

Odéon, Luxembourg: The Rue de l'Odéon, like the nearby Rue Monsieur-le-Prince, is lined with lovely 18C houses. The arcaded *Théâtre de l'Odéon* was erected 1779–82 and the ceiling of the auditorium was painted by André Masson in 1965; it consists of an elegant semicircle of four 18C buildings. Marie de Medici had the

Palais du Luxembourg built because she found the Louvre uncomfortable. It was started in 1615 by Salomon de Brosse, modified by Jean Chalgrin, and enlarged in the 19C. It contains some remarkable paintings by Jordaens and Delacroix and houses the Senate, which owns the Jardin du Luxembourg (laid out in the 18C for Marie de Medici). The *Medici Fountain* between the Palace and the Rue Médicis, is possibly the work of Salomon de Brosse.

The gardens of the Avenue de l'Observatoire are an extension of the Jardin du Luxembourg, and are decorated with a very beautiful fountain (1875) by Davioud, which has tortoises and sea-horses (Frémiet) and with the *Quatre Parties du Monde*; this group includes an armillary sphere by Carpeaux.

Denfert-Rochereau, Catacombes: The replica of Bartholdi's Belfort Lion dominates the Place Denfert-Rochereau on the edge of which are two 1784 Ledoux *toll houses* from the Fermiers Généraux town wall. The *Catacombes* are former quarries and contain bones from thousands of skeletons exhumed in the 18C from the old Cimetière des Innocents.

Jardin des Plantes, Salpêtrière: Buffon enlarged and improved this garden, which is in the French style, adding the maze and the alpine garden. On the edge are the galleries and buildings of the *Muséum d'Histoire Naturelle*. The *Hôpital de la Salpêtrière* at 47 Boulevard de l'Hôpital was built at the end of the 17C by Le Vau and the church was added by the architect Libéral Bruant (1670–7).

Gobelins Factory:: The modern façade hides quasi-monastic old buildings. The Royal Tapestry Workshops were founded by Henri IV and merged with the carpet factory of the Savonnerie and more recently with the Beauvais factory. The factory is still in use.

PRINCIPAL MUSEUMS

(The number after the address refers to the arrondissement.)

Musée de l'Affiche (16 Rue de Paradis 10): Collection of posters past and present housed in an old faience shop with astonishing decor. Some of the exhibits were avant-garde when created.

Musée de l'Armée (Hôtel des Invalides 7): History and techniques of warfare, an extraordinary collection of weapons and armour, lead soldiers and models. Exhibits from the swords of prehistory to the German 'Big Bertha', from arquebuses to the sophisticated artillery of the last two wars. Everything is well presented and clearly labelled.

Musée des Arts Africains et Océaniens (296 Avenue Daumesnil 12): Art and civilization from Maghreb, black Africa and Oceania. There is a large aquarium in the basement.

Musée des Arts Décoratifs (107 Rue de Rivoli 1): This exciting museum has some 50,000 exhibits on the subject of the decorative arts from the Middle Ages to the Belle Époque. The history of French, European, Turkish and Oriental decorative art is attractively presented in chronological order (furniture, woodwork, tapestries, secular and ecclesiastical silverware, ceramics, etc.).

Musée d'Art Moderne de la Ville de Paris (11 Avenue du Président-Wilson 16): Changing exhibition of 20C works.

Luxembourg, Fontaine Médicis

'Seated Nude' by Picasso

Musée des Arts et Traditions Populaires (6 Route du Mahatma-Ghandi, Bois de Boulogne): A collection on pre-industrial civilization in a modern building. It includes agriculture, stock breeding, crafts, domestic life, religious creeds and customs, games, popular theatre and art, history of puppets.

Musée de Baccarat (30 bis Rue de Paradis 10): Crystal and glass; exhibits from the 200-year-old Baccarat crystal factory.

Musée Balzac (Maison de Balzac) (47 Rue Raynouard 16): This is the garden 'cabane de Passy' where Balzac lived from 1840–7. It exhibits some of the writer's possessions, documents relating to his career, portraits, caricatures and statues.

Musée Bourdelle (16 Rue Antoine-Bourdelle 15): This maze of courtyards and studios was the home of the sculptor Antoine Bourdelle from 1884–1929. There are drawings, gouaches, paintings, statues, original plaster casts and a strange collection of busts of Beethoven.

Musée Carnavalet (Musée de l'Histoire de Paris) (23 Rue de Sévigné 3): This varied museum in a remarkable 16C hôtel (Marais) presents the history of daily life in Paris from the time of Henri II to the present day. There are innumerable documents, models, flags, fine Louis XIV, Regency and Louis XV furniture, paintings and engravings of the capital over the centuries.

Musée de Céramique de Sèvres (Place de la Manufacture, Sèvres (a nearby W. suburb): splendid collection of ceramics from many countries and periods.

Musée Cernuschi (Musée d'Art Chinois de la Ville de Paris) (7 Avenue Velasquez 8): Chinese art, including pieces from the 16C BC, Han Dynasty funerary statuettes, (3C BC) to T'ang Dynasty (8C), Buddhist sculptures, 8C paintings on silk (*Chevaux et Palefreniers*).

Musée du Cinéma (Cinémathèque Française) (Palais de Chaillot 16): History of the cinema from Émile Reynaud and the Lumière brothers to contemporary directors.

Musée Georges-Clemenceau (8 Rue Franklin 16): This is in the flat where Clemenceau lived for 34 years, and is devoted to the great statesman and his love of ancient art and modern painting.

Musée de Cluny (6 Place Paul-Painlevé 5): The Gothic residence of the abbots of Cluny now houses an admirable collection of medieval arts and crafts: sculpture, fur

Musée de Cluny, tapestry of the Lady and the Unicorn

niture, silverware, armory, ironwork, pottery, games. There are some fine tapestries, including the *Dame à la Licorne* series (late 15C). The museum extends into the ruins of the Gallo-Roman baths adjacent to the hôtel, and houses the *Autel des Nautes* (1C), a monument dedicated to Jupiter by the boatmen of that time.

Musée Cognacq-Jay (25 Boulevard des Capucines 2): This exciting and varied museum is arranged like an 18C house. It has thousands of precious objects, paintings and sculptures (such as *l'Anesse de Balaam* by Rembrandt, works by Greuze, Boucher, Chardin, Quentin de La Tour, Watteau, Fragonard, Tiepolo, Guardi, Lemoyne and Clodion).

Palais de la Découverte (Avenue Franklin-D.-Roosevelt 8): Devoted to the popularization of science with reconstructions of famous experiments. The *Planetarium*, showing accelerated star movements, was one of the attractions of the 1937 Exposition Universelle.

Musée Delacroix (6 Rue Fürstenberg 6): devoted to the painter and located in his flat and studio.

Centre Georges-Pompidou (Plateau Beaubourg): Built at the instigation of President Pompidou by architects Renzo Piano and Richard Rogers, the futuristic glass and metal building rises incongruously from the heart of old Paris; it is a great attraction today, but many were strongly against it when it was opened in 1977. It contains a large collection of modern and contemporary art, but it is far more than just a museum; it is a meeting place and centre of work and culture. Inside the enormous steel and glass structure with its appropriately gigantic entrance hall ('Op' portrait of Pompidou by Vasarely) there is a public library with audio-visual aids, the Institut de Recherche et de Co-ordination Acoustique-Musique, directed by Pierre Boulez and the Centre de Création Industrielle. There are various temporary exhibitions.

Musée Grévin (10 Boulevard Montmartre 9): Waxwork models of historical figures, distorting mirrors—a very amusing museum.

Musée Guimet (6 Place d'Iéna 16): The splendour and refinement of the East are on show in this museum devoted to Indian, Indo-Chinese, East Indian, Central Asian, Tibetan, Chinese and Japanese art, and it contains some 55,000 exhibits, including large bejewelled Buddhas and lacquered porcelain.

Louvre, 'The Dance' by Carpeaux

Musée Gustave Moreau (14 Rue de la Rochefoucauld 9): Numerous works by the symbolist painter.

Muséum d'Histoire Naturelle (Jardin des Plantes 5): Outstanding mineralogical and entomological collections (latter 45 Rue Buffon).

Musée de l'Homme (Palais de Chaillot 16): This is a remarkable anthropological museum dealing with the evolution and culture of the human race. It is highly informative, without being boring. There is an excellent pre-history section; other exhibits include superb African statues and masks, charming works of popular art and carnival characters).

Musée Jacquemart-André (58 Boulevard Haussmann 8): A 19C hôtel full of treasures including paintings, sculptures, tapestries, furniture and objets d'art from the Renaissance to the 18C. Of special interest are works by Tintoretto, Tiepolo, Botticelli, Carpaccio, Mantegna, Uccello, Van Dyck, Rembrandt, Rubens, Hubert Robert, Watteau and various sculptors.

Jeu de Paume (Musée de l'Impressionnisme) (Jardin des Tuileries, Concorde entrance 1): An annexe of the Louvre, this museum is devoted to the Impressionists, with works by the greatest and the less well-known members of the movement. It includes the principal Impressionists, like Monet, Sisley and Pissarro, and also some pre- and post-Impressionists.

Musée du Louvre: A truly vast collection covering miles of rooms, galleries and stairways. This museum in a palace has been extended and reorganized constantly since 1791. It contains the collections of the

Louvre, the Mona Lisa (Leonardo da Vinci)

former Kings of France and numerous other works of art.

Greek and Roman antiquities: Terracotta with friezes, vases with jewels, etc.—an extremely varied collection. The *Winged Victory* or *Nike of Samothrace*, a Greek masterpiece from the 3C or 2C BC; *Venus de Milo* from the 2C BC; also fragments of the frieze from the Parthenon, 5C BC.

Oriental antiquities: Finds from digs in the Near East, including the *Statue of the Intendant of Mari, Ebih-II* from the middle Euphrates, 3rd millennium BC; and the *Codex of Hammurabi,* a block of basalt with inscriptions from the 2nd millennium BC.

Egyptian antiquities: This department, created by Champollion and extended by Mariette, contains great works of art and countless ordinary daily objects (from the Thinite period, beginning in the 4th millennium, onwards.) There is a colossal granite *Sphinx,* probably from the Old Empire (3rd millenium); the *Mastaba,* or tomb of an Egyptian dignitary, a little edifice decorated with informative scenes of daily life, which dates from the middle of the 3rd millenium; three pink granite columns from the 5th Dynasty; and the *Scribe accroupi* a small limestone figure of a scribe sitting cross-legged from the old Empire. There are also sarcophagi, funerary furnishings, and jewellery.

Objets d'art and furnishings: This very varied department shows objets d'art and furniture from the Middle Ages to the 19C. There are enamels, Renaissance bronzes, fine furniture by Charles-André Boulle, a collection of boxes and snuff boxes, and silver-gilt toilet articles which belonged to Marie Leszczynska. The famous diamond, *Le Régent* (137 carats) and the *crown jewels* are exhibited in the *Galérie d'Apollon* on the first floor of the *Petite Galérie* (vault painted by Delacroix).*Paintings:* A very important department occupying numerous rooms and the *Grande Galérie.* The breathtakingly varied collection has very

few gaps. It includes works from the 14C to Impressionism. A major attraction for many is the *Mona Lisa* with her enigmatic smile; this work, protected by bullet-proof glass, was bought by François I and is the only undisputed portrait by Leonardo da Vinci; it is said to represent Mona Lisa Gherardini, the young wife of a Florentine doctor. There are two other pictures by da Vinci in the Louvre: *Madonna and Child with St.Anne* and the *Virgin of the Rocks.* The various Italian schools are very well represented: in particular by Cimabue, Giotto, Simone Martini, Fra Angelico, Paolo Uccello, Sandro Botticelli, Vittore Carpaccio, Andrea Mantegna, Perugino, Veronese, Tintoretto, Correggio, Raphael, Giovanni Battista Tiepolo, Francesco Guardi and Domenico Tiepolo. There are also a great many French paintings from the *Portrait de Jean le Bon* (about 1360) to Delacroix, Corot and Courbet (very fine works from the Fontainebleau School of the 17&18C). There is a large collection of *Dutch and Flemish Painting*: the paintings for the Palais du Luxembourg by Rubens, works by Rembrandt, and the famous *Lacemaker* by Vermeer. The *Drawing Department* is one of the most varied in the world (frequent temporary exhibitions). *Sculptures*: Romanesque, Gothic, Renaissance and other works up to the second half of the 19C: in particular, there are works by Donatello, Jean Goujon, Germain Pilon and Michelangelo.

Musée de la Marine (Palais de Chaillot 16): Navigation and the history of the navy, with works of art, paintings, spectacular models and instruments.

Musée Marmottan: (2 Rue Louis-Boilly 16): Wonderfully colourful paintings including works by Monet and a general overview of Impressionism.

Musée des Monuments Français (Palais de Chaillot 16): Reproductions of

The Petit Palais

Musée Rodin, 'The Kiss' by Rodin

great examples of French architecture and sculpture.

Musée Nissim-de-Camando (63 Rue de Monceau 8): A hôtel set out as the house of an enlightened 18C art-lover.

Musée de l'Orangerie (Place de la Concorde, Tuileries entrance 1): Two huge compositions by Monet, *Nymphéas*, painted 1890–1921; temporary exhibitions.

Musée du Petit-Palais (Musée des Beaux Arts de la Ville de Paris) (Avenue Winston-Churchill 8): Beautiful and varied collections, the greater part devoted to French 19C painters (Ingres, Géricault, Courbet, Bonnard, Vuillard and Renoir).

Centre Pompidou, see under **Centre Georges-Pompidou**

Musée Postal (34 Boulevard de Vaugirard 15): The history of the postal service and philately.

Musée Rodin (in the fine Hôtel Biron, 77 Rue de Varenne 7): Numerous sculptures and works by Rodin; many objets d'art.

Musée du Seita (12 Rue Surcouf 7): The Seita (Service d'Exploitation Industriel des Tabacs et des Allumettes) opened this museum in 1979 and it covers the history of tobacco and its world-wide use. It exhibits all the paraphernalia of the smoker; some very fine objects and some surprising ones.

Musée des Techniques (292 Rue Saint-Martin 10): Linked with the Conservatoire des Arts et Métiers, this educational museum deals with technical and scientific innovations of all sorts, from gear systems to

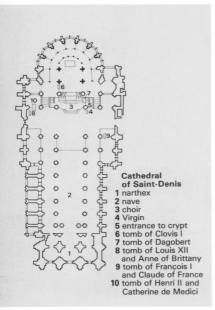

Cathedral of Saint-Denis
1 narthex
2 nave
3 choir
4 Virgin
5 entrance to crypt
6 tomb of Clovis I
7 tomb of Dagobert
8 tomb of Louis XII and Anne of Brittany
9 tomb of François I and Claude of France
10 tomb of Henri II and Catherine de Medici

television, from Pascal's calculating machines to aviation. There are clocks, pendulums, automatic machines, models of locomotives, and an exhibition of transport from the horse onwards.

Palais de Tokyo (13 Avenue du Président-Wilson 16): Post-Impressionists and Belle Époque objets d'art. Works by Braque, Laurens, Rouault, Dunoyer de Segonzac.

Maison de Victor-Hugo (6 Place des Vosges 4): Exhibits concerning Victor Hugo's literary, political and family life, including furniture and his drawings.

Musée du Vieux Montmartre (17 Rue Saint-Vincent 18): A charming presentation of Montmartre's past.

Environs: Château de Vincennes: This vast military and residential complex on the edge of Paris was a royal city, became a prison and then deteriorated when the army took it over. The *Tour du Village* (Avenue de Paris entrance) was the governors' residence in the Middle Ages. The superb square *keep* (160 ft. high) is a remarkable 14C defensive structure housing a small *Musée Historique*. The *Sainte-Chapelle* with its late Gothic façade was begun about 1387 and consecrated in 1552 (restored 16C stained glass, carved frieze inside, tomb of the Duke d'Enghien, who was shot in 1804 in the Vincennes moat). The *Pavillon du Roi* and the *Pavillon de la Reine* are by Le Vau and were built from 1654-61. The *Arc de Triomphe* is also by Le Vau.

Saint-Denis Cathedral: This famous basilica is in Saint-Denis, an expanding industrial suburb near Paris. It became a cathedral in 1966. It replaced churches built by Dagobert and Pepin the Short and is essentially the work of the Abbot Suger (12C) and of Pierre de Montreuil (13C). Begun in 1136 (façade, beginning of the nave), it was the first example of emerging Gothic art. At the end of the 18C it was in a deplorable state and underwent its first, rather clumsy, restoration. Work was re-started under Viollet le Duc who was in charge of operations from 1858 until his death. The cathedral, entered through a 350 ft. pronaos between the two towers, was used as a funerary chapel by the Kings of France (most of the French kings—from Dagobert to Louis XVII—were buried at Saint-Denis). The desecrated tombs were saved by Alexandre Lenoir, who took them to Paris during the Revolution; they were probably replaced in the basilica in 1816 on the orders of Louis XVIII. Saint-Denis houses the remarkable *tombs* of Kings, Queens, royal children, other celebrities and superb Renaissance *mausoleums*. There is a very beautiful painted Romanesque wooden *Virgin* at the side of the choir. The crypt is the burial chamber of the Bourbons. The former abbey building

Parthenay, Porte Saint-Jacques

Parthenay, church of Saint-Pierre

date from the 18C. In the Place de la Légion d'Honneur is a *Musée d'Art et d'Histoire*.

Parthenay	(13,040 inhab.)
79 Deux-Sèvres	p.418☐F 9

Parthenay, an old stopping place on the route to Santiago de Compostella, spreads out on the granite slopes of the Gâtine on the edge of the Thouet region. Formerly protected by a double line of ramparts, it was a powerful fortress. It became a Royalist stronghold and was captured by the Republicans in 1793. A 13C bridge and the 13C *Porte Saint-Jacques*, with twin machicolated towers, lead to the medieval town. Thousands of pilgrims passed along the Rue de la Vau-Saint-Jacques, which is

lined with picturesque half-timbered houses from the 15&16C and which leads to the little Place du 14 Juillet where the old 13C ramparts can be seen. The *Porte de l'Horloge*, a massive Gothic structure used as a belfry in the 15C, marks the entrance to the citadel.

The **Church of Sainte-Croix** is 12C and there is a 15C tomb of a Parthenay nobleman and his wife in the Angevin choir. Only the lower part of the façade remains of the church of **Notre-Dame-de-la-Couldre**, which was sold off as a national asset in the Revolution. The sculpture on the triple doorway is a marvellous example of Poitevin Romanesque art (there are prophets, apostles, fantastic animals, warriors etc.). The **Church of Saint-Laurent** from the 13C has been refurbished. It is dominated by a 240 ft. high bell tower and contains some fine capitals, a 15C Burning

of Jeanne d'Albret and a gilded wooden
17C altarpiece. The 11&12C **Church of
Saint-Pierre-de-Parthenay-le-Vieux**,
in the suburbs, has a perfect Poitevin façade. Inside you will find fine carvings
'Constantine the Horseman', Samson con-
fronting the lion and imaginary scenes and
animals.

| **Pau** | (85,860 inhab.) |
| 64 Pyrénées-Atlantiques | p.422 □ F 15 |

Pau, Henri IV's town, ('Nouste Henric'
as the Béarnais say), has a spectacular view,
ending in the distance with the peaks of the
Pyrénées. It was a modest little Gallo-
Roman town which grew up around a
manor and owed a great deal to Gaston
Phoebus in the 14C. It became the capital of Béarn in 1464, and expanded in the
16C before the Wars of Religion threw the
region into bloody turmoil. It was rejoined
to France, along with Béarn, at the beginning of the 17C, and Louis XIII set up a
Parliament here. Louis XIV made it a seat
of provincial government and today it is the
principal town of the Département of the
Pyrénées-Atlantiques.

Château and Museums: This impressive château, which was rather over-
zealously refurbished by architects under
Louis-Philippe and Napoleon III, is situated at the edge of a promontory overlooking the Gave (a mountain torrent). It has
a disfigured keep dating from about 1370
and has been constantly changed and altered over the years, in particular by
Gaston de Foix in the 15C and Henri d'Albret and Marguerite d'Angoulême in the
16C. It houses the *Musée National* and the
Musée Henri IV as well as the old-fashioned
Musée Béarnais (natural history, local
trades, history, folklore and local art). In
particular it contains some very fine and
varied 19C furniture, Gobelin and Flem-

Pau, the château

ish tapestries, numerous religious paintings going back to Henri IV's time, and a
turtle's shell said to have been his cradle.
'Henri IV's bedroom' is a 19C reconstruction. Near the château, and part of the
huge 18C Navarre Parliament building, is
the bell tower of a former church. **Musée
Bernadotte** (Rue Tran): In 1763 Jean-
Baptiste Bernadotte, the future Marshal of
France and King of Sweden, was born in
this Béarnais house, which has a small exhibition concerning his life. **Musée des
Beaux-Arts** (Rue Mathieu-Lalanne): This
houses paintings of the area by Eugène Devéria who died in Pau in 1865, a very fine
painting by Degas—*Le Bureau de Coton à
la Nouvelle-Orléans* (1873), works from the
16C to the present day, and a coin exhibition.

Environs: Lescar (7.5 km. NW): This

Lescar, Notre-Dame, capital

little town was originally called *Beneharnum* and is perched on the edge of a plateau above the Gave valley; it was the first capital of Béarn and gave the area its original name. The former *Cathedral of Notre-Dame* was built mainly in the 12C but it has been much interfered with, rebuilt and restored. However, the apse has preserved its Romanesque purity. It contains some interesting decorated capitals, a 12C mosaic, funerary stones (it was a burial place for princes in the 15&16C) and some Renaissance stalls.

Penmarc'h   (6,920 inhab.)
29 Finistère   p.412 □ A 6

The village of Penmarc'h is an outpost of the Bigou country and the centre of a large,

far-flung community. Its *church* is dedicated to Saint Nonna and is an elegant Flamboyant building begun in 1508. Its plan is simple, with a flat apse and three windows; it has all the main characteristics of Breton Gothic: poor elevation of the triple nave with its panelled vault and a pierced bell tower with side turrets. An impressive (unfinished) tower on the W. façade is decorated with carved boats and fish, which bear witness to a vanished prosperity.

Chapel of Notre-Dame-de-la-Joie: A little way away from the Eckmühl lighthouse lies the chapel of *Notre-Dame-de-la-Joie-au-Péril-de-la-Mer*. Built in 1897 beside a little 15C fortified church, this 15C building washed by the waves, has a blind gable with bell tower and turrets on its W. side. Its nave contains an interesting collection of ex voto offerings (models of boats) and some old statues. There is a pretty Pietà on the base of the 1588 calvary.

Environs: Saint Guénolé (3 km. W.): The *Musée Préhistorique de Saint Guénolé* was founded in 1920 to house the many local archaeological discoveries. A series of megaliths surround the building, and inside there are extensive collections of tools, weapons, pottery and jewellery from different prehistoric periods, including the Gallic and Gallo-Roman periods. In one room there are two reconstructed burial places (Saint-Urnel and Roz-en-Tre-Men).

Périgueux   (37,670 inhab.)
24 Dordogne   p.419 □ G II

The capital of Périgord and the Préfecture of the Dordogne is encircled by a loop of the river Isle. Dominated by the famous domes of its churches, the city abounds in a mixture of architectural periods. The town has kept the name of the Gallic

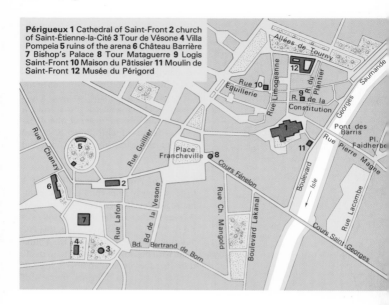

Périgueux **1** Cathedral of Saint-Front **2** church of Saint-Étienne-la-Cité **3** Tour de Vésone **4** Villa Pompeia **5** ruins of the arena **6** Château Barrière **7** Bishop's Palace **8** Tour Mataguerre **9** Logis Saint-Front **10** Maison du Pâtissier **11** Moulin de Saint-Front **12** Musée du Périgord

Périgueux, aerial view

Petrocorii who founded a fortress here on the left bank of the river. Although these people were allied to Vercingétorix, they did well out of the Roman rule and the beautiful town of *Vésone* replaced their fortified camp. After a period of prosperity it was ruined by barbarian invasions and then eclipsed by the town which grew up around the nearby Abbey of Saint-Front in the Middle Ages. The two, rivals for a long time, were joined in the 13C, and became prosperous thanks to the Moulins de l'Isle, and fairs and pilgrimages, but then suffered greatly in the Hundred Years War, the Jacqueries (peasant uprisings) and the Fronde. The town was improved in the 16C and in the 18C given its majestic panoramic terrace by the Intendant Tourny, who also did much for Bordeaux. The town walls were pulled down in the 19C. Today there is relatively little industry but Périgueux is well known for its gastronomic special-

ities, such as truffles and foie gras, which are famous all over the world.

Saint Étienne de la Cité: This 11&12C church stands in the 'Cité' (that part of Périgueux descended from the Gallo-Roman *Vésone*). The cathedral until 1669, it is much more interesting archaeologically than Saint-Front, in spite of having been partly destroyed in 1577 by the Huguenots and having undergone major rebuilding in the 17C. It once had four domes and a bell tower (which contained the porch). Now it only has two bays with domes; that in the nave is massive, rough and sombre and that in the choir high, light and ornate. The nave would seem to date from the end of the 11C, and the choir from the second quarter of the 12C. On the S. wall there is a paschal table, which shows the dates of Easter between the years 1163 and 1253. To the left of the nave there

Périgueux, cathedral of Saint-Front

is a prettily carved 12C arch, beneath which there is the tomb of a bishop.

Remains of Vésone: There are substantial remains of Vésone, even though the Gallo-Roman town was used as a quarry by medieval builders. The strange *Tour de Vésone*, gutted, decapitated, and minus its former covering of red and green marble, is still impressive. It was the *cella* of a 2C temple dedicated to a tutelary god. The remains of the nearby 1C *Villa Pompeia* are arranged in the classical manner around a patio. The remains of the arenas, which have been made into a small park and are also 1C, show the importance of the elliptical amphitheatre (with a capacity of 20,000 people). Nearby there are the remains of the *Château Barrière*, a fortified medieval house with a keep, which probably dates from the 12C, and which is still

in the form of a tower from the 4C Gallo-Roman town wall. The Bishop's Palace was also built on the remains of the ancient defences.

Old Périgueux: The *Cité de Puy-Saint-Front*, the rival of *Vésone* until the 13C, has largely survived. Its old quarters by the cathedral still look medieval with their narrow cobbled streets, winding alleys with central gutters, fine houses and Renaissance hôtels. The massive *Tour Mataguerre*, machicolated and with arrow-slits, was rebuilt in 1477 and was part of the Puy-Saint-Front fortifications set up in the 14C. One of the most beautiful houses in old Périgueux, the *Logis Saint-Front*, is at the corner of the Rue de la Constitution and the Rue du Plantier; its main section is 15C and it has an elegant staircase tower. At 1,3, and 5 Rue Limogeanne there are

Périgueux, the Logis Saint-Front

lovely Renaissance houses, and at 17 Rue
Éguillerie a 15&16C hôtel called the 'maison du pâtissier'. On the water's edge near
the Pont des Barris there are some picturesque houses; the Moulin de Saint-
Front is a pretty half-timbered house on the
Quai de l'Isle.

Musée du Périgord: Allées de Tourny.
This important museum is housed in a
magnificent Belle Époque house, and has
very interesting collections of ethnography,
paintings and faience, but it is above all a
prehistoric and Gallo-Roman archaeological museum. There are numerous finds
from the prehistoric burial places in the
area, including the famous skeleton of a
Magdalenian man found in 1888 in Chancelade, and some very fine Gallo-Roman
mosaics and stele found in the Périgord
area.

Péronne	(9,420 inhab.)
80 Somme	p.411 □ J 3

The pools and marshland near this town
(the capital of the Vermandois) give it its
particular character. Ravaged by war—the
Somme battlefields are close by—it none
the less still has some relics of its turbulent past. When Louis XI was the prisoner
of Charles the Bold, he was probably kept
in one of the four massive towers of the
13C *château*; the building is enclosed by
the colossal 17C brick bastion. Only the
Porte de Bretagne (1602) remains of the old
town wall, and it still has its drawbridge
and outer defences. The *Musée Danicourt*
in the Hôtel de Ville shows Gallo-Roman
and Merovingian jewellery and has a
remarkable collection of ancient coins, in-

cluding a priceless gold piece with what is thought to be the effigy of Vercingetorix.

Pérouges (530 inhab.)
01 Ain p.421 □ M 10

Pérouges is an extraordinary fortified medieval village set on the top of a hill. At the beginning of the century it was in a very poor state. However, it has since been successfully restored. The half-timbered houses along its narrow cobbled streets are mostly late 15C or 17C. The church is a curious fortified building by the *Porte d'En Haut*; it was built from the 13C–15C (the bell tower is 19C). There are finely worked keystones on the vaulting of the nave.

Perpignan (107,970 inhab.)
66 Pyrénées-Orientales p.424 □ J 16

The citadel of the Palais des Rois de Majorque still watches over this city of the plain,

which has now broken loose from its encircling ramparts and spread out on to the left bank of the river Têt. The former capital of Roussillon, it is Catalan in spirit and lively and original in character. Its considerable expansion is due to its trade in wine, fruit and vegetables, to its development as an administrative centre and to the growth of its university. Originally it was a small Roman city, *Ruscino* (hence Roussillon), which declined as a result of the barbarian invasions. The city figured in history in the 12C, during which time Roussillon returned to the Aragon crown. King Jaime I of Aragon, who landed near Palma and recaptured the Balearic Islands from the Moors, shared his possessions between his two sons, so Perpignan became the capital of a hybrid kingdom comprising Montpellier, Roussillon and the Cerdagne, as well as the Balearic Islands. The Kingdom of Majorca only had three kings before the Balearics were joined once more to Aragon, but they left their mark on the city. Perpignan was occupied by Louis XI, Charles VIII restored it to the Catholic monarchs Ferdinand and Isabella, and in

Perpignan, Palais des Rois de Majorque

1642 it was retaken by Louis XIII. In the mid 17C it was finally restored to the French Crown along with Roussillon. The great portraitist Hyacinthe Rigaud was born here in 1659, and it has attracted a number of 20C artists e.g. Picasso, Dufy, Lurçat and Salvador Dali among others. (The latter liked to imagine that Perpignan station was the centre of the world.) Perpignan has two of Aristide Maillol's best female statues (he died here in 1944): *Méditerranée* (1905 in the courtyard of the town hall) and *Vénus* (1928 in the Place de la Loge).

Cathedral of Saint-Jean: Begun by the second King of Majorca in 1324 but not completed until about 1507; it was consecrated in 1509. It is Gothic with a southern flavour. The wide nave has chapels set into the interior buttresses, the transept is quite short, and there is a large apse between two apsidal chapels. The rectangular façade is flanked by a square tower (the bell tower on top of this dates from the 18C). The cathedral contains some fine altarpieces from the late 16–17C. The altar-

Perpignan, cathedral, the Dévôt Christ

piece de la Vierge de l'Espérance was painted by two Catalan-inspired artists in about 1500 at a time of strong Italian and Flemish influences. It is also known as de la Magraña and can be found in the S. apse; there is a modern Virgin and Child in the centre. The marble altarpiece on the high altar (1618–30) is by Claude Peret, of Burgundian origin, and the Catalan Onuphre Salla. A passage beneath the Flamboyant organ chest leads to the *Chapelle de la Vierge dels Correch* (of the ravines), the transept of an 11C Romanesque church, Saint-Jean-le-Vieux. Outside (leave by the right side door) in a chapel is a touching and realistic *Dévot de Christ*, a 14C Crucifixion in carved wood, probably of Rhenish origin.

Church of Saint-Jacques: This 14C church is adjacent to the Miranda garden; beneath its S. porch is a large Cross of Shame (bearing the Instruments of the Passion). Inside are statues, altarpieces and a monumental high altar. The nave is prolonged to the W. by the 18C chapel of the Confrérie de la Sanch (Holy Blood) which for the past five hundred years has held a Good Friday procession rather like the one at Seville.

Castillet: The Castillet is a fine fortified gate which was turned into a little fortress in about 1480; it has crenellations and machicolations and was part of the town wall, which has since been demolished. Inside is the *Casa Pairal*, a museum of Catalan arts and traditions.

Place de la Loge, Loge de Mer, Hôtel de Ville: This square has pink marble flagstones and a charming statue by Maillol, and is the tourist centre of Perpignan. The Loge de Mer was built in the late 14C and enlarged to the W. in the 16C; its function was the same as the Lonja and the Consulat de la Mer in Palma di Majorca i.e. it was the stock exchange and commer-

Perpignan **1** Cathedral of Saint-Jean **2** chapel **3** church of Saint-Jacques **4** Jardin Miranda **5** Castillet (Casa Pairal) **6** Loge de Mer, Hôtel de Ville **7** Citadelle, Palais des Rois de Majorque **8** Musée Rigaud

Perpignan, ceiling of the town hall

cial centre. The Hôtel de Ville, next to the Loge, has some medieval parts but is essentially 16C&17C. The bronze arms on the façade stand for the Nobility, the Clergy and the Third Estate. The former Députation building by the Hôtel de Ville is 15C and has a façade of finely worked stone and a doorway with large keystones.

Citadelle, Palais des Rois de Majorque: The 16C fortifications, modified by Vauban, enclose the Palais des Rois de Majorque, which is 13&14C. The whole is a rectangle and built of a mixture of river pebbles and brick, decorated with marble. An unusual chapel overlooks the E. side of the main courtyard. It has two storeys and is an early 14C Gothic building with a Romanesque doorway.

Musée Rigaud (former university): There

are many pictures by the local artist Rigaud, primitives from Roussillon and Catalonia and 17,18&19C works.

Environs: Elne (14 km. SE): The *cloister* here, whose elegance much impressed Mérimée and Viollet-le-Duc, is more or less intact. The S. walk, which backs on to the church, is 12C; the rest of the buildings are 13&14C. The later additions have not impaired the overall harmony of the cloister; the different periods are only apparent from the sculpture, e.g. the hooked capitals in the S. walk. The capitals are decorated with floral or zoological motifs and religious scenes. There are various funerary monuments in the cloister. The former *cathedral* of Elne (the bishop and chapter abandoned it in 1602 and moved

Perpignan, cathedral, retable

The Fort de Salses

Pézenas, Hôtel Lacoste

to Perpignan) was rebuilt in the 11C and fortified in the middle of the following century. It follows the ground plan of a basilica and is bare and rather severe inside and out. Its massive S. bell tower with arches was finished in 1415 by the Majorcan architect Guillaume Sagrera. Chapels were added on the S. side; the first was built by Bishop Raymond Costa (who died in 1310) and houses his sarcophagus. The capitals have floral decoration with human figures among the foliage. **Castelnou** (18 km. SW): The impressive Mount Canigou overlooks this remarkable feudal site with its massive 10C *fortress*, which was restored in the 19C. **Monastir del Camp** (16 km. S.): Legend has it that this former priory was founded by Charlemagne. It is a peaceful haven, with an 11C single-aisled *church* and a *cloister* finished in the early 14C; the convent buildings date mainly from the

13C&14C. **Salses** (16 km. N.): The massive *Fort de Salses*, built in 1497 by Don Sanche de Castile, is remarkable for the harmony of colour of its stone and brick.

Pézenas   (8,060 inhab.)
34 Hérault   p.424☐K 14

Pézenas was formerly the fortified Roman city of *Piscenae* and its inhabitants still call themselves Piscénois. In the Middle Ages the town grew rich from trade and fairs, and had a golden age when it became the seat of the Languedoc government. In this period noblemen lived here, among them was the flamboyant Armand de Bourbon, Prince de Conti. He was host to a number of artists and writers, including Molière. The town has many 16&17C buildings and

Pézenas, Hôtel de Flottes, detail

today is a flourishing centre of the wine and spirit trade. It is picturesque and unusual, with a fine array of houses, hôtels and shops now occupied by craftsmen. Especially interesting are the Rue de la Foire, Cours Jean Jaurès, Rue Conti and Rue Saint-Jean.

Old Pézenas: In the Rue François-Oursin is the 15&16C Hôtel Lacoste, and in the Place Gambetta the Renaissance and late 17C *Maison Consulaire.* In the Rue Alfred-Sabatier the Hôtel de Flottes-de-Sébasan is a mixture of periods from the 14C–18C and has a pretty Renaissance corner niche. In the Rue Denfert-Rochereau the *Hôtel Malilbran* and in the Rue de Conti the *Hôtel d'Alfonce,* where Molière performed, are both interesting and date from the 17C. Molière lived in the Maison du Barbier Gély which today houses the Syndicat

d'Initiative. The *Porte Faugères* was built in the late 16C and leads to the old part of Pézenas with its medieval quarter (in particular the Rue de la Juiverie and the Rue des Litanies).

Churches: *Saint-Jean* is 18C and faces a former command post of Saint-Jean-de-Jérusalem, which is probably 16C. The mock Gothic *church of Sainte-Ursule* (opposite a 16C hôtel) is 17C.

Musée Vulliod-Saint-Germain (Rue Albert-Paul-Alliés): Housed in a hôtel from the 16&18C, it contains a reconstruction of an old Piscénois interior; there are also sculptures, 17C Aubusson tapestries, two fine Louis XIII cupboards, memorabilia of Molière, flags, banners, paintings and faience.

Pfaffenhoffen (2,310 inhab.)
67 Bas-Rhin p.417□O 4

The fame of this large N. Alsatian village is due mainly to its delightful *Musée de l'Imagerie.* The varied collection includes old, vividly-coloured pictures under glass, ex-voto offerings, 'canivets' (very fine cut-out pictures), pictures of saints, confirmation souvenirs, baptismal greetings, some 'little Strasbourg soldiers' painted and carved by hand and also exhibits concerning Alsatian folk art of the 18&19C.

Phalsbourg (4,350 inhab.)
57 Moselle p.417□O 5

This former fortress on the road to Nancy was besieged three times in the 19C. There are still traces of the 17C fortifications by Vauban (Portes de France and d'Allemagne). The *museum* in the Hôtel de Ville is devoted to the history of Phalsbourg, where Émile Erckmann, the literary collaborator of Alexandre Chatrian, was born in 1822. The two published several novels under the name of Erckmann-Chatrian, including the popular *l'Ami Fritz*.

Pierrefonds	(1,720 inhab.)
60 Oise	p.411 □ J 4

This village, on the edge of the Forest of Compiègne and near a small lake, has retained an old and very much restored *church* (bell tower with Renaissance top). The place is not especially interesting; its fame being due to its massive medieval fortress, or rather the reconstructed version by Viollet-le-Duc. This imposing edifice overlooks the village, which had a château as early as the 11C.

Château: This is a fortress and also a residence. Viollet-le-Duc tried, not without imagination, to restore its original appearance. It was built in the late 14C and during the first ten years of the 15C for Louis d'Orléans, the brother of Charles VI and master of Valois. It belonged to the poet-prince Charles d'Orléans and was occupied by the English and members of the Sainte-Ligue and given by Henri IV to the father of his mistress Gabrielle d'Estrée. Her brother took arms against the crown and the château was captured by Louis XIII's troops and soon pulled down. Napoleon I bought the ruins and Napoleon III commissioned the reconstruction from Viollet-le-Duc. He was faithful to the original, but put his personal stamp on the chapel, the main staircase and the paintwork and carving. The rebuilt château, flanked by high towers with double crowns and statues, is almost square in form and surrounded by walls with two parapet walks; these are particularly striking when seen from the road running along the bottom of the moat. After the *Grandes Lices*, as the first terraced courtyard is called, comes a little gatehouse governing the bridges and postern-gate which lead to the *main courtyard*. The entrance to this is dominated by the imposing *keep* on the

Pierrefonds, the château

right; this was used as a residence, and much of it survives.

The chapel has an elegant façade with a statue of Saint Jacques le Majeur on the pier (whose features are very like those of Viollet-le-Duc himself). In front of a majestic corner flight of steps is a 19C statue of Louis d'Orléans. You can visit Napoleon III's many apartments; one of of these, called 'des preuses', has statues of Charlemagne and his companions; heroines from courtly romances are depicted over the monumental fireplace, (one of them has the features of Empress Eugénie). The large guardroom contains fragments of old sculptures.

Environs: Morienval (7.5 km. SW) The *church* is the former abbey church of a monastery said to have been founded by King Dagobert. It has three bell towers and is a late-11C/early-12C reconstruction. It was ahead of its time when it was built (rib vaulting in the ambulatory) and along with Saint-Denis is one of the first examples of Gothic art in the Île de France, although it is still Romanesque in parts. It contains

funerary slabs 6f abbesses and 15C carved stalls; it was modified in the 17C and then restored.

Plessis-Bourré (château)
49 Maine-et-Loire   p.413☐ F 7

This château standing amid lovely countryside and reflected in its moat, seems almost to have been invented by the illustrator of some fairy-tale or courtly romance. Previously a manor house occupied the site. The château was built 1468–73 (in light stone from the Angers area) by Jean Bourré, a rich financier and associate of Louis XI and Charles XVIII. Half fortress, half summer residence, it exhibits the transition from a robust medieval style to the first graceful touches of the Renaissance. Built with the intention of being attractive, it also had a defensive function; the narrow terrace around it between the walls and the moat allowed grazing fire by the artillery (then an innovation). The outbuildings were rebuilt in the 18C. It has survived time and the Revolution without

Morienval, the church

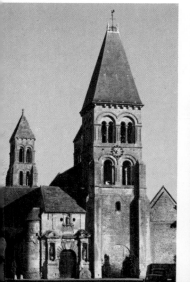

Plessis-Bourré, the château

Plessis-Macé, the château, detail of the balcony

suffering too much and you can still see some fine beautiful Louis XV and Louis XVI woodwork. The château is beautifully furnished and decorated and there is a collection of fans in the library. The large guardroom on the first floor has a curious painted ceiling with strange allegories and some licentious scenes (the paintings may be connected with alchemy and occultism, in which Jean Bourré was interested).

Plessis-Macé (château)
49 Maine-et-Loire   p.413☐F 7

This château, surrounded by enormous trees, still has wide moats, a largely intact 12C wall and a ruined 15C keep. The massive defences are in stark contrast with the fine main wing and the long outbuildings,

which were built in the mid 15C by Louis de Beaumont, a favourite of Louis XI. A balcony at the corner of the elegant residence is a masterpiece of delicacy. The interior has been largely restored in its original form and has many 17&18C tapestries. The Flamboyant chapel attached to the main building was consecrated in 1472 and has some beautiful open-work wood carving and a 15C altar. Several kings have stayed here. The château belonged to the du Bellay family and then the de Serrant family, who also own the Château de Serrant (q.v.)

Pleyben   (3,480 inhab.)
29 Finistère   p.412☐B 5

Pleyben, in the valley of the Aulne, is

Pleyben, calvary

grouped around its Grand-Place (Place Charles-de-Gaulle), with a magnificent *parish close* to the N. This shows traces of three centuries of work, the most recent part is the monumental gateway (1725) leading to the former cemetery. The ossuary (1550), originally intended to hold exhumed bones, is a separate Flamboyant building (see Guimiliau).

Church of Saint-German: This remarkable 16C church has two bell towers: the imposing square tower with dome and lanterns contrasts with the Gothic tower with its graceful spire linked to a corner tower by a catwalk. Near the S. transept there is an unusual sacristy (1719) with a dome and lantern. The S. side has a doorway with statues of the Apostles, each one carrying a phylactery with his personal symbol. Inside, the 16C panelled vaulting is sup-

ported by brightly coloured carved beams painted with great imagination by unknown artists (scenes from daily life, Breton saints, mythological characters, imaginary animals). The altarpiece on the high altar and the stained glass in the apse depict the Passion and are 17C.

Calvary: This is thought to have been built in about 1555. It is unusual in that the lower part (with statues) is in the form of a triumphal arch. Around the Cross there are four small angels, two at the feet and two at the hands, collecting the blood of Christ, whilst the fifth angel is kneeling at the top of the Cross. The Virgin and Saint John appear on the cross piece. Behind, the good thief is placed next to an angel and there is a demon on the bad thief's scaffold. On the dais are the Entombment, the Resurrection and the De-

Pleyben, parish close

Plougastel-Daoulas, calvary

scent into Hell. Friezes depict scenes from the Life of Christ, including the Nativity and the Passion.

Environs: Brasparts (11 km. N.): At the edge of the Arrée hills Brasparts also has a remarkable parish close, which dates from the 16C. On the calvary, a touching Pietà is surmounted by St.Michael subduing the dragon. On the ossuary is the figure of Ankou (Death). The church has a bell tower and spire with turret and a Renaissance porch with lanterns. It contains a Vierge de Pitié in painted wood, a stained-glass window showing the Passion (16C) and an altarpiece of the rosary (17C).

Ploërmel	(7,020 inhab.)
56 Morbihan	p.413☐D 6

This historic town consists of a group of very old houses around the interesting 16C *church of Saint-Armel* which has a fine N. doorway and Renaissance stained glass. It is dominated by an 18C tower, and contains several funerary statues. The educational innovator Abbé Jean-Marie de Lammenais, the brother of the philosopher, founded the Institut des Frères de l'Instruction Chrétienne (1817).

Plombières-les-Bains	(1,090 inhab.)
88 Vosges	p.417☐N 6

This well known spa is situated in a narrow valley surrounded by forests and waterfalls. The Romans built the first baths here and there are underground remains of the pool and bath house. Later on, the place found favour with European intelligentsia and royalty, including Napoleon III. The town has been tastefully modernized; the Maison des Dames du Chapitre de Remiremont (1733) is still interesting, and

Daoulas, cloister of the former abbey

the *Maison des Arcades* (1761), with its fine wrought-iron balcony and Stanislas' arms carved on it, is like a small palace. Under the arches the Source du Crucifix, 'endowed with healing warmth' according to its inscription, is rather vulgar.

Plougastel-Daoulas   (8,220 inhab.)
29 Finistère   p.412□A 5

This little town is situated on a peninsula which has many charming 15C chapels in which there are polychrome wooden statues and other fine woodcarving. The first visible sign of Plougastel-Daoulas is its 1604 *calvary*, which stands on its own beside a rather uninteresting church. Built after an epidemic of the plague, it is rather similar to the calvaries in Guimiliau and

Pleyben; it has a square base with buttresses and more than 150 statues. In front of it there is an altar with statues of St. Peter, St. Sebastian and St. Roch, erected as a protection against epidemics. The frieze and platform have particularly solemn depictions of the Lives of Christ and Our Lady. On the central upright there are two horsemen, a Holy Woman, Mary Magdalene and Our Lady of Pity. The two thieves have an angel and a demon on their crosses.

Environs: Dirinon (8 Km. NE): The *church* here has a fine two-storey Renaissance bell tower with balustraded balconies and a thin spire. The façade is decorated with a little statue of St. Nonn, the patron saint of the parish, whose life is depicted in the modern stained glass in the choir. A chapel nearby contains the

16C tomb of the saint with a recumbent figure and statues of the apostles. **Daoulas** (10 km. E.) This little estuary town has a former *abbey* with a 12C cloister, which is a remarkable example of the Romanesque architecture of Lower Brittany. The 32 arches are supported by small columns with capitals decorated with geometrical motifs. An octagonal fountain basin also has remarkable Romanesque decoration. Beside it is the parish *close*; its 16C porch is decorated with statues of the Apostles. The *church* was built in the 12C and has a sacristy in the 16C ossuary. The Renaissance *Chapel of St.Anne* is separated from the cemetery and has an attractive 17C doorway.

Plouha	(4,190 inhab.)
22 Côtes-du-Nord	p.412 □ C 5

Plouha, set back from the steep cliffs of the coast where St.Brieuc landed from Britain with his followers in the 6C, is a good centre for visits to some interesting churches.

Environs: Kermaria-An-Isquit (3.5 km. NW): In a green area S. of the village is a former seigneurial chapel called the 'Maison de Marie-Qui-Guérit'. Built in the 13C, it has been renovated many times. Above the 14C S. porch is the elegant balcony from which the Seigneur dispensed justice. The interior is lavishly decorated with 15C alabaster bas-reliefs showing the life of Our Lady, a fine group of wooden statues, 15C murals including a magnificent Dance of Death with 47 figures, in which the circle of the living (a mix of all social types) mingles with the cicle of the dead. Above the high altar is a 14C carved figure of Christ. **Lanloup** (7 km. NW): The 16C village church has an attractive porch on its S. side with niched buttresses and a statue of St.Lupus. There is a 14C Virgin on the tympanum of the doorway. **Lanleff** (11 km. W.): The 'Temple' on the right bank of the Leff is a source of controversy. Long thought to be a Roman temple, it is now held to have been rebuilt in the 11C on the model of the Church of the Holy Sepulchre in Jerusalem. The sanctuary includes two rotundas separated

Plougastel-Daoulas, apostles, parish close of the abbey

by an ambulatory; one of them has twelve semicircular arches. The capitals and bases of the columns are decorated with geometrical or representative motifs. **Saint-Jacques** (12 km. W.): The 16C village chapel here has a strange statue of the Virgin and Child and St.Anne.

Poissy (37,710 inhab.)
78 Yvelines p.428□I 4

A former royal residence on the Seine in which St.Louis was baptized. It was the site of the livestock market for Paris until the last century; now it is a centre of car manufacture. The town is surrounded by enormous modern buildings. It was the setting for the 1561 'Colloque de Poissy' in which Catholics and Protestants stated their doctrines and tried—in vain—to avoid armed conflict.

Notre-Dame: The former collegiate church is essentially Romanesque (12C bell tower with porch and central bell tower), but was rebuilt in the 15C and then heavily restored by Viollet-le-Duc. The 15C S. side porch has a Flamboyant double doorway; one tympanum is decorated with foliage and scrolls, and the other with a vase with a stem of fleur-de-lys, the symbol of the Virgin, and rays issuing from a cloud, the symbol of the Holy Spirit; together the symbols form an allegorical representation of the Annunciation. The rib-vaulted nave is Renaissance in the first two W. bays. One chapel contains the fonts said to have been used for the baptism of St.Louis. There are also ancient statuettes and a 16C Holy Sepulchre.

Former Abbey: Only the fortified entrance remains; there is a park on the site of the 'Colloque de Poissy'. There is a *toy museum* in the grassy area where the 'fireman' painter Meissonier had a house.

Villa Savoye (Parc du Lycée): This villa on piles was built 1929–31 by Le Corbusier for the Savoyes, a rich Parisian family. A fine example of modern architecture, it has been in ruins since André Malraux classified it as an 'ancient monument' in 1965.

Environs: Grignon (13.5 km. SE): The former château of the 17C financier Law is now occupied by an agricultural college.

Poitiers (85,470 inhab.)
86 Vienne p.419□G 9

The old quarters and monuments of Poitiers, on the edge of the Paris basin and Aquitaine, are built on a promontory; the city has churches and civil buildings from all the great historical and artistic periods. *Limonum*, the main town of the pictish Gauls, was very prosperous and became an important religious centre in the 4C thanks to its bishop, St.Hilary. After Charles Martel drove back the Arabs at the Battle of

Poissy, church of Notre-Dame

Grignon, the château

Poitiers in 732 the town was much favoured by the Carolingians. The capital of the Duchy of Aquitaine, it was fought over for many years by the French and the English. It grew richer thanks to Jean de Berry, and Charles VII often held court here. He founded a high court and a university, which soon became famous. Since the Renaissance it has been an intellectual centre, but it suffered great bloodshed during the Wars of Religion. From 1654 onwards, the Intendance of Poitou had its seat here. It is now the capital of the Poitou-Charentes region and has a lively university. Since 1960 it has been heavily developed.

Religious Buildings: Notre-Dame-la-Grande: This 11&12C building can barely be seen above the rooftops, and was probably called 'La Grande' to distinguish it from another Notre Dame, 'La Petite' which once stood close by. The decoration on the façade is exuberant, a wonderful expression of the medieval imagination and a fine example of Poitevin Romanesque. It is framed by two side turrets with conical spires. The ground floor has a central doorway with blind arches on either side; the first floor has a central window between two rows of arches with figures of saints and apostles. Bas-reliefs are undoubtedly illustrations of an 11C liturgical play, the *Drame des Prophètes*.

This frieze, which once had paintings as well, shows from left to right: *Christ's Temptation, Nebuchadnezzar, the Annunciation, the Visitation, the Tree of Jesse,* and *the Nativity*. The gable has Christ in Glory.

Poitiers, Notre-Dame-la-Grande

Poitiers, church of Sainte-Radegonde

Interior: Sadly this was whitewashed in the 19C, but it is typical of Poitevin Romanesque, having a nave flanked by tall side aisles. The choir is above a crypt, which is decorated with late-11C wall paintings. Chapels were added to the squat ambulatory and the side aisle in the 15&16C. The Gothic chapel S. of the choir contains an *Entombment* (1555).

Cathedral of Saint-Pierre: Begun in 1166, it is a compact building with thick buttresses. The 13C W. façade is framed by asymmetrical towers with Angevin arches. There are three doorways: in the centre the *Last Judgement* is portrayed, on the left the *Death and Coronation of the Virgin* and on the right the *Story of St. Thomas.* On the arch mouldings there are saints, prophets and apostles. *Interior:* There is a three-aisled Plantagenet-style nave with pronounced rib vaulting running the whole length of the church. The delicate arcades on the walls are reminiscent of those in the Palais des Comtes (Palais de Justice). There is some fine 13C *glass* (Crucifixion) in the straight wall of the apse. The choir contains some 13C stalls decorated with depictions of trades, animals and a smiling Virgin and Child.

Church of Sainte-Radegonde: This church in a little square full of trees is a mixture of Romanesque and Gothic. The fine octagonal bell tower is set on a square tower which forms a porch with a Flamboyant doorway. The Gothic nave with four bays is characteristic of the Plantagenet style. The Romanesque choir with ambulatory is 11C, and there are decorated

Poitiers, cathedral, portals

columns and radiating chapels around the crypt, which contains the tomb of St. Radegonde.

The Saint-Jean Bapistery: Built in the mid 14C, it is one of the oldest Christian buildings in France. It consists of a vast rectangular hall and a narthex with two vestries. The inside is disposed around an octagonal pool for baptism by immersion; this is fed by a Roman aqueduct. The Roman origins are obvious from the arches on the grey marble columns and the white marble capitals. There are Roman frescos on the dividing walls: the peacock, symbol of immortality, an Ascension, a Christ in Majesty and four Imperial Horsemen. The baptistery houses a *Museum of Merovingian Archaeology*.

Church of Saint-Porchaire: Gothic

from the 11&16C. It has a sturdy Romanesque bell tower, which contains the porch and has three tiers of arches.

Church of Saint-Hilaire-le-Grand: This complex 11C church has a nave with narrow side aisles, a bell tower (which was originally detached), a long transept, and a sanctuary with ambulatory and radiating chapels. The choir is striking for its delightful curves and fine buttresses; the capitals, corbels and metopes form a continuous sculpted frieze. The nave has a series of domes each with eight unequal segments. Under the choir a crypt contains the tomb of St. Hilary, whose death is depicted on a capital in the N. crossing. There are traces of 12C paintings of local bishops on the columns.

Poitiers, church of Saint-Hilaire

Poitiers, baptistery of Saint-Jean

Church of Saint-Jean-de-Montierneuf:
This church is contemporary with Notre-Dame-la-Grande and was reconstructed in the Gothic, Renaissance and classical periods. The Romanesque choir is extended by a Gothic superstructure.

Hypogée des Dunes: This underground 7C chapel is at the centre of a former burial place (pagan, then Christian), and contains some Merovingian sculpture.

Church of Saint-Hilaire-de-la-Celle:
12C; the choir and the crossing with a fine rib vaulted dome survive.

Secular buildings. Palace of the Counts of Poitou: Now part of the Palais de Justice, it replaced an earlier Merovingian building. The *Tour Maubergeon* was built by the Counts of Poitou and made

into a residence by Jean de Berry. It is early 12C and has a Gothic hall; the corners of the towers have corbels decorated with prophets. The great hall of the 'lost steps' was built at the end of the 12C and later reconstructed; its walls have fine arches on three sides (14C), and three fireplaces with a balcony and vast Flamboyant stained-glass windows above. Right at the top are four remarkable statues by Guy de Damartin.

Hôtel Berthelot (Rue de la Chaîne): This fine Renaissance building, the former residence of the mayor of Poitiers, is decorated with scrolls and busts above the staircase doorway. *Hôtel Fumé* (Rue Descartes): This is now the philosophy faculty of the university. It is Flamboyant and has watch-towers and machicolations above the entrance to the courtyard with its late-15/early-16C half-timbered galleries. *Hôtel Jean-Beaucé:* 16C. The Renaissance exterior is broken by a Gothic staircase tower. *Sainte-Croix Museum* (Rue Jean-Jaurès): The archaeological section contains Gallo-Roman collections including the famous 1C or 2C white marble *Minerva* discovered in Poitiers, and Romanesque and Renaissance sculptures. The fine art section has Limousin enamels, paintings from the 15–20C, and a remarkable set of 12C Dutch paintings on copper showing the life of Christ.

Environs. Former Abbey of Ligugé, Church of Saint-Martin (8 km. S.): Gallo-Roman remains have been brought to light in front of the doorway of the parish church and under the nave; they include a 4C martyry, the apse of a primitive 4C basilica built by St.Martin, and some 5&6C Merovingian tombs. The 16C Church of Saint-Martin has an elegant façade and a fine Flamboyant bell tower. **Nouaillé-Maupertuis** (10.5 km. SE): The Benedictine *abbey*, the successor to a modest 7C monastery, has been ruined and rebuilt on many occasions; it has a fortified wall, moats, an elegant 15C abbot's residence by the N. door and some medieval buildings. *Abbey Church:* The important 12C bell tower, which contains the porch, has a fine octagonal dome comparable with that of Saint-Hilaire-de-la-Celle in Poitiers. The N. wall of the nave is 11C; the sanctuary was rebuilt in the 17C. Behind the high altar is the 11C tomb of St. Junien, on which the painting appears like oriental cloth. The choir stalls, rood screen and lectern are fine examples of 17C carving.

Poitiers, Hôtel Fumé

agriculture and vine growing. There are several very old houses. The 15C *Church of Saint-Hippolyte* has a remarkable collection of Burgundian statues, and a beautiful wooden Pietà. The *Church du Mouthier-Viellard* has a Romanesque bell tower with four turrets around the spire over the crossing. The deconsecrated 13C *Church of the Dominicans* has a Renaissance doorway. The 17C *Hôtel Dieu* has a refectory and kitchens, which are both vaulted, and a superb pharmacy.

Poligny (4,890 inhab.)
39 Jura p.421□M/N 8

This little fortified village, dominated by cliffs, has become a prosperous centre of

---

Pommiers (320 inhab.)
42 Loire p.420□K/L 10

Pommiers, a picturesque fortified village, grew up around a Benedictine priory. The very plain 11C *church* has good proportions

Pommiers, the fortified village seen from the old bridge

and its three aisles are separated by two series of cruciform pillars. The main altar rests on a stone base, the former sarcophagus of St. Pève, and there is a 16C wall painting in the N. apsidal chapel which depicts the Life of Christ. The *Prior's Residence*, now used as the presbytery, has remained intact since the 15C. The convent buildings, which have been restored and partly rebuilt, still have 14C elements.

Pons	(5,420 inhab.)
17 Charente-Maritime	p.418☐F 10

This town, overlooking the peaceful valley of the Seugne, spreads out on a rocky headland dominated by the fortress of the Lords of Pons. It was said, 'If the King of

France cannot, the Lords of Pons will...', which gives some indication of the power of these lords who ruled over sixty towns and villages and six hundred parishes. This was once one of the most formidable fortresses in Saintonge.

Château of the Lords of Pons: The keep, which is about 90 ft. high, is a massive square block with corner buttresses, crenellations and unusual watch-towers (which date from early this century). The keep has three storeys of vaulted rooms. The other buildings date from from the 15–17C. The Hôtel de Ville occupies the old Pons family residence. To the NE of the area, under the Saint-Gilles chapel, there is a passageway which crossed the fortified château compound; its entrance has a Romanesque gate beside a Renaissance

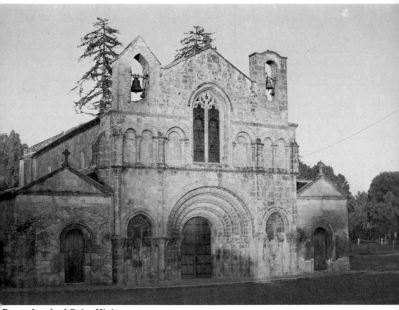

Pons, church of Saint-Vivien

façade. The defences were taken down in 1622.

Church of Saint-Vivien: Built in a suburb of the lower town, the 12C façade has a vast doorway with five archivolts. The central bay was replaced in the 16C by a tall Flamboyant window.

Hospice des Pèlerins: On leaving the town the road runs underneath a strange rib-vaulted porch; this was a shelter for travellers and pilgrims on their way to Santiago de Compostella, and formed part of the 'Hôpital Neuf' consisting of church and hospice buildings. In the middle of the corridor and facing each other are two lovely late-12C gates with decorated archivolts. Graffiti scratched on the walls by the pilgrims can still be seen.

Environs: Usson (1 km. S.): The château, formerly a few kilometres away was moved stone by stone to its present position. There are three buildings around the courtyard, the one at the back being the most interesting with arcaded galleries and lavish decoration (medallions and busts). Inside there are delicate Regency wood-carvings which came from Choisy-le-Roi. **Chadenac** (9 km. SE): The 12C church is remarkable for the lavish decoration of the façade which illustrates the struggle between Good and Evil (Wise and Foolish Virgins). **Marignac** (8.5 km. S.): Of note here is the apse of the little 12C church: the variety, skill and realism of the corbels is outstanding. **Échebrune** (7.5 km. E.): The 12C church was restored in the 15C; the façade has a wide doorway with five archivolts. There is a magnificent cornice with corbels supporting a row of high arches. (The central one is many-lobed.)

Pont-à-Mousson   (15,060 inhab.)
54 Meurthe-et-Moselle   p.417☐N 4

This industrial town on the Moselle is a bridgehead, and was ravaged by two world wars. It has had a lively university since 1572 and was something of a religious bastion, taking an active part in the defence of Catholicism against reform (hence the abundance of religious buildings). The main courtyard of the Jesuit College is framed by rebuilt buildings, and is now very attractive. The Premonstratensian Abbey, mainly restored, recalls 18C monastic architecture with its emphasis on order and clarity.

Church of Saint-Martin (14&15C): The façade is flanked by two octagonal Flamboyant towers. Inside, apart from the rich furnishings, there is a splendid 15C Entombment with thirteen figures. The fa-

çade of *Saint-Laurent* is 19C, but the choir and transept go back to the 15&16C, and the church contains a fine 16C wooden altarpiece and a moving depiction of Christ carrying the Cross, which is thought to be by Ligier Richier.

In the heart of the town, note the 17C houses with arches: in the Place Duroc the *Maison des Sept Péchés Capitaux* has caryatids (16C), the Château d'Amour is flanked by a Renaissance turret and the Hôtel de Ville of 1788 has a pediment.

Pontarlier   (18,840 inhab.)
25 Doubs   p.421☐N 8

At the entrance to this busy little tourist town there is an 18C triumphal arch in honour of Louis XV. Nearby is one of the most beautiful cluses (tranverse valley) in the Jura. The *Chapelle des Annonciades* (17C) is a pleasant building with a rib-vaulted nave and Renaissance doorway. The church of Saint Bénigne, a composite building, was rebuilt in the 17C; the Flam-

Chadenac, the church, wise virgin

Fort de Joux, the fortress

boyant doorway survives, but the façade has been rebuilt.

Environs: Fort de Joux (4 km. S.): This fortress (originally a 10C château) is situated on a rock about 3,500 ft. high and controls a route into Switzerland. It is protected by a series of tiered walls. Once a state prison, it now houses a *Musée d'Armes.*

Pont-Audemer	(10,010 inhab.)
27 Eure	p.410☐G 4

The name Pont-Audemer comes from a bridge over the Risle, which was built in the Merovingian period by one Aldomar or Odomar. The town was badly bombed in 1940 and 1944 but some picturesque streets and old houses, such as the 17C *Auberge du Vieux Puits*, have survived.

Church of Saint-Ouen: Lack of funds meant that this church was never completed; the choir is late 11C and the façade

with one uncompleted tower 15&16C; the large, unusual, essentially Flamboyant nave also dates from this period, but it has some Renaissance features. Lovely old windows were installed at the time of Louis XII, François I and Henri II; there are also modern works by Max Ingrand.

Church of Saint-Germain: This plain, severe church in the suburb of Saint Germain-Village dates from the late 11C.

Pont-Aven	(3,560 inhab.)
29 Finistère	p.412☐B 6

This little Breton town in the charming Aven valley owes its fame to Paul Gauguin, who stayed here on several occasions between 1886 and 1889 with a group of young painters such as Émile Bernard, Sérusier, Maurice Denis, Maufra and Meyer de Haan. In the square which bears his name there is a commemorative plaque on the former Pension Gloanec where the artists used to stay. The *Musée Gauguin*

Pont-Audemer, windows in the church of Saint-Ouen

in an annex of the Town Hall has exhibitions of the Pont-Aven School.

Environs: Chapelle de Trémalo (1 km. NW): This chapel is on the edge of the Bois d'Amour. It was often painted (*Le Talisman* by Sérusier, *Madeleine au Bois d'Amour* by Émile Bernard) and contains the great 16C polychrome wooden crucifix which may have inspired the famous *Christ Jaune* by Gauguin in 1889. **Nizon** (2 km. NW): The village *calvary* here, near a well-restored church, has a very unusual Pietà, which was used by Gauguin as a model for his *Breton Calvary (le Christ Vert)* in 1889. **Château de Henan** (4 km. S.): This lovely house on the Aven was built in the 15C. It is fortified and has a doorway with a turret complete with arrow holes. Adjoining the main wing is an elegant hexagonal tower with a pepper-pot turret, a delicate open gallery and a staircase turret with the corners cut off. The other parts of the château are later, indeed, some are quite recent (e.g. left wing).

Pont-Croix (1,870 inhab.)
29 Finistère p.412□A 6

The sloping streets of this little town on the right bank of the Goyen have several lovely old houses. Its church, dedicated to Notre-Dame-de-Roscudon, has a magnificent 15C bell tower with a tall spire and four smaller corner spires—this inspired the addition of two towers to Quimper Cathedral in the 19C. The S. doorway (late 14C) has elegant pointed gables with rose-windows. The oldest interior features are 13C; there are semicircular arches and pillars with columns. Furnishings include a 17C pulpit, baptismal fonts with carved panels, altarpieces of the same period and some fine old statues. On the lower part of the altar in the 16C apse is a 17C Last Supper.

Environs: Confort (5 km. E.): The village *church* was built in the 16C and has a beautiful window in the apse showing the Tree of Jesse. In the nave is one of the last 'wheels of fortune' in Brittany. Only the base of the Calvary is 16C; the statuary was reworked in 1870. **Notre-Dame-de-Kérinec** (7 km. NE): This little *parish close* in a charming setting has a chapel which is 13C in part and the work of the Pont-Croix school, a 16C fountain, and a calvary above a circular pulpit which is supported by a telamon. **Saint-Tugen** (11 km. SE): This *chapel* on the jagged coastline is dedicated to St.Tugen (16C) who cured rabies and toothache. It is interesting in that it has a small side alcove called 'the prison' where parishioners suffering from rabies were locked up; beside the painted baptismal fonts is a fireplace to warm the faithful during their vigils beside the dead. Note the decorated beams, the 17C altarpieces and the statue of Saint Tugen, and also the little 17C catafalque decorated with statues of Adam and Eve. **Cléden-Cap-Sizun** (14 km. W.): The church has a fine 16C bell tower with spire and a staircase turret. The S. doorway dates from the late 16C, and has unusual carved decoration (fishing boats and monsters).

Pont-de-L'Arche (2,880 inhab.)
27 Eure p.410□H 4

This old fortress, once the 'key to Upper Normandy', lies on the edge of the lovely Forest of Bord; practically no traces remain of its extensive fortifications. The *Church of Notre-Dame-des-Arts* is 16C and has very fine 16&17C windows (one of them represents a boat pulled in under the bridge). There are also 18C choir stalls which came from the former abbey of Bonport, a Cistercian abbey founded by

Pont-Croix, church porch

Pont-du-Gard, Roman aqueduct

Richard the Lionheart in 1190. A few surviving buildings from this foundation are on private property to the W. of the village; the church and cloister no longer exist. The name Pont-de-l'Arche comes from a bridge which Charles the Bald had built in the 9C; Massenet composed his *Werther* here.

Pont du Gard
30 Gard   p.425☐L 13

The famous Pont du Gard, really an aqueduct, was built about 19 BC on the orders of Agrippa, the son-in-law of the Emperor Augustus. It crosses the Gard near Remoulins, and was intended to supply Nîmes with water. About 900 ft. long it consists of three superimposed sets of arches and stands about 150 ft. above the water.

Pontécoulant (château)
14 Calvados   p.413☐F 4

This charming little château is situated in the heart of the Suisse Normande in the Condé-sur-Noireau region. It has an artificial lake, and dates mainly from the 18C. It was restored after the last war, and now belongs to the Département. It still looks like a family house, and is very well furnished.

Pontigny   (680 inhab.)
89 Yonne   p.415☐K 6

The Cistercian Abbey of Pontigny, a daughter abbey of Cîteaux, was founded in 1114 by a follower of Saint Bernard and

Pontigny, abbey church

his fellow monks. It was enlarged in the mid 12C, and three Archbishops of Canterbury visited it: Thomas à Becket, the preacher and university teacher Stephen Langton, and St. Edmund. It was powerful for a long time, and only declined after the Wars of Religion; the palace was destroyed in the Revolution, but the church was spared.

Abbey church: The large 12C chalk-white church is 350 ft. long and about 65 ft. high. It is very bare, as required by Cîteaux tradition, and was refurbished inside after the Wars of Religion. A somewhat theatrical screen in the choir rather spoils the perspective (17&18C stalls). The choir is surrounded by elegant 18C grilles and is dominated by the monument to Saint Edmund, built at the end of the Ancien Régime. The saint's reliquary is 19C.

There is a fine and unusual statue of the Virgin shielding praying figures under her cloak (dating from the 16C or 17C, it can be seen in the right arm of the transept).

Pontivy (14,320 inhab.)
56 Morbihan p.413□C 6

This town, founded in the 6C by St. Ivy, is full of surprising contrasts. To the N. it is a network of old narrow streets and little squares (like the Rue du Fil and the Rue du Pont), lined with 15&16C gabled and overhanging houses, while in the S. the rather severe geometrical Napoleonic town is built round the imposing Place A.-Briand.

Château des Rohan: This was built by

Jean II de Rohan at the end of the 15C. He was also Lord of Josselin, and the château is a massive fortress with pepper-pot turrets on its towers. The high walls have elegant dormer windows which alternate with little machicolated openings. The recently restored buildings are now used for cultural functions (museum, exhibitions and library).

Church of Notre-Dame-de-la-Joie: Built in Flamboyant style in the 16C, it lies in the heart of the old town. It has a tower with a spire and polygonal staircase turret. Inside it has interesting 17&18C furnishings.

Environs: Stival (4 km. NW): This village church was built in honour of Saint Mériadec in the 16C and contains some fine 16C stained glass showing the Tree of Jesse (in the choir) and the Passion (right transept). A copper bell said to have belonged to the saint is reputed to cure deafness. **Noyal-Pontivy** (7 km. E.): The former cemetery has an ossuary and the tomb of Saint Mériadec, and a 15&16C *church* with a fine S. porch and 16C stained glass.

2 km. N. of Noyal Pontivy, in the hamlet of **Sainte- Noyale**, there is a Gothic fountain which stands under the protection of the saint, a large calvary and a simple cross with 15C figures. The chapel has a porch topped with a 17C bell tower and slate spire. Inside there are 17C paintings on panelling and these depict the life of St. Noyale, which is also shown in the little neighbouring oratory. **Quelven** (11 km. SW): This picturesque and somewhat isolated village has some old houses, and the *Chapel of Notre-Dame-de-Quelven* (late 15C), which has a very attractive bell-tower (with porch) with a Flamboyant rose-window and a spire about 250 ft. high. On the S. side the porch with delicately carved archivolts and the doorway with eaves and a staircase turret and spire are very fine. In the chapel there is an alabaster bas-relief showing the Coronation of the Virgin and also two 16C stained glass windows depicting the Tree of Jesse and the Apostles. There is a 15C statue of the Virgin at the

Pontivy, Château des Rohan

side of the choir; this can be opened and contains 12 pictures of the Passion. There is also a 'Scala sancta' used on the day of the Pardon (15 August) and a monumental Flamboyant fountain (16C).

Saint-Nicodème (12 km. S.): The *chapel of Saint-Nicodème* in the Blavet valley is 16C and is the size of a church. It is a harmonious blend of Flamboyant and Renaissance styles. An imposing bell tower (with porch) leads into the nave, which has beams carved with angels, monsters and musicians. The furnishings include some striking 17C altarpieces. Nearby, one of the holy fountains is quite remarkable; it has three niches with finely carved gables (17C). **Melrand** (16 km. SW): The main attraction of this town lies in its calvaries. The most important is on the road to Guémené-sur-Scorff, and has one upright decorated with the heads of apostles (identifiable by an inscription), surmounted by the Cross, God the Father and the Holy Spirit. The sculptures in bas-relief on the base are of the Passion and there are statues of the Virgin and St. John.

Pont l'Abbé	(7,820 inhab.)
29 Finistère	p.412[?]A/B 6

This regional capital figures in *Le Cheval d'Orgeuil* by the Breton writer Pierre Jakès-Hélias. It is a quiet little estuary port with a 13&18C château, which has a large oval tower and a main wing housing the *Musée Bigoudien* (history, arts and traditions of the region). The *Church of Notre-Dame-des-Carmes* on the same side of the river dates from the 14&17C and has two gables with rose windows and a vast nave with old statues.

Environs: Chapel of Notre-Dame-de-la-Tréminou (2 km. W.): The chapel is in a rural setting and has an annual Pardon procession on the fourth Sunday in September; the building is squat and has a certain charm. The openwork bell tower has a stone spire with gables. You can see signs of the many alterations inside; there are modern cylindrical pillars in the 17C transept alongside 13C pillars with multiple

Saint-Nicodème, detail of one of the fountains

Pont-l'Abbé, the harbour and château

N.-D.-de-la-Tréminou, the chapel

small columns. The exterior pulpit bears a simple cross. **Château de Kerazan** (4 km. SE): This château on the banks of the river has been owned by the Institut de France since 1929 and its two wings at right angles date from the 16&18C; these have exhibitions of paintings, drawings, pastels and engravings (works by Flandrin, Maurice Denis, Cottet, Steinlen etc.). **Loctudy** (6 km. SE): A fishing port frequented by holidaymakers, it has an astonishingly well-preserved Romanesque *church* from the early 12C; the façade was rebuilt in the 18C. The church has no transept, and consists of a nave with five bays and cruciform pillars, a choir and groin-vaulted ambulatory with three half domed radial chapels opening off it. The capitals are decorated with geometrical patterns or figures of animals etc. and some of the bases show naked men and women. In the cemetery is

a Christianized lech (Celtic monumental stone). **Notre Dame de Tronoën** (9 km. W.): Tronoën, splendidly isolated on a wind-swept dune, has a marvellous calvary, the oldest in Brittany (1450–1470). On a simple rectangular base there are two layers of sculpture in relief or in the round, which illustrate the life and death of Christ. The main surface has two baptismal scenes above a console which forms an offertory table. To the N. the lower frieze depicts an astonishing *Nativity*: The Virgin is shown lying on a willow couch with loose hair and naked breasts, with the almost adolescent boy Jesus to one side and St.Joseph sleeping in a sitting position on the other. The central upright carries the crucifix and this is framed by two angels without wings, which lift chalices to receive the blood of the crucified Christ. Beside this is a Gothic chapel with an elegant openwork bell tower

N.-D.-de-Tronoën, calvary

flanked by turrets. The S. side with buttresses has two delicately ornamented doorways. There are old statues in the nave and an impressive monolithic altar (about 16 ft. long).

Pont-l'Évêque (3,760 inhab.)
14 Calvados p.410 □ G 4

A little town in the Auge which gave its name to a famous Normandy cheese. It suffered greatly in 1944 but still has some old half-timbered houses from the 15,16&17C, e.g. the elegant *Hôtel de Brilly* in Louis XV style (now the Mairie) and the *Hôtel de Montpensier*, begun in 1624. *Saint-Michel*, Flamboyant in style, dates from the late 15/early 16C.

Pontoise (29,120 inhab.)
95 Val-d'Oise p.410 □ I 4

Pontoise, the former fortress of the Vexin Français against the Duchy of Normandy, was a favourite residence of the Kings of France and the refuge of Mazarin and the young Louis XIV during the Fronde. Pissarro also found it enchanting. He stayed here from 1872 – 4 and introduced the young Cézanne to the town. Both painted several views of the area. The twisty streets of the town, which is now part of greater Paris, rise in tiers above the Oise and the Viosne. The new town of Cergy-Pontoise is part of the complex. The château was destroyed in the Revolution and nothing remains but the high supporting walls.

Cathedral of Saint-Maclou: One of the

most important Gothic churches in the Ile de France, it was begun in 1140, shortly after St.Denis, but building continued until the 16C, with major rethinking in the 15C—hence the presence of Flamboyant and Renaissance elements. The transept, choir, ambulatory and apsidal chapels are essentially 12C with the exception of the vaulting (fine Romanesque capitals). The decoration in the choir is 17C. The Chapelle de la Passion by the N. tower contains an important mid-16C Saint-Sépulcre with eight figures.

Notre-Dame: This was rebuilt in the late 16C and is rather uninspired. It has Gothic vaults but its general appearance is Renaissance. A modern chapel contains the 13C statue of Notre-Dame-de-Pontoise and has ex-votos on the walls. Under an arch to the right of the nave is the 12C tomb of St.Gautier.

The **Musée Tavet-Delacour** is housed in a charming late-15C Flamboyant hôtel and features paintings, drawings, sculptures, local history and paintings by Jouy.

Saint-Ouen-L'Aumône is a suburb of Pontoise on the other bank of the river, and has the remains of the chapterhouse and tithe barn of the once prestigious **Abbey of Maubuisson**. The church, originally Romanesque, has been much restored.

Environs: Auvers-sur-Oise (7 km. NE): Daubigny, Cézanne and Pissarro all worked in this large village. Van Gogh committed suicide here in July 1890 and he is buried next to his brother Theo in the cemetery. Near the school in the public park is the monument dedicated to Van Gogh by Zadkine (1961). The *church*, somewhat modified in the 16C (chapelle de la Vierge), dates from the 12&13C and was once the chapel of a manor house which has since disappeared. Its bell tower

with a saddleback roof inspired one of Van Gogh's most famous paintings.

Pont-Saint-Pierre   (1,160 inhab.
27 Eure   p.410☐H 4

Pont-Saint-Pierre is spread out in the Andelle valley a few km. from the panoramic Côte des Deux-Amants with its famous view over the Seine. The Andelle runs through the park of a picturesque late-15C *manor house*. The *church* is 11&12C and contains interesting furnishings from Fontaine-Guérard.

Environs: Abbey of Fontaine-Guérard (3.5 km. E.): The remains of the once powerful abbey blend attractively with the green of the landscape. The 12C monastery, sold as a national asset at the time of the Revolution, was pillaged. The 15C chapel of St.Michel survives along with the lofty ruins of the abbey church (consecrated 1218) and the 13C chapterhouse.

Porta (La): see **Corsica**

Porto-Vecchio: see **Corsica**

Port-Royal-des-Champs
78 Yvelines   p.428☐I 5

This green valley is the spiritual home of Jansenism. What little remains of the abbey does not tell us much, but the setting is just as Mère Angélique and 'those Port Royal gentlemen' knew it in the 17C. The monastery of Notre-Dame-de-Porrois (the

'The Church of Auvers/s/Oise', van Gogh (Paris, Musée de l'Impressionnisme)

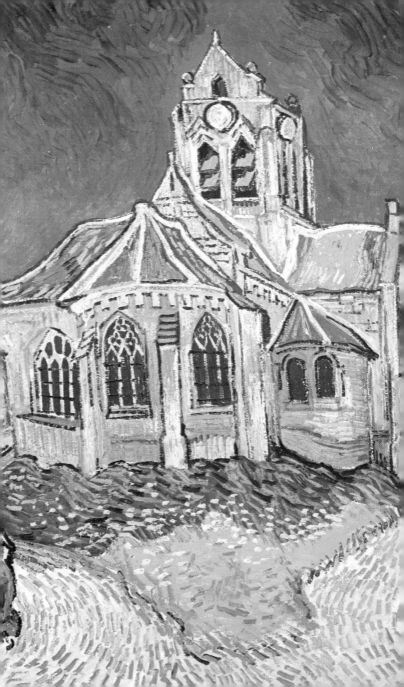

name was changed to Port-Royal) was founded in 1204. The original Cistercian rule and severity were forgotten when Jacqueline Arnauld, a lawyer's daughter, became abbess at the age of 11. However, after an illness she had a change of heart about her duty and, at the age of 17, decided to re-establish the closed order and institute a radical reform of her abbey. She went down in history under her nun's name of Mère Angélique. The community of women which she directed had to move to Paris and the new abbey of Port-Royal (today a large maternity hospital). Subsequently the deserted buildings in this unhealthy, marshy area were refurbished and inhabited by the austere disciples of Jansenism. These were rigid, ascetic moralists who rejected the values of the leisured classes. The 'solitaires' were the object of violent attacks by the Jesuits and by those in power, but they made Port-Royal famous. When Mère Angélique returned with her nuns in 1648 they settled on a hill at the 'Granges' and created the 'petites écoles' and an entirely new form of education. The young Jean Racine studied here and Blaise Pascal wrote the first of his *Provinciales* (violent attacks on the Jesuits) here in 1656. However, Louis XIV gave in to the opponents of Port Royal, and after a lot of persecution the 'solitaires' were forced to disband. The nuns were expelled in 1709 and the abbey was pulled down soon afterwards.

Remains of the Abbey: Practically nothing remains of the illustrious abbey; lime trees, lawns and a few stones mark the place where the cloister, the church and the desecrated cemetery used to be. An *oratoire-musée* was built on the site of the dismantled abbey choir in the late 19C. This is devoted to the history of Port-Royal, Mère Angélique, her nuns, and Pascal.

Musée National de Port-Royal: To the N. of the abbey on high ground it is housed in the buildings erected by the 'gentlemen of Port-Royal' in the mid 17C (which also formerly housed the 'petites écoles'). This important Jansenist museum has paintings, drawings, engravings, various original documents as well as pictures by

'Two nuns with Port-Royal in the background', Philippe de Champaigne

Philippe de Champaigne and his followers. From the first floor there is a view of the Solitaires' farm and the deep well which the versatile Pascal equipped with a winch so that large buckets of water could be raised quite easily.

Near to the 3C *church* at **Saint-Lambert-les-Bois** (1.5 km. S. from the abbey) is the cemetery where the bones dug up at Port-Royal were flung into a communal grave, 'le carré de Port-Royal'.

Environs: Magny-les-Hameaux (3 km. E. of the Granges): the choir of the church here is 12C and the nave 15C. The parish church of the abbey of Port-Poyal, it contains remains of the former convent, stalls from the Abbey of Vaux-de-Cernay and tombstones from the desecrated cemetery. The cemetery has a monument to the poet Albert Samain, who died at Magny in 1900.

Dampierre (5 km. SW): The château, with a large park designed by Le Nôtre, is built of brick and stone on the site of a previous building by Jules Hardouin-Mansart, the architect of Versailles. Built 1675–83, it was restored in the 19C and is richly decorated and furnished. The building can be seen from the road through the beautiful 18C railings at the end of the main courtyard.

Pouzauges	(5,560 inhab.)
85 Vendée	p.418☐E 8

The old quarters of Pouzages are overlooked by the grey mossy ruins of the former 12C château. The keep, which has rounded buttresses, stands in the middle of the rectangular line of the fortifying walls, of which only the bases of ten towers remain. The memory of the sinister Gilles de Rais (or de Retz) still clings to the place. An ally of Joan of Arc, he became a criminal and inspired Perrault to write his famous *Barbe-Bleue*. *Saint-Jacques* dates from the 12&15C. It is a squat granite building with a square crossing tower and a huge Flamboyant choir. The charming Romanesque *Notre-Dame-du-Vieux- Pouzages* is

Dampierre, the château

also in granite and stands about 1 km. S. of the former cemetery, between the hosanna cross and cypress trees. It has several tombstones and on the N. wall of the nave some outstanding 12C frescos depicting the life of St. Joachim and the childhood of the Virgin.

Environs: Le Boupère (7 km. NW): The 13C *church* is mainly remarkable for its 15C fortifications. There is a parapet walk around the building and the bell tower is topped by a guardroom. **Les Épesses** (14 km. N.): The *château* of Puy-du-Fou dates from the 16C. The fine Renaissance pavilion has mullioned windows, porticoes and tall roofs. A pool reflects the rear façade.

| **Prades** | (6,870 inhab.) |
| 66 Pyrénées-Orientales | p.423□ 16 |

Prades, the former capital of the small Conflent region, stands among orchards beneath the mass of Mount Canigou. A great deal of its fame is due to the great cellist Pablo Casals (1876–1973). Exiled from Spain after the Civil War, he settled here and founded a major music festival (the concerts take place in Saint-Michel-de-Cuxa). The old quarter of the town is built in local pink marble; there is a Gothic *church* with a Romanesque bell tower and a fine late 17C altarpiece by a Catalan artist on the high altar.

Environs: Abbey of Saint-Michel-de-Cuxa (3 km. S.): The huge and beautiful abbey with its crenellated tower and reconstructed cloister stands in sharp relief against Mount Canigou. Some of the buildings are occupied by a Benedictine community of the monastery of Montserrat. From 1000 the abbey was the most important religious and artistic centre in Roussillon. It was sold off as a national asset in the Revolution after a long period of decline and was scandalously divided up in the late 19/early 20C—the Metropolitan Museum of New York now owns part of it, and the cloisters have been rebuilt in the Hudson valley (though the present cloister of Cuxa still includes part its predecessor). The *abbey church*, badly damaged in the last century, has pre-Romanesque and 11C features and shows signs of the local Visigoth tradition, as well as the influence of Andalusian Islam in the horseshoe arches. The dark, circular Chapelle of the Vierge-de-la-Crèche seems to be incomplete. It has an annular vault supported by a heavy round pillar. Formerly reserved for the Marian cult, it seems to have escaped the vicissitudes which Cuxa has suffered since the 11C. **Corneilla-de-Conflent** (19.5 km. S.): The last capital of the Comté de Cerdagne (*c*.1100). A modest Lombard-style bell tower is attached to an interesting Romanesque church, which was altered in the second half of the 12C. It has a fine doorway with a decorated tympanum, rich furnishings, three Romanesque seated Virgins and

Pouzauges, ruined castle

a 14C Virgin and Child. Parts of a piece
of Romanesque ironwork have survived.

Prémontré
02 Aisne   (590 inhab.)
     p.411 ☐ K 3

In the 12C St.Norbert founded this monastery in the woods and from it grew the
famous Premonstratensian order. The *abbey*, rebuilt in the 18C, is majestic and
stern; there are three buildings at right angles with a garden in the French style. The
façade of the main building is decorated
with pilasters, and there is a pedimented
avant-corps. One of the side buildings has
an ingenious oval staircase.

Provins
77 Seine-et-Marne   (13,100 inhab.)
     p.411 ☐ K 5

This picturesque town set among cornfields has maintained its rural character. It
is peaceful, provincial, steeped in history

Prades, abbey of St-Michel-de-Cuxa

St-Michel-de-Cuxa, the cloister

Provins, the ramparts

and full of roses; one of its ancient rulers Edmund of Lancaster (13C) made the red rose grown here famous; Edmund, the brother of the King of England, took it as the emblem of the House of Lancaster, while the House of York adopted the white rose. Provins became busy and prosperous in the Middle Ages because of its two long annual fairs patronized by merchants from all over Europe.

Ville-Haute: This part of the town, dominated by the massive Tour de César, occupies both sides of the straight Rue Saint-Thibault (houses with projecting upper storeys) on a promontory surrounded by 12&13C ramparts. In the centre of the town, the old well, the cross and the old houses in the *Place du Châtel* form a charming group. *Saint-Quiriace:* This former collegiate church, begun in 1160 on the site of a Roman temple, is unfinished; the nave only has two bays and a 15C façade. The crossing dome is 17C, and the choir with ambulatory late 12C (primitive Gothic). *Tour de César:* This massive keep is about 140 ft. high and dates from the early 12C; the upper part and roof are 16C. The first floor has a guardroom with an opening in the high vaulting which enabled the soldiers on the upper level to be supplied with ammunition and food. The turrets all had cells in them with the exception of the one used by the governor as a bedroom. *Tithe barn:* This austere 12C military building was turned into a warehouse. It is built over a room where several underground passages meet. *Porte Saint-Jean:* This impressive gate from the 12&13C is at the far end of the upper town. It has two towers and

St-Ayoul, angel musician

Provins, church of Saint-Quiriace and the Tour de César

is made of ashlars. The defences also included drawbridge, portcullis and a gate. The *ramparts* and towers between the Porte Saint-Jean and the Porte de Jouy (12C) are extremely well preserved .

Ville-Basse: The upper town was the citadel and the lower town was the commercial centre, crowded at fair times, when the money changers set up in the Place Saint-Ayoul. *Saint-Ayoul:* This former abbey church is 12C but has been much altered, particularly in the 16C. Now restored, several Romanesque features, including the transept and a damaged doorway with headless statues, have survived. The large altarpiece at the end of the nave and the woodcarving in the Chapelle de la Vierge are 17C, and there is an attractive 16C statuette of the Virgin. *Tour du Cloître Notre-Dame-du-Val:* This now contains the

Saint-Ayoul bells and is all that remains of a former collegiate church and cloister. *Sainte-Croix:* This was enlarged and decorated in the 13C to house a piece of the true cross brought back from the Crusades. It burnt down in the 14C and was rebuilt in the 16C. One Romanesque tower, with a modern spire, still survives. The façade doorway is Renaissance and the N. doorway is Flamboyant. The *Chapelle des Fonts* to the left of the entrance contains 13C carved font. There is a fine Louis XV grille in the 16C choir, which is surrounded by a double ambulatory; its outer part was modified to incorporate chapels. *Hôtel-Dieu:* This former palace is 11&12C and has been largely rebuilt, but still retains some old features; its cellars communicate with a network of underground passages. *Former Convent of the Cordeliers:* This was founded in 1248 by Thibaud IV, Count of

Champagne, known as the 'songmaker'. Two sides of the 14&15C cloister survive along with the rib-vaulted chapterhouse and the chapel (small 13C funerary monument containing Thibaud's heart). The lower town has many old houses.

Environs: Saint-Loup-de-Naud (8 km. SW): Perched on a ridge, this pretty little village has an 11&12C *church* which clearly shows the development from Romanesque to Gothic. The early Gothic porch has a very remarkable door reminiscent of the Portail Royal at Chartres (Christ in majesty and symbols of the Evangelists on the tympanum, Virgin and apostles on the lintel, statues of St.Loup on the piers and statue columns on the jambs). The original frescos, which were badly damaged, were marvellously recreated rather than restored in the 19C. The right apsidal chapel contains a 14C stone Virgin and the church also has a strange 12C baptismal font.

Nogent-sur-Seine (11 km. SE): This has half-timbered houses upstream on the right bank of the Seine, a 15&16C church and a small museum.

Provins, church of Saint-Ayoul, Virgin

Punta (château de La) see Corsica (Ajaccio)

Puy (Le)	(29,030 inhab.)
Haute-Loire	p.420□K 11/12

Le Puy is not so much a town as one of the most exceptional landscapes in France: a vast limagne with plateaux on its horizons and volcanic obelisks carved by erosion in the centre. The red tiled roofs of this amazing town line up in tiers on a ridge, at the top of which stands the immense and pompous statue of the Virgin and Child. Le Puy, famous since the 12C because of the cures effected by a 'fever stone', became even more well known when the Virgin was brought here by St. Louis in 1254 (probably from the Crusades). Thousands of pilgrims on the route to Santiago di Compostela came to this holy place to worship the statue in the magnificent cathedral. The town has also been known since the 15C for fine hand-made lace; this industry underwent major expansion in the 17C, when some 70,000 Velay peasants were involved, knotting the threads with tireless patience and incredible manual dexterity on needles stuck into cushions held on their knees. Today there are a few lace-making factories which use a mechanical process derived from the traditional one.

Cathedral of Notre-Dame: In spite of many vicissitudes, this 11&12C building is still one of the most beautiful and origi-

Le Puy, cathedral of Notre-Dame   *Le Puy, the black Virgin*

nal in the Midi. The cathedral, which has Islamic features, is largely built on a rock (the last bays of the nave were added at the end of the 12C and were built on piles to compensate for the steep slope). The part directly on the rock was built in stages: the apse, the transept and two bays of the choir date from the end of the 11C; the third and fourth bays of the nave were built in the mid 12C. *W. Façade:* This has five levels of polychrome masonry arches at the top of a large staircase. The staircase continues under the porch and through the late-12C bays. At the level of the second bay are the two carved wooden Romanesque doors of the side chapels. The staircase ends in the landing on to which the Porte Dorée opened until the 18C; from here seventeen steps led to the centre of the nave, which caused people to say that 'one enters Notre-Dame de Puy by the navel and leaves by the two ears'. The 'fever stone' is on show in front of the Porte Dorée.

INTERIOR: The cathedral consists of a nave with six bays, each with an octagonal dome on pendentives, groin-vaulted side aisles, a transept and a square apse. The remarkable pulpit is 18C. The famous Virgin on the high altar replaces the original statue burnt by revolutionaries in 1794. The frescos decorating the twin chapels under the N. gallery represent the Holy Women at the Tomb (mid-12C) and the martyrdom of St.Catherine of Alexandria (mid-13C). The gallery wall in the N. transept is decorated with a vast, beautifully coloured St. Michael. The reliquary chapel (third bay of the N. side aisle.) has a magnificent late 15C fresco depicting the liberal arts.

Treasure: This includes several valuable pieces: a head of Christ in beaten copper,

Le Puy, cathedral, W. façade

Le Puy, capital in the cloister

a reliquary, silverware, a 15C Pietà and the remarkable 9C Théodulphe Bible, the work of monks from St.Benoît-sur-Loire.

Bell tower: This is detached from the church and about 175 ft. high with seven slightly recessed storeys, each one in a different architectural style.

Porche du For: This is a magnificent piece of late-12C architecture and although Romanesque has the oldest rib vaulting in the region and shows Arab influence in its embossed columns and pierced arches.

Porche Saint-Jean: This leads to the N. transept through a Romanesque doorway and gives access to the **Saint-Jean baptistery,** which consists of a nave with two bays and an apsidal chapel with five niches framed by Gallo-Roman columns.

Cloister: This 13C Moorish-Spanish building with polychrome arches and mosaics formed from red, yellow, black and white lozenges was restored in the 19C and is the marvel of Le Puy. Rectangular, it has five arches on the N. and S. and ten on the other two sides; they are supported by magnificent pillars each surrounded by four columns. The subjects featured on the capitals are extremely varied; the cornice too is extraordinarily rich. The passage leading to the Cathedral has a fine Romanesque grille. *Chapelle des Morts:* The former chapterhouse, it has been used as a funerary chapel since the 14C. It is decorated by a large 13C mural of the Crucifixion.

OTHER MONUMENTS:

Chapelle des Pénitents: This has an elegant 17C door. The single aisle has a painted coffer ceiling and the chapel con-

Le Puy, cloister of the cathedral

tains a number of paintings by local artists, as well as processional objects.

Saint-Laurent: This former Dominican chapel is 14&15C and has one vast aisle and a five-sided apse with narrow bays. Under the recumbent figure in the choir are the remains of the Constable du Guesclin, who died in 1380. The chapter-house N. of the church is rib vaulted with two pillars.

Chapel of Saint-Michel d'Aiguilhe: Perched on a 260 ft. high volcanic peak overlooking the town, it dates from the 10&11C. The 12C Romanesque door opens on to a staircase carved out of rock, which leads to a parapet walk round the church. You can see oriental influence here too in a doorway with a large trilobed arch and two sirens on the lintel. The upper

Le Puy, cloister, polychrome arch

Le Puy, Musée Crozatier, lace

part of the façade, decorated with mosaics, has five semicircular arches. The other parts of the building, nave, ambulatory, façade and bell tower are all disposed around a primitive 10C oratory with frescos. *Chapelle Saint-Clair:* This 12C slightly recessed octagonal chapel has exterior arches and lozenges typical of the Velay area.

Musée Crozatier: This extensive provincial museum has collections of stones and ancient paintings; there is also a local history room, which deals with lace-making and exhibits the work of spindle and needle from the 16–20C.

Old houses: The street leading from the Tour Pannesac has many 15,16&17C houses. In the narrow alley called 'du Charmalenc' is the 17C Maison des Cornards, the meeting place of the le Puy company; there are inscriptions over two masks.

Quesnoy (Le)   (5,370 inhab.)
59 Nord   p.411☐K 2

This charming little town has been fortified since the 13C and is a an important
example of military architecture. Its fortified walls are still intact and the defensive
system designed by Vauban is displayed in
all its perfection. Glacis, demilunes,
ditches and bastions, some from the time
of Emperor Charles V, are laid out impres-
sively; the pink brickwork is striking.

Environs: Château de Potelle (2 km.
E.): This medieval moated fortress was
built in 1290 and renovated in the 16C.

Quimper   (60,510 inhab.)
29 Finistère   p.412☐B 6

Quimper is an ancient city at the confluence of the Steir and the Odet; it was
raised to the rank of capital of Cornwall in
the late 5C by King Gradlon and its history is linked with the famous legend of the
town of Is. Today it is the Prefecture of
Finistère. Its twisty old streets have fine
houses with projecting upper storeys, some
of them are clad in slate (Rue Kéréon) or
decorated with caryatids (Rue Guéodet).

Cathedral of Saint-Corentin: This was
dedicated to the first Bishop of Cornwall
and is a majestic 13–15C Gothic building.
The spires were only placed on the high
towers with twin bays in 1856 (they were
modelled on the Pont-Croix bell tower).
The façade has an equestrian statue of
King Gradlon at spire level and a large
doorway with finely carved archivolts. The
long nave is out of alignment with the
choir, for reasons which are not clear—perhaps there were building difficulties, or
perhaps it was an attempt to integrate an
existing chapel or to symbolize the inclined
head of Christ on the Cross. The problem
is still being debated. The church has fine
15C stained glass and a carved pulpit with
panels illustrating the life of St.Corentin
(1679), an 18C organ chest, statues and altarpieces of different periods, four 15C
recumbent figures and some modern
frescos.

Breton Museum: Next to the cathedral
a fine 16C spiral staircase leads to the the
former bishop's palace (16–18C), which
has housed this interesting museum of history, archaeology and ethnography since
the beginning of the century. Exhibits include Gallo-Roman objects found in the
area, a Breton interior, a collection of
historic wood carvings (furniture, statues,

Quimper, cathedral of St-Corentin

Quimper, the cathedral, portal

panels), tombs including that of Troïlus de Mondragon (16C), traditional costume and Quimper faience.

Beaux-Arts Museum (Place Saint-Corentin): This museum is housed in part of the Hôtel de Ville and has an important collection of paintings, particularly foreign 16&17C works (Carracci, Rubens, Jordaens) and 18&19C French works (Boucher, Fragonard, Oudry, Corot, Chassériau, Boudin). The Pont-Aven school is represented by Émile Bernard, Maurice Denis, Paul Sérusier *(La Vieille du Pouldu),* Meyer de Haan and Maxime Maufra. One room is devoted to Max Jacob, who was born in Quimper.

Notre-Dame-de-Locmaria: At the end of the avenues on the left bank of the Odet is a former Gallo-Roman village. Only the

courtyard and the church with its large, square 12C tower remain of its 9C abbey. The 15C porch leads to a nave with a panelled ceiling and arches with cruciform piers which probably date from the early 11C.

Environs: Chapel of Kerdévot (9 km. E.): This 15C chapel in the nearby hamlet of Kerdévot-en-Ergué-Gaberic has a 16C *calvary* with Flamboyant niches. One of the altarpieces in the nave, depicting the Life of Our Lady, is 15C Flemish and particularly interesting. **Quilinen** (11 km. N.): The little parish close at Quilinen is mainly notable for its *c.*1550 calvary. The base consists of two inverted pyramids, and this and the unusual disposition of the figures gives the whole group an extremely strong vertical line continued by the crucifix, which has the risen Christ on the reverse. The Apostles with their attributes are depicted on the platform. The figures on the central shaft are supported by corbels carved in the shape of angels' heads. The thieves, contorted with suffering, make a striking impression. The 15C chapel has an elegant bell tower with spires and a Virgin surrounded with angels on the S. doorway. Inside there are old statues and a glory beam.

Saint-Vennec (16 km. N.): This hamlet has a 1556 *calvary* constructed in a similar but less mannered fashion to the one at Quilinen. The Gothic chapel next to it has 15&16C statues and a polychrome stone group of 'St.Gwenn with the three breasts' and her sons Guénolé, Jacut and Vennec. An elegant fountain with pinnacles completes the group of buildings. **Guengat** (15 km. NE): the *parish close* has sacred fountains, a 1557 ossuary, a simple calvary with a Pietà and a fine 15&16C Gothic *church*. The choir has magnificent Gothic windows depicting the Passion, the Entombment and the Resurrection.

Quimperlé, N.-D.-de-l'Assomption

Quimperlé	(11,710 inhab.)
29 Finistère	p.412☐B 6

Quimperlé, set in a steep valley at the confluence of the Ellé and the Isole, has one of the masterpieces of Romanesque architecture in Brittany, **Sainte-Croix**, which stands beside the ancient houses in the Rue Brémond-d'Ars and Dom-Morice (Low Town). The church, which was carefully restored in the last century after the collapse of the tower, was built in the 11C on the plan of the Church of the Holy Sepulchre in Jerusalem, like the church at Lanleff (see **Plouha**). It has a central rotunda with two apsidal chapels and a porch. The apse survived the collapse of the tower and

has a crypt and a choir with remarkable capitals decorated with animals, scrolls and leaves. There is a fine altarpiece of 1541 at the main entrance.

The Rue de Brémond-d'Ars, which runs beside the church, was the showpiece of the town.

Notre-Dame-de-l'Assomption and Saint-Michel: This 13&15C building dominates the Upper Town; the bell tower now has no spire. The finely decorated Gothic porches lead to a 13C nave with panelled vaulting and carved beams. In the square 15C choir there is a fine 16C statue of Our Lady of the Annunciation on one of the extremely sturdy pillars which support the square tower.

Rambouillet

Rambouillet	(20,050 inhab.)
78 Yvelines	p.410☐I 5

Situated on the edge of a vast forest with enormous clearings and lakes, the asymmetrical **château** of Rambouillet stands amid formal French gardens and water gardens. L-shaped owing to the demolition of the left wing by Napoleon I, it encloses a large 14C tower, known as François I's

Rambouillet, the Queen's dairy

tower (François I died here in 1547). The present building was built by the Comte de Toulouse, one of Louis XIV's sons by Mme de Montespan. He rebuilt the château in 1706 and also improved the park, which had been laid out around 1700 by the financier Fleuriau d'Armenonville. The Jardin Anglais (English Garden) was laid out by his son, the Duc de Penthièvre. In 1783 Louis XVI bought the property and created an experimental farm. The Laiterie (dairy) was built to amuse Marie Antoinette but, it seems, to little effect; her nickname for the château was the 'toad-hole' ('la crapaudière'). In the 19C Rambouillet became a sort of funfair, until Napoleon III removed the booths from the gardens and the pleasure boats and fake gondolas from the canals. Félix Faure made it a summer residence of the French presidents. Like Chambord, it is a favourite venue for presidential hunting and shooting parties.

INTERIOR: Parts of the château can be visited when the President is not in residence. It has some fine 18C woodwork. Dating from 1807, Napoleon I's bathroom is frescoed in the style of Ancient Rome. It adjoins the bedroom where he spent the night of 29–30 June 1815—an unplanned halt on the long journey to St.Helena. The

Salle des Marbres (marble room) on the ground floor was part of the old château. The walls were faced with coloured marble in 1556 by the Marquis de Rambouillet, Charles d'Angennes.

GARDENS AND PARK: Around the château there are parterres (formal flower beds) and a water garden. The latter consists of canals and little artificial islands—the Îles des Festins and the Îles des Roches—where parties and elegant picnics were organized. These in turn are set in a well laid out park, crossed by small roads with parking areas. The *Laiterie de la Reine* (Queen's Dairy, 1785), curiously resembling a small temple, has a marble rotunda (the milking parlour!) and a hall with an artificial grotto at one end. From Louis XVI's experimental farm there has now evolved the *Bergerie Nationale* (national sheep farm). The merino sheep imported from Spain by Louis XVI were originally kept in the open air; later, under the Empire, special buildings were built for them. The 'Rambouillet merinos' now have a worldwide reputation as splendid wool producers. In the *Jardin Anglais* paths and streams meander amongst beautiful, rare trees. The delightful *Pavillon des Coquillages* (pavilion of shells) was built around 1778 by the Duc de Penthièvre for his daughter-in- law, the Princesse de Lamballe: the interior is completely covered with shells and fragments of mother-of-pearl.

Rampillon (410 inhab.)
77 Seine-et-Marne p.411 ☐ J 5

This small village on the Brie has a 13C *church* with a fine main door—an excellent example of the sophistication achieved in sculpture in the first Gothic phase. Surrounding Christ in Judgement in the tympanum are angels, the Virgin, and St.John. On the lintel is a resurrection of the dead, with St.Michael weighing souls. On the centre post we see Christ teaching, while on either side of the doorway are the twelve Apostles. The tympanum above the small door on the right contains a Coronation of the Virgin. An attractive triforium lightens

Rambouillet, the château

Nangis, the château

the interior; there is a polygonal choir. Formerly attached to a commandery, the church contains tombstones of Knights Templar. At the end of the right aisle is a fine 16C carved retable with a 14C statue of the Virgin.

Environs: Nangis (4.5 km. NW): A large country town, now quite industrial, with a church of 13C origin. The Town Hall is in a wing of the old château, which still has two medieval towers.

Redon   (10,760 inhab.)
35 Ille-et-Vilaine   p.413☐D 7

A crossroads for both road and river traffic, Redon flourished for several centuries. The abbey was founded in the 9C and

rebuilt after the Norman raids; from the 11C it was a great intellectual centre. All that now remains from this period is the abbey church of **Saint-Sauveur**, with a magnificent Romanesque bell tower over the crossing (12C), built in variously coloured stone, with triple-tier arcading and rounded corners. At the end of the 18C a fire destroyed part of the Romanesque nave, thus isolating the tall Gothic tower and turreted spire. The Gothic choir, dating from the 13C, has a beautiful high altarpiece of 1636, which was presented by Cardinal Richelieu. Some traces of Romanesque frescos were discovered in 1950. On the S. side the monastic buildings (including a 17C cloister) house a religious college.

Environs: Rochefort-en-Terre (25 km. NW): Perched on a promontory, with a wild, steep approach, Rochefort was once a military stronghold. All that remains of the medieval castle and walls now, however, are a few ruins and the gateway of the Porte Cadre. The outbuildings of the château (17C) have been pleasantly converted into a Renaissance-style dwelling. Among the houses fronting on to the spruce streets and little squares of the town are a number dating from the 15&17C, with attractively decorated doors and windows. A 16C *Calvary* stands beside the *church* of Notre-Dame-de-la-Tronchaye (16 –17C). The corners of the tower (thought to date from the 12C) feature charming carvings of oxen. Inside there are a 16C wooden rood screen, oak choir stalls of the same period, some old stone retables and the greatly venerated statue of Notre-Dame-de-la-Tronchaye (discovered in the 12C inside a tree trunk, where it is thought to have been hidden from the Normans).

Reims

	(183,610 inhab.)
51 Marne	p.411 □K 4

Reims was an important city in Roman Gaul and had some 80,000 inhabitants at the beginning of the 3C. The cloth trade brought increased prosperity in the Middle Ages and, much later, champagne production brought further wealth. With centuries of continuous expansion behind it, Reims is now one of France's most important cities economically, politically and culturally. It has always been historically significant: Clovis was baptized here by St.Remi in 496, and most kings of France were crowned here (one of the most famous coronations being that of Charles VII, in the presence of Joan of Arc). With Épernay, Reims is the 'Champagne capital' (champagne having been invented by a monk of the abbey of Hautvillers, Dom Pérignon). The history of this great wine is often linked with families who came

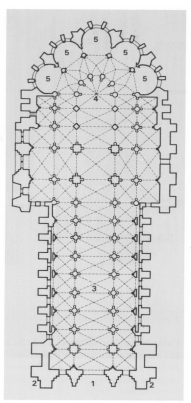

Reims - cathedral of Notre-Dame 1 Main façade **2** towers **3** nave **4** choir **5** radiating chapels

from the E.—the Krugs from Hesse, the Heidsiecks from Westphalia and the Mumms from the hills of Johannisberg. Already successful in the 18C, champagne gained vastly in popularity in the 19C. Reims suffered terribly in 1914, with thousands of houses destroyed and many buildings severely damaged. Almost a ghost town at the end of the Great War, it is now a modern metropolis, with a motorway around it—some would say uncomfortably closely.

Reims, the cathedral, the portals of the façade

Cathedral of Notre-Dame: Architecture and sculpture combine to make Notre-Dame a perfect example of a 13C Gothic cathedral and a supreme witness to the Christian faith. Begun in 1211 on the site of a Romanesque church, it was completed in the 14C (except for the towers, which are 15C). Superbly constructed in shelly limestone, it has survived despite being set ablaze by German bombs in 1914, having undergone an extensive restoration from top to bottom. Like the Parthenon, it is still a magnificent testimony to the art of the past and is one of the greatest achievements of the medieval creative vision.

EXTERIOR: The lavishly decorated W. front is magnificent and perfectly balanced. It is superbly composed around the main entrance to the building, with a large rose-window above the porches and two open-work towers. The window is surmounted by the Gallery of the Kings, with its gigantic statues, some 165 ft. up. The towers continue the vertical movement of the façade as they soar on upward. With the zigzag line of five gables and with the richly ornamented arches, the sumptuous decoration of the lower level is a masterpiece in itself. The theme of the carvings around the central portal concerns the Virgin. The various episodes in her life, from the Annunciation and Visitation to her Coronation, are depicted in sculpture of great dignity, some of it classical in inspiration. The portal on the right is devoted to Christ and the Prophets and has a great mass of figures, motionless and solemn, carved in the stone. Accompanying the Crucifixion in the left portal is a host of saints and martyrs; next to the decapitated St. Nicaise is a guardian angel with mischievous face,

Reims, 'Cavalcade of Louis XV', by Martin le Jeune (Versailles)

known as the 'Angel with the smile' ('l'Ange au sourire')! This, like the angel of the Annunciation on the splay of the main door, is a work of the 13C Champenoise school, characterized by simple, yet subtly modulated young bodies, at once sensual and serene. In the tympanum of one of the doors of the N. transept there is a strikingly human, motherly Virgin. The wonderful side elevations end in a remarkable, complex apse. Everything here testifies to the technical brilliance, vigour, and rich imagination of Gothic architecture. Reims has been called 'the cathedral of angels', and angels are indeed everywhere—adorning the abutments supporting the flying buttresses and taking the place of a weather vane atop a little 16C clock tower.

INTERIOR: The dimensions inside are as befits royal ceremonial: some 500 ft. long, with vaulting approximately 125 ft. high. However, after the richness of the exterior, the plainness inside is surprising. The interior consists of three storeys, the main bays of the arches at the bottom, a triforium, and immediately above that a clerestory. The lightness of the construction, the pointed arches and ribs lend the vaulting grace and movement. Finally, one of the most remarkable features of the cathedral is the internal decoration of the W. elevation: the stained glass in the great rose-window and the tympanum above the central portal, framed by some fifty statues in niches one on top of the other, forming an exceptional ensemble (mid 13C). The 13&14C glass has been well restored in places by Jacques Simon, who has also added some glass of his own, in keeping with the earlier style.

Reims, Place Royale

Palais du Tau: Next to the cathedral, this is the ancient residence of the archbishop, where kings stayed when they came to be crowned. The two-storey Palatine Chapel (13C) is reminiscent of the Sainte-Chapelle in Paris. The Gothic Salle du Tau is especially interesting. Built at the end of the 15C, it offered a sumptuous setting for the festivities that followed a coronation. Rebuilt after 1918, it still preserves a monumental chimney-piece (1498). Today the famous cathedral *museum* is housed in the former archbishop's palace. The collection includes statues and casts, and some superb 15C arrases (tapestries from Arras), the two most notable of which depict in vivid detail 'the history of strong King Clovis'. Taking pride of place in the treasury, alongside a number of 12&13C reliquaries, is the coronation chalice, made of gold, enamel and precious stones.

Basilica of Saint-Remi: This former abbey was built in the 11–12C over the tomb of the venerated 6C bishop of Reims, St. Remigius. Heavily damaged in 1914–18, it has been carefully restored. The real originality of the building has been preserved and the happy medley of styles retained. With Gothic vaulting on an originally Romanesque structure, Saint-Remi includes elements from every period of sacred architecture.

EXTERIOR: The additions of each century are clearly visible on the outside of the basilica. The imposing W. front, with statues of St. Peter and St. Remigius on Gallo-Roman columns flanking the door, is essentially Romanesque. The two square towers are topped by turreted slate spires; only the S. tower, however, is genuine (11C). The semicircular choir (apse) and

ather primitive flying buttresses are early, somewhat tentative Gothic, while the S. levation of the transept reveals the full lory of Flamboyant Gothic.

NTERIOR: The unusual length of the nave some 400 ft.), and its relative narrowness reate striking effects of perspective, enanced by a superb 'crown of light'—96 vindow lights high up in the vaulting illustrating the long life of St.Remigius. The Romanesque origins of the nave are visible in the round arches with their enormous galleries; the Gothic roof vaults and he clustered shafts of the columns supporting them date from the end of the 12C. n the four-storey choir we find all the richless and delicacy and fine sense of balance of true Gothic. This part of the church is nagnificent, with its radiating chapels eparated from the ambulatory by a light,

elegant colonnade, and its numerous fine windows (some still containing 12C glass). Behind the high altar is the tomb of St. Remigius with 16C statues. A chapel in the right transept has a fine Holy Sepulchre with eight figures (1531).

Abbey: Adjoining the church are the 12&13C abbey buildings (altered in the 17&18C), an architecturally rich and varied complex. The chapterhouse has some 12C arcading with fine capitals. Here too is the *Musée Historique* and the treasury of Saint-Remi.

Other religious buildings: In a garden behind the apse of Saint-Remi are the ruins of the church of Saint-Julien (11C). *Saint-Jacques,* begun *c.* 1190 and altered in the 13&15C, is one of Reims's oldest shrines. Architecturally interesting, it also has some beautiful contemporary stained glass. The *Basilica of Saint-Clotilde,* with its curious central dome, is an unusual example of late-19C religious architecture. The *Chapelle Foujita* was designed and decorated by the Japanese painter Foujita. In this quiet chapel stylized stained glass and frescos give a gentle affirmation of the artist's Christian faith.

Old Reims: A number of Gallo-Roman remains bear witness to the early existence of this capital of the Second Belgium. In the Place du Forum some 2C cryptoporticuses (underground galleries originally used as warehouses) have been discovered. Marking the N. entrance to the city is the *Porte de Mars.* Some 108 ft. long, this grand tripartite triumphal arch (3C) still retains some of its carved decoration. The more recent past survives in various houses and monuments, such as the 13C Gothic Maison des Comtes de Champagne (House of the Counts of Champagne) or the Hôtel de la Salle, with its fine Renaissance façade of 1545. The stately façade of the Hôtel de Ville, which has columns and pediments, is 17C. Begun in 1758, the *Place Royale* forms a charming square; the houses, built over arcades and with balustraded roofs, provide a strong horizontal emphasis to the architecture. The W. section was completed only shortly before the Great War.

Musée des Beaux-Arts: The range and quality of the works of art exhibited in the former abbey of Saint-Denis make it one of France's leading provincial galleries. Of special note are works by the Cranachs, Philippe de Champaigne, Nicolas Poussin, the Le Nain brothers and Fragonard. 19C French painting is well represented; there are a number of works by Delacroix, some twenty Corots, pre-Impressionist (Jongkind, Boudin) and Impressionist (Pissarro, Sisley, Renoir) works.

Musée du Vieux-Reims: Housed in the 15C Hôtel Le Vergeur. The courtyard contains a somewhat startling frieze depicting bizarre battles. Inside there is a superb 13C Gothic hall. The history of Reims is brought alive in a series of fascinating documents. There are also valuable engravings by Dürer, including *The Apocalypse* and the *Great Passion.*

Bibliothèque Carnegie: Both pleasant and well suited to its function, this library houses rare manuscripts (10&11C) and incunabula, book bindings, and prints. Also important works by great caricaturists, including Daumier.

Remiremont   (11,500 inhab.)
88 Vosges   p.417☐N 6

This attractive town, with pleasant views of wooded hillsides, boasts a thousand-year-old history. The main buildings include those of an important house of canonesses (17&18C), a delightful arcaded main street and a number of beautiful fountains. The church of **Notre-Dame** formerly the abbey church of Saint-Pierre, was begun in 1300. The light floods into the noble Gothic nave and the grandeur of the church is further enhanced by an enormous retable above the high altar, in black marble and white limestone (17C). In a niche, behind a fine gilded wooden grille, is Notre-Dame-du-Trésor—a delicate 11C wooden statue. Beneath the choir there is a remarkable crypt with three vaulted aisles. This is the oldest church in the Vosges (1049). The *Palais Abbatial* beside Notre-Dame has a graceful 18C façade. The small *Musée Municipal* is a museum of local history and traditions; it also has paintings, including two by Greuze. The *Musée Friry* is a museum of religious art.

Rennes   (205,730 inhab.)
35 Ille-et-Vilaine   p.413☐E 6

The historic capital of Brittany and an important administrative, commercial and cultural centre. A fully industrialized city,

Rennes, Hôtel de Ville, façade

it has developed continuously since World War 2, with large modern suburbs spreading into the surrounding countryside. Founded by the Celtic Redones tribe, at the point where the Ille and the Vilaine meet, Rennes had by the Middle Ages become a prosperous and well fortified town. Before being crowned in the cathedral, the Dukes of Brittany would make a solemn entry into the city through the Porte Mordelaise (15C). In 1561 it became the seat of the Breton parlement — this famous parliament opposed the absolutism of the monarchy and later also the authority of the Constituante (1789–1791), claiming the privileges given to Brittany by the treaty of 1532, when it was 'joined' to France. However, few buildings remain from this era. In 1720 a great fire raged for six days in part of the city, claiming 100 lives and destroying almost 900 houses. Rebuilding was the work of Robelin and then Jacques Gabriel. Based on three squares—the Place du Palais, the Place de la Mairie, and the Place de la République—and close to old narrow streets lined with beautiful 16&17C houses, the new town features straight avenues of symmetrical classical buildings (blocks of flats and hôtels) with arcades and Mansard roofs.

Palais de Justice: The former home of the Breton parliament, in the beautiful Place du Palais (so-named after this building). It was built 1618–55, to the designs of Salomon de Brosse, the architect of the Palais du Luxembourg in Paris. Jacques Gabriel altered the façade in the 18C, replacing the massive double flight of steps in the courtyard with an Ionic portico and two bas-reliefs. Behind this splendid façade the rooms are lavishly decorated by leading exponents of the decorative arts (Jouvenet, Coypel, Errard) from the 17C. The Grand-Chambre, where sessions of the Supreme Court of Brittany were held, is a superb achievement, with its coffered and painted ceiling, gilded wainscoting, and elegant loggias. Modern Gobelins tapestries depict important events in Brittany's history.

Hôtel de Ville: One of the finest buildings of the 'new' town. Designed by

Rennes, the Palais de Justice

Gabriel, the façade is partly baroque, with a large niche in the centre and an onion dome bell tower, its base concealed by a pediment. Before the Revolution the large central niche housed a bronze sculpture of Louis XV surrounded by allegorical figures. In 1911 a controversial sculpture was placed here; it represented the union of Brittany with France (with Brittany portrayed kneeling). This work met with no better fate than its predecessor for in 1932 it was blown up by separatists. The 19C theatre has an interesting modern ceiling fresco (1913) showing Breton dances.

Cathedral of Saint-Pierre: Destroyed more than once and almost completely rebuilt in the 19C, Rennes cathedral is a large building, which is rather over-decorated inside (1880). A side chapel on the right has a fine 16C Flemish altarpiece depicting the life of the Virgin. The area around the cathedral still exudes its old charm.

Basilica of Saint-Sauveur: 18C. Close to the cathedral, with a graceful crossing tower. Pilasters, entablature, and pediment lend the façade considerable dignity. Of note inside are the fine pulpit (made by a local ironworker in 1781) and the gilded wooden canopy over the high altar.

Saint-Germain: 15&16C Flamboyant, with a double door and, inside, an 18C organ case and a 16C carved pulpit. There is some 16C stained glass; the modern glass is by Max Ingrand.

Palais Saint-Georges: This grand, severely classical building was for Benedictine nuns of noble birth. Overlooking a formal French garden, a long arcaded walk extends across the front between two corner pavilions. Carved on the arcading is the name Magdelaine de la Fayette (the nun who rebuilt the convent in the 17C). A large curved pediment bearing the arms of Brittany surmounts the three dormer windows in the centre.

Notre-Dame: An old abbey, originally dedicated to St.Melaine (bishop and patron saint of Rennes), Notre-Dame dates from the 14–17C, although parts of the nave and transept are 11C Romanesque. In the last century the tower acquired an octagonal, domed crown, with a statue of the Virgin. The adjoining monastic buildings (17C) are built around an elegant cloister with decorated arcades.

Toussaints: On the far bank of the Vilaine, this church (1624–51) used to be attached to the Jesuit College. It is an excellent example of Counter-Reformation architecture. A striking 17C retable on the high altar combines marble, calcareous tufa and gilt, and incorporates a picture of the Virgin taking the Society of Jesus into her protection.

Palais des Musées: Quai Émile Zola. The palais is occupied by two museums. On the ground floor the *Musée de Bretagne* offers a general introduction to Brittany—imaginative displays giving a stimulating picture of Breton history, folk art and traditions (with a wonderful collection of furniture and traditional dress); one room is devoted to the social and economic problems of Brittany today. Upstairs, the *Musée des Beaux-Arts* contains a remarkable collection of paintings. Many great artists are represented, including Tintoretto, Veronese, Jordaens (*Christ on the Cross*), Le Nain (*Virgin with Glass of Wine*), Guercino, Annibale Carracci (*Rest on the Flight into Egypt*), Rembrandt (*Bathsheba at her Toilette*), Philippe de Champaigne, Rubens (*Tiger and Lion Hunt*), Chardin and, in particular Georges de La Tour (the famous *New-Born Baby, c.* 1630). Alongside Gauguin's *Still-Life with Oranges* and his *Vase of Flowers* are other paintings from the Pont-Aven school (Émile Bernard, Verkade,

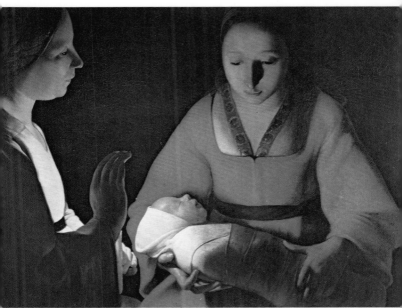

Rennes, Musée des Beaux-Arts, 'The Newborn', by Georges de la Tour

Sérusier), a fine selection of works from the Impressionist era (Jongkind, Boudin, Caillebotte, Sisley), and some modern pieces (Utrillo, Vlaminck, Delaunay, Picasso). The gallery also possesses important drawings by Vouet, Puget, Watteau, Botticelli, Leonardo da Vinci, Dürer, and Rembrandt. There are several showcases of French ceramics from the 17–19C, as well as Egyptian, Greek, and Etruscan objects.

Hôtel de Blossac: 6 Rue du Chapitre. Spared by the fire, this 18C aristocrat's house in the picturesque cathedral quarter was the official residence of the governors of Brittany. The entrance hall is arcaded and has a splendid stone staircase with a beautiful wrought-iron bannister.

Maison 'de Du Guesclin': 3, Rue Saint-Guillaume. The French Constable Bertrand Du Guesclin is said to have stayed here, but in fact this fine 16C house postdates him. The façade is a bewildering composition of half-timbering, small columns and carved entablatures. Flanking one of the doors are two charming wooden figures.

Environs: Les Iffs (26 km. NW): 14&15C, the village *church* stands by the small cemetery, its elegant tower topped by a modern spire. Flamboyant in style, it has a huge W. porch. Superb stained glass lights the choir and side chapels. There are a 17C high altar, polychrome woodwork and 15C holy water stoup and font. **Château de Montmuran** (1 km. from Les Iffs): A 12C castle dominating the surrounding countryside and of rather stark appearance. Of the original castle, there re-

Rennes, the Maison de Du Guesclin

Rennes, Hôtel de Blossac, staircase

main only two massive towers with conical roofs. A more recent domestic wing links them with the 14C fortified entrance, which has fine machicolations and drawbridge. A stained-glass window in the Flamboyant chapel portrays scenes from Du Guesclin's life. Du Guesclin is reputed to have been knighted here in 1354 and also to have married Jeanne de Laval, his second wife, here.

Réole (La)   (5,150 inhab.)
33 Gironde   p.422☐F 12

Perched above the Garonne, La Réole is a small town of ancient foundation named after a 10C monastery—or rather, after the rule (*regula*) of life followed in the monastery. Now a quiet farming town, its past has

not always been so peaceful. Its strategic position made it a fiercely contested town during the Anglo-French wars and it later became a Protestant stronghold during the Wars of Religion.

Saint-Pierre: The old Benedictine priory church, dating from the late 12/early 13C. Vandalized by the Huguenots, it was then restored and altered in the 17C. Fine Flamboyant N. door from the 14C or 15C; interesting capitals and a mixture of Gothic and Romanesque in the apse. There is a *Marriage of the Virgin* (1666) by Jean de Batse and a *Madonna and Child with Angels* which is possibly by Correggio.

Monastery: This exquisite early-18C building now houses various public offices. The ironwork is by a local craftsman. The elegant wrought-iron cloister gate (1756) opens into the Place Rigoulet.

La Réole, the town and the Garonne

The old Hôtel de Ville dates from about 1200, with 15&16C alterations. La Réole still has many old houses, as well as remains of the medieval castle of the 'Quatre sos' (the Trois Soeurs—three sisters), which was demolished in 1629. The synagogue (Rue Blandin) dates from the 12&13C. There are still substantial traces of the three town walls (13&15C).

Ribeauvillé	(4,410 inhab.)
68 Haut-Rhin	p.417☐O 6

Miraculously unscathed by the fighting of December 1944, Ribeauvillé is a picturesque little town, typical of old Alsace, still retaining a ruined castle and walls. Set amid undulating vineyards at the foot of the Vosges, these ruins preserve the memory of the powerful Ribeaupierre family —the annual summer 'Pfiffertag' festival recalls the minstrels who came to pay them homage each year. The monastic *church* (belonging to the Augustinians) is early 15C; the Gothic *parish church* was built 1282–1473. The 18C French-style Hôtel de Ville has a pretty fountain in front of it and houses a small *museum* (good collection of flagons and tankards). One of the most attractive of the old houses is now a 'wistub' (a typical Alsatian café-cum-wine-bar, more commonly known as a 'winstub' in Strasbourg). A low half-timbered building, it is called the *Maison de l'Ave Maria* because of the beautiful wooden carving on the oriel.

Castles: Round the lycée there are the remains of the great castle which stood against the walls to the NE. In the 15C it became the residence of the local lords when they abandoned their medieval eyries of *Grand-Ribeaupierre* (the *Château de Saint-Ulrich*) and *Haut-Ribeaupierre* (or *Altenkastel*). Proud vestiges of these earlier fortresses can still be seen.

Riceys (Les)
10 Aube   (1,530 inhab.)   p.415☐L 6

This little town in the heart of a famous wine-growing area has three distinct districts, each with a 16C *church*. Ricey-Bas has a large church with a tall square central tower. Flamboyant elements combine with characteristic features of the Renaissance architecture of Troyes. The interior is richly decorated; 16C glass, late-15C wooden Christ and 18C woodwork. The church of *Ricey-Haute-Rive* has a beautiful apse and, inside, a magnificent Louis XV wooden pulpit. An amalgamation of two buildings, the church of *Ricey-Haut* has a holy water stoup and a statue of St. Bridget, both from the 16C.

Richelieu
37 Indre-et-Loire   (2,530 inhab.)   p.419☐G 8

This quiet town, built as a unified whole by Cardinal Richelieu in the 17C, seems almost unreal in its strict classical symmetry. Richelieu already had a château here (of which only the park and the outbuildings survive) and he commissioned Jacques Lemercier to plan an orderly square new town with walls and moats. Work stopped when the Cardinal died and the town remained as it was: uniform hôtels, two neat squares, church (by Lemercier, 1625–38) and a fine market. There is a small *Musée Historique* in the Town Hall.

Riom
63 Puy-de Dôme   (17,960 inhab.)   p.420☐J 10

A rival to Clermont in the 16–18C, this ancient capital of the Duchy of Auvergne

Ribeauvillé, traditional Alsace houses

as the home of magistrates anxious to impress on the world the dignity of their status. Of the many hôtels in the old town the most noteworthy are the *Maison des Consuls* (16C), with its fine, pure Renaissance façade, the Hôtel Guimoneau and the *Hôtel de Ville* with its superb spiral staircase. The *Saint-Amable* has a 12C nave and transept, 13C choir, and 18C façade; the sacristy has good 17C woodwork. *Notre-Dame-du-Marthuret* dates from the 14&15C and has fine 15C glass, as well as the splendid 14C *Virgin with a bird,* formerly on the centre-post of the porch (where there is now a copy). Rebuilt in the 19C, the courthouse stands on the site of the 14C *Palais de Justice* built by Jean de Berry (of which the *Sainte-Chapelle* survives, with 17C wall hangings and beautiful 16C glass).

Museums: *Musée Jeanne-d'Arc:* In the Hôtel de Ville. On display is the original letter sent to the inhabitants of Riom by Joan of Arc in 1429. *Musée Mandet:* Works by 17&18C painters and local Auvergnat artists, housed in a 17C hôtel. *Musée*

Régional d'Auvergne: Local folk art and traditions illustrated by a good collection of everyday objects, furniture and costume.

Environs: Mozac (1 km. W.): *Saint-Pierre,* 12C; largely destroyed by an earthquake in the 15C. However, there still survive some exceptionally fine Romanesque carved capitals of classical and Oriental inspiration. The sacristy, has the fine 12C reliquary of St.Calmin, a work in enamel from the Limoges school. **Ennezat** (9.5 km. E.): With one of the oldest churches in the Auvergne; 11C nave, with great purity of line and a 13C Gothic choir. The capitals feature favourite motifs of the Auvergnat sculptors—in particular, miserliness. The choir has two 15C frescos.

Riquewihr	(1,200 inhab.)
68 Haut-Rhin	p.417☐O 6

The vineyards covering the hillsides around Riquewihr come right up to the

Richelieu, gate in the ramparts

Riom, church, the Virgin with a Bird

double ring of walls around the town. This unique village (granted town status in 1320) is one of the sights of Alsace. All the houses demonstrate the place's wealth and with three quarters of them dating from before 1630, the unspoilt appearance of the original *cité* is jealously preserved. Damage from the last war is not obtrusive. The houses — with balconies thick with flowers—nearly all have plaques indicating their age and history. Everything seems to harmonize, giving a perfect expression of the prosperity enjoyed by the vine growers of Alsace in the 16&17C. The picturesque *Grand-Rue* (high street) and adjacent side streets have a delightful succession of building styles with half-timbering, quarried stone, fine doorways, oriel windows, and galleried courtyards.

The old fortifications are still mostly extant and include the 13C Porte Dolder and the 16C Obertor. *Musée des P.T.T.:* A (restored) Renaissance building *c.* 1540, houses a charming and intriguing museum of the postal service, stretching back to the Gallo-Roman period—from the early runners and post-horses to the postage stamp, the invention of the telephone, and the Imperial German post, and modern telecommunications. The Porte d'En-Haut, or Dolder, houses the little *Musée de Riquewihr*, which has armaments, old locks, door knockers, Alsatiques (books of art from Alsace), everyday objects from the past, and exhibits from the two World Wars.

Roanne
42 Loire   (56,500 inhab.)
                                            p.420☐K/L 10

A commercial town between Beaujolais and the Massif Central, with the famous restaurant of the Troisgros brothers on the Lyons road. Roanne began life as the Gallic village of *Rodumna*. The *Musée Joseph-*

Déchelette, 22 Rue Anatole-France, named after the local archaeologist who excavated Gergovie and Corent, has an excellent display of finds mostly from Roanne and the neighbouring areas, as well as an exhibition of archaeological methods.

Rocamadour
46 Lot   (710 inhab.
                                             p419☐H 1⁚

The rather mournful dry plateaux of the Causses boast wonderful underground sights (e.g. the famous Padirac caves), and above ground, clinging spectacularly to the side of a plunging gorge, with shrines built into the rock face, the town of Rocamadour. A place of pilgrimage since the late Middle Ages, the town takes its name from the semi-legendary early Christian hermit St Amadour, whose undecayed body was said to have been discovered in the 12C. From all over Christendom, princes, prelates and kings (Louis IX, Philip III, Philip the Fair, Charles VII, Louis XI and Henry Plantagenet) came to venerate Our Lady. This unique town gradually expanded over the centuries, notably in the 11–15C. Medieval Rocamadour had somewhat the appearance of a small fortified city. Its fortunes waned with the decline of pilgrimages in the 17&18C and also with the Revolution. Its former splendour was only brought back through 19C restoration. Now it ranks as the second most important sight in France, after the Mont-Saint-Michel.

Military and civilian buildings: Dominated by a heavily restored château (now the house of the chaplains), Rocamadour nestles against the cliff, below the chapels. The 13C or 14C Porte du Figuier (Gate of the Fig-Tree) leads into the long high street with its numerous ancient houses. One of

Mozac, reliquary of St-Calmin, detail

Riquewihr, detail of a house

the finest of these houses (13&15C) was burnt down in 1925, but has been remarkably well restored. Known as *La Couronnerie* — after the makers of rosaries (couronnes)—it is now the Town Hall and the tourist office. The large room with mullioned windows on the first floor has two Aubusson tapestries of scenes of Causse designed by Lurçat. In the *Rue de la Mercerie,* the oldest street in Rocamadour, pilgrims used to buy religious badges to wear in their hats. The 13C *Maison de la Pomette,* roughly in the middle of this street, was altered in the 15C. With a central pillar supporting the ceiling, it is typical of the old houses in Rocamadour.

Chapels: The 'Grand Escalier', the *Via Sancta* which pilgrims would climb on their knees as they said their rosaries, leads

to a second level. Passing under a heavily restored 14C structure, you then reach the square around which the pilgrim chapels are grouped. The 12C *Chapelle Saint-Amadour,* with modern paintings on the subject of the legendary St.Amadour, lies beneath the basilica of *Saint-Sauveur* (late 12C, early Gothic in style). Saint-Sauveur has two tall aisles and a large 16C crucifix. Leading from it is the *Chapelle Miraculeuse,* built into the rock in 1479 to replace another chapel which had been destroyed by a landslide. Here are numerous ex-votos, an ancient bell and the fetters of prisoners freed after making the pilgrimage to the mirculous Madonna and Child—the 'primitive' statue (probably late 12C) above the altar. Altered in the 19C, the Chapelle Miraculeuse has a 15C fresco, in poor condition, on the outside. It gives on to another square, the Parvis Notre-Dame, overhung by the cliff face. A 'sword of Roland' is stuck in the stone. Legend has it that this great hero of Charlemagne's army threw it here from Ronceveaux as he lay dying. Opposite the Chapelle Miraculeuse, or Notre-Dame, is the *Chapelle Saint-Michel,* with fairly well preserved 12C frescos (Annunciation and Visitation). Partly built into the cliff side, Saint-Michel also has paintings within, but these have not survived so well.

Rochechouart	(4,200 inhab.)
87 Haute-Vienne	p.419☐G 10

The first one sees of this small hilltop town of the Limousin is the broad fronted château, which is now the sub-prefecture (a deep moat still separates it from the square, with its shady plane trees). Apart from the 13C keep, the Tour de la Décube, it dates from the 15C. The main courtyard was altered in the 17C and two sides now

Rocamadour

Rochechouart, the château

have columns with figures. A fresco in the Salle des Chasses (Hunting Room) depicts the life of a 16C seigneur—mainly hunting scenes. The château houses the Musée Municipal (prehistoric and Gallo-Roman exhibits).

Roche-Courbon (château)
17 Charente-Maritime   p.418☐F 10

This 15C château, altered in the 17C, was saved from ruin by Pierre Loti, who lived here and immortalized it as the castle of the Sleeping Beauty. The property, entered through the monumental Renaissance Porte des Lions, overlooks stepped terraces and formal French gardens. The rectangular machicolated keep, housing the small *Musée de Préhistoire*, formed part of the old

walls. The graceful garden front (altered in the 17C) is reflected in a small lake. The beautiful interior is 17C throughout. The bathroom is decorated entirely with painted panels.

Rochefort
17 Charente-Maritime   (32,880 inhab.)
     p.418☐E 10

A commercial port and former naval base, Rochefort was developed by Louis XIV and Colbert. The town has all the formal regularity of the Grand Siècle, with streets at right angles to each other. The old arsenal—once the largest and most magnificent in France—was badly damaged in 1944. The Place Colbert in the town centre has a large 18C fountain with sculptures representing the Atlantic and the Charente. Built like a triumphal arch, the Porte du Soleil (Gate of the Sun) dates from 1830, and forms the main entrance to the arsenal (which is not open to visitors). The surviving arsenal buildings are beautiful, if rather severe, e.g. the quartermaster's store).

Museums. *Musée Naval:* Housed in the 17C Hôtel de Cheusses, this museum records Rochefort's great naval past and has miniature 17C ships, models and much documentation. *Musée Municipal des Beaux-Arts:* Local history exhibits and drawings by French and foreign artists. *Musée Pierre-Loti:* Pierre Loti was a naval officer who became a novelist. This, the house where he was born in 1850, contains his various collections. The simplicity of his bedroom contrasts with the exotic décor of the other rooms (mosque-style, Turkish salon, Arabian drawing room, etc.).

Environs: Échillais (5 km. S.): Charming Saintonge Romanesque *church* from the 12C. The richly decorated façade takes the form of a triumphal arch cut in two by a corbelled cornice. To the left of the door

La Roche-Courbon, the château

a large, typically Saintonge gargoyle appears to be swallowing the column. **Moëze** (5 km. SW): The *church* with a tall Flamboyant belfry was formerly a landmark for sailors. *Temple de Moëze* (16C): This 'Croix Hosannière' in the form of a Greek temple is probably incomplete. **Fouras** (13 km. NW): On a long peninsula opposite the Ile d'Aix, protecting the mouth of the Charente, Fouras was fortified by Vauban in the 17C with a triple ring of walls. The 15C keep houses a small *Musée d'Histoire Locale et Maritime.*

Rochefoucauld (La)   (3,780 inhab.)
16 Charente   p.419□G 10

Built of white stone and with slate roofs, his château from the 12&16C rises above

the river and is reminiscent of those of the Loire. Owned by the descendants of François de la Rochefoucauld—the author of the famous *Maximes*—it can only be admired from the outside. Behind the fine Renaissance façade there is a superb courtyard with three tiers of arcades similar to certain Italian palaces.

Rochelle (La)   (81,880 inhab.)
17 Charente-Maritime   p.418□E 9

La Rochelle's medieval towers, its harbour full of brightly painted boats, and the orderly houses glimpsed through a forest of masts have been painted by artists as varied as Joseph Vernet, Corot (who called La Rochelle, 'that pretty character in blue'), Signac and Marquet. Architecturally the

Moëze, temple of Moëze

Fouras, the château

town is remarkably unspoilt with buildings dating from various eras reflecting an interesting (though also troubled) past. La Rochelle's prosperity came originally from trade in salt and wine. A busy port (built in the 14C), protected by solid walls, and enjoying privileges granted in the 13C by Eleanor of Aquitaine (which, in the 12C, permitted the Rochelais to form a free commune), La Rochelle grew prosperous and influential. In the 16C, adopting the ideas of the Reformers, with whom its trading links with Northern countries brought it into contact, the city became a centre of Protestantism. A Huguenot refuge—a western 'Geneva'—after the St. Bartholomew Night massacre, it was the focus of violent religious strife. The siege of 1572 ended in a compromise, the Calvinists being allowed to continue their form of worship. Then came Richelieu's famous siege of the town (1627–8); he built an enormous mole, cutting it off from the open sea, which was held by the English. When the town eventually capitulated, only 5,000 of the original 28,000 inhabitants were still alive. Though the former privileges were withdrawn, La Rochelle once again became prosperous through trade with Canada and the West Indies. The comfortable 18C hôtels in the Old Town which belonged to shipowners reflect a well-off and cultivated society. One of France's first Orientalists, Eugène Fromentin, the great traveller, painter and writer, was born here in 1820. Sponsored by the town authorities and a very active Maison de la Culture, there is now an annual summer festival of modern art (the *Rencontres Internationales d'Art Contemporain*).

Old Harbour: Two formidable towers

protect the entrance to the harbour. Dating from the 14C the *Tour Saint-Nicolas* rises some 90 ft. or more on the S. side, guarding the harbour mouth and one of the quarters of the town. Pentagonal with corner turrets, it is a veritable fort, having a large square keep-like structure on top. It is a fine example of military architecture, comprising three octagonal rooms one above the other, and numerous annexes. Contemporary with it is the *Tour de Chaîne* — so named after the enormous chain strung between two towers at night to close the harbour. In the 17C this tower had its top removed. The Tour de Chaîne now houses a large model of medieval La Rochelle. Adorned with a tall, octagonal, crocketed spire, the 15C *Tour de la Lanterne* was once a fort and a lighthouse.

The Town: Through the 13&18C *Porte de la Grosse Horloge* (Gate of the Large Clock) you reach the *Rue du Palais*, the town's main artery along with the Rue Chaudier. The architecture here — porticoes with shops—is typically Rochelais. *Hôtel de la Chambre de Commerce:* Symbolic of the prosperity of the 18C traders, it has an arcaded street elevation and two wings linked by a colonnade giving on to an inner courtyard. The sober decoration consists of ships' prows and a variety of naval trophies. *Palais de Justice:* Late-18C, it has a heavy classical façade with Corinthian columns and a carved frieze. *Maison Henri II:* Rue des Augustins. The house of a wealthy 16C citizen. The attractive façade has arches and a balcony. The *Rue des Merciers* has typically 16C houses; the street elevations are decorated with busts and ornate dormer windows.

Cathedral of Saint-Louis: Designed by Jacques Gabriel and his son Jacques Ange in the 18C. The façade remains unfinished (two towers were originally planned). One of the side chapels has some fine 16&18C ex-votos.

La Rochefoucauld, the château

La Rochelle, Tour de la Lanterne

Hôtel de Ville: 15&17C. Machicolations and corner turrets give the building the look of a fortress. The main residential block is in the courtyard. A 'prestige' building erected by Henri IV, the ground floor is arcaded, with rather short columns. Above, Corinthian columns alternate with broad windows and niches containing statues of the cardinal virtues. The elevation giving on to the Rue des Gentilhommes features a bossed door and a triangular pediment. The building has a certain amount of furniture, as well as mementoes of Jean Guiton, the mayor who resolutely opposed Richelieu.

Place du Marché: Two old houses survive: one is timber-framed and 15C; the other is stone and 16C. *Rue de l'Escale:* Still paved with round stones which served as ballast on ships returning from Canada, this street has a number of interesting 18C houses. *Maison du Médecin Venette:* The façade of this 17C house sports busts of six celebrated doctors from Antiquity and the Middle Ages. *Saint-Sauveur:* Only the Gothic belfry survives of what was once

one of the most beautiful churches in the town. 12C front, leading into a 13C nave.

Museums: *Musée des Beaux-Arts:* Housed in the former Bishop's Palace (18C), this gallery has paintings ranging from Early Flemish to modern, with works of special note by Corot, Fromentin, and Chassériau. *Musée d'Orbigny-Bernon:* Local history, and some interesting ceramics. *Muséum Lafaille:* Remarkable ethnographic and natural history collections. Well worth seeing is the curious natural history cabinet of the Rochelais Lafaille (18C).

Environs: Esnandes (12 km. N.): The typically Poitevin Romanesque façade of this church gained 14&15C fortifications, along with a crenellated and machicolated parapet walk.

Rochepot (La)   (260 inhab.)
21 Côte-d'Or   p.420□L 8

The Romanesque village church has been extensively altered. The *château* where the Seneschal of Burgundy, Philippe Pot, was born in 1428 is beautifully sited atop a small wooded hill. Picturesque and very 15C in its appearance, it is, however, not as it seems. La Rochepot was badly damaged during the Revolution and stood empty for a long time. Its careful restoration (and partial rebuilding) was undertaken by President Sadi Carnot's son. It now contains some beautiful furniture and works of art (dining-room).

Environs: Nolay (4 km. W.): Next to a 17C church (restored after a fire) are impressive medieval *market buildings,* with beams covered with 'lauzes' (roofing stones, characteristic of the S. of France).

La Rochelle, church of Saint-Sauveur

La Rochelle, aerial view

Esnandes, fortified church

La Rochepot, the château

Roche-sur-Yon (La)　　(48,050 inhab.)
85 Vendée　　　　　　　　　p.418□E 8

Burnt down by the Republicans during the Vendée uprising, this city was resurrected by Napoleon in 1804, as a strategic centre in what was still a recalcitrant area. The present city dates from that time, with its regular layout of streets intersecting at right angles around the Place Napoleon —a huge esplanade lined with neo-Gothic buildings and with an equestrian statue of the Emperor in the middle. In the *Museum* is a Salle Napoléon, a display devoted to the Vendée wars, and a number of local Gallo-Roman archaeological exhibits.

Environs: Apremont (8 km. E.): Of the magnificent 16C château of Admiral Philippe de Chabot, only two large towers

and the chapel built on the old walls survive. **Les Essarts** (20 km. NE): Two circular towers flank the entrance to this ruined castle, which has a drawbridge and portcullis. Known as the Tour Sarrazine, the huge keep is thought to date from the 11C. Across the courtyard are the remains of the 15C château. **La Chabotterie** (24 km. N.): A fortified manor (16&17C) of some renown, being the place where the Royalist leader Charette was captured.

Rocroi　　　　　　　　　(2,910 inhab.)
08 Ardennes　　　　　　　p.411□L 3

On the plain of the Ardennes, close to the Belgian frontier, this industrialized village still retains the fortifications built in the style of Vauban in 1691. Forming a pen-

Apremont, the château

tagon, the outer perimeter is a superb bastioned star-shape structure, within which the town is oriented around the central Place d'Armes, with radiating streets. Rocroi is associated with Le Grand Condé who, as the Duc d'Enghien, won a decisive victory over the Spanish in 1643.

Rodez	(28,170 inhab.)
12 Aveyron	p.424☐J 13

Situated in the heart of the Rouergue, of which it is the capital, Rodez is splendidly placed on top of a hill skirted by the Aveyron. Clustered around the cathedral, the town is a fine illustration of the medieval rivalry between Church and State; the squares of the old Cité and Bourg divided by tall fortifications.

Cathedral of Notre-Dame: 13&16C. The red sandstone façade, flanked by still incomplete towers, dominates the Place d'Armes, the bustling centre of the town. Once part of the city's defences, it is strikingly military in appearance. Only the upper sections were decorated (Flamboyant rose-window and Renaissance coping). On the N. side, contrasting with the severity of the façade, is a five-storey belfry (early 16C), the three top storeys of which are lavishly decorated. A lantern at the top forms a pedestal for a statue of the Virgin.

INTERIOR: The nave, which is 360 ft. long, is plain and impressive, with 27 beautifully furnished side chapels. Above the Renaissance altar in the third chapel (which has an ornate early-16C screen) there is a large painted stone retable of the Entombment (16C). The 15C retable in

Rocroi, aerial view   *Rodez, cathedral of Notre-Dame*

the next chapel depicts Christ on the Mount of Olives. The remains of the great rood screen have been reassembled at the end of the S. transept. White marble sarcophagi (6C) are displayed in the ambulatory, off which side chapels containing the tombs of the bishops of Rodez open. The choir stalls and organ chest (choir and N. transept) are superb examples of 17C wood carving.

Numerous old houses still survive in the streets around the cathedral, many with Gothic and Renaissance features (Rues du Bosc, du Touat, Penavayre, the Place d'Estaing, etc.).

Saint-Amans: Behind the 18C façade is a beautiful 12C Romanesque interior with carved capitals and 16C tapestries telling the story of St. Amans.

Musée Fenaille: Housed in two hôtels, one Gothic, the other Renaissance, this is a museum of prehistory (menhir-statues), Gallo-Roman archaeology, (Gallic gods, 1C pottery), and medieval and Renaissance sculpture.

Musée des Beaux-Arts: The work of local sculptors and painters up to the present day.

Romans-sur-Isère	(34,200 inhab.)
26 Drôme	p.421 □ M 11

France's main production centre for high-quality footwear, Romans nestles against the side of a hill in the heart of the Drôme region. It was here in 1349 that Dauphiné was officially proclaimed part of France.

Romans-sur-Isère, church of Saint-Barnard

Saint-Barnard: A soldier turned monk, Barnard founded the abbey around which Romans was to grow in 837. The old abbey church is a fine building with bare façade, a massive yet elegant apse and solid belfry. Several Romanesque features survive. The door and lower portions of the nave date from the mid 12C, the transept and choir from the 12C, and the belfry from the 14C. The side chapels were added later. The cloister was demolished when the quai along the river was created. A beatiful doorway typical of Provençal Romanesque remains from a former belfry-porch. The broad single aisle retains its arcaded Romanesque walls (with Gothic upper sections). There are some fine capitals. On the vaulting of the dark 15C chapel of the Blessed Sacrament are traces of frescos. The hangings were worked from cartoons by a 15C Flemish painter.

The area behind the apse of Saint-Barnard is particularly picturesque (Place aux Herbes, the Rue des Trois-Carreaux, with the former Hôtel of the archbishops of Vienne, and the Rue des Clercs). The pedestrian precincts of old Romans lead to the *Jaquemart* — a 14C tower surviving from the old city walls, now a belfry.

Musée de la Chaussure et d'Ethnographie Régionale: 4,000 years of fashions in footwear, from late antiquity to our own day. The other section of this museum is devoted to the history and folklore of both the immediate vicinity and the whole of Dauphiné.

Environs: Saint-Donat-sur-l'Herbasse (12 km. NW): An old town with a finely-sited collegiate church, well known for its organ. Originally 11&12C, the church was

çade, is the superb *Maison du Carroir Doré* (1480, with carved posts). Attached to this is a small *Musé Archéologique et Historique*.

Environs: Château du Moulin (13 km. W.): Just outside the Sologne village of **Lassay-sur-Croisne** (late-15C church with frescos) stands the delightful moated Château du Moulin. A beautiful late feudal residence, in an area of forests and lakes, it was built 1480–1502 and has now been restored and refurnished.

much altered in the 15C (choir); the furnishings are 18C.

Romorantin-Lanthenay	(17,040 inhab.)
41 Loir-et-Cher	p.414☐ I 7

Situated in a part of the Sologne where the river Sauldre is dotted with small islands, Romorantin has many old houses (Rue de la Résistance, most notably) and the remains of a 15&16C château where François I spent his youth. The Town Hall houses a *Museum of Sologne*, which provides an excellent introduction to a very distinctive region (with exhibits relating to everyday life, agriculture, crafts and folklore of the area). Near the Renaissance *Hôtel de la Chancellerie* and the *Hôtel Saint-Pol*, with its remarkable glazed brick fa-

Ronchamp	(3,090 inhab.)
70 Haute-Saône	p.417☐ O 7

This large industrialized village is famous for the chapel built here in 1955 by Le Courbusier. Standing on one of the very last slopes of the Vosges massif, **Notre-Dame-du-Haut** is like a beautiful grey and white balloon held down on the ground by three cylindrical towers. With superb technical brilliance, it exploits all the potential of building in concrete, with sweeping curves and a graceful balance of architectural mass that fit perfectly in this hillside setting. The windows are so set in the thick walls that the light inside is at once glowing and tranquil.

Roquebrune	(11,250 inhab.)
06 Alpes-Maritimes	p.426☐ P 14

Built in the 10C by a Count of Ventimiglia on a spur of the mountainside formed by an earthquake, Roquebrune was once a fortress village inhabited by soldiers, craftsmen and peasant farmers. These inhabitants lived around the *keep*, which by the 15C had come to be referred to generally as a 'château'. A fief of the princes of Monaco, it was then proclaimed part of Alpes-Maritimes at the Revolution; Roquebrune was returned to Monaco in 1814. In 1848 it declared itself a free town, and then voted to become part of France. Restored to its 12C state, the 'château' affords excellent views. On the third floor there is a small furnished residence.

Roquebrune-sur-Argens (5,040 inhab.)
83 Var   p.426☐O 14

A charming little town on a rocky hill above the Argens plain. The 15C *church* contains four altarpieces dating from the 15&16C. A 17C chapel and monastic building survive in the hilltop convent of Notre-Dame-de-Pitié.

Roquetaillade (château)
33 Gironde   p.422☐F 12

At once imposing and graceful, the castle of Roquetaillade rears its crenellated keep above surrounding woods, fields and vineyards. Restored and slightly 'altered' by Viollet-le-Duc in the last century, it has a perhaps somewhat too authentically medieval air. Built at the start of the 14C by a cardinal (a nephew of Pope Clement V), its chapel—Saint-Michel—has undergone many alterations. The nearby village of Roaillan has a Romanesque church with an old statue of St.Eutrope.

Rouen   (118,330 inhab.)
76 Seine-Maritime   p.410☐H 3/4

The beautiful and historic capital of Normandy stands on the Caux plateau, straddling the Seine. A major river- and maritime-port and industrial centre, it has expanded W. in recent years. However, within 'Greater Rouen' the old city centre

Romorantin, the Carroir Doré

is of exceptional interest. Despite the horrific fires which ravaged it during the last war, it still retains wonderfully ornate soaring spires and belfries; the streets are still lined with attractive timber-framed houses, and the museums and galleries are still full of art treasures. For all the post-war concrete reconstruction, it remains a superb example of what a city can be, its pedestrian precincts redolent of two thousand years of history. Historic Rouen, on the right bank, grew to prosperity in the Gallo-Roman era. It had some important bishops (Prétextat, who was assassinated by order of Frédégonde; St.Romain and St.Ouen), and it was here that Rollo, the Viking who became official ruler of Normandy in 911, was baptized. The kings of France tried to wrest the city from the dukes (who were also English lords). But although besieged and occupied on more than one occasion,

Roquetaillade, the château

it did not finally fall to France until 1449. Taken by the Burgundians and sold to the English, it was here that Joan of Arc was interrogated, tried by an ecclesiastical court, and burned at the stake in May 1431. A modern church and memorial now stand in the Place du Vieux-Marché, close to where she died. At the same time Rouen also figures prominently in French literary history. The playwright Corneille was born here in 1606, and lived here until 1662; several of his plays were written here, while he was working as a professional lawyer (his first play, *Mélite,* was inspired by a local beauty). His nephew Fontenelle, who published his *Entretiens sur la Pluralité des Mondes* here, was also a native of the city. The young Pascal spent a number of years in Rouen, where he perfected a machine for helping his father do arithmetic calculations. He conducted his first experi-

ments here in the empty Faubourg Saint-Sever, and it was here too that he discovered Jansenism. A surgeon's son, the novelist Gustave Flaubert was born in a wing of the Hôtel-Dieu in 1821, and lived and died at Croisset, beside the Seine. Rouen and the surrounding region are beautifully evoked in *Madame Bovary* (1857).

Cathedral of Notre-Dame: A masterpiece of Gothic art, the vast, airy cathedral of Rouen is one of France's best known religious buildings. The spot on which it stands has been used for worship since the 4C, but the present structure is a completely remodelled version (started in about 1170) of an original Romanesque cathedral. Largely complete by the mid 13C, it has, nevertheless, been continually embellished over the ages. Side chapels were

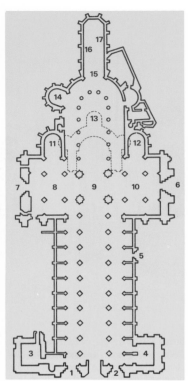

Rouen - cathedral of Notre-Dame 1 Portal of Saint-Jean **2** portal of Saint-Étienne **3** Tour Saint-Romain **4** Tour de Beurre **5** Portail des Maçons **6** Portail de la Calende **7** Portail des Libraires **8** N. transept **9** lantern tower **10** S. transept **11** chapel of the Blessed Sacrament **12** chapel of Joan of Arc **13** crypt **14** chapel of Saint-Pierre et Saint-Paul **15** Lady Chapel **16** tombs of the Brézé **17** tombs of the Cardinals Amboise

added in the late 13C, the Lady Chapel dates from the early 14C, and the so-called Tour de Beurre (Butter Tower) was built 1485–1506. The highly daring spire, visible for miles around, was begun in 1825. An example of 19C technological enterprise, it is made entirely of cast iron. Fortunately the Department of Historic Monuments removed the fine stained glass

from the windows in 1939 (the good glass in the other churches of Rouen was similarly placed in safety). Notre-Dame was partly burnt down in June 1940, when the Germans arrived, and was seriously damaged in April and June 1944. Threatening complete collapse, it was extensively restored, the restoration work being more or less finished by 1980. Now the worry concerns air pollution which is destroying the stone carvings around the entrance. The front was superbly caught by Monet at different hours of the day and in different weather conditions. Oriented in the traditional manner towards Jerusalem and the rising sun, the cruciform cathedral is some 450 ft. long and the remarkable, austere 15&18C Archbishop's Palace forms a kind of extension.

CATHEDRAL SQUARE (PARVIS), W. FRONT AND TOWERS: Now a pedestrian precinct, the 'parvis' in front of the cathedral contains the former Office of Finances (a surprisingly ornate building dating from 1509, now the Tourist Office), and a decidedly silly modern Palais des Congrès, incorporating the remains of a Renaissance hôtel destroyed in the bombing. Two circles on the ground denote the diameter of two old bells christened Georges d'Amboise and Jeanne d'Arc. The sumptuous W. front, with its three doors, is a breathtaking vision of carved stonework. Erected by Roulland le Roux in the early 16C, the large central doorway is surmounted by a free-standing gable with a host of statues, large and small. In the tympanum is a Tree of Jesse by the Rouennais sculptor Pierre des Aubeaux. Flanking this door are two delicately carved, slender spires and some statues in niches amid otherwise empty niches. The Portail Saint-Jean on the left and the Portail Saint-Étienne on the right probably date from 1170–80. A tympanum set into the former in the 13C features two tiers of sculptures, of St.John the Evangel-

Rouen, the cathedral, façade

Rouen, N.-D., Portail de la Calende

ist and St.John the Baptist. Making a superb tableau in stone, the infamous banquet of Herod is depicted with a delightfully acrobatic Salome dancing on her hands. The portions of the front above the side doors were adapted to the new Flamboyant style in the late 14C. The lower part of the substantial *Tour Saint-Romain* on the left of the façade is early 12C, the middle dates from the 1160s, and the top from the 15C. The original roof was destroyed in the war. The *Tour de Beurre* on the right resembles the Tour Saint-Romain structurally, but is Flamboyant (late 15C) in decoration, with light pinnacles and a delicate balustrade at the top. As its name recalls, this tower was built with money raised by dispensations allowing consumption of butter and other dairy produce during Lent. It houses a carillon of 56 bells hung in 1920, which are used for both religious and secular music.

N. SIDE (Rue Saint-Romain): The Cour d'Albane at the corner of the cathedral is named after the medieval college built by one Cardinal d'Albano, an archbishop of Rouen. From it one is able to admire the soaring cast-iron steeple (some 495 ft. high, it is the tallest in France). Running alongside the cathedral is the picturesque medieval *Rue Saint-Romain*. Lined with old timber-framed houses, it leads to the 15C outer portal, the 13–15C courtyard, and the *Portail des Libraires* (mainly late 13C). This last door, designed by Jean Davy, and carved as sumptuously as a piece of jewellery, is covered with statues of angels, Apostles, and male and female saints. Set in the base are 150 medallions with vivid and immensely varied scenes taken from Sacred History and medieval fables. All in all, a veritable picture-book in stone.

S. SIDE (Rue du Change, Place de la Calende): This side of the cathedral suffered badly during the war, but the *Portail de la Calende*—symmetrical and contemporary with the Portail des Libraires—survives. Also an astonishing achievement, it was likewise the work of Jean Davy and a school of 'Ymagiers'; these sculptors filled every available space with carving. Standing between two fine 13C door towers, the Portail de la Calende boasts 230 medallion scenes of Biblical events and the lives of Rouen's most famous archbishops. In the three-tier tympanum are scenes of Christ's Passion and Resurrection. The arches are adorned with angels, prophets and martyrs.

NAVE AND SIDE AISLES: The early-Gothic nave (mostly 13C) is simple, light, and majestic. Above the Louis XV organ chest is the great rose-window. It was not possible to remove the glass from this, and it was completely shattered during the bombing.

Rouen, Musée des Beaux-Arts, detail of the Cathedral by Monet

The side aisles, lined with chapels, appear curiously tall: galleries were originally planned but were decided against at the last moment, hence the odd arrangement of small columns resting on the capitals (a remarkably successful readjustment of design). The base of the Tour Saint-Romain, at the end of the N. aisle, is now the baptistery chapel. There then follows a line of chapels, most with very beautiful glass (13C in the Chapelle Saint-Jean, and latter half of the 15C in the Chapelle Saint-Sever, to mention only the most outstanding windows). At the head of the right aisle, beneath the Tour de Beurre, is a large Flamboyant chapel. Gutted by bombs, the S. aisle has several modern chapels with contemporary stained-glass windows. One chapel that survived the war contains photographs taken in 1944, showing the devastated cathedral virtually at the point of collapse.

CROSSING AND TRANSEPT: Four massive piers carry the lantern-tower which forms the base for the spire. The effect is of a breathtaking great well of light. Largely 13C, the bare transept arms are richly decorated around the doorways with statues and canopies, crocketed gables, balustrades and rose-windows. The charming Flamboyant staircase in the left transept was begun in 1480 by Guillaume Pontifs. One of the chapels in this transept has Eustache Desplanche's fine Pietà (*c.* 1590). The 14C stained glass has been replaced in the N. rose-window. The S. transept contains a splendid 15C *Ecce Homo,* as well as superb 14C and Renaissance glass. The Chapelle Sainte-Jeanne-d'Arc has modern windows by Max Ingrand.

CHOIR AND AMBULATORY: Excellently restored since the war, the simple 13C choir has both old and modern furnishings, with a high altar surmounted by Christ flanked by two 18C angels. Around it runs an ambulatory with radiating chapels with blue and red 13C glass. The chapel of *Saint-Barthélemy,* known as the Chapelle du Revestiaire (Robing Chapel) because it was used as a vestry by the canons, is one of Guillaume Pontif's most beautiful creations (1479). There are several tombs and tombstones in the ambulatory. The *Chapel of Our Lady,* an axial chapel, is an exquisite example of Rayonnant Gothic. Built 1302–20, it is a veritable treasure house of 14C glass and sculpture. It contains the Gothic *tomb* of the Seneschal Pierre de Brézé, the spectacular Renaissance *mausoleum* of Louis de Brézé (1535–44), and the large *Tomb of the Cardinals of Amboise,* designed by Roulland le Roux in the early 16C and lavishly carved. Below the present choir the crypt survives from the 11C church; it has a well and a casket containing the heart of King Charles V.

Saint-Maclou: A jewel of Flamboyant architecture, dating from 1437–1517, this church was badly damaged during the war. Almost totally restored, it has now recovered much of its former splendour. The spire, almost 270 ft. tall, is 19C. The façade has a five-bayed porch projecting in front of it, with two ornate doors mostly attributed to the famous 16C sculptor Jean Goujon (who is also held to have created the N. door in the Rue Martainville, and to have decorated the columns supporting the organ chest (1521) on the inside wall of the façade). At the top of the nave there is a Flamboyant spiral staircase formerly attached to the rood screen.

Aître Saint-Maclou: The once insalubrious area of Saint-Maclou has been exceptionally well restored. Hidden behind timber-framed houses is a mysterious, seemingly timeless courtyard: the 16C arcaded parish cemetery of Saint-Maclou (the S. arcade, built about a century later, never received any corpses). Once colourfully painted, the carvings on the columns and the wooden frieze above the arches depict a dance of death with skulls, various bones, and gravediggers' tools.

Rouen, Saint-Maclou, door leaf

Rouen, Aître St-Maclou, detail

Saint-Ouen: A wonderful light, Gothic church with a highly decorated Flamboyant spire. A former abbey church, it was built between 1318 and the second quarter of the 16C. Despite this unusual slowness in construction (caused by the Hundred Years War and financial problems), the original concept was consistently respected and there is an overall stylistic unity, although the 19C saw fit to add a somewhat lacklustre façade. Once attached to the great abbey of Saint-Ouen, it is particularly interesting on the S. side, where the Porche des Marmousets shelters a door with a lavishly carved tympanum (scenes from the *Golden Legend*). It is worth standing back from the church to admire the subtle disposition of the apse and to see the central tower at its best.

INTERIOR: The long, graceful nave has good stained glass. The organ (the chest dating from 1630) is one of the best in France. Closed off by a marvellous 18C screen, the choir (1318–39) has beautiful 14C windows following on from those in the nave. This fine show of glass is completed by contemporary work by Max Ingrand. The windows (mostly 14C) in the radiating chapels around the ambulatory depict lives of the saints. The long apsidal Lady Chapel contains tombs with recumbent figures and numerous saints.

Other churches: *Saint-Éloi* is now a Protestant church. Though very dilapidated, it has a fine 18C organ. The 19C *Saint-Gervais* has a number of sarcophagi and a 4C crypt. *Saint-Godard* is late 15C; nave and two aisles have wooden vaulting and there are two remarkable 16C windows. *Saint-Nicaise* is partly a post-war reconstruction, but the choir and some of the windows are 16C. It has a good 17C altarpiece. 16C Flamboyant, *Saint-Patrice* has bright colourful windows dating from 1538–1625. A rather grand and cold late-17/early-18C church, *Saint-Roman* has 16C glass, adding a touch of warmth. There is a slightly precious looking organ and a painted dome. Unusually wide, *Saint-Vivien* (14&15C) has an interesting door, a late-16C organ chest, an 18C pulpit, and a fine altarpiece (1700). A fine Louis XVI structure grafted on to the classical Hôtel-Dieu 1758–80, *Sainte-Madeleine* is decorated both outside and in with carvings by the Rouennais sculptor Jaddoulle. Dedicated in 1979, the modern church of *Sainte-Jeanne-d'Arc* was designed by Louis Arretche. It is like a great cage of light (the windows were designed to accommodate the fine old glass from Saint-Vincent, a church destroyed in the war—see the later entry: Vieux-Marché).

Palais de Justice: Seriously damaged in the last war, the old courthouse has been meticulously restored to its former glory. Flamboyant in style, with touches of Renaissance elegance, it dates in part from the first half of the 16C (the main building was erected 1508 – 26). The superb courtyard elevation contrives to be at once austere and ornate: the delicately sculpted upper section is a riot of exuberant carving, despite the delicacy of the work. The impressive great Salle des Procureurs has been reconstructed along the old pattern and has magnificent panelling. In 1976, during the restoration work, remains of a Romanesque structure with Jewish characteristics were discovered—almost certainly an 11C or early-12C synagogue.

Hôtel de Bourgtheroulde: Place de la Pucelle. A curious building erected by Guillaume le Roux (a member of the aristocratic de Bourgtheroulde family) and his son, the Abbé d'Aumale. It gives on to

a square which despite much destruction still retains some fine timber-framed houses. Access into the courtyard of the Hôtel is through a restored vaulted pavilion. Begun in the early 16C, it combines Flamboyant Gothic (the end building) and Renaissance styles. The gallery and friezes on the left date from about 1520. The reliefs illustrate Plutarch's *Triumphs* and the famous meeting of François I of France and Henry VIII of England at the Field of the Cloth of Gold.

Tour Jeanne d'Arc: Rue Bouvreuil and Rue du Donjon. This huge, solid tower (the top is 19C) was the keep of the great 13C castle, of which it is now the only vestige. Before her trial Joan of Arc underwent more than one interrogation in the low ribvaulted chamber here.

Fierte Saint-Romain: Place de la Haute-Vieille-Tour. Backing on to some restored market buildings, this graceful Romanesque shrine was miraculously undamaged by the fighting that raged all around. It was

Rouen, the Palais de Justice

built to house the 'fierte' (reliquary) of Rouen's patron saint, St. Romain.

Place du Vieux-Marché, Gros-Horloge, Old Rouen: The old market place where Joan of Arc was burned at the stake in 1431 has retained its ancient timber-framed houses and residences such as have been demolished in other quarters of the city. Alongside these old façades, and blending well with them, there is also the modern complex consisting of the new church of *Sainte-Jeanne-d'Arc* and the long *Mémorial* dedicated to the Maid. Leading off from this square towards the cathedral, the *Rue du Gros-Horloge* cuts through the heart of both old and modern Rouen, passing under the carved arch of the Pavillon du Gros-Horloge, on each side of which is a huge clock face with a single arm. With a 14C bell tower (medieval bells) standing beside it, this wooden edifice dating from 1527 has become one of the symbols of the city. Many of Rouen's old houses were lost in the war, but at the same time hundreds of picturesque timber-framed façades have been stripped of their later overlays and now the old city centre seems to be full of them. Specially worth visiting are the *Rues Saint-Romain, Martainville, Damiette, Eau-de-Robec* and *Beauvoisine.*

Musée des Antiquités: Rue Louis-Ricard, 198 Rue Beauvoisine. Housed in a 17C convent, this very varied museum is devoted to the distant and not so distant history of the region. The following are of particular interest: a remarkable large Gallo-Roman mosaic discovered at Lillebonne, fine medieval exhibits, a 15C tapestry known as the tapestry of the Winged Deer, and carved fragments from now-demolished houses; there are also some beautiful carved ivories, delicate alabaster figures, and reliquary and processional crosses.

Musée des Beaux-Arts: Square Verdrel. This vast 19C building forms a world of its own, with a number of first-rate paintings, particularly from the 17C (two superb Poussins) and Impressionist (Monet, Sisley and Renoir). There is a beautiful sol-

Rouen, Rue Saint-Romain

Rouen, the Gros-Horloge

Rouen, Musée des Beaux-Arts, 'Diana Bathing', by Clouet

emn *Virgin and Saints* by Gérard David (*c.* 1450–1523) and a group sculpture verging on the obscene by the famous portraitist and horse painter Géricault. The nearby Hôtel d'Hocqueville displays a fine collection of faience, comprising hundreds of exhibits, all locally produced between the second quarter of the 16C and the end of the 18C.

Other museums. Musée Corneille: 4 Rue de la Pie. Dedicated to the 17C playwright Pierre Corneille, it is housed in the much-altered house where he was born. There is another museum in his memory in the family *Maison des Champs* in **Petit-Couronne**, 8 km. from Rouen. **Musée Flaubert et d'Histoire de la Médecine:** Hôtel-Dieu, 52 Rue Lecat. The 'surgeon's wing' (1755) has been refurnished as it would have been in Flaubert's day, and

there are numerous papers, etc. relating to this great 19C novelist and his family. The history of medicine is traced through a good number of interesting displays; the museum also possesses an 18C 'collection of curiosities'. On the ground floor there are statues of saints reputed to be healers. The memory of Gustave Flaubert is also honoured in the one surviving wing (Louis XV in style) of his house at Croisset, which is one of the inner suburbs of Rouen. This little museum has furniture and mementoes of the master. **Musée Jeanne d'Arc:** Place du Vieux-Marché. An entertaining museum of not totally convincing waxworks, with some interesting documents. **Muséum d'Histoire Naturelle, d'Ethnographie et de Préhistoire:** 198 Rue Beauvoisine. A curious museum, highly instructive, very varied, and sometimes rather surprising (strange collections of hand-embroidered eggs and monstrosities from the animal world). Though somewhat old-fashioned, the displays are clear, and cover geology as well as prehistory and ethnography. There is a good collection of stuffed birds. **Musée Le Secq-de-Tournelles** (ironwork): Rue Thiers, Rue Jacques-Villon. Some wonderful and most unusual ironwork displayed in a former church. Unique of its kind, this museum combines famous exhibits such as the 13C screen from the Abbey of Ourscamp, and keys and locks of all periods, with thousands of often amazing objects both functional and decorative.

Rouffach	(5,100 inhab.)
68 Haut-Rhin	p.417□O 6

A small town at the foot of the vineyards formerly owned by the bishops of Strasbourg. The home of Marshal Lefebvre (husband of the celebrated 'Madame Sans-Gêne'), it has many houses with oriel windows and step or scroll gables.

Notre-Dame: This magnificent church, built in an attractive patchwork of grey, beige and pink stone, was under construction from the 11C to the late 15C. Nevertheless, Romanesque (transept and initial bays of the nave) and Gothic are quite happily combined. Standing on a tall daïs in the broad nave is a 15C Madonna. On either side of the indifferent modern altar are stairs worked in stone (part of a now destroyed rood-screen). 18C carved choir stalls, and late-15C font lavishly sculpted in pink stone.

Alongside the church at the end of the square, the late-16/early-17C *Hôtel de Ville*, the *Tour des Sorcières* (Witch's Tower; 13C base), and the *cornmarket* (1569) together make a picturesque sight. Of the numerous monasteries that once existed here,

Rouffach, the Tour des Sorcières

only the 15C Franciscan church survives, with an unusual external pulpit, which is delicately carved.

Rouffignac	(260 inhab.)
24 Dordogne	p.419□H 11

Intentionally burnt down by the Germans in 1944, this rebuilt Périgourdin village is now more functional than attractive to the eye. Miraculously undamaged, the 16C Renaissance *church* has a curious bell tower façade containing an exquisitely carved porch (slightly damaged by the passage of time). The unusual interior has spiral columns set into the round piers. There are no capitals. On the inside wall of the front elevation is an attractive gallery. The modern choir is Romanesque in style.

Rouffignac, church portal

new town designed by Claude Ferret are the huge, domed concrete market building and, in particular, the church of Notre-Dame—a remarkable elliptical reinforced concrete structure.

Environs: Talmont (16 km. SE): One of the most delightful villages in Charente-Maritime, it is built on a promontory jutting into the estuary and has white houses, narrow streets full of hollyhocks, and the marvellous 12&15C church of Sainte Radegonde, on a rocky cliff with a graveyard around it.

Royat   (4,490 inhab.)
63 Puy-de-Dôme   p.420☐J 10

A spa since classical times, Royat stands on the slopes of the cool Tiretaine valley. In the spa itself remains of Roman baths have been found (there must have been several pools, decorated with mosaics). The name Royat derives from *Rubiacum*, 'the red place'.

Saint-Léger: A simple 11&13C church, with a latin cross ground plan, it was fortified in the 13C with buttresses supporting crenellations and machicolations. Two beautiful Gothic rose-windows adorn the apse and wall of the right transept. The apse is 19C. Inside, the columns abutting against the walls of the nave have interestingly modelled capitals. In the crypt the vault rests on columns with beautiful foliate and geometric capitals, and there is a Madonna which has been venerated locally for many years.

Royaumont (abbey)
95 Val d'Oise   p.428☐I 4

Founded by St. Louis in 1228 and richly

Environs: Grotte de Rouffignac (4 km. S.): Stretching for almost 10 km. (there is a little railway for visitors), these caves have numerous paintings of prehistoric animals dating from the mid- or late-Magdalenian period. **Château de l'Herm** (4 km. N.): The still-proud ruins of this 15C manor stand in almost total isolation. Moated and raised up on a slight hill, it must once have been quite attractive. Now sightless windows look out from a gaunt, empty shell of a building.

Royan   (18,700 inhab.)
17 Charente-Maritime   p.418☐E 10

Completely destroyed by the shelling of 1945, this sea resort stands at the mouth of the Gironde estuary. Of interest in the

endowed, the royal abbey of Royaumont
was one of the grandest medieval abbeys
in the Ile-de-France. Mazarin and a number of princes held the abbey at different
times. During the Revolution it was sold
as national property. Unhappily it fell into
unsympathetic hands; the church was
demolished, the relics, furnishings, and
works of art were sold and the monastery
buildings were turned into a factory. The
still significant remains of the abbey (now
restored) stand in a large park through
which the river Thève (which splits into
several arms at this point) flows. The property now belongs to the *Fondation Royaumont* and is used by seminaries, and for
courses, conferences, and cultural activities, especially concerts. What remains of
the 13C abbey church gives only an idea
of its original huge size. Virginia creeper
spreads over the beautiful great 13C cloister, whose huge arched walks with terrace
roofs enclose an attractive garden. In the
superb Gothic *refectory* (also of the same
period) is the tomb of the Comte d'Harcourt, carved by Antoine Coysevox, which

Royat, church of Saint-Léger

Talmont, church of Sainte-Radegonde

Royaumont, abbey, aerial view

was formerly in the church. The kitchens have been restored to their medieval state, and various works of art are exhibited there. The former monastic buildings now house the Fondation and its visitors. Now known as the 'Château de Royaumont', the small 18C abbot's palace stands in an adjacent property.

Rue	(3,120 inhab.)
80 Somme	p.410□I 2

Crowning the Hôtel de Ville of this quiet village is a solid looking turreted belfry (15C). The *Chapelle du Saint-Esprit*, once a place of pilgrimage, dates from the 15&16C. It is a exceptionally fine example of Flamboyant: the carved stone is like delicate lace, and the spectacular vaulting with pendent keystones is a work of rare perfec-

tion. The wonderful altarpiece harmonizes with the rest of the décor.

Ruffec	(4,670 inhab.)
16 Charente	p.419□G 10

Destroyed by fire, the church of *Saint-André* was rebuilt in the 15C around the fine Romanesque façade which had fortunately escaped the tragedy. Tall columns separate the main door from the richly carved arches which flank it. In the tympanum of the left arch there are Judith and Holofernes. Standing in the graceful arcading above are statues of the Apostles.

Environs: Lichères (18 km. S.): On its own in the open fields, the church of *Saint-Denis* was formerly attached to the Abbey of Charroux. The interior of the ele-

Lichères, Romanesque church of Saint-Denis

giant apse is arcaded. The Romanesque door has a tympanum with a magnificent arch around it.

Rugles (2,640 inhab.)
27 Eure p.410□G/H 5

The old established village of Rugles lies on the meandering river Risle. The castle has now been demolished. Drawing attention to itself with its huge Flamboyant tower, the composite church of *Saint-Germain* is 13–16C. *Notre-Dame-Outre-l'Eau*, across the river, is now redundant. Probably early 11C, it was altered in the 16,17&18C, and still has a 16C carved wooden ceiling.

Sabres (1,150 inhab.)
40 Landes p.422☐E 13

This village in the heart of the Landes de Gascogne natural park is hidden away in the immense maritime pine plantations which conceal the countryside from the main roads. It is typically Landais. The church, medieval in origin, was altered in the 16C and again later; it has a fine Renaissance doorway. Little old trains run on a piece of disused track and serve the Marquèze 'airial'. A very unusual ecological museum is devoted to life in the Landes through the ages. A typical hamlet has been reconstructed in the middle of the wood and the superb 19C house already there is now surrounded by other buildings which were dismantled and removed from abandoned 'airials'. A water mill with a threshing floor has also been rebuilt a short way off. Those running the natural park are determined to keep alive the activities of the now depopulated 'Grande Lande' and to preserve traditions of the past. Among other projects, they have established a museum of pine products at **Luxey** (22 km. NE of Sabres) in a pine resin distillery (operational 1859 –1954). There is a very beautiful Landes house of 1722, with a balcony typical of the area; simple workshops still contain some old equipment.

Saché (600 inhab.
37 Indre-et-Loir p.414☐G

The fine 15&17C manor house of Saché (with medieval foundations) is surrounded by a very attractive but simple park. I houses the *Musée Balzac*, which has autographs, corrected proofs and many other mementoes of the great writer who came from Tours. He was a friend of the manor house's owners and he stayed and worked here on many occasions (*Lys dans la Vallée* is set in the region). You can visit his bedroom, a rather cold and comfortless room where the 'galley slave of pen and ink' wrote for hours on end, either in bed or at a small desk.

Saint-Aignan (3,680 inhab.
41 Loir-et-Cher p.414☐H

This little town is dominated by a château (rebuilt under François I in Renaissance style) which stands on the side of a small hill by the Cher. **Collegiate church:** This

Saint-Aignan, crypt of the collegiate church

sturdy church with a superb bell tower is surrounded by houses. Begun *c.* 1080, work went on until the end of the 12C. It was later altered and decorated but then suffered in the Wars of Religion, in the Revolution and from a rather over-ambitious 19C restoration. Its windows are mostly modern (the old ones were shattered in 1940); its majestic choir contains some remarkable decorated capitals. *Crypt:* This follows the plan of the choir and has three apsidal chapels decorated with delicate and unusual capitals. There are also paintings from the 12–15C. The central part of the fresco covering the half-dome of the middle chapel is Romanesque. It depicts Christ in Glory with two saints bestowing divine blessings on the paralysed. The paintings around it are 15C.

Environs: Thésée (9 km. NW): There are ruins of an extensive Gallo-Roman establishment on the site of *Tasciaca*, a stage on the Roman road from Bourges to Tours.

Saint-Amand-les-Eaux　(16,950 inhab.)
59 Nord　　　　　　　　　　　　p.411□K 2

This historic town lies on the edge of a majestic forest and is the only spa in the Nord. Its architectural claim to fame rests with the ruins of a Benedictine abbey. The supremely elegant entrance pavilion or *Échevinage* is a masterpiece of Flemish Renaissance. Two octagonal sections have high sandstone basements and faces decorated with carved tablets around a doorway with columns. The whole is enhanced by a charming bell tower. Inside there are delightful Watteau paintings of 1782. Only the façade of the abbey church remains, together with the 260 ft. tower flanked by two turrets. This splendid group, built 1626–40, remains a fine example of the baroque despite its mutilation. It contains a museum devoted to bells and it also has a remarkable collection of local faience.

Saint-André
66 Pyrénées-Orientales   (1,020 inhab.)   p.424☐J 16

The church of *Saint-André-de-Sorède,* partially rebuilt in the 12C around the remains of an earlier building, has a remarkable, though crudely worked, lintel over the doorway. Depicting Christ in Glory in a mandorla, it has kneeling angels and Apostles set in arches. The window above the doorway is framed by carvings which originally came from elsewhere. The N. transept has an archaic altar table which is probably Spanish-Moorish from the 10C.

Environs: Saint-Génis-des-Fontaines (3.5 km. W): The church is partly pre-

Romanesque, although it was later extensively rebuilt (reconsecrated in the 12C). Its doorway has a remarkable marble lintel of 1020, which is clearly based on that of Saint-André-de-Sorède and shows Christ enthroned in a mandorla supported by two kneeling angels and flanked by Apostles in arches.

Saint-Benoît-sur-Loire
45 Loiret   (1,800 inhab.)   p.415☐I 7

The famous abbey church of Saint-Benoît stands a short distance from the Loire, its large, rather austere Romanesque outline dominating the countryside of orchards and farms. Benedictines still live near the massive basilica (the monastery was reinstated as an abbey in 1959) and the area is redolent of the long history of the religious community. When the first few Benedictine monks arrived and founded a monastery the site was known as Fleury, after a former Gallo-Roman owner. It became a focus of Christianity when the body of

St-André, church of St-André, façade

St-Benoît, bell tower and porch

St.Benedict was brought from Monte Cassino in Italy in 672. The abbey, a great centre of learning, was ravaged on three separate occasions in the 9C by Norman pirates, the relics being saved each time. Rebuilt and surrounded by walls, Fleury was at its height in the 10&11C under the great abbots St. Abbon and Gauzlin (a natural son of Hugues Capet). The abbey suffered in the Hundred Years War and in the Wars of Religion but it was revived in the 17C under Cardinal Richelieu, who introduced the Saint-Maur reform. It declined at the end of the 18C, being sold off in the Revolution and destroyed (only the church was spared). The poet Max Jacob, a converted Jew, found peace near the great abbey church before dying as a deportee in the Drancy camp.

Basilica: This vast grey and pink abbey church, about 370 ft. long, is visible from afar. Its long period of construction splits into three separate phases. The bell tower and porch appears to date from Gauzlin's tenure of office (1004–30), although certain experts think it is substantially later.

The choir and transept date from 1067 onwards and the nave was begun in about 1150; the church was consecrated in 1218.

EXTERIOR: An almost free-standing tower, whose original upper section was removed in 1529, now forms a narthex, although it was built as a separate tower. The solid, central bell tower above the crossing ends in a lantern. The apse has radiating chapels and the bases of two square towers which framed it until 1780 are still visible. The early-13C *N. doorway* is highly ornate; the tympanum depicts Christ teaching the Evangelists and the lintel shows the translation of the relics of St.Benedict.

INTERIOR: *W. tower:* Open on all four sides, this was added both for defensive purposes and to enhance the prestige of the abbey. Square ground plan. The bays of the ground floor have rib vaults (fine historiated and foliate capitals). The tall, upper chamber, which served as a chapel, has capitals depicting human figures. The *nave* has five bays and rib vaults; the aisles have groin vaults. Simple and pleasing, the body of the church appears almost Gothic

Saint-Benoît, capital in the basilica

Germigny-des-Prés, church, mosaic of the Ravenna school

at first sight. There are some fine 15C choir stalls at the crossing. *Choir, apse and transept:* The choir is a masterpiece of Romanesque architecture. Deep and high, it consists of a straight section leading to a raised apse with a colonnade, blind arcades in a false triforium and 15 windows in the clerestory. The pavement has a mosaic brought from Italy in the 16C. The transept is contemporary with the choir, having been finished in 1108; the crossing has a dome on pendentives above which there is the central bell tower. The stalls date from 1413 and there is a recumbent figure of Philippe I (d. 1108). The N. transept contains a gracious 14C alabaster statue of Notre-Dame-de-Fleury; the wall facing the chapels has an unusual mask which probably represents a Norman pirate. The much-restored right transept has a large 17C altarpiece. In all, the church has 550 capitals, twelve of which are outside; some of the most interesting are on the right in the upper part of the choir. *Crypt:* Beneath the apse and the ambulatory, a fine, highly restored 11C structure. At its centre, a hollow pillar houses the reliquary of St. Benedict. Subtly lit by windows it leads to the Chapel of Saint-Mommole, part of buildings predating the present church, and probably 10C.

Environs: Germigny-des-Prés (5 km. NW): This small village contains a pleasant surprise in the shape of a Byzantine church. Built in the early 9C by a Bishop of Orléans and friend of Charlemagne, it was restored in the 19C. It has a lovely 9C mosaic in its small E. apse. The only work of the school of Ravenna in France, it consists of 130,000 cubes of coloured glass, which depict the Ark of the Covenant surrounded by angels. The rustic group depicting St.Anne teaching the Virgin as a child is 16C. Near the church is the top of a 16C graveyard lantern.

Saint-Bertrand-de-Comminges
	(250 inhab.)
31 Haute-Garonne	p.423□G 15

Saint-Bertrand-de-Comminges, on the edge of the deep valley of the Garonne, retains some old ramparts and an imposing cathedral on an isolated crag. The site is superb and the village is one of the most picturesque in France. In classical times it was the site of *Lugdunum Convenarum*, where Herod Antipas and Herodias, the murderers of the John the Baptist exiled by Caligula in AD 37, probably died. After the troubles of the 5&6C it was abandoned and only revived from the 12C onwards with the building (on top of the hill) of the cathedral by Bertrand de l'Isle Jourdain, Bishop of Comminges. The remains of the Gallo-Roman town—theatre, temple, baths and basilica—have been uncovered on the plain. The upper town preserves several 15&16C houses.

Cathedral of Notre-Dame: Begun in about 1120, and again in 1304, it is partially Romanesque (façade, tower, first bay of the original building) but mostly Gothic. The second phase of building ended in about 1350 and the building was enlarged with the addition of chapels in the late 14&15C. Splendid woodwork and windows were added in the 16C. It is flanked by a cloister, three sides of which are Romanesque; the fourth, which runs along the church, dates from the 15&16C. The cloister contains sarcophagi (walk to the right of the entrance), carved capitals and a pillar with statues of the four Evangelists. *Interior:* The cathedral has some fine woodwork as a result of the generosity of

St-Bertrand-de-C., statues in the cloister

Bishop Jean de Mauléon: rood screen, choir screen, high altar retable (repainted), 66 fine, carved Renaissance stalls, bishop's throne (all completed by 1535). Behind the high altar there is the large shrine known as the mausoleum of St.Bertrand (15C). The Lady Chapel on the left has the tomb (with a recumbent figure) of Bishop Hugues de Châtillon (d.1532). There is a 16C organ in the short nave. One of the chapels and the former chapterhouse above the cloister have 16C Flemish tapestries, as well as copes and ecclesiastical ornaments.

Galerie du Trophée: A former Benedictine chapel near the cathedral and a stoneyard are used to house statues from a 1C imperial trophy which were found in the lower town; also milestones, a sarcophagus and other carvings.

Saint-Bertrand-de-Comminges, church, recumbent figure of Hugues de Châtillon

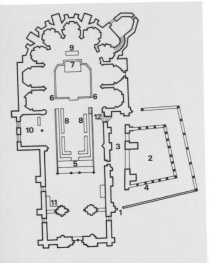

Saint-Bertrand-de-Comminges - cathedral 1 Entrance **2** cloister **3** sarcophagi **4** pillar of the Evangelists **5** rood-screen **6** choir enclosure **7** altar **8** stalls **9** mausoleum of St. Bertrand **10** Lady Chapel **11** organ **12** treasury.

Environs: Valcabrère (2 km. NE): Set amidst cypresses, the church of *Saint-Just* and its churchyard blend perfectly with their surroundings. 11&12C Romanesque, it has a strong, square bell tower and a strange apse. It was once the cathedral of Comminges. On the N. side there is a fine doorway from the late 12C which is framed by statues of St. Stephen, St. Justus, St. Pastor and, probably, St. Helen.

Saint-Bonnet-le-Château
(2,210 inhab.)
42 Haute-Loire   p.420 □ L 11

Saint Bonnet, pleasantly situated on a hill at the end of the Monts du Forez, is dominated by the mighty outline of its early-15C Gothic **collegiate church**. The simple bell towers are most impressive, with their large, mullioned bays. Entering through a Renaissance doorway, you come upon three aisles separated by short, octagonal pillars which lack capitals. The *monks' cellar* contains naturally mummified bodies, probably those of victims of the Wars of Religion, who were thrown in there alive when the town was captured. The crypt has wonderfully fresh wall paintings from the 15C; reminiscent of the Italian school, they depict New Testament subjects.

Saint-Brieuc	(56,280 inhab.)
22 Côtes-du Nord	p.412□C 5

The prefecture of the Côtes-du-Nord, it stands on a plateau between the Gouët and Gouëdic valleys. A few houses with overhanging upper storeys have survived (in the Rue Fardel and the Rue du Gouët in particular) around the austere **cathedral of Saint-Étienne**, which was built in the 12C and rebuilt in the 14&15C. It is both church and fortress, with massive towers, arrow slits and machicolations. There is a fine Flamboyant rose-window in the right transept. Inside there are numerous tombs, as well as some 15C tomb recesses, including that of the 13C St.Guillaume Pinchon, Bishop of Saint-Brieuc and the first Breton to be canonized (in a transept chapel). In the Rue Ruffelet there is a 15C fountain next to the chapel of Notre-Dame-de-la-Fontaine (altered in the 19C), which was built on the site where St.Brieuc and his followers established themselves when evangelizing the area in the late 5C.

Environs: Quintin (19 km. SE): This little hillside town on the banks of the Gouët still has some beautiful 16&17C houses (Place 1830, Grand Rue, Rue Notre-Dame, with its pretty 15C fountain). The *château* is unfinished and consists of a 17C pavilion and some 18C buildings. The basilica of Notre-Dame dates from the last century

and houses a statue of Notre-Dame-de-Délivrance once venerated by pregnant women.

Saint-Cirq-Lapopie	(170 inhab.)
46 Lot	p.423□H/I 13

This village occupies one of the most astonishing sites in Quercy, clinging perilously to the edge of a cliff above the Lot. It has a late-15C fortified church. From the reign of Louis XI until the last century the village was well known for its woodworkers. It is full of old-world charm and still has 14&15C timber-framed houses with overhanging upper storeys. The *Maison Rignault* contains the small *Maison la Gardette* which exhibits furniture and oriental objets d'art. Ruins of a 13C château.

Environs: Cabrerets (on the right bank of the Lot, in the Célé valley): Château from the 14&15C. Above it on the hillside are the **Peche-Merle** stalactite caves with

St-Brieuc, cathedral, recumbent figure

Saint-Cirq-Lapopie, aerial view of the fortified village and the site

paintings which may date from the Aurignacian period (mammoths, bison, horses, human figures, strange, stylized outlines). In one chamber there are the footprints of a prehistoric man or woman and child.

Saint-Claude   (14,090 inhab.)
39 Jura   p.421 □N 9

Built on a narrow terrace between two torrents, this tourist centre and, since the 19C, pipe capital was once an important place of pilgrimage. The **Cathedral of Saint-Pierre** is 14&15C and built in a variety of styles, beginning with the Gothic and ending in the 18C with a classical façade. The apse, fortified with watch towers, lends originality to the building.

Nave and two aisles are remarkably restrained and contrast with the ornate furnishing of the choir. There are superb choir stalls carved by Jean de Vitry (mid 15C) depicting the Apostles and Prophets. Fine 16C retable in the nave.

Saint-Dié   (26,540 inhab.)
88 Vosges   p.417 □O 6

Steeped in 2,000 years of history and surrounded by wooded hills, this is one of the oldest towns in the Vosges, as can be seen from the Celtic camp of Bure and the wealth of archaeological sites in the region. Jules Ferry, one of the pioneers of national education in France, was born here in 1832 and it has always been a cultural centre. In

Saint-Dié, cloister

Saint-Dié, cloister, detail

the 16C a team of local geographers, the 'Gymnase Vosgien', decided to name the newly discovered continent Amérique; the word appears for the first time in their *Cosmographiae Introductio* printed in Saint-Dié in 1507 and carefully preserved in the Bibliothèque Municipale (Town Library) beside a splendid illuminated gradual from the same period. The town was burnt by the retreating German army in 1944 but has been carefully rebuilt and includes a fine group of pink sandstone religious buildings. The **cathedral** lay in ruins after the war apart from its cold, solemn 18C façade and two square towers. The Romanesque nave (1155) had to be completely rebuilt, as did the choir and the transept, both 14C. There are some 13C stained-glass windows and about 40 vigorous Romanesque capitals. The small 12C

church of **Notre-Dame**, parallel to the cathedral, was miraculously spared. It is one of the most successful examples of Rhenish Romanesque in the Vosges. The façade is modest and has a separate bell tower, which with the porch forms a narthex. The simple, well-proportioned nave is groin vaulted and it has alternating sturdy and slender piers. The walls are plain apart from a frieze of billet moulding. There is a lovely white limestone statue of Notre-Dame-de-Galilée (14C). The open cloister links the two Romanesque churches and exhibits all the richness of the Flamboyant (15&16C). A curious 15C stone pulpit backs on to one of the walks outside.

A short way from the town centre stands the early-16C **Chapelle Saint-Roch** with a fine altar and a tall triptych by Claude Bassot (17C) as its altarpiece.

Saint-Émilion	(3,360 inhab.)
33 Gironde	p.418☐F 12

This, one of the great wine towns of Bordeaux, is built of pale, local limestone and, indeed, in parts, is built into the rock. The site is supposed to have attracted the Gallo-Roman poet Ausonius, after whom a fine wine has been named and who was reputed to have lived in a luxurious villa surrounded by vines. Emilion was a wandering monk of Breton origin who settled as a hermit in a cave, worked some miracles, gathered a number of followers and observed the rule of St.Benedict. The village grew up around the religious establishment and took the name of *Villa de Sancto-Emiliano* and then *Sainct-Milion*. Ramparts were added and, during the Revolution, it was the last refuge of the Girondins, who were finally captured and executed. The town, behind the unusual 'Mur des Dominicains', the remnant of a vanished convent, still has one of its old gates, sections of walls, and Romanesque and Gothic houses. It is all very picturesque

and at its centre is the charming Place du Marché. Note the unusual, ruined *Couvent des Cordeliers* (Franciscan Convent) and its 14&15C cloister.

Église Monolithe: The bell tower is partly 12C but the bulk is 16C and perches on the top of a cliff. It appears to have been part of a vanished church but the church does still in fact exist—below, at the foot of the cliff. Stripped of its contents, it occupies an underground chamber which was slowly excavated in the 11&12C from a series of small caves. It was once painted all over, but the walls were scraped when it was exploited for saltpetre. On one vault, however, you can see two angels with four wings which have the effect of an optical illusion—they appear alternately to be hollowed out and in relief.

Beside the church, note the defaced *Chapelle de la Trinité* with a polygonal 13C apse, and the dark *Ermitage de Saint-Émilion* (an underground cell and oratory),

Saint-Émilion, cloister of the collegiate church (14C)

as well as some catacombs. A steep lane leads from the Trinité to the 13C citadel known as the *Château du Roi*.

Collegiate church: The canons of Saint-Émilion thought the Église Monolithique too unrefined and had a collegiate church built in the upper part of the town. This, together with a large religious establishment, formed a group which is still known as the Doyenné. The church has a single 12C Romanesque aisle preceded by a bell-tower-porch. The choir and transept are Gothic (14–16C). In the nave there are wall paintings of the Virgin (12C) and of the Life of St. Catherine (13C). Next to the church there is a large 14C Gothic cloister and nearby there is a small 13C chapel for the chapter which houses a small museum.

Environs: Montagne (4 km. NE): Pretty 12C Romanesque church, much restored (ribbed dome over the crossing). **Petit-Palais** (12 km. NW): Late Romanesque (end of the 12C) church with a striking fa-

Saint-Émilion, église monolithique

St-Émilion, the Trinité, portal

Petit-Palais, Romanesque church

Petit-Palais, church, capital

çade with columns and arcades displaying Spanish-Moorish influence.

Saint-Étienne	(221,260 inhab.)
42 Loire	p.420☐L 11

Saint Étienne is an industrial, prefectoral and university town in the centre of the coal basin of the Loire and at the foot of the famous slag heaps. The coal, steel and textile industries have all contributed to the town's importance. Known as the 'ville noire' (black town) its appearance has been somewhat lightened by the building of new quarters, although the working-class nucleus of the the town has been much affected by the recent depression. The town's cultural life is focused on the Comédie de Saint-Étiennne, one of France's first provincial theatres.

Grande Église: Built in the 14C and deprived of its upper section by the Huguenots, its façade has a fine 15C door next to a heavy square bell tower. The choir has fine windows with 19C stained glass. The *Palais des Arts* houses the Musée des Beaux-Arts with works by Rubens, Le Brun, David and Gros in particular, and more modern paintings by Matisse, Henri Michaux, etc. The *Musée d'Armes* has a section on textiles and industry and recalls the trades of the town (in 1516 François I established a musket factory; the Manufacture Française d'Armes et Cyles has thrived here since 1885).

Saint-Fargeau	(3,290 inhab.)
89 Yonne	p.415☐J 7

This large village's history is inextricably

Petit-Palais, church, archivolts of the porch

linked with that of a fine château. Surrounded by water and greenery and built on the site of a medieval fortress the mainly 15C château takes the form of an extensive and sturdy pentagon with solid towers; it still has a medieval appearance, although with a touch of Grand Siècle (18C) magnificence. Mlle de Montespan came here during her exile (1652–7) and she refurbished and redecorated it. Later the property belonged to Le Pelletier des Forts, the member of the Convention who was murdered after having voted for Louis XVI's execution. Saint Fargeau's main street runs beneath a pretty brick and stone tower, which is actually a 15C fortified gate. The church dates from the 13&15C and has a lovely rose-window, a polychrome Pietà and a 15C triptych.

Environs: Saint-Sauveur-en-Puisaye

(12 km. E.): In the Rue des Vignes a plaque marks the Maison de Claudine. The novelist Colette spent her childhood here with her mother, the lowly and warm-hearted Sido (La Puisaye appears in 'La Maison de Claudine' and in 'Sido'). There is a 17C château with a large 12C tower and a church from the 12&16C.
Treigny (10 km. S. of Saint-Sauveur-en-Puisaye): There is a large 15&16C church and, some way off, an ivy-clad fortress, which now houses potters carrying on an old local tradition. The *Château de Ratilly* is from the 13&16C.

Saint-Ferme	(400 inhab.)
33 Gironde	p.422□F 12

On the borders of Entre-Deux-Mers and

Périgord is the small abbey church of a former Benedictine monastery. The church is Romanesque in origin but has been altered, especially in the 17C. It contains some remarkable historiated capitals (late 12C) at the entrance to the sanctuary and the apsidal chapels and on the little columns framing the windows. There are numerous workmen's marks on the walls.

Saint-Florent: see Corsica

Saint-Flour	(inhab. 8,830)
15 Cantal	p.420☐J 12

An episcopal and judicial town famous for its striking location. The old town clusters around the cathedral which was built some 3,000 ft. up on the edge of the planèze (basalt plateau). Within its ruined ramparts some fine hôtels line pretty streets, e.g. the Rue du Tuile.

Cathedral of Saint-Pierre-et-Saint-Flour: On the site of a former Cluniac monastery; building began in c. 1396 and continued until the 15C. The dark stone emphasizes the church's fortress-like appearance. The façade is crowned by strong square towers; the upper storey of that on the right was at one time used as a prison. The body of the church is broad with five aisles and no transept. Inside there is a large wooden 15C Christ—the 'Bon Dieu Noir' of Saint-Flour. The former collegiate church of Notre-Dame from the 14C has now been turned into a market. It is still very elegant in appearance with an apse pierced by bays.

Maison Consulaire: A Renaissance house with a pretty staircase turret in the courtyard. It houses the *Musée Alfred-Douet* which has Limoges enamels, furniture, paintings by Dutch masters and Aubusson tapestries. The *Musée de la Haute Auvergne*

occupies the former Bishop's Palace (17C). It has religious art from the Haute-Auvergne, including a polychrome wooden Saint-Pierre, a fine example of popular art; there are also folk exhibits and an archaeological section.

Saint-Gaudens	(inhab.12,830)
31 Haute-Garonne	p.423☐G 15

Saint-Gaudens, on the edge of a plateau overlooking the Garonne, faces the Pyrenees. It takes its name from a shepherd boy who was beheaded by the Visigoths in the 5C. This child saint has been venerated since the Middle Ages, especially by pilgrims to Santiago de Compostela. The collegiate church dates from the 11&12C and in structure is very similar to Saint-Sernin in Toulouse. To the N. is a Flamboyant doorway. The nave is flanked by high side aisles, which have galleries towards the choir. There are fine foliated or historiated capitals and 18C stalls and tapestries. The museum deals with local prehistory and history and exhibits 14&15C wooden statues, portraits of generals from the time of the Empire, porcelain and tools formerly used in the region.

Saint-Germain-en-Laye	(40,470 inhab.)
78 Yvelines	p.428☐I 5

This residential suburb of Paris lies on the edge of a lovely, flat expanse of mature forest. It has an express (RER) service linking it with Paris and, although modern building has increased, the old centre of the town has not lost its character and has retained fine 17&18C houses. Its history

St-Flour, St-Pierre, black Bon Dieu

Saint-Germain-en-Laye 1 Château-Vieux
2 keep 3 Sainte-Chapelle 4 pavilion of Henri IV
5 French parterres 6 English garden 7 Petite
Terrasse 8 rose garden 9 Grande Terrasse
10 church of Saint-Louis-Saint-Germain 11 town
museum 12 forest of Saint-Germain 13 church
of Saint-Léger

Saint-Germain-en-Laye, the château

was for long linked with that of the château, which developed from an early-12C fortress built to defend Paris. Kings often stayed here and Louis XIII and the exiled King James II of England died in the château. In 1862 the composer Claude Debussy was born in Saint-Germain.

Château and gardens: This royal palace—destroyed, rebuilt and altered over the years — consisted of the Château Vieux, which was rebuilt in the 16C and the Château Neuf, a country house begun by Henri II and finished by Henri IV. The latter building, in a very bad state before the Revolution, was razed. Louis XIV, fond of his native town before he became totally obsessed with Versailles, altered the Château Vieux; corner turrets were replaced by pavilions designed by Hardouin-Mansart, and Le Nôtre built the terrace, laid out the gardens and replanted the forest. After the destruction of the Château Neuf the abandoned Château Vieux housed a cavalry school and a prison and Charles X had part of the gardens divided up. Napoleon III restored it to its

16C appearance and he opened a *Musée des Antiquités Nationales de France* here in 1867. The Château Vieux had been rebuilt by François I who had retained only the large Charles V keep and the lovely *Sainte-Chapelle*, built by St.Louis, 1230–8. The château is an irregular pentagon and it follows the plan of the old fortress, whose basement is visible in the lower floors. The Italianate roof terrace, a great novelty when built, has balustrades and urns carved with the letter 'F' and the salamander—the emblem of François I. The Sainte-Chapelle, older than that in Paris, is a jewel of Gothic art. It soars upwards but sadly no longer has its stained glass. The keystones of the vaults are carved with figures, thought to be St.Louis, Blanche of Castile and their family. Le Nôtre's gardens were ruined when the railway was built but the French parterres are still as they were at the time of Louis XIV and lead to a pretty English-style garden. The Petite Terrasse, beginning with the Pavilion Henri IV (which with the Pavilion Sully is all that remains of the Château Neuf), extends beyond the Rond-Point du Rosarium and finishes in

St-Germain-en-Laye, Sainte-Chapelle

Saint-Germain-en-Laye, the terrace of the château

the *Grande Terrasse*, which was built in the early 1670s—7,500 ft. long, it has a very fine view.

Musée des Antiquités Nationales: Set up in the château by Napoleon III after he had more or less restored the building to its Renaissance appearance. (The Hardouin-Mansart pavilions were removed.) One of the world's major archaeological museums, it was reorganized in the 1960s and now has a collection ranging from remote prehistory to the Carolingian era (exhibited in chronological order). Exhibits include Stone Age tools, the famous *Venus of Bassempouy* and a *horse* from the Espelugues cave (both the latter came from the SW). The Gallo-Roman collections are very extensive (*Dieu de Bourray*, numerous statues, funerary stele, everyday objects, jewellery).

Town: The church of *Saint-Louis-Saint-Germain*, classical in style, is a reconstruction from the late 18/early 19C. It contains a pulpit which was a gift from Louis XIV, an early-18C organ chest, a 14C Virgin and the mausoleum of James II. The modern church of *Saint-Léger* is triangular and dates from 1960–1. The *Musée Municipal* is housed in an 18C house and its collection includes a well-known painting by Hieronymus Bosch (the Conjurer), numerous drawings and paintings, and three terracottas by Jean-Baptiste Lemoyne.

Saint-Gilles-du-Gard	(9,760 inhab.)
30 Gard	p.425□L 14

This little town on the edge of the Camargue bears the name of a miracle-working hermit who arrived from Greece in the 8C; legends about him abound and his tomb was greatly venerated. The former abbey church of **Saint-Gilles** was sacked in the Wars of Religion and much altered in the 17C, although its superb Romanesque façade remains intact. Many sculptors from Toulouse or Ile-de-France came to work on it (1180–1240). The three portals show the influence of Antiquity and depict the Life of Christ. He appears in majesty on the

Saint-Germain-en-Laye, church of Saint-Germain

tympanum of the central doorway along with symbols of the Evangelists. This, the oldest door, clearly shows the influence of Toulouse. The long crypt is a huge underground church and contains St. Giles's tomb and a small museum of masonry and inscriptions. The 'Vis de Saint Gilles', the remarkable staircase in the N. bell tower, has long been famous among stonemasons. The 'Maison Romane' (much restored) was the birthplace of Pope Clement IV.

Saint-Guilhem-le-Désert (270 inhab.)
34 Hérault   p.424☐K 14

This village, in the narrow gorge of the Verdus at its confluence with the Hérault, grew up near to a Benedictine abbey founded in 804 by a Duke of Aquitaine. Guilhem (or Guillaume) was the grandson of Charles Martel and a childhood friend of Charlemagne. When he gave up a life of war and politics for that of religion the Emperor offered him a relic of the Cross, which is still much venerated today. The

sizeable establishment here attracted pilgrims to Compostela, but now only two galleries of its cloister and the abbey church remain, the latter being mainly 12C. The church, with its well-balanced apse with two apsidioles, contains a Romanesque altar dedicated to St. Guilhem, a Gallo-Roman sarcophagus, a 6C or 7C sarcophagus and tombstones. The village still has the ruins of an old château and parts of the ramparts, as well as a few much-altered Romanesque houses.

Saint-Haon-le-Châtel (410 inhab.)
42 Loire   p.420☐K 10

This old fortified village has some historic houses within its ramparts. Passing through the 14C *Porte de l'Horloge,* with its studded wooden doors, you come to the *Hôtel de Jehan Pelletier* (15C, with a lovely Flamboyant door with carved tympanum) and then the *Maison du Cadran Solaire* (House of the Sundial, 16C). The modest 12C church with a 17C polygonal apse

Saint-Gilles, tympanum of the abbey church

Saint-Haon, Maison du Cadran Solaire

St-Jean-d'Angély, Fontaine du Pilori

contains interesting Forez furnishings. There is a large wooden Christ over a baroque wooden arch at the entrance to the choir.

costumes and beautiful panelling. There are also a few Impressionist paintings (Sisley, Monet, Renoir) and some Coromandel laquer.

Saint-Jean-Cap-Ferrat	(2,270 inhab.)
06 Alpes-Maritimes	p.426□P 14

Here, on the most residential of peninsulas and in an extraordinary park, there is a relatively unknown but very exciting museum. The Musée de l'Ile-de-France, set up in a building dating from 1911–12, brings together the rich and varied collections of Beatrice Ephrussi (née Rothschild). The 18C is particularly well represented: paintings by Boucher, drawings by Fragonard; Regency, Louis XV and Louis XVI furniture; as well as porcelain, tapestries,

Saint-Jean d'Angély	(10,320 inhab.)
17 Charente-Maritime	p.418□F 10

This town, in the heart of the hilly Saintonge countryside, is situated on a loop of the Boutonne. Ringed by boulevards and with narrow, white streets, it was a stage on the route to Santiago; in the 16C it was a Reformist stronghold. **Former abbey:** The church, known as 'Les Tours' is a strange, unfinished building. Begun in 1741, building was interrupted by the Revolution. There is an imposing façade which has a large porch with a dome and

St-Jean-d'Angély, the college

St-Jean-de-Côle, the church

lateral towers. Only two buttresses linked by a framework (used as the bell tower of the present parish church) remain of the Gothic abbey church destroyed in 1562 by the Huguenots. To the left of 'Les Tours' is a magnificent Louis XV portal which opens on to the courtyard of the former abbey (a fine classical building now occupied by a school). **Fontaine du Pilori:** In 1819 the delightful Renaissance well-head, which formerly covered the well in the old Château de Brizambourg, was re-erected in the centre of the little square named after the Canton of Pilori. **Tour de l'Horloge:** A former belfry dating from the early 15C, it has five storeys crowned by machicolations; its bell sounded the curfew, fire-alarm and call to arms. **Museum:** The Hôtel d'Hausen (18C) contains archaeological collections and souvenirs of the Citroën expeditions.

Environs: Fenioux (7 km. S.): The church of *Notre-Dame* is 12C but its Carolingian origins are evident from the small stones of the nave walls. The façade is typical of Saintonge Romanesque and the arches of the wide doorway depict the seasons, the signs of the Zodiac and the struggle between Good and Evil. The 12C graveyard lantern in the cemetery is very tall and consists of a cluster of eleven columns.

Saint-Jean-de-Côle (320 inhab.)
24 Dordogne p.419☐G 11

A pretty little Périgord village set in hilly countryside. A humpbacked bridge crosses the Côle. The church, a former priory church from the 11&12C, once had a vast

St-Jean-de-Luz, Maison de Louis XIV

St-Jean-de-Luz, Maison de l'Infante

dome over the nave but this has now been replaced by an ordinary ceiling. The building is rather crude from the outside and inside it exhibits a curious plan, which gives the appearance of it being unfinished or of having lost part of the nave. One of the capitals on the outside of the apse bizarrely depicts God forming the head of Man and breathing life into it. Two upper galleries of the priory have survived. The **Château de la Marthonie** is 15C and has a 17C wing.

Environs: Thiviers (7 km. E.): This busy and attractive little town has a Romanesque church (with alterations). It is unremarkable outside but inside there are lovely rib vaults over the choir and crossing, which also has fine Romanesque capitals on tall columns. The fortified manor behind the church has been altered on several occasions.

Saint-Jean-de-Luz	(12,060 inhab.)
64 Pyrénées-Atlantiques	p.422☐D 14

Saint-Jean, once full of pirates and whalers, is a seaside resort and fishing port today. Situated in a quiet bay, it is closely associated with Ciboure and has many typical Labourd-style houses (Labourd is the W. part of the Pays Basque). The town is full of character with its lively quays, charming little streets and marvellous church. The Sun King, who solemnized his marriage here in 1660, stayed in the house now known as the *Maison de Louis XIV* (built 1643; next door to the Town Hall of 1635). Before the marriage Maria Theresa stayed in the hôtel with square turrets, which is still known as the *Maison de l'Infante*.

Saint-Jean-Baptiste: Rebuilt in Gothic

St-Jean-de-Luz, St-Jean, retable

Saint-Jean-Pied-de-Port, old houses along the Nive

style in the 14&15C, it was enlarged in 1649 and altered in the 18C. A large church, it is plain outside and ornate within. Typical of the region, the vast nave is covered with painted panelling and has three storeys of galleries. It has a fine 17C organ; other furnishings include a striking gilded retable with numerous carved figures (*c.* 1670) and a small 18C altarpiece by Restout.

Ciboure: (Linked to Saint-Jean-de-Luz by a bridge.) In 1875 Maurice Ravel was born in a Dutch-looking house on the Quai de la Nivelle (No. 12). The church of *Saint-Vincent* is dominated by a strange octagonal bell tower, which has small pinnacle turrets on top, and presents a rather fortress-like appearance. Untypical of the area, it does, however, have traditional galleries (in Labourdin churches these were formerly

reserved for men) in the nave, which was finished about 1579 and later enlarged. The *Fort de Socoa* was built in Henri IV's reign and altered by Vauban.

Saint-Jean-de-Maurienne

(10,420 inhab.)
73 Savoie   p.421 □ N 11

Once the capital of the Maurienne — a 'province of the Duchy of Savoy'—today it is an industrial town. The Romanesque **cathedral**, altered in the 15C, has an 18C porch. Inside it contains some superb carved stalls and a delicate 15C alabaster ciborium. To the left, the elegant *cloister* with alabaster arches typical of the region leads to a very old crypt. The 11&12C free-standing tower on the parvis was formerly the bell tower.

Saint-Jouin-de-Marnes, the church, carving of the archivolts

Saint-Jean-Pied-de-Port (1,890 inhab.)
64 Pyrénées-Atlantiques   p.422☐E 15

This village was formerly a major stage on the route to Santiago de Compostela for pilgrims crossing via Roncevaux. Today it is the capital of the Basse-Navarre (a region of the Pays Basque) and it owes its intriguing name to its nearness to the pass or 'port' of Ibaneta. In the summer it is full of tourists—for the upper town is very picturesque (surrounded by 15C walls, with a newer part inside 17C town walls). The Porte Notre-Dame, opening under the bell tower-keep of the solid church of *Notre-Dame-du-Pont,* a much altered red sandstone building, leads to the *Rue de la Citadelle,* which is lined with 16&17C houses. The citadel, occupying a vantage point with fine views, dates from 1668 with

alterations by Vauban, who was commissioned to strengthen the town's defences because it controlled one of the routes to and from Spain.

Environs: Saint-Jean-le-Vieux (4 km. E.): This was on a Roman road, which later was also the route to Compostela, the church has a Romanesque porch. **Mendive** (11.5 km. SE): The church has a Romanesque portal and discoidal stele in the cemetery.

Saint-Jouin-de-Marnes   (750 inhab.)
79 Deux-Sèvres   p.418☐F 8

This village is grouped around an important abbey founded in the 4C by St.Jouin. The Benedictines who rebuilt the church

Saint-Leu-d'Esserent, church

Saint-Lô, church of Notre-Dame

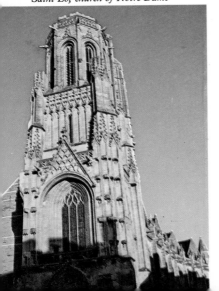

left one of the most impressive monuments in Haut-Poitou. The abbey, taken over by followers of the St.Maur reform in the 17C, was at that time a splendid complex. However, only a rather imposing 17C building and the 15C S. walk of the cloister now remain. **Church:** Built in the 12C and fortified in the 14&15C, it has a strikingly but majestically simple façade with two clusters of buttress columns framing this lovely piece of Romanesque art (capitals, decorated arches, embedded reliefs and a Last Judgement). Above the crossing there is a dome with a two-storeyed bell tower. The long nave, revaulted with Angevin rib vaulting, leads to the choir and ambulatory; beautiful 17C lectern and fine choir stalls.

Saint-Léonard-de-Noblat

87 Haute-Vienne

(5,540 inhab.)

p.419☐H 10

A charming little town overlooking the Limoges countryside. It has some 13,15&16C houses around the church of **Saint-Léonard**, which is itself a fine building from the 11&12C and is Limoges Romanesque in style. It has a tall, six-storey bell tower, whose base forms a porch flanked by pillars with capitals (leaves, figures, animals). The choir has an elegant and light ambulatory; there is a dome over the crossing. The church contains some 15C oak stalls and the tomb of St.Leonard.

Saint-Leu-D'Esserent (4,400 inhab.)
60 Oise p.428☐I/J 4

A small town on the banks of the Oise, it is dominated by the magnificent church of **Saint-Nicolas,** whose location high above the river increases the impact of this pure and unified early Gothic building. The façade dates from the 1150s (the porch forms a sort of narthex); much of the rest is 12C (nave, choir and ambulatory). (There is no transept.) The impressive apse is on the edge of the cliff. The church has contemporary stained glass (choir windows and rose-window by Max Ingrand) and in one of the radiating apsidal chapels there is a 13C statue of St.Leu. During the post-1944 restoration, remains of an earlier chapel and sarcophagi were discovered. A fortified gate, two walks of the 12C cloister and a very old underground room are among the remains of the Benedictine priory served by the church.

Saint-Lizier	(1,310 inhab.)
09 Ariège	p.423□H 15

This quiet town, formerly the regional capital, dates back to a Gallo-Roman foundation. It is rather unexceptional apart from the former cathedral, which dates from the 12C with 14C alterations (rib vaults and the Toulouse-style central bell tower). The 12&15C cloister is also interesting. Extensive remains of the ancient town wall were somewhat damaged in the Middle Ages.

Saint-Lô	(25,040 inhab.)
50 Manche	p.413□E 4

Saint-Lô, the Préfecture of the Manche Département, is surrounded by bocage and grassland. It was devastated by bombing just before the Liberation. Today, a modern town without much character, it is still partly ringed by walls. However, it has saved what remained of the superb church of **Notre-Dame**, which dates from the end of the 13C and the beginning of the 14C and was altered in the 15&17C. The present façade, an extensive green shale wall, is embellished by three beautiful contemporary bronze doors by Jean Bernard. It has a strange exterior pulpit on the N. side and contains a large 18C Christ by the entrance to the choir, and a statue of Notre-

Saint-Macaire, medieval houses

Dame du Pilier (venerated since the 15C).

The Hôtel de Ville, dominated by a tall concrete tower, houses a **museum** with fine tapestries and paintings (Jordaens, Corot, Millet, Boudin, Gros).

Environs: Torigni-sur-Vivre (14 km. SE): This little town suffered severely in 1944 but has rebuilt its 17C château, which was formerly a shell. There are tapestries and fine furniture inside. **Château de l'Angotière** (10 km. S. of Torigni): This is a charming 15&19C manor house set in the bocage. Inside you will find large fireplaces and 17&18C furniture.

Saint-Macaire	(1,680 inhab.)
33 Gironde	p.422☐F 12

Saint-Macaire looks out over the Garonne to the Sauterne region through the fortified gates of its former defences. It has a timeless charm with its maze of narrow

St-Maixent, stalls in the church

streets, medieval houses (like the 13C Maison de Lanau) and its pretty arcaded square. The church of **Saint-Sauveur** stands on a terrace with a wide view and is 12C (apse), 13C (nave) and 14C (hexagonal bell tower). It has a very fine Romanesque nave, a curious dome over the crossing and restored 14C paintings in its apse.

Saint-Maixent-l'École	(9,620 inhab.)
79 Deux-Sèvres	p.418☐F 9

This town has become famous for its military academy (founded in 1880); it also preserves some lovely houses, such as the Hôtel de Balisy (Renaissance), a 15C house which once belonged to an apothecary and bears the inscription 'hic valetudo' (here is health). **Saint-Maixent**, Romanesque in origin, is a former abbey church which was rebuilt in Gothic style by the Normandy architect Leduc (known as Toscane) after the Wars of Religion. There are several features from the earlier building: Romanesque narthex and walls of the side aisles, straight-ended 13C apse, 15C bell tower. The 17C nave with its stellar vaulting is majestic and light. The rich furnishings are mainly 17C and include among other things a rood screen, now around the main door, elegant stalls and a good 17C painting from the French school. There are the sarcophagi of St. Maxentius and St. Leger in the Romanesque crypt.

Saint-Malo	(46,270 inhab.
35 Ille-et-Vilaine	p.413☐D 5

Saint-Malo is perched on a rock at the mouth of the river Rance, and only a narrow causeway known as the 'Sillon'—itself once liable to be submerged—links it to dry land. It is this unusual position that has governed its history and the character of its inhabitants. In the 8C the population of Aleth (Saint-Servan) fled to the small island and fortified it, first against the Franks and then the Normans. In the 6C, the monk Malo landed here, coming from Britain to spread Christianity in the region. Quite soon the town became fiercely independent and, very jealous of its privileges, such as the right to 'guard itself', which it did with the famous and dreaded 'corps of watch-dogs'. It strongly resisted the French, English and local dukes, and Anne of Brittany provoked a rebellion when she strengthened the château. Ever since then, one of the towers has borne the inscription, 'Quic en groigne, ainsi sera, cer tel est mon plaisir' (if anyone complains, let him, for I shall do as I please). The château was besieged at the end of the 16C during the Ligue wars, and then the town established an independent republic for four years, even sending ambassadors to foreign courts. Saint-Malo's maritime prosperity began with Jacques Cartier's expeditions to the New World and to the St. Lawrence (1491 – 1557). Behind the powerful ramparts, ship owners and merchants raised fine hôtels and in the surrounding countryside they built luxurious houses with elaborate gardens. In order to damage enemy trade, particularly that of the English, they armed privateers and put daring local raiders in command, such as Duguay-Trouin and Surcouf who had royal 'lettres de course' giving them a free hand. Centuries of incessant fighting left Saint-Malo intact but the last world war devastated it in a few days in August 1944, when three-quarters of the town was reduced to ashes, although the greater part of the ramparts survived. Some very good rebuilding followed which retained the previous layout and respected the individual character of the traditional houses.

Château: This ducal, and subsequently royal, château in the Place Chateaubriand is reached through the Porte Saint-Vincent. A fine 15C fortress (the Galère was added in the 17C), it has four massive towers. The small keep was built in about 1395 and formed part of the ramparts. The famous *Tour Quiquengrogne* abuts on to this

Saint-Malo, the ramparts

keep; it was built by order of the Duchess Anne and now houses a small *waxworks museum* devoted to the great men of Saint-Malo. The Musée Municipal in the large keep (1424) is devoted to a number of famous figures (Cartier, Duguay-Trouin, La Bourdonnais, Surcouf, Chateaubriand, Lamennais), the history of the town, and the role of its sailors; the Tour des Moulins deals with fishing in the New World.

Ramparts: These majestic ramparts, altered many times and completed in the 18C by Garanjeau to plans by Vauban, date in part from the 12C (the *Petit Murs,* between the *Bastion de Hollande,* 1674, and the *Tour Bidouane,* 1652). The bastions have a small public garden and statues of Surcouf (1903; his finger pointing towards England), Jacques Cartier (1905) and Duguay-Trouin. To the S., facing the Avant-Port (outer harbour), there are a few splendid 18C hôtels which dominate the line of ramparts. From the parapet walk you can see the lovely roadstead strewn with rocks and islands which Vauban fortified. The Ile du Grand-Bé can be reached

at low tide; this is probably where the Celts laid out their dead and now it is the site of the simple, solitary *tomb of François René de Chateaubriand,* born in 1768 in the Hôtel de la Gicquelais (3, Rue Chateaubriand).

Cathedral of Saint-Vincent: This was built in the 12&17C and has been recently restored. It is a composite building and since 1972 has been crowned with a tall granite spire. The Renaissance and classical façade rises up in front of the 12C ribvaulted nave. The 13C choir is set lower down in order to follow the slope of the rock. It contains some sparkling glass by Jean le Moal; some other windows are the work of Max Ingrand. The cathedral contains a 12C holy-water stoup decorated with figures, an old Virgin, damaged in 1944, an 18C baptistery, and the tombs of Jean de Châtillon (12C), the first bishop, and that of Jacques Cartier, whose head was buried here in 1972, shortly before the transfer of the remains of Duguay-Trouin.

Saint-Servan: This town was joined to

Saint-Servan, Tour Solidor   *Saint-Malo, cathedral, rose-window by Jean le Moal*

Saint-Malo in 1967 along with **Paramé**. Situated on a rocky headland, one of its landmarks is the beautiful *Tour Solidor*. This is really three towers joined together, complete with arrow-slits and machicolations. It houses the *Musée International du Longcours-Cap-Hornier,* which is devoted to voyages of circumnavigation by the great sailing ships. Nearby, the Fort de la Cité (18C) was made into a bastion by the Germans in the last war.

Environs: The countryside all around is dotted with sumptuous country houses, known as 'malouinières'—small châteaux built in the 17&18C by the rich Saint-Malo ship owners and fitters. For example, the powerful family, Magon de la Lande, owned **Le Bosq** (towards Saint-Jean-des-Guérets), **La Balue** (in Saint-Servan), where Chateaubriand's mother lived, **Le Montmarin** (at Pleurtuit), with an Italianate roof, and **La Chapaudière**, built near Paramé to plans by Garanjeau and with a garden designed by Le Nôtre. The ship owner Le Fer de la Sauldre built the large and sumptuous **Château de**

Saint-Martin-de-B., church of St-Georges

Bonaban en la Gouesnière in the 18C (11 km. SE of Paramé).

Saint-Martin-de-Boscherville
(1, 190 inhab.)
Seine-Maritime   p.410□H 4

The large, pale church of **Saint-Georges-de-Boscherville** lies on the edge of a straggling village, and was the church of a small Benedictine abbey. A fine product of Norman Romanesque, it dates essentially from the first half of the 12C. Its façade is simple in line and enlivened by a doorway with luxuriantly decorated arches; the apse is particularly successful. During major restoration, the nave was almost too zealously cleaned and is of a dazzling whiteness. There is an open gallery supported by a column at either end of the transept and numerous fine capitals. The large *chapterhouse* (12C), with complicated vaulting, is surmounted by a 17C structure.

Saint-Martin-de-Ré
(2,190 inhab.)
17 Charente-Maritime   p.418□E 9

Saint-Martin, the capital of the flat, sandy island of Ré, retains its Vauban fortifications. Two very attractive gates open in the town walls: the *Porte Toiras* and the *Porte des Campani*. They are preceded by ravelins and have royal crests on their tympana. The 17C *citadel* (where Mirabeau was imprisoned) was used as a prison for many years. The *Hôtel de Clerjotte* near the port was once an arsenal. It is a late Gothic/early Renaissance building, whose galleried inner courtyard has an elegant Flamboyant doorway. Inside, there is a *Musée Naval*. The *Hôtel des Cadets* (Place d'Armes) is a fine late-18C building, and the *Musée Ernest-Cognacq* has some rare pieces of

Delft and documents connected with the history of Ré. The Hospice Saint-Honoré was founded in the 12C and enlarged in the 17C; it has a remarkable 18C pharmacy.

Saint Martin: This fine 15C Flamboyant church was ruined by the Anglo-Dutch fleet when the island was captured in 1692. The W. façade and the tower above it are 18C. The fortifications which once protected the church are still visible in the N. transept.

Saint-Martin-du-Canigou

66 Pyrénées-Orientales   p.424□I 16

Perched like an eyrie at an at an altitude of 3,590 ft., this abbey church commands a superb view. Benedictines in search of an isolated, beautiful site established themselves here at the beginning of the 11C under the patronage of a Count of Cerdagne. A church had already been built by this time (or was in the course of being built). The present one is on two levels, one above

the other. The lower church with its massive pillars was possibly consecrated in 1009, and became the crypt of the slightly later upper church, which is archaic in style with swollen, monolithic columns, semicircular vaults and roughly-hewn walls with meagre openings. To the N. of the choir, the solid, severe bell tower is dominated by a crenellated platform, which was rebuilt after an earthquake damaged the building in 1428. The cloister had largely been destroyed but was somewhat freely rebuilt in the early 20C (Romanesque capitals and the S. walk). Nearby is the 11C tomb which the Count of Cerdagne had hollowed out of the rock for himself.

St-Maximin-la-Ste-Baume

                            (4,030 inhab.)
83 Var   p.425□N 14

This small town occupies the former bed of a lake (in between the source of the Argens and that of the Arc) which has been

Saint-Martin-du-Canigou, cloister

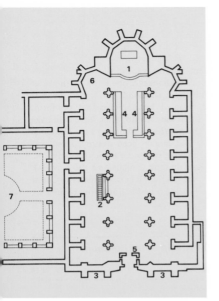

Basilica of Saint-Maximin-la-Sainte-Baume
1 Apse 2 crypt 3 side portals 4 stalls 5 organ 6 altarpiece of the Passion 7 cloister

dried up for thousands of years. Originally a Gallo-Roman township, it became famous in the 13C when tombs, presumed to be those of St.Maximin and Mary Magdalene, were discovered. The town is dominated by its N. Gothic **basilica**, inspired in part by that of Bourges. It has no transept or ambulatory, and is simple, yet imposing, from the outside. It was built in three stages: 1295/6 – 1316 (apse, initial bays); 1404–12 (sixth bay, crypt bay) and 1508–32 (W. bays). The two lateral doorways of the façade are 16C. The church itself, nearly 240 ft. long, is richly decorated and furnished, and ends in a polygonal apse which was rather over-decorated in the 17C. Inside the church there are some fine 17C stalls and a remarkable organ (1772). One side chapel contains an altarpiece of the Passion (1520) by Antonio Ronzen. The 4C crypt contains Gallo-Roman sarcophagi, four engraved slabs from around 500 and a reliquary dating from 1860. The former royal monastery adjoining the basilica, once occupied by Dominicans, forms a beautiful Provençal Gothic complex.

Saint-Maximin-la-Sainte-Baume, the basilica

Saint-Menoux   (790 inhab.)
03 Allier   p.420☐J 9

This quiet village clusters around one of
the most beautiful churches in the region,
the former abbey church of a Benedictine
nunnery, founded on the tomb of St.
Menoux. **Saint-Menoux**. Part of the
original 11C church, the narthex houses a
Musée Lapidaire which contains a 12C bas-
relief of Christ in Glory. The 13C nave has
capitals with elegant and varied carving
reminiscent of Burgundian art. The fine
Romanesque choir precedes a deep apse
surrounded by an ambulatory with alternating fluted pilasters and pillars. The
tomb of St.Menoux, behind the high altar,
has a cavity in one of its faces known as the
'débrédinoire' where the weak-minded
placed their heads in order to be cured.

Saint-Michel-de-Frigolet
13 Bouches-du-Rhône   p.425☐L 14

The abbey of Saint-Michel-de-Frigolet,
which features in Alphonse Daudet's story
L'Elixir du Père Gaugher, nestles in a valley of La Montagnette. It is now occupied
by Premonstratensians. The name Frigo-
let is derived from *ferigoulo,* meaning
thyme, and the whole place is fragrant with
Provençal herbs. Still a major place of pilgrimage, the abbey was founded in the
10C, then altered and surrounded by a
medieval wall in the 19C. The chapel of
Notre-Dame-du-Bon-Remède (11C) forms
the apse to the *abbey church's* nave; this latter, built in the last century, is highly ornate. There are gilded wooden carvings
and paintings by the school of Nicolas
Mignard. The simple church of *Saint-
Michel* (11C) has a cloister built in the early
12C.

Environs: Barbentane (5 km. N.): This
large agricultural village in the N. of La
Montagnette has two fortified gates, a
'Maison des Chevaliers' with a
Renaissance façade and an old keep, the
Tour Anglica. The elegant *château* was
built in the second half of the 17C and
dominates a series of terraces. It was lux-

Saint-Michel-de-Frigolet, the abbey

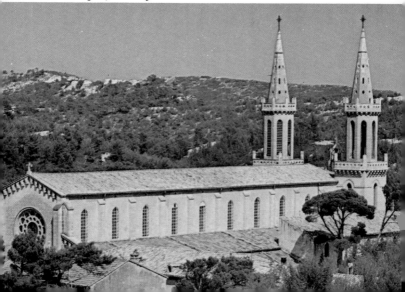

uriously decorated in the 18C and has some fine Louis XV and XVI furniture. Built for a Marquis of Barbentane, it is rather reminiscent of the Ile-de-France architecturally, although the interior and the park are very Italianate.

Saint-Nectaire (682 inhab.)
63 Puy-de-Dôme p.420☐J 11

The old village of Saint-Nectaire-le-Haut lies above the spa of Saint-Nectaire-le-Bas and possesses a magnificent Romanesque **church**, as well as one of the best views in the Auvergne. The smallest of the major Limagne churches (12C) stands on a high, rocky shelf and its bare façade contrasts with the magnificent arrangement of its apse. The fine group of historiated capitals in the choir are amongst the most complete in the Auvergne. Their subjects are mostly taken from the Old and New Testaments and are depicted with vigour; the figures are full of life despite being rather out of proportion. The treasure includes

a splendid reliquary bust of St. Baudime (12C), and a polychrome wooden Virgin in majesty, also 12C.

Saint-Nicolas-de-Port (7,300 inhab.)
54 Meurthe-et-Moselle p.417☐N 5

This large industrial village contains a surprising 15&16C church dedicated to **St. Nicholas**, the patron saint of Lorraine. Severely damaged in 1940 but now restored, it exhibits daring Flamboyant experimentation: a large façade with high towers, and a soaring nave with tall columns. It has also retained its 16C stained glass and, on the pier of the central portal, a marvellous 16C statue of St. Nicholas.

Saint-Omer (17,990 inhab.)
62 Pas-de-Calais p.410☐I 1

This ancient town lying between Flanders and Artois is surrounded by fertile marsh-

Barbentane, the château

land. It grew up around a monastery founded in the 7C by Omer. The ramparts are 17C and now provide the site for a remarkable public garden. A prosperous town, it has fine 18C residences lining quiet streets full of provincial charm. Many historic buildings have survived despite the fierce battles that have been fought in the area. They include the church of *Saint-Denis* (splendid 13C tower and rich furnishings), the church of *Saint-Sépulcre* (14&15C, tall stone spire), and the former Jesuit chapel (17C baroque façade).

Basilica of Notre-Dame: This is by far the most appealing building in Saint-Omer. It has a robust 13C choir, a 14&15C nave and a strong tower built in the 15C and decorated with arches. Inside, the broad, high nave is very restrained whereas the 17C polychrome marble screens to the chapels are magnificent. The basilica, a museum in itself, is full of works of art: tombs of St.Omer (13C) and Eustache de Croy (16C), both of which are strikingly realistic, a simple and moving carved group, the *Grand Dieu de Thérouanne* (13C)

Saint-Nectaire, Romanesque church

Saint-Omer, basilica of N.-D., the Grand Dieu de Thérouanne

Saint-Omer, the Musée Sandelin

and an astonishingly complicated astronomical clock (1558).

Musée Sandelin: Housed in an elegant classical hôtel (1766), this rich museum contains a few masterpieces by Boilly (1761–1845) along with Flemish, Dutch (17C) and French (18C) paintings. There is an outstanding ceramics collection featuring local products and an extensive display of Delftware. Also note the gold and enamel pedestal of the cross of St. Bertin, a precious piece of goldsmith's work from the 12C.

The library has some rare manuscripts and incunabula, including a *Life of St. Omer* (11C) and a *Gutenberg Bible*.

Environs: Aire-sur-la-Lys (14 km. SE): This ancient stronghold has altered little over the years: it still retains its narrow, noisy streets and a well-proportioned main square with an 18C belfry. Note the pretty Renaissance guardhouse (early 17C). The powerful 15–17C collegiate church of Saint-Pierre is Flamboyant in style and contains a marvellous organ chest (1633).

Saint-Paterne-Racan	(1,720 inhab.)
37 Indre-et-Loir	p.414□G 7

Situated on the banks of the willow-lined Escotais, **Saint-Paternes-Racan** has a terracotta Adoration of the Magi (16C) with a lovely Virgin and Child. Some distance away, the **Château de la Roche-Racan** was begun in 1634 by a local master mason, an ancestor of the great architectural family of Gabriel. It preserves mementoes of the poet Racan, the friend of Malherbe.

St-Paul-de-Vence (1,980 inhab.)
06 Alpes-Maritimes p.426☐O/P 14

This large village's defences were rebuilt by order of François I in the 16C. It stands on a spur between two valleys, and its medieval parts contrast with the ultra-modern *Fondation Maeght,* set amidst a pine forest. The Rue Grande offers both 16&18C houses and some fine views. Cobbled alleys lead off it and there is a walk following the lines of the ramparts, begun in 1537.

The former collegiate church dates from the 12&13C, although its vaults and bell tower have been rebuilt. It has a modern Stations of the Cross and some interesting paintings, in particular St. Catherine of Alexandria by Tintoretto. In the sacristy here are silver and silver-gilt statues and reliquaries. The Provençal museum consists of a reconstruction of the interior of a 16C house.

Fondation Maeght: This was established by Aimé and Marguerite Maeght, and it brings together a sizeable collection of paintings, sculptures, ceramics, tapestries, drawings and graphics from the 20C. Many artists collaborated with the Latin American architect José Luis Sert in incorporating their works in the low, light complex, topped by concrete coifs. In the park here are works by Miró, Calder and Giacometti. As well as the permanent exhibition (Braque, Miró, Chagall, in particular), here are also temporary ones. There are windows by Braque and Bazaine in the chapel of Saint-Bernard.

Environs: Vence (5 km. N.): Known in antiquity as *Vintium,* it has a medieval at-

St-Paul-de-Vence, Fondation Maeght

mosphere—alleys, tiny squares and fountains. The *former cathedral* seems to be partly 11C but was greatly altered in the 17C. It contains several works of art and some beautiful stalls (15C, by a local artist). The *Chapelle du Rosaire,* a dependency of a Dominican convent, was designed and decorated by Henri Matisse (drawings, stained glass).

St-Paul-Trois-Châteaux (4,350 inhab.)
26 Drôme p.425☐M 13

Once the capital of the Tricastins (a people whose name was corrupted to 'Trois Château'), old Saint-Paul, with its white stone buildings is still protected by the remains of ramparts (partly 12C). The seat of a tiny bishopric, the town spreads out

Saint-Philbert-de-Grand-Lieu, nave of the abbey church

at the foot of its former cathedral (11&12C), which has a superbly arranged façade. A powerful, balanced building, it is one of the finest examples of Provençal Romanesque architecture (the bell tower is 17C). The nave is well-lit, barrel-vaulted and has half columns with capitals and torsos engaged in the pilasters. It is lavishly carved and there is a remarkable unfinished frieze. Arcades of large semicircular arches separate it from the narrow side aisles. Over the crossing there is a fine dome, rebuilt in the 19C; the central apse has a half-dome and Corinthian capitals. When the high altar was moved in the last century, a large mosaic with a picture of Jerusalem in the centre was revealed.

Environs: Saint-Restitut (3 km. SE): The little and rather simple late-12C Romanesque church here is embellished with fine carving. There is an elegant S.porch with a pediment beneath a powerful archway. The 'funerary tower' to the W. of the church was erected on the site of St.Restitut's tomb; his relics were burnt by Protestants. Adjoining the church, but separate from it, this tower is probably 11C. About a quarter of a mile outside the town is the small hexagonal chapel of Saint Sépulcre, which dates from the 16C.

St-Philibert-de-Grand-Lieu

(3,630 inhab.
44 Loire-Atlantique   p.418☐E

Saint-Philibert-de-Grande-Lieu, between the Loire and the Vendée and to the S. of a large lake, possesses one of the oldest churches in France: it was built in 836 by

Saint-Pierre-sur-Dives, the market

the monks of Noirmoutier, who were fleeing from the Norman invasion. They brought the heavy 7C marble sarcophagus of the founder of the abbey, St. Philibert, and installed it in the lofty crypt, where it is to this day. A few years later the monks were again in flight; they took the saint's relics on a wandering journey which finally brought them to Tournus (see entry). The monks didn't return to Grand-Lieu (formely *Déas*) until the 11C and the saint's relics were only replaced in the sarcophagus in 1937.

Abbey church: This was partly rebuilt in the 11C, and restored at the end of the 19C after a long period of deconsecration. The interior is a rare example of Carolingian architecture (massive cruciform pillars of alternating brick and white stone). The choir is above a small arcaded crypt which was intended to house Philibert's tomb and allow access to pilgrims.

St-Pierre-sur-Dives	(4,310 inhab.)
14 Calvados	p.410☐G 4

This lively little town on the edge of the Pays d'Auge has an annual Easter fair and a number of important markets; it also has a beautiful Gothic *church*, a former abbey church whose S. tower is Romanesque (the N. one was rebuilt in the 14C and the lantern tower over the crossing is 13C). The church replaced an earlier one which was burnt down in 1107 and the greater part of it is 13C. Only two 17C wings of the abbey survive. The 11&12C **market buildings**, dwarfed by their vast roofs, were burnt down in 1944 but were subsequently

Saint-Pol-de-Léon, cathedral, window

rebuilt in strict accordance with the old methods.

Saint-Pol-de-Léon (8,750 inhab.)
29 Finistère p.412□B 5

Saint-Pol, inland from a rocky coastline, lies in the centre of a vast area of market gardening, the 'golden belt', which is famous for artichokes and cauliflowers, fields of which surround the town. Once the seat of a bishop, the town was founded in the 6C by the Welsh monk Paul Aurelian and became highly prosperous, as can be seen from the fine granite houses with pretty dormer windows or projecting turrets. The 14&15C **Chapelle Municipale du Kreisker**, was used for meetings of the 'General Assembly of the Nobles,

Citizens, Villagers and Inhabitants'. It has a magnificent monumental bell tower (about 253 ft. high) which is the pride of the Saint-Politains and which surpasses the one it was modelled on (that of Saint Pierre-de-Caen). Standing above the crossing, it consists of a square tower pierced by bays and capped by a pointed spire with pinnacle turrets.

Cathedral: Next to the 16C canons' house and the former bishop's palace (18C). It is 13–16C and is reminiscent of that of Coutances in its elegance and the white Normandy stone used in its building; the master-builders were inspired by the great churches of the Cotentin peninsula. The 13C façade, flanked by two bell towers with spires, has a porch with a platform above it for the bishop's blessing. There is a small side door which was once kept for lepers. The 15C choir has some fine 16C carved stalls and the high altar has a carved wooden palm tree (17C) which carries the pyx containing the Host. There is a delicate 15C rose-window in the right arm of the transept, and two Renaissance stained-glass windows; it also contains a 17C organ-chest, a Romanesque sarcophagus used as a holy-water stoup, several tombs and St. Pol's relics enshrined in bronze.

Chapelle Saint-Pierre: This 15C Flamboyant building adjoins the cemetery, the walls of which contain small ossuaries. The war memorial is the work of Quillivic.

Environs: Roscoff (5 km. N.): Opposite the island of Batz, Roscoff was the port for Saint-Pol-de-Léon. There are some fine decorated granite façades along the quais (16C). On the ramparts there is a watchtower known as the Tourelle Marie Stuart; adjacent to which is the house where the

Saint-Pol-de-Léon, cathedral, retable

future queen stayed as a child in 1548. The church of *Notre-Dame-de-Croaz-Baz* has a fine mid-17C bell tower with balconies crowned by lanterns. There are two 17C ossuaries in front of it, and the pictures of boats and cannons on the walls indicate the main activity of Roscoff at the time of the privateers. There are several altarpieces inside, including a late-15C alabaster one, as well as some fine wood carving. The *Institut Biologique de Roscoff*, attached to the University of Paris and the Centre National de la Recherche Scientifique, includes the Charles Perez aquarium, which displays the main species found in the Channel. **Château de Kerouzéré** (8 km. W.): Early 15C, it was built by Jean de Kerouzéré, whose tomb is in the nearby church of Sibiril. The castle is well defended; three round, machicolated towers flank the main residence, from one façade of which a small chapel with a Gothic window juts out. **Manoir de Tronjoly** (11 km. W.) This manor in the commune of **Cléder** is 16&17C and has an elegant façade facing the main courtyard, a mixture of Flamboyant and Renaissance decoration, and an adjacent tall, square tower.

Saint-Pons

(3,420 inhab.)
34 Hérault   p.424 □ J 14

Set amidst green mountains, this small town was the seat of a bishop until the Revolution and its former Benedictine abbey church (late 12C) served as a cathedral. The building preserves a Romanesque doorway from the original façade, but was greatly altered in the 18C, when it also acquired some fine furnishings.

Saint-Quentin

(69,150 inhab.)
02 Aisne   p.411 □ J/K 3

This historic town in a bend of the busy Somme is still in Picardy but it also has a Flemish atmosphere. It has suffered severely as a result of war and much of the heritage of its prosperous past has been destroyed.

Saint-Pol-de-Léon, the Chapelle du Kreisker

The massive collegiate church of **Saint-Quentin** is 13&15C, but has been rather ravaged by time. However, it is still a fine and attractive Gothic building. The W. front has been reduced to a solid, restrained bell tower and porch (14C) on a Romanesque foundation, but the apse, with triple sets of flying buttresses, is an impressive piece of architecture. The interior is strikingly wide and there is a gigantic 13C choir and five elegant radiating chapels. The lovely glass dates from 1230 and the marvellous organ-chest (1700) is by Jean Berain. The 4C tomb of Saint Quentin lies in the altered crypt.

Hôtel de Ville: Begun in the 14C, its façade dates from 1509 and is exuberantly Flamboyant in style. Highly ornate, there is an arcaded portico supporting a gallery with glazed-in bays and three triangular gables. It is further enhanced by a pretty 18C bell tower with a carillon.

Musée Antoine-Lécuyer: This museum is devoted to the works of Quentin de la Tour, who was born here in 1704. There are 90 pastel portraits by him which capture the spirit of his age.

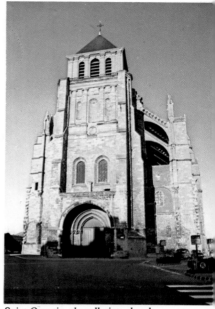

Saint-Quentin, the collegiate church

of art from America before Colombus, from Africa and Asia.

Saint-Rambert-sur-Loire (4,560 inhab.)
Loire   p.420☐L 11

This old village stands on the side of a small hill at the mouth of the gorges of the Loire. The modern town has grown up on the left bank of the river. Old quarters still have houses from the 15,16&18C. The massive church dates from the 11&12C and has two bell towers. The barrel-vaulted nave gets progressively wider from the entrance to the transept and this gives a feeling of spaciousness. The former priory buildings house a museum, which has exhibits concerning the town and has works

Saint-Rémy-de-Provence
                                         (7,970 inhab.)
13 Bouches-du-Rhone   p.425☐M 14

Old St-Rémy, encircled by boulevards, still has the tight irregular plan of a medieval town. The church of Saint-Martin, rebuilt in 1827, is dominated by a 14C bell tower. The Musée des Alpilles in the Hôtel Mistral de Mondragon (16C) has popular art and exhibits concerning Mistral and the great astrologer Nostradamus. An elegant Renaissance house, it is linked to the old Hôtel de Sade (15&16C)—a sort of archaeological storehouse of objects found at Glanum, with examples of Celto-Ligurian art, fragments of masonry, marble portrait

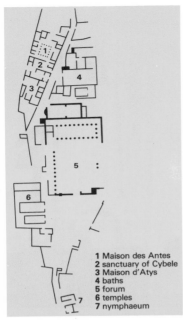

1 Maison des Antes
2 sanctuary of Cybele
3 Maison d'Atys
4 baths
5 forum
6 temples
7 nymphaeum

Saint-Rémy-de-Provence (excavations)

Saint-Rémy-de-Provence, the antiquities

heads of Octavia and Julia (sister and daughter of Augustus), jewellery and domestic objects. One room has finds from the digs of the Greek and early Christian site of **Saint-Blaise**, near Istres.

The town hall occupies a former convent (17C). The chapel of Notre-Dame-de-Pitié (15–17C) has a beautiful carved marble Virgin (18C).

Environs: Plateau des Antiques (1 km. S.): Here, under the natural ramparts of the Alpilles and in a beautiful situation, are two of the best-preserved Roman monuments in France, and the extensive remains of ancient Glanum. The site was inhabited from the 6–2C BC by Hellenized Ligurian Celts and then by the Romans. The town, near a sacred spring, was a major staging post and trading centre. *Mausoleum:* This is a quarter of a century later than the Arc Municipal adjoining it, and would seem to date from the dawn of the Christian era. Supremely elegant, this three-storeyed cenotaph is some 60 ft. high. The base has bas-reliefs of battle and hunting scenes. The next storey has an arch on each face

which were probably intended for funeral urns. The whole is surmounted by a circle of columns supporting a cupola under which two restored male figures in togas stand. *Municipal Arch:* This was erected outside the ancient town — probably in about 20 BC — on the road from Italy to Spain. It is badly damaged (barely two-thirds of the original monument remain) and was restored in the 15C by some monks. However, the nicely carved arch with a coffered vault has survived. **The Glanum Excavations:** A town — originally the Gallo-Greek Glanon, which became the Gallo-Roman Glanum—has been uncovered at the foot of the jagged Alpilles. It developed around a holy spring which was an important religious site and it prospered for centuries, until the German invasions of *c.* 270 began its decline. Building appears to date from three separate periods: the first phase is totally Greek (6 –2C BC); the second shows Roman influence (*c.* 105 BC); and the third, Gallo-Roman (46 BC–3C AD). The nymphaeum, on the edge of the area, marks the site of the sacred spring which attracted the founders of the city; the shrine has a Hellenistic base with a Roman part above. The E. slope of the valley has tiers of a modern theatre on top of the remains of a Hellenistic one. **Saint-Paul-de-Mausole:** The name of this old priory derives from 'mausoleum'. It is situated near the antiquities and became an asylum in the 18C. In an avenue in the park there is a bust which commemorates the fact that van Gogh was treated here from May 1889 until May 1890. Pictures he painted here dramatically reveal his inner turmoil—indeed, he committed suicide two and a half months after leaving for Auvers-sur-Oise. The 12C Romanesque church had a new façade in the 18C; the side chapels are additions. The lovely bell tower on the S. side of the nave can best be appreciated from the cloister, which is also 12C and is decorated with fine carved capitals.

Saint-Riquier	(1,210 inhab.)
80 Somme	p.410□I 2

A very appealing village, it has a 16C bel-

Glanum, the excavations

Saint-Rémy-de-Provence, 'A Road to Saint-Rémy' by van Gogh

fry, an 18C Hôtel Dieu with an ornate chapel and an impressive Gothic **abbey-church** from the 15&16C. The latter, the finest building in the town, is cathedral-like; the square Flamboyant tower, which serves as a façade, is lavishly carved and full of statues. The interior is beautifully simple and contains some splendid items, including a wooden Christ by Girardon, a splendid Renaissance baptistery and some striking wall paintings in the 16C treasury.

Saint-Sauveur-le-Vicomte
(2,200 inhab.)
50 Manche   p.413 ☐ E 4

This little town, rebuilt after the last war, is greatly enhanced by the remains of a strong 14C fortress, which was itself se-

verely damaged in 1944. This *château* houses the *Musée Barbey-d'Aurevilly*. The author of the *Diaboliques* was born very near here in 1808. The *church* (13&16C) was altered in the last century and contains a statue of St.James of Compostela (15C) and an Ecce Homo dating from 1532. The modern monastery just outside the town has an 18C residence.

Saint-Savin
(1,320 inhab.)
86 Vienne   p.419 ☐ H 9

Saint-Savin, on the Gartempe, between Berry and Poitou, has a church with a splendid Gothic spire. Inside the church there is the most beautiful set of Romanesque frescos in France; there is also the tomb of the anchorite St.Savinus, who gave his name to the town.

Saint-Sauveur-le-Vicomte, the château

Abbey church: Supposedly founded by
Charlemagne, there is, however, doubt as
to the exact date of construction of the present church—it is thought to be 11C. The
apse is sober and has many curved lines.
A long nave of nine bays is flanked by side
aisles and ends in a bell tower and porch.
The capitals are carved with leaf designs,
tracery and animals. The porch, gallery,
nave and crypt all have wall paintings,
which afford a fine example of the blending of art with architecture. These unique
frescos date from the 12C, are sober in colour, show lightness and vivacity of execution and reveal characters of great life. The
paintings in the *porch* illustrate the Apocalypse and have a white background. Those
in the *gallery* are large-scale depictions of
Christ's Passion and Resurrection. The left
side of the *nave* is devoted to scenes of the
Creation, while the right side depicts Gen-

esis, the story of Noah and that of Joseph.
The *crypt* has scenes from the life of St.
Savinus and St. Cyprien.

St-Seine-l'Abbaye   (350 inhab.)
21 Côte-d'Or   p.416☐L 7

This small village's name is not a reference
to the nearby sources of the Seine, but to
Sigo or Seigne, the abbot who founded a
monastic community here in the 6C. The
former abbey church is typical of Burgundian Gothic, and there is a real unity of
style, even though building continued
from the early 13C to the 15C. The 18C
stalls back on to two stone screens with
Flamboyant upper sections—the walls have
some remarkable paintings on the other
side. The N. screen on the left retells the

story of St. Seine (1504) and the S. one, painted about twenty years, shows a Tree of Jesse, the presentation of a Burgundian knight to the infant Christ, and the litanies of Our Lady. There are also several tombstones.

Environs: Sources de la Seine (9 km. NW): The source of the Seine, a clear stream, is protected by an artificial cave built by Napoleon III. The remains of a Gallo-Roman temple have been found, as well as statues and statuettes, and ex votos, all of which are now in the Musée Archéologique in Dijon (the Seine was deified as Sequana).

Saint-Sever (4,800 inhab.)
40 Landes p.422☐F 14

Saint-Sever on a plain of the river Adour, grew up around a Benedictine abbey, on the site of a Roman camp. The church faces an arcaded square with 18C houses; it was begun in 1008 and was certainly the finest Romanesque building in the Landes until it was ravaged by the Protestants in 1569. It was partially rebuilt and heavily altered, but preserves Romanesque capitals showing a marked Spanish-Moorish influence. The former Dominican abbey was rebuilt in the 17C; the church is crowned by an elegant turret, the cloister has been altered in Languedoc Romanesque style.

Saint-Sulpice-de-Favières (260 inhab.)
91 Essonne p.428☐I 5

This humble village, once a place of pilgrimage, has a surprisingly large church — a very fine Gothic building begun in 1260 and finished in the first half of the 14C. The large portal in the façade has sadly been defaced, but the choir is won-

derfully balanced, with three tiers of windows and a remarkable saddle-back bell tower. The nave has wooden barrel vaulting in the opening bays and then rib vaulting, and has side aisles and a gallery which pierces the buttresses and continues in the choir. There are several old stained-glass windows, and the raised choir has some 16C carved stalls. In the chapel of Saint-Sulpice, to the left, there is a 17C altarpiece. A staircase leads from the left aisle to the Chapelle des Miracles, a legacy from a 12C church where St. Sulpice's relics were venerated.

Saint-Thégonnec (1,990 inhab.)
29 Finistère p.412☐B 5

This Haut-Léon village owes its fame to a majestic parish close (see Guimiliau) built in the 16&17C in honour of Tigernach, a follower of St. Pol about whom little is known. The triumphal gateway (1587) has semicircular arches crowned with lanterns. The sober calvary (1610, three crosses) tells

Saint-Sever, the church

the story of the Passion. There is a small offertory table against the base carrying the statue of the patron saint of the parish, depicted traditionally with his cart laden with stones.

Ossuary chapel: This is later (1676) and is regarded as one of the finest pieces of Breton Renaissance building. Its façade is relieved by Corinthian colonettes, arched windows and shell-shaped niches. Above the door is the statue of St.Pol between two caryatids. A carved frieze runs all round the building. Inside there are a few statues, a 17C altarpiece and the church's treasure (silver 17C Virgin, an 18C silver-gilt cross). In the crypt is a striking Entombment in polychrome oak (1702), carved by the Morlaix artist Jacques Lespaignol.

Church: Built in the 16C, largely rebuilt in the 17&18C, it stands by the old cemetery, with the former bell tower (1563) and its own striking Renaissance bell tower inspired by the one at Pleyben. The porch, surmounted by the statue of St.Tigernach, with an Annunciation and the statues of St.John and St.Nicholas, now contains just four statues of the apostles (James, Thomas, Peter and John). The interior decoration includes some fine wood, the best being the pulpit of 1683.

Saint-Thibault	(160 inhab.)
21 Côte-d'Or	p.415☐L 7

Near to this little Auxois village are the remains of a large church built in the late 13C to house the relics of St.Thibault. It fell down in 1686 and only a bold, light choir of cathedral-like dimensions remains, adjoining a humble 18C nave, as well as a magnificent doorway from the old transept. On the tympanum appear the Death, Assumption and Coronation of the Virgin; on the archivolts the wise and foolish virgins, along with figures from the Old and New Testaments. In the early 14C statues of St. Thibault (on the pier), various benefactors and a bishop of Autun were added. The 30 panels of the door leaves (late-15C) depict the life of St.Thibault and his

Saint-Thégonnec, the calvary

Saint-Thégonnec, the church

14C reliquary is in the Chapelle Saint-Gilles to the left of the choir.

Saint-Tropez	(5,440 inhab.)
83 Var	p.426☐O 15

This charming little harbour, rebuilt after the war, suffers from an excess of fame. The old town, once fiercely independent and repopulated by the Genoese in the 15C is unbelievably crowded in the summer. The *Musée de l'Annonciade* in the former Chapelle des Pénitents-Blancs, has a remarkable collection of neo-Impressionist, Fauvist and modern paintings (Signac, Bonnard, Matisse, Marquet, Dunoyer de Segonzac, to name a few). The 16&17C citadel houses a naval museum.

Environs: Grimaud (10 km. W.): This Provençal village has lots of character, a ruined château, Romanesque church and the medieval Maison des Templiers. **Chartreuse de la Verne** (20 km. W.): Built of serpentine in the 12C, the char-terhouse has risen from its ruins and occupies a lovely Maures site (Maures comes from the Provençal word 'Mauro' meaning 'dark wood'). **Collobrières:** A monumental 17C gateway leads through to a large courtyard with 17C buildings all around. There are some fine remains of a small and a large cloister and of a Romanesque chapel.

St-Vaast-la-Hougue	(2,270 inhab.)
50 Manche	p.413☐E 3

A small resort, fishing port and marina on the Cotentin, Saint-Vaast once found favour with the Norman Duke Rollo. Attacked on many occasions up until the end of the Wars of Religion, it was later protected by fortifications designed by Vauban (Fort de la Hougue, Ile de Tatihou). The little *Chapelle des Marins* consists of the choir and apse of a Romanesque church partially demolished in the last century. N. of Saint-Vaast, the church of **Réville** is a mixture of Romanesque and Gothic and

'The Gulf of Saint-Tropez at Sunset' by Bonnard (Musée d'Albi)

has been greatly altered. The nearby **Manoir de la Crasvillerie** is a rather severe 16C building, built by an ennobled privateer.

Environs: Quettehou (3 km. E.): The massive, beautiful church of Saint-Vigor is 13C, with a powerful 15C tower.

St-Valéry-en-Caux   (3,350 inhab.)
76 Seine-Maritime   p.410☐H 3

This old harbour town was once arranged around a convent founded by St.Valéry, but it was almost completely flattened during the last war. Hardly any relics of the past survive; there is a lovely Renaissance house with carved beams and a rather uninteresting Gothic church in Vieux-Saint-Valéry. The *Chapelle de Notre-dame-du-Bon-Port* (1963) is highly original with its huge slate roof.

Environs: Cany-Barville (12 km. SW): 16C *church* with 13C bell tower. At some distance, the *Château de Cany*, built 1640–6 in Louis XIII style.

Saint-Wandrille   (1,270 inhab.)
76 Seine-Maritime   p.410☐H 3

Surrounded by trees and pasture land, the abbey of Saint-Wandrille is still occupied by Benedictine monks. Wandregesilus, its founder, was an official of King Dagobert. It was ravaged by the Normans in the 9C but it soon revived and became very prosperous in the Middle Ages, after which it declined and fell into ruins. Its restoration this time was the work of the Benedictines of Saint-Maur. Sold off at the time of the Revolution, it was rented for several years by the writer Maurice Maeterlink; then in 1931 the Benedictines reoccupied

it and the relics of St.Wandregesilus, which had been in Belgium for ten centuries, were returned to their rightful place. Through the fine *Portail de Jazente*, between two pavilions with carved pediments, you can see lawns in the main courtyard and buildings of various periods. Of the former 13C abbey church only some impressive ruins remain (it was a mixture of Norman and Ile-de-France styles). The new abbey church was built by the monks themselves, as was the chapel of Notre-Dame de Caillouville. They used the beams and stones from a 13C tithe barn (fine roof) which was demolished in the Eure. The cloister is 14C, as is the statue of Notre-Dame de Fontenelle. The chapel of Saint-Saturnin, on the side of a little hill, would seem to be 10 or 11C. The village church is Romanesque in origin and in one chapel is the statue of Notre-Dame de Caillouville (about 1300).

Ste-Foy-la-Grande   (3,580 inhab.)
33 Gironde   p.419☐G 12

This 13C former bastide has retained its regular plan and a certain picturesque quality: the remains of the ramparts, the arcaded square, the Tour des Templiers (13C) and old houses. The 14C church seems to be an old oratory built by Conques (Aveyron) monks which has been totally transformed. The great geographer Élisée Reclus was born in Sainte-Foy in 1830.

Ste-Mère-Église   (1,430 inhab.)
50 Manche   p.413☐E 3

Sainte-Mère-Église, a quiet town in green countryside, won its place in history on 6 June 1944 with the daring American parachute drop prior to the Utah Beach land-

Saint-Wandrille, the abbey church

thousands of pilgrims have climbed up to this famous monastery. The establishment owes its origins to a convent of which St. Odile, a daughter of a duke of Alsace, was abbess in the 7C. Because of a terrible fire in the 16C, there are few reminders of its long past; only a 12C stela, the *Chapelle de la Croix* (11C) and the *Chapelle de Sainte Odile* (Romanesque/Gothic). The convent church dates from 1687. There is a small path leading to the spring from which St. Odile obtained healing water and to the Neidermünster (lower monastery), burnt in 1542. The vaulted porch, tower walls and columns remain of the Romanesque abbey church.

ings. The church, made famous by the film *The Longest Day*, is 12C (tower and nave), 14&15C (choir). It still bears the marks of machine-gunning, and its two modern stained-glass windows depict one of the decisive phases of the last war. The *Musée des Troupes Aéroportées,* beneath a huge dome like a concrete parachute, is entirely devoted to the fighting.

Sainte-Odile (Mont)
67 Bas-Rhin   p.417☐O 5

Mont Saint-Odile, Alsace's holy mountain, is covered by dark vegetation and is flanked by the remains of a prehistoric wall which runs for about ten kilometres. There is a marvellous view of Alsace from here. Goethe, Taine, Barrès and thousands upon

Saintes
17 Charente-Maritime

(28,400 inhab.)
p.418☐F 10

This Roman and Romanesque town is the capital of the Saintonge region, and its history goes back over twenty centuries. The pink rooftops of the ancient centre of the town rise in tiers from the river Charente, hiding quiet walled gardens and courtyards shaded by plane-trees. After conquering the Gauls, Caesar made this town of the Santones a flourishing capital of the South-West. An idea of the scale of the Roman *Mediolanum Santonum* can be gained from the Roman remains. St.Eutrope converted the town to Christianity, and in the Middle Ages there was a spate of religious building, and Saintes became an important stage on the route to Santiago de Compostela. English and then French during the Middle Ages, the town later witnessed fierce struggles between Catholics and Protestants in the Wars of Religion. In the 17C many improvements were made, and further alterations were made in the 18C by engineers and administrators; the town dis-

Saint-Odile, the monastery

Saintes, the arena

plays the classical taste of the provincial nobles of the period in their luxurious hôtels.

Roman remains: *Amphitheatre:* Dating from the 1C, this is in a natural depression slightly outside the town. It could hold 20,000 spectators in its arena measuring 209 ft. by 128 ft. Performances are held here each summer. *Arch of Germanicus:* Until the middle of the last century, this stood on the old Roman bridge at the entrance to the Roman port, but it was then taken down and moved stone by stone to its present position. It was built in the year 19 in honour of Tiberius, and it consists of two large arches supporting the architrave, with fluted pilasters and fine Corinthian capitals at the corners of each pier. *Baths of Saint-Saloine:* Only a thick wall with half-domed niches remains of these baths.

Abbaye aux Dames: Founded in the 11C by Geoffroi Martel, Count of Anjou and lord of Saintonge, it was richly endowed convent and was administered by abbesses from the most noble French families; the future Madame de Montespan was one of its inmates. After the Revolution, it was turned into a barracks and only became a convent again in 1942. The church, a fine example of Saintonge Romanesque, is dominated by a bell tower with the purest of lines. *Façade:* This is 12C and on the ground floor has a vast semicircular doorway and two false doors; on the first floor is a window crowned with a large arch and framed by two blind bays. The Carving on the portal is abundant: starting from the bottom on the archivolts there are six adoring angels, the Pascal lamb and the symbols of the Evangelists, scenes of martyrdom, and the 54 elders of the

Saintes, the Arch of Germanicus

Saintes, St-Eutrope, capital

Apocalypse. The interior has magnificent proportions and a dome on pendentives over the crossing.

Saint-Paul: This church was for long dependent on the Abbaye aux Dames, and it bears the name of Palais or Pallade, a 6C bishop of Saintes. The nave is 12C, the rib-vaulting 13C and there is a large 15C Flamboyant bay in the square-ended apse.

Saint-Eutrope: This is one of the town's major buildings and it has a distinctive and powerful Gothic bell tower. The church was one of the stages on the pilgrimage route to Santiago de Compostela, but unfortunately its nave was removed in the early 19C, so that it now consists of the transept and apse of the Romanesque building, altered in the 15C. Inside, the clustered capitals of the pillars support the

dome and the effect is most striking. The designs of the capitals include tracery, imaginary beasts, Daniel in the lion's den and the weighing of souls. *Crypt:* This is the oldest religious building in Saintonge; it dates from the end of the 11C or early 12C and was built using masonry left over from earlier buildings. Its plan is an exact replica of the choir above it. There are three aisles and the groin vaulting rests on piers with columns and capitals inspired by antiquity. St. Eutrope's relics are kept in a 4C sarcophagus. There is a 160 ft. deep well in a former chapel which provided the water for the baptism of the first Christians and to one side there is an 11C font.

Saint-Pierre: This former cathedral is a major 15C building. Not very much remains of the Romanesque one built in 1137 by Pierre de Confolens (bases of walls,

Saintes, the church of Saint-Eutrope, the crypt

domes over the transept). The church was rebuilt in the 15C, finished and restored in the 16C, and now it dominates the lower quarters of Saintes. There is a porch in the massive bell tower with its polygonal dome and pinnacled buttresses. The Gothic doorway is a masterpiece, and features a multitude of figures: saints, apostles, bishops. The nave and aisles were rebuilt in the 16C, and the former ends in a wide apse with a series of radiating chapels. An elegant spiral staircase inside a narrow turret leads to the vaults of the nave. There is a very fine organ-chest in the gallery with wooden statues decorating it (17C). Next to the church, the remains of the cloister have been uncovered and restored.

Chapelle des Jacobins: The magnificent Gothic window (15C) taking up the entire E. wall of this chapel is one of the gems of the Gothic architecture of the South-West.

Museums: *Musée Archéologique:* This is close to the Arch of Germanicus and is full of relics from the ancient *Mediolanum Santonum* (rows of columns, capitals, bas-reliefs, torsoes of statues). *Musée Dupuy-Mestreau:* This is in the Hôtel Monconseil (18C), whose façade overlooking the river has a beautiful wrought-iron balustrade. Ceilings and panelling from the Châteaux of Romegoux and Tonnay-Charente have been adapted to the original apartments. The collections are of regional furniture, costumes, head-dresses, sets of ceramics (including 16C dishes by Bernard Palissy, who discovered the secret of his glaze in Saintes). *Musée des Beaux-Arts:* The former

Saintes, the church of Saint-Pierre

Hôtel du Présidial (17C) houses collections of paintings, including the superb *Allegory of the World*, by Jan Brueghel, and Saintonge ceramics. *Musée Éducatif de Préhistoire:* This deals with prehistory by means of tables, diagrams, displays of tools and so on.

Environs: Le Douhet (12 km. N.): The late-17C, early-18C château was a residence of the bishops of Saintes before the Revolution. Its elegant and sober façades are set in a fine park, enhanced by pools with balustrades still fed by a Roman aqueduct. **Romanesque churches.** Saintonge is one of the richest areas in France for Romanesque monuments. It was on the route to Santiago de Compostela and there are hundreds of simple little churches in lovely white stone. Generally, they are single-

aisled, with a circular or polygonal choir and arcaded façades. The archivolts of the single doorways, framed by two blind arcades, express all the exuberance and skill of the Romanesque sculptors. **Corme-Royal** (10 km. E.): This was built in the late 12C by an abbess of Saintes, a former abbey preserving a remarkable two-storey façade, lavishly decorated. The S. façade is fortified. **Retaud** (12 km. S.) This 12C church is famous for its apse, divided into eight sections by highly ornate column buttresses. There are a number of grotesque modillions. **Rioux** (15 km. S.): This church is very like Retaud and is also 12C. The polygonal apse is very elaborate indeed. The carved arcade surrounds a lovely Madonna and Child in a mandorla. **Écoyeux** (14 km. N.): The village church is a magnificent example of a 12C fortified

Retaud, church portal

Rioux, church, Madonna and Child

church. Its façade is framed by two pepper-pot corner turrets.

Saintes-Maries-de-la-Mer
(2, 120 inhab.)
13 Bouches-du-Rhône   p.425☐L 14

The gypsies (gitans) still flood into Saintes-Maries-de-la-Mer during their famous May pilgrimage: they venerate Sarah, their patron saint, and also Mary the mother of John and James, whose relics were discovered in 1448 during excavation beneath the church. Provençal tradition has it that they were brought here with Mary the sister of the Blessed Virgin and Lazarus (who was raised from the dead) in about the year 40.

The fortified church of Saintes-Maries is

visible from afar. It overlooks the Camargue and the sea, which has been getting nearer to the town ever since the Middle Ages. It was built in the second half of the 12C and it was used for defence prior to its fortification in the 14C and its subsequent alteration in the 15C. The present church does not appear Romanesque from the outside, apart from the Lombard bands on the apse, above which were built the chapel containing the relics of the three Marys and the keep. There are two marble lions on the 15C right flank, which once guarded a porch. After having been destroyed by lightning, the bell tower was rebuilt in 1903. The single aisle is austere and ends in a soaring choir. In the half-dome there are marble colonettes with arches and eight carved capitals (leaves, masks and human busts depicting the Incarnation and the Sacrifice of Abraham). The crypt (which is later than 1448) houses the shrine containing the relics of Sarah.

Musée Baroncelli: This is in the former town hall and bears the name of the Marquis Folco de Baroncelli, a cattle dealer who was in love with the Camargue and a friend of Mistral (who set the denouement of *Mireille* at Saintes-Maries). The museum covers various aspects of Camargue life (cowherds, traditions, animal life).

Saintes-Maries-de-la-Mer, the church

The **Place Tyssandier-d'Escous** is somewhat theatrical with its 15C lava houses and projecting turrets. Along the narrow streets are a succession of medieval and Renaissance façades, including the Maisons du Baillage, de Bargues, de la Ronade, des Templiers, the last of which houses an exhibition devoted to Salers's past.

Salers	(540 inhab.)
15 Cantal	p.420□J 11

The old medieval town is superbly situated on a basalt plateau almost 3,300 ft. high. Behind its ramparts there are noble, gabled and turretted houses, evidence of a prosperous past. The church, rebuilt in the 15C, retains a fine porch flanked by arcades from an earlier building. There are numerous works of art inside, in particular some old Aubusson tapestries and a remarkable 15C Entombment in polychrome stucco.

Salon-de-Provence	(35,590 inhab.)
13 Bouches-du-Rhône	p.425□M 14

Surrounded by shady courtyards, Salon, once a possession of the archbishops of Arles, has a timeless quality in its ancient centre. In the past it was encircled by ramparts but only two gates, one 14C the other 17C, survive from these. The church of

Salers, the gables, roofs and turrets of the old houses

Saint-Michel dates from the first half of the 13C. Although the portal has Gothic colonettes, Saint-Michel's builders re-used a Romanesque archivolt and tympanum (12C); the square bell tower of the façade is 15C. Inside there is a fine gilded altar with a 17C altarpiece. The former collegiate church of **Saint-Laurent**, on the outskirts of the town, was begun in 1344 and completed in 1480. It contains a marble bas-relief and the tomb of Nostradamus, the famous 16C astrologer, who ended his life in Salon (there is a small museum devoted to him in what was his house, near Saint-Michel). **L'Emperi:** A vast château with some 12C sections, its entrance gateway was rebuilt in 1585 and the guard house is 17C. Since 1967 it has housed the *Musée National d'Art et d'Histoire Militaire*, which has extensive collections of arms, uniforms and colours—collections which were assembled by Jean and Raoul Brunon.

Environs: Château de la Barben (12 km. E.): Originally a feudal fortress, it was transformed into a country seat in the 16&17C. It contains fine 17&18C furniture. Its white towers overlook a wildlife park.

Sarlat-la-Canéda (10,880 inhab.)
24 Dordogne p.419☐H 12

In spite of being cut in two by a long straight road built by an 'enlightened town council' in the last century, Sarlat is still

La Barben, the château ▶

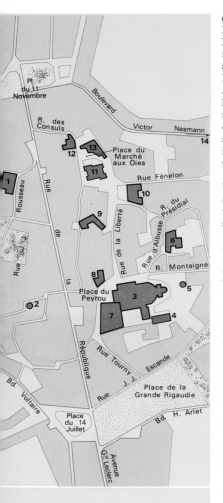

Sarlat-la-Canéda 1 Chapelle des Pénitents Blancs **2** watchtower **3** cathedral of Saint-Sacerdos **4** Chapelle des Pénitents Bleus **5** funerary lantern **6** Présidial **7** former Bishop's Palace **8** Maison de la Boétie **9** Hôtel Maleville **10** Hôtel de Ville **11** former church of Sainte-Marie **12** Hôtel Selve de Plamon **13** Hôtel de Glisson **14** Chapelle Notre-Dame-de-Temniac

one of the most astonishing towns in France. An open-air museum of medieval, Renaissance and 17C architecture, it has retained many of its old doorways, turrets, arches and passageways. As with Saint-Paul-de-Vence, Pérouges and Mont-Saint-Michel, time appears to have stood still here since the Revolution. Built in a golden stone, and with a colourful market and crowds of tourists in the summer, it is also a lively town. Having gained importance in the Carolingian period, it won the right to self-administration in the 13C; from 1317 until the Revolution, it was a bishopric. It was fortified and frequently attacked in the Hundred Years War and it was in English hands for a time. It also suffered badly during the Wars of Religion. In the 17&18C it prospered and the lesser aristocracy and newly rich citizens built fine houses. However, due to its rather out-of-the-way position it stagnated in the 19C. There was little modernization and consequently its historic heritage is well preserved. The law on historic monuments passed in August 1962 led to a major renovation programme. Now a beautiful town with interesting shops, it is renowned for its truffles and foie gras—the two great gastronomic specialities of Périgord. Modern industry has been kept outside the ring of boulevards surrounding the town; these follow the line of the old defensive ditches, which were filled in in about 1750. There are several important buildings but the town's main charm is to be discovered by simply strolling in the streets off either side of the Rue de la République. The *Rue de la Liberté* (formerly the Rue Bourgeoise) is the heart of old Sarlat; the *Place du Peyrou* is nearby. The part of the town crossed by the Rue Jean-Jacques Rousseau still has character, with its splendid pointed arches and watch-towers, its former convents, the *Chapelle des Pénitents Blancs* (1615–28, housing a small Musée d'Art Sacrée), its hôtels and the *Tour du Guet* (15C). But the most appealing area, with the cathedral and the finest hôtels, lies on the other side of the Rue de la République.

Cathedral of Saint-Sacerdos: A mixture of different styles, this 16C cathedral replaced an earlier abbey church, of which the magnificent façade tower and a number of Romanesque elements survive. The simple 17C doorway, with damaged medieval statues above, leads into a groin-vaulted room, which forms a kind of narthex. The interior is mostly 16C (though the pentagonal choir and apse are older in style), with 17C choir stalls and an 18C organ-chest. The former chapterhouse (two naves and 14C rib vaulting) is now the sacristy. Where the large Cluniac abbey once stood there are now two picturesque courtyards (entered from the right aisle). Next to the canon's chapel is the lovely *Chapelle des Pénitents Bleus*—12C Romanesque altered in the 17C by a confraternity of Penitents. A passageway and staircase lead to the unusual crowned 'lanterne des morts', an intriguing medieval tower with a conical top, said to commemorate St. Bernard's visit in 1147. There is no other tower like it in the region. Nearby is the elegant **Présidial**, the seat of royal justice in the 16&17C.

Former Bishop's Palace, Maison de la Boétie: In the delightful Place du Peyrou and in front of Saint-Sacerdos are the former Bishop's Palace, with its restored Renaissance gallery and Gothic windows, and the Hôtel de la Boétie, an unusual early-16C house, the birthplace of the poet and philosopher Étienne de la Boétie (b. 1530), a Councillor of the Bordeaux Parliament and a great friend of Montaigne. The arcaded Rue de la Liberté runs from the cathedral bell tower to the splendid Place Maleville and Place de la Liberté.

Hôtel Maleville: This superb house, built by a Superintendent of Finances un-

Sarlat, the Maison de La Boétie

der Henri IV, has a beautiful façade on the Rue de la Liberté (Renaissance doorway, tall staircase tower, with wings on either side). The rather less impressive rear elevation is reached via a vaulted passageway. The somewhat odd shape of the building reflects the layout of the houses which originally occupied the site. **Hôtel de Ville:** Early 17C, it incorporates remains of the medieval Commune house. Its little belfry looks on to the lovely Place de la Liberté (old hôtels).

Sainte-Marie: The remains of 14&15C parish church stand between the Rue de la Liberté and the Rue des Consuls. The church became redundant and was partly demolished after the Revolution.

Rue des Consuls: A particularly pretty street lined with 16&17C houses; the very

Sarlat, old houses

Saulieu, St-Andoche, capital

fine **Hôtel Selve de Plamon** is older (14&15C). The 16C **Hôtel de Gisson** is the main building in the charming Place du Marché-aux-Oies. Rather severely graceful, it consists of two wings linked by a slender but solid hexagonal staircase tower. On the N. boundary of the Commune (2 km. from the centre) lies the **Chapelle Notre-Dame-de-Temniac**. This much altered Romanesque church, standing on a hill, still attracts pilgrims. The nave has two domes.

Sartène: see Corsica

Saulieu	(3,160 inhab.)
21 Côte-d'Or	p.415□L 7

This town, the last before Morvan, is

famed for its gastronomic delights. (Madame de Sévigné got drunk here for the first time!) It also has a charming, slightly old-fashioned little museum with very varied exhibits relating to the locality.

Saint-Andoche: This became a collegiate church when the monks were replaced by canons. Dating from the early 12C, it suffered greatly in the Hundred Years War and the Wars of Religion. Much damaged and vandalized, it has an 18C choir but is only relatively interesting architecturally, although it does exemplify the Cluniac style (see **Cluny**). What makes it worth more than just a cursory visit, however, are the beautiful and imaginative Romanesque capitals (all kinds of plant motifs, strange fauna, Biblical scenes). The church contains the sarcophagus of St.Andoche—one of the first missionaries to Burgundy—and

Saulieu, Château de Thoisy-la-Bercherie

also a beautiful Virgin and Child donated by Madame de Sévigné. The stalls, which have carved elbow-rests, date from the late 14C. The animal sculptor Pompon (1855 –1933) came from here and is buried near the old 15C church of *Saint-Saturnin*. Some of the museum displays concern him and his work and the large statue of a bull in one of the town squares is his.

Saumur	(23,600 inhab.)
49 Maine-et-Loire	p.413☐F 7

The great château of Saumur towering above both town and river is exactly as depicted in the famous *Très Riches Heures du Duc de Berry*. At first a possession of the Angevin Princes and the Kings of England, Saumur reverted to France in the 12C, remaining loyal to it throughout the Hundred Years War. It became a Huguenot centre at the Reformation and there was a famous Protestant academy here. The walls were demolished in 1623. It remained loyal to the Crown during the Fronde, but suffered when, with the Revocation of the Edict of Nantes, many Protestants were forced to leave. It picked up when it became a garrison town and a large Riding School was established. Balzac's *Eugénie Grandet* is set in Saumur. The town was heavily shelled in June 1940, when the pupils of the Cavalry School made a heroic but vain attempt to halt the German advance.

Château: Graceful but still very much a fortress with strong walls, it sits firmly on a promontory overlooking the Thouet and the Loire. Though partially rebuilt, altered

Saumur, the château and the Loire

and much restored, it still looks more or less as it did in the second half of the 14C (it was built by Duke Louis I of Anjou in about 1367 on the site of an old fortress, which was probably 10C). The NW side completing the square no longer exists and in its place there is now a terrace affording fine views. The four solid towers, still with machicolations, survive in all their splendour thanks to extensive restoration (the castle was abandoned for years, then used as a prison and then a barracks). There is a lovely main staircase in one turret, and museums in the NE and SE sides. **Musée des Arts Décoratifs:** Of most note are the medieval and Renaissance works, tapestries, pottery and furniture. There are also extensive Gallo-Roman exhibits. The **Musée du Cheval** covers the history of riding through the ages—Saumur was for years a great riding centre, its

famous Cadre Noire boasting some superb horsemen.

Notre-Dame-de-Nantilly: Originally Romanesque (mainly 12C) and formerly attached to an abbey, this church was considerably altered under Louis XI (the Flamboyant right aisle). Imposing and somewhat austere, it contains a 12C wooden Madonna in an apsidal chapel to the right of the choir. The fine tapestries are 15&16C, apart from those woven in Aubusson in the 17C. There are interesting capitals and a late-17C organ-chest.

Saint-Pierre: 12C (transept and choir), with a sharp, pointed spire soaring above the old houses round about. The original façade collapsed and was rebuilt in the 17C. The right transept has an attractive

Saumur, Musée des Arts Décoratifs

Romanesque door, and there are two fine sets of tapestries (16C).

Notre-Dame-des-Ardilliers: Standing at the upstream end of the town, this 17C church has a somewhat incongruous rotunda whose vault was reconstructed in concrete. Built by the Oratorians with financial help from Mme de Montespan (whose sister was the Abbess of Fontevraud), it contains a statue of the Virgin —discovered in 1454 near a 'miraculous spring'—and a monumental altarpiece. Incorporated in the sacristy are remains of a former pilgrimage chapel.

Secular buildings of interest include the **Hôtel de Ville** (the left part is 16C; the small chapel, 13C), which the Loire used to lap against and the **École de Cavalerie** (18C), the history of which is presented in a museum in the building.

Environs: Bagneux (2 km. SW) The largest megalithic monument in Anjou, it is more a covered walk than a normal dolmen. It is now on private land. **Brézé** (11 km. SE): A much restored Renaissance château with a moat.

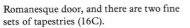

Sauve-Majeur (La)	(840 inhab.)
33 Gironde	p.418

Of the vast forest of *Silva Major* (hence the name Sauve-Majeur) in the heart of the Entre-Deux-Mers region only patches still remain. It was cleared by the monks from a once famous Benedictine abbey founded

La Sauve-Majeur, abbey church

of the fast-flowing river Oléron, which passes under an arch with a slender defensive tower (known as the 'bridge of the legend'). The *church* is a solid 13C building, combining Romanesque (pillars and half-domed apsidal chapels) and Gothic (rib vaults); the open porch is 19C, with a much restored Romanesque doorway. The *keep of Monréal* (12&13C) towers above the still impressive ruins of the rest of the castle.

Environs: Château de Laàs (9 km. E.): A large 17C manor in marvellous parkland. Externallly it is of no great architectural interest but the interior is sumptuous and contains treasures collected by a rich art connoisseur (wood-carvings, furniture, numerous objets d'art, drawings, paintings)—the luxurious home of a man of taste rather than a mere museum.

in 1079 by St.Gérard. The **abbey church** (12&13C), repaired in the 15&16C) stands on a large terrace. It declined and was then totally abandoned at the Revolution. Now, though only a fine ruin with its collapsed tunnel vaulting and fallen walls, it is still an interesting example of Romanesque (the apse is remarkably developed and there are magnificent capitals). In front of this shell there is the Gothic church of **Saint-Pierre**, with a late-12/early-13C square-ended apse (restored 13&16C wall paintings, large Romanesque capital used as a holy-water stoup).

Sauveterre-de-Béarn	(1,670 inhab.)
64 Pyrénées-Atlantiques	p.422□E 14

This charming old town stands on a bend

Saverne	(10,430 inhab.)
67 Bas-Rhin	p.417□O 5

A pleasant town at the mouth of a valley on the plain of Alsace, it has some fine old houses. Once a staging post, it still has three hotels (the name of the town actually derives from *tres tabernae*). It was here that the great 16C revolt of the Alsace peasants came to its tragic end, with their massacre at the hands of the Duke of Lorraine's troopers. From the 13C until the Revolution it was the favourite resort of the bishops of Strasbourg; and indeed they lived here for more than a century until the Reformation drove them from their See. The château was destroyed by a fire in 1779 and rebuilt by the extravagant Cardinal Louis René de Rohan (shortly afterwards he was rather naïvely compromised in the 'affair of the Queen's necklace', which resulted in his disgrace). In November 1944 the liberation of Saverne by General Leclerc's tanks opened up the road

Saverne, the château

to Strasbourg after a diversionary ma-
noeuvre which deceived the Germans.

Château: Described by Goethe as 'an ecclesiastical outpost of a powerful monarch'.
An imposing structure in pinky-red sandstone, it was not quite finished when the
Revolution broke out. It was eventually
completed under Napoleon III, who had
decided to house the widows of civil servants here. It has a fine park, and a splendid garden front with columns and
pilasters. It houses a **Musée d'Archéologie et d'Histoire**.

Parish church: 14&15C, with a partly
Romanesque bell tower. Very richly decorated and furnished: Christ Entombed
(15C) in a recess, a beautiful pulpit (from
the 1490s by Jans Hanvier), a white marble
group of Christ, Mary and John (16C),

tombs, wooden panel paintings (15C), and
a 16C Pietà. The 15C rood loft is now used
for the organ. There are Gallo-Roman and
Frankish remains in the garden. To the
right of the church, the 17C Vieux
Château houses the Sous-Préfecture.

Cloître des Récollets: Once part of a
convent (now converted into a college) this
is a fine Gothic structure (early 14C), with
17C wall paintings.

Environs: Château du Haut-Barr (4
km. SW): Perched some 1,476 ft. up on
three rocks and surrounded by a single vast
wall, this has been called 'the eye of Alsace'.
Romanesque, with Lombard friezes in the
chapel, it was the residence of the Bishop
of Strasbourg, Jean de Manderscheidt,
who restored it in the 16C. In the Thirty
Years War it was damaged, and it was sold

Sceaux, the château

off as national property in the Revolution.
Neuwiller-lès-Saverne (14 km. N.): The
former abbey church of *Saint-Pierre-et-
Saint-Paul* dates from the 12&13C.

| **Sceaux** | (19,960 inhab.) |
| 92 Hauts-de-Seine | p.428☐I 5 |

The lovely park of Sceaux, belonging to
a château destroyed early in the 17C, was
landscaped by Le Nôtre after the property
was bought by Colbert in 1670; parts have
since been sold off, and the remainder has
been landscaped afresh. At the entrance
gate there are two groups of animals by
Coysevox, and there is a beautiful 17C
Orangerie by Hardouin-Mansart, the *Great
Cascade* (reconstructed), a magnificent
pond called the *Octogone*, a large canal and

elegant pavilions. The 19C château is
rather commonplace, but it houses a rich
Musée de l'Ile de France (paintings,
drawings, sculptures, tapestries, earthenware and porcelain from the old Sceaux
factory, models, books and cards).

| **Sedan** | (25,430 inhab.) |
| 08 Ardennes | p.416☐L 3 |

This former strongpoint on the banks of
the Meuse, where Turenne was born in
1611, suffered terrible damage in the last
war. Despite this, it possesses some typical 17&18C houses. The *Palais des Princes
de Sedan*, built in the 17C and still known
as the Château-Bas, is most attractive. On
a rocky outcrop dominating the town and
protected by enormous stone walls, it is one

Sedan, Palais des Princes de Sedan, aerial view

of the largest fortresses in Europe. It was begun in 1424 (the two entrance towers) and altered at various times to keep up with changes in the art of warfare (squat 16C bastions).

Environs: Bazeilles (3.5 km. SE): This village boasts a majestic 18C château consisting of a main block with a decorated pediment flanked by two pavilions; a wrought-iron gate stands in front of the buildings. In 1870, the French army suffered a terrible defeat in Sedan after fierce fighting, and the *Maison des Dernières Cartouches* — portrayed in a very popular painting—has made Bazeilles famous. **Mouzon** (17 km. SE): This large village still has some of its 14&15C fortifications, including the Porte de Bourgogne. The splendid 13C Gothic church was substantially altered in the 19C. Over the cen-

tral door there is a pretty carved tympanum (13C). The nave is remarkably high with galleries and a triforium; the choir is beautifully arranged with five radiating chapels.

Sées	(5,240 inhab.)
61 Orne	p.410☐G 5

Rising above this peaceful town is the tall spire of one of the most beautiful religious buildings in Normandy. A major ecclesiastical centre, the town has seminaries, colleges and an abbey (it first had a bishop in the 4C). Several churches preceded the cathedral of **Notre-Dame** (or Saint-Gervais-et-Saint-Protais), which was begun in the late 13C on rather flimsy foundations. The 14C façade had to be reinforced in the 16C. The nave is light

Sées, window in the cathedral

and soaring and the choir airy and unusually big (all the clergy of the town had to be able to be accommodated) with some lovely late-13C glass. The transept, almost contemporary with the choir, is all elegance and vertical lines. There is a 13C or 14C marble Virgin in the right transept and an 18C marble 'Beau Dieu'.

There are two museums in Sées, one of sacred art, and the other a museum of folklore. The former Bishop's Palace was built about ten years before the Revolution, during which it was stripped of all its treasures. The church of *Notre-Dame-de-la-Place* is much damaged but contains a Renaissance organ loft and some 16C basreliefs.

Environs: Château d'O (8 km. NW): This oddly-named château (called after an old noble family) is surrounded by a large moat. Started at the end of the 15C, it is distinctly Renaissance in style, though with a fine Gothic pavilion; the S. wing is 16C (important restoration work was undertaken in the W. wing in the 18C).

Sélestat	(15,750 inhab.)
67 Bas-Rhin	p.417☐O 6

The dull outskirts of this town do not prepare one for the delightful cluster of narrow streets and tiny squares in the centre, where there are two totally dissimilar churches.

Sainte-Foy: A former abbey church with an elegant spire, stylistically it reflects the influence of both Lorraine and Burgundy. Rebuilt in the second half of the 12C, and restored and 'completed' (rather badly) at the end of the last century, it is nevertheless striking in its architectural balance and the richness of its décor. Outside, the best preserved parts are the façade with two towers (very elegant door), the graceful apse with carved decorations, and the tall octagonal tower over the crossing which has attractive ornate arcading. Inside, the capitals are very varied and lavish (plant decoration, ribbon and rope motifs). Beneath the crossing is the crypt.

Saint-Georges: This church with its square tower, is a complete contrast to Sainte-Foy's luxuriant Gothic. It has an extended narthex with a pretty S. door and dates from the 13&15C (19C restoration). Along with numerous old windows, it has some modern glass by Max Ingrand.

Secular buildings: The *Tour des Sorcières* is part of the fortifications rebuilt by Vauban. Near the church of Saint-Georges is the *Hôtel d'Ebermunster* an early example of Renaissance architecture in this region. **Musée et Bibliothèque**

Sélestat, houses with flowers

Humaniste: In the 15&16C Sélestat enjoyed a literary heyday with some brilliant historians and theologians. Its Latin School of the time had a very rich library, whose treasures as well as some works of art, are preserved in a decidedly dull corn-market (converted in the 19C). This library and museum displays manuscripts and books from the 7–18C. Two of its proudest possessions are the *Merovingian Lectionary* (late 7C) and the *Book of Miracles of St.Foy* (12C). It also contains two altarpieces and a beautiful Head of Christ (15C), various sculptures and some pottery. The *Tour de l'Horloge* is 14&17C.

Selles-sur-Cher	(4,660 inhab.)
41 Loir-et-Cher	p.414 ☐ H 7

This little town on the Touraine-Sologne-Berry border developed around an abbey which owed its existence to *St.Eusice* (6C). The church of **Saint-Eusice** is Romanesque in origin (most of the façade, bell tower, S. aisle and capitals), but it has undergone much alteration and restoration. The interesting apse is decorated outside with two curious carved friezes illustrating the New Testament and the life of St. Eusice. Among the treasures is a 14C ivory triptych. The tomb of St.Eusice is in the crypt. The cloister of the former abbey (a 17C reconstruction) is occupied by a **Musée de la Pierre à Fusil** (working with flint had for a long time been a local industry). The château on the Cher is completely surrounded by water. Built in the 13C on the site of a demolished fortress, it acquired some pretty pavilion towers, linked by a gallery with oculi, in the 16&17C. It is a happy mixture of brick and tufa. The interior has coffered ceilings, huge fireplaces and some 16&17C furniture.

Semur-en-Auxois   (5,370 inhab.)
21 Côte-d'Or   p.415☐L 7

A picturesque town, the capital of Auxois, one of the regions of Burgundy, Semur was said to have been founded by none other than Hercules. History, however, more prosaically stresses the influence of the dukes, who made it an important military centre and gave it the cathedral. Quite medieval-looking with walls, the remains of a castle, and the Porte Sauvigny (14C), the town lies in a loop in the river Armançon. It is best first to get an overall view from across the river and then to enter the town, preferably via the short Rue Buffon —a street lined with venerable old houses.

Notre-Dame: Founded in the 11C by Duke Robert I, rebuilt in the 13&14C, altered, then extensively restored by Viollet-le-Duc. Either side of the 13C façade are two heavy square towers. In front is a large 15C porch with crocketed pinnacles. The pretty decorated 13C *Porte des Bleds* (i.e. des blès, the corn door) is on the N. side: in the tympanum is the legend of St. Thomas, entertainingly accompanied by two stone snails climbing up one of the columns (recalling the days when snails were plentiful in the region, and restaurants did not have to buy them from elsewhere). *Interior:* In spite of various modifications, Notre-Dame remains a very good example of Burgundian Gothic, especially the choir (interesting capitals in the apse). The chapels on the left (mainly late 15C) have an Entombment of 1490 and some fine windows showing medieval butchers and drapers. Near the Porte des Bleds is a tall ciborium (15C), obelisk-shaped and crowned with an ornate pinnacle turret.

Tour de l'Orle d'Or: A vestige of the castle demolished on Henri IV's orders, this now houses a small museum belonging to the Société des Sciences Historiques et Naturelles de Semur. The former Dominican house also contains an interesting museum, and a library of precious manuscripts and incunabula.

Environs: Château de Bourbilly (9 km. SW): This former strongpoint belonged to the family of St.Jeanne de Chantal and Madame de Sévigné.

Senlis   (14,390 inhab.)
60 Oise   p.411☐J 4

A quiet sous-préfecture dating back to Gallo-Roman times, Senlis was a royal possession from very early on—Hugues Capet was crowned here in 897. It was then gradually neglected by the kings of France (except that they stayed here on their way from Reims after the coronation). It has, however, known bloodshed: the Burgundians in 1418 and, five centuries later the Germans in 1914, massacred hostages here. The delicate spire of the cathedral is a permanent feature of the town. Some of the old walls survive, and the centre has considerable charm, with buildings ranging in date from the Middle Ages to the 18C.

Notre-Dame: Senlis was a bishopric until 1790. The cathedral, though modest in size, is extremely beautiful. Started in the 12C, ten years before Notre-Dame in Paris, building proceeded slowly; in the 16C it had to be partly rebuilt after a fire. The sober late-12C façade looks on to a quiet little square. The right tower has a tall 13C spire. The remarkable, much imitated *central doorway* is dedicated to the Virgin (a Dormition appears on the lintel and her Coronation on the tympanum). On the

Semur-en-Auxois, aerial view

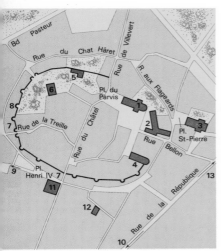

Senlis 1 Cathedral of Notre-Dame **2** former Bishop's Palace **3** church of Saint-Pierre **4** church of Saint-Frambourg **5** Château Royal **6** Musée de la Vénerie **7** Gallo-Roman wall **8** towers of the Gallo-Roman wall **9** arena **10** Collège Saint-Vincent **11** Hôtel de Ville **12** Musée de Haubergier **13** Abbaye de la Victoire

right is another beautiful and interesting door, also devoted to the Virgin; it is the work of Pierre Chambiges (responsible for the reconstruction in the 16C). *Interior:* The nave is long, tall and narrow and has side aisles with galleries. The choir, with ambulatory, is ringed by monolithic columns, two of which still have capitals with floral decoration. The church contains several statues: including a Madonna and St.Louis (14C) in the apsidal chapels. The chapterhouse dates from the late 14C or the 15C and has a strange carving of a lunatics' party on the capital of the central column. The former **Bishop's Palace** is 13C, although it was altered during the Renaissance and in the 17C. It incorporates a tower and remains of the Gallo-Roman town wall in the apse of the cathedral. The deconsecrated church of **Saint-Pierre** was converted into a market

some time ago. It dates from the 11&16C. The left tower is Romanesque with a Gothic spire, the S. tower is Renaissance and the façade is Flamboyant. The former church of *Saint-Frambourg,* near the Bishop's Palace, is late 12C and was restored by the great pianist Giorgy Cziffra having been used as a coachbuilder's workshop. A fine building with Carolingian elements, it now functions as a centre for music.

Château Royal: Standing on the site of a Gallo-Roman castrum, this is a mixture of periods, notably Romanesque and Gothic. The park has the buildings of a priory founded by St.Louis. The *Musée de la Vénerie* (hunting museum) was set up in one of the priory buildings (18C). The displays include hunting dress, buttons of various hunts, horns, hunting knives, trophies, paintings and prints.

Gallo-Roman wall: This runs beside the base of the château. Now partly hidden in private properties, it had 28 towers and some substantial ruins of these still survive. 3C Gallo-Roman arenas.

Collège Saint-Vincent: Housed in the former Royal Abbey of Saint-Vincent and the former Convent of the Visitation, it has a 12C bell tower and a classical cloister. The Hôtel de Ville is mainly a very late 15C reconstruction. There are some fine hôtels (16,17&18C) around the long Place Gérard-de-Nerval (named after the poet who wrote about Senlis and the region). The Hôtel de Saint-Simon in the Rue Bellon belonged to the family of the great diarist of that name.

Musée du Haubergier: This museum housed in a 16C hôtel with a hexagonal staircase turret, is dedicated to regional history and has varied collections (prehistory,

Senlis, cathedral, façade

Gallic, Gallo-Roman, medieval and Renaissance). Of particular interest are the ex-votos from a temple in the Forest of Halatte and a prophet's head (late 12C or early 13C) which came from the cathedral.

Environs: Abbaye de la Victoire (3 km. SE): The ruins of this abbey founded by Philippe Auguste are set in a park. The abbey château is 18C. **Montépilloy** (8 km. E.): The name comes from *Mons speculatorum* (watcher's mountain). Remains of a 12&15C fortress. **Saint-Christophe** (8 km. N.) Encircled by the Forest of Senlis, this village still has the ruins of a medieval priory and its church.

Sens   (27,460 inhab.)
89 Yonne   p.415□K 6

This was the capital of the powerful Senones (a Gallic tribe, from whom the present name of the town comes) and then of a Gallo-Roman province. It was surrounded by thick walls, and became an important archbishopric. By the 9C the prelates of Sens had gained considerable power and, having the title of Primate of the Gauls and of Germania, their authority extended over Paris, Chartres, Orléans and Meaux right up until 1622. (Though much smaller now, it still remains a large diocese.) In 1234, St. Louis was married here; St. Loup, Archbishop of Sens, condemned Abélard from here. At the same time, Sens was developing commercially, helped by its location between the Ile-de-France and Burgundy. There are still remains of the Gallo-Roman defences and some lovely old houses (Maison Abraham (16C) Rue de la République). However, the outstanding feature of the town is the cathedral, which is one of the most beautiful Gothic buildings in France.

Cathedral: Nearly as old as Saint-Denis, it was begun in about 1130 by Archbishop Henri Sanglier, a friend of St. Bernard. The choir was already completed when the building was consecrated (1164), and work on the nave finished in about 1175–80. The architect Martin Chambiges erected the great transept at the end of the 15C, and

Senlis, park of the château, Diana the huntress

chapels were added in the 16&18C. This marvellous church, one of the prototypes for the Gothic cathedral, has three aisles, an arrangement which is reflected in the remarkable triple façade.

PORTALS: The left door is the oldest (final years of the 12C) and recounts the story of St.John the Baptist. The scene of Herod's feast has a young-looking Salomé in a tight-fitting garment. The central doorway has a superb statue of St.Stephen on the centre post; his life is depicted in the tympanum (13C). The right door, which would seem to be no earlier than about 1300, has statues of the prophets and, in the tympanum, the Dormition of the Virgin. The late-12C N. tower, the *Tour de Plomb* (Lead Tower) had a belfry which was destroyed in the last century. The S. tower, the *Tour de Pierre* (Stone Tower), fell down after the cathedral was finished and was only replaced in the 16C. The doorways and façades of the transept arms are fine examples of Flamboyant.

INTERIOR: Superb early Gothic: no gallery but a wide nave with alternating pillars and twin columns beneath markedly curved vaults. The windows date from the late 12C to the 17C, so differ considerably in style. The rose-windows in the transept are among the largest in the world after that in the cathedral of Palma. The choir has a magnificent wrought-iron *screen* (Louis XV style), a gift from the Cardinal of Luynes in 1762. It bears his coat-of-arms, and is the work of the Parisian metal worker Guillaume Doré. The high altar, with canopy, is by Servandoni (1742). The ambulatory has radiating chapels containing numerous works of art. The 18C *Chapelle de Sainte-Colombe* contains the tomb of the Dauphin, Louis XV's son; it originally stood in the middle of the choir. In the next chapel, the exquisite glass with its wonderful dominant blue is the work of Guillaume Coustou and dates from the 12C. The oldest chapel in the cathedral is that of John the Baptist, whose capitals are still Romanesque in inspiration. *Treasury:* In spite of repeated pillaging, this is one of the largest in France. Of great interest are the pieces of silk cloth used for wrapping relics (some are as old as the 6C). There are also lovely ivories, enamels, religious plate and 15&16C tapestries.

Palais Synodal: Also called the **Officialité,** it is an elegant 13C building and was formerly an ecclesiastical court, abutting on to the cathedral. Restored by Viollet-le-Duc, it contains a *Musée Lapidaire* with some fine tapestries. The synodal room has a tomb with a recumbent figure of a 16C bishop. To the right of the Palace, in the Rue de la Résistance, is the *Archbishop's Palace,* with 16&17C buildings and a Renaissance doorway.

Other churches: *Saint-Pierre-le-Rond* is 13C (nave) and 16C; the former abbey church of *Saint-Jean* is 13&17C (interesting apsidal chapel); *Saint-Savinien,* on a site called the Champs-des-Martyres (Martyrs' Field), is the oldest church in Sens, parts of which are 11C.

Sens, cathedral, central portal

Sens, cathedral, glass

set up here in 1082 under the patronage of the Bishop of Elne. The rather basic 11C *church* was enlarged in the 12C, and contains some of the best Romanesque sculpture in Roussillon (unusual lion capitals and delicate decoration on the pink marble gallery which was probably once a rood-loft).

Serrant (château)
49 Maine-et-Loire   p.413☐F 7

This stately, symmetrical château stands amid lawns and meadows and is reflected in the water of its wide moat. It has a quiet, rather severe elegance. The overall impression is one of unity, although construction went on from the late 16–early 18C. The well ordered use of shale and tufa adds to this feeling. The chapel, attributed to Jules Hardouin-Mansart, was erected after 1700; it contains the imposing *tomb of the Marquis of Vaubrun,* designed by Charles Le Brun and carved by Coysevox. The apartments are well furnished (large library, large drawing room with a fine ceiling hung with tapestries of trees and plants).

Sézanne   (6,550 inhab.)
51 Marne   p.411☐K 5

This little agricultural and industrial town on the Ile-de-France and Champagne border has a 15&16C church (the tower finished in the 17C). Parts of the old fortifications also survive. Incorporated in the hospital is a 17C convent chapel.

Musée Archéologique et des Beaux-Arts: 5 Rue Rigault. This is interesting and varied, with major Gallo-Roman exhibits (mosaics, funeral slabs, inscriptions) and many 17&18C paintings; also mementoes of Napoleon.

Environs: Fleurigny (16 km. NE): The elegant Renaissance château was built about 1520 on the site of a demolished fortress, some of whose features it incorporates. The chapel has a painted coffered ceiling.

Serrabone (priory)
66 Pyrénées-Orientales   p.424☐J 16

Serrabone ('Bonne montagne' — good mountain) is in wild and bleak country in the Aspre region; a religious community

Silvacane (abbey)
84 Vaucluse   p.425☐M 14

This abbey, together with Sénanque and

Sens, cathedral, rose-window

Serrant, the château

Le Thoronet (see Gordes), is one of the 'three Cistercian sisters' of Provence. It stands on the banks of the Durance and its name comes from the 'forest of reeds' (*sylva canae*) which originally covered the site (this incidentally gives a further link with Cîteaux, whose name derives from 'cistel', meaning reed). Founded in 1144, and made important by the Lords of Baux, it became famous and then fell into decline; it was finally taken over by the chapter of Aix cathedral in the 15C. It was sold off as a national asset in the Revolution and, in 1846, the fine typically Cistercian abbey church was almost lost for ever—there was a serious plan to demolish it and use the stones to surface nearby roads! It was, however, saved and restored for future generations to admire. In its design it follows the Burgundian ground plan of Fontenay. The badly damaged cloister is still Romanesque, while the advent of Gothic can be seen in the chapterhouse. The refectory has four bays and dates from 1420.

Sion-Vaudémont	(70 inhab.)
54 Meurthe-et-Moselle	p.417☐N 5

The architecture here hardly does justice to the splendour of the location or the memories which haunt it. From time immemorial, this 'antique mountain' in the shape of a horseshoe, with the villages of Sion and Vaudémont at either end, has been a place of pilgrimage. A spot over 1,640 ft. up, it affords views of a vast sweep of sky and land, taking in the extensive ruins of the **Château de Vaudémont,** the family seat of the Dukes of Lorraine. The

Sion-Vaudémont, church, Virgin

church of Sion is 18C, with an imposing 19C tower; the choir is authentic Gothic (14C) and has a gilded statue of the Virgin (15C). There is a *Musée d'Histoire Locale* in a neighbouring convent.

Environs: Haroué (10 km. NE): This small village boasts a superb château built by Boffrand in 1720; a moat from an earlier castle adds considerably to the atmosphere. It has paintings by Hubert Robert and sumptuous 18C furniture.

Sisteron   (7,440 inhab.)
04 Alpes-de-Haute-Provence   p.425□N 13

Sisteron, the Roman *Segustero*, was once a Bishop's See and belonged to the kingdom of Arles. After changing hands on several occasions, it was finally ceded to France in the 15C. The towers of the old town wall survive, together with a powerful 11C citadel (the fortifications date mainly from the late 16/early 17C). Its strategic position in a narrow valley of the Durance meant that it was fiercely contested in the Wars of Religion.

Notre-Dame-des Pommiers: Probably dating back to the third quarter of the 12C, this former Romanesque cathedral stands near a classical burial place. A distinctive Romanesque building, it is majestic and bare outside. An octagonal dome rises in front of the choir, the arches and the barrel-vaulting of the nave are slightly pointed, and the apses are half-domed. It was altered in the 14&17C when the present bell tower and the chapels were added.

Dominican church: A mid-13C building in the Baume quarter, it reflects Cistercian influence (although the little bell tower has Lombard Romanesque decoration).

Sizun   (1,870 inhab.)
29 Finistère   p.412□B 5

The little town of Sizun, between Élorn and Monts-Arrée, an area dotted with chapels and calvaries (see **Guimiliau**), has a *parish close* with a remarkable triumphal gate (1590) consisting of three round arches with columns and Corinthian capitals. A platform above the arches has a balustrade with places for lanterns, a small altar and a simple calvary with attendant figures. The façade of the adjacent ossuary (similarly late 14C) has little arched windows with caryatids, fluted columns and niches containing statues of the Apostles. The mainly-17C *church* has a perforated bell tower with a tall octagonal spire (18C). The S. side has an ornate 16C porch. The interior is panelled throughout, has carved beams, several altars with altarpieces and a 17C canopied font.

Environs: Locmélar (7 km. N.): The *parish close* here is less grand than others in the area. However, the 16&17C church is interesting and has paintings illustrating the life of St.Hervé and St.Mélar, the patron saint of the parish. Nearby is a simple cross with figures (16C) and a 17C ossuary. **Commana** (10 km. E.): A beautiful 16&17C *church* perched on a little hill. The cemetery in which it stands has a monumental gate, two crosses and an ossuary chapel. Beside the choir, with its decorative woodwork, are two imposing altarpieces dating from 1682 and dedicated to St.Anne and the Five Wounds of Christ. The font (also 1682) has a canopy supported by five statues representing the theological and cardinal virtues.

| **Soissons** | (32,110 inhab.) |
| 02 Aisne | p.411 □ K 4 |

Once the capital of the Suessiones (Gauls), then a Roman garrison, Soissons was conquered in 486 by Clovis, thus bringing about the beginning of the Frankish era. Any French schoolchild will know the story of the Vase of Soissons as related by Gregory of Tours (according to Gregory —although it is probably only legendary —Clovis broke the skull of one of his warriors who had deliberately broken a vase that was to have been returned to the Bishop of Reims). Soissons, the capital of the kingdom of Neustria, shared the fate of the rest of the Ile-de-France. Standing on the route of invading armies in 1870 and in the two World Wars, it had to be almost completely rebuilt and its great monuments restored. Still recognizable by the lofty spires of Saint-Jean-des-Vignes, Soissons is today primarily an agricultural, market and industrial centre.

Cathedral of Saint-Gervais-et-Saint-Protais: Begun in the 12C (S. transept), but built mostly in the 13C (choir, nave, side aisles), this cathedral was not finished until the 14C (N. transept and the fine E. door). The façade was altered insensitively

Sizun, triumphal gateway of the parish close

in the 18C, but some careful restoration was undertaken after World War 1. A church of graceful simplicity, it contains elements of every phase of Gothic: the S. transept has galleries; the rest of the building is in the three-storey style; and the interior decoration is distinctly more elaborate in the N. transept. *Interior:* The bare, elegant nave has tall handsome, twinned windows above the triforium. The choir, finished in 1212, is one of the first examples of decorated Gothic. The S. transept, started in 1177, is wonderfully balanced with ambulatory and upper-storey galleries (reminiscent of so many of the Rhineland churches). Leading off this transept, and contemporary with it, is the two-storey Chapelle de la Résurrection, the upper floor communicating with the galleries. The N. transept has a lovely rose-window and contains an *Adoration of the Shepherds* by Rubens, which the painter gave to the Franciscans of Soissons to thank them for looking after him.

On the other side of the Place Fernand-Marquigny, in a quarter which was de-

stroyed in 1918, are the ruins of the Romanesque *Saint-Pierre-au-Parvis*, now a memorial to deportees.

Former Abbey of Saint-Léger and museum: The abbey was founded in the mid 12C. Sacked by the Protestants, it suffered further damage centuries later in the Great War. The 13C church was partially rebuilt in the 17C. The cloister is 13C, as is the apse, although the sanctuary rests on a 12C crypt. Now restored, the monastic buildings house a *Musée d'Archéologie et d'Art,* a museum of local history: with Gallo-Roman objects, including a fine silver dish; and works by Houdon, Largillière, Courbet, Boudin and local artists. The chapter-house is 13C and contains sculptures. Near Saint-Léger is the Hôtel de Ville, in the former Palais de l'Intendance (18C).

Former Abbey of Saint-Jean-des-Vignes: Founded in the 11C, and richly endowed by successive kings, princes and prelates. Damaged by war on several occasions, it also suffered at the hands of a philistine bishop, who had the large abbey

Soissons, cathedral of Saint-Gervais, aerial view

Soissons, cathedral, façade

Soissons, cathedral, transept

church demolished in order to use the materials for the restoration of the cathedral (early 19C). Because of the public outcry, he refrained from demolishing the 13&14C façade and the later towers, and these are now an odd sight, with a rose-window and other windows opening on to a void. Of the great monastic buildings, there survive sections of the large and small cloisters, the fine 13C refectory and the cellar beneath, as well as a residential block (16C) where some statues are now displayed.

Former Abbey of Saint-Médard: On the right bank of the Aisne. An important abbey in the Merovingian and Carolingian periods, there now remains little more than the pre-Romanesque crypt, which contained the tombs of St. Médard and two descendants of Clovis.

Environs: Septmonts (7 km. SE): The ruins and keep of a 14C castle set amid huge trees create a somewhat ghostly scene.

Oulchy-le-Château: (20 km. SE): Remains of a castle and a church of Romanesque origin (capitals).

Solesmes	(1,000 inhab.)
72 Sarthe	p.413□F 6

A quiet village on the Sarthe, made famous by the Benedictine **abbey** of Saint-Pierre —an impressive 19C granite building, with some lesser 18C buildings. Though of ancient foundation, the community had declined and finally been destroyed by the Revolution. Its revival was due to Dom Guéranger (born at nearby Sablé in 1805), who made it a great religious centre, contributing to the renaissance of Gregorian chant. The **abbey church** dates from the 11,15&19C (19C choir) and can be visited. It contains some superb carved groups of *Saints of Solesmes* (15&16C), a monumental Entombment of Christ (1496) and a rather overdone 16C Entombment of the Virgin.

Solignac	(1,120 inhab.)
87 Haute-Vienne	p.419☐H 10

The monastery founded here by St. Eloi in the 7C was the cradle of the great silver- and enamel-working tradition of Limousin. The **abbey church of Saint-Pierre** was rebuilt in the early 12C and the proportions of its majestic, multi-domed nave are surprising. The choir, with many sculpted capitals and richly carved 15C stalls, still retains some of its 15C glass. At the entrance, a 15C fresco depicts St. Christopher and the Christ Child. The abbey suffered many vicissitudes from the 10C on, but was fully restored in the 18C.

Solutré	(370 inhab.)
71 Saône-et-Loire	p.420☐L 9

The high chalky escarpment of Solutré now overlooks the rows of vines producing the dry white wine Pouilly-Fuissé. A natural fortress, 1,624 ft. up, it has been used as such since the dawn of history. A refuge, it also had a plentiful supply of flint for making weapons and tools. Because of the quantity and variety of tools found around here, one period of the Upper Palaeolithic is known as the Solutrian (18,000 – 15,000 BC). This vast deposit,

Solignac, abbey church of Saint-Pierre

found in 1866 at the foot of the 'rock', is an incredible sequence of layers, all resting on a Mousterian (Middle Palaeolithic) base. An intermediate level is made up of broken horse bones 1 ft. 3 in.–6 ft. 6 in. thick. (One theory is that hunters 15,000 or 20,000 years ago cornered herds of wild horses and forced them to throw themselves off the top of the cliffs. However, this idea of equine mass suicide is far from being proven.) The results of the excavations and archaeological research are displayed in the Musée des Ursulines at Mâcon (see **Mâcon**).

Sorde-l'Abbaye	(620 inhab.)
40 Landes	p.422☐E 14

Vestiges still survive of the 13C fort built

here at the edge of the cascading river Oloron. The former Benedictine abbey church, somewhat ravaged by time, has been much restored; the Romanesque features are interesting, as are the sizeable fragments of Gallo-Roman mosaic in the choir. The *Logis de l'Abbé,* near the apse and oddly disembowelled by excavations, is an unusual house, which incorporates the remains of a Gallo-Roman building (mosaics and tombs).

Environs: Peyrehorade (4 km. NW): This, the 'capital' of the small Landes region of Orthe, is dominated by a ruined castle keep. The so-called Château de Montréal (late 15C, in rather poor condition) is reflected in the waters of a river formed by a confluence of the two Gaves.

Cagnotte (7 km. NW of Peyrehorade): An interesting, carefully-restored church of Romanesque origin, formerly the burial place of the Viscounts of Orthe. It contains a marble sarcophagus dating from the 5C or 6C and another strange sarcophagus hollowed out of the trunk of a beech tree.

Sorde, the abbey church

Sospel	(2,160 inhab.)
06 Alpes-Maritimes	p.426□P 13

This is an attractive Alpine resort about 20 km. from the Mediterranean. It has an old bridge with a tower (11C, rebuilt after being badly damaged in 1914) and old houses clustering along either side of the Bévéra. The 17C church of **Saint-Michel** stands on a pretty square lined with medieval arcaded houses. It was built as a cathedral, which explains its size. Along with this classical church is a Romanesque bell tower, surviving from a now-demolished building.

Souillac	(4,370 inhab.)
46 Lot	p.419□H 12

Souillac grew up around a Benedictine abbey built on former marshland ('souilh'=mire). A small commercial town in the upper Quercy near the Dordogne (a region of rocky cliffs, woods of walnut trees, truffles and foie gras), it seems rather uninteresting when approached from the main road, which allows only the barest glimpse of the bell tower of the former church of Saint-Martin (16C with 12C tympanum) behind the town hall. It is only when exploring the narrow streets of the town that you discover what must be one of the finest monuments in Périgord and Quercy, the church of **Sainte-Marie**, which belonged to a community said to have been founded by St.Benedict. Mostly 12C, though started in the late 11C, it is now a parish church. Mined by the Protestants, it remained standing, whereas Saint-Martin was brought down (1573). During the Revolution it was closed and found to be in a dreadful state when the long work of restoration began.

EXTERIOR: Domes rise behind a strong,

squat tower, pre-Romanesque in origin, heightened in the 14C and having a 17C door. This bell-tower-porch of Carolingian type (now restored and strengthened) was left intact in the 11&12C reconstruction work. It is a graceful, sober structure in somewhat severe grey stone which leaves the restoration work clearly visible. It has a superb apse with a fine half-dome (there are three polygonal apsidal chaples, and two others adjoining the transept arms).

INTERIOR: The airy nave with its three magnificent domes gives an impression of width and verticality, although compared with the cathedral of Cahors, on which the nave is modelled, the dimensions are not large. The dome over the crossing is larger than those over the nave, and since it has been cleaned, the perfect craftsmanship of the masons who built it can be fully appreciated. Apart from the ornate inner door the church is soberly decorated inside (palms and foliage, birds carved beak to beak, and various other carvings). *Inner door:* Though the Protestants did not destroy the building they did pillage it, seri-

ously damaging this door. During the 17C restoration, parts of it were 'turned around' and set at the head of the nave. The reconstituted door (five fragments) is a masterpiece, showing the influence of Moissac. Constructed like a triptych, the door is framed by statues of the prophets Hosea and Isaiah (the latter on the right is particularly fine and has a bas-relief above). It tells the story of Theophilus, who, having signed a pact with the Devil, was overcome with remorse and saved by the Virgin. The pillar supporting this bas-relief (possibly once an engaged pier) is carved with wonderfully entangled monsters of mysterious and ferocious appearance. On the right of what we presume to have been the centre post there are three representations of an old man and a young man; on the opposite side is the Sacrifice of Abraham. A piece of carving similar to the pier has been reused symmetrically, creating something that may approximate to the original appearance.

Environs: Château de la Treyne (6 km. S.): This little château set in lovely park-

Souillac, the church of Sainte-Marie

land above the Dordogne is mostly 17C, though begun in the 14C. It is prettily furnished and decorated, and contains various works of art.

Soulac-sur-Mer	(2,390 inhab.)
33 Gironde	p.418☐E 11

Soulac, a large village on the Aquitaine coast, developed from the Roman port of *Noviomagnus* (the Gironde town of Ys destroyed by the encroaching Atlantic). It is not only the ocean that encroaches on this coastline—there is also a sea of sand, as the wind whips the constantly advancing dunes. The 11C, 12C (choir) and 14C former priory church of *Notre-Dame-de-la-Fin-des-Terres* was in fact buried in sand for some time. Eventually uncovered and restored, it had lost most of its transept, so that it now appears to have only one bay of the nave (possibly built in about 1079).

Environs: Phare du Cordouan: This tall lighthouse on the Pointe de Grave (whence La Fayette set out for America in 1777) has a Renaissance base (1584–1601) and an 18C tower. Standing between the two navigable channels of the Gironde, its most notable feature is its domed chapel.

Souterraine (La)	(5,510 inhab.)
23 Creuse	p.419☐[H 9

The lovely **Porte Saint-Jean** (once part of the fortifications), which leads into the town is a tall 14C structure flanked by two overhanging machicolated turrets. **Notre-Dame-de-l'Assomption:** The present building was begun in the mid 12C with the three W. bays. The transept, choir and bell tower (13C) were paid for by Richard the Lionheart. In the 19C, the church was restored by Abadie. At the entrance there are two columns with limestone capitals illustrating the Annunciation and the Visitation. The nave has three different kinds of vaulting: barrel, pointed-barrel and ribbed. *Crypt:* Altered in the 11C and extended in the 13C. It leads into a mysterious cavern with classical granite columns and a well—probably relics of the *cella* of a Gallo-Roman temple.

Souvigny	(2,120 inhab.)
03 Allier	p.420☐J 9

Standing amid the tall-roofed old houses of Souvigny is the finest religious building in the Bourbonnais.

Saint-Pierre: Famous because two abbots of Cluny died here—St.Mayeul in 994 and St.Odilo in 1049—this monastery was the wealthiest daughter-house of Cluny. Several Dukes of Bourbon chose to be buried here and it was dubbed the 'Saint-Denis of the Bourbons'. In the 15C a new façade was grafted on to the original 11&12C Romanesque structure, of which only the left door survives. *Interior:* The huge nave, with four side aisles, is impressive. Of the many capitals which betray Cluniac influence, one depicting the minting of money recalls the concession once granted to the monks of Souvigny. The *Chapelle Vieille,* containing the 15C tomb of Louis II of Bourbon and his wife, is closed by a delicate Flamboyant stone screen. The *Chapelle Neuve*—also Flamboyant—houses the magnificent marble tomb of Charles I of Bourbon and his wife (15C). Underneath the vast 18C sacristy is a room converted into a **Musée Lapidaire,** with the superb Romanesque 'calendrier de pierre' (stone calendar), showing the signs of the zodiac and the labours of the months (12C). **Cloister:** Only one side of this remains (late 15C), with an interesting fivefold arrangement of

Souvigny, the church of Saint-Pierre

Souvigny, Musée Lapidaire

the keystones. **Former priory:** This leads into the square through a fine gate (late 17C) framed by pilasters.

Strasbourg (257,300 inhab.)
67 Bas-Rhin p.417☐P 5

Strasbourg has a distinctive character. It is a major economic and intellectual centre, at once typically Alsatian, eminently French and supremely European. One of the largest ports on the Rhine, it also has a very active university, and is the headquarters of the Council of Europe. It extends way beyond the branches of the Ill which encircle its historic centre. Though the rather jumbled outskirts are overrun by mediocre concrete blocks of flats, the historic heart of the city has been respected

and lovingly restored, and large areas have been turned into pedestrian precincts. For centuries the symbol of the city has been its breathtaking cathedral. Yet the rest of the city fully lives up to this symbol: it is a great centre for music and the arts, has many museums, is both traditional and lively, and has managed to preserve its picturesque old charm and the very varied heritage of its great past. Half-timbering and wrought-iron—the domestic and the aristocratic—mingle in a plethora of styles: Rhenish, Ile-de-France, Alsatian Renaissance, Versailles, 18C French, Modern, together with German town planning. These styles do not clash but form a special Strasbourgeoise character. Only modern architecture is poorly represented (designs by Le Courbusier were turned down). There are a few buildings of moderate interest, like the new Synagogue, but

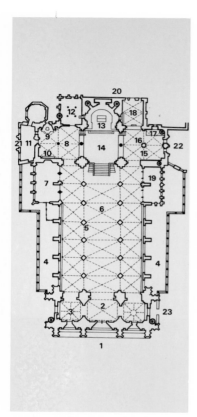

Strasbourg - cathedral of Notre-Dame 1 Façade **2** narthex **3** tower with spire **4** gallery **5** pulpit **6** nave **7** Chapelle Saint-Laurent **8** N. transept **9** font **10** Mount of Olives **11** sacristy **12** Chapelle Saint-Jean **13** choir **14** crossing **15** S. transept **16** angel pillar or pillar of the Last Judgement **17** astronomical clock **18** Chapelle Saint-André **19** Chapelle Saint-Cathérine **20** cloister **21** portal of Saint-Laurent **22** portail de l'Horloge (clock doorway) **23** access to the platform

civil centre, often destroyed and abandoned during invasions. Then *Strateburgum* ('road town'), appeared in the Frankish era on the ruins of the classical city, subsequently passing from the counts to the increasingly powerful bishops. It continued to expand around its cathedral (first Carolingian, then Romanesque): Holy Roman Emperors came to the city and St. Bernard also visited it. The citizens were strong in their prosperity and obtained freedom and privileges, soon freeing themselves from episcopal authority and taking over many of the bishop's powers themselves (notably the guardianship of the 'Oeuvre Notre-Dame'). A sort of aristocracy evolved, then later the merchant and artisan classes gained ascendance. With the advantage of its port, Strasbourg had become a rich city and European trading counter. It then acquired from the Emperors the status of a free town and the right to self government as a republic (the Corporations elected aldermen, who formed Councils). The home of Rhenish mysticism in the 14C, and ever open to technical and intellectual innovation (Gutenberg lived here), the city was rapidly won over to the Reformation. In the Thirty Years War it was weakened by religious strife and declined. Joined to France and administered by Intendants, it flourished anew, but then went through turbulent times in the Revolution. It was here that Rouget de L'Isle composed the Marseillaise. A thriving city again in the 19C, it became German, with the rest of Alsace in 1870 and remained so until November 1918. The population was evacuated in 1939 and the city once again reverted to Germany. Badly bombed, it was finally liberated in November 1944. The HQ of the Council of Europe since 1949, by 1968 it had developed into a major urban conglommeration. The city is now particularly famous for its music (the Opéra du Rhin) and its numerous museums and galleries.

most of the new building is mediocre and, luckily, in the outskirts. A river crossroads and natural focal point, Strasbourg has been inhabited since the Bronze Age, first by the Celts and then the Romans. *Argentorate* became an important military and

Strasbourg, tympanum and archivolts of the cathedral portal

Cathedral: An unmistakable façade, with its daring spire and delicate stone tracery. The mixture of traditional Rhineland architecture, Ile-de-France Gothic, and its own very individual spirit is somewhat bewildering. Rebuilding of the rather grandiose 11C basilica started in the 12C and proceeded in stages. Gothic made its mark in the 13C with the arrival of master builders trained in the Ile-de-France. The W. front — on which the great masterbuilder Erwin de Steinbach worked—was erected 1277 – 1384 (when the belfry aligned with the side towers was put in place). The spire, designed by the architect of Ulm Cathedral, was finished in 1439. In the 19C Gustave Klotz began a very incompetent restoration: a ridiculous tower was built over the crossing. The financing and upkeep of the cathedral were assured by the Oeuvre Notre-Dame, of which more below.

EXTERIOR: *W. front and spire:* The façade was partly carried out according to Plan B, preserved in the Oeuvre Notre-Dame. Unlike traditional façades, it does not reflect the structure of the building as a whole but is like a separate piece of decoration. Its doorways surrounded with statues are striking, as are the unusual airy 'toothed arches' standing away from the bare walls, which they mask. Equally striking is the superb great rose-window with sixteen radiating petals. The late-13C portals owe their iconography to Albertus Magnus. The *central doorway* is richly decorated with statues and bas-reliefs, and has a tympanum with four sections (the first three 13C, the top one modern). The sculptures

Strasbourg, cathedral, detail of the façade

in the arches are 19C, as the medieval ones were broken during the Revolution. The piers bear prophets, and Solomon appears beneath a Virgin and Child on the gable. The right door illustrates the parable of the Wise and Foolish Virgins (some statues are copies), and the left one has 14C statues of the Virtues laying low the Vices. The upper platform affords marvellous views over Strasbourg. The delicate openwork spire is nearly as high as that at Rouen (about 465 ft.). The side aisles are flanked with neo-Gothic arches, erected in the 18C to hide the shops lining the sides of the cathedral. The 13C *Portail de l'Horloge* on the right is the oldest entrance into the church; between its two doors (Romanesque) is a restored statue of Solomon. On either side are very good copies of that 'admirable couple, the Synagogue (with eyes blindfolded) and the Church Triumphant'.

A superb Dormition of the Virgin in the tympanum of the left door shows Byzantine influence (about 1225). The *Portail Sant-Laurent* on the other side is late 15C. Heavily restored in the last century, it depicts the Martyrdom of St. Sebastian. Originals of the other statues are now in the Oeuvre Notre-Dame.

INTERIOR: The cathedral is 340 ft. long, and has a Latin cross ground plan. The W. end has three bays corresponding to the outside portals. Both the three-storey nave and the wide side aisles have beautiful 13&14C glass (princes and emperors of the Holy Roman Empire in the N. aisle). The *pulpit*, extravagantly modelled and carved with niches and statues, was commissioned by the great Geiler de Kaysersberg (1485),

Strasbourg, Musée de l'OEuvre N.-D.

and is the work of Hans Hammer. The present organ chest is late 15C and very ornate, resting on a most impressive, carved pendent keystone (note the moving *Rohraffen* — little sculptures which the clerks could play with while apparently attending their office). The *Chapelle Sainte-Catherine* (*c.* 1340) opens at the E. end of the right aisle. It has some very fine 14C glass and a beautiful bas-relief of the Death of the Virgin (1480). The *Chapelle Saint-Laurent* to the N. dates from the early 16C (altar, 1698). *Right transept:* In the centre is the astonishing *Angel Pillar or Last Judgement*, with the Evangelists (at the bottom), angels blowing trumpets, and Christ in Judgement—a superbly delicate and original 13C work by an anonymous artist who was obviously very familiar with Chartres. Leaning his elbows on the choristers' gallery is a little stone man (1495) who eternally contemplates this unique pillar (perhaps it is a self-portrait of some architect). The present *astronomical clock* is quite a curiosity; though the case is still mostly 16C, it was given a new movement in 1838). It is half an hour slow (it chimes midday at 12.30 p.m.), has a perpetual calendar, and has a crowd of little animated figures. To the left of the clock is a 13C stained-glass window of a huge St.Christopher. The transept leads to the Chapelle Saint-André (late 12C), which in turn leads to the cloister (14&15C glass from the former Dominican church, sculptures, religious objects, tapestries). *Choir:* Built above a large crypt dating almost certainly from the early 11C and quite high up at the top of steps, it markedly separates the two arms of the transept. The arches and painted decoration are modern. In the apse (vaulted by a half-dome) is a window by Max Ingrand, donated by the Council of Europe in 1956. Its subject is the Virgin, the patron saint of Strasbourg. Here and there on the choir staircase are altars with triptychs (16C). *Left transept:* The N. transept arm was transformed and com-

Strasbourg, cathedral of N.-D., window

pleted 1220–5. It preserves some elements of the original basilica and a monumental niche erected about 1200, and has a wonderfully carved Flamboyant *font* by Jodoque Dotzinger (1453). Opposite these is the enormous late-15C *Christ on the Mount of Olives*. This transept leads to the *Chapelle Saint-Jean-Baptiste,* built about 1230 (sculptures contemporary with the Angel Pillar and the tomb of Bishop Conrad of Lichtenberg).

Place de la Cathédrale: Just in front of the cathedral is the important *Pharmacie du Cerf,* a half-timbered house with a stone ground floor (15&16C). To the left of the cathedral is the superb *Maison Kammerzell,* owned by the Oeuvre Notre-Dame and now a restaurant patronized by tourists and locals alike. It bears the name of a former owner, and dates from 1467

Strasbourg, cathedral of Notre-Dame, rose-window

(ground floor) and the 16C (overhanging upper storeys). There are numerous carvings on the façade and amusing murals in the inside rooms (1910). There are many old houses around here, especially in the *Rue Mercière* (16&17C) and *Rue du Maroquin* (the name from the old-time shoemakers), the *Place de la Grande-Boucherie* and *Place du Marché-aux-Cochons-de-Lait*. The former Jesuit College (18C) forms one side of the Place du Château, on to which fronts the Museum of the Oeuvre Notre-Dame, and the Rohan château-museum.

Oeuvre Notre-Dame: No visit to the cathedral is complete without a visit here. A rich organization, owning a considerable amount of property, it still finances the cathedral. The very fine *Museum* occupies a group of medieval and Renaissance buildings, comprising a part on the left with 14C stepped gable volutes and a late-16C right wing with a gable with volutes, the former Hôtel des Cerfs (14C), and reconstructed sections of demolished timber-framed houses. There is a strange lopsided doorway in the façade and an original Renaissance spiral staircase in the entrance hall. The museum is extremely varied and, while it constantly reminds one of the cathedral, it is far from being exclusively devoted to it. Of particular interest: the well-displayed glass, including one of the oldest known stained-glass windows, the 11C 'Wissembourg Head', some silver, 15C Rhenish sculptures, paintings, a beautiful work by Konrad Witz (*St. Catherine and Mary Magdalene*), miniatures and local furniture. There are numerous statues on show which were originally part of the cathedral, including the marvellous Synagogue and Church Triumphant (1230)

Strasbourg, glass in the Oeuvre N.-D.

and the drawings of master-masons of the cathedral (including the famous 'Plan B' which was the inspiration for the façade).

Main religious buildings: Saint-Thomas. A beautiful large Gothic church, very severe externally, dating mainly from the 13&14C. It contains the tomb of Maurice de Saxe by Jean-Baptiste Pigalle (1776), and in one chapel is the tomb (*c.* 1130) of Bishop Adeloch. **Saint-Pierre-le-Vieux:** Both Catholic and Protestant, this church dates partly from the early 13C (major work in the 15C). It has carved panels dating from 1501, and late-15C painted panels of the Passion. **Saint-Pierre-le-Jeune:** This became Protestant at the beginning of the Reformation. It is a complex building in lime-treated brick, dating from the 12&13C (choir) and the 14C (nave). It has a fine rood screen,

painted in 1620. The modern cloister has some 11C elements.

Petite France and Ponts Couverts: The quarter known as Petite France lies between the church of Saint-Thomas and the Ponts Couverts. It was the domain of fishermen, tanners and artisans. Wonderfully pretty, it has been well restored and is full of many old houses of great character quite often with a touch of Alsatian Renaissance: a picture postcard scene of half-timbering, balconies and gables, huge roofs and spacious courtyards. Typical of the area is the *Maison des Tanneurs* (1572, with later rebuilding and additions), now a restaurant serving regional food. The name 'Petite France' is a reference to the 'mal français' (the French disease), syphilis, which used to be treated in a hospital nearby. The *Ponts Couverts* (covered bridges — in fact a line of three bridges) have kept their name despite having lost their roofs in 1784. They span the Ill, and are watched over by the massive towers from the old city walls (14C). A splendid view of the bridges can be had from the *Barrage Vauban* or *Grande Écluse* (large lock); built to designs by the famous military architect Vauban at the end of the 17C. It controlled the entrance to the town, and could be used to flood the S. side.

Place Kléber: General Kléber (b. Strasbourg, 1753) is buried beneath the statue of him carved by the local sculptor Philippe Grass in 1840. Designed in Louis XV's reign by Jacques François Blondel, this vast square has been rather ruined since. The Aubette building (begun in 1765) burned down in 1870, along with the collections of the museum it housed. The new building is rather uninspired and the interior décor by Théo Van Doesburg, Jean Arp and Sophie Taeuber-Arp — a

Strasbourg, 'the Wissembourg Head

Strasbourg, Petite France

remarkable 1920s geometric and abstract creation—was destroyed by the German occupying forces in the war. To the Nazis it was the epitome of 'decadent' art. **Place Gutenberg:** The large Chamber of Commerce building, begun in 1582, Renaissance, extended on the S. side in 1867. David d'Angers' statue of Gutenberg was unveiled in 1840. **Place Broglie:** Named after Marshal de Broglie who made a promenade here in 1740. The Hôtel de Ville, built in 1730–6, by the architect Joseph Massol was once a nobleman's house. The town theatre is 19C. **Place de la République:** Dominated by the enormous and somewhat pompous *Palais du Rhin,* formerly the Palais Impérial, this square (formerly the Kaiserplatz) reflects the ideas of late-19C German town planners—Haussmann-type logic and a taste for the monumental.

Bishop's Palace: 16 Rue Brûlée: (doorway at No. 3, Rue Parchemin). The first Strasbourg hôtel to reflect Parisian taste (1720s). A fine building, it has been the Bishop's Palace since 1855. Its 'garden' façade faces the 18C Rue Brûlée, one of Strasbourg's most interesting streets (beautiful *Hôtel du Préfet,* the formerer Intendance, behind a magnificent doorway at No. 19).

Museums: Apart from the Oeuvre Notre-Dame near the cathedral, Strasbourg has a number of other remarkable museums, very varied and well laid out. They are in the S. part of the old town, near the Ill. **Château des Rohan, Musées des Beaux-Arts, des Arts Décoratifs et Archéologique.** This sumptuous palace named after the first of four Rohans who were bishops of Strasbourg before the

Strasbourg, the Château des Rohan

Revolution stands close to the cathedral, and is reflected in the waters of the Ill. Itself an elegant, noble building, built 1731–42 by Joseph Massol to plans by Robert de Cotte, it has been a museum since the Belle Époque. It forms a huge sandstone square arranged around a main courtyard, its main doorway almost directly opposite the S. door of the cathedral. Beautifully proportioned, with balanced vertical and horizontal emphases, it, nevertheless, inside reflects a showy luxury catering for the tastes of a prelate who adored Versailles and wanted to dazzle. **Musée des Beaux-Arts:** 14C to late-18C works, with a few 19&20C canvases. A superb collection, particularly of Italian (Botticelli, Filippo Lippi, Correggio, Guercino, Tiepolo, Guardi, etc.), Flemish and Dutch (Lucas van Leyden, Rubens, van Dyck, Jordaens) and 17&18C French schools.

The famous portrait by Nicolas de Largillière, *La Belle Strasbourgeoise* (1703), shows a lady in local costume with a strange 'chapeau à cornes' (cocked hat). **Musée des Arts Décoratifs:** Some superb exhibits especially from the 18C; an important collection of ceramics, with fine pieces from the local Hannong factory, founded in 1721. **Musée Archéologique:** Finds from various excavations in Strasbourg and Alsace displayed in the basement of the château. All kinds of objects and works of art Palaeolithic to Merovingian, plus a remarkable Gallo-Roman section. **Musée Historique:** Housed in the converted *Grande Boucherie* (late-16C) near the Pont Corbeau, this museum retraces Strasbourg's history, with numerous documents and objets d'art. There are amusing regiments of 'little Strasbourg soldiers', painted and cut out (19C), a vast collection

Strasbourg, wall painting, Rue des Bateliers

of uniforms and a very charming room full of mechanical toys from the 19C and early 20C. **Musée d'Art Moderne:** Opposite the Musée Historique, part of the reconstructed Ancienne Douane (Old Customs House). Some charming 19&20C works, with a few avant-garde contemporary pieces. There are paintings by Monet, Sisley, Renoir, Boudin, Monticelli and Degas, a major work by the local artist Jean Arp and Sophie Taeuber-Arp, works by Magnelli, Herbin, Hartung and Lindner. Strange works by the Alsatian François Rupert Carabin, who died in Strasbourg in 1921, including an entertaining Surrealist armchair supported by nude women and with cats as arm-rests. **Musée Alsacien:** Alost opposite the Ancienne Douane, this is on the Quai Saint-Nicolas, alongside 16&17C houses (including the restaurant *A la Canette d'Or*, with an oriel

window dating from 1600). Representative of the whole of Alsace, it is a marvellous mish-mash of exhibits: local folk art, customs and traditions, trades, agriculture and viticulture. The collections are in perfect keeping with the décor. There are signs, conscription souvenirs, paintings under glass, finely decorated baptismal greetings, popular ceramics, furniture, domestic items and objects relating to Judaism.

Sully-sur-Loire	(5,180 inhab.)
45 Loiret	p.415☐l 7

Upstream from the 'Val des Châteaux', Sully is a peaceful little town on the Sologne border, pleasantly rebuilt after the war. It owes much to the skilful adminis-

Strasbourg, Musée Rohan, Jan Brueghel I

Sully-sur-Loire, the château

trator Maximilien de Béthune, created Duke of Sully by Henri IV, who modernized it, at the same time enlarging and re-organizing the crude 14C fortress controlling the passage of the Loire. The Château de Sully was pillaged in the exodus of 1940, shelled, and used first as the German staff headquarters and then for refugees...after which it underwent major restoration. It is in a variety of styles: the section facing the Loire is medieval and is flanked by two towers. At right angles to it is the late-16C **Petit Château**, which was altered by Sully and to which he added the large Tour de Béthune. The **Vieux Château** has a splendid chestnut roof (1363). The Petit Château contains the study and bedroom of Sully (fine ceilings painted at the beginning of the 17C).

Collegiate church of Saint-Ythier: 16C

and early-17C, this church retains two fine stained-glass windows from the 1590s, one is in the S. aisle and the other is in the central apse (Tree of Jesse). There is a statue on the façade of the great prelate, Maurice de Sully, a native of the region, who built Notre-Dame in Paris. In the centre of the town there is a fine Renaissance house.

| **Surgères** | (6,500 inhab.) |
| 17 Charente-Maritime | p.418 □ F 9/10 |

In the N. of the Saintonge, this small town is a centre of the Charente dairy industry. It was once the fief of the counts of Surgères and their castle suffered numerous sieges in the course of the centuries. Only the remains of the curtain wall, one round tower and the moat survive from it. **Notre-**

Surgères, the church of Notre-Dame, detail of the cornice

Dame: An interesting 12C church with a restored façade buttressed at either corner by groups of columns. It is richly decorated with the signs of the zodiac and the labours of the months on the modillions of the cornice, highly carved archivolts and niches containing statues of knights which even experts cannot identify with certainty. An unusual octagonal tower forms the lantern and the bell tower is over the crossing.

Talcy

41 Loir-et-Cher

(230 inhab.)
p.414☐H 7

This village in the Beauce near Blois, is reached via the appropriately named Route de la Rose (a road bordered with roses). The impressive keep of the **château** stands amid vast cornfields and farms. It was rebuilt in the 16C by a wealthy Florentine, Bernardo Salviati, whose daughter Cassandre was beloved of the poet Ronsard, and whose granddaughter Diane inspired an intense passion in the Calvinist poet Agrippa d'Augbigné. The delightful first courtyard has retained a canopied well. The second courtyard has a large, excellently preserved 16C dovecote with 1,500 nesting holes and swivelling ladders. The luxurious furniture (17C Directoire) inside the château contrasts markedly with the feudal austerity of the rooms themselves.

Tanlay (château)

89 Yonne

p.415☐K 6

A wonderfully unusual château, Tanlay was begun in the mid 16C, but was not finished until the 1640s by Pierre Le Muet, partly because of the intervention of the

Wars of Religion. The result is a charming mix of French Renaissance and classical styles. Broad moats and a wooded park complete the enchantment of the place. Tanlay is entered through a Louis XIII-style gatehouse, the *Petit Château*. The *Grand Château*, with a fine entrance, domes and steeply pitched roofs, houses superb furniture and works of art. A spirit of delightful eccentricity pervades the house. On the first floor the great gallery

Tanlay, the château

is decorated with remarkable trompe-l'oeil grisaille work: only close-up do you realize that the pilasters, niches and statues along the walls are just painted illusions. The dome of the Tour de la Ligue has a strange fresco from the school of Primaticcio, an enigmatic work featuring leading figures from the time of Henri II in various states of undress. Among those who are completely naked, Queen Catherine de Médicis reveals a strong back and a distinctly robust rump, the Cardinal of Lorraine receives full frontal treatment and a number of gracious ladies are grouped in attendance. There is still no universal agreement about this painting, though it is sometimes taken to be a political allegory.

| **Tarascon** | (10,670 inhab.) |
| 13 Bouches-du-Rhône | p.425☐L 14 |

Tarascon—the *Tarouscôn* of the Greek geographers—has a long history. Originally a Massalian trading counter and then a Roman military base, it protected Provence from Beaucaire and Languedoc. It is also associated with the legendary Tarasque, the fearsome monster vanquished by St. Martha. In 1469 King René inaugurated a festival to commemorate this and every year at the end of June a carcase representing the Tarasque is carried through the town. The writer Alphonse Daudet brought the town further fame in 1872, when he created the naïve braggart Tartarin de Tarascon.

Château: Situated beside the Rhône and on the site of the *castrum*. This powerful fortress was begun in the 12C, though it is mostly 14–15C and was completed under King René. With corner towers and a wide moat it is an impressive sight. It consists of a virtually unassailable seigneurial residence and less well defended outbuildings in the 'basse-cour'. The apartments give on to the well of the main courtyard, their mullioned windows set in elegant façades. The upper chapel, above the *chapelle basse*, contains the former oratories of the king and queen. From the terrace there is a fine view of the Rhône. The river has now been tamed by the great Vallabrègues dam, opened in 1970.

Church of Sainte-Marthe: Consecrated in 1197, this stylistically varied church acquired a new nave in the 14C and a bell tower in the 15C (it was enlarged after receiving the putative relics of St.Martha, which have since been lost). The original Romanesque S. porch is similar to the 'Porte de France' in Nîmes, with a monumental arch and gallery of small columns and pilasters. The carvings are reminiscent of Saint-Trophime in Arles.

Environs: Beaucaire (right bank): The twin of Tarascon, on the other bank of the Rhône, this town became part of France in 1271 and owed its prosperity to a famous Fair that survived until the 19C. (Napoleon had a long political debate with the

Tarascon, the château

traders here; this inspired his pamphlet *Le souper de Beaucaire.*) Nowadays rather less busy, it is dominated by the triangular *keep* and ruined walls of a 13–14C castle (the simple Chapelle Saint-Louis was founded by King Louis in 1254). *Notre-Dame-des-Pommiers* is a well proportioned 13C church by Jean-Baptiste Franque. The outer wall of the S. transept has a Romanesque frieze of the Last Supper and the Passion. Fine 17–18C houses in the Rue de la République. On the Fourques road (1.5 km.) there is an early 15C Gothic cross.

Tarbes   (57,770 inhab.)
65 Hautes-Pyrénées   p.422☐F 15

A commercial town at the end of a valley in the Pyrenees, Tarbes is the ancient capital of the *comté* of Bigorre. The *cathedral* (Romanesque with later alterations) has interesting 18C furnishings. In the 19C the former director of the Versailles *Orangerie*, Placide Massey, laid out the beautiful

gardens (with Gothic cloister), which were named after him. His house is a *museum* with paintings, folk exhibits and displays relating to the Tarbais hussars and horses (Tarbes has a famous stud).

Environs: Ibos (6 km. W.): Interesting 14C church.

Tende   (2,060 inhab.)
06 Alpes-Maritimes   p.426☐P 13

Clustering above the modern town, the old quarter of Tende is dominated by a terraced cemetery and the remains of the ruined château of Vintimille-Lascarès. Ceded back to France only in 1947 by plebiscite (the town had been separated from the *comté* of Nice when Nice became French), Tende has an interesting late 15/early 16C *church* in a mixture of Renaissance and imitation Romanesque styles.

Environs: Notre-Dame-des-Fontaines (by Saint-Dalmas and La Brigue): In a

Beaucaire, ruined fortress

lonely valley, some 2,840 ft. up, this pilgrim chapel stands by a stream and has springs all around. Simple outside, the interior has beautiful 15C *frescos* by Jean Canavesio (or Canavesi) and Jean Beleison (or Baleisoni). **Vallée des Merveilles** (Valley of Wonders, Massif du Bégo, via the D.91): An area of lakes, the hillsides worn away by glaciers. The region has thousands of prehistoric carvings and graffiti—over 100,000 according to the latest count. The oldest of these mysterious pictures dates from about 1700 B.C. and depicts early Bronze Age weapons. The later pictures are of other weapons, curious 'horned rectangles', anthropomorphic figures, chequer patterns and circles.

Thann	(8,520 inhab.)
68 Haut-Rhin	p.417☐O 6

An old town, at the foot of the Vosges and at the mouth of a valley, it was much damaged in both World Wars. The ruins of the *Château de l'Engelburg* (destroyed in

Thann, collegiate church, stalls, detail

1674, one side having collapsed) are curious; the remains of the circular keep stare up into the sky and have given it the nickname, the Witch's Eye.

Collegiate church of Saint-Thiébaut: Rather pompously called 'the Sainte-Chapelle of Alsace', this superb Gothic church is mostly 14–15C (with a very slender tower from the 16C). The great *W. door* is decorated with a host of heavenly and earthly figures; these fill every arch, the two small tympana above each door and cover the doorposts. The main tympanum features scenes from the life of the Virgin. The fine N. door is 15C Flamboyant. The main interior features are the beautiful 15C carved *choir stalls* (with foliation, monsters, and some human figures), a 16C pulpit, the superb *Virgin* of the vine growers' guild (15C polychrome wood sculpture), and the late-15C gilded wooden statue of St. Thiébaut. Some 15C glass. The old cornmarket (1519) is by the architect from Basle who completed the collegiate church. It now houses the *Musée des Amis de Thann*, a museum which documents the town from its foundation in the 13C. The *Tour des Sorcières* (Witches' Tower) was part of the old fortifications.

Thiers	(17,830 inhab.)
63 Puy-de-Dôme	p.420☐K 10

Clinging to the mountainside above the valley of the Durolle, Thiers owes its fame to the cutlery which has been produced here since the 14C. There are many old houses (half-timbered and with overhanging storeys) like the 15C *Maison du Pirou* or the *Maison des Sept Péchés Capitaux* (House of the Seven Deadly Sins) with its seven decorated beams. The Rue du Bourg, the Rue Grenette and the Rue Durolle have fine medieval secular architecture. Over the crossing of the 11C church of **Saint-Genès** there is a huge dome. The gable of the S. transept has interesting polychrome decoration. The **Musée Fontenille-Mondière** covers the history of the cutlery trade as well as regional folklore.

Thoiry (château)
78 Yvelines   p.428☐I 5

This 16C château is well furnished, has tapestries and paintings and a good library. There are 18C French gardens, English gardens and a Safari park.

Environs: Maule (7 km. NE): Church with Renaissance bell tower and 11C crypt.

Thonon-les-Bains
74 Haute-Savoie   (25,230 inhab.)   p.421☐N 9

The former capital of Chablais, it was owned by the House of Savoy. Today it is a holiday and spa resort overlooking Lake Geneva. **Saint-Hippolyte** (rebuilt in the 17C, but with a Romanesque crypt) is incorporated into the 19C neo-Gothic **Basilique du Doctorat de Saint-François-de-Sales** (paintings by Maurice Denis). The **Musée du Chablais** covers local history and folklore. The glass and aluminium **Maison de la Culture** (early 1960s) is by the marine architect Maurice Novarina. **Château de Ripaille:** A fine, solid, typically Savoyard building surrounded by vineyards; used as a convent. Its appearance has rather suffered over the years. Dating from the 15C, it has a classical doorway. The old kitchen survives; there is a small *museum*. **Environs: Château des Allinges** (7.5 km. S.): Ruins of two medieval castles. Incorporated in the walls of the old Château-Neuf is the very ancient *Chapelle des Al-*

linges, with a very early Romanesque fresco (Christ in Glory, Virgin and St. John).

Thoronet (abbey)
83 Var   p.426☐N 14

A sister foundation of Sénanque (see-**Gordes**) and Silvacane, this admirably spare Cistercian abbey nestles in a wooded valley. Founded in 1146 on land given by one of the Counts of Toulouse, it never had more than a handful of monks. It was almost empty by the time of the Revolution, when it was sold as national property. Restored in the second half of the 19C and again in our own century, it consists of a large, austere church (18C decoration now removed), a cloister and the 12C monastic buildings. The vaulted chapterhouse is a superb example of Burgundian Gothic.

Thouars
79 Deux-Sèvres   (12,630)   p.418☐F 8

On a bend in the Thouet, the town of

Thiers, view

Thouars, church of Saint-Médard, frieze on the right portal

Thouars extends along a promontory into the river. One night in 1372 the victorious Du Guesclin passed through the 13C *Porte au Prévost* in the N. of the old town. Further on, the *Tour du Prince de Galles* (Prince of Wales's Tower), used as a prison under the Ancien Régime, recalls the long years of English rule in Poitou. Two sinister wooden cages are on display. The Hôtel des Trois Rois (where Louis XI stayed on a number of occasions) has a fine bartizan above the entrance. The hôtel of President Tyndo features an elegant hexagonal turret.

Saint-Médard: 12C. This church has an arcaded façade with fine frieze, an excellent example of Poitou's Romanesque sculpture. Flamboyant rose window over the door. Multifoil N. door is Moorish in style.

Saint-Laon: Romanesque tower and Gothic doorway (15C), pillars, and windows. Delicate 17C stone retable.

Château: 17C, noble and regular in design, built by Marie de la Tour d'Auvergne, Duchesse de La Trémoille. Now a lycée. At one end a 16C chapel combines Gothic vigour of line with Renaissance elegance of décor.

Museum: Good collection of ceramics and fine prehistoric and Gallo-Roman finds.

Environs: Oiron (13 km. E.): This quiet village has two buildings which deserve more attention. On a par with some of the royal residences in the Loire Valley, the 16–17C château has a central section with 17C pediment, a Renaissance wing with an arcaded gallery—decorated with medallions—and a 17C wing. Some of the rooms are sumptuously decorated. There is a long gallery with frescos of scenes from the *Aeneid* (16C) and a coffered painted wooden ceiling. The Cabinet des Muses has reliefs and paintings. In the 16C *church* (formerly the chapel of the château) are the Gouffier family tombs. The château was built in 1515 by a member of this family who was a former governor under François I.

Thury-Harcourt	(1,410 inhab.)
14 Calvados	p.413☐F 4

Situated on the edge of that area of Normandy known as 'la Suisse normande' (Norman Switzerland), this village was rebuilt after the war. Earlier buildings include the partially rebuilt 12–13C *church* and the remains of a 17C château, with a charming 18C pavilion.

Tiffauges	(1,120inhab.)
85 Vendée	p.418☐E 8

Romantic ruins overgrown with ivy and brambles evoke the sad memory of Gilles de Rais (or Retz). Towering over a ruined barbican, the 12C *keep* contrasts strikingly with the nearby remains of the choir of a 13C chapel (magnificent 12C crypt). The Tour du Vidame, overlooking the Sèvre, is a fine 16C structure with an interesting acoustical curiosity—through the hollow column of the spiral staircase orders could be transmitted from one floor to another.

Tonnerre	(6,520)
89 Yonne	p.415☐K 6

Rising out of the huddle of brown roofs sloping down to the Armançon are the

Oiron, the château

churches of **Saint-Pierre** (11C, with a little Romanesque door) and **Notre-Dame** (mostly 15C with Renaissance façade), together with the immense roof of the hospital founded in 1293 by the sister-in-law of St.Louis, Margaret of Burgundy. The **Old Hospital**—which received the sick until 1650 and served for a time as a necropolis—is a vast hall with a remarkable oak roof. The hall terminates in a triple-vaulted stone apse, once separated off by a rood screen. Margaret's tomb is a 19C restoration. That of the Duc de Louvois from the late 17C is by François Girardon and Martin Desjardins. The Hospital has a 14C polychrome Virgin and a most impressive Holy Sepulchre (1454) with life-size figures.

Hôtel d'Uzès: Now a thoroughly respectable bank, this is the birthplace of Charles

Tiffauges, the 12C keep

de Beaumont (b.1728), the mysterious transvestite Chevalier d'Éon, known as 'La Chevalière' (a courageous soldier when necessary, he was 'reader' to the Czarina Elizabeth). The large round pool of the deep Fosse Dionne dates from the 18C.

Touffou (Château)
86 Vienne   p.419☐G 9

Superbly situated above the fields on the left bank of the Vienne, the building was originally a 12C double keep. This acquired windows in the 15C along with a rectangular outer wall, which was demolished in the 17C. The Renaissance wing has attractive pedimented dormer windows. One of the rooms in the keep has a curious heraldic decorative motif. The château is furnished and has many hunting trophies.

Toul
54 Meurthe-et-Moselle   (16,830 inhab.)
                                     p.417☐N 5

An ancient stronghold with a stormy history, it was particularly badly damaged during the two World Wars. However, the 17C walls, some 16–17C houses (including one Renaissance house with gargoyles) and two fine ecclesiastical buildings in the Gothic style of the Champagne school have survived.

Cathedral of Saint-Étienne: 13–16C; considerably restored after 1944. The 15C façade, with two 213 ft. octagonal towers, is a masterpiece of Flamboyant. Inside there are two exquisite Renaissance chapels on either side of an austere nave; also some beautiful 13,14&15C glass. The large three-tier cloister with enormous bays dates from the 14C.

Church of Saint-Gengoult: 13–15C, with a graceful 15C W. door. Short nave, with no triforium; 13C glass in the apsidal chapels around the choir. The *cloister* has beautiful stellar vaulting (16C), elegant Flamboyant motifs, and rich decoration, which is both imaginative and sophisticated.

Toulon
83 Var   (185,050 inhab.)
                                  p.425☐N 15

A great naval port with docks for shipbuilding, it occupies a natural harbour at the foot of steep mountains. In Roman times it prospered through the manufacture of purple dye extracted from shellfish. The city gained in importance under Louis

Toulon, aerial view of Mont Faron

XIII and Louis XIV. After its royalist inhabitants handed it over to the English,
Napoleon captured the city in 1793 and
punished it through the Convention.
When the Germans broke the Armistice
in 1942 the French fleet was scuttled, thus
blocking the port for some considerable
time. Severely damaged by the fighting in
August 1944, Toulon was rebuilt in a
rather dull fashion. Nevertheless, its old
picturesqueness survives in the undamaged centre and in the 'rues chaudes'
literally, 'hot streets'), which could almost
have been built as a realist film set. The
harbour front is now just uniform modern
blocks, the only vestige of the past being
the two superb caryatids by Pierre Puget
on the façade of the modern Musée Naval.

Cathedral of Sainte-Marie-Majeure:
11-12C, but with much from the 17C and

the façade and tower from the 18C; the
great nave is Gothic.

The 'Grosse Tour' or 'Tour Royale':
This tower on the Pointe de la Mitre, on
the Mourillon promontary, defended the
entrance to the 'Petite Rade'. Built 1514–
24, it served as a prison; in 1870 the Bank
of France's gold was stored here. Now the
chilling blockhouses and gloomy galleries
contain ships' figureheads and old canons.

Museum of Art and Archaeology:
Boulevard du Général-Leclerc. Antiquities, Oriental collections, and paintings
from 13–20C (Carracci, Fragonard, David,
Vuillard, Maurice Denis, Vlaminck, and
Friesz). **Museum of Old Toulon:** 69
Cours Lafayette. Historic Toulon,
weapons, models of boats, paintings,
prints and drawings. **Naval Museum:**

Quai Stalingrad. Recognizable by Puget's caryatids, it contains some splendid figureheads, spectacular model ships and many paintings and engravings of Toulonnais and naval history.

Memorial Museum of the 'Débarquement': This museum of the Liberation of the SE by the Allies is housed in a small fort and has annexes up on the magnificent vantage point of Mont Faron. There are audio-visual displays, film documentaries and dioramas.

| **Toulouse** | (383,180 inhab.) |
| 31 Haute-Garonne | p.423□H 14 |

A lively city animated by a constant bustle and congested by horrendous traffic jams. A city of the arts, it has a university and is the home of *Caravelle, Concorde* and the *Airbus*. Toulouse lives in both the past and the future. The fourth leading city in France and the metropolis of the Midi-Pyrénées region, this modern descendant of ancient *Tolosa* is both an open-air museum and a vigorously expanding centre (Toulouse-Le Mirail, which is mostly the work of Georges Candilis, is one of the most important new cities in Europe). Toulouse lies in flat open ground where the majestic River Garonne veers sharply W. The Romans preferred this spot to the Celto-Ligurian oppidum of **Vieille-Toulouse** (Old Toulouse, 8 km. S.) because there was a ford here. The Gallo-Roman poet Ausonius praised it as highly as Bordeaux and Martial described it as 'palladian' (Pallas Athena—Minerva—was the goddess of wisdom, war, science, and the arts). In the 5C the Visigoth King Alaric made Toulouse his capital and issued his famous legal *breviary* from here. Ostensibly part of the Kingdom of France, it was for many years governed by highly independent counts, but this situation changed after the cruel Albigensian Crusade, which quelled the Cathar heretics. Now wholly attached to the Crown, it nevertheless enjoyed many privileges and was quite liberally governed by municipal magistrates known as *Capitouls*. Prosperity came through the trade in woad (a plant producing a blue colorant) and the Renaissance saw the city's fortunes at their height. Europe's oldest literary society, the *Compagnie du Gai Savoir*, was founded here in 1323. In 1762 the whole of France was shaken when the death sentence was passed on the Protestant Calas for killing his son to prevent him becoming a Catholic—after a campaign led by Voltaire and the Encyclopédistes, Louis XV reviewed the case. Toulouse became a centre of aviation at the beginning of the 20C, with the airmail service inaugurated by Latécoère, Daurat, Mermoz, and Saint-Exupéry.The buildings are a harmonious combination of brick and stone, indeed Toulouse is known as 'La Ville rose', the Pink City. It has fine churches and cloisters, beautiful tower houses (e.g. those of the *Capitouls*) and aristocratic hôtels of parliamentary deputies. There are some excellent museums. There is also a great tradition of classical music and opera: the old cornmarket is now a concert hall, and the Grand Orchestre Régional du Capitol draws audiences of up to 2,500 people. The horrific rush-hour snarl-ups of traffic are now less tiresome for pedestrians since the medieval and Renaissance quarter (centred on the bustling Place Esquirol) is now a pedestrian precinct. The main square is the imposing **Place du Capitole**, the Capitole being the 18C Town Hall (whose name derives from 'chapter' —*capitulum*, whence also *capitoul*). This brick and stone building, some 390 ft. long, encloses a 16 – 17C courtyard and boasts a number of modern works of art. The nearby church of **Notre-Dame-du-Taur**, with its fortified façade from the 14C, stands where it is said the bull drag-

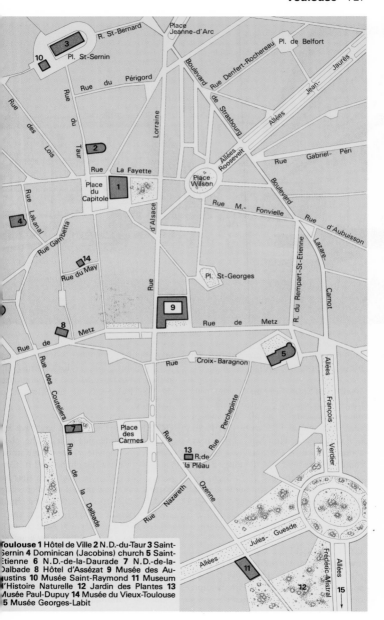

Toulouse 1 Hôtel de Ville **2** N.D.-du-Taur **3** Saint-Sernin **4** Dominican (Jacobins) church **5** Saint-Étienne **6** N.D.-de-la-Daurade **7** N.D.-de-la-Dalbade **8** Hôtel d'Assézat **9** Musée des Augustins **10** Musée Saint-Raymond **11** Museum d'Histoire Naturelle **12** Jardin des Plantes **13** Musée Paul-Dupuy **14** Musée du Vieux-Toulouse **15** Musée Georges-Labit

Toulouse, Place du Capitole

ging the martyred St. Saturninus (or Serninus) stopped (c. 250).

Basilica of Saint-Sernin: A grand, beautiful church restored by Viollet-le-Duc and one of the largest of all Romanesque edifices (only *Cluny III* was bigger). Begun in stone c. 1080 and finished in brick, it was a major place of pilgrimage, which accounts for its size: 377 ft. long, 210 ft. across the transept and 69 ft. high. Formerly run by canons (for some time by Benedictines), it stands over the burial vault of St. Saturninus—though the tomb itself has been transferred to the apse.

EXTERIOR: The splendidly tiered 12C tower (heightened in the 13C and much copied in Languedoc) rises above the apse and apsidal chapels. There are two notable S. doors: the Porte Miegeville—*mieja vila* (middle of the town)—with carvings (*c.* 1150); and the Porte des Comtes (11C) at the end of the transept, so called after the nearby tombs of the Counts of Toulouse.

INTERIOR: The tall 12-bay nave has galleried double side-aisles. The choir (similarly with gallery) has a large ambulatory with radiating chapels off it. Consecrated in 1096, the great high altar has been restored and moved to the crossing. Though dating from 1670, the choirstalls are Renaissance in style; the gates are 16 –17C. Over the tomb of St. Saturninus in the centre of the apse there are striking 18C furnishings. There are seven 17C marble reliefs in the ambulatory. The restorations undertaken by the Department of Historic Monuments have brought some Romanesque wall paintings to light, notably in the left arm of the transept. The transept has three aisles, with very beautiful capitals (the carving in this church is by a workshop closely linked to that of Moissac).

Church of the Jacobins: This curious and splendid Dominican church from the 13–14C has a kind of massive elegance from the outside. Internally, there are two tall aisles divided by seven slender pillars, which soar up to complex vaulting. The last pillar spreads like a palm tree, with a network of delicate ribs forming star patterns in the roof. The tower (1294) is the pride of Toulousain Gothic. The early-14C cloister is vast and rather cold but, together with the church itself, the chapterhouse and the Chapelle Saint-Antonin (with damaged frescos), it makes a remarkable ensemble.

Cathedral of Saint-Étienne: Motley in style, combining typical features from 11–17C with an imposing 16C rectangular tower. The single nave (c. 1100) and the choir (13–14C) follow different axes and seem quite randomly juxtaposed. Erected c. 1200, the daring Gothic nave vaulting marks the arrival of Gothic in the Midi. In the centre of the first vault are the arms of the Counts of Toulouse, which then became those of Languedoc (a cross with twelve pearls). The severe nave is enlivened by 16–17C tapestries. There is old glass in the ambulatory; one window (in the chapel to the right of the axial chapel) shows King Charles VII. Used as an army depot during the Revolution, the beautiful large Romanesque cloister was demolished in 1798. Some carvings from it survive in the Musée des Augustins.

Basilica of Notre-Dame-de-la-Daurade: 13C, with a Madonna—Notre-Dame-la-Noire — venerated by pilgrims. Though of little architectural interest, it is a much-loved church in Toulouse. It stands

Toulouse, basilica of Saint-Sernin

on the site of an early Christian church, whose gleaming mosaics (dorata) gave it its name. Some remarkable capitals from the cloister are now in the Musée des Augustins.

Notre-Dame-de-la-Dalbade: Erected in the first half of the 16C on the site of an earlier church. Restored after the tower collapsed in 1926 and with the tympanum over the Renaissance door restored, this brick structure is once again a very beautiful example of S. French Gothic. The Rue de la Dalbade has some fine 18C parliamentarians' hôtels, as well as older houses.

Hôtel d'Assézat: In the Rue de Metz (which leads to the 16–17C Pont-Neuf), this hôtel was built in the mid 16C by a *Capitoul* who had made a fortune in the woad trade. A distinguished, elegant building, it is now the premises of a number of learned societies. It was designed by Toulouse's most famous Renaissance architect, Nicolas Bachelier. Apart from this, the most beautiful house in the city, there are also many other early- and late-Renaissance houses.

Musée des Augustins: Housed in a former Augustinian monastery, near the Place Esquirol. There are fine paintings (Rubens, Philippe de Champaigne, Largillière, Gros, Corot, Delacroix, and Toulouse-Lautrec) but it is above all famous for its collection of Romanesque sculpture from demolished cloisters in Toulouse. These are displayed in the former chapterhouse, the large 14C cloister and the small 17C cloister.

Musée Saint-Raymond: This 16C college building near Saint-Sernin houses a very fine collection of Romanesque sculpture (from Toulouse and elsewhere in Languedoc), ancient pottery and various exhibits from early times to the Carolin-

gian era. The important **Natural History Museum** stands in the Jardin des Plantes (Botanic Garden) and has a good prehistoric section. Close by the Place des Carmes (Hôtel du Vieux-Raisin, 1530), the **Musée Paul-Dupuy** traces the history of the applied arts from the Middle Ages to modern times and has exhibits relating to pottery, glassware, clock and watch making, numismatics, etc. Occupying a 16–17C hôtel in the Rue du May, the **Musée du Vieux Toulouse** covers the history of the city and local traditions. Oriental and Egyptian art can be seen in the 19C 'Moorish villa' of the **Musée Georges-Labit**.

Environs: Pibrac (15 km. W.): 16C Renaissance brick château; the modern basilica is an important place of pilgrimage.

| **Tour-du-Pin (La)** | (6,840 inhab.) |
| 38 Isère | p.421 □M 10/11 |

Once the seat of an important barony,

Toulouse, Musée des Augustins, Romanesque capital

whose lords became the masters of Dauphiné, the main feature of this little village is the 19C neo-Gothic church, which contains a most interesting *triptych* by a pupil of Dürer, dating from the early 1540s. The Renaissance Maison des Dauphins is 16C.

Tournoël (château)
63 Puy-de-Dôme   p.420 ☐ J 10

Looking out across the Limagne from its rocky outcrop, Tournoël was once a powerful castle. Its imposing ruins, which so caught the Romantic imagination, testify to different periods of construction. The square Romanesque keep is 13C; the 105 ft. tall round tower and the thick triangular walls are 14C; and the domestic buildings were rebuilt in the 15C, when the castle became a residence rather than a fortress. Within the walls, the staircase tower (against the keep, and leading to the hall of honour and the private chapel) has

Toulouse, Musée des Augustins

carved lava stone decoration in rich Flamboyant style.

Tournon   (9,560 inhab.)
07 Ardèche   p.421 ☐ L/M 11

The houses of Tournon cluster between the waters of the River Rhône and the vine-growing slopes of Tain-l'Hermitage. The collegiate church of **Saint-Julien** is 14–15C with 17C tower. Flamboyant predominates. 15C frescos of the Life of Christ in the Penitents' Chapel; a 16C Resurrection in the baptistery chapel; and a wooden triptych of the same era at the end of the right aisle. The 15 – 16C **château** forms a small *Musée Rhodanien*, a museum of local history. The 16C college building is the lycée where the poet Mallarmé taught.

Tournus   (7,340 inhab.)
71 Saône-et-Loire   p.421 ☐ M 9

Skirted by the N6 Tournus stands beside the Saône and overlooks the lush countryside of Bresse. Rising above the huddle of tiled roofs, the two dissimilar stone bell towers of Saint-Philibert herald one of the most beautiful and remarkable Romanesque churches in Burgundy. Descended from a Roman castrum, the town contains many old buildings, including the interesting 17C **Hôtel-Dieu** with a pharmacy with attractive woodwork and a splendid collection of earthenware. There are two museums. Not far from Saint-Philibert the folk **Musée Perrin de Puycousin** recreates the everyday life of the past (the writer Albert Thibaudet spent his childhood here and wrote several works in the beautiful 17C residence which is now the museum's home). The **Musée Greuze** is pleasantly established in a former convent in the Rue du Collège. It has portraits and drawings by Jean-Baptiste Greuze (b.Tournus, 1725) and works by Primitives and the Impressionist Ziem (a native of Beaune). It also has a most varied collection of local archaeological finds, medieval statuary, Oriental art, etc.

Abbey church of Saint-Philibert: In 875 monks fleeing from the Norman raids, and bringing with them the relics of St. Philibert, settled in the monastery founded near the tomb of St.Valérien (martyred in Tournus— *Trenorchium*—in the late 2C). Sacked by the Magyars in 937, it was then rebuilt and carefully fortified. The church was finally dedicated in 1120. Work had begun at the end of the 10C but there had been many interruptions. The interim years also saw the birth and evolution of Romanesque. Taken over by canons in 1627, Saint-Philibert became a collegiate church; having been spared in the Revolution, it then became a parish church. The exterior was plain but graceful, with typical early Romanesque friezes and arcading in the façade. Flanking the façade are towers, one with a saddle-back roof, the other with a spire (probably early 11C). The square crossing tower is 12C. There is a magnificent *fortified narthex*, the powerful lower level of which has an almost barbaric beauty. It supports a large chapel—almost a church in itself—accessible by a spiral staircase in a corner tower. The airy, beautifully vaulted upper level has a large arch on which there is an inscription (after which it is called 'the arch of Gerlannus'). There are also impressive, though crude, sculptures — one curious figure gives a blessing with his right hand and holds a hammer in his left. The great 11C nave is a marvellous sight, being slender, light, pinkish in colour, and with great soaring pillars and unusual transverse barrel vaults spanning the bays. The transept and choir are somewhat detached from the nave, but still beautifully in harmony with

it; in white stone, they were completed (with many alterations) in the late 11/early 12C. The compact barrel-vaulted ambulatory is 11C. The apse follows the outline of the late 10C crypt below (access via the N. transept), which has excellently preserved capitals.

Cloister of Saint-Ardain: S. side of the church, with a 13C door. The beautiful rib-vaulted chapterhouse dates from the first half of the 13C. The cloister court is bordered by the 12C cellar, at right angles to the refectory of the same period. In the Place des Arts, outside the cloister, is the charming residential part of the abbey (15C Flamboyant).

Tours	(145,440 inhab.)
37 Indre-et-Loire	p.414□G 7

A large and graceful city between the Loire and the Cher. A prefecture, archbishopric, and university town, Tours is a privileged city in a naturally privileged area. Always an important centre, the ancient city of the Turons (*Urbs Turonum*) crops up frequently throughout history. Catholicism, introduced in the 3C by St.Gatien, was imposed here by the celebrated bishop of Tours, St.Martin (b.316 by the Danube, d.397 in Candes). Another famous bishop of Tours, Gregory (6C), wrote a *History of France* in Latin. Alcuin (advisor to Charlemagne, and inaugurator of the first schools of theology and philosophy in France) was abbot of Saint-Martin in the 8C. Throughout the Middle Ages Tours was a great religious centre and place of pilgrimage. Most kings of France from St. Louis to François I stayed here, Louis XI finding it especially congenial (his principal residence was at Plessis-lès-Tours). After suffering during the Wars of Religion it expanded again in the 18C, when the roads were improved. The railways came in 1846. Severely affected by the last War,

Tours, Hôtel de la Croix Blanche

Tours, the Tour de Guise

it has been successfully restored and expanded, to form an 'urban district' with the surrounding *Communes*. Famous natives of Tours include the painters Jean Fouquet (*c.* 1420) and François Clouet (*c.* 1515), Balzac (1799), who often describes the city in his writing, and Georges Courteline (1858).

Cathedral of Saint-Gatien: The evolution of Gothic, from the early 13C to pre-Renaissance, is visible in this building. First to be built was the choir and the different styles of Gothic then proceed chronologically to the Flamboyant at the *W. front*. The latter façade is flanked by towers and built in the local calcareous tufa, a soft stone, which sadly is not very weather-resistant. Although almost all the original statues were removed in the 16C, it is still a marvel of delicate stone tracery,

with an abundance of apertures and festoons, leaf-work, niches, and crocketed pinnacles. The N. (15C) and S. (16C) towers are both topped with elegant Renaissance-style domed lanterns. *Interior:* The nave is later than the choir, but fits perfectly with it. The side aisles have chapels opening off them. The beautifully proportioned 13C choir has glorious stained-glass windows of the same period. Counterbalancing each other at the ends of the transept arms are two 14C rose windows; that in the nave is 15C. In a chapel off the S. transept is the tomb of the children of Charles VIII and Anne of Brittany (early 16C). The *Cloister of Saint-Gatien* or *Psalette* afforded a covered walk for the canons of the cathedral. A fine 15–16C structure, it was for a time converted for residential use (one of the characters in Balzac's *Curé de Tours* lived here).

Tours, Musée des Beaux-Arts, 'Crucifixion' by Mantegna

In the quarter behind Saint-Gatien there are Gallo-Roman remains.

Other churches: **Saint-Julien:** (13C); built on the site of the former abbey church of a community founded by Clovis. Of the original building only the belfry and porch (11C) survive. The glass is modern. Beside it are the abbey ruins: cloister with a 16C wine press, Gothic chapterhouse and cellar (12C, now housing the Museum of the Wines of Tourain). **Notre-Dame-la-Riche**, on the W. edge of the old city. Frequently altered; interesting 16C glass in the choir.

Prefecture: A converted 18C convent. The main courtyard used to be the cloister. **Place Foire-le-Roi:** Old houses, including the charming 16C *Hôtel Babou de la Bourdaisière* (No.8). The 12C *Tour de Guise* is all that survives of the castle which once defended the nearby bridge (Quai d'Orléans). **'Pont de Pierre' (Stone Bridge):** Officially named, 'Pont Wilson', it was partially destroyed by the Loire in spate. In 1979 it was voted that a new bridge be built and that it should be identical to the original of 1765–79.

Old Tours: Counterpart to the cathedral quarter on the other side of the Rue Nationale. Formerly it was rather decayed and had suffered severely in bombing. After very problematic restoration and much successful reconstruction work, this area, dating from the 15–18C, once again has great charm. The *Place Plumereau*, with beautiful gabled houses, is delightful. The Hôtel Gouin stands on Roman foundations; burnt down in 1940, it still has an attractive 16C façade. There are fine

Tours 1 Cathedral of Saint-Gatien **2** cloister of Saint-Gatien **3** Gallo-Roman remains **4** Tour de Guise **5** church of Saint-Julien **6** church of Notre-Dame-la-Riche **7** Préfecture **8** Hôtel Babou de la Bourdaisière **9** Hôtel Gouin **10** Tour Charlemagne **11** Tour de l'Horloge **12** cloister of Saint-Macaire **13** Musée des Beaux-Arts **14** former abbey of Saint-Julien **15** priory of Saint-Cosme **16** Château of Plessis-lès-Tours **17** Abbaye de Marmoutier **18** Grange de Meslay

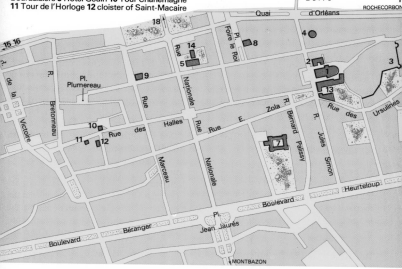

houses in the Rue Paul-Louis-Courrier, the Rue du Change and the Rue Briçonnet. The Romanesque and Gothic *Tour Charlemagne* (once the tower of a church) half collapsed in 1928, but has been well rebuilt. The *Clock Tower* (formerly part of the front elevation of the same church) from the 11–13C has a 19C dome. Nearby, the cloister of Saint-Macaire has a 16C arcade (virtually on the site of the previous church there is now a modern one, in Romano-Byzantine style).

Musée des Beaux-Arts: Housed in the former Bishop's Palace (17–18C), which abuts on to a wall dating from the time of St.Martin. The collection was built around works seized during the Revolution and there are paintings of all periods from Primitive to Modern (an outstanding Crucifixion by Mantegna, *Head of a Monk* by Jean Foucquet, *Flight into Egypt* by Rembrandt and other paintings by Delacroix and Degas). Panelled rooms contain fine furniture and sculpture.

Musée du Compagnonnage: 8 Rue Nationale. An engaging and rather unusual museum lodged in the monks' dormitory of the former abbey of Saint-Julien. It records the history of the *compagnons* of the old guilds, explaining particular techniques and traditions; virtuoso exhibits illustrate the degree of craftsmanship demanded of a master. **Musée des vins de Touraine:** An important museum of wine production in the region. It occupies the abbey cellar, which has a superb vaulted roof.

Environs. Priory of Saint-Cosme, Château of Plessis-lès-Tours (3 km. W.):

Formerly on an island in the Loire (the river has since altered its course), this partly ruined priory had the poet Ronsard as its abbot. His remains were discovered in the ruined church before the war. Plessis-lès-Tours (15C), occupying the site of an older castle, is hardly very impressive in its present state. Nevertheless, it evokes the memory of Louis XI, who greatly contributed to the formation of the State of France and who was particularly fond of the building (he died here in 1483). The surviving residential wing houses a museum dedicated to Louis; there is also a section which covers the traditional local silk industry.

Abbey of Marmoutier (4 km. E., right bank): Alongside the new convent buildings are the remains of the great monastery founded by St.Martin in 372 and fortified in the Middle Ages (fine 13C door, outer walls, ruined church and underground cells). Slightly upstream, the village of **Rochecorbon** is partly built into the rock face; the main feature of interest is an attractive watch tower (the lantern). **Grange de Meslay** (10 km. N.): Old tithe barn of the Marmoutier monks. This vast hall with a magnificent 15C chestnut roof frame is used for concerts during the Touraine annual music festival. **Montbazon** (12 km. S.): During the last century the great rectangular keep (12C) in this village on the Indre acquired a huge, incongruous copper Madonna.

| **Tréguier** | (3,720 inhab.) |
| 22 Côtes-du-Nord | p.412☐C 4/5 |

At the junction of the valleys of the Jaudy and the Guindy and just within range of the highest tides is the small regional capital of Trégor. Its wonderful Gothic **cathedral** (14–15C) was built in honour of the 6C St.Tugdual, founder of the city and of the bishopric (suppressed at the Revo-

lution). Of the previous building there survives the Romanesque Hastings Tower, with round-arched apertures in the N. transept. The transept has three towers altogether—that to the S. has bells in its 18C spire. Apart from the Bell Porch, there are two other finely ornamented doors. The clerestory glass is modern (1970); underneath, the triforium has a sculpted frieze. 17C organ. In the choir forty-six Renaissance choir stalls (1508) carry edifying scenes from the lives of saints Tugdual and Yves (the tomb of the latter, rebuilt in 1890, stands in a side-chapel by that of John, 5th Duke of Brittany, which was also vandalised during the Revolution). There is a beautiful old stained-glass window in the right transept, where there is also a sculpted wooden group representing St. Yves (patron saint of lawyers) between the rich and the poor. **Cloister:** 15C, on the N. side of the church, with graceful Flamboyant twin arches with quatrefoil tops and slender buttresses. The panelled arcades have tomb figures from the 15&17C.

Ernest Renan's house: The house where Renan was born in 1823 has retained its attractive half-timbering. In 1947 it became a State *museum* with various mementoes of the famous philosopher, a statue (1903) of whom stands in the Place du Martray.

Environs: Minihy-Tréguier (2 km. S.): The birthplace of Yves Héloury de Kermartin (1253–1303), one of the most popular Breton saints. Late-15C church on the site of the former chapel of the family manor house. In the little cemetery next door there is a stone altar beneath which pilgrims walk on their knees on the great day of the Pardon of St.Yves (19 May).

| **Triel-sur-Seine** | (6,970 inhab.) |
| 78 Yvelines | p.428☐I 4 |

Once a large farming village, it is now an

Tréguier, the cathedral

La Possonnière, the manor, detail

expanding small town. Fine 13 – 16C *church*. Mixed Gothic (nave) and Renaissance (good 16C glass in the choir). Attractive 15C Flamboyant entrance on the right.

Trôo	(300 inhab.)
41 Loir-et-Cher	p.414 □ H 7

A curious old village with an ancient collegiate church, Trôo is built into the hillside above the Loir. Many attractive house fronts. As well as the houses, there are also 'caforts', or fortified caves, built into the soft tufa. Part of the medieval defensive walls still survives. For many years pilgrims to Compostella passed through here, staying at the lazar-house of Sainte-Catherine (of which one wall with Roman-esque arches is visible from the Montoire road). The 11C collegiate church of **Saint-Martin** was altered in Angevin style in the 12C, and acquired a new choir in the 14C. Fine square tower and Romanesque apse with Gothic windows; interesting historiated Romanesque capitals, 15C choir stalls and communion table, and a 16C statue of St.Mamès. Nearby, under an old shingle roof, is the ancient 'talking well'. This well is almost 150 ft. deep and echoes at the slightest sound. About a hundred yards away are the ruined chapel of **Notre-Dame-des-Marchais** (*c.*1124) and a 16C prioral residence. Across the Loir, the church of **Saint-Jacques-des-Guérets** has remarkable 12C *wall paintings*, some of which still have beautifully vivid colours. Most notable are those in the apse portraying the life and Passion of Our Lord.

**Environs: the manor of La Posson-
nière** (13 km. SW, near Couture-sur-Loir):
The poet Pierre de Ronsard was born in
this modest early-16C manor house in
1524. A delightful, airy, part Renaissance
house, both it and the outhouses are inscribed with curious Latin sayings and
maxims ('The eye of God is watching',
'Sustain yourself and abstain', 'Take care
to whom you give', etc.). A pedimented
dormer window at the top of a small tower
bears the Ronsard family arms with the
motto, 'The future belongs to merit.' The
manor is sometimes called La Poissonnière
('poisson' = fish, and the coat-of-arms features three fish), though its name actually
derives from 'posson' ('poinçon' = awl, a
standard measurement.

Troyes	(75,500 inhab.)
10 Aube	p.415□K 6

A well-known industrial centre, the capital of the hosiery trade and a city of considerable cultural importance. Many
factors contributed to its growth: politically, the Counts of Champagne wished to
beautify their sovereign city; economically,
the regional fairs of the Champagne area
made it one of the great commercial centres
of Europe, situated as it is midway between
the North Sea and the Mediterranean; and
finally culturally, the ancient capital of
Champagne enjoyed exceptional artistic
patronage. Throughout the 16C it was a
meeting place for leading architects,
stonemasons, wood carvers, and glass workers. Many treasures survive from this brilliant past. The 'city of the hundred towers'
presents a superb townscape, which has
sometimes earned it the accolade of 'a little Rome'.

**Cathedral of Saint-Pierre-et-Saint-
Paul:** Building, which began with the apse,
continued for over four centuries (1208–

1640). Though somewhat lacking in unity
it is nevertheless one of the greatest reli
gious buildings in the Champagne region
its huge size, lofty nave, lavish decoration
and resplendent stained glass contribute to
this uniqueness.

EXTERIOR: The beautiful, massive W
front is the work of the great 15C builder
Martin Chambiges. Powerful buttresses
support the square tower (220 ft. high)
Despite its size, this highly ornate façade
—with three doors surmounted by steep
pierced gables—is not at all ponderous
The vandalism of the Revolution has left
some large gaps, but the lovely curving
tracery of the great rose window and the
bands of fleur-de-lys ornamentation at the
foot of the gables are a triumph of Flamboyant work. The sculptures of the '*beau
portail*', in the N. transept, reflect the
whole range of medieval symbolism; above
this door there is a spectacular 15C rose
window.

INTERIOR: The nave is well proportioned, light and airy, with three storeys
(including a pierced triforium) rising to the
magnificent vaulting. A number of original stained-glass windows have survived
and these have been carefully restored. The
development of stained glass—ever more
complex in composition, and with greater
clarity of detail—can be followed from the
13C Tree of Jesse in the ambulatory to the
17C Mystic Wine-Press in one of the nave
chapels. The treasury, well laid out in a
charming 13C vaulted room, includes an
11C ivory box and a wonderful collection
of chased enamel work (12C).

Church of Saint-Urbain: Begun in 1262
by Pope Urban IV, a native of Troyes. It
is one of the finest examples of Champenois Gothic.

EXTERIOR: The W. front (only com-

Troyes, the cathedral

Troyes, the cathedral, glass

pleted in the 19C) has a 13C door, whose tympanum has a Last Judgement. The transept doors have graceful early-14C porches, and together they form a subtly composed ensemble. Slender flying buttresses, delicately carved pinnacles, charming little turrets and amusing gargoyles combine to make a rare visual treat. The heavily traceried windows not only fill the building with light but also emphasize the vertical thrust of the design.

INTERIOR: Glorious stained glass. The 13C windows in the choir depict Christ and the prophets; they are almost like tapestries, the tracery so fine as to be virtually no more than a framework. The exquisite *Virgin with a Grape* in one of the side chapels is a masterpiece of local 16C sculpture; her lovely oval face and slightly slit eyes are beautifully expressive.

Church of Sainte-Madeleine: Mid 12C, the oldest church in Troyes. Successive alterations have left it with a Gothic door (1525) and a Renaissance tower (finished in 1560). The rood screen, at the entrance to the choir, takes the form of a suspended triumphal arch. Carved 1508–17 by Jean Gailde, it appears as a luxuriant stone 'hanging' with three arches. In marked contrast is the famous statue of St.Martha beside one of the piers of the crossing; a moving image of truth and humility, this is the work of an anonymous 16C sculptor known as the Master of the Sad Faces. Enormous and magnificent 16C windows in the apse are similarly fine products of the Champenois school.

Other religious buildings: Troyes boasts a number of other beautiful, if less remarkable, churches and here and there some su-

Troyes, cathedral, glass (fourth chapel, right aisle)

perb stained glass. **Saint-Remy**, begun in the 14C, has a splendid bronze Christ by Girardon. **Saint-Jean** (14–15C) is badly-weather beaten and has only recently been restored. It has a beautiful slender Renaissance choir (1534), and fine altar-pieces at the high altar (1667) and the apsidal altar (1693). There is a magnificent early-16C stone sculpture of the Visitation. **Saint-Nicolas** (16C) has an imposing staircase leading up to the Calvary Chapel, a curious gallery with loggia and balustrade. The famous *Christ at the Pillar* and the two statues in the beautiful doorway of Saint-Nicholas are attributed to the Troyes sculptor, François Gentil. **Saint-Nizier**, with its fine glazed tile roofs, is late Renaissance in style. Inside there is a late-16C Holy Sepulchre and a profoundly tragic Christ of Sorrows. In **Saint-Pantaléon** (16–17C), some sixty statues,

including a charming St. Barbe and a startlingly simple Charity, offer an impressive survey of 16C Troyen sculpture.

Secular buildings: Small cobbled streets and ancient houses form a magical old city centre, the medieval façades calling up memories of another age. Half-timbering, steep gables, projecting upper storeys, cob walls, and the occasional cantilevered corner turret make streets like the Rue Champeaux or the narrow Rue des Chats an endless delight. From the less distant past, the marble columned façade of the Hôtel de Ville is pure Louis XIII; the superb gate of the Hôtel-Dieu is 18C.

Museums and library: The **Municipal Library** — the main room of which has about thirty stained glass windows by Linard Gontier — has a very old collection in the 'Champenois chequer' pattern. The *Maison de l'Outil et de la Pensée Ouvrière*, a museum of manual work and ideas of the labour movement, has a remarkable collection of several hundred woodworking tools.

Tulle	(21,640 inhab)
19 Corrèze	p.419□| 11

Tulle, the old capital of Bas-Limousin, straggles along the deep, narrow valley of the Corrèze. Off the major roads it has expanded less than its rival, Brive.

Notre-Dame: The cathedral pinpoints the city centre with its tall spire. Built in the 12C, it was badly damaged in the 18C when the transept and choir collapsed. The nave was then closed off by a straight wall. The graceful belfry, about 246 ft. tall, has three storeys of different dates (12&13C with a 14C granite spire). Under the porch the columned door is of characteristic Limousin design, with a multifoil archivolt. The nave has pillars with imbedded columns and rib vaulting; here too is a much venerated St.John the Baptist (16C) and a 15C polychrome stone Pietà. The *treasury* includes two large copper and silver reliquaries (12&13C). Of the cloister of the old abbey, the double-arched arcades of the E. and W. sides still survive.

Nearby is the **Archaeological Museum**, which has old firebacks, weapons, wood carvings and Limoges porcelain. Traces of paintings are still visible on the walls of the 13C chapterhouse.

Old houses: The steep, winding streets of the old city have some interesting medieval and Renaissance secular buildings, the most notable being the 15C *Maison de Loyac*, which has prettily ornamented windows. The Rue de La Tour Maîsse, the

Troyes, church of Saint-Urbain

of manuscripts, incunabula, and bindings dating back to the 7C. One of the most valuable treasures is a richly illuminated 14C Troyen missal. The **Musée des Beaux-Arts** has an exceptional collection of monumental sculptures, including one in honour of Girardon (a native of Troyes). Among the paintings are works by Mignard, Watteau, and Hubert Robert. Housed in the Hôtel de Vauluisant—a superb achievement of mid-16C architecture —are the **Museum of Historic Troyes and Champagne** and the **Hosiery Museum**. These museums exhibit sculptures, everyday objects, and machinery and products relating to the hosiery business.

Hôtel de Mauroy: Dating from 1560, this house is a good example of the Renaissance architecture of Troyes, having half-timbering and alternating brick and stone

Tulle, cathedral of Notre-Dame

La Turbie, the Trophée des Alpes

Rue de la Porte de Chanac, and the Rue de la Porte Riche are typical of old Tulle.

Turbie (La)	(1,830 inhab.)
06 Alpes-Maritimes	p.426□P 14

A hillside village with a fine view of the Mediterranean coast and Monaco, La Turbie owes its existence to the important *Via Julia*, the great Roman road linking Genoa and Cimiez (Nice).

The village clusters charmingly around an interesting 18C baroque *church* (which contains many pictures, including a *Madonna* by Louis Bréa and a *Female Saint* by Ribera). **Trophée des Alpes:** After Caesar's death, Pax Romana was threatened by the turbulent and warlike peoples of the Alps. Augustus managed to subdue them and to commemorate this the Senate erected a vast monument in his honour. Ravaged by the barbarians, it was rebuilt, converted into a fortress, and looted of its marble. Today this majestic tower has been partially re-erected (originally it stood 165 ft. high and was crowned with a large statue of Augustus). Nearby a small *museum* displays a model of the Trophy as it would have looked in the first century A.D.

Turenne	(700 inhab.)
19 Corrèze	p.419□H 11

Towering above medieval houses with overhanging tiers, an impressive *keep* looks out across an extensive and hilly landscape. (This privileged Vicomté was made fa-

Turenne, view

mous by Henri de la Tour d'Auvergne, known as 'Le grand Turenne', who governed it in absentia in the 17C). **Château:** On top of a small hill, the ruins of the castle of the Viscounts of Turenne are guarded by two fine towers. The Clock Tower (the 13–14C keep with flat buttresses) has large vaulted rooms; there is a superb view from the top of Caesar's Tower (12–13C). **Church:** Begun in the 16C and continued in the 17C; rather austere, built against the side of the hill. Good altarpiece.

U

Ussé (Château)
37 Indre-et-Loire   p.419☐G 7/8

This fairytale castle with pointed roofs, tall dormers, turrets, and chimneys is set amid lush green countryside. It is said to have provided Charles Perrault with inspiration for his 'Sleeping Beauty'. The old white stone building and its terraces rise up from the Indre, backing on to the hills of the

Ussé, the château and the Indre

great Forest of Chinon. It combines a number of different aspects, e.g. an almost military severity (16C outer façades) with Renaissance grace (the seigneurial residence in the main courtyard). Originally a four-sided structure, the N. wing was demolished in the 17C to create a better view and the Renaissance W. apartments were extended by the addition of a pavilion. There is a magnificent *internal staircase* (17C); the décor includes furniture, pictures, tapestries and weapons. Some distance away in the park, there is a pretty Renaissance *chapel* with fine choirstalls. The initials C and L, used as decorative motifs, recall a former owner of the château, Charles d'Espinay, and his wife Lucrèce. (The chapel and courtyard apartments were built by the great d'Espinay family, who were particularly in favour under Louis XI and Charles VIII.)

Ussel
19 Corrèze   (11,150 inhab.)
                 p.419☐I 11

On the edge of the plateau of Millevaches, the old town of Ussel has narrow streets and many ancient buildings, most notably the fine Renaissance *Hôtel de Ventadour*. The 12C church of *Notre-Dame-de-la-*

Chabanne incorporates many later alterations. The granite Roman eagle in the Place Voltaire was discovered on the site of an oppidum. The bronze copy of this eagle (outside one of the schools) is by the modern sculptor and painter Pierre Chieze.

Uzerche	(3,220 inhab.)
19 Corrèze	p.419☐H 11

A delightful Limousin town on a hill encircled by the Vézère. It has a number of 15–16C houses with towers. On a different scale is the **Château Pontier**, of whose 14–15C walls the fortified Porte Bécharie still survives. Built over one of the oldest crypts in Limousin (11C), the 12–13C church of **Saint-Pierre** has a four-storey belfry, which soars high above the old slate roofs of the town. It also has a massive tower, which remains from the defences constructed in the 14C. Inside, three large capitals—one decorated with human heads and lions—have been converted into holy water stoups.

Ussel, the Hôtel de Ventadour, detail

Uzerche, the Château Pontier

Uzès	(7,390 inhab.)
30 Gard	p.425☐L 13

An interesting old town and the seat of a bishop before the Revolution. It has an ancient foundation and was France's first duchy. Set in the middle of the Garigues, it has a very fine town centre with old houses, elegant hôtels and a picturesque arcaded square (the *Place de la République*); boulevards follow the line of the former walls. **'Duché':** The fortified ducal residence is a square building dominated by a tall, mighty 12C keep. Of most interest are the 14C tower, the restored Gothic chapel and the beautiful Renaissance wing. The apartments (also restored) are furnished and hung with portraits of the d'Uzès family (large Louis XV salon, with plasterwork). Beside the medieval bulk of

the Duché is the fine Hôtel de Ville, which pre-dates the Revolution.

Saint-Étienne: A good 18C church with an elegant curved façade with flame ornaments. On one side there is a medieval tower, which was probably part of the old fortifications. The 17C **Cathedral of Saint-Théodorit** acquired a new façade in the 19C. It is classical in style; inside it has a fine organ. The Romanesque belfry by the porch, the *Tour Fenestrelle*, is unusual for a 12C tower in that it is round.

Museon di Rodo: On the Nîmes road (Av. du Maréchal-Foch). A 'museum of the wheel', which opened in 1960. It exhibits old cars, marvellous model trains (running on close to a quarter a mile of track), many cycles and other items, including posters.

Uzès 1 Duché **2** Hôtel de Ville **3** church of Saint-Étienne **4** cathedral of Saint-Théodorit **5** Tour Fenestrelle **6** Museon di Rodo **7** fortifications

Uzès, the Tour Fenestrelle

Vaison-la-Romaine

(5,210 inhab.)

84 Vaucluse   p.425□M 13

A historic town on the border of Drôme and Vaucluse, between the mountains and the plain and on the meandering River Ouvèze. It is now a centre for festivals and music. The capital of the major Celtic tribe of the Voconces, *Vasio* was a wealthy town in the Gallo-Roman period. Administered by clergy after the barbarian invasions, it then passed to the Counts of Toulouse (who owned the 12C hilltop castle), and subsequently came under the Holy See. The Roman ruins and excavated sites extend to the edge of the modern town (begun in the 18C). The medieval upper town clusters beneath the keep of the old castle of the Counts on the left bank of the Ouvèze (spanned by a Roman bridge, which has more or less retained its original appearance).

Roman monuments. Puymin quarter:
Excavations have revealed a considerable number of buildings arranged in four sections. The large *Maison des Messii*, reminiscent of the beautiful houses of Pompeii, gives a clear outline of a Roman villa. *Pompey's Portico*, where some of the columns have been set upright, was a covered walk.

Archaeologists have found remains of simple houses with atriums, parts of small buildings which would have provided rented accommodation as well as various other structures. The cleverly designed modern *museum* houses finds from the digs and has good statues (most notably, an emperor in armour and a marble head of Venus), everyday objects and quite a hoard of imperial coins. Cut into the N. side of the hill is a 1C *theatre*, to which the inhabi-

Vaison-la-R., museum, Roman statue

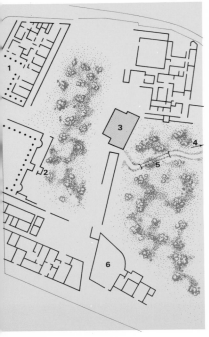

Vaison-la-Romaine, excavations of the Puymin quarter 1 House of the Messii **2** portico of Pompeii **3** museum **4** theatre **5** gallery **6** nymphaeum

tants of the Puymin quarter had access through a gallery dug into the promontary. Half cut out of the rock, it has a partially re-erected colonnade. **La Villasse quarter:** This site has the remains of a commercial street and the *House of the Silver Bust* (named after the effigy of the owner discovered there—now in the musuem).

Church of Notre-Dame: This cathedral (11,12,&13C) stands on the site of a Merovingian church, of which parts (the apse) survive. There are tombs and, in front of the bishop's throne, a pre-Romanesque high altar. Below the cornice on the N. side there is an enigmatic in-scription in 'neo-Latin'. Visible from the 11 – 12C Romanesque cloister, it defies translation. The cloister houses a *Museum of Christian Art* (sarcophagi, altar, a 15C double-sided cross with Christ and the Virgin, and sculptures). At some distance to the N. of the cathedral is the chapel of *Saint-Quenin* with a bizarre triangular apse, which is possibly 12C.

The upper town: The feudal town up the hill has preserved a distinctive medieval character in its narrow cobbled streets. It is entered through a 14C fortified gate (with 18C belfry). The 15C *church* was enlarged and altered in the 17-18C. The *castle of the Counts of Toulouse* (12&15C) crowns the hill. In ruins, but still impressive, the square keep towers above a precipitous drop.

Valençay	(3,170 inhab.)
36 Indre	p.419☐H 8

A small town in the lush border area of Berry, it produces a popular cheese not unnaturally called 'valençay'. However, it is famous above all for its extraordinary **château**, which was built in the 16C by the wealthy d'Étampes family. The château is surrounded by a zoo park, where deer, llamas, peacocks, and flamingoes stroll peacefully. Terraces overlook the Nahon valley. Building continued in the 17C (S. wing) and the 18C (the New Tower, domed like the enormous Old Tower). It has decorative fortifications and in style combines different types of elegance (Renaissance and pre-classical). In the early 19C it was sumptuously furnished by the astute and cunning Talleyrand, who then owned it. A *museum* commemorating the great diplomat is housed in the outhouses.

Environs: Nouans-les-Fontaines (23 km. W.): The 13C church houses the beau-

Vaison-la-Romaine, remains of the Roman town

tiful *Pietà de Nouans*, a sober, powerful painting on wood, attributed to the workshop of Jean Fouquet (15C).

Valence   (70,310 inhab.)
26 Drôme   p.421 □ M 12

On the borders of Provence, Vercors, and Vivarais Valence was always a commercial and administrative centre, and is now quite industrialized. The old centre and the 19C quarters, rather swamped by modern buildings, are lamentably cut off from the Rhône by the motorway. *Ventia*, or *Valentia*, was a Roman colony in which Christianity was quick to establish itself. Created a bishopric in the 4C, during the Middle Ages it was ruled by prelates who shared their power with the kings of France. Louis

XI founded a great university here, at which Rabelais studied. Pope Pius VI, who had condemned the Civil Constitution of the clergy and been obliged to accept the annexation of the Comtat Venaissin by Revolutionary France, ended his days here in 1799 after a month's imprisonment in the citadel. After leaving the Military School at Brienne, the young 'cadet' Napoleon Bonaparte then completed his military training at the local artillery school (1785–6).

Cathedral of Saint-Apollinaire: This cathedral was consecrated in 1095 (while still being built) by Urban II, who had come to preach the First Crusade. Restored after the ravages of the cruel Baron des Adrets (whose men destroyed the vaulting), it was then 'modernized' in 1730. The old Romanesque tower collapsed due to age in

Valence, Maison des Têtes, detail

the last century, and a neo-Romanesque replacement was built. The 18C porch at the corner of the S. transept conceals traces of an earlier door. Light comes into the spacious barrel-vaulted nave (Auvergnat Romanesque) from the side aisles; the transept is unusually prominent for the region. On the N. side is the *Pendentif*, a curious Renaissance structure marking the grave of a canon. Classical in inspiration, it takes its name from the bellied vault above it, reminiscent of the pendentives of a dome.

House of Heads: A strange, somewhat damaged house (1532) at the top of the Grand-Rue. It has a delightful street front combining Flamboyant and Renaissance styles. The heads, in medallions, have been sculpted in the round and there are a variety of figures, notably those representing the four winds. A rib-vaulted corridor leads

to the attractive courtyard. Hidden in the courtyard of the **Maison Dupré-Latour** (Rue Pérollerie) is a superb Renaissance stair turret, whose doorframe is delicately carved. **Saint-Jean-Baptiste** in the Place Belat has a fine 12C porch-belfry, but the soft stone has become very worn and its lines have lost definition. The huge nave was rebuilt in the last century.

Museum: At one end of a paved courtyard in the 18C bishop's palace, (built on the medieval city walls), this museum has a great variety of exhibits, ranging from stuffed birds and fish, mineralogical samples, paintings from the 16–19C, as well as contemporary works of art (Dufy, Lhote, Friesz). There is a fine Gallo-Roman gallery with mosaics, stone fragments and an enormous dolium, over 4 ft. high. On the first floor, there are 96 drawings—of ruins, collapsed arches and dilapidated temples — by the pre-Romantic painter Hubert Robert (1733 – 1808). The Gallery of Bishops has portraits of former bishops of Valence. The museum also covers local history and has some very good furniture.

| **Valenciennes** | (43,200 inhab.) |
| 59 Nord | p.411 □ K 2 |

Situated on the Escaut, in the heart of a heavily industrialized region, this pleasant medium-sized town has a proud cultural history. Sadly, however, this 'Athens of the North', as it was known, suffered badly during the wars. Behind a 19C façade, the church of **Saint-Géry** has a beautiful 13C Gothic interior, which has recently been carefully restored. With its tower and cusped gables, the *Provost's House* is a model of 15C elegance. Dating from 1601, the church of **Saint-Nicolas** has been greatly altered over the centuries; it contains a magnificent Renaissance organ loft in alabaster and black marble (17C). Next door, the former **Jesuit College** has a fine 18C brick façade with stone dressings and curiously decorated small circular windows surrounded by garlands. Upstairs there is a beautiful large vaulted room with paintings and oak panelling. As well as valuable illuminated manuscripts, the **Bibliothèque Municipale** (town library) boasts the *Cantilène de Sainte Eulalie* (881), one of the earliest documents written in French. The **Chapelle du Carmel** (1966), though built of rather inferior materials, creates excellent spatial effects. The wonderful **Musée des Beaux-Arts** has a whole room devoted to Rubens (1577–1640), including his famous *Landscape with Rainbow* (1637). Two famous natives of Valenciennes are also represented: Antoine Watteau (1684 – 1721), whose *Portrait of Antoine Pater* reveals a style less familiar than that of the famous *fêtes galantes* (also to be seen are his *Country*

Portrait of A.Pater by Watteau

Pastimes and *Open-Air Concert*); and Jean Carpeaux (1827 – 75), with some good sculptures, and a splendid collection of drawings.

Environs: Condé-sur-l'Escaut (13 km. NE): This old fortified town still has parts of its defensive walls, together with a fine 18C architectural ensemble consisting of a huge town hall, guard house, and the church of *Saint-Wasnon* (with an early 17C tower). The *Château de Bailleul* (1411), the residence of the Princes of Condé, has a magnificent sandstone façade, with projecting turrets.

| **Vallauris** | (18,820 inhab.) |
| 06 Alpes-Maritimes | p.426 □ O 14 |

A centre for pottery and ceramics since the

16C, this ancient association was revived after the last war, when Picasso settled in Vallauris. The bronze *Man with Sheep* (Place Paul Ismard) was a gift from Picasso to the town, along with the large *War and Peace* (1952–9) now displayed in the crypt of a Romanesque chapel.

Valognes	(6,080 inhab.)
50 Manche	p.413☐E 3

This little town used to be known as the Versailles of Normandy. Devastated in 1944, it has been reasonably well restored, here and there retaining the dignity and elegance which so appealed to the writer Barbey d'Aurevilly (who lived in the town and describes it in his *Diaboliques*). On the outskirts, by the composite *church of Alleaume* (ornate altar and retable), a number of Gallo-Roman remains testify to the town's long history. Fine 17&18C private hôtels. The church of **Saint-Malo** is largely a post-war reconstruction of raw concrete amid vestiges of Gothic. The restrained,

imposing **Hôtel de Beaumont** (Louis XV) was the source for the setting of one of Barbey's most disturbing works, *Le Dessous de Cartes d'une Partie de Whist*. It is richly furnished. Housed in an attractive 15C building, the interesting **Musée Regional du Cidre** traces the history of apple-growing and cider-making (old presses and tools, pottery, reconstruction of a rustic interior).

Valréas	(8,510 inhab.)
84 Vaucluse	p.425☐M 13

A hillside town (with a 12C rectangular keep), Valréas forms an enclave in the Département of Drôme, recalling its former status as a Papal town in Dauphiné. The old quarters survive, though the walls have been replaced by boulevards. Despite its Gothic main doorway, the church of *Notre-Dame* is basically 12C Romanesque. The majestic 17&18C **Château de Simiane** is now the Town Hall.

Valognes, Hôtel de Beaumont

Environs: Grignan (9 km. NW). An old Tricastin village. The great letter writer Madame de Sévigné lived and died in the 16C château owned by her son-in-law, the Comte de Grignan. Her tombstone can be seen in the 16C church of *Saint-Sauveur*. Housed in a 17C building is a museum devoted to her memory and that of the Grignan family (*Musée Faure-Cabrol*).

Vannes	(43,510 inhab.)
56 Morbihan	p.412 □ C 7

Situated on a small inland sea (in the préfecture of the Morbihan) dotted with reefs and islands (some with megaliths — Gavrinis, Er Lannic), this old town of the Veneti is now a tranquil port, accessible at high tide. However, more than once in the past Brittany's fate has been decided here. From Vannes, after a remarkable naval battle, Julius Caesar began his conquest of the Armorican peninsula. Breton independence (proclaimed by Count Nominoë in the 9C) formally ended here with an assembly of all the Estates in 1532.

Cathedral of Saint-Pierre: In the centre of the old city and flanked by defensive walls. The N. tower, dating from the 13C, has survived from an earlier building and is topped by a modern spire. On the left, next to a number of arches from the old cloister, there is an Italianate round chapel; there is also a fine Flamboyant door with Renaissance niches. The interior is a jumble of styles from different centuries. Of great interest is the *tomb* of the Spanish preacher St. Vincent Ferrer (d.Vannes 1419) in the chapel of the Blessed Sacrament. Good 17C tapestries depict scenes from the saint's life and his canonization. The *treasury* (in the 13C chapterhouse) includes a superb 12C marriage chest painted with scenes of medieval aristocratic life.

Château-Gaillard, Archaeological Museum: Rue Noé. This museum, housed in the former seat of the Breton parliament (a 15C building), has an excellent collection of prehistoric finds un-

Valréas, church of Notre-Dame

Vannes, cathedral of Saint-Pierre

Vannes, cathedral of Saint-Pierre, tomb of St. Vincent Ferrer

earthed in local digs (weapons, jewellery, pottery, and various domestic utensils). There are also Gallo-Roman, medieval and Renaissance exhibits. The natural history section contains birds and shells. An old half-timbered house on the street corner features two grotesque carved wooden effigies popularly known as 'Vannes and his wife'.

City walls: The walls have undergone many alterations since the 13C, and are now set in charming French formal gardens. Only three fortified gateways remain: the Porte Saint-Vincent (1625 & 1704), the Porte Poterne, or postern gate (1678), and the imposing 15C Porte Prison (which formerly had two towers in which the Royalists were imprisoned in 1795). To the S., past the 16C Tour Poudrière (powder tower) and the fine *Tour du Connéta-*

ble (14–15C), the walls incorporate the old Château de l'Hermine, built in the 14C by Duke John IV of Brittany. At the foot of the walls and following the curve of the river there are picturesque public washhouses with projecting slate roofs; there is also a small half-timbered house.

Place Henry IV: Lined with beautiful 16C houses, which have gables and overhangs, this litte square used to be a bird market. Nearby is 'La Cohue', the old city market (mainly 14&16C). **Hôtel de Limur:** Rue Thiers. Typical 17C building, housing the tourist office and a fascinating Oyster Museum, which exhibits the different techniques of oyster cultivation and the problems involved in this important regional industry. **Town Hall:** Place M.-Marchais. Standing in a huge square with a modern equestrian statue of

Saint-Gildas-de-Rhuys, former abbey church

the Connétable de Richemont (1393–1458), the 19C Hôtel de Ville has a Renaissance-style façade, crowned by a campanile. The monumental staircase has windows of the same period, depicting the marriage of Anne of Brittany to King Charles VIII.

Environs: Tours d'Elven (15 km. NE): Destroyed in 1488 by Charles VIII's army, the old castle of Largoët stood in woods beside a lake. The impressive remains which survive provided the inspiration for the 19C writer Octave Feuillet's *Roman d'un Jeune Homme Pauvre*. A massive six-storey 14C keep, now in ruins, adjoins the 15C fortified gate (a round tower capped by a steep-roofed structure, which was converted into a hunting pavilion). **Château de Suscinio** (24 km. S.): Inshore from beautiful beaches, this medieval fortress controlled access to the Rhuys peninsula. Built in the early 13C by Duke Pierre de Dreux (nicknamed Mauclerc), it lost two of its original eight towers at the Revolution. The moat was filled by water draining off the nearby marshes. The walled courtyard enclosed by the moat leads into the domestic quarters, which contain splendid fireplaces. **Saint-Gildas-de-Rhuys** (28 km. SW). The name of this village in the S. of the Armorican peninsula is derived from a saint who came from across the Channel, founding a monastery here in the 6C (later destroyed during the Norman invasions). In the 12C the famous theologian Abelard (1079–1142) was sent by the Duke of Brittany to reform this community, which, as he recounts in a letter to Héloîse, 'had no Rule other than to live without a Rule'. The monks proved intractable and after some years Abelard came

Varengeville, Braque, window

to fear for his life. This finally led him to flee the monastery. The former *abbey church* (11C, considerably altered at the end of the 17C) retains a superb Romanesque choir and St.Gildas's tomb. Some capitals have been removed—two now serve as holy water stoups. The sacristy houses one of the finest *treasuries* in Brittany. The Saint's relics are preserved in embossed and studded silver gilt reliquaries shaped like a head, an arm, a knee and a thigh (14–17C). The treasury also has two more reliquaries (14&18C), an embroidered mitre, and a Vermeil cross set with emeralds (17C).

Varengeville-sur-Mer (1,000 inhab.)
76 Seine-Maritime p.410☐H 3

A collection of hamlets scattered over a wooded landscape, Varengeville has attracted numerous painters (e.g. Isabey and Braque). At some distance, towards Dieppe, is the charming **Manoir d'Ango**, built 1530–45 by the local ship-owner Jean Ango. Named after an old priory, the *Parc des Moustiers* (*moustier* = monastery) is a wonderful garden which slopes down to the sea and is almost hidden by vegetation. The church (12&16C) on the crown of the cliff has a pillar carved with curious naïve figures. Georges Braque is buried in the graveyard; his grave is decorated with the distinctive bird-messenger which appears in his work. There is a fine blue stained-glass window by him in the church (the other window is by Raoul Ubac). Other glass by him can be seen in the *Chapelle Saint-Dominique*.

Vaucouleurs (2,550 inhab.)
55 Meuse p.416☐M 5

It was from here, in 1429, that Joan of Arc set out on her path to glory. The *Porte de France,* through which the Maid would have passed, still survives—a round arch beneath a square tower. Towers and stretches of wall still remain from the 13C defences. The Château of Baudricourt is now in ruins; in 1929 the chapel was rebuilt and the very beautiful late-13C *crypt* preserved (the statue of Notre-Dame-des Voûtes, which was venerated by Joan of Arc is housed here). A little two-room *museum* is devoted to Joan of Arc and Mme.Du Barry, who came from Vaucouleurs. The exhibits include a magnificent oak figure of Christ from the Abbey of Septfonds. With an imposing façade, Italianate painted vaulting, and carved woodwork, the 18C parish church is well worth seeing.

Environs: Château of Gombervaux (5 km. N.): Standing amid the ruins of this

Varengeville, the church and the sea

medieval castle is a highly unusual crenellated keep-gateway (14C).

Vaux-de-Cernay (abbey)
78 Yvelines   p.428☐I 5

In fine weather the rural tranquility of Vaux-de-Cernay is broken by Parisians doing the 'Chevreuse Valley excursion'. Most impressive among the overgrown ruins of this former Cistercian abbey (now on private land) are those of the 12C abbey church.

Vaux-le-Vicomte (château)
77 Seine-et-Marne   p.411☐J 5

An exquisite château, which is commonly supposed to have been the inspiration for Versailles. It was built *c.*1660 by Louis XIV's finance minister, Nicolas Fouquet, and the young King Louis was sumptuously entertained here by Fouquet (who was shortly to fall from favour), fabulous meals being prepared by the great chef Vatel. The first great palace of the 'Grand Siècle', Vaux-le-Vicomte is a supremely luxurious and elegant château amid completely rural surroundings. Enclosed by a moat, it has a vast entrance courtyard bordered by grandly conceived, ornate outhouses built in a combination of brick and stone. The château proper, with a pediment carved by Michel Anguier, is reached via a second, formal courtyard; the garden elevation, on the S. side, has a projecting central section with a colonnade and dome. The magnificently redecorated and furnished apartments are arranged around the high oval hall under this central dome.

Laid out in the style of Le Nôtre, after designs by Israël Sylvestre, the outstandingly beautiful *gardens* have a succession of ornamental lakes and fountains. Its terraces descend into a small river converted into a formal canal.

Environs: Blandy-les-Tours (5 km. E.): Ruins of a medieval castle, much altered and partly demolished; Romanesque crypt, remains of the baronial residence and 16C chapel, walls and towers. **Champeaux** (3 km. NE of Blandy): Large *church* with fortified façade from the 12C (transept), 13&14C; 16C carved choir stalls; tombstones.

Vénasque	(530 inhab.)
84 Vaucluse	p.425□M 13

A pretty village on the edge of a plateau, Vénasque still has a moat (now dry) and walls (of uncertain age). **Notre-Dame** (early 13C, with alterations) has a fine 17C retable in the choir and, in a side chapel, a Crucifixion painted in 1478. The **baptistery**—probably 7C, altered in the 11C—is one of the oldest religious buildings in France (apsidal chapels have either re-used classical, or Merovingian capitals). 2.5 km. N. is the chapel of **Notre-Dame-de-Vie**, containing the carved tomb of Bishop Boethius (d.604).

Vendôme	(18,550 inhab.)
41 Loir-et-Cher	p.414□H 7

The meandering river Loir divides into narrow channels around the ancient town of Vendôme, which grew up around the 11C abbey of the Trinity. With many military associations in the past (Rochambeau, the hero of American Independence, was born here), it was partially destroyed in 1940 but has been satisfactorily restored. The ex-abbey church of the **Trinity** incorporates different styles of Gothic; the church's most striking features are its splendid tower (12C) and the façade, which is an ornate Flamboyant masterpiece with

Vaux-le-Vicomte, the château

intricate carved white stone (designed in the early 16C by Jehan de Beauce, one of the architects of Chartres). The nave is 14&15C, the choir 14C (with curiously carved 15C stalls). Romanesque columns and capitals at the crossing. Of the 11C structure, only the transept arms survive. Restored 16C glass in the chapels around the choir; also a fine 12C window depicting the *Madonna and Child* in the axial chapel. A door at the foot of the tower leads to the 14C cloister (vandalized when the former abbey was used as a barracks). One of the old monastic buildings houses an interesting little *museum* (prehistory, Roman history, paintings, earthenware, reconstruction of a rustic house, and exhibits relating to local arts and crafts).

Church of the Madeleine: 15C, with a slender stone spire. Wooden barrel vault over the nave. Among the pupils of the former **Collège des Oratoriens** (now a lycée) was the novelist Balzac. Originally attached to a hostel for pilgrims en route for Compostela, it has a chapel with a little Renaissance bell tower. At the head of a bridge over one of the arms of the Loir the imposing **Porte Saint-Georges** dates from the 14C and was altered in the early 16C. A key feature of the town (on the site of an oppidum) is the ruined castle, which stands in a well laid out garden. The Porte de Beauce leading to it is a 17C addition to the medieval walls; the Tour de Poitiers dates from the 15C.

Verdun	(26,930 inhab.)
55 Meuse	p.416□M 4

An old town, strategically positioned to control the passage of the Meuse. Over the centuries, and particularly in World War 1, this meant that it bore the brunt of much heavy fighting. Destroyed in ten months, between February and December 1916, it took a decade to rebuild (1919–29); numerous buildings have survived only because of extensive restoration.

Religious architecture: The seat of a bishop since the 4C, Verdun has a pre-

Vendôme, the Trinité, Madonna and Child

Verdun, the Porte Chaussée

dominance of ecclesiastical buildings. At the top of the upper town is the composite cathedral of **Notre-Dame**, begun in the 11C, but subsequently much altered. Initially Romanesque and in typical Rhenish style, it had two transepts and two apses (still extant). The wooden roof was replaced by Gothic vaulting in the 13&14C. In the 18C the last vestiges of Romanesque were hidden by two balustraded square towers, which replaced the belfries, and by 'contemporary' doors (not until the devastation of 1914–18 did the originals come to light). *Exterior:* The powerful Romanesque buttresses of the magnificent E. apse are carved with groups of figures. The tympanum in the round arch of the 12C *Porte du Lion* has a superb carved Christ in Majesty in Burgundian style. *Interior:* Together, the great organ loft, the marble and carved oak canopy

over the high altar, and the stalls in the E. apse form a remarkable 18C ensemble. In the splendid *Salle du Sacraire* (1250) there is a small *cathedral museum*. Down in the great restored crypt—one of the best examples of Romanesque in Lorraine—there are some original 12C capitals. The S. side of the cathedral has a beautiful three-sided *cloister*, which is mainly 16C Flamboyant. Giving on to the Meuse, near the cathedral, the **Bishop's Palace** shows off 18C elegance at its best, the curvature of the central structure harmonizing with the circular entrance courtyard. In the town library, which occupies part of this building, there is the finely illuminated *Breviary of Hugues de Bar* (1352).

Military Architecture: Verdun has been a military centre since the Middle Ages. Looming over the Meuse, the 14C *Porte*

dun in December 1916, when the French retook the positions they had been forced to abandon ten months earlier under a terrific German attack. During this battle of ten months, villages—now wiped off the map—were taken and retaken as often as twenty times. The casualties on both sides were appalling: 360,000 French, and 335,000 German. **The Verdun Memorial** (10 km. N.): Opened in 1967, a 'museum' documenting the battle. **Fort Douaumont** (12 km. N.): An important military complex, still in good state of repair, and a small *war museum*. From the top of the fort, there is a good overall view of the battle area, a stretch of country irreparably scarred. **Ossuary of Douamont** (11 km. N.): Approximately 150 ft. high, the *Tower of the Dead* rises above the long vaulted gallery which forms the body of this vast necropolis. Under the central vault there is a richly decorated chapel, a place of stark solemnity.

Verneuil-sur-Avre, the Madeleine

Chaussée is a veritable fortress, with its massive round towers topped by crenellations and machicolations. Also surviving from the old city walls is the 15C Porte Châtel. Built by Vauban on the site of the Abbey of Saint-Vanne, the *citadel* has numerous underground chambers; somewhat oddly, it also incorporates a 12C tower from the old monastery. A sober *Victory Monument* (1929) in the town centre commemorates those who fought at Verdun.

Secular Architecture: The splendid *Town Hall* (1623) also houses a *war museum*. In the delightful Renaissance *Hôtel de la Princerie* (1525) there is a municipal *museum* (archaeology, and local arts and traditions).

Environs: The scene of the battle of Ver-

Verneuil-sur-Avre	(6,860 inhab.)
27 Eure	p.410☐H 5

Verneuil, on the border of the Duchy of Normandy, was an important military post, and the waters of a diverted arm of the Iton still lap the old town walls. Of the castle, only the massive, blank 12C grey tower survives. Walking around the walls, it is possible to see remnants of the outer fortifications. The church of the **Madeleine** appears almost crushed by its tall Flamboyant tower (late 15/early 16C). Incorporated into the façade is the Romanesque door of an earlier building. The delicate windows are 15&16C. Among a number of old statues are a 16C polychrome Virgin with an Apple and a fine 16C Holy Sepulchre.

Notre-Dame (originally Romanesque, much altered) contains a whole host of statues from different periods (an exquisite

Vernon, Château de Bizy

Vernon, Notre-Dame, glass

13C Virgin beside the pulpit steps; several 14C works). The town still retains a number of 15–18C houses.

Vernon	(23,560 inhab.)
27 Eure	p.410☐H 4

Beautifully situated on the Seine, at the edge of the forest. Shelled by the Prussians in 1870, and even more severely damaged in 1940 and 1944, it preserves its charm, despite the amount of reconstruction. With a light, slender façade (a mixture of Rayonnant and Flamboyant), the composite church of **Notre-Dame** dates from the 11–17C. The Romanesque arches in the transept and choir are from the first phase of construction; the nave was only completed in 1617. 16C organ chest, 17C tapes-

tries and a very beautiful 18C high altar taken from an old Charterhouse; the statue of Notre-Dame-de-Vernon at the end of the apse is 14C. The church stands among fine timber-frame houses.

In the outskirts of the town and on the right bank of the river lies **Vernonnet**, which has a Renaissance door in an old church. Beside the Seine there is a little fort, which was originally built to defend a bridge (now demolished). Just outside Vernon is the **Château of Bizy** — a 19C reconstruction in the style of an Italian palazzo. It has a beautiful wooded park with waterfalls, which stretches towards the town, and an attractive 18C courtyard with elegant outbuildings on either side.

Environs: Giverny (4.5 km., right bank). A quiet village on a hill, where Monet lived

from 1883 till his death in 1926. It was here that he laid out the garden with the water-lily ponds which he so loved to paint. The house and garden, as well as the water garden, were fully restored in 1978–9. **Gaillon** (14 km. NW): Only a beautiful doorway and a few ruins survive of this 'Renaissance Versailles', the château of the bishops of Rouen. A magnificent episcopal palace, it was torn down during the Revolution, then used as a prison barracks. 18C church, and some old houses, one dating from the 16C.

| **Versailles** | (97,140 inhab.) |
| 78 Yvelines | p.410□I 5 |

Versailles evokes all the splendour of the *Grand Siècle* (the French 17C), the supreme refinement and tragic upheavals of the 18C and some of the highlights of the republican era. Set in a brilliantly laid out park and gardens, beside the elegant town of Versailles, the château creates a world of its own. Am immense complex built by Louis XIV, it is constructed around a somewhat cramped little château erected by Louis XIII. In 1661 the Sun King commissioned the three great creators of Vaux-le-Vicomte (Le Nôtre, Le Vau, and Le Brun) to transform this already existing château. The project was further extended after 1668, the royal residence and the new, somewhat Italianate classical palace becoming ever more labyrinthine. While Le Nôtre designed the great vistas of the gardens and park, Le Vau practically enveloped the original modest building in grand 'extensions'. After his death François d'Orbay continued this work; Jules Hardouin-Mansart also worked on further additions (1678). Thousands of people had to be accommodated — the whole court, ministers, civil servants and employees of all kinds. Some 36,000 workmen were engaged in building the palace, which was

mostly completed by 1690. Hardouin-Mansart replaced the central terrace with the Galerie des Glaces (Gallery of Mirrors) and was responsible for the vast S. and N. wings,as well as various of the outbuildings. The chapel was finished before Louis' death (on 1 September 1715) by Robert de Cotte. Though essentially the creation of the Sun King, who took a close interest in every stage of its construction, the palace underwent a number of modifications later. Under Louis XV, most notably, came the addition of the opera house (designed by Gabriel). There was also a number of little 'satellite' palaces; to the late-17C Marble Trianon, or Grand Trianon, Gabriel then added the Petit Trianon and the whimsical Hameau (artificial hamlet), where Marie Antoinette played at being a peasant. Under Louis XIV, Versailles was a sublime palace where life was regulated by strict etiquette. In the 18C it developed into an increasingly luxurious and delightful royal home. Then in 1789 Louis XVI finally left it, when the Revolutionary Paris mob invaded it and forced him to return to Paris. Looted during the bloody period that followed, it was left untended until the reign of Louis-Philippe, who made it into a museum 'to the honour of all that is glorious in France'. After the defeat of France in 1870, Wilhelm I was crowned Emperor of Germany in the Galerie des Glaces. Under the Commune the National Assembly sat here, and Versailles remained the capital of France until 1879. In 1919, after the defeat of Germany, the signatories of the Armistice met here.

Still huge, though considerably smaller than they were, the grounds contain the château itself, the Small Park, the Orangery, the Grand and Petit Trianons with their respective outbuildings and gardens, the Large Park, the Large and Small Stables, the lake known as the *Pièce d'Eau des Suisses*, the old King's Kitchen Garden and the Parc Balby.

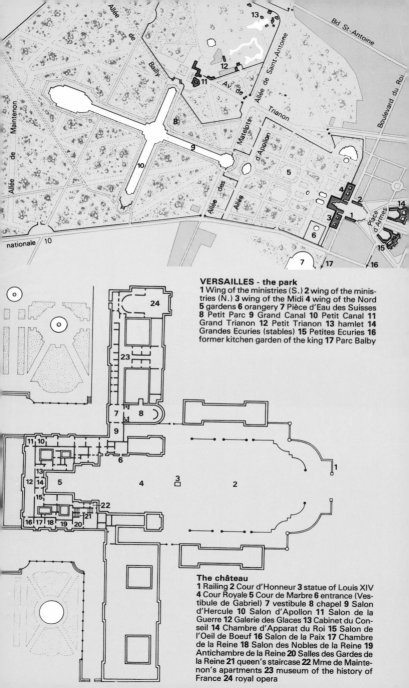

VERSAILLES - the park
1 Wing of the ministries (S.) **2** wing of the ministries (N.) **3** wing of the Midi **4** wing of the Nord **5** gardens **6** orangery **7** Pièce d'Eau des Suisses **8** Petit Parc **9** Grand Canal **10** Petit Canal **11** Grand Trianon **12** Petit Trianon **13** hamlet **14** Grandes Ecuries (stables) **15** Petites Ecuries **16** former kitchen garden of the king **17** Parc Balby

The château
1 Railing **2** Cour d'Honneur **3** statue of Louis XIV **4** Cour Royale **5** Cour de Marbre **6** entrance (Vestibule de Gabriel) **7** vestibule **8** chapel **9** Salon d'Hercule **10** Salon d'Apollon **11** Salon de la Guerre **12** Galerie des Glaces **13** Cabinet du Conseil **14** Chambre d'Apparat du Roi **15** Salon de l'Oeil de Boeuf **16** Salon de la Paix **17** Chambre de la Reine **18** Salon des Nobles de la Reine **19** Antichambre de la Reine **20** Salles des Gardes de la Reine **21** queen's staircase **22** Mme de Maintenon's apartments **23** museum of the history of France **24** royal opera

Versailles, aerial view of the château

EXTERIOR

Courtyards: Extending from the magnificent railings (restored under Louis XVIII) to the equestrian statue of Louis XIV (1835), the *Cour d'Honneur* is flanked by the long wings designed by Le Vau and Hardouin-Mansart to house the Ministries. Next, the *Cour Royale* has a 17C wing on the left, while its counterpart on the right was altered in the 18C. At the end and originally slightly raised is the *Cour de Marbre*, the focal point of the old Louis XIII château; it is now somewhat altered on this side and the other elevations are hidden by the 'envelope' of Le Vau's later construction.

W. elevations: These constitute the garden front, a grand and spectacular façade some 1,900 ft. long. Projecting forward towards the formal water gardens, the central section encases the original Louis XIII château (by Le Vau, with N. and S. wings by Hardouin-Mansart).

INTERIOR

Given the style in which the château was built, even a simple outline guide is necessarily complex. Its vast size, and the different opening and closing hours of the various sections, make it impossible to see everything in a single day. The main entrance is through the *Vestibule de Gabriel* on the ground floor of the Louis XV wing. Dedicated in 1710, the chapel (by Hardouin-Mansart and Cotte) has numerous sculptures and paintings. On the floor above is the balcony where the royal family sat for services. Here there is a graceful vestibule with pilasters and Corinthian

Versailles, statue of Louis XIV

columns, which opens into the huge *Salon d'Hercule* (a vast fireplace has a face of Hercules carved by Antoine Vassé; the ceiling was painted by François Lemoyne to the designs of Veronese).

The Grands Appartements: A succession of sumptuous rooms on the first floor at the heart of the château. There are paintings by P.A. Houasse, Le Brun, G.Blanchard, Simon Vouet, and particularly Philippe de Champaigne; fine 18C furniture, tapestries and sculpture. The *Salon d'Apollon*, named after the god Apollo to whom the courtiers flatteringly compared the Sun King, was the throne room; ceiling and arches painted by Charles de Lafosse. Built by Hardouin-Mansart and decorated by Le Brun, the *Salon de la Guerre* has bas-reliefs by Coysevox depict-ing Louis XIV's successful military campaigns.

Galerie des Glaces or Grande Galerie: Designed by Jules Hardouin-Mansart, the work was carried out by Charles Le Brun. Some 240 ft. long, 34.5 ft. wide and 40 ft. high, this majestic gallery leading to the King's apartments has seventeen windows looking on to the Parterre d'Eau (the formal water garden); palely reflecting mirrors hang opposite each window. In the décor, allegory combines with realism; the king is distinctly idealized and there is an evocation of historical events of the years 1661–78. With his masterly eye for detail, Le Brun also oversaw the lavish work of the sculptors (groups of children by Coysevox above the gilded plaster cornice). The scene of magnificent festivities under the

Versailles, Galerie des Glaces

Ancien Régime, the gallery originally had fabulous furniture in solid silver. Left in a dreadful state at the Liberation of France, it was exhaustively restored. Some of the original candelabra survived, from which exact reproductions were made.

Appartement du Roi (King's Apartment): The *Cabinet du Conseil* (Council Chamber) dates in its present form from 1775. It was here that the Treaty of Versailles was signed (18 June 1919), on the large, flat desk attributed to Cressent. Just to the E. of the middle of the château is the *Chambre d'Apparat du Roi* (King's bedchamber), which was completed for Louis XIV at the beginning of the 18C. The sculptures on the great alcove arch are by Coustou and Lespingola; *Magdalene* by Domenichino, and *Self-Portrait* and *Portrait of the Marquis de Moncade* by Van Dyck. Overwhelmingly luxurious, this bedroom (where Louis died) was the 'holy of holies' of Versailles. Those privileged to enter did so according to the strictest dictates of etiquette. The *Salon de l'Oeil-de-Boeuf* (1701) has royal portraits and an allegorical painting by Jean Nocret (the King, as Apollo, surrounded by his close family).

Grand Appartement de la Reine (Queen's Apartments): The S. section of the piano nobile, starting with the *Salon de la Paix* (Salon of Peace), which corresponds to the Salon of War at the far end of the Galerie des Glaces (ceiling by Le Brun, painting by F.Lemoyne over the fireplace). The *Chambre de la Reine* has gold and grisaille work, fine wood carving and beautiful Lyons silk. Superbly restored to its pre-Revolutionary state, this exquisite

Versailles, Salon de l'Abondance

room was the bedchamber of the last of the Ancien Régime queens. Le Brun's original décor was gradually transformed, at first with charming carved *panels*, after designs by Robert de Cotte. The work above the door is by Natoire and De Troy; ceiling cameos by Boucher. The bed has been rebuilt. A lovely jewel case belonged to Marie-Antoinette. *Salon des Nobles de la Reine:* Painted ceiling by Michel Corneille. The *Queen's Ante-Chamber* has now been restored after years of sad neglect. *Salle des Gardes de la Reine* (Room of the Queen's Guard): polychrome marble décor; paintings by N. Coypel. The *Queen's Staircase*, or *Marble Staircase*, was built by Hardouin-Mansart and enlarged in 1701.

Museum of the History of France: Occupying several levels of the N. wing (17C rooms), the central block (18C, Consulate,

and Empire), and the S. wing (Gallery of Battles), this museum, which was created by Louis-Philippe, follows the course of French history from the Crusades to the advent of the 3rd Republic. It also occupies the *Apartments of Mme. de Maintenon* (16&17C collections).

Private Apartments: Giving on to the marble courtyard and the inner courts these apartments were for the sovereigns, their queens and favourites. They include delightfully decorated studies and drawing-rooms (18C). *Royal Opera House:* By Gabriel, an enchanting auditorium, in blue, red, and gold, opened in 1770; delightful sculpture by Pajou (who also produced the striking groups in the foyer).

Orangery: Open to the public for exhibitions, this beautifully simple building is a masterpiece of stereotomy by Hardouin-Mansart (1684-6). Containing the nursery plants for the S. wing and the S. gardens, it also houses the pool from the old Bathing Apartments, together with (in winter) some 1,300 trees. The two vast stairways flanking the Orangery are called the *Cent-Marches* (100 steps), though they in fact have 103 steps. The nearby *Pièce d'Eau des Suisses* was dug in 1679.

Gardens, Small Park: The highly formal gardens and the skilfully laid out Small Park are the work of André Le Nôtre, and took more or less definitive shape in the 1680s. A number of changes were, however, made under Louis XV, Louis XVI, and Louis XVIII. With numerous statues and formal ponds, the park of Versailles acquires a fairy-tale beauty through its great network of fountains (607 all told; the machinery was designed by Florentine engineers.

Designed by Le Nôtre and built by Hardouin-Mansart (1683-5), the two large formal pools reflecting the central block

and the Galerie des Glaces are known as the *Parterre d'Eau* (literally, water flowerbed). On the terrace are a *Vase of War* by Coysevox, and a *Vase of Peace* by Tuby. The *bronzes* around the pools (the first one cast in 1687) are by the Keller brothers; figures symbolizing the various rivers of France are by Regnaudin, Tuby, Coysevox, and Le Hongre. Below the terrace, the *Parterre de Latone* (designed by Hardouin-Mansart) has statues in gilded lead by the Marsy brothers; the sculpture of *Leto and her Children* is by Balthazar Marsy. Stretching down to the *Bassin d'Apollon* (Fountain of Apollo, a group by Tuby, after Le Brun) is the immense green strip of grass known as the *Tapis Vert* (green carpet).

Grand Canal: The park's dominant feature, created in 1667–80 and measuring some 5,000 ft. in length, this great ornamental lake was the scene of superb boat parties, with fleets of miniature ships. Forming an extension to the gardens around this canal is the Small Park; the rest of the Versailles estate consists of the Trianon gardens and the Large Park.

Allée d'Eau, Bassin de Neptune: Facing the Orangery is the *Parterre du Nord* (with a charming *Kneeling Venus* by Coysevox). The *Pyramid Fountain,* with its great pile of separate bowls, was designed by Le Brun and constructed by Girardon. Also known as the *Allée des Marmousets* (alley of the little brats!), the Allée d'Eau is lined with small marble fountains with bronze sculptures of children. Begun by Le Nôtre under Louis XIV, the magnificent semicircular *Bassin de Neptune* was finished by Gabriel. With a host of statues reflected in its waters, this is the finest of all Versailles' fountains (to be seen working at the time of the 'grandes eaux').

The vast gardens of Versailles also include a number of 'bosquets' (groves), subtly combining trimly kept greenery, statuary, and a variety of architectural elements.

Grand Trianon: Built 1687–8 by Hardouin-Mansart, this elegant little pink palace consists of two wings joined by a peristyle (the work of Robert de Cotte). Somewhat neglected in the 18C, it was restored first by Napoleon, then by Louis-

Versailles, palace, royal opera

Philippe. Used to lodge visiting heads of state, the Grand Trianon has ante-chambers, drawing-rooms, and bedrooms, which are occasionally furnished in a rather heavy style. Styles of various periods appear in the right wing, where Louis XIV, Mme. de Maintenon, and Napoleon all stayed. The décor of the *Salon Rond* dates from the time of the Sun King, the luxu-rious *Salon de Famille* from the age of Louis-Philippe, and the *study* and *bed-chamber* from the Napoleonic period. The *Grande Galerie* has charming works by Cotelle depicting gardens and groves as Le Nôtre originally designed them. At the end of one arm of the Grand Canal, the Grand Trianon is surrounded by its own gardens and park. Hardouin-Mansart was respon-sible for the splendid marble fountain known as the *Buffet d'Eau* (sideboard of water), dating from 1703. Housed in a 19C building is the *Carriage Museum* (horse-drawn coaches, sedan chairs, etc.).

Petit Trianon, Hameau: Built by Gabriel 1762-8, the graceful Petit Trianon was commissioned by Louis XV at the re-quest of Mme. de Pompadour (who in fact died before it was finished; by then any-way the King had found another mistress in the person of Mme. du Barry). Major restoration has been undertaken on it re-cently. There is fine woodwork in the dining-room and beautiful furniture.

Laid out for Marie-Antoinette 1775-84, the attractive *park* of the Petit Trianon has a number of delightful follies (the *Queen's Theatre,* the *Belvedere,* and the *Temple of Love*), including an artificial village, designed by Mique in 1783. The *Hameau,* a miniature reproduction of a peasant farm, stands beside an ornamental lake.

Town of Versailles: Originally an annex to the château, the town of Versailles, where the court nobility, those working in the ministries and an entire population of artisans and tradesmen lived, is an elegant example of urban planning with a concern for symmetry and a certain uniformity, e.g. the roofs are not allowed to be higher than those of the original marble courtyard. The fine houses dotted about the present-day

Versailles, palace, Salon de Vénus

town date mostly from the 17C. Facing the château, are the symmetrical *Grandes* and *Petites Écuries* (large and small stables), begun in 1679 by Hardouin-Mansart. To the left of the entrance courtyard of the château, in the Rue de l'Indépendence-Américaine, is the enormous *Grand Commun* (also by Hardouin-Mansart, 1682–4). Next door are the *Hôtel de la Marine et des Affaires Étrangères* (Ministry of the Navy and Foreign Affairs), both 18C. The latter has an important library with historic documents and works by Dunoyer de Segonzac. The *Tennis Court,* in the Rue du Jeu-de-Paume, was where the deputies of the Third Estate met in June 1789 and swore to give France a Constitution. To the right of the château are the 18C *Hôtel de Pompadour* and *Théâtre Montansier.*

Churches: Versailles has two interesting churches, standing almost symmetrical in relation to the Avenue de Paris (on the main axis through the courtyards and the very middle of the château). Louis XIV laid the first stone of Hardouin-Mansart's neoclassical *Notre-Dame* in 1684. *Saint-Louis* (1743–54) was designed by that architect's grandson, Jacques Hardouin-Mansart de Sagonne. This large church is now a cathedral.

Along the Avenue de Paris there are several interesting buildings: the poorly preserved *Hôtel des Menus-Plaisirs,* the *Caserne de Noailles* (façade by Ledoux), and the *Hôtel de Mme. du Barry.*

Musée Lambinet: This pretty 18C hôtel houses a pleasantly old-fashioned museum with a varied collection, which includes works by Houdon, weapons made at Versailles, popular 19C statuettes, fans, copper print plates from the Jouy cloth factory, mementoes of General Hoche (who came from the area), and works by Dunoyer de Segonzac depicting Versailles.

Vertheuil	(750 inhab.)
33 Gironde	p.418☐E 11

Surrounded by the vineyards of the Haut-Médoc, this small village has an *abbey*

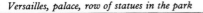

Versailles, palace, row of statues in the park

church of Romanesque origin with Gothic vaulting and 15–16C fortifications. It was much restored in the last century. A fine door in the Saintonge style is partially ruined. The remaining monastic buildings are 18C reconstructions.

Vervins	(3,260 inhab.)
02 Aisne	p.411 □K 3

Vervins, the little hillside capital of the Thiérache, has considerable charm with its cobbled streets and slate roofs,. It has had a turbulent history and although burnt down in 1552 it still retains traces of fine 15C walls. Built in an extraordinary medley of styles, the church of *Notre-Dame* is, nevertheless, a splendid edifice — 13C choir, 16C nave, and apse dating from 1870. 111 ft. tall, the impressive brick and stone porch tower was added in 1553. Inside: an enormous canvas by Jouvenet, and an 18C pulpit. 17C Town Hall. In the 16C Hôtel de Coigny, Henri IV signed the treaty concluding the war with Spain.

Versailles, Petit Trianon

Versailles, Grand Trianon

Environs: The Thiérache: A fertile area of gentle hills and valleys. Being border-country, it has suffered from invasion and war. In the 15&16C peasants would seek sanctuary in the local church from raiders, and fifty or so fortified churches survive, giving the region a distinctive character. Even in the smallest village the church always had a defensive armour of brick; sometimes there was a simple keep, sometimes the church was a veritable fortress, with towers, watch-towers and machicolations. With a well, a bread oven, and a large communal hall inside, even a siege could be withstood. **Prisces** (8 km. S.): A colossal square belfry-keep, 82 ft. high, with two turrets, gives the church the appearance of a Rhine castle. 12C nave and choir. **Burelles** (6 km. S.): Built in stone, the choir of the church disappears behind a fortified transept with bartizan and watch-tower in the left arm. On the upper floor there is a huge room which was used as a place of refuge. In place of a belfry there is a brick keep with a turret. **Plomion** (11 km. SE): Two round towers either side of a square keep make this beautiful late-16C church quite unique. In the keep there is a large room with a fireplace, which gives access to the upper part of the church (converted into a safety vault). **Montcornet** (20 km. SE): A large village with a splendid 13C church. This huge Gothic structure has a Renaissance doorway and a flat-ended choir. The transept and choir have cul-de-lampe watch-towers. Two turrets topped with fine red and black glazed brickwork flank the porch.

Vesoul	(20,080 inhab.)
70 Haute-Saône	p.417 □ N 7

On the borders of Lorraine and Franche-Comté, this industrial town stands at an important junction. Rising above it is the hill of La Motte, on the summit of which there is a statue of the Virgin (on the site of a medieval castle). A number of Gothic houses and 17&18C hôtels give the town a certain distinction. The church of **Saint-Georges**, with three aisles, is a classical building from the first half of the 18C. Of

Versailles, palace, façade

the same period, the interior décor includes superb woodwork. There are also some 15C statues and a 16C Pietà, as well as a Renaissance Holy Sepulchre. The Town Hall occupies a 17C hospital and has a small *museum* of local interest with works by the local painter and sculptor Jean-Léon Gérôme (1824–1904). The *Hôtel Thomassin*, near the church, is a good late-15C building.

Vétheuil (690 inhab.)
95 Val-d'Oise p.410☐I 4

Painted at sunset by Monet in 1901, Vétheuil is an attractive village beside the Seine. It has a 12C collegiate *church* on the hillside; Renaissance alterations include a highly ornate 16C W. front, and a fine S. door and porch (with a charming Virgin on the centre post). Inside there are several statues, mostly 16C. Behind a Renaissance carved wooden screen, the former chapel of the Confraternity of Charity, on the left, has wall paintings dating from the 16C.

Environs: Haute-Isle (4 km. NW) A village overlooking the Seine with cave dwellings. The little church is also cut out of the rock—only the miniature bell tower is visible. **La Roche-Guyon** (2 km. W. of Haute-Isle): First rebuilt in the 12C (the keep), this château underwent further alterations in the 13&18C; it was bombed in 1944 but has since been restored. The village square has a delightful fountain and an 18C market (the Mairie).

Vézelay (540 inhab.)
89 Yonne p.415☐K 7

One of the great centres of Christendom, Vézelay is situated on the border of the Morvan. The famous Romanesque basilica on the hill was one of the main gathering points for pilgrims to Compostela. St. Bernard preached the Second Crusade from here in 1146. Other visitors included Louis VII, Philippe Auguste, Richard the Lionheart, and St.Louis. As a holy place, its history began in the 9C with the foun-

Vétheuil, 'The Seine at Vétheuil' by Claude Monet

dation of a religious house in the valley, by Girart de Roussillon (a prince immortalized by the troubadour Chansons de Geste).

At first a convent, then a monastery, it was re-sited on top of the nearby hill for defensive purposes after being sacked by the Normans. It became well-known in the 11C when one of the monks was discovered to have brought the relics of Mary Magdalene from Jerusalem. Pious crowds flocked here until the end of the 13C (when it was admitted that the true relics were actually at Saint-Maximin in Provence). The Benedictine monks were replaced by canons and the near lifeless abbey was finally sacked by the Huguenots.

Basilica of Sainte-Madeleine: Unique in character, this immense, airy hilltop church has features of both mature Romanesque and Gothic. Damaged during the Wars of Religion and the Revolution, and struck by lightning in 1819, it was tumbling to ruin when the authorities were eventually alerted by Prosper Mérimée. When Viollet-le-Duc took on the task of restoration, it was no more than an amazing shell of a building. Today, with its breathtaking W. doorway, its sculpted capitals, and beautifully structured nave, it is one of the most remarkable sights in France. The church is a successful fusion of three distinct parts: the *Romanesque nave,* quickly erected after a terrible fire in 1120; the *narthex,* with the entrances—an impressive mid-12C structure; and the *Gothic Choir,* which is late 12/early 13C. The façade is now more than a reflection of the medieval original, having been reconstructed from ancient documents by Viollet-le-Duc (the central doorway is completely new). *Narthex and doors:* Built immediately after the nave, with superb historiated capitals, the vast porch is over 65 ft. wide. The famous *tympanum* above the central doorway needed no restoration; it shows Christ with extended hands filling the Twelve Apostles with the Holy Spirit. Accompanying this masterpiece of 12C Burgundian sculpture are numerous scenes carved in stone. The first arch has a strange calendar with the signs of the zodiac and depictions of the months. On

Vézelay, basilica, nave

the central post there is a statue of St.John the Baptist; a procession passes across the lintel; Apostles appear on the jambs. The *S. side door* depicts the childhood of Christ, while the *left-hand door* shows our Lord appearing to the disciples after His Resurrection, and the episode on the road to Emmaus. The *nave* is narrow and imposing, creating a magnificent architectural vista. It differs from that at Cluny, having no triforium and with a horizontal rather than vertical emphasis. Over 200 ft. long and almost 60 ft. high, with lower side aisles, it has a somewhat severe grace. White and pinkish-brown stones have been used in striking alternation. The ceiling is groin vaulted and there are some hundred or so capitals carved with superb freshness and vigour (Biblical scenes, lives of saints and depictions of Hell are along side such pagan themes as the education of Achilles and the abduction of Ganymede). The present *transept* and *choir* (early 13C) replaced the original Romanesque structure. One of the column shafts in the right transept contains the purported relics of Mary Magdalene. Enclosed by a broad ambulatory, the choir was built over a very old crypt (altered in the 13C: pre-Gothic capitals, perhaps reflecting Cistercian influence). Extending beyond the right arm of the transept is the former *chapterhouse* (late 12C), which opens into a reconstructed cloister walk.

Town: Vézelay still retains more than a mile of its 12C walls which formerly encircled the hill (*Porte Neuve*, 14&15C). Numerous old houses survive in the town, along with the 18C *Logis des Chanoines* (canons' house).

Environs: Saint-Père-sous-Vézelay (2 km. E.) Lying in a green valley at the foot of Vézelay, this quiet village is known particularly for its restaurant, *L'Espérance*. Somewhat overshadowed by the fame of the nearby basilica is the surprisingly

Vézelay, central portal

Vézelay, basilica, capital

Vézelay, bays of the nave

Vienne, church of Saint-Maurice

beautiful church of *Notre-Dame*. Dating from the 13,14&15C, it looks like a small cathedral from the outside. Inside, however, it is quite intimate. The fine façade has a porch with three doors, an attractive gable, and a graceful belfry. The 12C presbytery houses an interesting *museum* mainly displaying finds from Les Fontaines-Salées (carved flint, burial urns, ex-votos, pottery and coins). **Les Fontaines-Salées** (2 km. from Saint-Père): A remarkable archaeological site amid quiet hilly countryside. Bubbling salt water springs have been in use since the 6th millennium BC. Excavations have unearthed protohistoric water catchments, a field of burial urns (900 BC), a Celtic church, and the ruins of a major Gallo-Roman spa. Despite its out-of-the-way position, it was clearly inhabited throughout antiquity.

Vienne	(28,750 inhab.)
38 Isère	p.421 □ M 11

A motorway cuts insensitively between Vienne and the river Rhône. A former metropolis of the Allobroge Gauls, it was then an important Gallo-Roman centre and later a flourishing medieval town governed by powerful bishops. It thus combines classical, Romanesque and Gothic architecture. Beneath skies that already resemble those of Provence, dominated by the Mont Pipet, formerly protected to the N. by the castle of La Bâtie (demolished by Richelieu), and with remnants of its original Roman walls, Vienne is of interest both historically and culturally.

Saint-Pierre; Musée Lapidaire (museum of sculpture and mosaic): Originally outside the town walls, Saint-Pierre is one of the oldest churches in France. It has been much altered over the years. One can

Vienne, Musée Lapidaire, mosaic

only guess as to the appearance of the church destroyed by the Moors *c.* 735. It is hard to gain any clearer picture of the building erected in the 9C. Built partly on 4C foundations, and incorporating walls that possibly date from the 6C, this church was heightened in the 12C, when it also received a Romanesque belfry; it was then further altered in the 15C. Sold during the Revolution, it was subsequently bought back and restored in the 19C, when it came to house an interesting museum of sculpture. On display are mosaics, sarcophagi, stele, reliefs and a 2C marble sculpture of the goddess Tutela (discovered at Sainte-Colombe in one of the pools of the spa). The nave is floored with beautiful *mosaics* all from Vienne. In the apse is an exceptionally fine 6C bishop's *sarcophagus*.

Saint-Maurice: Standing on a terrace with an ornate balustrade, the old cathedral of Saint-Maurice has an elegant W. front with fine Flamboyant doors. Mainly Gothic, though with some Romanesque, it is built in the local limestone which sadly is not very weather resistant. Construction began in the early 12C and dragged on for several centuries: the choir is 13C; the Romanesque arches in the nave were revaulted in the 14C; and the upper section of the façade was not added until the 16C. In the 1560s the building was sacked by the soldiers of the Baron des Adrets. The N. tower, which was in need of repair because of the vibration and weight of its bells, burnt down in 1869. *Façade:* Flanked by two towers this is a fine elevation with three doors that remain impressive despite vandalism by the Huguenots. The 14C S. porch (on the right) is adorned with prophets and angels playing musical in-

Vienne, St-Maurice, central portal

Magi before Herod. A re-used Romanesque frieze runs above the N. porch, in which stand three large 12C marble statues (St.Peter, St.John and St.Paul). In the exterior tympanum is a re-used Roman statue.

Place Saint-Paul: The only surviving remnant of the cloisters and chapels that used to stand on this spot is the *Chapel of Virieu* (15C), now Saint-Théodore. The **Place du Palais** stands on the site of the *Roman forum;* the 17C tower was probably a firewatcher's tower.

Temple of Augustus and Livia: A graceful structure (1C BC) oriented E. and partially rebuilt after a fire. The Romans dedicated it to the Emperor Augustus and his wife. Some 79 ft. long, 50 ft. wide, and 55 ft. high, it later became a church. It became a temple of the goddess Reason during the Revolution, and was then successively a court and a museum. 19C restorations returned it to its original state, with free-standing columns.

struments. Dating from the 15C, the central doorway, with a steep gable, has more prophets, and scenes from the Old and New Testaments. The N. porch is also 15C. *Interior:* The first four bays of the nave were the last to be built, and are Gothic. Further E., the next seven bays have superb, massive Romanesque pillars with carved *capitals* (1107–40); the corresponding sections of the side aisles are similarly Romanesque. The chapels are 14&15C. In the Gothic choir is a carved marble frieze with red cement inlay. To the right of the 18C high altar is a tomb of two prelates, by Michelangelo Slodtz (1747). Dominating the canons' seats is a 13C bishop's throne. Of the fine stained glass that survives, the most remarkable is the great *Adoration of the Magi* in the chapel in the S. apse (16C). In the N. side aisle is a damaged 13C work representing the

Church, cloister and museum of Saint-André-le-Bas: With a 12&13C tower, this church still retains its 9C foundations and apse. Mostly, however, it is Romanesque (on one of the pillars is the name of the master builder with the date, 1152). The rib vaulting, supported by massive flying buttresses, is late 12C—i.e. early Gothic. There are some fine historiated marble *capitals*. In the 12C, when the abbey was in its heyday, a cloister was built on to the Roman walls. A masterpiece of Romanesque, with great variety in the capitals, it has a 15C wooden ceiling (N.). In the middle is a two-sided Carolingian cross; the cloister walks themselves have inscriptions carved in stone and memorial tablets (8–18C). The *Musée de l'Art Chrétien,* leading off the W. arm of the cloister, houses sculpture from chuches which have been demolished.

Vienne, church of Saint-Maurice, tympanum of the central portal

A busy shopping street in the Middle Ages, the *Rue Marchande* is lined with very old houses (most of them altered over the years). Some interesting houses survive in the *Rue des Orfèvres;* the *Place du Pilori* has a house with overhanging upper storeys and turrets.

Temple and theatre of Cybele: The temple and theatre of mysteries of the Eastern goddess Cybele (who was worshipped in Vienne from the 1C) were discovered just before the last war, when their foundations were unearthed during excavations. Of the Roman baths which stood beside the theatre there survive twin arches from a portico.

Roman theatre: An enormous theatre, with 46 banked rows of seats, at the foot of the Colline de Pipet. Sacked in the first barbarian invasions, it then fell to ruin, and was buried by earth. Now once again plays are performed here. Also discovered during the excavations (completed in the 1970s) was the odeum, which artisans had occupied after it was abandoned.

Art Gallery and Archaeological Museum: A great range of exhibits, from prehistoric objects to miniatures, including Roman coinage, some magnificent earthenware, and antique furniture.

The Saint-Romain site: Right bank. The huge archaeological dig of Saint-Romain-en-Gal began when construction of a school on this site was started, and extensive Gallo-Roman remains were discovered—the right-bank equivalent of the official Vienne across the river. Traces of luxurious villas with mosaics, and baths

Villandry, aerial view of the garden and the château

(formerly called the Palace of the Mirror) were found in the old Roman suburb of **Saint-Colombe**. The tower of Philippe de Valois is 15C; the church contains a 14C or 15C sculpture of the Virgin and St. Anne.

Villandry (château)
37 Indre-et-Loire   p.414☐G 7

Villandry, the most 'modern' of the great châteaux of the Loire, has retained the square keep of the old castle, which was demolished by François I's favourite, Jean le Breton. Built in the 1530s (after Chenonceau, Blois, Chambord and Azay-le-Rideau), it is a sober, elegant structure on the left of the Cher and on the bank of the Loire. Moated and built around a central courtyard, it has 18C panelling, some fine

old furniture, and many paintings. *Gardens:* Marvellously restored 16C gardens, with three terraces one above the other: a kitchen garden, with square beds of vegetables surrounded by fruit trees and hedges; a formal garden with intricate patterns of trimmed box and ornamental pools; and a water garden with a large pond feeding a canal. On the S. slope is an orchard, planted after designs by Androuet du Cerceau.

Villedieu-les-Poêles   (4,720 inhab.)
50 Manche   p.413☐E 5

A small town in the Sienne valley. Since the Middle Ages it has been a centre for the manufacture of pots and pans (poêle means frying pan); modern techniques are now used, but the same tradition still sur-

vives. A museum—the *Musée de la Poeslerie*—traces its history. *Notre-Dame* is a 15&17C church in dark granite, with a fine Flamboyant apse. The bell foundry continues a tradition dating back to the 12C. Superb examples of furniture of the region can be seen in the *Musée du Meuble Normand* in the Rue du Reculé.

Villefranche (7,260 inhab.)
06 Alpes-Maritimes p.426☐P 14

A charming port at the end of a well protected roadstead, Villefranche has many picturesque features: the curious *Rue Obscure* (largely covered), and a host of narrow alleys, passageways, staircases, and 17&18C houses. The modest chapel of *Saint-Pierre* on the quay was restored and frescoed by Cocteau. Its slopes have now been transformed into gardens. The 16C *citadel* is also worth visiting,

---

Villefranche-de-Rouergue
(13,670 inhab.)
12 Aveyron p.423☐I 13

Founded by St.Louis's brother in the 13C on the Rouergue-Quercy border, this characterful town occupies a dip of land surrounded by green hills. Retaining its original fortified layout, the town was built around a remarkable *square* with covered walkways. *Notre-Dame*, with a huge belfryporch (a veritable castle keep, with a tall doorway), is 14&15C. It is southern Gothic, with good choir stalls and a 15C stone pulpit.
The chapel of the **Pénitents-Noirs** (Black Penitents) in the N. of the town dates from the 17C. Across the Aveyron the former charterhouse of **Saint-Sauveur** is now a hospital. A remarkable Gothic complex, it includes a vast Great Cloister, from which there are some fine views, and a pretty

Flamboyant Little Cloister. The chapel has a large entrance porch and good woodwork inside (15C choir stalls).

Villefranche-Sur-Saône (30,700 inhab.)
69 Rhône p.420☐L 10

The farmers and vine growers of the Beaujolais area descend on the thriving town of Villefranche for its great traditional market. The town has a linear layout, for it grew up gradually along a stretch of the Rue Nationale (near a toll tower). As traffic increased, the lords of Beaujeu granted the town a number of privileges to encourage its development as a posting stop and market centre. These franchises (hence the name Villefranche) gained the town a certain prosperity. It became part of France with the rest of the Beaujolais region, and was industrialized as a result of the weaving trade (it is the manufacturing capital of the traditional French workers' overalls, known as 'bleu de travail'). Standing on the Rue Nationale are a church and several houses from the 15 – 18C. Beneath the houses are the very distinctive 'traboules' (a series of passageways, courtyards and staircases, which are typical of the Lyons region), worthy of Lyons itself.

Notre-Dame-des-Marais: A statue of the Virgin was discovered by the river in the 12C. Subsequently the banks of the river were drained and a chapel was erected on the site. This then became the present church. Originally Romanesque (though this is evident only from the top of the choir), it was enlarged in the 14C, given a belfry and Flamboyant façade in the 15C, and finally a tall spire in the 19C. On the N. side there is a bizarre carving of a goat and a witch.

Environs: Ars-sur-Formans (9 km. E.): Jean-Marie Baptiste Vianney was ap-

pointed Curé of Ars in 1817. Living a life of poverty, he became famed for his wisdom and counsel in the confessional. He founded a girls' school, and in 1830 achieved the revolutionary provision of free Sundays for servants. Described as a saint even during his lifetime, from the year 1828 he received some 25,000 pilgrims. When he died in 1859, 100,000 people visited Ars. Canonized in 1925, he became the patron saint of parish priests. His body rests in a gilded bronze shrine, donated by the Curés of France, in a modern basilica (designed by Bossan). An underground building with a terrace above (built 1959 – 61), it is like an immense bare crypt. Nearby, in the *Chapelle du Coeur*, a reliquary contains the Curé's heart and there is a statue of him praying. **Salles** (11 km. NW): A village with the ruins of a large religious house. The 11&12C church has a fine Romanesque door; there is a 12C cloister walk (opening into this cloister is a little Flamboyant door); the chapterhouse is 15C.

Villers-Cotterêts   (8,980 inhab.)
02 Aisne   p.411□J 4

A charming residential town on the edge of the Forest of Retz. The birthplace of Alexandre Dumas (1802), it grew in size with the construction of a royal **château** by François I (with later embellishments; the gardens and park, designed by Le Nôtre were laid out under Louis XIV). The château has a plain, elegant façade and inside there is a remarkable staircase with a coffered, vaulted ceiling. The first floor Salle des États has an attractive frieze combining floral motifs with the letter F and figures of salamanders (the initial and royal emblem of François I). The *church*, originally 12C or 13C, was altered in the 16&17C (doorway). The *Musée Municipal* has mementoes of the Dumas family.

Villesavin (château)
41 Loir-et-Cher   p.414□H 7

In the rural setting of the Sologne-Blésois border, this château combines Renaissance grace with a hint of classical sobriety. Finished *c.* 1537, it was the residence of the Superintendent of Chambord. Now restored, and with its steeply pitched roof repaired, its best features are the frescoed chapel and the old kitchen, which has a whole table service of pewter. In the courtyard there is a white marble ornamental bowl with delicate carving. There is also a large dovecote. One of the outbuildings houses old vehicles of various kinds.

Vire   (13,740 inhab.)
14 Calvados   p.413□F 5

Devastated in 1944, Vire is almost completely a modern town. The 13&15C *Porte-Horloge* was the main town gate in the old walls (several of the towers from these fortifications survive). The restored church of *Notre-Dame* is basically 13&15C.

Vitré   (12,320 inhab.)
35 Ille-et-Vilaine   p.413□E 6

A proud trading town, once famed for its textiles, it is situated on the Brittany border close to the hills of Vilaine. It has an impressive medieval castle and withind the ramparts there is a church with a tall modern spire. The narrow streets are lined with old houses which have porches and overhanging upper storeys.

Castle: Rebuilt in the 14&15C over the remains of an older structure, the plan of the castle follows the natural contours of the outcrop of rock . The E. side has a fine for-

tified entrance, with drawbridge and two machicolated round towers (the towers have stepped upper storeys and conical roofs). Three massive towers guard the corners of the outer walls. On the N. side of the triangular inner courtyard is the modern Hôtel de Ville. Opposite the entrance is a side tower with a small Renaissance apse, which is cut off at the corners and has carved decoration. A number of rooms in the towers house a *museum* of art and archaeology (wood carvings, tapestry, earthenware, pewter and prints), ethnography and natural history.

Notre-Dame: This 15&16C building is most notable for its S. side, which has a series of gables separated by pinnacled buttresses and pierced by Flamboyant windows. Attached to one of the buttresses outside is a delicately carved stone pulpit. The sacristy houses a magnificent 16C *triptych* of 32 Limoges enamel scenes depicting the Life of the Virgin.

Environs: Château des Rochers (7 km. SE): Built in the 14C and altered in the 17C, this picturesque manor house is famous for its association with the Marquise de Sévigné (known for her remarkable letters), who stayed here several times between 1654 and 1690. There are two residential blocks, which are joined together at right angles and have a corner turret. The domed chapel was built in 1671 by Mme. de Sévigné's uncle, the Abbé de Coulanges. The Cabinet Vert, which was Mme. de Sévigné's room, has some mementoes and a fireplace decorated with her initials. **Champeaux** (9 km. NW): A delightful village with granite houses around a square, in the middle of which there is an old well. The 15&16C collegiate church, founded by the lords of Espinay, has magnificent 16C canopied choir stalls, a window of the same period depicting the Crucifixion, and tombs (including that of Guy III d'Espinay and his wife

in white stone and polychrome marble with two naked figures).

Vitteaux	(1,080 inhab.)
21 Côte-d'Or	p.416□L 7

Remains of the castle, several old houses (including the fine 13C Maison Belime), and 14C market buildings have survived in this village. The church is Gothic and Renaissance. The late medieval 15C *Château de Posanges* lies a little to the N.

Vittel	(6,800 inhab.)
88 Vosges	p.417□N 6

Opened in 1854, this famous spa lies amid woods and hills. The park and Olympic stadium set a tone of relaxation and sport. The huge plant where the local mineral water is bottled is well worth a visit. **Saint-Rémy:** The three Gothic aisles of this 12C church survive intact despite 15&16C al-

Vitré, the château

Vizille, the château

terations. The baptistery chapel has a 15C stone calvary and a 17C wooden diptych. **Saint-Privat:** A richly furnished 16C church, with interesting stone statues in the chapel of Saint-Éloi.

floor and a 14C octagonal second floor and is now a bell tower. Of the many old houses it is worth noting the 16C 'Maison des Chevalier', so named after the bas-reliefs on the façade which depict a joust.

Viviers	(3,200 inhab.)
07 Ardèche	p.425□L 13

Overlooking the Rhône as it enters the gorge of Donzère, this small town (an episcopal see after which the Vivrais region is named) grew up around the **cathedral**. Of the Romanesque original, the façade and porch still survive. The choir is exceptionally spacious and has Flamboyant vaults with lovely tracery. In front of the cathedral stands a solitary *tower,* a vestige of the Château-Vieux; it consists of an 11C first

Vizille	(7,250 inhab.)
38 Isère	p.421□N 11

Standing at the mouth of the industrialized valley of the Romanche, where the Route des Grandes Alpes and the Route Napoléon cross, Vizille has claims to fame for being the meeting place of the famous Assembly of 1788 (portentous of the Revolution) and also the place through which Napoleon passed to great acclamation in 1815, on his return from Elba. A former Presidential residence, set on a rocky out-

crop, the **château** is only part of the original building (built in the 17C and later enlarged), which was ravaged by two fires in the 19C. It is now restored and has Louis XIII, Louis XIV, and Empire furniture. The park, with ancient trees, covers more than 250 acres.

Volvic	(3,250 inhab.)
63 Puy-de-Dôme	p.420☐J 10

A town famous for its pure water and unusual stone—the black volcanic stone from the lava flow of Nugère, in which all the towns and villages of the region are built. **Saint-Priest:** Entirely Romanesque. The apse incorporates an ambulatory with radiating chapels. Typically Auvergnat subjects are carved on many of the capitals and these include sirens, centaurs, griffins, etc. At the entrance to the axial chapel there is a fine Romanesque grille. The church contains a graceful 14C statue of the Virgin with a bird. Set up in an old quarry, the **Maison de la Pierre** explains the various phases of the volcanic evolution of the Auvergne area as well as documenting the local industry of quarrying and stone cutting.

Vougeot (Clos de)
21 Côte-d'Or	p.421☐M 8

The famous 'climat' (vine growing area) of Close de Vougeot is now shared amongst a considerable number of vineyard owners. Fine wines were first produced here by Cistercian monks in the 12C (a papal bull of the period mentions the 'Close de Vooget'). The *château*, built by a 16C abbot, once echoed to the plainchant of the monks. Noticeably Renaissance in style, it has a huge Romanesque cellar, and medi-

Vouvant, church, portals

eval wine presses in the fermenting room. It now belongs to the Confrérie des Chevaliers du Tastevin.

Vouvant	(840 inhab.)
85 Vendée	p.418☐F 9

A quiet village in the middle of the forest, a ruined *castle* evokes its feudal history. The **Tour Mélusine** (118 ft. tall) has two rooms one above the other, with pyramidal vaulting. **Notre-Dame:** The most striking feature is the N. transept façade which, unusually for the W. of France, is richly decorated and has two symmetrical doors with decorative foliage in the arches. The upper section of the gable (altered in the 14C) has two rows of carvings illustrating the Last Supper and the Ascension.

| **Wassy** | (3,230 inhab.) |
| 52 Haute-Marne | p.416☐L/M 5 |

In the pleasant Blaise valley, a traditional iron-working area, this large village has a rather old-world charm. Some remains of the old fortifications still survive (such as the **Tour des Vicaires**), together with attractive stone and timber-framed houses. **Notre-Dame** is a composite church. It was begun in the late 11C and altered after a fire around 1600. The building combines certain original Romanesque details (see the fine central tower) with Gothic additions, though the result is not always a complete success. The church contains 17C works of art. The 18C Hôtel de Ville boasts a remarkable 19C *astronomical clock*, which is at once functional and pleasing to the eye. The house in which the writer Claudel spent part of his childhood in the closing years of the last century stands near the site of a barn where, on 1 March 1562, many Protestants were massacred by soldiers of the Duc de Guise. Whether planned or not, this bloodbath was one of the incidents which led to the terrible Wars of Religion. Wassy was devastated by the Ligueurs in August 1591 and suffered severely from the Revocation of the Edict of Nantes.

| **Wissembourg** | (6,100 inhab.) |
| 67 Bas-Rhin | p.417☐P 4 |

Wissembourg (white castle), the northernmost town of Alsace, lies on the German border and grew up around a very old abbey. Stanislas Leszczynski (the exiled king of Poland) fled here in 1720. Most noteworthy of the old houses is the Maison Vogelsberger, built in 1540. With a fine Romanesque belfry at one side, the abbey church of **Saint-Pierre-et-Saint-Paul** dates from the second half of the 13C. It has a 14C cloister walk. The *Musée Westercamp* (mostly local history, traditions and crafts) occupies a 16C house which is built up against the town walls.

| **Wormhout** | (4,320 inhab.) |
| 59 Nord | p.411☐J 1 |

With its triangular Place and painted houses, this is a typical small town of the area (the fertile plain of Flanders, whose skyline is dotted with windmills). There is a pleasant 16C brick church, which has an attractive pulpit.

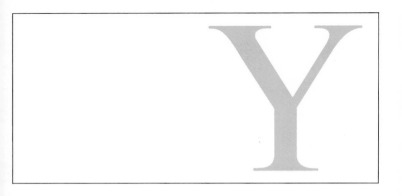

Yeu (island) (4,770 inhab.)
85 Vendée p.418☐D 8

10 km. long and 4 wide, the Île d'Yeu is an island of considerable contrasts: the magnificent wild coastline is rather like Brittany, while the villages are typical of Vendée, with their small limed houses. **Port-Joinville:** The island's capital and an important port for tuna fishing. Having been imprisoned in the fort of Pierre-Levée on 16 November 1945, Marshal Pétain died here on 23 July 1951. Romantically situated on the stark coast, with the waves beating against it, is the ruined *Vieux Château* (11&16C). **Saint-Sauveur,** the former capital of the island, has a Romanesque *church* with a square belfry roofed with round tiles similar to those on other churches in the wooded Vendée region.

Yquem (château)
33 Gironde p.422☐F 12

In the heart of the delightful Sauternais area, surrounded by its vineyard from which one of the most famous French wines comes, the château of Yquem was originally a medieval manor. It was then altered in the 16&18C. Now owned by the Lur-Saluces, it preserves the memory of the d'Eyquem family, to whom the essayist Montaigne was related.

Yvetot (10,940 inhab.)
76 Seine-Maritime p.410☐H 3

Built mainly of wood, this town burnt down on several occasions, and was virtually totally destroyed in the last war. The interesting church of **Saint-Pierre,** dating from 1956, is a huge rectangular structure with a tall square belfry. The walls consist of vast stained-glass windows by Max Ingrand, depicting the lives of the saints of Normandy. In the small *Musée Municipal* is a superb collection of ivories.

Yvoire (340 inhab.)
74 Haute-Savoie p.421☐N 9

A most picturesque village on a promontory jutting out into Lake Geneva, Yvoire still has its 14C walls (with *fortified gates*) and the solidly built *keep* of a castle of the same era. There are several old houses, including the 14C Maison de Beauvais. The *church* is 13&17C.

Glossary

Acanthus: Decorative element found especially on → Corinthian capitals; it developed from the stylized representation of a sharply serrated, thistle-like leaf.

Aedicule: Wall niche housing a bust or statue; usually with a → gable, → pillars or → columns.

Aisle: Longitudinal section of a church or other building, usually divided from other such sections by an → arcade.

Altar: Sacrificial table of Greeks and Romans. The Lord's table in the Christian faith. Catholic churches often have several side altars as well as the high altar.

Ambo: Stand or lectern by the choir screen in early Christian and medieval churches; predecessor of the → pulpit.

Ambulatory: A corridor created by continuing the side aisles around the choir; often used for processions.

Antependium: Covering for the front of the altar.

Apse: Large recess at end of the → choir, usually semicircular or polygonal. As a rule it contains the → altar.

Apsidiole: A small apsidal chapel.

Aquamanile: Pouring-vessel or bowl for ritual washing in the Catholic liturgy.

Aqueduct: Water pipe or channel across an arched bridge; frequently built as monumental structures by the Romans.

Arabesque: Stylized foliage used as a decorative motif.

Arcade: A series of arches borne by columns or pillars. When the arcade is attached to a wall (and is purely decorative), it is called a blind arcade.

Arch: A curved structure of support employed in spanning a space.

Architrave: Main stone member on top of the columns; lowest part of the → entablature.

Archivolt: The face of an arch in Romanesque and Gothic portals; often more than one.

Ashlar: Hewn block of stone (as opposed to that straight from the quarry).

Atrium: In Roman houses a central hall with an opening in the roof. In Christian architecture, a forecourt usually surrounded by columns; also known as a → paradise.

Attic: A (usually richly decorated) storey above the main → entablature; intended to conceal the roof.

Baldacchino: Canopy above altars, tombs, statues, portals, etc.

Baluster: Short squat or shaped column.

Balustrade: Rail formed of → balusters.

Baptistery: Place of baptism; may be a separate building.

Baroque: Architectural style from c.1600 – c.1750. Distinguished by powerfully agitated, interlocking forms.

Bartizan: A small corner turret projecting from the top of a building.

Base: Foot of a column or pillar.

Basket arch: A flattened round arch.

Basilica: Greek hall of kings. In church architecture, a type of church with nave and two or more aisles, the roof of the nave being higher than the roofs above the aisles.

Bastide: A fortified village, laid out with a regular grid of streets and an arcaded central square. They occur in SW France and were founded as strongholds by the English and French during the Middle Ages.

Bay: Vertical division of a building between pillars, columns, windows, wall arches, etc.

Blind arcade: → Arcade.

Blind tracery: → Tracery.

Bracket: A projection from the wall used as a support—for a bust, statue, arch, etc.

Calotte: Half dome with no drum.

Campanile: Bell tower; usually free standing.

Capital: Topmost part of a column. The shape of the capital determines the style or → order.

Cartouche: Decorative frame or panel imitating a scrolled piece of paper, usually with an inscription, coat-of-arms, etc.

Caryatid: A carved figure supporting the entablature.

Cella: Main room of ancient temple containing divine image.

Cenotaph: Monument to dead buried elsewhere.

Chapterhouse: Assembly room in which monks or nuns discuss the community's business.

Charnel house: House or vault in which bones are placed.

Choir: That part of the church in which divine service is sung. Shorter and often narrower than the nave, it is usually raised and at the E. end. In the Middle Ages the choir was often separated from the rest of the church by a screen.

Ciborium: Canopy over high altar; usually in the form of a dome supported on columns.

Classicism: Revival of Greek and Roman architectural principles.

Clerestory: Upper part of the main walls of the nave, above the roofs of the aisles and pierced by windows.

Cloister: Four sided covered walk (often vaulted) and opening inwards by arcades.

Coffered ceiling: A ceiling divided into square or polygonal pane[ls] which are painted or otherwi[se] decorated.

Column: Support with circular cros[s] section, narrowing somewhat t[o]wards the top; the type of colum[n] is determined by the → order o[f the] Pillar.

Compound pillar: Often found i[n] Gothic buildings. A central sha[ft] has attached or detached shafts [or] half-shafts clustered around it.

Conch: Semicircular recess with [a] half-dome.

Confessio: Chamber or recess for [a] relic near the altar.

Corinthian order: → Order wit[h] richly decorated →capitals; the ba[se] has two or more tiers and is simil[ar] to that of the → Ionic order.

Cornice: Projecting upper limit o[f a] wall; topmost member of the → e[n]tablature of an → order.

Cosmati work: Decorative techniq[ue] involving the use of marble inla[id] mosaics etc.; many Roman marb[le] workers had the family nam[e] Cosma.

Crocket: Gothic leaf-like decorati[on] projecting from the sides of pinn[a]cles, gables etc.

Crossing: The intersection of th[e] nave and transept.

Crypt: Burial place, usually unde[r] the → choir. Churches were ofte[n] built above an old crypt.

Curtain wall: Outer wall of castle[.]

Cyclops Wall: Ancient wall made [of] large rough blocks of stone of i[r]regular shape.

Dipteros: Temple in which portico[es] are connected by a double row [of] lateral columns.

Diptych: A painted hinged doub[le] (altar) panel.

Dolmen: Chamber tomb lined an[d] roofed with megaliths.

Doric order: → Order in which th[e] columns lack a base and bear fla[t] pad-shaped → capitals.

Dormer window: Window in slop[e] ing roof which projects and has i[ts] own gabled roof.

Drum: Substructure of a dome; as [a] rule either cylindrical or polygona[l.]

Dwarf Gallery: Romanesque featur[e] wall passage of small arches on th[e] outside of a building.

Entablature: Upper part of an →or[der]; made up of → architrave, →[ ]frieze and → cornice.

Exedra: Apse, vaulted with a hal[f] dome; may have raised seats.

Façade: Main front of a building, of[ten] decoratively treated.

Facing: Panelling in front of struc[]tural components not intended to b[e] visible.

Faience: Glazed pottery named afte[r] the Italian town of Faenza.

n vault: Looks like a highly decorated rib vault; Concave-sided cone-like sections meet or nearly meet at the apex of the vault.

filigree work: Originally goldsmith's work in which gold and silver wire were ornamentally soldered on to a metal base. Also used in a more general sense for intricately perforated carvings and stucco.

finial: Small decorative pinnacle.

flamboyant: French late Gothic architectural style characterized by long, curvilinear ornament.

flying buttress: Very large Gothic windows made it necessary to buttress or strengthen the outer walls by half-arches and arches. This support transmitted the thrust of the vault to the buttress.

foliate capital: Gothic capital in which the basic form is covered with delicate leaf ornaments.

fosse: Artificially created ditch; often separated castles from the surrounding land with access by a drawbridge.

fresco: Pigments dispersed in water are applied without a bonding agent to the still-damp lime plaster. While the mortar dries, the pigments become adsorbed into the plaster.

frieze: Decorative strips for the borders of a wall. The frieze can be two- or three-dimensional and can consist of figures or ornaments.

gable: The triangular upper section of a wall. Normally at one end of a pitched roof but it may be purely decorative.

gallery: Intermediate storey; in a church it is usually for singers and the organ. Arcaded walkway.

gobelin: Pictorial tapestry made in the Gobelins factory in Paris.

Gothic: Period in European art and architecture stretching from the mid 12C to the 16C.

grisaille: Painting in various shades of grey.

groin vault: Vault in which two → barrel vaults intersect at right angles. The simple groin vault is to be distinguished from the rib vault, in which the intersecting edges are reinforced by ribs.

half-timbering: Beams are used as supporting parts with an infill of loam or brick.

hall church: In contrast to the →basilica, nave and aisles are of equal height; no → transept.

hermitage: Pavilion in parks and gardens; originally the residence of a hermit.

Holy Sepulchre: Structure representing Christ's tomb as discovered by Constantine, who later encased it in a miniature temple.

iconostasis: In the Eastern church, a screen of paintings between the sanctuary and the nave.

Intarsia: Inlaid work in wood, plaster, stone etc.

Ionic order: → Order in which the columns stand on a base of two or more tiers; the → capital has two lateral → volutes.

Jamb: Vertical part of arch, doorway or window.

Keep: Main tower of a castle; last refuge in time of siege.

Lantern: Small windowed turret on top of roof or dome.

Loggia: Pillared gallery, open on one or more sides; often on an upper storey.

Lunette: Semicircular panel above doors and windows, often with paintings or sculptures.

Mandorla: Almond shaped niche containing a figure of Christ enthroned.

Mannerism: Artistic style between → Renaissance and → baroque (c.1530–1630). Mannerism neglects natural and classical forms in favour of an intended artificiality of manner.

Mansard: An angled roof in which the lower slope is steeper than the upper. The area gained is also called a mansard and can be used to live in. (Named after the French architect F.Mansart.)

Mausoleum: A splendid tomb, usually in the form of a small house or temple. From the tomb of Mausolus at Halicarnassus.

Mensa: Flat surface of the altar.

Mezzanine: Intermediate storey.

Miniature: Small picture, hand illumination in old manuscripts.

Monks' choir: That section of the choir reserved for the monks, frequently closed off.

Monstrance: Ornamented receptacle in which the consecrated Host is shown (usually behind glass).

Mosaic: Decoration for wall, floor or vault, assembled from small coloured stones, pieces of glass or fragments of other materials.

Mullion: Vertical division of a window into two or more lights.

Narthex: Vestibule of basilica or church.

Nave: Central aisle of church, intended for the congregation; excludes choir and apse.

Neo-baroque: Reaction to the cool restraint of → classicism. Re-uses baroque forms; developed in the last part of the 19C as a historicizing, sumptuous style with exaggerated three-dimensional ornamentation and conspicuous colours.

Neo-Gothic: Historicizing 19C style, which was intended to revive Gothic structural forms and decorative elements.

Net vault: Vault in which the ribs cross one another repeatedly.

Nuns' choir: Gallery from which nuns attended divine service.

Nymphaeum: Roman pleasure house, often with statues and fountains.

Obelisk: Free-standing pillar with square ground plan and pyramidal peak.

Odeum: Building, usually round, in which musical or other artistic performances were given.

Onion dome: Bulbous dome with a point, common in Russia and E.Europe; not a true dome, i.e. without a vault.

Opisthodomos: Rear section of Greek temple; behind the cella.

Orangery: Part of baroque castles and parks originally intended to shelter orange trees and other southern plants in winter. However, orangeries often had halls for large court assemblies.

Oratory: Small private chapel.

Order: Classical architectural system prescribing decorations and proportions according to one of the accepted forms → Corinthian, → Doric, → Ionic, etc. An order consists of a column, which usually has a base, shaft and capital, and the entablature, which itself consists of architrave, frieze and cornice.

Oriel: Projecting window on an upper floor; it is often a decorative feature.

Pallium: A cloak worn by the Romans; in the Middle Ages, a coronation cloak for kings and emperors, later also for archbishops.

Pantheon: Temple dedicated to all gods; often modelled on that in in Rome, which is a rotunda. Building in which distinguished people are buried or have memorials.

Paradise: → Atrium.

Pavilion: Polygonal or round building in parks or pleasure grounds. The main structure of baroque castles is very often linked by corner pavilions to the galleries branching off from the castle.

Pedestal: Base of a column or the base for a statue.

Pendentive: The means by which a circular dome is supported on a square base; concave area or spandrel between two walls and the base of a dome.

Peripteros: Greek temple in which the porticoes are connected laterally by single rows of columns.

Peristyle: Continuous colonnade surrounding a temple or open court.

Pilaster: Pier projecting from a wall; conforms to one of the → orders.

Pilaster strip: Pilaster without base and capital; feature of Anglo-Saxon and early Romanesque buildings.

Pillar: Supporting member, like a → column but with a square or polygonal cross section; does not conform to any order.

Plinth: Projecting lower part of wall or column.

Polyptych: An (altar) painting composed of several panels or wings.

Porch: Covered entrance to a building.

Portico: Porch supported by columns and often with a pediment; may be the centre-piece of façade.

Predella: Substructure of the altar. Paintings along lower edge of large altarpiece.

Pronaos: Area in front of ancient temple (also of churches); sides enclosed and columns in front.

Propylaeum: Entrance gateway, usually to temple precincts. The Propylaeum on the Acropolis at Athens, 437–432 BC, was the model for later buildings.

Prothyra: Railing before door of Roman house.

Pseudoperipteros: Temple in which porticoes are connected laterally by → pilasters and not → columns.

Pulpit: Raised place in church from which the sermon is preached. May be covered by a → baldacchino or → sounding board.

Putto: Figure of naked angelic child in → Renaissance, → baroque and → rococo art and architecture.

Pylon: Entrance gate of Egyptian temple; more generally used as isolated structure to mark a boundary.

Quadriga: Chariot drawn by four horses harnessed abreast.

Refectory: Dining hall of a monastery.

Relief: Carved or moulded work in which the design stands out. The different depths of relief are, in ascending order, rilievo stiacciato, bas-relief and high relief or alto-rilievo.

Reliquary: Receptacle in which a saint's relics are preserved.

Renaissance: Italian art and architecture from the early 15C to the mid 16C. It marks the end of the medi-

eval conception of the world and the beginning of a new view based on classical antiquity (Ital. rinascimento = rebirth).

Retable: Shrine-like structure above and behind the altar.

Rib vault: → Groin vault.

Rocaille: Decorative ornaments adapted from the shell motif; chiefly late → Renaissance and → rococo.

Rococo: Style towards the end of the → baroque (1720–70); elegant, often dainty, tendency to oval forms.

Romanesque: Comprehensive name for architecture from 1000–c. 1300. Buildings are distinguished by round arches, calm ornament and a heavy general appearance.

Rood screen: Screen between → choir and → nave, which bears a rood or crucifix.

Rose-window: A much divided round window with rich → tracery found especially in Gothic buildings; often above the portal.

Rotunda: Round building.

Rustication: Massive blocks of stone separated by deep joints.

Sanctuary: Area around the high altar in a church.

Sarcophagus: Stone coffin, usually richly decorated.

Scroll: Spiral-shaped ornament.

Sedilia: Seats for clergy; usually in the wall of the S. side of the choir.

Sgraffito: Scratched-on decoration.

Sounding board: → Pulpit.

Spandrel: The triangular space between the curve of an arch, the horizontal drawn from its apex, and the vertical drawn from the point of its springing; also the space between two arches in an arcade, and that part of a vault between two adjacent ribs.

Springer: The first stone in which the curve of an arch or vault begins.

Squinch: An arch or system of arches at the internal angles of towers to form the base of a round drum or dome above a square structure. → Pendentive.

Stela: Standing block.

Strapwork: Renaissance carved w▯ modelled on fretwork or cut leath▯

Stucco: Plasterwork, made of gy▯ sum, lime, sand and water, which ▯ easy to model. Used chiefly in ▯ 17&18C for three-dimensional ▯ terior decoration.

Synagogue: Jewish place of worsh▯

Tabernacle: Receptacle for the co▯ secrated host.

Telamon: Support in the form o▯ male figure (male caryatid).

Terracotta: Fired, unglazed clay.

Thermal baths: Roman hot-wat▯ baths.

Tracery: Geometrically conceiv▯ decorative stonework, particular▯ used to decorate windows, scree▯ etc. If it embellishes a wall, it ▯ known as blind tracery.

Transenna: Screen or lattice in ope▯ work found in early Christi▯ churches.

Transept: That part of a church ▯ right angles to the nave; → basilic▯

Triforium: Arcaded wall passa▯ looking on to the nave; between t▯ arcade and the clerestory.

Triptych: Tripartite altar painting▯

Triumphal arch: Free-standing ga▯ way based on a Roman original.

Truss frame: Frame of timbe▯ joined together to span a gap and ▯ support other timbers, as in a roo▯

Tunnel vault: Simplest vault; co▯ tinuous structure with semicircul▯ or pointed cross section uninte▯ rupted by cross vaults.

Tympanum: The often semicircul▯ panel contained within the lintel ▯ a doorway and the arch above it.▯

Volute: Spiral scroll on an Ionic cap▯ tal; smaller volutes on Composi▯ and Corinthian capitals.

Winged altar: Triptych or polyptyc▯ with hinged, usually richly carve▯ or painted, wings.

Index of major artists

List of places mentioned in the environs sections. The entry in which they appear is indicated by the → symbol.

PHOTOGRAPHIC CREDITS

The majority of the photographs in this edition were taken specially by photographers of the Société SCOPE:
Philippe BEUZEN, Hervé COATANER, Jean-Claude FAUCHON *(using a Leica R 3)*, Jacques GUILLARD *(using a Leica R 3)*, Michel GUILLARD *(using a Leica R3)*, Pascal OURY, Antoine SENNE
assisted by: Bruno CHAINE, Michel LABOILLE, Jacques LOMBARD and Jean-Daniel SUDBES *(Cap Théojac).*
Other photographs from the archives of: Beaujard/Nathan: pp. 26 - 31 - 84 - 100 - 105 - 111 - 159 - 186 - 208 - 225 - 249 - 282 - 315 - 323 - 362 - 389 - 407 - 467 - 509 - 552 - 587 - 590 - 608 - 618 - 677 - 678 - 683 - 687 - 697 - 718 - 766 - 782. Poupard/Nathan: pp. 26 - 209 - 337 - 372 - 604. Photos Musées Nationaux/Nathan: pp. 67 - 217 - 247 - 367 - 568. Higon/Nathan: p. 97. Walter/Nathan: p. 450. Tétrel/Nathan: p. 469. Duran/Nathan: pp. 514 - 61 Franz/Nathan: p. 715. Archives N than: pp. 51 - 332 - 397 - 785. Ci of Bayeux *(by special permission)*: 79. Simion/Ricciarini: pp. 20 - 1 - 445 - 498 - 501 - 599 - 734. Aeri views by Alain Perceval: pp. 40 293. Giraudon: pp. 545 - 546 - 57 - 658 - 662 - 751 - 775.